The Life of
Bishoi

THE LIFE OF BISHOI

The Greek, Arabic, Syriac, and Ethiopic *Lives*

Edited by Tim Vivian and Maged S.A. Mikhail

Contributors:
Apostolos N. Athanassakis, †Rowan A. Greer,
Robert Kitchen, Maged S.A. Mikhail, and Tim Vivian

Foreword by Mark N. Swanson

Saint Athanasius and Saint Cyril Theological School Press

The American University in Cairo Press
Cairo New York

First published in 2022 by
The American University in Cairo Press
113 Sharia Kasr el Aini, Cairo, Egypt
One Rockefeller Plaza, 10th Floor, New York, NY 10020
www.aucpress.com

Copyright © 2022 by Tim Vivian and Maged S.A. Mikhail

All rights reserved. No part of this publication may be reproduced, stored in a retrieval system, or transmitted in any form or by any means, electronic, mechanical, photocopying, recording, or otherwise, without the prior written permission of the publisher.

ISBN 978 1 617 97999 6

Library of Congress Cataloging-in-Publication Data

Names: Vivian, Tim, editor. | Mikhail, Maged S.A., 1974- editor. | Swanson, Mark (Mark N.), other.
Title: The Life of Bishoi: the Greek, Ge'ez (Ethiopic), Syriac, and Arabic Lives / edited by Tim Vivian and Maged S.A. Mikhail; contributors, Apostolos N. Athanassakis, Rowan A. Greer, Robert Kitchen, Maged S.A. Mikhail, and Tim Vivian; preface by Mark N. Swanson.
Identifiers: LCCN 2020037131 | ISBN 9781617979996 (hardcover) | ISBN 9781649030658 (epub) | ISBN 9781649030665 (pdf)
Subjects: Subjects: LCSH: Pshoi, of Scetis, Saint, active 4th century–5th century. | Coptic Christian saints—Biography. | Desert Fathers—Egypt—Biography. | Church history—Primitive and early church, ca. 30–600—Sources.
Classification: LCC BX139.P74 L54 2022 | DDC 270.2092 [B]--dc23

1 2 3 4 5   26 25 24 23 22

Designed by Adam el-Sehemy
Printed in the United Kingdom

In Memoriam
Rowan A. Greer
1935–2014
Priest, Scholar, Professor, Mentor
Yale Divinity School

Contents

Contributors	ix
Acknowledgments	xi
Abbreviations	xiii
Foreword	xv
Mark N. Swanson	
General Introduction: Saint Bishoi of Scetis	1
Maged S.A. Mikhail	
Bishoi's Name and Identity	2
Translation of Relics	4
Purgation in the Desert	6
A Textual History of the *Life of Bishoi*	8
A Note on Transliterations	18
1. THE GREEK *LIFE OF PAÏSIOS* IN TRANSLATION	29
Translated by Tim Vivian and Apostolos N. Athanassakis	
Introduction	29
Appendix: List of Three Key Terms in the *Life of Païsios*	46
The Greek *Life of Païsios*: The Life and Ascetic Practice of Our Holy Father Païsios Written by Our Holy Father John the Little	51
2. THE GREEK *LIFE OF PAÏSIOS*. BNF GREC 1093	131
Edited and transcribed by Tim Vivian and Apostolos N. Athanassakis	
3. THE GE'EZ (ETHIOPIC) *LIFE OF ABBA BSOY* IN TRANSLATION	195
Translated by Robert A. Kitchen	
Introduction	195
The Ethiopic *Life of Bsoy*	201

4	THE SYRIAC *LIFE OF ABBA BISHOI* IN TRANSLATION	237
	Translated by †Rowan A. Greer, Robert A. Kitchen, and Maged S.A. Mikhail	
	Introduction	237
	The Syriac *Life of Abba Bishoi*	239
5	THE ARABIC *LIFE OF BISHOI* IN TRANSLATION	281
	Translated by Maged S.A. Mikhail	
	Introduction	281
	The Arabic *Life of Bishoi*	283
	Appendix: Carrying Christ ¶v	323
	Bibliography	329
	Indexes	341
	Topics	341
	Authors	353
	Transliterated Names and Terms	356
	Geographical Names	362
	Scripture	363

Contributors

Tim Vivian is professor emeritus of religious studies at California State University, Bakersfield, and a retired priest of the Episcopal Church. He has published, among many books, *The Life of Antony* (with Apostolos N. Athanassakis, 2003), *The Holy Workshop of Virtue: The Life of Saint John the Little* (with Maged S.A. Mikhail, 2010), *Becoming Fire: Through the Year with the Desert Fathers and Mothers* (2009), and *The Sayings and Stories of the Desert Fathers and Mothers* (vol. 1, 2021).

Maged S.A. Mikhail is professor of history at California State University, Fullerton. His research and teaching focus on Coptic Christianity, late antiquity, and the Islamic Middle East. He is the author of *The Legacy of Demetrius of Alexandria* (2017) and *From Byzantine to Islamic Egypt: Religion, Identity and Politics after the Arab Conquest* (2014).

Rowan Allen Greer III (1935–2014), an Episcopal priest and Walter H. Gray Professor of Anglican Studies at Yale Divinity School, was the author of *Broken Lights and Mended Lives: Theology and Common Life in the Early Church* and *Anglican Approaches to Scripture: From the Reformation to the Present*.

Robert Kitchen is a retired minister of the United Church of Canada, living in Regina, Saskatchewan. He read for the D.Phil. (Oxford) in Syriac Language and Literature and has taught Syriac studies in Sweden and Austria.

Apostolos N. Athanassakis is professor emeritus at the University of California, Santa Barbara. He is well known for his translations of *The Homeric Hymns*, *Hesiod*, and *The Orphic Hymns*. He has made contributions to *The Orthodox Study Bible* and has translated the *Lives* of several of the early desert fathers.

Acknowledgments

The editors wish to thank the following translators who generously helped with this volume: Apostolos N. Athanassakis, †Rowan A. Greer, and Robert Kitchen.

We also wish to thank the following persons for their assistance and support: H.E. Metropolitan Serapion, H.G. Bishop Kyrillos, H.G. Bishop Metta'us, Stephen Davis, Ramez Mikhail, Nadia Naqib, The Saint Athanasius and Saint Cyril Coptic Orthodox Theological School, The Saint Shenoute the Archimandrite Coptic Society, Hany Takla, and Mark N. Swanson.

Special thanks to Emily Stuckey for doing the indexing and for catching some errors.

Finally, many thanks to our editor, Johanna Baboukis, for her painstaking work, patience, and counsel, especially with the proofs and, with them, especially with the Greek transcription. Thank you, Jody!

Abbreviations

AlphAP	*Apophthegmata Patrum*, Alphabetical Collection
BHG	Bibliotheca Hagiographica Graeca
BHO	Bibliotheca Hagiographica Orientalis
CPG	Clavis Patrum Graecorum
CSCO	Corpus Scriptorum Christianorum Orientalium
GCAL	Geschichte der christlichen arabischen Literatur
Lampe	Lampe, *A Patristic Greek Lexicon*
LSJ	Liddell, Scott, James, *Greek–English Lexicon*
LXX	Septuagint
NRSV	New Revised Standard Version
PG	Patrologia Graeca
PO	Patrologia Orientalis
POM	I.V. Pomialovskii (1902)
SOCC	Studia Orientalia Christiana Collectanea

Foreword
Mark N. Swanson

Tim Vivian and Maged S.A. Mikhail introduce this extraordinary volume by telling us that "Saint Bishoi of Scetis (d. ca. 417) enjoys tremendous popularity throughout the Christian East." For some readers, that may be news. The name Bishoi is not very well known among Western Christians. My own knowledge of the saint until not so many years ago was limited to the following: he was the Coptic St. Christopher (¶v, appendix); there was a monastery named for him in Egypt's Wadi al-Natrun (¶1); and there was a place within the ancient church of the neighboring Monastery of the Syrians (Dayr al-Suryān) where he was said to have tied his hair to a hook or peg in the ceiling in order to help him keep vigil at night (¶20). For many readers, indeed for me, a volume like this present one is an introduction to a new world—or better, a number of intersecting worlds.

At the historical level there is the world of Eastern Christianity, a world of diverse but deeply interconnected communities. In that world, stories of saints like Bishoi readily jumped linguistic and confessional barriers, "the same" story being refashioned in subtle (and not-so-subtle) ways so as to inspire awe, give hope, instill virtues, warn against demonic "thoughts,"[1] defend the faith, or simply provide entertainment—in a wide variety of cultural and political settings. The general introduction traces the journey of the *Life* through four languages, three major families of manuscripts, and (by my count) sixteen recensions—a testimony to painstaking and determined historical detective work! The presentation of results may be a bit daunting at first read, but I found myself repeatedly returning to this general introduction, with increasing profit, as I became more familiar with the texts themselves and began to think of them synoptically: for every individual anecdote, we are given four "snapshots" of its evolution through time and space.

Another world to which the texts point us is an imaginative world, a world of wonders: the Egyptian desert conceived of as a place where earth and heaven meet. There, saintly individuals can fast from physical food because they are fed with heavenly food (¶17);[2] Christ (e.g., ¶¶12–13, 69) or the prophet Jeremiah (¶9) or the emperor Constantine (¶¶35–40) might drop in for a visit; a Syrian saint can ride home on a cloud (¶52); saints can defeat Satan (e.g., ¶¶14–16, 59–62); and angels protect those who sleep (¶53A). This world of wonders may already be familiar from other literature of the Egyptian desert; *The Life of Bishoi* is a witness to its importance in the imaginations of Eastern Christians, an element in the resilience of Christian cultures that, even in the bleakest historical moments, have sustained the confidence that heaven can touch earth and that Christ dwells with the saints.

But not all is perfect in that imaginative world. *The Life of Bishoi* also reminds us that this is a *distant* world, a *strange* one, not to be too easily romanticized or made into a kind of utopia. Scholars of this ancient literature of the desert ascetics may be used to pointing out (for example) examples of anti-Judaism or misogyny as unfortunately typical. Newcomers to these texts,[3] however, may react to them with deep offense, to the point of wondering *why* they should be invited to read a text that includes something like, say, the story of the monk Isaac and the Jewish woman (¶¶64–67)—a story that became *more*, not less, misogynistic over the passage of time. Perhaps Content Warnings are in order?[4] As someone who loves the literature of the desert Christians and who has used it in teaching "spiritual formation" courses, I find in such passages a call to some soul-searching (and syllabus revision): perhaps in my teaching I have implied the quasi-canonical status of texts that cannot and should not be expected to bear that weight.

In spite of the strangeness of these texts about the ancient desert Christians, and increasing awareness of the ways in which they participate in human fallenness, I and many others have regularly been surprised by their capacity, across barriers of time and space and culture, to capture mind and heart with questions about what is truly important in a human life. What sticks with me about the portrayal[5] of St. Bishoi in the *Life* is not his feats of fasting or his mystical conversations, but rather his humility and care for others, some of whom have lost their way or "fallen into some kind of mental and spiritual depression."[6]

There is some irony in this portrayal. Bishoi had a "longing desire" (*eros* in the Greek *Life*) for God, to be lived out in "contemplative solitude" (*hēsychía*). In his introduction,[7] Tim Vivian has a fascinating discussion of the importance of this for a Christian reclamation of the category of the erotic. However, the *Life* is not finally a story about a solitary figure whose "heart was on fire" (¶69) with love for God, but rather a story about a person who, *despite* an intense desire for solitude, became a teacher, intercessor, guide, and head of a community (¶¶33–34, 48–49). It is not the solitary lover of God, but rather the one who "spiritually struggles *and ministers to others*," whom Christ calls "my son and heir" (¶49, Greek, my emphasis).

The ancient request made to the desert teachers was for "a word" to live by.[8] I heard "a word" to me in this call to teach and guide, in spite of desires to invest my time in "higher" (in my case, purely academic) things. Other readers of the literature of the desert ascetics have had similar experiences. So, I believe I can say: Read on, in the hope that, for all the text's distance and strangeness, you will hear "a life-giving word" about "problems . . . and disciplines . . . [that] are directly and profoundly our business."[9] Even if not, you'll gain insight into the faith that has sustained ancient Christian communities, from the time of the historical Bishoi down to our own day.

Notes

1. Note the treatment of anger (¶¶48, ϛ) and vainglory (¶77).
2. And note the account of a monastic "intervention" at ¶58.
3. I have in mind some of my own students, who have been formed by the Black Lives Matter and the Me Too movements, and who have known far too many instances of violence directed at faith communities.
4. This was the solution of one of my students in a report for my "Desert Discipleship" class during spring semester, 2019.
5. Or better, "portrayals." I note the way that the descriptions of Anba Bishoi and his teachings become more down to earth, as we move from the Greek to the other versions; see, for example, ¶63.
6. From the Introduction to the Geʿez *Life*, p. 200.
7. The introduction to chapter one, "The Greek *Life of Païsios* in Translation."
8. As in ¶63, Greek.
9. Rowan Williams quoted at the end of Tim Vivian's introduction to chapter one, p. 46.

General Introduction
Saint Bishoi of Scetis

Maged S.A. Mikhail

Our Righteous Father, the perfect man, the beloved of our Good Savior
—Coptic Diptych

Saint Bishoi of Scetis (d. ca. 417) enjoys tremendous popularity throughout the Christian East, and particularly among the Copts. "Bishūy" is a common name within that community, busloads of pilgrims visit the saint's monastery at Scetis (Shihēt/Wadi al-Natrun) every week, and his life has been made into a full-length movie. The saint and his monastery only increased in popularity since the 1980s as the late Coptic Patriarch, H.H. Pope Shenouda III (Patr. 1971–2012), established his patriarchal residence adjacent to the monastery, which rendered it the leading monastery in Egypt.

The historical Bishoi lived during what may be easily regarded as the Golden Age of Scetis, a remarkable era in which a litany of larger-than-life monastics lived and interacted with one another.[1] Even among such elite company, however, Bishoi stood out as the founder of one of the four great monasteries of Scetis: those of Macarius, John the Little, Bishoi, and the Roman Fathers (al-Barāmūs).[2] In fact, Bishoi is the patron of two monasteries at Scetis. As the Aphthartodocetic controversy ripped through anti-Chalcedonian ranks in Egypt during the first half of the sixth century,[3] pitting the followers of Severus of Antioch against those of Julian of Halicarnassus, monks from the Monastery of St. Bishoi likely founded the neighboring community, "the Monastery of the Mother of God of the Syrians of Abba Bishoi," which is best known as "the Monastery of the Syrians" *(Dayr al-Suryān)*. Soon, as the Aphthartodocetic controversy faded into the footnotes of the history of Christology, both monasteries flourished as monuments to the memory of the saint. Among other points of interest, ancient and modern visitors to the Monastery of the Syrians have always sought out

1

the cave where the saint tied his hair to the ceiling to force himself to stay awake praying (*Life of Bishoi* [*LBsh*] ¶20), and the Tree of Ephrem, which is associated with that saint's visit to Bishoi (¶¶50–51).[4] Moreover, several of the Syriac manuscripts of the *LBsh* discussed below came from the Monastery of the Syrians, which still retains the oldest known manuscript.

Sometime in 407, Scetis was sacked by barbarians, prompting many monastics, including John the Little and Bishoi, to depart for other regions.[5] At that juncture, Bishoi fled to Middle Egypt, where his legacy became intertwined with that of Paul of Tamma. The two saints lived together perhaps for as long as a decade (407–17) and their relics remain together until this day.[6] Eventually, as detailed in greater length below, their relics were translated to what would become known as Dayr Anba Bishoi at al-Barsha in Antinoë/Ansina, and, subsequently, they were brought to Bishoi's monastery at Wadi al-Natrun in the ninth century.

In spite of Bishoi's prominence, his biography has received only sporadic, scattered attention. It survives in Greek, Syriac, Ethiopic, Arabic, and Garshuni[7] recensions, though, oddly, no Coptic text survives. The goal of this study is to make the various recensions of his hagio-biography more accessible to both scholars and the general public,[8] particularly those interested in early Christian and monastic spirituality or Egyptian (Coptic) Christianity. Another goal is to provide discussions and commentary on the literary and historical heritage of these texts, several aspects of which may be appreciated only by contrasting the various recensions. Finally, the volume presents new editions and translations for *LBsh* based on the oldest accessible manuscripts. The Greek text provided in chapter two, though not intended to be a critical edition as such, is based on four of the earliest accessible manuscripts, only one of which has been edited, by Pomialovskii in 1902, and none previously translated. Similarly, the English translation of the Syriac recension is based on an unpublished manuscript that provides a far more reliable textual witness than the sole edition published by Paul Bedjan in 1892. An edition of that manuscript is forthcoming. In a similar vein, the Arabic translation is based on the oldest accessible manuscript for that recension. The Ge'ez (Ethiopic) version of the *Life*, the first translation into English, is based on the critical edition published by Gérard Colin in 2002. The remainder of this general introduction focuses on the meaning of the saint's name and identity, the translation of his relics, a controversial pericope in the *Life*, and the textual history of *LBsh*.

Bishoi's Name and Identity

The saint is known by various names throughout history. Not only has his name changed somewhat as various scribes translated his hagio-biography from one language into another but, at least in Syriac and Arabic, fluctuations in orthography and the phonetic pronunciation of the name are well attested. Moreover, confusion as to the different figures who share the name "Bishoi" persists among the laity and within scholarly literature, along with uncertainty surrounding the meaning of his name.

Attempts at discerning the meaning of the saint's name often beg a basic question: which of the dominant forms—Gr. Paîsios, Cop. P[i]shōi, Syr. Bishoi [Byshwyhy], Eth. Bsoy, Ar. Bishūy, Bishiyyah, and Bishāy—should be considered original and which are derivatives? The etymology would be preserved in the original form of the name, but not necessarily within its variants. To that end, Evelyn-White forwarded a problematic etymology of Paîsios that calls for reading this Greek form, which is not attested in any non-Greek manuscript, according to a mixed, Greek–Coptic, etymology: *pa*-Isis, "he who belongs to Isis." Reading the name as Coptic, however, resolves this oddity. The original etymology is likely closer to "Pa-Shai," i.e., "he who belongs to Shai"—the popular Egyptian god of fate. Unconcerned with linguistic accuracy per se, *LBsh* provides an etymology of the name in ¶7 by way of a ubiquitous hagiographic trope that underscores the meaning of a saint's name.[9] The passage maintains that Abba Amoi (Gr. Pambo/Syr. Bemoi) called the saint "Sunrise," or "the Shining Father." Behind the gloss is a wordplay that understands *shoi* as a synonym for the verb *shai*, "to rise," which also designates "dawn."[10] Confusion between *shoi* and *shai* is reflected in the common Arabic variant for the saint's name, "Bishāy," which is also attested in Syriac.[11]

Given that the wordplay is intelligible only in Coptic, the form "Pshōi" should be considered original. This passage (¶7) is attested in the Arabic, Syriac, Garshuni, and Ethiopic recensions, but the extant Greek manuscripts (see below), while retaining the structure and wording of the trope in part, fail to comprehend the wordplay and do not retain it. This, among other clues (discussed below), indicates that the accessible Greek recension, while preserving early readings and passages of *LBsh*, is not the oldest. Regardless of which language *LBsh* was originally drafted in, whoever penned the autograph must have understood the wordplay on the saint's name in Coptic.

The popularity of the name and its cognates has led to a great deal of confusion within the historical record.[12] Here, the first three figures discussed shared the same name in Greek (Paîsios), Coptic (Pshoi), Ethiopic (Bsoy), Syriac and Arabic (Bishoi, Bishay; but also, Ibshāy, Bīshā), while the other four shared one or more variants of it. (1) The first and most famous bearer of the name is our saint, Paîsios or Bishoi of Scetis (d. ca. 417), the focus of this study. Commemorated on 8 Abib (July 15), this saint was born in Egypt and never left the province. Moreover, there is no evidence that he spoke a language other than Coptic, or was ordained to a clerical rank. Most likely, this saint also carried the designation "Bishoi of Jeremiah."[13] *LBsh* records that the saint was particularly fond of the Book of Jeremiah; he memorized it, and the prophet would come and explain it to him (¶9). (2) A second figure is Païsios/Bishoi of Constantinople, the author of the *Life of Maximus and Domitius*. This Bishoi was a Greek-speaker and a citizen of Constantinople, who came under the guidance of Macarius the Great. In the manuscript record, he is identified as "the Archdeacon of Constantinople, who became the first Archdeacon in the desert of Scetis."[14] (3) A third saint with an identical name is Bishoi of Akhmim (or Sohag), the founder of the famed Red Monastery, who was associated with Saint Shenoute of Atripe. He is commemorated on 5 Amshir (February 12).

Other saints are more marginal, but have also been conflated with one or more of the above-named saints. (4) One figure is Bishoi Anub (Bishay Anub), a martyr commemorated on 19 Ba'ūna (June 26), though confusion here seems to be minimal, given that "Anub" is typically given as part of his name. (5) Another Bishoi (Bishay) was also a martyr; he is commemorated on 29 Ba'ūna (July 6). (6) The final Egyptian figure sharing this name is Saint Pshōi of Tud, a seventh-century monastic in Upper Egypt, who was the patron saint, or possibly the founder, of a monastery.[15] He is commemorated on 25 Kiyahk (January 3). (7) Outside of Egypt, phonetic similarity led to confusion between Bishoi of Scetis and the late eighth-century East Syrian Saint Beh Isho', whose biography is a version of *LBsh*.[16] Having distinguished the various saints who shared this name, the focus now shifts to the traditions surrounding the translation of the saint's relics to Scetis/Wadi al-Natrun.

Translation of Relics

It is essential to delineate the two translations of the relics of saints Bishoi and Paul of Tamma (¶79). The sequence of these events is hopelessly confused in the *Synaxarium* and most modern studies,[17] though they inform how we may read and date various recensions of *LBsh*. Two details are consistent across all texts: the saints died at different times, and at different locations. Moreover, the pattern of translation is nearly identical across most manuscripts, though the proper names of the individuals involved and the location where the relics were deposited differ. The following description is based on Manuscript *Family B* [MS *FamB*] and *Family C* [MS *FamC*] (see below for the manuscript families and recensions); the account in MS *FamA* retains the same overall pattern parsed here, though it forwards a problematic reference addressed separately below in the context of *LBsh*'s textual history. Notably, the long recension of the *Life of Paul of Tamma* places the death of Paul at Aswan rather than Antaiopolis/Qaw, as proposed below.[18] In general, while the *Lives* of Bishoi and Paul maintain that the saints were buried together,[19] the details in Paul's *Life* are irreconcilable with those in *LBsh*. Moreover, while Bishoi appears in two passages in the *Life of Paul*, the close relationship between the two saints carefully cultivated in *LBsh* is lacking in that text.[20]

Bishoi passed away ca. 417, at what *Recension WN2 Ar1* identifies as Minyat al-Saqr (or al-Saqar); it, along with the Ethiopic Mukyāduḥ and the Syrian Mounēya Duwany, remains unidentified. "Minya" is most likely a port district,[21] perhaps that of Panopolis or Hierakonopolis.[22] Regardless, the details of the account position that location south of Antaiopolis/Qaw.[23] After Bishoi's death, Paul of Tamma relocated to the north and passed away a few months later. Hearing of Bishoi's passing, an abbot from a monastery at Antinoë/Ansina traveled south on a boat to procure his relics.[24] The Arabic *(Rec. WN2 Ar.1)* identifies the abbot as "Athanasius" of Ansina, while the Syriac, Garshuni, and Ethiopic texts identify him as [S-y-r-w-s] "Siyrwūs" or "Siyrawes" of Ansina. (The Greek recensions' identification of "Isidoros" is discussed below). Athanasius is otherwise unknown, but Siyrwūs is likely the "Sūrus" of Ansina and Asyut, referred to in the *Life of Paul of Tamma*,[25] and is likely synonymous with the Apa Soures (or Sourous) attested in several Coptic inscriptions alongside Bishoi and Paul—though those inscriptions are farther north, at Saqqara.[26]

The abbot acquired Bishoi's relics, but on the trip back north to Ansina the boat halted near the location of Paul's burial. Two days later, an anchorite Jeremiah—whose name is consistent across all recensions—informed the crew that the bodies of Bishoi and Paul must remain together. Jeremiah is likely the noted anchorite, and perhaps the founder of the Monastery of Jeremiah, that is, Dayr Anba Harmina, near Antaiopolis (Tkoou/Qaw al-Kabir).[27] Once the crew brought Paul's remains on board, the boat sailed, and the abbot proceeded to deposit the remains of both saints at his monastery, where they remained until the 840s. This monastery is almost certainly Dayr al-Barsha, near Antinoë/Ansina. This first translation of relics occurred within the fifth century, though the *Synaxarium* does not cite it. Still, it grafts the account of the immovable ship onto the narrative of the later translation from the second quarter of the ninth century.

The second translation proceeded during a unique historical juncture—the late eighth to early ninth centuries—during which several monasteries were renovated and the relics of many saints were translated to Scetis/Wadi al-Natrun.[28] These translations included the relics of saints who had left the wadi in the fifth century due to violent barbarian raids. Hence, at the end of the eighth century, the remains of John the Little were translated to his monastery at Wadi al-Natrun,²⁹ but Bishoi's and Paul's relics had to wait. The second and third decades of the ninth century were extremely turbulent. In 817, the Fifth Sacking of Scetis devastated the monasteries of the region, and the Fourth Fitna (civil war) between al-Amīn and al-Ma'mūn for control of the caliphate, and its turbulent aftermath, along with the ensuing Bashmūric Revolt in the Delta, brought a great deal of chaos and violence to Lower Egypt.³⁰ With great effort, the government restored order in the mid-830s, and by the 840s the *History of the Patriarchs* reports that the monasteries prospered and an era of "grace and peace" commenced.³¹

Sometime in the 840s, Patriarch Yusāb I (Joseph: 830–49) called for the second translation of the relics of Bishoi and Paul.³² (One manuscript provides an exact date: 4 Kiyahk AM 558/30 November AD 841.)³³ Thus, the relics were translated from Ansina to the Monastery of St. Bishoi at Wadi al-Natrun; it is this translation that is recorded in the *Synaxarium*.³⁴ As demonstrated below, the drafting of the exemplar for *LBsh* MS *FamB* almost certainly occurred prior to this event, though the normative shape of the recension at the core of that family came about in the wadi. On the whole, the monastic centers at Ansina had been in decline since the late eighth century, and the Coptic patriarch instigated the translation of the relics. Moreover, beyond the fame and antiquity of the monasteries of Wadi al-Natrun, the wadi was quickly developing into one of the preeminent centers of ecclesiastical authority in the Coptic Church.³⁵ The procurement of relics bolstered that prestige.

Later, by the early fourteenth century, the Monastery of Anba Bishoi had fallen into disrepair, and suffered from what appears to have been a major termite infestation. Patriarch Benjamin II, who visited the wadi in AD 1330, spearheaded the restoration efforts, which included the consecration of a church (though, perhaps, only an altar).³⁶ The renovation proceeded so swiftly that we are told that "if not for human weakness, [the workers] would have seen angels aiding in the restoration."³⁷ Significantly, the earliest reference to the tradition of the incorruptibility of Bishoi's body dates to the fourteenth century (see below), and at least one source directly links it to the patriarch's visit.³⁸

Purgation in the Desert

Undoubtedly, the most sensitive account in *LBsh* is in ¶¶22–31. In that detailed narrative, Bishoi's intercessions with Christ on behalf of a fallen monk result in the latter's release from "Gehenna." Previously, he was supposed to remain in punishment there until the "Lord returns upon a cloud." Resoundingly, the pericope is disquieting in the East today, but it is imperative to note that the medieval audiences who heard the account, and the scribes who copied the Greek, Arabic, Syriac (including two different abbreviated recensions), Garshuni, and Ethiopic versions of *LBsh*, were clearly not as disturbed by it; hence, they retained it in all these recensions and manuscripts. Premodern audiences focused on the saint's intercessory powers, not the purgation aspect per se.

Nonetheless, though attested in all the Arabic manuscripts surveyed, the account is lacking in every modern Arabic publication[39] save one, which appends a scolding footnote stating that the account is "contrary to divine justice, logic, and the Holy Bible."[40] We see a similar attitude in P. Bedjan's edition of the Syriac *LBsh*,[41] in which he transcribed the first three lines of BnF Syr. 236 fol. 25v, but then placed a series of ellipses and shifted the focus to an account based on another manuscript, and then commenced with fol. 26v. He must have read, and decided to forgo, the remainder of fol. 25v and all of fol. 26r—which preserve the account in question. All indications are that he intentionally omitted this account. A more malicious approach may be observed in the unpublished BL.Or. (Syr.) 963 [Add. 14,732.8], where the pertinent folio (116r–v) was hastily torn out of the manuscript, leaving behind only a thin sliver of the torn folio still attached to the binding.

Regrettably, the hypersensitivity around this issue, heightened in the modern era due to the East's various encounters with the Roman Catholic Church, is largely misplaced. Purgation is not the same as Purgatory. The latter is a specific Roman Catholic doctrine that, by most accounts, developed in the later twelfth and early thirteenth centuries, gaining its dogmatic articulation at the Second Council of Lyon in 1274.[42] Nonetheless, while the Christian East rejects the doctrine of Purgatory, the Orthodox, Roman Catholic, and Anglican communions are in agreement that prayers for the dead are efficacious (see Job 1:5; 2 Macc 12:42–44), and that on its journey to heaven a soul is prepared or conditioned for the heavenly realm and the encounter with God's glory. In the East, as J. A. McGuckin notes, theological "speculation" on these matters, though common, never achieved the doctrinal status it gained in the West.[43] Moreover, the East tends to conceive of purgation in terms of the purification of the soul in anticipation for the encounter with God as opposed to a notion of judicial punishment per se.

On the whole, references to purgation (as opposed to Purgatory) are not rare in early Christian, patristic, or medieval writings.[44] Such references are scattered throughout the literature of the East in general, and certainly within the writings of the Coptic Orthodox Church:[45] from early references in the writings of Clement of Alexandria, Origen, and Athanasius to the annual Kneeling Prayer (*ṣalāt al-sajdah*), which retained unambiguous references to purgation until 29 May 1999, when the Coptic Holy Synod removed the three most obvious references.[46] In all, the Western doctrine of Purgatory, which interjects specific concepts of time and space in the hereafter, is not accepted in the Christian East, but purgation is a different matter. In the East, there is a long history of speculation on the soul's journey to heaven and how it is purged of "sin that does not lead to death" (1 Jn 5:16–17). Here, the hagiographic account is not commenting on doctrine. Rather, its primary focus is the incredible intercessory power of Saint Bishoi (see also ¶21), God's "chosen one," as the *LBsh* reminds us on at least fifteen different occasions.

A Textual History of the *Life of Bishoi*

Largely unknown in the West until the modern era, the manuscript evidence leaves no doubt as to Saint Bishoi's renown among Christians in the East; pro-Chalcedonians (Greek Orthodox), anti-Chalcedonians (Coptic, Ethiopian, and Syriac Orthodox), and East Syrians (the Church of the East) celebrated his sanctity and reflected on the core of his biography. In Egypt, three monasteries and a host of churches and altars were named after the saint, while his *Life* circulated in several recensions. Among Syriac-speaking Christians, Bishoi's biography transcended the West/East Syrian divide, inspired religious poetry,[47] and provided the textual basis for commemorating an East Syrian saint.[48]

With few exceptions, the extant manuscripts of the *Life of Bishoi* [*LBsh*] are far removed from the recensions they document, each text preserving a fossilized form of multi-tiered, evolving recensions that are not easily disentangled. Nonetheless, keeping in mind the above discussion of the two translations of the saint's relics, the textual history of *LBsh* may now be written in broad strokes. This analysis clusters the available manuscripts and recensions into three text families, or types, and provides tentative dates for the emergence of each family. Notably, while two families are dominated by manuscripts in the same language, allegiance to a family is, nonetheless, based on textual similarities, not language per se. Hence, MS *FamB* is attested in Syriac, Garshuni, and Ethiopic manuscripts, and, doubtless, an Arabic version existed as well.

The archetype [Ω]

As often noted, John the Little's purported authorship of *LBsh* is an impossibility given that he died before Bishoi, and that they separated later in life. At best, John would have been able to comment only on Bishoi's stint at Shihēt/Scetis. For their part, medieval scribes accepted the traditional attribution, but also attempted to account for the narratives they penned (see ¶79). Be that as it may, the accessible manuscripts conceal Ω quite well: hence, the language of original composition remains obscure, and while the complete absence of a Coptic *Life* for the saint remains enigmatic, and a Coptic original is not inconceivable, the evidence suggests a Greek exemplar. Demonstrably, all manuscripts postdate Ω by several generations and present longer versions of that autograph.

Ω survives in recensions that adhere to three text families. Distinctive readings and pericopes establish the direct reliance of MS *FamC* on *FamB*; the link between MS *FamA* and *FamB*, however, and their relationship to Ω remain ambiguous. To be sure, the two manuscript families address the same figure and share a great deal with regard to structure and content. Nonetheless, a pericope from a *FamB* manuscript may forward an abridged or an embellished version of the parallel passage in a *FamA* text. Overall, while the exemplar for MS *FamB*, that is, *Rec. β*, developed before the AD 840 translation of relics, the distinctive readings and features attested in the available manuscripts point to a ninth-century date and the immediate environment of Wadi al-Natrun (hence a date post-AD 840—see below). Here, the reconstruction presumes the primacy of the exemplar for MS *FamA*, *Rec. α*, and maintains that the exemplar for *FamB*, *Rec. β*, was most likely a heavily reworked manuscript from that family. Hitherto, the earliest manuscript witness for *LBsh* is a tenth-century Syriac manuscript belonging to MS *FamB* (see below), though MS *FamA* recensions must have also been in circulation by that juncture.

MS *Family A*
BHG 1402–3; CPG 2503
(Rec. Gr α, Gr1, and Gr2)

MS *FamA* is hitherto exclusively attested in Greek manuscripts,[49] and appears to present an early form of the *Life*, though the extant manuscripts are several generations removed from Ω and are not older than the exemplar for MS *FamB (Rec. β)*. *FamA* manuscripts retain the normative structure of *LBsh*, and read: ¶¶1–80. Thus far, this recension is attested in thirty-three manuscripts,[50] some of which retain the entirety of the biography, while others are incomplete or preserve only excerpts. The exemplar for this family, *Rec. α*, was likely drafted sometime between the seventh and early ninth centuries,[51] though the earliest witness to the extant recension, *Rec. Gr.1*, is the incomplete BnF suppl. gr. 759, which dates to the late twelfth century. It is one of the manuscripts included in the critical apparatus for the Greek text and translation forwarded in this volume.

The priority of MS *FamA* is likely, given that several pericopes lacking in this Family (that is, ¶¶α–ν) are better interpreted as later amendments rather than intentional omissions, and that its reading of ¶¶41 and 53B ff., discussed below, is likely earlier than that presented in the other families.

Another characteristic of *Rec. Gr1* is that while various aspects position it squarely within the Egyptian hagiographic tradition,[52] the recension is, nonetheless, loosely grounded in Egypt's topography. By contrast, MS *FamB* (and, by extension, *FamC*) typically replace generic designations (e.g., "city") with the names of specific Egyptian towns.[53] Moreover, *FamB* appends references to well-known hagiographic accounts (e.g., the Tree of Obedience and Macarius' encounter with Hieracas; ¶¶8, 41).[54] What emerges in MS *FamA* is a saint whose association with Egypt is incidental, while in the other families Bishoi and his *Life* are thoroughly Egyptian.

Rec. Gr1 also retains a unique tradition that explicitly places the relics of Bishoi and Paul of Tamma outside Egypt,[55] in Pisidia in Cappadocia (modern Antalya, on the southern coast of Turkey).[56] It is unlikely that *Rec. α* forwarded this problematic reading. No other source maintains that the saints' relics were housed at, or translated to or from, that region. Moreover, it is not readily apparent why the otherwise unattested Isidore of Pisidia would travel to Middle Egypt (Antinoë/Ansina) to recover the relics of two Egyptian saints who, at that point, were relatively unknown beyond the province or to the Greek tradition.[57] A variant tradition, *Rec. Gr2*, cited by some secondary sources, but hitherto not directly read in the manuscripts, attempts to resolve this tension by identifying "Isidore" as Isidore of Pelusium (d. ca. 450)—a saint recognized by pro- and anti-Chalcedonians. Nonetheless, that tradition faces similar challenges: Isidore appears suddenly in the narrative, and there is no tradition for the translation of the saints' relics to or from Pelusium.

It is possible that ¶79 in *Rec. Gr1* is primarily concerned with positioning the saint (and his divine patronage) within a pro-Chalcedonian context, rather than with historicity per se.[58] Another possibility is that the recension conflates Païsios (Bishoi) of Scetis (clearly the subject of this biography) with Païsios (Bishoi) of Constantinople, the author of the *Life of Maximus and Domitios*, discussed above.[59] The confusion is common enough. Notably, other than who procured the remains of Bishoi and Paul, and where they were deposited, all the miraculous details associated with the translation of the relics—attested in the three manuscript families—follow a well-established Egyptian topos: the divinely guided ship.[60]

MS Family B
BHO 181–182
(Rec. β, WN1 γ, SA δ, SA Syr1, SA Syr1–Short1, SA Syr1–Short2, SA Syr2, SA Eth, SA Gar)
This is the most linguistically diverse manuscript family. It constitutes the "Semitic" recensions of *LBsh*; that is, the Arabic, Syriac, Garshuni, and

Ethiopic versions of *LBsh* that circulated among Christians living under Islamic rule. Many surviving Greek manuscripts doubtless circulated under Islamic rule as well, but MS *FamB* appended new traditions to *LBsh*, redrafted existing pericopes to address Islamic polemics (¶¶41 and 53B–56), and introduced two declarative passages focused on intracommunal tensions at Wadi al-Natrun (¶¶ι and κ).

Structurally, while retaining the same order of accounts as MS *FamA*, *FamB* exhibits several distinctive features:

A) It interjects new pericopes, ¶¶α–μ, in the following order: ¶¶1–29, 31–37, 39–67, α–ε, 68–75, ζ–μ, 76, [77A, 78A, 77B, 78B], 79–80. Later, some *FamC* manuscripts also appended ¶ν. Several of the new additions present autonomous pericopes, though a few are carefully interconnected to other parts of the *Life*, especially ¶μ and the details of the translations of the saints' relics in ¶79. The additions are:

 α. A Lesson about Theft
 β. Instructions to Monks on Attending Festivals and Visiting Shrines
 γ. Bishoi and John Flee Scetis after a Barbarian Invasion
 δ. Bishoi Instructs on Dogma, Sacrament, and Love
 ε. Bishoi Tests the Brothers; Isaac Answers Correctly
 ζ. Bishoi Teaches about Anger
 η. Bishoi as an Abbot
 θ. Bishoi Teaches a Disgruntled Monk about Work
 ι. The Hierarchy of the Four Great Monasteries
 κ. On the Position of Bishoi's Monastery in Wadi al-Natrun
 λ. The Healing Well at Bishoi's Monastery
 μ. Bishoi and Paul Accept a Disciple
 ν. Bishoi Carries the Lord (see appendix)

B) Paragraphs 77 and 78 are rearranged in the following manner, ¶¶77A, 78A, 77B, 78B.
C) It lacks ¶¶30 and 38, which are likely later additions to *Rec. G1*.
D) ¶79 clearly positions the relics of Bishoi and Paul of Tamma in Egypt, in anti-Chalcedonian hands, and forwards an extended narrative focused on the translation of their remains to what may be identified as Dayr al-Barsha, near Antinoë/Ansina.
E) Several passages were redrafted to better resonate within a post-Umayyad (AD 661–750) socioreligious setting (¶¶41, 53B ff., 65).[61]
F) Saint Macarius and his monastery are repeatedly cited.

This final aspect is striking. References to Saint Macarius and his monastery are entirely lacking in MS *FamA*, yet high praise and extended passages focused on both are scattered throughout MS *FamB* (¶¶12, 41, 51, 1), and an additional reference is appended to the concluding paragraph in *FamC* manuscripts.

MS *FamB* originated prior to the mid-ninth century; that much is certain. In a crucial passage near the end of ¶79, the author states that the bodies of Saints Bishoi and Paul continue to perform miracles up to his day, and that he is assured of this from "faithful, trustworthy people who came from the city of Ansina."[62] Unambiguously, this passage places the saints' relics in Antinoë/Ansina rather than at Wadi al-Natrun; hence, MS *FamB Rec. β* must predate the translation of the saints' relics to the wadi in the 840s.

Other features of MS *FamB* also point to a ninth-century provenance. Thematically, while the *LBsh* consistently associates Bishoi with John the Little, Bishoi is entirely lacking in the eighth-century *Life of John the Little* by Zacharias of Sakhā. His omission from the lengthy list of monastic saints at the conclusion of the first paragraph of that *Life* is particularly glaring. On the whole, Zacharias appears to have been unaware of *LBsh*, though the authors of *Rec. α* and, with more certainty, *Rec. β* were acquainted with the *Life of John the Little*.[63] Another clue is the above-mentioned redrafting of pericopes to function as implicit Christian apologetic. *Rec. Gr1* ¶41 forwards a brief defense of the doctrine of the Trinity, which was routinely attacked by Jewish and, later, Muslim polemicists. In MS *FamB*, Bishoi's terse response morphs into a lengthy, scripturally based defense.

Even more revealing, where in *Rec. Gr1* ¶53B a Jewish merchant argues that Jesus was not the awaited messiah, in MS *FamB* his comment is replaced with the prevalent Islamic assertion, based on Qur'ān 4:157, that Jesus was not crucified but rather someone who resembled him.[64] (Placing Islamic critiques and polemics on Jewish lips is a common literary strategy in Christian Arabic literature.) The account then proceeds to detail the dire spiritual consequences for accepting such a claim (¶¶54–57). Documenting the polemic and couching a response in a hagiographic text, which would have been read by—and, more importantly, to—the laity rather than theologians, *mutakallimūn*, points to an era of increased contact between Christians and Muslims in Egypt. Such a dynamic hardly existed under the Umayyads, but is easily reconciled with the socioreligious environment that prevailed under early Abbasid rule (post-750).[65] Finally, one finds Arabic toponyms (e.g., Fustat, ¶64) and terminology ('*āmil*, ¶14) across all recensions of this family. Consistently, the ninth century emerges as the most likely period for the genesis of the extant recensions of MS *FamB*.

Leaving aside the question of "when" and turning to the question of "where" *Rec. β* was drafted brings us back to the authorial gloss in ¶79: "I have learned [these things] from faithful, trustworthy people who came from the city of Ansina. They came to the Monastery of Saint Abba Shenoute, prayed in it, and informed us concerning all things." This positions the drafting of *Rec. β* at a "Monastery of St. Shenoute." This gloss is crucial in delineating the two major branches of this family (*WN1* and *SA*), and in tracking the circulation of *LBsh* in Egypt. Now, this specific Shenoutian reading is from MS *FamC*, which likely emerged in the 1300s, when the saint's relics had long been deposited at Wadi al-Natrun; hence, the assumption that the gloss is a carryover from the much earlier MS *FamB Rec. β*. (Less likely, though still possible, is that this is the location in which the exemplar for MS *FamC* emerged.) Here, we proceed with the most likely scenario: namely, that MS *FamB Rec. β* was drafted at a "Monastery of Saint Shenoute." But which one? The monastery in question may have been the famed White Monastery near Sohag, which had a steady stream of pilgrims throughout the Middle Ages, or, less likely, the saint's monastery in Ansina.[66] Still, the little-known Monastery of St. Shenoute in al-Fayyum provides another alternative.[67] Al-Fayyum had several manuscript-copying centers, including the famous Touton, which provided manuscripts to the monasteries of Wadi al-Natrun.[68]

The contents of the lost archetype, *Rec. β*, drafted before the translation of relics ca. 840, remain hypothetical. It certainly retained the tradition of the translation of relics to Dayr al-Barsha (Ansina) and likely appended ¶¶α–ε, and perhaps ¶¶ζ, η, and θ as well. As that text made its way to Wadi al-Natrun, perhaps alongside or shortly after the translation of the saints' relics, the normative recension that lies at the core of MS *FamB*, that is, *Rec. WN1*, emerged. It is possible that *Rec. β* and *WN1* γ are one and the same, though that seems unlikely. Whether drafted in al-Fayyum, Ansina, or Atripe, it is doubtful that *Rec. β* would have: 1) repeatedly interjected Saint Macarius and his monastery at such great length and detail into the biography (¶¶12, 41, 51, ι); 2) weighed in so decisively on the contentious issue of the hierarchy among the monasteries of Wadi al-Natrun, as in ¶¶ι and κ[69] (pre-ninth century hagiography lacks this aspect altogether);[70] or 3) included a tradition that is exclusive to Bishoi's monastery at Wadi al-Natrun (¶λ). These same reasons also argue against the priority of the Saint Antony recensions (*SA*), below, as opposed to that of *WN1*. A *Rec. WN1* must have existed, though, hitherto, it remains unattested among the manuscripts surveyed.

At some point prior to the late tenth century (the date of Syr. Monast. 30D), a manuscript belonging to *Rec. WN1* made its way to the Monastery of Saint Antony, where the second major recension—*Rec. SA* δ—developed.

Rec. SA δ is primarily distinguished by the crucial scribal gloss at ¶79, which was altered to read: "as we were told by faithful, trustworthy people who came from the city of Ansina *to the Monastery of Saint Abba Antony.*"

Rec. SA δ retained this distinctive Antonite reading and served as the basis for six closely related recensions. One is an Ethiopic translation: *Rec. SA Eth*. Gérard Colin edited and translated two fifteenth-century Ethiopic manuscripts of this recension into French; he believed that the texts reflected two different Arabic manuscripts.[71] Robert Kitchen has translated Colin's Ethiopic text into English in chapter three, below. In general, monks at St. Antony's Monastery translated a long list of Christian Arabic literature into Ethiopic from the early 1200s until the monastery's destruction in 1484, and again after its restoration in 1540. These translation projects included the *Synaxarium*, *Kitāb al-bustān*, and al-Ṣafī ibn al-'Assāl's *Nomocanon (al-Majmū')*, to name but the most prominent texts.[72] Given the date of the manuscripts Colin utilized, *Rec. SA Eth* must have been completed during the first phase, prior to 1484. Notably, among several unique readings, the recension retains a tradition at the conclusion of ¶ε that identifies Bishoi's successor as the monk Isaac (the subject of ¶¶ε and 64–66).

Rec. SA δ is also attested in Syriac:[73] *Rec. SA Syr1*. The earliest surviving version of this recension is also the earliest known manuscript within the whole dossier: the tenth-century Monastery of the Syrians Syr. MS D.30, fols.139r–166r. Caution is required here, since only the first and last folios (139r and 165v–166r) are accessible.[74] Nonetheless, this manuscript retains the Antonite reading and a comparison with BL.Or. (Syr.) 971 (see below) yielded only a few, insignificant variants. Hence, at the moment, the earliest surviving manuscript for *LBsh* is a Syriac manuscript based on an Antonite recension preserved at the Syrian Monastery in Wadi al-Natrun.

In itself, this is significant. The history of the Monastery of St. Antony is not well documented from the eighth to the twelfth centuries, though the meager evidence suggests that the monastery had a strong Syrian presence—if it was not entirely under Syrian leadership for much of that period.[75] This manuscript reflects the existence of a channel of communication and exchange between the Syrian monks at St. Antony's by the Red Sea and those at the Syrian Monastery in Wadi al-Natrun. Notably, the manuscript resists identifying the "Syrian elder" who visited Bishoi as St. Ephrem (¶¶50–51), though he is noted on the margin.[76] In fact, only the Salomon Manuscript, below, identifies the elder as Ephrem in the main text of *LBsh*, and only one recension of the *Life of Ephrem* mentions the encounter.[77]

The complete *Rec. SA Syr1* is attested in an unpublished thirteenth-century manuscript, BL.Or. (Syr.) 971 [Add. 14,735], fols. 24v–50v, in what W. Wright described as a "rather inelegant hand."[78] It is translated here into English (chapter four), and an edition of the Syriac text is forthcoming. It reads: ¶¶1–29, 31–37, 39–67, α–ε, 68–75, ζ–μ, 67–76, [77A, 78A, 77B, 78B], 79–80. *SA Syr1* is also attested in a Garshuni manuscript *(Rec. SA Gar)* at the Syriac Orthodox Monastery of Saint Mark in Jerusalem: MS 199A, fols. 66r–a – 80r–b. In AD 1733–34, Bishāra of Aleppo had completed this translation at Dayr al-Zaʿfarān. Its colophon (fol. 750v) maintains that the translation is of a Syriac manuscript dated AD 1178/9 (AG 1490).[79] Of the two *SA* recensions discussed thus far,[80] *Rec. Gar* consistently agrees with the structure and wording of *SA Syr1* more than any other manuscript or recension surveyed here, with *SA Eth* constituting the next-closest relative.

MS *FamB*, *Rec. SA Syr1* served as the basis for three subsequent recensions. The first, *Rec. SA Syr1–Short1*, is represented by BnF Syr. 236, fols. 21r–33r (AD 1193–94).[81] P. Bedjan used this manuscript as the basis for his 1892 edition of the Syriac *LBsh*, but, regrettably, he fundamentally misinterpreted this manuscript and poorly represented it in his edition. Bedjan read Syr. 236 as a text filled with lacunae, which he supplied from a private manuscript placed at his disposal by his friend M. Salomon. Nonetheless, Syr. 236 is a complete manuscript that retains an intentionally abridged recension of *LBsh* (see the introduction to the Syriac *LBsh*, below). It reads: ¶¶1–29, 31,[82] 35–37, 39–40, 47–48,[83] 53A–57, 64–67, 69A–74, η–*short*, 78B, 80. A second dependent recension is also "short": MS University of Cambridge Add. 2016 *(SA Syr1–Short2)*. Similar to Syr. 236, while the accounts appear whole, passages of various lengths, from words to whole pericopes, are excised. Nonetheless, it is undoubtedly a work independent of Syr. 236. The manuscript reads: ¶¶1–13, 17–29, 31–37, 39–40, 44–48, 50–57, 59–67, α–ε, 68–75, η–μ, 76, [77A, 78A, 77B, 78B], 79–80. Neither of the short recensions retains ¶ζ, but *SA Syr1–Short2* does retain versions of all the other distinctive pericopes of MS *FamB*.

A third recension dependent on *SA Syr1* is *SA Syr2*, which is attested in another thirteenth-century manuscript, BL.Or. Syr. 963 [Add. 14,732.8], fols. 113r–129v (written in a meticulous west-Syrian hand), and the "Salomon Manuscript" used by P. Bedjan. Both texts follow the same structure as *SA Syr1*, but their contiguous text unknowingly jumps over a large gap from the end of ¶52 to the middle of ¶60; hence, this recension reads ¶¶1–29, 31–37, 39–52 || 60–67, α–ε, 68–75, ζ–μ, 67–76, [77A, 78A, 77B, 78B], 79–80. In his edition of the Syriac *LBsh*, Bedjan made a serendipitous error. On page 595, which purports to transcribe BnF Syr. 236, which lacks this textual anomaly, Bedjan quietly switched to the Salomon Manuscript, the contiguous text of which jumps from ¶52 to mid-¶60, thus permitting the classification of the Salomon Manuscript as a second witness to *SA Syr2*. Still, if Bedjan's transcription is accurate, the Salomon Manuscript likely represents a later generation of that recension. It is the only text that identifies the Syrian elder in ¶¶50–51 as Saint Ephrem in the main text.

MS *Family C*
GCAL I: 539
(Rec. ε, WN2 Ar1, WN2 Ar2)

None of the extant Arabic manuscripts surveyed conforms to MS *FamB*, though such a text surely existed, and likely served as the basis for the Saint Antony recensions (cf. *SA Eth*). Rather, all Arabic manuscripts identified thus far belong to MS *FamC*, which is easily recognized due to its radical reshuffling of pericopes: ¶¶1–19, 35–37, 39–44, 50–57, 20–29, 31–34, 45–46, 68, 58, η–θ, 59–65, 67, α–γ, 69–75, ζ, ι–μ, 76, [77A, 78A, 77B, 78B], 79–80. All Arabic manuscripts read lack ¶¶30, 38, 47–49, 66, δ, and ε (this is the only manuscript family lacking ¶66). Moreover, ¶¶ζ and η are presented in rather short recensions, and there are sentences in ¶¶34, μ, and 78B that reflect a misreading of the Arabic (perhaps Syriac) exemplar for this family. The enigmatic reshuffling might have resulted from the quires of the exemplar manuscript falling out of order and being reassembled with only the introductory and concluding quires as guides. Whatever the case may have been, the exemplar for this family most likely emerged in the fourteenth century at Wadi al-Natrun: *Rec. WN2 ε*.

One of the distinctive readings in this recension is an enigmatic clause (in italics here) introduced in ¶11: "*But if you desire to surpass Moses*, let us keep vigil this whole night." Significantly, the odd phrase is rendered intelligible in the context of a stanza from a fourteenth-century ode from Wadi al-Natrun: "I will liken the face of a man unto our Father Abba Bishoi: for he spoke with Christ, like Moses the Lawgiver."[84] The theme of the saint's ability to speak with God in person and at will is ubiquitous in *LBsh*. Another aspect denoting a later period is the manner in which this recension refers to geographic designations. Earlier readings favor Greek toponyms, but as time went on and Arabic nomenclature became more common, it became necessary to gloss certain terms. Hence, beginning in tenth-century manuscripts, "Antinoë" is often qualified as "Antinoë, that is, Ansina" (see Syriac text ¶¶γ, 71, 79; and Syr. Monastery 30D). Yet, by the time MS *FamC* emerged, "Ansina" altogether replaced "Antinoë."

The oldest identifiable manuscript for this recension is dated AD 1363 (AM 1079). In 1957, Fr. Mīṣā'īl Baḥr published a five-page summary of that manuscript in his study of the *Life* of John the Little.[85] Regrettably, he did not clearly identify the manuscript, though it unambiguously reflects *Rec. WN2 Ar1*, save for a single discrepancy: the placement of ¶β. Still, it is not clear if this is due to an oddity in the manuscript or, more likely, if it was a mistake introduced by Fr. Mīṣā'īl; ¶*y* and all other pericopes cited by him adhere to that recension's peculiar structure.

When *Rec. WN2* emerged and how it came to displace the earlier *Rec. WN1* are not altogether clear. Perhaps this resulted from the reintroduction of the *Life* to the libraries of Wadi al-Natrun after the various devastations of the first half of the fourteenth century. At two junctures (without parallel in any other family or earlier manuscript), this recension notes the public recitation of *LBsh* during the saint's annual commemoration (¶¶1 and ι). Most likely, this was a mid-fourteenth-century phenomenon. The monastery was restored at that juncture, and the traditions surrounding the incorruptibility of Saint Bishoi's body gained popularity and—we may presume—attracted a greater number of pilgrims at that point. The incorruptibility tradition found its way into the Ethiopic *Synaxarium* ca. AD 1400, though, significantly, it is lacking in the Coptic Arabic *Synaxarium*, which achieved its normative wording and structure by 1300. As noted in the above discussion of the translation of the saint's relics, the discovery of the saint's incorruptibility is associated with Benjamin II's patriarchal visit to the monastery in 1330.

A slightly expanded version of *WN2 Ar1* also emerged, *Rec. WN2 Ar2*, which introduced a new account (¶v) in which the saint unknowingly carried his Lord (see the appendix). This incredibly popular tradition serves as the inspiration for much of the saint's modern iconography in the Coptic tradition,[86] though it is unattested in any of the recensions or manuscripts surveyed here. Nonetheless, this pericope is attested in some of the later manuscripts read by the late Fr. Ṣamū'īl al-Suryānī (the later Bishop Ṣamū'īl of Shibīn al-Qanāṭir), a manuscript published by Fr. Ibrāhīm from the monastery of al-Anbā Bishūy,[87] and yet another which the late Fr. Bishūy Kāmil of Sporting, Alexandria, used as the basis for his booklet on *LBsh*.[88] Regrettably, none of these manuscripts is clearly identified. Notably, however, although habitually overlooked, the incorruptibility tradition is foundational to the newly introduced ¶v—*Rec. WN2 Ar2*. A more thorough discussion of the manuscripts and partial editions for *Rec. WN2* is provided in the introduction to the English translation of the Arabic text.

Finally, a note on the public performance or recitation of *LBsh*.[89] While all the available Arabic manuscripts reference this practice (¶¶1 and ι), BnF Ar. 4796 goes on to append a lengthy prayer at the conclusion of the text for the blessing of the congregation. A manuscript from the Church of Our Lady Mary in the village of Kafr al-Saʿidi, read by B. Pirone (identified as *Codex S* in his study), has a similar, though shorter, ending.[90] Here, the recitation and hearing of hagiography is transformed into liturgy.

A Note on Transliterations

Greek transliterations in this volume adhere to the guidelines in the *SBL Handbook of Style*, which have been supplemented with acute and grave accents as well as umlauts to better reflect the Greek original. Syriac transliterations follow the guidelines of *Hugoye: Journal for Syriac Studies*. Transliterations from Ethiopic adhere to Thomas Lambdin's *Introduction to Classical Ethiopic (Ge'ez)*; the Arabic conforms to the guidelines of *International Journal of Middle East Studies*.

Notes

1 William Harmless, *Desert Christians: An Introduction to the Literature of Early Monasticism* (Oxford: Oxford University Press, 2004); H.G. Evelyn-White, ed. Walter Hauser, *The Monasteries of the Wadi 'N Natrun*, 2 vols. (New York: Metropolitan Museum of Art, 1926–32; repr. Arno Press, 1973).

2 Today, most of the laity would omit the Monastery of John the Little and substitute that of the Syrians. Nonetheless, until its abandonment in the fourteenth century, the Monastery of John the Little was undoubtedly second only to the Monastery of St. Macarius in size and number of monks. The order of the monasteries is not neutral, but something of a hierarchy. The same order is maintained in liturgical prayers, including the Diptych/Communion of Saints, and the hymn *pinishti*.

3 The traditional accusation against the Aphthartodocetists, or Phantasiasts, led by Julian of Halicarnassus (d. after 527), is that they taught that the body of Jesus was like that of the pre-Fall rather than the post-Fall Adam. See Yonatan Moss, *Incorruptible Bodies: Christology, Society, and Authority in Late Antiquity* (Berkeley: University of California Press, 2016); Pauline Allen and C.T.R. Hayward, *Severus of Antioch* (New York: Routledge, 2005); Evelyn-White, *Monasteries*, 2:315–16.

4 As discussed below, however, the identification of the Syrian visitor as Ephrem is late.

5 Evelyn-White, *Monasteries*, 2:151–53, 154–60.

6 Earlier in his career, Bishoi had lived with John the Little after Abba Amoi's death (¶8). On being joined at death, see ¶¶μ, 79; Claudia Rapp, *Brother-making in Late Antiquity and Byzantium: Monks, Laymen, and Christian Ritual* (Oxford and New York: Oxford University Press, 2016), 152–57. The *LBsh* provides incompatible details about how long Bishoi resided at Scetis and in Middle Egypt; cf. ¶¶78A and 78B.

7 Arabic written in the Syriac script.

8 On the permeable divide between hagiography and biography, see Patricia Cox, *Biography in Late Antiquity: A Quest for the Holy Man* (Berkeley:

University of California Press, 1983); Stephanos Efthymiadis, ed., *The Ashgate Research Companion to Byzantine Hagiography*, 2 vols. (Burlington, VT: Ashgate, 2011–14); Arietta Papaconstantinou, "Hagiography in Coptic," in *The Ashgate Research Companion to Byzantine Hagiography*, ed. Stephanos Efthymiadis, 1:323–43; Tomas Hägg and Philip Rousseau, eds., *Greek Biography and Panegyric in Late Antiquity* (Berkeley: University of California Press, 2000).

9   See the references in Maged S.A. Mikhail, "A Lost Chapter in the History of Wadi al-Natrun (Scetis): The Coptic *Lives* and Monastery of Abba John Khame," *Le Muséon* 127, no. 1–2 (2014): 171–74.

10 See the discussions in W.E. Crum, *A Coptic Dictionary* (Oxford: Clarendon Press, 1939), 543b–544b. Interestingly, it is not understood in light of *shōi*, "what is high," "above," "elevated" (Crum 550a).

11 See MS Cambridge University Add. 2016.

12 E.g., Édouard René Hambye, "Pishay, anachorète: une commémoraison peu connue du calendrier de l'Eglise syrienne d'Antioche," *L'Orient syrien* 7 (1962): 255–59.

13 See *LBsh* ¶9; Long Recension of *Life of Paul of Tamma* ¶¶84–93, esp., 128; Alin Suciu, "Sitting in the Cell: The Literary Development of an Ascetic Praxis in Paul of Tamma's Writings. With an Edition of Some Hitherto Unknown Fragments of *De Cella*," *Journal of Theological Studies* n.s. 68, no. 1 (2017): 146. For contrary views that read Bishoi of Jeremiah and Bishoi of Scetis as two distinct figures, see Suciu, n. 18.

14 The description is in MS Syrian Monastery (Syr.) 30, fol. 24v; Sebastian P. Brock and L. van Rompay, *Catalogue of the Syriac Manuscripts and Fragments in the Library of Deir al-Surian, Wadi al-Natrun (Egypt)* (Louvain: Peeters, 2014), 223.

15 René-Georges Coquin, "Pshoi of Tud," *CE* 6:2030; René-Georges Coquin and Maurice Martin, "Dayr Anba Abshay," *CE* 2:718b–719a.

16 Monica Blanchard, "Beh Ishoʻ Kamulaya's Syriac Discourses on the Monastic Way of Life: Edition, English Translation, and Introduction" (PhD diss., Catholic University of America, 2001), 4–5 and n. 47; Johannes Sanders, "Introduction to the Life of Mar Bishoi (Siglum MB)," *The Harp* 8–9 (1995–96): 277–88.

17 Cf. *Synaxarium*, 7 Babah/7 Teqemt/18 October with *LBsh* ¶79.

18 *Life of Paul of Tamma* (Ar. Long Rec.), ¶126; also see Suciu, "Sitting in the Cell," 142–48.

19 *Life of Paul of Tamma* (Ar. Long Rec.), ¶127.

20 The second reference to Bishoi in the *Life of Paul* (Ar. Long Rec.), ¶127, seems to render the earlier reference in ¶¶84–93 a later interpolation. Bishoi is not attested in the Short Recension of this *Life*.

21 Ar. *minyā* may be also a "garden" or "valley."
22 Although that would require reading the *sīn* as a *ṣād*; hence, Madīnat al-Ṣaqr, "Hawk City," Hierakonopolis (Nekhen), modern al-Kawm al-Aḥmar in the Aswan governorate.
23 Most modern publications in Egypt place the location near Dayr al-Barsha, but that is highly unlikely given the details of the account.
24 The proper name is not consistent across any of the recensions. Nonetheless, he was an abbot, not a bishop, as some literature claims. In the Coptic Church, combining the roles of bishop and abbot became normative in the 1970s, not before.
25 *Life of Paul* (Ar. Long Rec.) ¶60. It is uncertain if the abbot knew of Paul's passing; he is depicted as a disciple to both saints in ¶µ.
26 Evelyn-White, *Monasteries*, 2:112, nn. 6–7; Suciu, "Sitting in the Cell," 147–48.
27 Maurice Martin, S.J., "Dayr Harmina," *CE* 2:808. The *Life of Abba Harmina*, based on BnF. Ar. 4748, has been published by Makarī of the Monastery of Saint Macarius, *Sīrat al-qiddīs al-ʿaẓīm al-Anbā Hirmīnā al-sāʾiḥ* (Cairo: Dār Yūsuf Kamāl lil-ṭibaʿā, n.d. [after 2012]). That text does not mention Bishoi or Paul.
28 Maged S.A. Mikhail, *From Byzantine to Islamic Egypt: Religion, Identity, and Politics after the Arab Conquest* (London and New York: I.B. Tauris, 2014), 207–10, 226–28, ch. 6.
29 *Life of John the Little* (Mikhail and Vivian, trans.), 296–99.
30 Mikhail, *From Byzantine to Islamic Egypt*, 123–27.
31 B.T.A. Evetts, ed. and trans., *History of the Patriarchs*, PO 10.5: 652–53.
32 De Lacy O'Leary, *The Saints of Egypt* (London: SPCK, 1937; Amsterdam: Philo Press, 1974), 107. Often cited as AD 841; e.g., Zakariyā al-Baramūsī, *al-Qiddīs al-ʿaẓīm al-Anbā Bishūy: tārīkh dayrahu wā athāruh bi-Anṣinā maʿa sīratuh ḥasab al-naṣṣayn al-yūnāni wā al-ʿarabī* (Cairo: Markaz al-Diltā lil-ṭibaʿah, 2002), 89, though without reference. Mattā al-Miskīn, *al-Rahbanah al-qibṭiyah fī ʿaṣr al-qiddīs Anbā Maqqār*, 3rd expanded ed. (Wadi al-Natrun: Maṭbaʿat Dayr al-Qiddīs al-Anbā Maqqār, 1995), 234–35, simply states that the translation was during the patriarchate of Yusāb. There is a short reference in H. Ferdinand Wüstenfeld, trans., *Synaxarium, das ist Heiligen-Kalender der coptischen Christen* (Gotha: F.A. Perthes, 1879), Kiyahk 5. Here, it simply states that Bishoi's relics came from Upper Egypt. The short entry is not in the manuscripts surveyed by René Basset in his edition of the *Synaxarium*. Also see Evelyn-White, *Monasteries*, 2:302, 395–96, appendix 5, fol. 113a.

33 There is an extended account of this translation in Fr. Zakariyā's *al-Qiddīs al-'aẓīm al-Anbā Bishūy* (91–93), but it is unclear which manuscript he is referencing.
34 The remains of both saints are accounted for in the 1088 census of relics at Wadi al-Natrun taken by Mawhub ibn Mansur. HP II.3: fol. 179r, Ar. p. 227/Eng. p. 359; Evelyn-White, *Monasteries*, 2:365.
35 Always important, the prestige and authority of the Monastery of St. Macarius, even in matters pertaining to the whole Coptic confession in the Middle Ages, was particularly striking from roughly the ninth to the twelfth centuries. See Mikhail, *From Byzantine to Islamic Egypt*, 204–13; *Synaxarium*, 27 Baramhāt (Basset, 260). Twenty-nine Coptic patriarchs came from this monastery, and most patriarchs from the ninth to the fourteenth century were buried at it.
36 The restoration of the Monastery of St. Bishoi from his personal funds is one of the few things mentioned about this patriarch in the *History of the Patriarchs*: A. Khater and O.H.E. Khs-Burmester, *History of the Patriarchs of the Egyptian Church*, 3.3 (Cairo: Publications de la Société d'Archéologie Copte, 1970), 233. This is most likely the context for the brief note in the Ethiopic *Synaxarium*: I. Guidi, *Le synaxaire éthiopien: les mois de sané, hamlé et nahasé*, PO 7.3 (Paris: Firmin-Didot, 1907), s.v. Hamle 13, pp. 308–309. The visit is summarized in Evelyn-White, *Monasteries*, 2:395–96, based on BnFArabe 100, fols. 46r–69r; see especially 54v–56r.
37 BnF Ar. 100, fols. 46r–69r, "Book of the Consecration of the Mayrūn," at fol. 56r.
38 Ethiopic *Synaxarium*, Hamle 8 (Guidi, PO 7.3:259); see the appendix, 323–27, below.
39 Notably, it is lacking in the editions by Makarī al-Bahnasawī, Ṣamū'īl al-Suryānī, B. Kāmil, M. Baḥr, Y. Ḥabīb, and in *Firdaws al-abā'*; all are discussed at length below.
40 Zakariyā al-Baramūsī, *al-Qiddīs al-'aẓīm al-Anbā Bishūy*, 31 n. 40. This Arabic text is a translation of the edition by Papadopoulos and Lizardos; see n. 49, below.
41 Paul Bedjan, *Acta Martyrum et Sanctorum*, vol. 3 (Leipzig: Otto Harrassowitz, 1892), 583. The omission, which was assumed to be in BnF Syr. 236, was later supplied by V. Scheil based on a private manuscript: "Restitution de deux textes dans le récit syriaque de la vie de Mar Bischoi (ed. Bedjan)," *Zeitschrift für Assyriologie und verwandte Gebiete* 15 (1900), 104–106.
42 Jacques Le Goff, *The Birth of Purgatory*, trans. Arthur Goldhammer (Chicago: University of Chicago Press, 1986); Eileen Gardiner, "Hell, Purgatory, and Heaven," in *Handbook of Medieval Culture*, vol. 1, ed. Albrecht Classen (Berlin: De Gruyter, 2015), 653–73. The Eastern

reaction to the rise of this doctrine is discussed in Dragos Mirsanu, "Dawning Awareness of the Theology of Purgatory in the East: A Review of the Thirteenth Century," *Studii Teologice* 4 (2008): 179–93.

43 John Anthony McGuckin, *Westminster Handbook to Patristic Theology* (Louisville, KY and London: John Knox Press, 2004), 286–87.

44 Isabel Moreira, *Heaven's Purge: Purgatory in Late Antiquity* (Oxford: Oxford University Press, 2010); Nicholas Constas, "'To Sleep, Perchance to Dream': The Middle State of Souls in Patristic and Byzantine Literature," *Dumbarton Oaks Papers* 55 (2001): 91–124; Constas, "An Apology for the Cult of Saints in Late Antiquity: Eustratius Presbyter of Constantinople, *On the State of Souls after Death* (CPG 7522)," *Journal of Early Christian Studies* 10 (2002): 267–85.

45 E.g., *Life of Macarius*, ¶6 (Vivian, esp. 115–18); *Life of Paul of Tamma* (Ar. Long Rec.) ¶¶85–92; (Pseudo-) John III, *Les "Questions de Théodore": Texte sahidique, recensions arabes et éthiopienne*, ed. and trans. A. Van Lantschoot (Vatican City: Biblioteca Apostolica Vaticana, 1957), Third Question; Agostino Soldati, "Some Remarks about Coptic Colophons and Their Relationship with Manuscripts: Typology, Function, and Structure," *Comparative Oriental Manuscript Studies Bulletin* 4, no. 1 (2018): 115–19; Fr. Shenouda [/Imīl] Mahir Ishaq, *al-Khalāṣ al-ladhī nuntaziruh*, vol. 2, *Ḥālat arwāḥ al-rāqidīn*, 3rd printing (Cairo: al-Anbā Rūways al-Ufset, 2002), 66–70, 82–112.

46 See nn. 42 and 44, above. For the synodal decree, see Secretarial Committee, *al-Qararāt al-majmaʿiyah fī ʿahd ṣāḥib al-qadāsah al-Bābā Shinūdah al-thālith*, 3rd printing (N.p.: al-Markaz al-Thaqāfī al-Qibṭī al-Urthūdhuksī, 2011).

47 He is part of Timothy of Gargar's long metric *maymra* on Egyptian monastics: MS Mingana Syr. 83, 55v–105v; MS Deir al-Zaʿfarān, cod. pap. 71 (Dolabany).

48 See n. 16, above. Blanchard, "Beh Ishoʿ Kamulaya's Syriac Discourses," appendix 1, contains a translation of the Syriac *LBsh* according to the Bedjan edition. Although Beh Ishoʿ and his *Discourses* likely date to the late eighth century, his *Life*, which is a reworking of the *LBsh*, is later and survives in a manuscript dated 1900. As Blanchard notes, similarities between the two names—Bishoi and Beh Ishoʿ—may have led to confusion. St. Bishoi is not explicitly referenced by Beh Ishoʿ. The possible parallel Blanchard notes between the *Discourse* of Beh Ishoʿ and the Syriac *LBsh* proper (22–23; cf. 28) speaks to monastic themes in general, but does not demonstrate Beh Ishoʿ's acquaintance with the *LBsh*.

49 E.g., BnF Grec 1093 and the Greek *Synaxarion*. Leonidas Papadopoulos and Georgia Lizardos translated the *Life* based on the Greek *Synaxarion*: *Saint Païsios the Great by Saint John the Dwarf of Egypt* (Jordanville, NY:

Holy Trinity Monastery, 1998). This English translation was rendered into Arabic by Fr. Zakariyā al-Baramūsī *(al-Qiddīs al-'aẓīm al-Anbā Bishūy)*. His study comments only on the Arabic *LBsh*, but it does not have the text for that recension.

50 See the Pinakes database: http://pinakes.irht.cnrs.fr/; search, BHG 1402–1403, *Vita S. Paisii*.

51 The text may be earlier, but its use of *eros* and other terms of affection (see the introduction to chapter one) is not typical of an earlier era, though this correlates well with the seventh-century linguistic shift and emphasis discussed by Claudia Rapp in *Brother-making*, ch. 4.A.

52 E.g., referencing the Nile as the "sea." Such references are common in Egypt and persist until today. Moreover, it should be noted that Paul is never identified as "of Tamma" in the Greek text, yet the identification can hardly be erroneous. Associating Bishoi and Paul demonstrates knowledge of the Egyptian hagiographic tradition. "Tamma" would have been unidentifiable to a reader outside of Egypt, and the designation would be somewhat useless given that Paul of Tamma is completely unknown to the Greek tradition.

53 Compare ¶41 in *Rec. Gr1* with the others. Also, in ¶64 "a city" in *Rec. Gr1* is "Fustat" in the other recensions. In *Rec Gr1* ¶79, the only geographic location is "Pisidia" (in modern Turkey), while in the other recensions Antinoë/Ansina occurs in three passages in that same paragraph.

54 In case of the tree, a specific location seems to be implied—a location that would have been known to those who visited or lived at Wadi al-Natrun.

55 Isidore is said to have "wanted to enrich his homeland" (¶79).

56 The city appears in one of the accounts in the *Life of Maximus and Domitius*: Tim Vivian, "The Bohairic *Life of Maximus and Domitius*," *Coptic Church Review* 26, no. 2–3 (2005): 44. Significantly, this *Life* is frequently attributed to Bishoi of Scetis in error. As discussed above, it is the work of a Bishoi (Paîsios) of Constantinople.

57 Evelyn-White cites what appears to be a passing Greek reference to Bishoi (*Monasteries*, 2:112). Paul was unknown to the Greek tradition.

58 Interestingly, Bishoi/Paîsios is glossed at several websites as a "Greek," though his name is very much Coptic and there is no evidence that he read, spoke, or wrote anything in Greek.

59 See nn. 14 and 56, above.

60 E.g., *History of the Patriarchs*, PO I.2:495, 498–501; 8 Ṭūba, the attempt to steal the head of Saint Mark (one modern edition places the account on 30 Bābah); 28 Hatūr, Martyrdom of Serapion (Sarabamūn) of Nikiou; 12 Baramhāt, Martyrdom of Bishop Macrobius; 22 Abīb, Martyrdom of Macarius son of Basilides. Cf. 15 Tūt, Translation of the Relics of Saint

Stephen the Archdeacon; 10 Kiyahk, Transferring the Body of Patriarch Severus of Antioch.

61 An additional development is the elevated misogynistic tone of ¶65 in the Semitic recensions; cf. Maged S.A. Mikhail, *The Legacy of Demetrius of Alexandria: The Form and Function of Hagiography in Late Antique and Islamic Egypt* (New York: Routledge, 2016), 66–69. This incident was excised and circulated independently of the *Life*: Ms Berlin, Königliche Bibliothek, Syr. 201 (Sachau 165), fols. 12v–16v. Other passages that circulated independently in Syriac include BnF Syr. 234, fols. 1–9; Damascus Patriarchate 12/17, fols. 1–2.

62 Cf. ¶78B. Trying to account for evidence by alluding to accounts from visitors, or pilgrims, is not uncommon in this literature; e.g., *Life of John the Little*, ¶82; *Life of John Khame*, passage recovered in Mikhail, "A Lost Chapter," 181, 185.

63 Cf. *LBsh* ¶¶ 8, 53A, γ with *Life of John the Little*, 25, 55, 76–77. *FamA* does not note the flight from Scetis as do *FamB* and *FamC*.

64 Itself echoing passages in the Gnostic *Apocalypse of Peter* and the *Second Treatise of Seth*. Also see Mahmoud M. Ayoub, "Toward an Islamic Christology II: The Death of Jesus, Reality or Delusion (A Study of the Death of Jesus in Tafsīr Literature)," *Muslim World* 70 (1980): 91–121.

65 See Mikhail, *From Byzantine to Islamic Egypt*, chs. 4–5; Sidney H. Griffith, *The Church in the Shadow of the Mosque: Christians and Muslims in the World of Islam* (Princeton, NJ: Princeton University Press, 2008); Samir Khalil Samir and Jorgen Nielsen, eds., *Christian Arabic Apologetics during the Abbasid Period (750–1258)* (Leiden: Brill, 1994).

66 The monastery in Ansina is mentioned in B.T.A. Evetts, *The Churches and Monasteries of Egypt and Some Neighbouring Countries* (Oxford: Clarendon Press, 1895; repr. Gorgias Press, 2001), 244 (fol. 87r). If it were the monastery in Ansina, the author would have had firsthand knowledge of the traditions he recorded; rather, he states that he is depending on the accounts of pilgrims.

67 The monastery in al-Fayyum is mentioned by al-Nabulsī: B. Moritz, ed., [*Ta'rīkh al-Fayyūm wā bīlāduh*] *Description du Fayoum au VIIme siècle de l'Hégire par Abou 'Osmân il Naboulsi iṭl Ṣafadi* (Cairo: National Press/al-Maṭba'ah al-Ahliya, 1899), 161; M. Georges Salmon, "Répertoire géographique de la province du Fayoum, d'apres le Kitāb Tārīkh al-Fayyoām d'an-Nāboulsī," *Bulletin de l'Institut Français d'Archéologie Orientale* (1901): 66.

68 René-Georges Coquin, "Tutun," *CE* 7:2283a–b.

69 Within the context of ¶κ, "this holy place" is clearly a reference to the Monastery of St. Bishoi at Wadi al-Natrun.

70 E.g., Coptic versions of the *Life of Macarius*, *Life of John the Little*, *Life of Maximus and Domitius*. See also Mikhail, "A Lost Chapter," 179–85; Evelyn-White, *Monasteries*, 1:122, 2:97–98.

71 Gérard Colin, ed. and trans., *La version éthiopienne de l'histoire de Bsoy: Édition critique et traduction française*, PO 49.3 (Turnhout: Brepols, 2002).

72 Ute Pletruschka, "Some Observations about the Transmission of Popular Philosophy in Egyptian Monasteries after the Islamic Conquest," in *Ideas in Motion in Baghdad and Beyond: Philosophical and Theological Exchanges between Christians and Muslims in the Third/Ninth and Fourth/Tenth Centuries*, ed. Damien Janos (Leiden: Brill, 2016), ch. 3; Gawdat Gabra, "Perspectives on the Monastery of St. Antony: Medieval and Later Inhabitants and Visitors," in *Monastic Visions: Wall Paintings in the Monastery of St. Antony at the Red Sea*, ed. Elizabeth S. Bolman (New Haven, CT: Yale University Press, 2002), ch. 10, esp. 176; Otto F.A. Meinardus, "Aethiopica in Aegypto," *Journal of Ethiopian Studies* 3, no. 1 (1965): 23–35.

73 There is a possibility that *Rec. SA* δ may have been a Syriac text. Hopefully, once MS Syrian Monastery 30.D is accessible, this aspect will be clarified. As is, the opening sentences of *WN1 Syr1*, edited in the *Catalogue* by Brock and Van Rompay, and *SA Syr1* are identical save for one word, but it is impossible to draw any conclusions based on that alone, especially since the beginning of hagiographic lives is often quite formulaic.

74 The first folio is published in Brock and Van Rompay's *Catalogue*. Upon request, the authorities at the Syrian Monastery, H.G. Bishop Metta'us and the manuscript librarian, permitted Profs. Stephen Davis, Mark Swanson, and Ramez Mikhail to take a picture of the last folio for use on this project. We are thankful to all of them.

75 Gabra, "Perspectives," 175–76.

76 Brock and Van Rompay, *Catalogue*, 225. The Garshuni manuscript, discussed below, also identifies Ephrem in a marginal note.

77 All recensions of the *Life of Ephrem* (*LEph*) bring him to Egypt (¶¶21–24), but only one (attested in two manuscripts written at Wadi al-Natrun, the earliest dating to AD 1100) records him meeting Bishoi: see Joseph P. Amar, ed. and trans., *The Syriac "Vita" Tradition of Ephrem the Syrian*, 2 vols., CSCO 629 and 630, Scr. Syr. 242 and 243 (Louvain: Peeters, 2011); on manuscripts, see CSCO 629: vi–viii, xv; on the meeting, chs. 22.B, 24.A; Amar, "Byzantine Ascetic Monachism and Greek Bias in the Vita Tradition of Ephrem the Syrian," *Orientalia Christiana Periodica* 58 (1992): 143–48. Even in that recension (Vat. Syr. 117), however, the narrative is disjointed. All recensions of *LEph* maintain that a bilingual disciple functioned as Ephrem's translator in Egypt (chs. 21.A, 22.A); yet all recensions of *LBsh* emphasize that the saints could not initially

communicate since neither spoke the other's language, rendering their miraculous communication a re-enactment of Acts 2:7–11. Moreover, *LBsh*(¶52) maintains that Ephrem returned home after spending a week with Bishoi; yet *LEph* (ch. 24.A) states that he remained another eight years in Egypt. The account of the visit was reinforced by the tradition that the relics of Ephem were translated to the Monastery of Bishoi in the thirteenth century (Evelyn-White, *Monasteries*, 2:114, 143 and n. 2). A late version of *LEph* (or so it is described) also mentions the "Tree of Ephrem" at the Syrian Monastery. The account maintains that Ephrem left his walking stick outside Bishoi's cell, but when he came out, it had grown into a large tree.

78 This manuscript is used as the base text for the upcoming textual edition of the Syriac *LBsh*. On the manuscript, see W. Wright, *Catalogue of the Syriac Manuscripts of the British Museum*, vol. 3 (London: Longmans/British Museum, 1872).

79 See https://hmmlorientalia.wordpress.com/page/12/?iframe=true&previe w=true%2F for a summary of this long manuscript. "AG" *Anno Graecorum* ("Year of the Greeks"), or *Seleucid Era*, or *Era of Alexander*, was a calendar inaugurated by the Seleucids. It was maintained by Syriac-speaking Christians long after (AG 1 = 1 October 312 BC).

80 There are differences among them; for example, the Garshuni text forwards a unique tradition that identifies Bishoi's parents as Iraqis (fol. 66r–a), which would make it likely that his parents were Syriac-speaking Christians.

81 This is presumed at the moment. The abridged nature of this manuscript, which lacks ¶79 altogether, makes it difficult to definitively classify it. What is certain is that it was not derived from *SA Syr2*, which lacks several of the paragraphs attested in that recension.

82 Only one sentence from this lengthy paragraph is retained in this recension.

83 Only the opening laudatory sentence of ¶48 is retained, which the scribe likely read as the conclusion of ¶47, rather than the beginning of ¶48. The remainder of that pericope is omitted.

84 Evelyn-White, *Monasteries*, 1:122.

85 [Al-Qummūṣ/Hegumen] Mīṣā'īl Baḥr, *Tārīkh al-qiddīs al-Anbā Yūḥannis al-qaṣīr wā manṭiqat Anṣinā* (n.p.: n.p., 1957), 134–39.

86 Otto F.A. Meinardus, "St. Bishoi: A Coptic Christophorus," *Orientalia Suecana* 48 (1999): 67–73.

87 I have not been able to find this publication; the assertion that it reflects *WN2 Ar2* is based on the notes about this publication in Fr. Zakariyā's study.

88 In addition to summarizing the manuscripts at their disposal, Fathers Miṣā'īl and, especially, Bishūy directly quote sizable portions of the manuscripts they utilized. The adherence of their manuscripts to *Rec. WN2* is beyond doubt.
89 Introduction to the *Life of John the Little* (Mikhail and Vivian, trans.), 50–52.
90 Bartolomeo Pirone, ed., "Anbā Bishoy," *SOCC* 45 (2012): 11–12.

1

THE GREEK *LIFE OF PAÏSIOS* IN TRANSLATION

Introduction: A Spirituality of Desire: The *Life of Païsios* vis-à-vis *The New Asceticism* by Sarah Coakley[1]
Tim Vivian

> To reproach mystics with loving God by means of the faculty of sexual love is as though one were to reproach a painter with making pictures by means of colors composed of material substances. —Simone Weil[2]

Part 1: Preface

The word "love" occurs twenty-seven times in the *Life of Païsios*, "lover" eleven times.[3] It may surprise most readers (it did me) that ἔρως / *érōs*, usually thought of as erotic, sexual love, outnumbers ἀγάπη / *agápē*, "warm regard for and interest in another," fourteen to nine.[4] As I was working on a transcription and revised translation of the Greek *Life of Païsios* for this volume, I happened to be reading *The New Asceticism* by Sarah Coakley, a theologian and Anglican priest, and I quickly realized that Coakley offers a fresh perspective on early monastic asceticism and its spirituality of desire.[5] Here, after a brief discussion of history and story (part 2), I will offer a summary of and reflection on Coakley's and others' ascetic exegesis and its contemporary importance (part 3), and then apply her perspective and insights with my own to the *Life of Païsios* (part 4).

Part 2: Païsios of Scetis: History and histories

The English word "story" comes from Greek *historía* which, at its root, means "inquiry, research," "result of research, information, knowledge," "telling, exposition, account, history."[6] Its cognate verb *historéō* makes verbal these nouns: "to seek to know oneself, inform oneself, do research, inquire," "interrogate," "examine, explore, observe." *Historía*, smiling, sits side-by-side on a vernal park bench with the Delphic Oracle's "Know thyself." *Historía/historéō* later came to mean "to come to know or inform oneself through history."[7]

In the literature of early Christian monasticism, Païsios goes by a number of names, thus histories; he is a different figure within each tradition—Greek, Arabic, Syriac, and Ethiopic—that tells (and, thus, in translating retells and reshapes) his story, as Maged Mikhail details in the general introduction. He is Païsios (Greek), Pshoi (Coptic), Bishoi or Bishoy (Arabic), Bishoi (Syriac), and Bsoy (Ethiopic). With this volume, we hope to give speech to each language and tradition's storytelling.

The *Life*, in Hippolyte Delehaye's classification, purports to be "the *accounts of reliable eye-witnesses* or of well-informed contemporaries reporting the recollections of other eye-witnesses."[8] But, Delehaye continues, agreeing with Evelyn-White, since John died before Païsios, this narrative device is a fiction. If this is so, then the difficulty for modern (at least Anglo-European) readers is to discern fact from fiction. Or are they so easily discernible? Are miracles and theophanies ipso facto "fiction"? If so, why? A skeptic might shelve the *Life* under Delehaye's fourth classification: "Acts whose basis is not a written source at all; they result from the arbitrary combination of a few real particulars within a purely imaginary framework, in other words they are *historical romances*."[9]

"Arbitrary" and "purely imaginary" are condescending and even dismissive. Who decides what are "real particulars"? And based on what criteria? Lest one think this is much academic ado about nothing, the discussion that Delehaye's methodology prompts applies also to study of the Bible and to any sacred text. Coptic hagiographers, we need to remember, like the writers of the Gospels, were not interested in "facts," historicity, and journalism; their goal was to show estimable—and imitable—spiritual truth.[10] Native Americans may help us here, showing us a people, like the ancient Copts and the Gospel writers, with a different reality, an "other" way of understanding the world and the way it works. In *Neither Wolf nor Dog*, Dan, a Lakota elder, in speaking to his interlocutor, excoriates "white" history: "It is a funny kind of history, where the most important thing is what happened. You want to know everything about what happened.... That's all-important to you. The more you know, the more history you think you have." For [whites], Dan concludes, it's all and only about "facts." Dan ends with an apt analogy: "It's like studying all the parts of the body and then saying you understand about life."[11] One Native elder states the reality of storytelling: "What I'm about to tell you may not have happened, but it's true."

The, or one, truth is that for around 1,500 years a monastery in Scetis has borne the saint's name. Although our historical footing is uncertain, we can say that certain objects, if not facts, are discernible in the near, not far, distance:

- Païsios (Bishoi) belongs to the fourth–fifth centuries, probably dying in the early fifth century.
- He settled in the renowned monastic settlement of Scetis/Wadi al-Natrun at some time in the fourth century.
- He followed the monastic pattern of apprenticing himself, as it were, to an "old man" or elder.
- Again, following the monastic pattern, at some point of spiritual and practical maturity (mature praxis), instead of staying at a monastic settlement, like many others, almost all lost both to history and hagiography, he went out on his own to become an anchorite or semi-anchorite.
- He has connections with several famous monks of the time.
- The tradition venerates him as a holy man, persevering in ascesis and wise in counsel.
- After his death it seems that his body was translated to one of the monasteries in Ansina and subsequently to his monastery at Wadi al-Natrun.
- At some point, one of the four founding monasteries of Scetis was named after him in his honor.

The "facts" in the above bullet points are, however, skeletal. What we require is flesh and blood, *and* mind, heart, soul, and spirit. Dan, the Lakota elder quoted above, stands side by side with the author of the *Life of Païsios*; both look us straight in the eyes: "See, none of what we know is history to you. Our sacred stories are just legends to you. The powers we were given by our ancestors you think are superstitions." And, he pointedly emphasizes, "The responsibilities, too."[12] In Dan's terms, and as Sarah Coakley understands (see below), the *Life of Païsios* is a work of responsibility. At the very least, the *Life* (or *Lives*) *of Païsios* spoke to the monks of later centuries. Historical facts can take us only so far, whether in hagiography or in history itself. The breath and spirit—the *ruah* and *pneûma*—of the *Life* reside, abide, in the stories, in their mythologies of desire.[13]

Part 3: Sarah Coakley and a spirituality of desire
Introduction: The erotics of desire
"[O]nly a revived, purged—and lived—form of 'ascetic life,'" Sarah Coakley urges in *The New Asceticism*, "will rescue the churches from their current theological divisions and incoherences over 'sexuality.'"[14] Coakley thus joins

Virginia Burrus who, intrepid, seeks to find "the place of eroticism in the salvific transformation of human subjects, even of the cosmos itself."[15] With *Toward a Theology of Eros*, Burrus and her colleagues work hard at drafting coherence (or coherences) about eros. Their volume, like Coakley's *New Asceticism*, "seeks new openings for the emergence of desire, love, and pleasure, while also challenging common understandings of these terms."[16]

The *Life of Païsios*, though, just may attest that incoherence, common understandings, and misunderstandings are neither quintessentially modern nor quaintly ancient. In ¶59 of BN Grec 1093, the manuscript used for this volume, "a certain young novice who lived alone in the desert leading the life of an ascetic," "[t]ormented by thoughts that fiercely rose up against him," comes to see "the divine Païsios" for counsel. Païsios, like Antony the Great, ever-discerning, observes that the monk is "following his own will" and "pursuing the wily demon of [wickedness] and self-conceit."[17] Another manuscript, however, instead of "wickedness," *ponērías*, has the similar-sounding *porneías*, "sexual immorality."

Such linguistic and, possibly, exegetical confusion can hypostasize for us our own need for clarity about asceticism and its adversaries, ancient and modern. Thus, we badly need Coakley's "core argument" for our modern spiritual and moral disarray: "only the same authentically 'ascetic life' will be demanding enough to command the respect of a post-Christian world saturated and sated by the commodifications of desire."[18] Demanding. How dare Coakley, arms crossed, defiant before the concomitant exalting and reifying of self and the empty satiation of the spirit, make such demands! She hopes that her presentation "necessarily brings God into the picture as the source and goal of all human life."[19] For her, the ascetic life develops out of desire *(érōs)*, but not desire that is "so heavily sexualized in the modern, post-Freudian period as to render its connection with other desires (including the desire for God) obscure and puzzling."[20] Sacred desire, birth mother of asceticism, is not something locked away distantly in monasteries or non-offensively sequestered in some out-of-the-way museum on a dusty bottom shelf in a dimly lit basement.

But first, for Coakley—and for us—what is asceticism?[21] "Asceticism" comes from the Greek athletic term *áskēsis*, "training." For the early monks, ascesis represented the training, often the bridling, usually the (re)education of body, soul, mind, and spirit. A question I often ask my students: Why, in our culture, do we lavish such adulation and emolument on professional trainers—athletes—while, at the same time, we give such little attention to *spiritual* training: prayer, silence, liturgy, lectio (reflective reading), contemplation, hospitality, care for the poor, and, for ascetics like Thomas Merton, Dorothy Day, and Daniel Berrigan, social justice? In our society, lavishing (on whatever) and spiritual attention are inversely proportional. The monastic offices, then, spiritual and corporal fitness centers, most likely inspired by Judaism, embody the genius of a religion, as do Islam's *salat*, the five daily mandated prayers, perhaps borrowed from Christian monasticism. Aristotle Papanikolaou summarizes well the idea(l) behind ascesis:

> I emphasize an understanding of the God-world relation in terms of *theosis*, which I prefer to translate as divine-human communion.[22] Practices like prayer and fasting were not developed to prove something to God or to score points with God. They are time-tested practices that rewire the body to make it available to the always-on-offer presence of God.[23]

Papanikolaou's "divine-human communion" comes about through desire—God's desire, and humanity's. I find most suggestive and usable—and, dare I say, inspirational?—Coakley's exegesis of "desire." For this former Cambridge theologian, modern society, partly through gratuitous hypersexualization, has corrupted desire. For her, desire, *érōs*, is, as the *Life of Païsios* attests, "a profound allure," "no less that which continually animates us to God." Coakley continues: sacred desire "allures us, liberates us, [and] gives us the energy and ecstasy of participation in the divine life." Coakley's unusual use of "allure" ("allures us") as a transitive verb and "animates" with an indirect object ("*to* God") should focus our attention: they show that she is, happily, bending language in order to flex and extend boundaries. Language is always liminal, theological vocabulary even more, the language of the Spirit superliminal.

Any attempt, therefore, to explicate "participation in the divine life" should do no less than what Coakley suggests. Alluding to Paul (Rom 8:38–39), she declares the opposition between the "passions" and sacred desire. A rephrasing of and a metaphor about the biblical and monastic understanding of the "passions" may be of use. The 1928 Book of Common Prayer of the Episcopal Church indirectly terms the passions "the devices and desires of our own hearts"; metaphorically, the passions, like a tractor, drag us, usually willingly, but also hypnotized, from God, from the Sacred. Sacred desire, however, the *Life* insists, "makes us humans 'fully alive' for whom nothing in the created world—as also in the divine compassion—can be 'alienated' from the same God of love."[24]

Here, as elsewhere, Coakley shows, and gratefully acknowledges, her indebtedness to Gregory of Nyssa.[25] This Cappadocian bishop (ca. 335–ca. 395), Coakley declares, "provides a potential hermeneutical key for reading other forms of ascetic literature against the grain and across traditional disjunctions": "ascetical *practices* are means of transformation and of the indispensable spiritual power of a person from whom one may *mimetically* 'catch the halo,' as Gregory puts it, of rightly ordered desire."[26] Anthony Meredith observes a line of succession from Plato in the *Symposium* through Origen to Gregory: the Cappadocian, like Origen, "assumes desire, *erōs* or *pothos*, to lie at the root of human craving for God.[27] It is a theme that finds expression in all his ascetic writings."[28] What each human, through ascetic practice, must do is work toward *rightly-ordered* desire.

Before we can proceed, however, with a discussion of *érōs* and *póthos* in Coakley's work or in the *Life of Païsios*, we must first very briefly look at Anders Nygren's seminal book *Agape and Eros* that began the modern discussion. We must look also at other scholars' demurrals. Burrus questions, correctly, Nygren's "binary opposition of divine love and human desire"; he states that "Eros and Agape belong to two entirely separate spiritual worlds."[29] Coakley disagrees, and the *Life of Païsios*, as I hope to show in part 4, refutes Nygren. As McGinn points out, *agápē* "was not a Christian creation, but it was a rare word until the early Greek-speaking Christians adopted it as the special designation for the love which God directs toward us and which we, through his grace, can in turn address to him."[30]

Agápē occurs 116 times in the New Testament and *agapáō* (the verb) 141 times.[31] Jesus uses *agápē* only twice in the Synoptic Gospels (Mt 24:12 and Lk 11:42) but seven times in John, and uses the verb *agapáō* numerous times in each Gospel. That these two words occur over 250 times in a relatively short book should inform us that the spirituality and soteriology of the New Testament are very much realized: with love, the Kingdom is in our midst, or within us (Lk 17:21).[32] All the commandments, after all, depend on loving God and loving one's neighbor.[33]

When one studies Nygren and many of the essays in *Toward a Theology of Eros*, one sees that, at least with regard to the discussion of eros, in the beginning was Plato, especially the Plato (and Socrates) of the *Symposium*.[34] In *Toward a Theology of Eros*, Daniel Boyarin argues that the *Symposium* has a "bottom line": it entirely transforms Greek eros "from the attraction to beautiful bodies into the interaction of souls through dialogue."[35] Boyarin's assertion fits the *Life of Païsios*—up to a point. In the *Life*, Païsios and Abba Pambo live out "the interaction of souls," but do so not through dialogue but through ascesis, ascetic practice. And Païsios' spiritual journey, like those of the ammas and abbas in the *Apophthegmata*, is one long interaction between his soul and God's.

At the end of his essay, Boyarin very briefly discusses "Christian celibate eros," finding that it "is neither the antithesis nor yet the product of heavenly Greek love, but finds its genealogy rather in the total break with sex and the city initiated by Platonic love."³⁶ The "total break" with both sex and the city *(tò kosmikón)* that Boyarin sees finds full expression in the *Life* (discussed below). A person reading this might well ask if she too has to make this "total break," almost demonizing "sex and the city." In general, early monasticism says "yes," but not always: "To Abba Antony it was revealed in the desert: In the city there is a certain person like you, a doctor by profession, who gives his excess income to those in need, and every day he sings the Trisagion with the angels."³⁷ The "yes," moreover, is not the focus of the *Life*; the *Life* emphasizes, rather, the oppositional *and* the appositional (discussed below).

In her afterword to *Toward a Theology of Eros*, Catherine Keller speaks of the volume's "ambiguous evaluation of the decorporealizing Platonic eros itself."³⁸ Does the *Life of Païsios* "decorporealize"? No. In the *Life* we see very dramatic spiritual, and physical, combat. As I hope to show below, the *Life*, in fact, in*corpor*ates the *psyché* ("soul, vital principle in creatures") with the *sôma* (body), not just in an adversarial fistfight but in an appositional dance.³⁹ I refer below to the "psycho-somatic" qualities of ascetic practice in the *Life*. However one views this, Keller rightly insists that "the *cosmos* of eros matters."⁴⁰ In contrast with Nygren, in agreement with Origen and Gregory, and with the *Life*, she concludes that eros and agape are symbiotic: "Eros without agape is little more than a greedy grasp; agape without eros issues straightaway in moralism."⁴¹

The ascetical long haul

Rightly ordered desire. This phrase could easily provide the subtitle for the *Life of Païsios* (see below). Rightly ordered desire, Coakley asserts, "rightly channeled *eros*, whether married or celibate, is impossible without deep prayer and ascetic perseverance." Ascetic perseverance, often against steep odds, is a key theme in the *Life*, but such sacred steadfastness, Coakley tells us, and the *Life* models, "is even more impossible, interestingly, without shining examples to emulate."⁴² "Shining Example," with Païsios as *imitator Dei* and, consequently, both the subject and object of *imitatio Dei*, could well be a title for the *Life*, as could Gregory's "Catch the Halo." Coakley's argument is neither newfangled nor highfalutin; as her allusions to and inspirations from Gregory show, Coakley is well-planted, -watered, and -nurtured in the fertile soil of early Christian asceticism and monasticism. Coakley wants to reclaim eros. She doesn't want to desexualize it but rather desires to pull us back from its sexualized suzerainty and idolatry—omniscient, omnipresent, and all-powerful. We have, she says, "so much individualized and physicalized desire that we assume that sexual enactment somehow exhausts it."⁴³ Perhaps "Exhausted" (Latin: "emptied out, drained out") could title the biographies—and, of course, autobiographies—of *homo consumptor*. As Aldous Huxley so clearly foresaw seventy-five years ago:

> But it is upon fashions, cars, and gadgets, upon news and the advertising for which news exists, that our present industrial and economic system depends for its proper functioning. For . . . this system cannot work unless the demand for non-necessaries is not merely kept up, but continually expanded; and of course it cannot be kept up and expanded except by incessant appeals to greed, competitiveness, and love of aimless distractions, which are the original sin of the mind.[44]

To put all this into a North American context, as Huxley does, sacred asceticism is the Native American, while "individualized and physicalized desire" is the Anglo-European conquistador: in the late nineteenth century, John Oberly, commissioner of Indian affairs, opined that "the Indian must be imbued with the exalting egotism of American civilization, so that he will say 'I' instead of 'We' and 'This is mine,' instead of 'This is ours.'"[45] This analogy is sobering because European-Americans perpetuated at least cultural genocide. What somatic and spiritual genocide, we must ask, do modern hyper-individualism, anything-goes capitalism, incestuous patriotism, and idolatrous militarism wreak?

By contrast with the simultaneous modern fetishizing and hamstringing of eros, Coakley reminds us that the ancients in faith (our grandfathers—and -mothers—as Native Americans say) still very much have something to say. "For Origen" (ca. 184–ca. 253), she says, "*agape* simply *is eros*, by any other name," whereas for Gregory, "*eros* is *agape* (as he puts it) 'stretched out in longing' towards the divine goal."[46] So, with regard to *érōs* and *agápē*, in Michelangelo's *Creation of Adam* who is reaching out to whom? As we stand before the great painting, perhaps we can imagine here, and thus use, the Classical Greek dual number (rather than singular or plural) where a noun or pronoun indicates two objects or persons acting as a single unit or in unison. As noted earlier, *érōs* ("loving desire") and *erastés* ("lover") together occur twenty-three times in the *Life of Païsios* (see the discussion in part 4 below). As we know all too well, though, from Genesis 2:4–3:24, from the whole of the Bible, and from looking around us and within, Adam and Eve and God will often be in conflict, if not in bloody spiritual conflagration.

Coakley and the *Life of Païsios* tell us of the manipulation of our desires. Such manhandling, she observes, is both conscious and unconscious: "the desire to dominate, to subjugate, to consume and own, and to control—sexually, racially and in other ways." In modern terms, "the pervasive effects in Western society of advertisement" are both: "advertisements affect us subconsciously, and they come from the manipulations of conscious actors."[47] In the *Life of Païsios*, one might say that conscious manipulations—machinations—come from the outside world ("the world," in monastic terms, a theme in the *Life*); subconscious or unconscious manipulation, if we use "insightful modern psychoanalytic accounts," appear in the form of demons and the Devil—and, as the *Life* wisely observes, from the obstreperous and insubordinate human will.[48]

Coakley, as we have seen, is an admirer of Gregory of Nyssa; she can also, helpfully, adduce Sigmund Freud to offer a hermeneutical password to some troubling dissonance, even violence, in the *Life of Païsios* (see part 4 below).[49] We don't want to bowdlerize, and thus sentimentalize, the *Life of Païsios* and its citizens. Sentimentalizing crafts caricature and, thus, inadvertently or deliberately, evasion. By contrast, Coakley tells us that in "a striking correspondence in 1932 between Freud and Albert Einstein," the former "can express the astonishingly optimistic view," given the rise of fascism and Hitler, that "Erotism" (Freud's term), the love instinct, "could finally triumph over Hate [sic] and war and aggression (Thanatos), by a sort of *direct* transference of the energies of hate."[50] The Bible, perhaps ironically for Freud, teaches this transference. Both Freud and the Bible show us that love, given our world and our selves, can be adversative. The *Life of Païsios* demonstrates this to the full. Mark's Gospel (1:12–13) offers no details about the temptation of Jesus by Satan; Matthew (4:1–11) and Luke (4:1–13), by contrast, have fuller and similar narratives—filling in Mark's chasmed silence with a terrifying and yet victorious myth.[51] But Luke, unlike Matthew, finishes his story with perhaps the most frightening line in the New Testament (4:13): "When the Devil had finished every test [or "temptation," *peirasmós*], he departed from him until an opportune time."

The *Life of Païsios*, as it were, like the *Life of Antony* and much early monastic literature, resumes the Devil's "opportune time," his depredations upon the faithful. However one understands "the Devil," it is undoubtedly more realistic to say that the Devil always assumes himself into human reality, beside, and within, us. He waits in the wings; it's as though Fortinbras stays off the murderous stage at the end of *Hamlet* and the play's surviving characters have to discern for themselves what evils still lurk in Denmark. In an irony that should terrify, the Devil's "opportune time" in Luke (*kairós*) is also the *kairós*, "the right, proper, favorable time" in other biblical passages.[52] Telling us the obvious, except that we need constant reminding, Freud insists that love and hate, whether from psychoanalytic couch or gospel pulpit, "must always," in Coakley's words, "go together, so that one—love—can modify or redirect the energies of the other—hate."[53] What we try to do, Freud concludes, sounding monastic, "is to *divert it*

[hate] into a channel other than that of warfare."[54] Is this not the gospel hope and imperative: that love (eros and agape) will now, both sublunary and in "heaven"—Jesus' Kingdom of God includes both—overcome the power of Thanatos, "death," not narrowly but broadly construed?[55]

But rather than look to Freud for our template, Coakley borrows from traditions of mystical theology in Christian thought and practice; she cites the purgative, illuminative, and unitive levels ("levels of spiritual engagement") of ascent to God.[56] One could profitably fit this template over the *Life of Païsios* and discover where the fit is neat and where it is not (see below in part 4). As Coakley notes, the first stage, the purgative, can be "largely oppositional, and the 'practices' remain somewhat legalistically construed: Christian *ethike* is being established."[57] The *Life of Païsios* often frames this opposition as a psycho-somatic tug of war between the world *(tò kosmikón)* and the monk in the desert, the wiles and seductions of the city *(pólis)* versus the contemplative quiet *(hēsychía)* of the monastic way of life *(politeía)*. Linguistically, the *Life of Païsios*, like a refiner's fire,[58] transmutes *pólis* (the city, the world) into *politeía*, a (holy) way of life: it is *érōs* and *agápē* that guide the ascetic through the purgative to the illuminative and on to the unitive (see below, part 4).[59]

As Coakley concludes her first chapter vis-à-vis the contemporary "ecclesiastical crisis" over homosexuality (and sexuality in general), she has shown that the subject of love/desire and asceticism are both timeless (the *Life of Païsios*) and timely (the various ancient and modern onslaughts against love/loving desire adduced in her book and in this essay).[60] We must, she tells us, "re-imagine theologically the whole project of our human sorting, taming, and purifying of desires within the crucible of *divine* desire. Such is the ascetical long haul set before us, in which faithfulness plays the indispensable role endemic to the demands of the primary love for God."[61] The *Life of Païsios*, then, with Sarah Coakley's *vade mecum*, despite coming from a very distant time and place, culture and latitude, can help those who endeavor the ascetic, both narrowly and broadly understood, to do so, both fearlessly and fruitfully. As Rowan Williams insightfully teaches:

> Look at the monastic fathers [and mothers, I would add] of the Egyptian desert.[62] They managed to combine two things that we often pull apart: they are absolutely rigorous towards themselves, they do not allow themselves any illusions or false pictures of who they are; they do not allow themselves as we say to "get away" with anything. They look, with a very cool eye, at the fantasies and ambitions and the consoling stories that they—like other people—tell themselves, and they lay them bare before God. They are very clear about the difference between truth and falsehood, sin and grace.[63]

Paul Evdokimov makes a startling claim: "Humanity is different before and after the Incarnation." He then continues with an even more startling assertion: "It can also be said that human consciousness is different before and after the ascetic of the desert."[64] Yes, as Coakley affirms, it's a long haul, but we can, Evdokimov tells us, not just at the end but along the way, catch the halo.

Part 4: A Spirituality of Desire in the *Life of Païsios*

Any explorer of the spiritual and theological terrain of the *Life of Païsios* must face a key tripartite question: Is its spirituality of desire a map shared by other early monastic literature definitely or likely dated to the fourth to sixth centuries, such as the *Apophthegmata, Historia Monachorum,* and *Lausiac History*? Is it better to search for parallels in the writing of later hagiographies? Or is the *Life*'s "erotic" guide and guidance sui generis, anchoritic (so to say) rather than cenobitic? The paradigm of early monastic hagiography, Athanasius' *Life of Antony*, uses *érōs* only twice, both positively: as in the *Life of Païsios*, the monks love monastic ascetic disciplines and virtue. "Lover," however, does not occur.[65] The Bohairic Coptic *Life of John the Little*, which has no extant Greek text, uses "lover" only once, and there the word more accurately means "adulterer."[66] The *Life of John* uses *agápē* and its Coptic equivalents sixteen times; *érōs* does not appear.[67] The main Greek texts for Abba Daniel of Scetis use "love" only in compounds with *philía* except once where almsgiving equals *agápē*.[68] These early monastic sources suggest that the *Life of Païsios*' spirituality of desire may in fact be unique.

With this foregrounding, and with Coakley's understanding as a guide in part 3 above, we can now look in some detail at the first paragraph of the *Life of Païsios*, part of the work's Exordium. Here is that section, with key Greek terms transliterated in parentheses:

> 1. The delightful things of life [*tà térpna toû bíou*], although subject to change and dissolution, by distorting through a lust [*érōta < érōs*] for inferior pleasure [*mikràs hēdonḗs*][69] a person's understanding of what loving desire [*érōta*] is and by making the intellect [*noûn < noûs*] incline toward the passions [*páthē < páthos*], know how to attract to themselves those attracted to loving desire [*érōta*]. As a result, understanding and intellect not only despise the good things promised by God,[70] but also—amazingly!—turn away from the Creator of true life [*tês óntōs zoês*][71] and prefer life's pleasures [*taúta* refers to *páthē*, the passions, above] rather than the good things that come from God [*tôn kalôn ekeínou*].[72] By doing this, they are willingly enticed to an eternal and bitter death.

In the same way, proportionately, divine affection [*ho theíos póthos*][73] works on those who are lovers [*erastás* < *erastḗs*; see *érōs*] of the things to come and of those things grounded in hope. To be sure, remembrance of the reward for labors performed here and of the magnificent prizes in the world to come for those purified here customarily teaches them to despise not only what is ephemeral and vain but also their lives and their wives, whom they naturally love [*philouménēn*], as was said by Christ in the divine Gospels.[74]

They procure for themselves the longest and most painful death [*thánatos*], borne each day; by means of myriad labors and endurance and by means of ascetic practice [*askḗsei* < *áskēsis*] and various struggles[, however,] they fight against invisible forces and, by always constraining nature [*phýsis*], with incorporeal forces [*asōmátois* < *sôma*], they contend with the body [*sôma*].[75]

As discussed above, Sarah Coakley views *érōs*, "desire" (or as we translate it in the *Life*, except for two occurrences, "loving desire") as oppositional. *The Life of Païsios* puts *érōs* front and center: in the very first sentence of the *Life* the author presents a boxing card with *érōs* vs. *érōs* (with two subordinate participles in Greek offering no doubt as to who will win): "The delightful things of life, although subject to change and dissolution, by distorting through a lust [*érōta* < *érōs*] for inferior pleasure a person's understanding of what loving desire [*érōta*] is . . . know how to attract to themselves those attracted to loving desire [*érōta*]." Opposition becomes *especially* true, Coakley says, when a person joins desire with practice (praxis): "Much of the emphasis is on setting one's life in a direction *different* from that of the 'world.'" Because of this, she continues, "the rhetoric [as cited in the *Life* immediately above] may be largely oppositional."[76]

Building on Coakley's insight, I wish to suggest that such opposition, given human nature, is not merely adversative but *appositive*: to place—or, in this case, *be*—in apposition is "the act of placing together or bringing into proximity; juxtaposition."[77] In other words, the Garden's serpent doesn't mythically and only adversatively invent desire;[78] it is already appositively there.[79] Such opposition, and apposition, I would argue, and as Coakley in her book deftly shows, is not a facile, and escapist, dualism that sees everything not merely as quotidian blacks and whites but as resplendent divine light versus—always versus—to borrow from William Blake, dark satanic mills that take good wheat and grind it down into a caliginous flour.[80]

The dualistic tendency of the Exordium, then, its *Tendenz*, is at odds with its narrative. The greatest adversative, even adversary, in early monastic literature, as the *Life* shows, is not Satan *but the monks themselves*. And the irony of early Christian monasticism, cruel and exemplary, and saving, is that these monks are *precisely the people who dare to take on human contrariness*, the "erotic" pull and decision-making of "desire"/"lust" and "loving desire." If monastic Lives, and lives, did not have superlative conclusions (there is too much struggle, and too many battlefield dead, for the endings to be "happy"), reading these *Lives* would be like closing a good book of noir detective fiction where not only does the hero not catch the murderer but he or she in fact gets killed and the now double-murderer gets away to commit yet more homicide.

The author of the Exordium to the *Life of Païsios* thus inherits a stage already prepared and furnished with an existential, even soteriological, understanding; the author's job is now to populate the stage not immediately with the incarnation of the virtues, but with a prologue (¶1) that details both oppositional and appositional language and themes. One could say that language and themes function as the incorporeal lighting now readied, as it were, for the protagonist's entrance later in ¶2. "The delightful things of life," the Exordium immediately emphasizes, are transient, "subject to change and dissolution." As a Baptist minister and student once said to the class, "Ain't no U-Haul following the hearse." Although impermanent and evanescent, however, these desires nevertheless have, adversatively and appositionally, the countervailing ability, power, "through a lust [*érōta* < *érōs*] for inferior pleasure, to make the intellect incline toward the passions."[81]

The quotation immediately above is one of only two places in the *Life* where *érōs* is negative. The rest of the hagiography, through the life and example of holy Païsios, transforms this, essentially false, desire—false in its very essence *(óntos)*—into a true loving desire (also *érōs*) for God and a holy way of life. Origen had spoken earlier of transformation of *érōs*.[82] But before metamorphosis, a warning: the "delightful things of life," with "pleasure" as their advance guard, bend one "toward the passions."[83] One could say they make one *lust* for the passions. "As a result," the Exordium threatens, the "understanding and intellect not only despise what is good" ("the good things," *tôn kalôn*, with its echo of Socrates and Plato, *tò kalón*, "the good"),[84] but "turn away from the Creator of true life himself."[85] Such miscreants, "attracted" to the passions, are thus now "enticed to an eternal and bitter death."

But now the lighting, previously dim, comes on full force, like someone in darkness turning on stadium lights before the big game. Proportionally—that is, inversely—the Exordium now pivots from dangers and threat to God's grace: "divine affection": "In the same way, proportionately, divine affection [*ho theíos póthos*] works on those who are lovers [*erastás* < *erastḗs*; see *érōs*] of the things to come and of those things grounded in hope." *Póthos*, "affection" or "desire," occurs eight times in the *Life*, and is always positive. Emulating the apostle Paul, the author affirms that divine affection "works on those who are lovers of the [good] things to come and of those things grounded in hope." "Hope" here could well be an allusion to what the Apostle in 1 Corinthians 13:13 declares will abide: faith, hope, and love.

"Lovers" here, and throughout the *Life*, translates *erastḗs*, cognate with *érōs*, that is, those with "loving desire." *Erastḗs*, like *póthos* and *érōs* (except for the two exceptions noted above and below), is always positive. For example, Païsios becomes "a lover of the virtues" (4) and then strengthens his fellow monastics "and with his teaching . . . makes them imitators [*mimētás*] and lovers of his holy way of life [*politeía*]" (33). Becoming a lover of God and of a holy way of life thus involves, indeed requires, mimesis, sacred emulation—and then, vitally, becoming emulatable.[86]

Mimesis in the *Life* can be a part of, lead to, repentance. A "certain brother," instead of "adhering to the desert and its good practices," follows his own will instead of God's—an important cautionary and realistic theme in the *Life*—and forsakes his monastic way of life (64). In a city, often in early monasticism the adversarial, appositive, lair of temptation and iniquity, he becomes "consumed with erotic love" (*érōti* < *érōs*). This is the second of only two times in the *Life* that *érōs* occurs with negative significance, and the occurrence here draws us back to its first appearance, in the Exordium: "The delightful things of life . . . distorting through a lust [*érōta* < *érōs*] for [or: love of] inferior pleasure a person's understanding of what loving desire [*érōta*] is . . . know how to attract to themselves those attracted to loving desire [*érōta*]." Thus "consumed with love," this brother's consumption (play on words intended) is for—double jeopardy—a Jewish woman.[87] Thus, using a seemingly counterfactual metaphor—she impregnates him—the *Life* tells us that "he conceived suffering and gave birth to transgression."

The author here echoes James 1:15: "one is tempted by one's own desire [*epithymía*],[88] being lured and enticed by it; then, when that desire has conceived, it gives birth to sin, and that sin, when fully grown, gives birth to death. Do not be deceived, my beloved [*agapētoí*]." James, quite appropriately, emphasizes that it is one's own desire that tempts a person. Thus, if we extend the metaphor, the monk impregnates himself. So, "separated from the Christians" and "cast down into the depths of his own impiety," one day nevertheless—or because of his fall—he, like Paul in Acts, receives "the illuminating light of divine providence."[89] That is, God's saving will triumphs over the monk's apostate desire (erotic in the negative sense).

After he repents, he sees some monks from where he "had long ago practiced the ascetic life." The fallen monk's heart, like the lovers in the Song of Songs, is "wounded" and he "remembers" the "ancient and holy community" he once forsook.[90] And, thus, now daily forsakes. Temptations, like a lion always lurking nearby (1 Pet 5:8), occur throughout the *Life*. The "chameleon-like Enemy" (that is, the Devil, in a monastic topos) tempts Païsios with wealth (14). The saint, like Jesus, defeats the Devil and devotes "himself to difficult spiritual practices" that differ "in no way from those of the incorporeal beings" (16). Thus Païsios becomes *isángelos*,[91] equal to God's angels.

Païsios, like Jesus, must oppositionally—*appositionally*—be tempted before he can overcome temptation and offer God's grace to others. Throughout the rest of the *Life* he becomes, then, not Christ's equal, *isóchristos*, but the Savior's stand-in, *sýnchristos*, the bearer of grace, absolution, and redemption.[92] Like the great Antony, "by the grace of God" Païsios offers throngs "of people, both lay persons and monastics," "drink flowing from the ever-flowing and divine fountain"; he teaches those "whom love [*érōs*] had inflamed to live in contemplative solitude" (19). But, with Satan always lurking, biding his opportune time, and attacking, fallenness, as with each human being, recurs in the *Life*.

- So Païsios rescues, although at length and, one should note, with difficulty, "a disobedient and insubordinate monk" from Hades (¶¶21–31).
- He defends the divinity of the Holy Spirit against a heretical monk who has fallen because of ignorance (41–43).
- He rescues "a certain disciple" from apostasy (53B–57).
- He helps a young anchorite defeat the Devil (59–62).
- He intercedes with God on behalf of another apostate monk (64–66).
- He prays on behalf of an impudent priest (68).
- He intervenes to absolve two young monks of false charges (75).

Païsios, therefore, with monastic mimesis emulates the life of Antony: he receives grace, through grace he overcomes temptation, he thus advances in the spiritual life, then he teaches others how to defeat ever-present demonic forces (whether one views these as exterior or interior, or both); thus enlightened and sacrally engaged, he dies a holy death. Païsios, therefore, within the monastic community, has in ministry acted as God's public defender. Is all this, we might ask, hagiographic stereotyping—or cliché? Or is it a very realizable monastic, and non-monastic, *politeía*, way of life?

Filled with grace ("grace" occurs twenty-four times in the *Life*), Païsios and Paul of Tamma thus become "agents of salvation for everyone" (76).[93] Païsios can reach this climax only through grace *and* loving desire, as a holy lover: the saint "is inflamed with loving desire" (*érōs*) (69); he teaches, and incarnates, "being wounded by the divine loving desire" (*érōti*) for obedience (69).[94] To use later monastic and mystical terms, Païsios, *and with him the reader*, in mimesis, passes therefore from the purgative stage to the illuminative and unitive stages.[95] The purgative stage, as discussed above, is oppositional. Using the *Rule of Saint Benedict*, Sarah Coakley suggests that the illuminative path is practice, which "will re-modulate beliefs" and "cause us to find Christ."[96] Coakley says, correctly, that such a path helps us to find Christ "in new and unexpected places." The *Life*, however, appears to be saying that Christ dwells in *expected* places: fellow monks, the monastery, the monastic way of life. In a holy workshop of virtue ("virtue" or "virtues" occurs eighteen times in the *Life*),[97] Païsios is like John the Little: While "in this holy workshop of virtue [John] progressed in two ways," by emulation and through grace: "in the doctrine of his teacher [Abba Amoi], and through the generosity of the blessings of heaven, as he grew, advancing and being illuminated [*efči ouōini* = Greek *phōtízō/phōtismós*] through the fruits of the Holy Spirit, so that (to put it concisely, according to the preaching of our Savior) 'it is sufficient for the disciple to be like his teacher'" (Mt 10:25//Lk 6:40).[98]

Through praxis, practice, the learner learns from a master; the village or city workshop has moved thence, like early monasticism, to the desert.[99] The *Life of Païsios*, like the *Rule of Saint Benedict*, as Coakley adduces it, shows that the illuminative is emulative, and that emulation can lead to illumination:

- Païsios learns from Pambo: "After Païsios had been mystically instructed[100] with these edifying words of his teacher and became filled with a yearning to work for God, he followed his teacher's instructions" (¶¶5–6).
- The Savior instructs Païsios about fasting, visiting others, anger, zeal, spiritual struggle, and ministry: "'The person who spiritually struggles alone is my disciple, but the person who spiritually struggles and ministers to others is my son and heir'" (48–49).[101]
- Thus instructed, ministering to his neighbor, Païsios teaches John, who is "suffering greatly because of his ascetic abstinence," about true fasting (58).
- Païsios teaches his disciple about the fruits of disobedience and obedience (69).

Illumination, through spiritual practice (*áskēsis*, asceticism), can foster holiness. We are now far removed from the boxing ring at the beginning of this introduction: the monk, the ascetic, the trainee, moves from *érōs* to *érōs*, the "lust" of the monk for the Jewish woman (see above) to "loving desire" for God, for oneself—and for others. Such holiness, thence, can lead to union, "theological insights," Coakley affirms, "available *only* through practices."[102] She concentrates in chapter 4 "on that minority strand in Christian theology and spirituality which has claimed that it is possible in this life to be *incorporated* into the life of the Trinity."[103] The *Life of Païsios* teaches exactly such incorporation. With a novelist's deft foreshadowing, the author has the holy man, with a three-handled basket that he crafts, teach about the unity of the Trinity: because, the saint says, "I am a friend and lover [*phílos* . . . *erastḗs*] of the supremely holy Trinity, it is incumbent upon me to represent through my work the persons of the Trinity and to praise the Trinity in a three-fold fashion by making these three signs representing it" (41–43).

With Païsios as both *didáskalos*, teacher, and *erastḗs*, one filled with loving desire *(érōs)*, the *Life of Païsios* uses implicit sexual language (and, thus, metaphor) to show that Païsios transmutes sexual eros not to the asexual nor the trans-sexual, but rather—meant very positively here—the hypersexual, where Greek *hypér-*, contrary to its usual sense in modern English of excessiveness ("hyperbolic"), embodies a whole range of meanings: "over, beyond," "in defense of, on behalf of," "for, instead of, in the name of," "for, because, by reason of," "exceeding, beyond," and, oppositionally, even "for the purpose of preventing or avoiding."[104] Here, loving desire and the active illuminative (illumination through action) join with practices that can bring union, emulating the unity of the Trinity. Such union often identifies as or with contemplative solitude, *hēsychía*:

- Païsios is "possessed by a love [*érōs*] for contemplative solitude [*hēsychía*]" (¶11).
- The monks' "loving desire" [*érōs*] has "inflamed" them to live in contemplative solitude *(hēsychía)* (19).
- Païsios is "made fervid in his endeavors by the love [*agápē*] of Christ" (20).
- Poemen is seized with the desire *(póthos)* to see Païsios (45).
- Païsios as "a lover" "desired [*érōn* < *eráō*, cognate with *érōs* and *erastḗs*] intimacy with God" (67).
- Païsios is inflamed with loving desire *(érōs)* (69).
- In solitude Païsios is a lover who desires *(érōn* < *eráō)* intimacy with God and divine ascent while in community his loving desire *(érōn* < *eráō)* is for his neighbor's salvation (77).

Thus Païsios at the end, like Francis, Teresa of Ávila, John of the Cross, and, within our own time, Thomas Merton, is both of the community and moving beyond it, to "intimacy with God and divine ascent": "Accordingly, having already reached a great old age, the great Païsios, shining resplendently in his way of life and famous for his virtues, came to the end of his earthly labors, called from here to heavenly blessedness" (68). As the apostle

Paul declares with great, even universalist, enthusiasm, "And all of us, with unveiled faces, seeing the glory of the Lord as though reflected in a mirror, are being transformed into the same image from one degree of glory to another; for this comes from the Lord, the Spirit."[105] Sarah Coakley illustrates this with a different image: "the goal is a progressive purification of the self so as to become transparent to the divine."[106] From glory to glory.[107]

The *Life of Païsios*, at its best, models such reflective, transformational, and "progressive purification." By doing so, it makes itself necessary. To return to Rowan Williams: "The great saints of the monastic tradition, the Desert Fathers [and Mothers] of Egypt, and St. Benedict and his followers, read to us now as deeply contemporary. The problems they identify and the disciplines that they suggest are not archeology, not museum pieces, they are directly and profoundly our business."[108]

Appendix
List of Three Key Terms in the *Life of Païsios*, with Quotations: "Pleasure/Pleasures" *(τερπνα / térpna)*, "Love" (ἀγάπη / *agápē*) and "Loving Desire" *(ἔρως / érōs)*, and "Lover" (ἐραστής / *erastés*)

The list is by section number (¶), with the Greek words transliterated.

Pleasure/pleasures (τερπνά / *terpná*)
- 1: "Desire for inferior pleasures" *(terpná)*, opposed to "loving desire" *(érōs)*; the desire for inferior pleasures, "by making the intellect incline toward the passions [*páthē*] know how to attract to themselves those attracted to loving desire" [*érōta < érōs*].
- 17: While he is praying, Païsios soars "to heaven. Filled with joy," he first sees "the delights of paradise" *(paradeísou . . . terpná)*.
- 19: Païsios fills the monks "with pleasure" *(hēdonḗs < hēdonḗ)*. "With divine eloquence," he wins over a vast multitude of monks and tells them "to delight in life's pleasures" *(bíou terpnoís)*.
- 39: The monks look down "on pleasures and all of life's delights [*terpnôn*] and instead of all these" receive God. They consider "what is pleasing *to God* to be wealth and pleasure" *(hēdonḗ)*.

Love and loving desire (ἔρως / *érōs*); desire (πόθος / *póthos*); love (ἀγάπη / *agápē*); love (στοργή / *storgḗ*); love (φίλτρον / *phíltron*; φιλία / *philía*)
- 1: With desire, the inferior pleasures, "by making the intellect incline toward the passions [*páthē*] know how to attract to themselves those attracted to loving desire [*érōta < érōs*]."

- 1: "Divine affection [*ho theíos póthos*] works on those who are lovers [*erastás* < *erastḗs* (*érōs*)] of the things to come and of those things grounded in hope."
- 4: Paísios is a "lover" (*erastḗs*) of the virtues; "wounded by both loving desire [*érōti* < *érōs*] for and fear of God, he fell in love [*érōti* < *érōs*] with the monastic way of life."
- 7: Pambo is hastening toward the numerous blessings he desired (*epóthei* < *pothéō* < *póthos*)
- 8: A loving desire (*érōs*) for other, loftier, spiritual disciplines takes possession of Paísios.
- 9: Paísios explicates the secret parts of Jeremiah's prophecy and stimulates his mind through the hidden meanings to a loving desire (*eis érōta* < *érōs*) for the good things promised by God.
- 10: Paísios' "loving desire [*érōti* < *érōs*] for contemplative solitude [*hēsychía*] became inexhaustible."
- 11: Paísios is "possessed by a love [*érōti* < *érōs*] for contemplative solitude" (*hēsychía*).
- 19: The monks' "loving desire" (*érōs*) has "inflamed" them to live in contemplative solitude (*hēsychía*).
- 20: Paísios is "made fervid in his endeavors by the love [*agápēs* < *agápē*] of Christ."
- 21: Paísios desires more than anything (*potheinóteron* < *póthos*) to have the Savior appear while he is praying.
- 21: The "extraordinary love" (*storgḗs* < *storgḗ*) of Christ.
- 31: Divine providence will not overlook Paísios' entreaties or "the great love" (*phíltron*) he has demonstrated for his disobedient disciple. Paísios has emulated the surpassing love (*agápēs* < *agápē*) that God has for human beings.
- 45: Poemen is seized with the desire (*póthō(i)*) to see Paísios.
- 45: The fame of Paísios "spread throughout the world" and "incited those whose souls love virtue [*philarétous*] to see him and receive his prayers."
- 47: A monk, "like an athlete, fasts on his own; inflamed with desire [*póthō(i) phlegómenos*], he allows himself to suffer beyond his ability to do so."
- 47: Paísios asks the Lord about those who walk "according to your commandments" and visits "those who love [*agapôsi* < *agapáō*] you."
- 47: Christ exclaims to Paísios, "How wonderful is the generosity of my servant, who emulates my love [*agápēn* < *agápē*]!"
- 50: Paísios is someone who "submits himself to humility and love [*agápēs* < *agápē*] for God."

- 53A: A monk leaves Païsios, "blessing and praising God and those who love [*agapṓntas* < *agapáō* < *agápē*] him."
- 64: A certain monk is consumed "with erotic love" (*érōti* < *érōs*) for a Jewish woman.
- 67: The Savior says to Païsios, "How wonderful is the generosity of my servant, who emulates my love!" (*agápēn*)
- 67: A monk, "after living in obedience and living a holy and chaste way of life with his behavior founded on a love of virtue [*philáretos*]," departs this life and goes to the Lord.
- 69: The narrator exclaims, "How merciful and compassionate you are, good Lord! With the love [*phíltron*] you have for those who love you [*erastás* < *erastḗs*], how you reach down to those who desire [*potheínos* < *póthos*] you!"
- 69: The holy Païsios is inflamed with loving desire (*érōs*).
- 69: Païsios speaks to a monk about "the error of disobedience" and not "being wounded by the divine loving desire [*érōti* < *eros*] for obedience."
- 72: A monk wants to "hear loving details [*axierásata*, literally "worthy of love," related to *érōs* and *erastḗs*] about Païsios."
- 74: The narrator speaks of "wonderful things for those who love God" (*philothéois*).
- 75: Two "brothers by birth," "both accomplished in contemplative quiet" (*hēsychía*), receive permission from Païsios "to set out upon a life of solitude." So they withdraw to the solitude they desire (*pothouménē* < *pothéō* < *pōthos*).
- 77: Païsios spends "his time wisely, both his time in community and his time in contemplative solitude [*hēsychía*]: in solitude he was a lover who desired [*erôn* < *eráō*, cognate with *érōs* and *erastḗs*] intimacy with God and divine ascent while in community his loving desire [*erôn* < *eráō*] was for his neighbor's salvation."

Lover (ἐραστής / *erastḗs*)
- 1: "Divine affection [*ho theíos póthos*] works on those who are lovers [*erastás* < *erastḗs*] of the things to come and of those things grounded in hope."
- 4: Païsios becomes "a lover [*erastḗs*] of the virtues."
- 33: Païsios' teaching strengthens the brothers and with his teaching he makes them imitators and lovers (*erastás* < *erastḗs*) of his holy way of life.
- 34: When Païsios goes to the monks, his arrival does not escape the notice of those who fervently love (*erastás* < *erastḗs*) the good things that he has to offer.

- 36: Constantine proclaims "the good news of divine benediction" to Paḯsios, who enkindles the lovers *(erastás < erastḗs)* of the holy monastic way of life.
- 41: Paḯsios declares that "I am a friend and lover [*phílos . . . erastḗs*] of the supremely holy Trinity."
- 69: The narrator exclaims, "How merciful and compassionate you are, good Lord! With the love [*phíltron*]) you have for those who love you [*erastás < erastḗs*], how you reach down to those who desire [*potheínos < póthos*] you!"
- 69: Paul of Tamma is Paḯsios' "fellow lover" *(sunerastḗs < erastḗs)*.

Sigla
[]: translators' addition or gloss
<>: an addition or correction from another text
{}: deletion

Index to some key monastic terms in the *Life of Paḯsios*
The numbers following the terms refer to section numbers (¶).
Ascetic(ism)
    Áskēsis / ἄσκησις 1, 40, 41, 53 (2x), 59, 65
    Agṓn / ἀγών 1, 76
Ascetic discipline(s) (*agōgḗ* / ἀγωγή) 1, 8, 76
Ascetic labors (*pónoi* / πόνοι) 78
Ascetic practice (*politeía* / πολιτεία) *see* Way of life
Ascetic struggles (*agōnízomai* / ἀγωνίζομαι) 61
Athlete (*athlētḗs* / ἀθλητής) 47 (2x)
Chosen (*eklektós* / ἐκλεκτός) 3, 5, 13, 14, 28, 47, 69, 77
Command(ments) (*entolḗ* / ἐντολή) 3, 4, 13 (2x), 48, 72, 74
Contemplative quiet/solitude/insight (*hēsychía* / ἡσυχία) 10, 11 (3x), 19 (2x), 51, 75, 76 (2x), 77
Delightful things (*terpná* / τερπνά) 1, 17
Desire (*póthos* / πόθος) 7, 21, 45, 47, 69, 75
Grace(s) (*cháris* / χάρις) 4 (2x), 5 (2x), 14, 17, 19, 22, 24, 34, 47, 50, 51, 53, 54, 61 (3x), 64, 65, 66, 70, 75 (2x)
Love
    agápe / ἀγάπη 13, 20, 31 (3x), 48, 50, 53A, 67
    érōs / ἔρως (including forms of *eráō* / ἐράω, "to love") 1 (3x), 2, 4, 9 (2x), 10, 11, 19, 20, 64, 69 (2x), 77
    philía / φιλία (and words built off of *phil-*) 1, 2, 13
    phíltron /φίλτρον 31, 69
    storgḗ / στοργή 21

Lover (*erastḗs* / ἐραστής) 1, 4, 33, 34, 36, 41, 69, 76, 79
Miracle(s), wonder(s) (*thaúma* / θαύμα) 2, 3, 30, 49, 67, 74, 78 (2x), 77, 79, 80
Mystery (*mystḗrion* / μυστήριον) 35, 36, 40
Passions (*páthos* / πάθος [sing.], *páthē* / πάθη [pl.]) 1, 68, 77
Power (*dýnamis* / δύναμις) 3, 5, 14, 15 (2x), 18 (3x), 36, 60, 74, 75, 79
Virtue(s)
    aretḗ / ἀρετή 2, 3 (2x), 4, 5, 7, 12, 13, 14, 19, 34, 50, 51, 68, 76, 77
    philáretos / φιλάρετος (lover of virtue) 45, 67
Way of life (*politeía* / πολιτεία) 1, 2, 4, 5, 8, 10, 11 (2x), 12, 14, 23 (2x), 36 (2x), 38, 67 (2x), 77 (2x), 78
Will (*thélēma* / θέλημα) 11, 13, 19, 59, 64
Wonder *see* Miracle
World(ly) (*kosmikós* / κοσμικός) 1, 67, 68 (2x)

The Greek *Life of Païsios* in Translation
The Life and Ascetic Practice of Our Holy Father Païsios
Written by Our Holy Father John the Little[109]
Manuscript Family A
Recension GR1
Translated by Tim Vivian and Apostolos N. Athanassakis

Exordium[110]
1. The delightful things of life,[111] although subject to change and dissolution, by distorting through a lust[112] for inferior pleasure[113] a person's understanding of what loving desire[114] is and by making the intellect incline toward the passions,[115] nevertheless know how to attract to themselves those attracted to loving desire.[116] As a result, understanding and intellect not only arrogantly despise the good things promised by God,[117] but also—amazingly!—turn away from the Creator[118] of true life and prefer life's pleasures rather than the good things that come from God. By doing this, they are willingly enticed to an eternal and bitter death.

In the same way, proportionately, godly affection[119] works on those who are lovers[120] of the things to come and of those things grounded in hope. To be sure, remembrance of the reward for labors performed here and of the magnificent prizes in the world to come for those purified here customarily teaches them to despise not only what is ephemeral and vain but also their lives and their wives, whom they naturally love,[121] as was said by Christ in the godly Gospels.[122] They construct for themselves the longest and most painful death, borne each day; by means of myriad labors and endurance and by means of ascetic practice and various struggles[, however,] they fight against invisible forces and by always constraining nature with incorporeal forces, they contend[123] with the body.[124]

2. With regard to such noble and godly men,[125] one whose birth and upbringing and especially magnificent life—Païsios was the man's name—will be offered here, let no one, hearing of those miracles that transcend nature, disbelieve the narrator because of them,[126] nor think that I, on account of the honor or love[127] I hold for such an eminent and belovèd father[128] as this, am adding anything elevated and insurmountable that ascribes glory to this man besides what I saw with my own eyes and heard with my own ears.[129] That man was far beyond the reach of any human glory and self-importance.[130] On account of this, therefore, the person being praised by the angels in the heights does not need base praises, but for the benefit of those who listen and for those who deliberately choose to imitate that man's virtue, I will recount in full the praiseworthy things about this man.[131]

Païsios' birth and parentage

3. Egypt, therefore, brought forth the great and famous man.[132] It was she who long ago produced Moses, the most eminent of the prophets,[133] who saw God;[134] through his relationship with God, Moses became famous in the Scriptures[135] for his surpassing miracles. Not long afterward, she demonstrated her glory through the shining example of the virtues of the holy Païsios, which greatly enriched his name.

Both of Païsios' parents were devout, fearing the Lord,[136] blamelessly walking in God's commandments and possessing all goodness.[137] To them were born seven children who possessed the same virtues. Their parents were sufficiently wealthy to supply the needy with a generous and open hand, offering each person what he needed; to be sure, as much as they distributed their possessions to the hands of the poor, God's unstinting largesse gave them back even more in return. As a result, their lives prospered in everything.[138]

The death of Païsios' father; an angel appears to his mother

Because no one among mortals lives without tasting death, the father died and the care of the children fell to his most noble wife who suffered alone. Of all the children, the youngest was Païsios and, because of his age, he gave his mother the most concern; as a result (there is no doubt), a kind-looking angel of the Lord appeared in the middle of the night. "God, the father of orphans,"[139] he said, "has sent me. Why do you appear so downhearted?" he said. "Is it because you have to care for the children and think that you alone are responsible for them and God does not care about them? Do not be discouraged. Dedicate one of your sons to God Most High, and through him to God's ever-glorified and all-holy name."

She said, "All my children are God's. May he take whoever pleases [him]."

The angel who appeared to her took Païsios by the hand and said, "This one pleases the Lord."

She said, "He's not capable of serving God; he's too young. Take one of the bigger children instead, whoever's old enough."

The godly angel said to her, "No, most noble of women, God's power is accustomed to manifesting itself through the weak.[140] This one is the Lord's chosen;[141] he will please God."

Having said these words, he disappeared.

Païsios goes to Scetis

4. She awoke from sleep and, astonished at the godly order given to her in the vision, offered[142] hymns of thanksgiving to God, saying, "May your mercy be upon me,[143] Lord, and upon your servant Païsios."[144] She spoke

these words and other words of thanksgiving like them; praying for her child, she presented him to God as a consecrated offering.[145]

Godly Païsios became a lover[146] of the virtues[147] and increased both in age and in grace: wounded by both loving desire[148] for and fear of God,[149] he fell in love[150] with the monastic way of life. After some time had passed, then, during which it was necessary for him to keep the godly commandments,[151] by godly grace he entered the desert of Scetis like a spotless lamb[152] and was guided to the godly and great Pambo,[153] the shepherd of the spiritual flock.[154]

Païsios, as Pambo's disciple, advances spiritually

5. The godly father, receiving him with all holiness and joy,[155] clothed him in the holy monastic habit. Pambo was not lacking in godly knowledge but had been instructed, rather, through a heavenly vision concerning [Païsios'] future. Because Païsios was a chosen vessel of grace and was guided by godly grace, he was directed to every suitable[156] virtue. He first achieved the characteristics of obedience,[157] willingly doing everything his father saw fit to order and doing it perfectly.[158] He later added to these by advancing in perfection, taking on a harder way of life. When our godly father saw Païsios imposing these mightier endeavors on himself, he said to him, "Païsios, my son, it isn't right for a combatant[159] who's a beginner to look someone directly in the face; instead, he should always keep his eyes looking down at his feet, with his mind continuously looking above[160] with discerning eyes in order to perceive what is real: the spiritual beauty of the ineffable glory of God. By doing this, he glorifies and sings hymns of praise to the all-powerful goodness of the Creator."[161]

6. After Païsios had been mystically instructed[162] with these edifying words of his teacher, therefore, and became filled with a yearning to work for God, he followed his teacher's instructions.[163] At that time, for three years he would carry out the godly father's order to the letter, not looking into the faces of the saints at all;[164] instead, he devoted himself completely to reading the Holy Scriptures and searching out their meaning. He would irrigate with their flowing streams his own soul[165] and was, if I may use the words of David, "like a tree that, flourishing when planted beside streams of water, bears ripe, sweet fruit in due and proper season."[166] As a result I may also speak this way.[167] "How sweet are your words to my throat, sweeter than honey to my mouth!"[168] Thus he was someone who prayed unceasingly, as the Apostle commands,[169] with fasts and all-night vigils,[170] reining in and instructing[171] his body, faithfully keeping in his heart whatever any wise person said.[172]

7. When this godly elder[173] saw how Païsios was advancing in spiritual discipline[174] and, like a father, observed him progressing in the godly virtues, he even more assiduously offered him his hand, rousing him and

moving him forward; and so, quickly guiding him and leading him into all knowledge and action, he rightly proclaimed him tried and tested.

The time for the spiritual elder's death was drawing near, summoning him to his appointed place in heaven. Holy Pambo, hastening toward the numerous blessings he desired,[175] proclaimed Païsios worthy and, prophesying at length and in detail concerning him, departed from this life for life eternal.[176] In this way he gloriously received the good things hoped for in heaven.[177]

After Pambo's death, John remains with Païsios

8. I, humble John, remained with the holy Païsios, the two of us sharing the same roof. We were of one mind,[178] living together and together carrying out the way of life laid down in the rule[179] we received from our father: we strengthened one another and, as David rightfully says, lived intentionally as brothers, with the same goal in mind,[180] attending to our own souls. After we had lived together for some time, yoked together in this fashion, a loving desire[181] for other, loftier, spiritual disciplines[182] took possession of Païsios, so we had to separate, as I will describe for us in full.

Païsios' spiritual disciplines

9. These, then, were the spiritual contests undertaken by Païsios, who was always fervent in the Spirit: he did not eat bread[183] all week. On Saturday his food was bread and salt; the rest of the week, instead of actual bread, he would enjoy spiritual bread. He used to continuously recite the prophecy[184] of the godly Jeremiah and, they say, the prophet would often appear to him, explaining the secret parts of the prophecy and stimulating his mind through the hidden meanings to a loving desire[185] for the good things promised by God.

10. Since he was always pushing forward to what lies ahead,[186] he was not content with his former practices but insisted on finding other ones: to his former practice of fasting for one week he added another; fasting for two weeks, at the beginning of the third he would partake of a little bread with salt as his food. Even more remarkable is the fact that no one knew about his way of life,[187] equal to the angels, except God alone, who sees what is hidden and has the unknown right before his eyes. And so his loving desire[188] for contemplative quiet[189] became inexhaustible, but what he held dear seemed to be to offer prayers in solitude to God alone, to converse with him and be reconciled with the Supreme Judge and draw near to him through illuminations received in solitude.

Païsios and John the Little separate

11. Knowing that he was wholly absorbed with such thoughts as these, although I could not bear the idea of separating from him I attempted

to find out about this contemplative quiet[190] that he was planning as a way of life, to see whether it was in accordance with God or was something of his own devising. "Brother Païsios," I said, "I see that you're possessed by a love[191] for contemplative quiet. You know very well that I'm also held captive by its spell, but I don't understand what sort of thought it is or where it comes from.[192] Come, then, let's entreat God's mercies and without hesitation follow his will for us: either the two of us persevere together in this way of life or we live apart, separate from each other."

Païsios replied, "You're right, belovèd. Let's do as you suggest, so our zeal for contemplative quiet may be acceptable and beyond suspicion."

After saying these things,[193] we spent the night in prayerful vigil, entreating God not to overlook our supplications to him and to show us his goodness and compassionate mercies.

12. About the time for early morning prayer, a godly angel stood beside us and said, "You will be separated by God, with each of you having his own dwelling. You will no longer live together in the same community; instead, each of you will follow his own way of life. You, John, will persevere here, and will be a guide leading many to salvation. And you, Païsios, servant of Christ, will leave here for the western part of the desert. 'Countless numbers of people will be assembled around you,' says the Lord, 'and a monastery will be built there by godly decree, and my name will be glorified there through you.'"

Having said these things, the angel disappeared from sight. We obeyed his command and went our own ways. I resumed my life there, as I had been commanded, while Païsios went off at some distance, as had been determined: going to the west, he dug a cave and lived in it.[194] He became so close to God through his surpassing purity and the ascetic disciplines God showed him that even Christ would often appear to him, guiding and leading him into virtue,[195] as the following account will show.

The Savior appears to Païsios

13. One day, then, as Païsios sat in his cave with a godly hymn on his lips,[196] the Savior appeared to him, saying, "Peace be with you, my beloved servant Païsios."[197]

Païsios got up, filled with fear and trembling.[198] "Christ, who loves us,"[199] he said, "behold your servant.[200] What about me is good, Lord, when compared with your goodness? What is the reason for your condescending to come to me?"

The Lord said to him, "Do you see this desert, in all its length and breadth? Through you I will fill it with monks glorifying my name."[201]

Païsios, the Lord's chosen,[202] fell to the ground and said, "All things, Master,[203] are subject to your mighty hand and have their being at the same time as you will it. I entreat Your Goodness: Tell me who will provide those bivouacking[204] in this desert[205] with what they need?"

He said, "Believe me, I am telling the truth. If I find that they hold love[206] as the mother of virtues and keep my commandments, no one will lack anything.[207] I will take complete care of them."

Then the godly man[208] said to the Lord, "Once more I shall ask Your Goodness: How will they be able to avoid without difficulty the snares of the Enemy and his fearful assaults?"[209]

The Savior said, "If, as I told you, they keep my commandments with humility[210] and a humble heart,[211] not only will I make them immune to evil plots and the warfare that threatens them, I will also proclaim them inheritors of the eternal kingdom in the heavenly habitations."[212]

Having said these words, the Savior ascended[213] with glory into heaven while holy Païsios from that time forward was seized with even greater fear, standing in awe of the Savior's condescension toward him.

A rich ruler, suborned by the Devil, comes to Païsios with money

14. The Father of Envy and Misanthropic Enemy, seeing Païsios safely avoiding his ambushes, invincible against his wiles, and victorious against his plots, gnashed his teeth[214] in anger. Unable to approach him because of the godly power[215] Païsios had received from God, he treacherously contrived to overcome him by other means. He thought Païsios could be easily defeated through greed for material possessions and hastened to put forward the pretext of almsgiving so that if by this means Païsios lapsed from his life of poverty, a way might be found to commit terrible deeds against him.

On account of this, the chameleon-like Enemy approached one of the rulers of Egypt, a proud and rich man, and in the form[216] of an angel the Wretched One[217] appeared and said to him, "You, leave. Go to the desert, and you'll find a poor man by the name of Païsios. Although poor, his way of life is rich; he is resplendently adorned with the virtues, and is a chosen vessel of God's grace. When you find him, kindly lavish all your money and praise on him."[218]

15. That ruler, not suspecting the demonic scheme but instead believing that the power appearing to him was angelic, took cargo consisting of all kinds of goods and went to see the holy man. The godly power surrounding Païsios revealed the plan, however, telling him in detail how the Enemy was using the ruler's gifts to plot against him. The godly man immediately arose and went to meet the ruler. When he met him, he was asked by him, "Who might this Païsios be, and where does he live?"

Païsios responded, "And why are you looking for him?"

The ruler said, "I have brought goods, and gold. I want to give them to him to distribute to the monks."

Païsios said, "Forgive me, my Christ-loving friend. If we want to live in this desert, gold or silver is of no use to us. Come now, no one living here will accept anything from you. So go, and don't be sad: God has accepted your gift, if you distribute what you have brought to the poor and needy; there are a lot of needy in the villages of Egypt, both orphans and widows.[219] If you provide for them in God's name,[220] you will have your reward."

Persuaded above all by the words of the holy man, he gave everything to the destitute and the working poor and, dividing up the goods, ordered that all this be done for those in need.[221]

Païsios defeats the Devil and enjoys spiritual communion

16. When Païsios returned to his cave, the Devil appeared to him and said, "What violence you do me, Païsios! Why don't the plans I contrive against you work? You ward them all off! I am leaving, then, to wage war against others. I have been beaten; I am never coming back to attack you!" The godly man rebuked him. "Be quiet!" he said. "You're full of evil."

Put to shame and chased off, the Devil no longer shamelessly dared[222] to come near him. Païsios returned to the inner desert: there he dwelled in the flesh but in the spirit he lived side by side with the heavenly beings and conversed with their Lord and Master, devoting himself to spiritual practices that differed in no way from the spiritual practices of the incorporeal beings.[223] <So the Holy Spirit, who dwelled in him,>[224] was pleased to make Païsios a witness to heavenly treasures and to the joy that the righteous share in heaven.

17. While he was praying, he soared to heaven. Filled with joy, he first saw the delights of paradise,[225] then he observed the Church of the First-born[226] in heaven. Partaking of the immaterial food provided by the spiritual teaching[227] above, he was deemed worthy to receive the gift of fasting and abstinence. Once a week he shared in the Holy Communion on the Lord's Day and would fast until the following Sunday, and this grace stayed with him because he was so enriched by the nature of God[228] of which he partook.[229]

18 (17).[230] Let no one who obeys the godly law doubt that I bear witness to the truth, for everything is subject to godly command. I will tell the truth: after the fear-instilling partaking of Holy Communion, he went without eating for seventy days—and this is not at all remarkable if one considers the unimaginable might possessed by godly power. The partaking of foods completes the natural cycle; it is a force that empties the body

which then needs these foods to effect growth and change. But the creative power[231] of God, which is not subject at all to natural law, fully and unstintingly gives to those of the highest spiritual qualities the ability to transcend nature,[232] for we know that on earth the creative power of God also preserved the lives of ill-fed children[233] in Ephesus for three hundred years and more[234] and will maintain Elijah in heaven[235] until the last <day>.[236] But these examples will have to suffice.[237]

Païsios' pastoral care

19 (18). Throngs of people, both lay persons and monastics, by the grace of God flowed to the godly Païsios like a river overrunning its banks, desiring to remain with him. Buzzing around him like a swarm of bees, they were insatiable as they eagerly <sought>[238] the sweet honeycombs with their godly honey.[239] Offering them drink flowing from the ever-flowing and godly fountain, sweeter than every kind of earthly honey and honeycomb, Païsios filled them with pleasure.[240] With godly eloquence,[241] he won over a vast multitude of monks[242] and told them to delight in life's pleasures;[243] because he took upon his shoulders the yoke of Christ in accordance with the gospel,[244] their numbers grew significantly every day.

Those whom loving desire[245] had inflamed to live in contemplative quiet[246] he taught to keep company with God through prayer while those who were used to a blessed way of life[247] he ordered to live in accord with one another and to live together in a brotherhood.[248] For some he also appointed manual work, doing this so they would not be slack and untrained in the virtues[249] and so they would not only eat <their>[250] bread from the sweat of their own labor,[251] but would also demonstrate loving affection[252] for those in need. He set down this rule above all others:[253] not to do anything—nothing at all—in accordance with one's own will but to accomplish[254] everything with the advice and knowledge of one's spiritual father.[255]

These were Païsios' instructions and the care and concern he showed for his neighbor. With regard to what he taught about contemplative silence[256] and solitude,[257] no account can adequately or accurately describe it. But out of the many examples one could adduce, here are a few, one after another.

The Savior appears to Païsios

20 (19). It happened one time that the godly Païsios went into the inner desert and, finding a cave, lived in it three years. When the hair on his head became very long, he drove some kind of stake into the upper part of the cave; by doing so, he devised a way to tie up his hair, which was the most practical way for him to pray.[258] By night and by day he devoted himself there to numerous ascetic struggles and labors, made fervid in his

endeavors by the love[259] of Christ,[260] considering it rest and refreshment from his toils.[261] And, indeed, the Savior appeared, as it is said in the holy Gospels, and stood before him.[262]

21 (20). The Savior appeared to Païsios when he was at prayer—something Païsios desired[263] more than anything. Unable to bear to look upon the Savior's appearance, Païsios fell to the ground, overcome with awe and fear.[264] Then the Savior stretched out his hand to him[265] (What extraordinary love[266] and affection you have, Christ our King, for those who worship you!),[267] took hold of him, and raised him up, saying, "Peace be with you, my servant.[268] Do not be overwhelmed by fear, nor let <alarm>[269] take hold of your heart. My goodness takes great delight in such things[270] and your prayer[271] is most acceptable to me. Rejoice, therefore, and receive the most resplendent reward in return for your deeds. See! I am giving you this great gift: whatever you ask in my name will be given to you. Furthermore, whatever sins you intercede about for those who sin will be forgiven."[272]

Saint Païsios said, <"Wretch that I am,>[273] I beg to be worthy of such great grace from your goodness, merciful Christ and God, that I may ask for everything <I need>[274] to allow me easily to finish walking your saving pathways and come to a good end, for without your providence it is impossible for us to do anything good. You poured out your precious blood for us and accepted death and burial, through your resurrection bestowing on us salvation.[275] How much suffering and how many deaths[276] ought we to endure for you!"

After Païsios said these things, the Savior blessed him and ascended to heaven. What follows, account by account, will demonstrate the truth of what we have said.

Païsios intercedes with God on behalf of another's disciple
Concerning the death of an elder's disciple[277]

22 (21). It happened that a disciple of one of the elders died. Seized[278] through the deceit of the one who always envies human beings,[279] he left this life disobedient and insubordinate and, what is in fact worse, having sunk into error before his death, he departed this life unrepentant. The elder, therefore, often begged to know where the soul of this indolent disciple had ended up. He saw this disciple in Hades being punished with harsh tortures.[280] Because of this, he was heart-stricken about the disciple and did not stop entreating God with tears and added a new regimen of fasting to his previous fasts until he went without eating for forty days. At that time he heard a voice saying, "It is necessary[281] that that soul for which you beg so fervently stay in Hades until my coming on the clouds with angels and trumpets;[282] then he will receive the payment he deserves for his actions."[283]

23 (22). When the elder heard that his request had been denied, he was filled with sorrow and dejection. He added another forty days of fasting to the fasting he had already undertaken, exhausting himself even more with entreaties to God, but he heard nothing except the original denial. And now he heard:[284] "There will be no remission for him yet; let him, rather, remain in Hades until my coming upon the clouds."[285]

Because the elder was not able to persuade the godly compassion[286] nor was able to hear anything different from what he had already heard (perhaps godly providence was managing things so Païsios[287] would attempt to redeem the disciple), he hurried to the inner desert[288] to see Païsios[289] because he knew that the saint had the freedom to speak openly[290] with God.

Therefore he anchored all his hopes on him, believing that he had the ability to propitiate God on behalf of his disciple.[291]

24 (23). Païsios, knowing through grace about the elder's arrival, met him[292] as the elder was coming to him. Embracing one another with an appropriate greeting, they formally recognized each other. Then Païsios said, "Father, why have you come, distressed like this, to see me, worthless sinner that I am?"

The elder answered and told him why, explaining about his disciple, whom he despaired of, how he had entreated God about him but accomplished nothing, and what he had heard from the godly voice that had declared to him that his disciple would suffer in Hades until the coming of the Lord. He added, "I've come as a suppliant to entreat Your Holiness to feel my sorrow, wretch though I am, that with your supplications to God you may become a suppliant for my miserable disciple; I'm confident that God will be exhorted by you when you entreat him. So, then, I beg of you, do not allow me to remain hemmed in by sorrow; otherwise, it will be impossible for your humble servant to leave here."

25 (24). After speaking like this in detail, the good elder,[293] with tears rather than words, persuaded the great Païsios to appeal to God's mercy and compassion. Païsios said, "It isn't possible for me, holy father,[294] to accomplish such an undertaking. This was something you undertook, even though God has just now rejected your magnanimous request, making unfathomable judgments that he alone <understands>.[295] Nevertheless, so I don't oppose what you've asked me to do, I'll offer myself as a suppliant to God along with you. May whatever he decides come to pass. You remain here, persevering with your prayers, while I go to the inner desert, and together we will entreat God at length."

After saying these words, he went off to the interior desert and stood in prayer. Raising his hands together with his thoughts to heaven, he opened them to the creator of the universe:[296] "Look upon our supplications, we who are your unworthy servants,[297] and, because you are good, cause the soul of the elder's disciple[298] to be freed from the bonds of Hades."

26 (25). Having said these and similar words to our merciful God while praying, he was not going to fail to get God's true promise but the one who stands ready to help everyone and who is unapproachable with bodily eyes immediately made himself visible to Païsios and asked, "What is it that you are asking for yourself at such length, Païsios my servant?"

27 (26). He said, "God who alone understands all things, compassionate one, have mercy on the elder's wretched disciple who had no regard for obedience and who fell into unnatural activities and now, I believe, endures the punishments of Hades. Therefore, do not allow the sufferings of your servant to be regarded as worthless, nor disregard us as we entreat your mercy and compassion."[299]

The Savior said to him, "No, I have already handed down my judgment, which is incontestable: I have determined that he is to enjoy [in Hades][300] his reward for his disobedience and unnatural activities.[301] I will allow no remission for him from his sufferings until I come upon the clouds."[302]

28 (27). But the Lord's chosen, Païsios, responded supplicatingly and said to him, "What, Lord of all, is *not* subject to your godly command and does not comply with whatever you wish? It is easy for you, master of the ages, who have brought everything into being from nonbeing, to come even now the same way as at your second coming."[303]

29 (28). After Païsios had spoken, the Savior disappeared from his sight and ascended into heaven. Then, with frightful majesty, with angels and archangels and trumpets,[304] together with choruses of the righteous and all those things appointed for the last day,[305] he came down from heaven upon the clouds. Afterward, thrones[306] took their positions too, and a fearful judgment seat[307] was displayed and the soul of the dead disciple, summoned from Hades, was placed in Païsios' hands. <Then his soul was entrusted to the elder>,[308] for he was praying where Païsios had left him and was in agony at that hour. (The two of them had agreed that both would pray.)

Suddenly[309] a voice was heard from above. "Receive through the hand of my servant Païsios," it ordered, "the soul of your disciple, which has been delivered from the depths of Hades. You will no longer see him in torment but rather enjoying rest and peace."[310]

Then the soul of the disciple came[311] and stood before the elder and spoke to him, confessing, "I endured many evils in Gehenna because of my disobedience. Disobedience was the cause of my fall and because of it I endured terrible things. But through your intercessions and those of the godly Païsios, God, who loves us,[312] appeared to me[313] and freed[314]

<me>[315] from Hades' chains. Look! I am now being transferred among the humble."[316] After saying these things, the disciple was transferred right before the elder's eyes to the abode of the righteous.

30 (29). These things were seen by the elder at the time appointed for prayer. Because he was convinced and no longer had doubts <about>[317] his disciple's salvation, he went as quickly as he could to the great Païsios and, coming to where Païsios was, found him[318] offering hymns of thanksgiving[319] for the salvation of the dead disciple. Then the elder recounted[320] in detail everything that had taken place in his vision and Païsios described in full the fearful presence of the Lord along with everything he had seen and done.[321] Together the two of them declared their thanksgivings[322] to God, who alone accomplishes such great wonders.[323]

31 (30). Then the elder said to Païsios, "I offer you my deep thanks, godly Païsios. Through your prayers you saved not only my disciple, of whom I despaired, but also my own soul, which was in danger of succumbing to terrible despondency. But now I beg Your Magnanimity, through what marvelous conduct and ascetic struggles have you been considered worthy of such great spiritual gifts? I'd like to know what they are."

The great Païsios said to him, "Forgive me, honorable father, nothing makes me, with my modest abilities, worthy of any sort of grace,[324] but godly providence, which bestows such assistance on those who ask with all their soul,[325] was <not>[326] about to overlook your entreaties or the great love[327] you demonstrated for your disobedient disciple. By doing what you did, you emulated the surpassing love[328] our compassionate God has for us human beings who, because of our disobedience, have been banished[329] from paradise and, through the deceit of the Evil One, have become enemies of God.[330]

"He[331] was born and grew up and suffered, and through his suffering has set us free.[332] He declared that nothing is greater than pure and unalloyed love,[333] through which we willingly lay down our life for another.[334] This love[335] was the cause of your disciple's salvation, as has been said; otherwise, it would not have been possible to speak on <his>[336] behalf. I am a sinful man by nature.[337] I am aware that nothing in me makes me worthy of God's spiritual gifts. Come, then, holiest of souls, forgive me, and let us offer thanks and praise to our compassionate and merciful God, and to him alone."

After humbly offering this advice to him, he joined the elder in singing praises to God, who bestows all gifts.[338] Then they prayed for each other and said goodbye to one another and each returned to his own dwelling.

The Savior tells Païsios to strengthen and teach the brothers

32 (31). Our father Païsios was always zealous about the Apostle's precept[339] "forgetting what lies behind and straining forward to what lies ahead,"[340]

devoting himself to other, more severe, spiritual struggles.³⁴¹ He moved around the waterless desert,³⁴² eager to escape people's notice, in order that all the good he did might be done in secret³⁴³ and that he might at the same time enjoy undisturbed the fruits of quiet solitude. And so he acted thus.

33 (32). But God, because he did not want Païsios alone to be saved but wanted others to be saved through him,³⁴⁴ did not think he ought to leave this lamp shining all by himself³⁴⁵ while others were deprived of the brilliant light he radiated. Therefore he ordered Païsios to leave where he was and go to the outer desert in order to strengthen the brothers there and to teach them and with his teaching make them imitators and lovers³⁴⁶ of his holy way of life, which was equal to that of the angels.³⁴⁷ Païsios said, "Lord, what will I gain if I abandon my way of life here, where I have had the great pleasure to enjoy your supervision, and leave to supervise others over whom I am not yet competent to exercise supervisory authority?³⁴⁸ Lord, I am afraid that,³⁴⁹ if I am charged with supervising others, I will not be able to do what you have ordered—which seems likely—and will be blamed for my negligence."³⁵⁰

34.³⁵¹ When Païsios said these things, asking for permission to stay there, the Savior said to him, "To be sure, your labors on behalf of others will not be considered equal <to those you do here,>³⁵² but you will receive³⁵³ double the compensation, and even more, in the city above because of those who are being saved through your teaching."³⁵⁴ Having said these things, the Savior disappeared from Païsios' sight and this marked the end of the godly command he gave Païsios near the desert that had been shown to him. When he went there, his arrival did not escape the notice of those who fervently loved³⁵⁵ the good things that that man had to offer, for a multitude were rushing to him, thirsting for the virtue he possessed: he was an ever-flowing fountain providing everyone with the flowing waters of immortality.³⁵⁶ I too wanted to see him because it was possible to share in his grace just by beholding him.

Emperor Constantine appears to Païsios³⁵⁷

35. Once when I went to see him, before I reached the door of his humble dwelling I heard him talking with another man. I waited respectfully outside, standing at the entrance. When I uttered a soft cry, summoning him to appear, the honorable father came out of his cell and when he saw me embraced me and joyfully greeted me. I too greeted him, as was fitting. Then, when I went inside his dwelling, I did not see anyone inside. I had no idea who might have been talking with the father a short time before so I looked with curiosity all around the room. He said, "Why are you so curiously looking all around the room? Do you think you're going to see something unusual?"

I answered, "Yes, I think there's something strange and unusual going on here and I have no idea what it is. Just now, as I came up to the door, I heard another man's voice; he was talking and conversing with you—and now I don't see anyone. Why this might be, I have no idea. I beg Your Holiness to explain this strange mystery[358] to me."

36. In reply the holy man[359] said, "John, God wants to reveal a godly and astonishing mystery to you today, just as he now arranged your arrival,[360] and that makes it appropriate for me to tell you what His Goodness[361] has ordained for us. That person, my excellent friend, whom you heard speaking with me, was the great Constantine, lord of all those who bear Christ's name: he just now came to me from heaven and spoke to me, saying, 'Blessed are you (pl.) who have been considered worthy to follow the monastic way of life. Truly, you deserve the Savior's pronouncement of blessing.'

"Then I said, 'And who are you, my lord, who says these things and so greatly blesses us?'

"He responded to my question, saying, 'I am Constantine the Great. I have come from heaven to proclaim the glory and authority that those who take on the yoke of Christ[362] have in heaven.[363] And to you, who enkindle the lovers[364] of this holy way of life, I proclaim the good news of godly benediction.[365] But as for myself, I censure myself, as a penitent, because I failed to attain such a lofty rank. The <memory>[366] of its loss is too much for me to bear!'

"I spoke again, saying, 'Why do <you>[367] accuse yourself, admirable sir? Do you not share in that eternal glory and godly illumination?'

"'No,' he said, 'I do share with the monks in heaven in the smallest way the right to approach God. I am in no way equal to them in honor.[368] 37. I saw certain monks, with their souls, having departed from <their>[369] bodies, confidently ascending to heaven like swiftly flying eagles in flight.[370] At the time of their departure they grow wings as they swiftly ascend and advance <as far as the holy walls of the heavenly Jerusalem,>[371] which lies far above them, all powerful and honored, opposing and resisting the strongest assault. Then I saw them reach the holy[372] gates of that city and go inside the entrance; the fearful doorkeepers in no way prevented them from being seen with the heavenly King. <They>[373] also had the confidence to stand before the godly throne. 38. Marveling at this position of worthiness you monks have in heaven, I come forward to pronounce you blessed but I find fault with myself[374] for being unworthy of such good things. Would that I had forsaken all the things of life and the purple robes of the temporal kingship and the royal diadem and sought instead poverty and rough clothing and whatever else the monastic way of life requires!'

39. "I in turn said to him, 'You have spoken well in recounting all these things, most venerable emperor, and by doing so you have offered <us>[375] encouragement. Such judgments, however, are entirely appropriate for our good God to make in his righteousness. How else could one speak about our God's judgment?[376] How could it be otherwise? Our just God, using a balance that weighs justice,[377] repays each person for everything in just measure and offers compensation in exchange for a person's labors. Your life did not entail the same sufferings as a monastic's; it was different from a monastic's life, seeing that you had a wife to help you and children and slaves and various <luxuries.>[378] These monks, however, looked down on pleasures and all of life's delights[379] and instead of all these received God. They considered what is pleasing *to God* to be wealth and pleasure[380] and delight and they were, as the Apostle says, "in need, afflicted, mistreated," and so on, <"wandering in deserts and mountains and caves and holes in the ground>."[381] How could you be considered equal to them?'"[382]

40. "While we were having this exchange, brother John, you suddenly and <propitiously>[383] arrived and the emperor parted from me and ascended into heaven. As a result, it's now been clearly demonstrated to you, if you want to know, how ascetic labors and suffering produce so many good fruits.[384] Go, then,[385] and strengthen the brothers, trusting in this mystery[386] you just witnessed."

When I heard these words, I offered great thanksgivings <to> God. Then, after talking with Païsios to my satisfaction, I got myself ready and went on my way, joyful and rejoicing. This is what happened. My account intends to demonstrate[387] this man's fiery zeal for the faith.

Païsios defends the divinity of the Holy Spirit
Concerning a brother who in ignorance was led astray
and fell into unbelief[388]

41. A certain elder, living in a village near the borders of Egypt,[389] fell because of ignorance. He was <asserting>[390] that the duality of the Holy Trinity should be worshiped, that is, the Father and the Son, but that the Spirit should not be called "God."[391] A large number was following him in thinking this way. God, however, did not want the elder's ascetic labor and sweat to be vainly squandered so he revealed the elder's ideas to the godly Païsios,[392] as well as showing him the region[393] where the elder lived.

Païsios immediately got up and made a number[394] of large baskets with three handles. He went to see that man and, when he found him, pretended to be a stranger. Many of the simpler people who associated with him shared the elder's ungodly opinion.[395] When those with him saw the three-handled baskets, not knowing who Païsios was or where he was from, they were utterly astonished and had no idea how the baskets had been made. They asked him what they were and what he planned to do with them. "I want to sell them," he said.

"Then why," they then asked,[396] "did you make them with three handles?"

"Because," he said, "I am a friend and lover[397] of the Holy Trinity,[398] it's incumbent on me to represent through my work the persons of the Trinity and to praise the Trinity in a threefold fashion by making these three signs representing it. That one Nature expresses itself in three Persons. If someone understands this differently, that person does not think correctly and shouldn't hold such an opinion. Each basket has one nature with three *hypostases*:[399] in each of the three handles the entire essence of each basket manifests itself equally. In this way, then, the immaterial Nature and superessential Godhead is [manifested][400] in three forms or persons—the Father with the Son and the Holy Spirit—and the whole essence abides in each.[401] Concerning the three, neither more nor less is spoken of, [seeing that one is not greater or lesser in nature than the other.]"[402]

42. After Païsios had spoken these words in a brief speech, <the men,>[403] along with that monk, saw the truth. They stood in awe of Païsios and were ready to listen. "Tell us, wondrous one," they said, "still more very clear[404] things about orthodox belief, and use other tangible demonstrations. We've been astonished at what you've said so far."

43. The godly Païsios, like a champion and an experienced speaker,[405] filled with the Holy Spirit, mocked all the blasphemous words of the heretics;[406] he showed that what they were saying was weaker than a spider's web and revealed to them the orthodox faith in greater detail. Painting a picture of the orthodox faith and imprinting it on their hearts,[407] he delineated[408] the truth for them. Citing[409] numerous examples about the Holy Spirit from the God-inspired Scriptures,[410] he brought them to true knowledge.[411] Afterward, admonishing them and teaching all of them to confess <their> ignorance,[412] and directing them to repent of their intoxication with heresy, he returned to the desert, offering up hymns of thanksgiving.[413]

An angel assures Païsios of God's care

44. When he returned to the desert, a resplendent light shone before his eyes.[414] Gazing into it, he saw ranks of angels filling the desert; marveling at what this might be, he had no idea what this phenomenon was. Suddenly, the angel accompanying him spoke to him, "Both when you are here and when you are away, Païsios, we watch over the monks here, just as the God of All promised you." So, with songs of thanksgiving he glorified God, who diligently cares for everything.[415]

Paul and Poemen come to visit Païsios

45. This concludes these matters. The discourse will now set forth the prophetic gifts that the godly Païsios possessed.

Because the fame of this holy man had spread[416] throughout the world and had incited those whose souls love virtue[417] to come see him and receive his prayers, Poemen, who was great among the fathers, was not going to go see him without an invitation. Although he himself was still young at that time, he was seized with the desire[418] to see him.

Concerning the great Poemen[419]

So he went to Saint Paul[420] and entreated him to accompany him to see the great one, for Paul was accustomed often to visit Païsios.

Our father Paul <said,>[421] "Since you're young, child, I'd be ashamed to take you to the great one. He's a lofty man; we don't simply go visit him nor do we go see him without giving it great consideration. No, we go reverently, and we don't go whenever we want but when it's appropriate and will be to our benefit."[422]

"But," Poemen said, "when I go I'll stand outside <his>[423] cell with you and the pleasure I receive from hearing his godly voice as he talks with you will be without measure. I'll consider this such a wonderful gift—if, that is, I'm able to do it. If, however, this can't be easily done but seems to be bothersome, even if I just touch his cell, wretch that I am,[424] I'll be saved. What's more, when you come out, I'll embrace your feet that have entered within the sanctuary and have walked on the same ground that his beautiful feet have trod. By doing this, I'll enjoy a bountiful blessing."

46. The godly Paul admired Poemen for saying these things out of humility and great faith so he took him with him and went to the great one. When they reached the saint's cell, Paul alone went inside. Païsios welcomed him in a friendly and fatherly manner and asked him about the young man,[425] <"Where is your child and traveling companion?">[426]

Paul said, "Outside, father, by himself; he has the highest respect for the holy entrance to your dwelling."

So Païsios urged him to come in, saying, "It isn't good to prevent such people who come to see us from coming inside. Our Savior has ordered that such people as these come in readily."[427]

Having said these words <he took hold>[428] of the young man with his own hands, embraced him, and blessed him, saying, "Believe me, Paul, my beloved friend, this child will save the souls of many and through him <many>[429] will be considered worthy of the joys of paradise; the hand of the Lord is with him, leading him on the godly paths, guiding him and teaching him with great care."[430]

After saying these words, he[431] laid hands on Poemen and blessed him and sent him off with the holy Paul, and Poemen greatly blessed and glorified God.[432]

The Savior visits Païsios and teaches him about acceptable good work Concerning the Lord's oversight and what the Savior recounted to him[433]

47. It happened one day when the holy Païsios had fasted for twenty-<two>[434] days that Christ came to him and said, "Païsios, since you suffer so much on my behalf, I want you to be my chosen one."[435]

Païsios said, "What is my suffering, good master? Why, nothing at all. Every perfect gift comes from you,[436] who give me strength."

The Savior said, "Every good work is acceptable to me and I will repay the worker full wages for his work.[437] Come, then; follow me."

Païsios followed the Savior into the desert until they came to a certain cave.[438] Then the Savior said to Païsios, "Go inside and you will see a man who is a true champion."[439]

When Païsios went in, he saw a man rolling on <the> ground, rubbing his mouth and face into the dirt. Perplexed at this man's excessive struggle, he immediately went outside to find out from the Savior the reason for the man's wild struggle. The Savior said, "Did you see how many labors my athlete[440] endures for me?"

Païsios said, "I did see, Lord, and I was horrified at the pain and suffering caused by his labors, but since it is not clear to me why he is making these efforts, will Your Goodness[441] explain it to me?"

The Savior said, "He has completed only two days of fasting and look how he has wasted away[442] with hunger and is parched with thirst."

Then Païsios said,[443] "And how can I have gone without eating for twenty-two days without suffering any of these terrible things?" He in turn inquired this of the Savior.

Once again the Savior <answered>[444] him, "Because you are strengthened by my grace, you fast with strength and perseverance.[445] That fellow, however, like an athlete, fasts on his own in spiritual struggle; inflamed with desire,[446] he allows himself to suffer beyond his ability to do so."

Then he asked, "What sort of reward will such a person receive from Your Goodness for his two days of fasting?"

And the Savior,[447] "I will repay him with the same reward for two days as I will you for twenty-two,[448] and <that Gospel saying>[449] will apply to both of you: 'Enter into the joy of your Lord'[450]—to you, who have received five talents, and to him, who has received two,[451] for both of you have been seen equally doing what is good and you have both been zealous to the best of your ability."

After the Savior said these things, he left.

Christ again appears and teaches Païsios about the nature of asceticism

48. Our father Païsios from that time added[452] even greater spiritual struggles, always importuning God to rise above the need for food. Food for him was partaking each Sunday of the body and blood of our Lord Jesus Christ. The Savior once again in his compassion appeared to his servant and said,[453] "Why are you still making requests about food when you do not eat anyway? You should use this time to ask for other things."

Païsios said, "Lord, when I leave the desert here to go visit the brothers, I want to return as quickly as possible."[454]

He said, "Do not be sad about this. When you are away from the desert here, I have not left you."

Then Païsios said, "Free me from anger, Christ."[455]

"<If>[456] you want to defeat anger and rage," he said, "do not rebuke anyone. <Do not hate anyone.>[457] Do not denigrate anyone.[458] If you guard yourself against doing these, you will not get angry."

Païsios said, "Compassionate Master and patient Lord, if someone walks according to <your>[459] commandments and visits those who love[460] you in order to care for <them,>[461] will he gain or lose because of <his> zeal?"[462]

The Savior said, "Just as the worker who goes out to the field to work will be paid by the landowner without delay,[463] so too will I reward those who do good or teach or assist me. I will repay such persons as these with resplendent rewards in the heavenly Jerusalem."[464]

49 (48).[465] Then Païsios again asked, "If someone struggles safe and sound[466] and ministers to others, while another person struggles and does not minister to others, how does the reward differ for each person?"

The Savior said, "The person who spiritually struggles alone is my disciple, but the person who spiritually struggles and ministers to others is my son and heir."[467]

Païsios again said, "If someone is serious about ministering to others and spiritually struggles as much as possible but does not find himself at all the equal of those who only spiritually struggle because his care for others prevents him from taking on more exacting spiritual struggles, will he receive equal payment?"

"Yes," the Savior said, "he will ascend to heaven."

With these events about the godly Païsios told, our narrative will now press ahead, proceeding[468] with his astounding miracles.

A Syrian monk visits Païsios
Concerning the man from the north[469]
50. There was a certain man to the north[470] adorned with a variety of virtues. While he was praying, a thought occurred to him: he wondered whether he had become the equal of any of those most pleasing to God.[471] While he was pondering this, he heard a godly voice from above: "Go to Egypt,"[472] it was saying, "and you will find a man by the name of Païsios who, like you, submits himself to humility and love[473] for God."

The venerable elder ignored the distance of the road before him, setting out on foot as quickly as possible for Egypt. When he reached the monastic community[474] of Nitria,[475] he asked where Païsios was. Since Païsios' name was known by all, the elder soon found out where his dwelling was located; nor was Païsios unaware of the elder's arrival, having been informed of it by divine grace.[476] As the elder approached Païsios' dwelling, Païsios[477] immediately went out to greet him and the two met one another in the desert. They joyfully embraced each other, each wrapping his arms around the other.

Later, they went inside the holy Païsios' dwelling and, after praying, sat down.[478] The elder began talking to the godly Païsios in Syriac but Païsios, being Egyptian, knew only the language of the Egyptians.[479] He was sad and distressed that he was unable to profit from the words of an elder such as this. Immediately raising his eyes to heaven and sighing and groaning[480] from the depths of his heart,[481] the blessèd one said,[482] "Son of God and Word, allow me, your servant, to understand the force of this elder's words."[483]

51. As soon as he said these words, Païsios, <being instructed alone by the godly Spirit>[484] (what a sudden visitation!), was able to think and converse in Syriac. Then the two elders took great delight in telling one another about the spiritual gifts and contemplative insight[485] that each had been considered worthy to have, and each declared to the other which of the fathers he had come in contact with and what their virtues were. Both[486] of them were filled with pleasure after being together for six days.[487] After they finished their conversation, the elder was about to leave for home, so Païsios summoned all his disciples who were there with him and said to them, "Look, my beloved children, a man holy and perfect,[488] filled with graces and the Holy Spirit! All of you, welcome his prayers as a guard tower with its watchmen against the enemies that stand against you."[489]

After Païsios said these words, all of them fell to the ground and venerated the elder, as was appropriate, fervently asking that they might be worthy of his prayers and benedictions. Praying on their behalf, the elder blessed them and, saying goodbye to all of them, set out on the road home.

Coda: Païsios sees the Syrian monk borne home on a cloud
52. Shortly thereafter, after the visitor had left, a certain anchorite came to see the great Païsios. His disciples[490] said, "Sir, if you'd come to visit us a little earlier, you would've benefited enormously. A godly man came to us from Syria, resplendent in mind and heart, who strengthened us with his words."[491] But he just left. If you want to catch up with him, he hasn't gone far. He's still close by. Hurry! You can catch up with him!"

But the godly Païsios spoke to the anchorite as the latter eagerly prepared to set out on foot to overtake the elder, "Stop! Right now! That man's already gone more than eighteen miles, borne home on a cloud."[492] After Païsios spoke these words, everyone glorified the true God.[493] They were astonished.[494]

An angel watches over Païsios
53A. A certain brother came to our father Païsios, wanting to see him, and found him asleep, with a beautiful angel standing guard at his head. Astonished, he said, "Truly, God protects those who put their hope in him."[495] And he left, blessing and giving glory to the one who gives glory to those who love[496] him.[497]

Païsios' disciple is deceived by a Jew[498]
Concerning the elder's disciple[499]
53B.[500] The holy Païsios had a certain disciple, simple and unsuspecting by nature, who readily obeyed his superiors. He left for Egypt[501] to sell his handwork and met a certain Jew and traveled with him.[502] When the Jew recognized the monk's simple nature, with his bloody and defiled tongue he poured out poison that the soul-destroying serpent[503] had lodged in his heart, saying to the monk, "Sir, why do you so naively and carelessly believe in the crucified one when he is not the Expected One?[504] [The Messiah][505] will be someone else, not this fellow."

The monk, due to his guileless way of thinking and unsuspecting nature, was won over by the Jew's argument and replied, "Maybe it *is* just as you say."

After he said these words (what happened to him is horrible to relate!), he immediately[506]—alas!—fell from the grace of baptism, as we will make clear in what follows.

Païsios rebukes and teaches the monk
54. When the monk returned to the desert and Saint Païsios saw him, the latter would not come near <him>;[507] in his teacher's eyes, he was now

without grace.[508] Païsios would <not>[509] come near him at all but turned his back on him and listened as little as possible to anything about him. After a while, the disciple saw that the elder was ignoring and avoiding him and had no idea why. He was upset that Païsios was doing this and grieved over his misfortune. Then, going to Païsios, he fell at his feet, saying, "Why do you turn your beneficent countenance away from me, father, and ignore your wretched disciple? You never treated me like this before. In turning away from me, you seem to be treating me as an abomination."[510]

The elder said, "And who are you, fellow? To be sure, I don't recognize anything about you. <I> don't know <you> at all."[511]

The disciple said, "And what do you see in me, father, that's so strange that you don't recognize me, and shun me?[512] Aren't I your disciple, someone you know?"

The elder said, "That person I used to know was a Christian and possessed baptism. You're not him. If you're really that disciple, you've lost your baptism and the identifying marks that make you a Christian. What happened to you?[513] Explain to me as clearly as you can the attack that took place. What won you over on the road?"

"Nothing at all happened."[514]

"Get away from me, child—as far as you can get! I cannot bear to hear the speech of someone like you who rejects God. If you were that disciple I used to know, I'd recognize you just as you used to be."

The disciple groaned and shed tears that moved the elder to compassion. <He said>[515] he was that same disciple and not somebody else, he had no idea what he was being accused of, and swore that nothing <shameful>[516] had happened.

55. The great one said, "Who did you speak to on the road?"[517]

He said, "With some Jew. No one else."

Then Païsios said, "What did he say to you and what did you say to him in reply?"

The disciple said, "He didn't say anything to me except 'The one whom you worship is not the Christ;[518] the Christ is someone else who is going to come.' I said, 'Perhaps it's as you say.'"[519]

56. In response the elder said, "<What>[520] could be worse or more shameful than what you've said, you wretch?[521] You miserable person! With your words you both denied Christ and stripped yourself of your godly baptism. Get out of here! Weep for yourself as much as you want. You and I have nothing to do with one another! Your name is written with those who have denied Christ, and with them you will face the same punishments in Hell."[522]

Wailing and lamenting, the monk raised his voice to heaven, saying, "Have mercy on me, father, wretch that I am, and forgive my soul.[523] I don't even know what I've become: through <carelessness>[524] I've abandoned[525] godly illumination[526] and have become an object of ridicule for ruinous demons. But it is you, after God, who I make my refuge.[527] Please, do not disregard me, wretch that I am!"[528]

57. In similar fashion, the monk entreated Païsios and, with tears more than with words, he propitiated the elder and moved him to compassion. Païsios said, "Be patient, child. I must entreat on your behalf the mercy and pity of God, who is merciful and compassionate."

After saying these words, he acted as an ardent suppliant before God on behalf of that monk, asking God to forgive him his offense. God did not ignore this request but immediately complied with what the saint asked. The object of Païsios' supplication was to release the monk from his debt[529] <and> restore[530] godly baptism for him. The elder saw the Holy Spirit like a dove enter the disciple's mouth,[531] demonstrating that the gift of the Spirit had returned, while the spirit of blasphemy came out like smoke and dissipated in the air.[532]

After he saw these things, believing without a doubt that his request had been granted, he turned and said to his disciple, "Give glory and thanksgiving to God with me, my child. Look! The unclean spirit of blasphemy is leaving and in its place the spirit of regeneration, a gift from God,[533] which will restore you, is entering quickly. So then, watch out for yourself from now on[534] and do not fall into the snares of impious behavior through carelessness and laziness, nor deliver your soul, through a ruinous blunder, to be burned in the fires of Gehenna."

With these events now concluded, I will proceed[535] to another topic.

Païsios assists John the anchorite with his fasting
Concerning John, who came to visit Païsios[536]

58. There came one time to the holy Païsios one of the elders, named John, who had been in the desert many days and had been assiduously <practicing>[537] ascetic labors. He was suffering exceedingly because he had at that time gone without food and any kind of rest. Once he and Païsios had talked with each other and delighted in one another's graceful and accomplished conversation, Païsios knew that John was suffering greatly because of his ascetic abstinence and needed to eat; he told his disciple, who was present, "Quickly prepare the table and bring food so that today we may feast together with the father."[538] So the disciple quickly prepared the table.[539] Then the elder urged John to eat, saying, "Because of your severe abstinence and lack of food, permit yourself something to eat."

But John said, "Forgive me.[540] Today is a fast day and I have to fast on account of my many sins."

The elder, marveling at John's steadfast resolve, immediately got up and, looking to heaven, said from the depths of his heart, "Lord, look to your servant John, who struggles so mightily on behalf of your holy name."

Then he prayed, and at the end of the prayer the Lord bestowed a good and astounding gift: right then John was seized by the {evil} Spirit[541] and seemed to see a young man[542] who, with food and drink in his hands, came to John and offered it to him. When John came to himself, he was filled with pleasure, having eaten his fill. Because he had not needed material food, he was filled with angelic nourishment. He rose before God and the godly Païsios, offering them thanks, then he returned once again to the desert, fasting, adding another fast to the previous one. He was always saying to himself, "With pleasure I ate; now I must fast with all eagerness." Thus this noble elder contended and was victorious, recovering his strength through the prayer of the holy Païsios.

Our discourse in its zeal now wishes to point out another man, who was inexperienced: assisted by the prayer of godly Païsios, he became a trophy-bearing champion.

Païsios helps a young anchorite to defeat the Devil
Concerning the man who was being harassed by [his] thoughts[543]

59. There was a certain young novice who lived alone in the desert leading the life of an ascetic.[544] Tormented by thoughts that fiercely rose up against him, he came to see the godly Païsios and said to him, "I entreat Your Holiness to mention my worthless self in your holy prayers. I'm being fiercely attacked by demons!"

When Païsios discerned,[545] however, that the monk was following his own will and was pursuing the wily demon of <wickedness>[546] and self-conceit, wishing to prevent the young man from being licentiously swept away, he said to him, "Child, it's not what you think: you're not being fought by a demon,[547] seeing that they haven't yet sensed that you've come to the desert. No, you're being fought by your own thoughts. Go, then, be a fighter; entreat always God's godly help[548] to keep watch over you. You're going to be tempted <and> fiercely attacked; then you will really know what it is to be attacked by demons and what sort of grievous assaults those who are being assailed by them submit themselves to."

Having said these words, he sent the young man home. Afterward, he prayed at length on behalf of the young man, asking God to keep him unharmed.[549]

60. But the leader of the demons appeared and, face to face, roaring like a lion,[550] said, "What violence you do me, Païsios![551] What do you and

I have to do with one another?^552 You completely wrong me while I do not fight against you at all!"

The elder said, "Leave the young monk alone. Don't bother him by arousing him with wicked thoughts."

[The Evil One] immediately disappeared.^553 The demon haughtily and boastfully responded, "Believe me, I didn't know whether the fellow had come to live in the desert.^554 No, he's being besieged by his own laziness.^555 From now on, though, he'd better be prepared to withstand my frightful abuses."^556

The elder said, "May God rebuke you, hated enemy of the truth, and <cast you>^557 into eternal fire!"

After Païsios said these words, the Evil One disappeared, but the Devil's servant [and beloved]^558 did not set aside his evil plans but put into action what he had said he would do, attacking the young monk and employing every evil device he had in his arsenal. The young man, tempted by thoughts brought on by the demon and unable to withstand the Enemy's terrible assaults,^559 fled once again to that unshakable pillar, the great Païsios, and told him about all the unbearable assaults of the Evil One, that he could barely endure the demon's ferocious attacks.

The saint said, "Didn't I tell you, my son, that the demon didn't know that you'd come to the desert here?" Then he admonished him and encouraged him and, turning to prayer, said, "Lord, Son of God and Word, do not neglect the one whom you fashioned with your own hands, allowing him to be swallowed up by the Enemy, but offer him a helping hand from heaven to assist him, for your might is unassailable and all things are subject to your power."

61. After he said these words and as he continued praying, a godly angel immediately stood near him, holding the Devil bound in chains. He said, "Take this wicked fellow and question him as you wish. Look at him! He who, through his varied machinations, has held numerous people bound in chains, is now being handed over to you as a prisoner."

In response the Devil said to the elder, "Oh, these prayers of yours, Païsios! How long are you going to mistreat me and torture me with all your prayers? How long are you going to protect the inhabitants of this desert? It will only make me wretched if I stay here talking with these people! I'm leaving, and that's a fact! I'm moving as far as possible away from here!"^560

Païsios focused his attention on him and said, "Apostate and enemy of the human race, why have you devoted yourself to fighting this young man so ferociously? Why do you maniacally wage war against those who are beginning their ascetic struggles?"^561

In response, Beliar^562 said to him, "I do not approach <the novices>^563 when they first begin their struggles because grace in no way allows me to come near these beginners who struggle so fervently. But when grace withdraws[564] because of their indolence and apathy, I immediately approach them since they are now easy prey, playthings ready for me to seize.[565] I now do whatever I want with them. This is the reason I choose not to fight them in the beginning: I can see that I will get burned to a crisp by their fervor. In the expectation that they will later became lazy, I ignore them, waiting my turn.[566] Whenever I see them fervently[567] making progress, I do not direct any assaults at them lest, in their tireless zeal for spiritual struggle accompanied by good works and, united with grace, they become invincible and invulnerable."

Having spoken <thus,>[568] the Devil left—but not willingly.

62. The saint said to the angel, "Take this prisoner; get the enemy of truth ready for the terrible things prepared for him in the fires of Gehenna."[569] From that time on, the monk was free from the demon's disturbances: the latter did not have the ability[570] to appear to the former or do battle against him. The monk completed his monastic life in a manner pleasing to God and, supported by the prayers of the holy Païsios,[571] died a good death.[572]

John tells about Païsios' insight
Concerning the monks who came to see Païsios[573]

63. While I was seated with him one time, some monks came to him wanting to hear[574] edifying words from him. "Tell us, father," they said, "a life-giving word."[575]

The elder said, "Go, safeguard the tradition[576] of the fathers, and don't seek to do more than you're ordered."[577]

Again they spoke: "Tell us something else suitable for us that will benefit the soul."

The godly man, with his discerning eyes, saw the thoughts and reflections of their souls and explained to them in turn what they were thinking, which of their thoughts were good, and which were hostile, and where they originated. They marveled very much at this and said to me privately, "Truly, Father John, [Abba Païsios] explains to us all the sufferings[578] of our hearts, each and every kind, things known only to God."[579]

And I said to them, "He's done the same with me on a number of occasions when I had passed through trials and temptations.[580] <Believe me, I'm not telling you anything but the truth about him! Since we await the Judge,[581] who seeks the truth itself for us, as it is written in the Holy Gospel, 'By your words you will be justified and by your words you will be condemned,'[582] and 'We will have to give an account for a [single] careless word,'[583] let me speak about the future trials that we're going to undergo and that we'll have to defend ourselves against at that fearful and unbearable

tribunal that God has prepared for us. And woe to those found there on that day—and I count myself among them! Woe! Woe! Those who have condemned themselves will be sent to punishment, having absolutely nothing to say in their defense.

"Nevertheless, putting off this subject a bit, let us proceed with the heavenly discourse and let the truth itself be set out in detail for us. I am telling you about the truth>[584] because you will believe me, that he has courteously shown me both what I have inwardly considered[585] and what I have done on my own, meeting <me>[586] face to face, going through everything with me as though he had been present with me."

They were saying,[587] "'Marvelous is God in his saints.'"[588] They left him.[589]

The discourse wishes now to point out a work of obedience and what sort of <baleful consequences>[590] disobedience causes the disobedient.

Païsios intercedes with God on behalf of the apostate monk Isaac
Concerning the monk who followed his own wishes[591]

64. A certain brother who followed his own will forsook the desert and its good practices and went and lived near a city. Since he often went into <that>[592] city to sell his handiwork, it happened that he saw a certain woman who belonged to the Jewish race; he was on fire, consumed with erotic, satanic, love for her.[593] Through demonic collusion and the deceiving snare that thoughts create, the monk—alas!—was caught in her trap. Because of this, he conceived suffering and gave birth to transgression[594] and—what is worse (shameful to say!)—he apostasized from his own faith and embraced the Jewish religion.

Living with this woman and conversing with her, he became so much like her that he wedded himself to her way of thinking, so much so that he came to be a partner in her impiety and seemed to agree with her insolence. That thrice-accursed wench[595] sank into such an abyss of perdition and shamelessness that she would often take the head of that wretch[596] <to> her lap and, opening his mouth, with a piece of wood in her hands would scrape <his> teeth lest—what atheism!—some remnant of the undefiled Communion remain stuck in his teeth![597]

I know how pained you [pl.] are to hear this, just as I am astonished at God's forbearance, but in the account that follows, which I will narrate, you too will marvel at the astounding compassion and heavenly oversight and godly help[598] that God has for those who marvel at him without measure.[599]

65. That man, who through disobedience was separated from the Christians because of his own impiety,[600] enlightened by <the> illuminating light of godly providence, after a long time condemned himself: it

happened that some monks from the desert where the man had long ago practiced the ascetic life[601] came to that city for something they needed and passed by <that> woman's treacherous dwelling by the side of the road. When the man saw them, his heart was wounded and he remembered that ancient and holy community.[602] He questioned them, asking who they were and where they had come from and why they had come there.

They said, "We're from Nitria and are disciples of Païsios.[603] We've come to the city for something we need."

He fervently entreated them to ask the great one to offer supplication on his behalf so the great one with his entreaties might propitiate the Lord so he would be freed from the machinations of the Enemy.[604]

They said, "We'll do as you wish and will remind him," and they promised to entreat the elder to pray on the man's behalf.

So, when the monks returned, they told the godly father about the man. When the elder heard about the painful events[605] surrounding the former monk, he groaned deeply and said, "Oh, my beloved children, how many of the most virtuous have fallen from godly grace on account of women! Holy Scripture, which we have from heaven through our forefathers, offers us reminders of them.[606] The Enemy cannot possibly have at his disposal any device more suitable than woman.[607] By employing this weapon,[608] which is difficult to overcome, he usually prevails—as you know—over great men such as the great David and his forefathers and descendants.[609] Therefore, we too must pray[610] to be delivered from such machinations as these."

Having said these words, he prayed on behalf of the man, saying, "Lord, Son of God and Word, do not allow what your hands created[611] to be swallowed up forever in the depths of perdition but rather in your forbearance look down from your heavenly habitations and accept our[612] prayers being offered to you on behalf of him who once denied you but who has now returned to his senses.[613] I beg Your Goodness to call him to repentance."

Praying this way for many days, he did not stop asking God for mercy and compassion. The Savior, won over in his godly mercy and compassion by these entreaties, did not think it right to ignore such requests, so he appeared to him. The Omniscient One asked the reason for his request, saying, "Is my servant Païsios acting on behalf of him who denied me and forsook his monastic order? The wretch who, led astray, consorted with my enemies? The one who was formerly a monk but who now has become a Jew?"

Païsios said, "Yes, Christ, you who love us,[614] because I look to your acts[615] of mercy and compassion (you always call people to repentance and do not wish the death of a sinner but await his conversion),[616] I have dared to propitiate Your Goodness on his behalf. Propitiated, therefore, be patient with him and [call back]⁶¹⁷ your wandering sheep.⁶¹⁸ Be kind to him."

66. Païsios spoke these words. The Savior said, "If you want me to call him back and have mercy on him who made breaking the law his own and who through his foul deeds deserted my flock,⁶¹⁹ you must agree to give up most of the prizes you have won through your sufferings and in turn act as judge and apportion compassion on him who deserves ten thousand punishments."

The great Païsios said, "Yes, good Christ, I gladly agree to this. But I do not know whether anything I do will be pleasing to you; rather, from your own goodness—I confess that it is through your goodness that I am acceptable due to your grace each day⁶²⁰—pour out upon him your mercy. In order for him to be saved, permit me to undergo his punishments in his stead rather than enjoy your benefits and have him lost."

67. Immediately the Savior said to him, "How wonderful is the generosity of my servant, who emulates my love!⁶²¹ For the sake of this sinner's salvation, you have preferred <punishment>⁶²² for yourself. As a result, you will not suffer any diminishment in the least. Instead, your request that he be saved will be granted."

After saying these words, the Savior ascended into heaven.⁶²³ Not long afterward, once that dreadful wench, because of God's wrath directed at her, died in the middle of life, Isaac (for this was his name) returned to the desert and was instructed like a catechumen by the great man: Isaac embraced first his former faith and then the angelic way of life;⁶²⁴ after living in obedience and living a holy and chaste way of life with his behavior founded on a love of virtue,⁶²⁵ he departed this life and went to the Lord.⁶²⁶ These things happened for him through the intercessions of the holy Païsios and we, hearing about such marvelous wonders, <must> glorify and exalt that saint's God.⁶²⁷

Païsios prays on behalf of an impudent priest
Concerning a priest thinking about worldly matters⁶²⁸

68. There was a certain priest in the desert⁶²⁹ who had a worldly⁶³⁰ way of thinking. This fellow, whenever the monks went to our father Païsios to hear his edifying words, would go with them to listen to him. He, however, did not receive any benefit at all from the elder's godly words. Inasmuch as he possessed neither a good spirit nor deep soil bearing the fruit of good words, he would make fun of the elder's words⁶³¹ and, making use of other words that the worldly are accustomed to use, would corrupt the rules that the elder was laying down.

As a result, the monks, annoyed and angry, went to a certain God-loving elder and were complaining about the priest. The elder went with them to the great Païsios. After they left, the priest[632] also followed along behind them. The elder, however, went to the godly Païsios by himself and said, "You should know, father, that this priest is a cause of scandal; he's a hindrance to the brothers. You must prevent his unprincipled attacks and censure and correct him."

The great one replied, "In truth, I would've done this a long time ago if I thought it would do him any good. You can see that the Devil stands ready to summon him to perdition. If [the priest] hears harsh and disagreeable words from me, however, he'll leave the brotherhood[633] and return to the world. I, then, who am responsible for him, would be held accountable to God and would in part be the cause of his perdition because I was unable to put up with a brother whom the Enemy was waging war on. Instead of what you propose, then, we need to pray about the passions besieging such a person."

Having said these words, he prayed on behalf of the priest and at once caused the demon of impudence to flee. The priest was immediately pricked with fear-inducing stings of repentance; with his conscience deeply troubling his soul, confessing with tears rather than with words his change for the better and asking for forgiveness for all his heedless acts, he was kind and gentle from that moment on and became a pupil of the godly words. With pleasure he listened to the elder's words and with pleasure he put into practice the good those words taught. As a result, he surpassed many in the practice of the virtues[634] and became a tried and tested anchorite through the assistance of the godly Païsios' prayers.

We must now narrate another story, one that tells about the most awe-inspiring and astounding of wonders.[635]

Païsios washes Christ's feet
Concerning the authority of the Savior with two angels[636]

69. One time, while Païsios was praying in his cave, the Savior visited him with two angels, as he had the patriarch Abraham,[637] and said, "Greetings, Païsios! Today we will be enjoying your hospitality if you oblige and welcome us."[638]

Païsios eagerly welcomed them, becoming someone who emulates [the hospitality][639] of that patriarch. He did not busy himself with food and drink, however, but rather possessed a pure disposition.[640] <So>[641] he welcomed the Omnipresent One; then, putting water <in>[642] a basin, he washed your undefiled feet in imitation of you.[643] (How merciful and compassionate you are, Christ![644] What great love[645] you have for those who love you,[646] how you reach down to those who desire[647] you!) Païsios[648] eagerly busied himself with showing hospitality while the Lord, demonstrating his love for humankind,[649] [accepted] his hospitality. (Nothing that a person does in offering hospitality[650] shows more kindness and forbearance than to wash the feet of those who come to visit.) "Peace be with you, my chosen one,"[651] said the Savior, and then he disappeared.

Païsios' disciple learns about the fruits of disobedience and obedience

The holy Païsios, inflamed with loving desire,[652] in doing this was emulating Cleopas: his heart was on fire and he could hardly restrain himself.[653] So he ran to the water, which the Savior had left as something great and worthily propitious,[654] and gladly drank it, leaving a little for his disciple. And this was that <Christ>-loving[655] man's intention: to take the good not for himself alone but also to reserve some for his neighbor.[656] So when his disciple returned from his travels (he had been in Egypt), completely exhausted from the journey, the great one swooped down on him and gave him the reserved water to drink,[657] saying, "Go to the basin, child, and drink the water: it will slake your thirst caused by the heat."

The disciple said, "I will do just as you say, father." While the answer was still in his mouth,[658] he was thinking the opposite: "Why's the elder inconsiderately ordering me to drink this nasty water on account of the heat when I've just returned? He should have sent me to the spring to drink cold, clear water."

While the disciple was pondering such thoughts as these to himself, the elder spoke again: "Go, child, drink."

The disciple said, "As you command," but for the second time he did not go. Yet a third time the elder told him to drink and, once again, he did not obey.

Then the elder said to him, "The reward you've received for your disobedience, child, is the loss of spiritual gifts."[659]

When the disciple heard these words, his heart and mind were stricken and he ran to the basin but found it empty. He said to the elder, "Father, I don't find any water to drink."

The godly[660] Païsios said, "How could you find something that you made yourself unworthy to find? Disobedience drives away a spiritual gift just as obedience obtains it."

That disciple, very troubled at hearing these words, asked what that great gift might be and in what way and why and how it might be restored.

The great man said, "Christ, the King and Lord of all, appeared to me with two angels who looked like strangers, just as he appeared long ago to the patriarch Abraham.[661] I rushed to him and dared to wash his feet. The audacity of my base and unworthy hands![662] Then heaven received him and welcomed him back, and the water, more precious than all wealth, was left for me. I gladly drank it, leaving some for you, my like-minded disciple. But because you sank into the error of disobedience and were not wounded by the godly loving desire[663] for obedience but instead persisted in the disobedience you were already practicing—although commanded[664] to drink, you refused—an angel just now came down from heaven; with all reverence taking that holy water into his hands, he ascended again into heaven and pointed out that you're unworthy to partake of that water since he saw that you were filled with disobedience and <madness>."[665]

When the disciple heard these words, he was seized with shuddering and fear and was unable to speak for a long time, shaking at this explanation. Later, he came to himself and, in a loud voice, bitterly <lamented>[666] his bad luck: "Woe is me," he plaintively wailed.[667] "Wretch that I am!" he said.[668] "What goodness I have robbed myself of![669] What envy, caused by the most evil of demons, bewitched me, not allowing me to enjoy such good things?"

70. With these words, therefore,[670] he bewailed his misfortune like a tragic actor, coming to repentance,[671] and with tears instead of words, he sought mercy and called out to the compassionate elder. In response, the godly man said to him, "Child, because of disobedience, Adam fell from paradise and, instead of eternal life, acquired death.[672] Because he was unworthy of primal glory and was banished from the things that transcend glory, he became an exile. In the same way, because you refused to do what I commanded, falling from the grace[673] you were meant <to enjoy,>[674] you incessantly[675] complain about it. <You seem to regret what you have lost; having it in your grasp not long ago, you didn't care enough about it to protect it.>[676] But because you've raised yourself up in repentance and obedience, however, fervently propitiating God, and have diligently asked for forgiveness for your lapses due to disobedience, God in compassion[677] is moved to pity for those who repent and bestows mercy on those who ask."[678]

Païsios sends his despondent disciple to a holy man

71. The <disciple,>[679] comforted by the elder's encouragement, endured for a short time, but then, held captive by the memory of the tragic events that had transpired, was afflicted with sorrow and despondency and did not know what would become of himself. So he went to see the godly elder[680] and said, "Father, <my>[681] thoughts give me no rest; I've sunk to the depths of despair. I'm always thinking about that gift and bewail my terrible misfortune. I don't know what will become of me. Let me go see someone who seems to you to be one of the more experienced elders. Maybe, finding release from my thoughts, I'll be freed from what is distressing me."

The elder took a little bread and gave it to his disciple, saying, "Take this bread and go to this city: at the walls of the city to the right you'll find a poor man[682] sitting on a certain dunghill being stoned and mocked by children. Place this bread in his hands and you'll hear what is pleasing to God and seems to concern you."

Taking the bread, he left quickly.[683]

72. He reached that city and saw the godly man. Holding the bread in his hands, he was waiting for the right moment when the children <would give up to him>[684] the elder they were using as a plaything. The godly man did not wait, however, but said, "Come here, up beside me, right now, and give me the blessed bread sent with you."

When the disciple went up to him, the man <took>[685] the bread in his hands, kissed it, and inquired, "How is the holy Païsios? I have very much wanted to hear loving[686] details about him. And you, child, why do you hesitate and not put your trust in him?[687] Don't you know that because of your disobedience you were deprived of the godly water and the spiritual gift it bestowed? Why do you still cling to <your>[688] disobedience and flee to another without waiting for Païsios' advice? You seem to me like someone who holds clear water in his hands yet <goes around>[689] hither and yon looking to quench his thirst. Go, then, submit yourself to the great father;[690] the person who refuses to place his trust in him will also oppose the Savior and refuse to obey *his* commandments."

After the disciple heard these words, he returned, glorifying and praising God, determined to follow, in obedience, the wishes of the holy Païsios.

The disciple goes to see the holy man again

73. Not long afterward, he was once again reminded of that gift and mourned its loss, so he again begged the great one[691] to allow him to go see that man who had taken on the appearance of a poor person. But the great one admonished and rebuked him since he had not been able to persuade him—the visitor was besieged with thoughts and wished to visit that man frequently. The godly Païsios said, "That man, child, has gone to the Lord, but I see that you've anchored all your hopes in him alone and, trusting in his advice, are eager to submit yourself to it. Go, therefore, to the northern part of the city where you will find a great tomb. Go inside; you'll see lying there the bodies of three saints who were found worthy of prophetic gifts.[692] They foresaw the end of their lives: when it came time for them to die, each of them entered the tomb and went to his rest there.[693] <Say>[694] to the one lying in the middle, 'Païsios, the servant of Christ, through him who raised Lazarus, dead four days,[695] commands you to get up so you can say something appropriate for me.'"[696] These were the words of the godly man.

74. The disciple went as fast as he could and reached the city. Looking for the aforementioned place and finding it, he entered the tomb and said to the dead person, "Païsios, through the power of Christ who raised the dead, <commands>[697] you: Arise, and tell me what I should do so I may get some relief from the thoughts that bother me."

Even as the disciple spoke, the dead man immediately got up—what an amazing occurrence!—and said, "Why didn't you believe me, fellow, when I told you earlier to obey the father[698] and do what he commands you? Go, therefore, and be obedient to him without hesitation and listen to what he says, if you want to be saved. Truly, the person who disobeys his words opposes the [commandments] of Christ."[699]

After the dead man said these words, he once again fell asleep.[700] The disciple returned[701] and from that time on regained through humility of thoughts the good things he had lost, and advanced and made spiritual progress.

This is what took place concerning him.[702] Our narrative has now recounted for those who praise God the events concerning the disciple and the dead man.[703] With regard to the rest, how shall I keep silent?[704] Let me run through for us without undue omissions the rest of that man's miracles and, after I have related in my account some troublesome matters,[705] then recounting two or three more stories, I will conclude my account.

Païsios intervenes to absolve two young monks of false charges
Concerning two brothers by birth[706]

75. Two brothers by birth came to the godly Païsios and lived together in his brotherhood.[707] After completing a sufficient amount of time in obedience, they would often ask the great one[708] to live by themselves in the desert. Seeing their burning zeal and observing that they were both accomplished in contemplative quiet,[709] he gave them permission to set out upon a life of solitude. So they withdrew to the solitude they desired,[710] where they proved themselves to be zealous and steadfast, driving away the assaults of their adversaries. The Enemy, however, subtle and ever envious of those who are good, waged war against <them>[711] with craftily devised machinations through those who shared their goals.

It so happened that some possessions were stolen from one of those living in the desert and the monk was investigating who the thief might be who stole his things. After searching everywhere without finding anything, he heard[712] about a certain elder who had the power to reveal the thief to him. He went to him and asked to know where the things that had been carried off were. That elder, however, did not have true prophetic insight given by grace but "prophesied" through demonic activity,[713] so he slandered[714] the two monks, saying to that monk, "Those two who just recently came to live in this desert committed the theft all by themselves. Once you get hold of them, do not let go of them until they return your possessions."

When that monk heard these words, he went as quickly as he could to the superior of the laura.[715] Taking a strong right arm from there[716] with him, he went off to find the brothers who lived as solitaries; after beating them and tying them up, he led them back to the laura. Then the two, punished by being shut up in prison, were condemned as the worst sort of thieves. But through grace our father[717] came to know about the abuse done to the brothers and immediately arose and went to them. When his arrival became known to everyone,[718] seeing that no one was considered more eminent than he, everyone got together and went to him. Accompanying them was also that elder held captive by error.

After everyone formally greeted him, the great father said to them, "Brothers, what have you done to those young men living in solitude?"[719]

They said, "They're thieves, father, and for this improper act they've been thrown into prison."

He said, "And who told you they're thieves?"

They answered, "This elder, who has prophetic insight."

Then the great Païsios asked the elder if what they had said about him[720] was true and the elder said that his prophecy was true and according to God. Then the holy Païsios said, "If your spiritual gift[721] were from God and were godly and were not the opposite, demonic error, the Devil would not appear in your mouth."

When they heard these words, the monks became confused and were gripped with fear; the words from Païsios' mouth truly seemed to everyone to be completely beyond dispute. So they hurled reproaches at the elder and persuaded him to seek forgiveness. Gripped with fear, he fell at Païsios' holy feet,[722] saying, "Forgive me, holy father, and pray for me. I've been deceived." When Païsios prayed for him, immediately the demon of self-conceit came out of the elder's mouth in front of everyone, looking like a pig.[723] When the demon came out, mad with rage, it charged the righteous one, wanting to rip him apart with its teeth, but the godly man[724] rebuked it and cast it into the abyss.[725]

When the elder not only realized that he was free from his error but also saw that the error had left him, he accused himself and very much bewailed his actions; rolling about on the ground, he would not stop importuning Païsios for forgiveness for his transgressions. In like manner, those who had been deceived because of him blamed themselves and asked for forgiveness.

Then, summoning those young men whom they had calumniated and whom they like drunkards had reviled and against whom they had sinned, they asked the young men's forgiveness. Our fair-minded father Païsios, showing care and consideration for all of them, exhorted all of them in what was appropriate behavior. Then, taking aside the head of the laura, he showed him where the stolen articles were. He did not, however, reveal who had stolen them.[726] Then he strengthened the monks with <his>[727] teaching and prayed for them and returned to the desert.

"Agents of salvation for everyone": The godly Païsios and the holy Paul[728]

76.[729] When Païsios heard about the holy Paul and what sort of things God had manifested to the people through him, he went to see him and after they met they became inseparable. Each helped the other.[730] Like a strong and secure city, the two of them brought forth [the] good things[731] of contemplative quiet,[732] devising each day new labors and loftier ascetic disciplines.[733] The holy[734] Païsios had gone well past old age, was ancient in days,[735] and was about the same age as the godly Paul, and his soul was <thoroughly>[736] alive. Because of this, he used to say to Paul, "Let us always rouse one another to the toil and labor of spiritual discipline while we still have time; while we're alive our Lord refuses to allow us to put off doing our work and it will be both fearful and disgraceful for us if we're found negligent at the time of our departure from this life."

These words the godly Païsios spoke. The holy Paul gladly listened to his godly advice and responded, "See, most noble[737] of the fathers, I follow your most noble advice[738] because, with <your> prayers[739] providing us with assistance, I have faith that God, in accordance with your advice, will grant us the ability to attain perfection of this life." 77. So the two of them, acting independently, were wonderworkers,[740] deliverers from the passions, experienced healers of souls, as they prayed for everyone. <They were called>[741] "agents of salvation for everyone."

Païsios' lofty way of life

The stories about the holy Paul are many while those of the godly Païsios are much more than many, uncountable even. Of the many, these few have been chosen to incite thanksgiving and longing imitation.[742] No words can adequately describe that man's lofty way of life. Because of his profound humility, he did not like his virtuous deeds being made known to others. To those who were always asking which of the virtues[743] are the loftiest, he would say, "What's done in secret."[744] Asked the same question on another occasion, he said, "To follow the will of others and not one's own will."[745]

Accordingly, he spent his time wisely, both his time in community and his time in contemplative quiet:[746] in solitude he was a lover who desired[747] intimacy with God and <godly>[748] ascent while in community his loving desire[749] was for his neighbors'[750] salvation. But what is more remarkable is that he never allowed anyone in the cenobium to get an idea of his way of life, but when he was about to be praised for something he was doing, he would immediately stop doing it and would occupy himself doing something else. By doing this, what he was doing earlier would be preserved. And when I asked him, "Why have you resolved to act this way?"[751] he would elegantly say,[752] "So that the things I have done in the past may be preserved unharmed and not be ruined by praise. Truly, great is the danger caused by people's praise. The gain from praise, then, is small for most people and few are those who are saved by it. As a result, <many are harmed by praise.>[753] It was well said by the Lord,[754] 'Do not let your left hand know what your right hand is doing.'"[755]

The narrative will now forego the details about his many teachings.[756] Now the discourse wishes to come to the end of his life.[757]

The deaths of Païsios and Paul
Concerning the death of Saint Païsios[758]

78. Accordingly, having already reached a great old age,[759] the great Païsios, shining resplendently in his way of life and famous for his virtues, came to the end of his earthly labors,[760] called from here to heavenly blessedness. A multitude of monks laid his body away in the earth[761] with honor while his spirit enjoyed eternal life above.[762] Not long afterward, the famous Paul also departed from this world to eternal life; he too crossed over and went to dwell with the saints in resplendent glory, where he shared Païsios' company: just as their blessèd souls had together delighted in ascetic labors, so too did they delight in heavenly repose.[763] Not only that, but <their>[764] bodies, separated for a short while in different places, were brought together and united in the following manner. (But one must attend to the narrative and indeed the treatise will recount in full <the>[765] very astounding miracles.)

Païsios and Paul are buried together; the translation of the relics[766]
Another miracle of the holy one after his death[767]

79. After Païsios had already left this life, the godly Paul went to the inner desert and not long afterward concluded his life there and was buried with honor where he died.

Concerning Saint Païsios after his death[768]

When our father Isidore heard about the death of the great Païsios, he boarded ship and crossed the sea and came to where the body of the godly

Païsios was buried. With great honor he took the body, embraced it, and placed it in a case, since this great item was more valuable than every kind of riches. By bringing the body with him, he wanted to enrich his homeland.[769] They boarded <ship>[770] and completed a good part of <their>[771] journey across the sea, hastening home with hymns and great joy. When they came opposite the desert where Paul's precious body lay, the ship would not move from the spot; instead, as though it had a mind of its own and were straining forward in the direction of Paul's desert, it pointed toward the long-time friend of the holy Païsios, who was looking for him.

The sailors tried to force the ship to move forward but were not able to at all.[772] After spending two days trying to move the ship backward or forward but without any success, they realized that their <being held fast>[773] came from God and nowhere else. Not knowing what to do, they let the ship proceed unpiloted wherever it might go. The ship, guided by an invisible hand, came to shore and stood motionless, awaiting its cargo. Those on board were perplexed and despondent at these events but a certain elder from among the fathers,[774] called Jeremiah, appeared from the desert, <came down>[775] to the beach, and said, "Why, men, do you fight against that which transcends nature? The godly Païsios is summoning his fellow lover Paul;[776] he wants him to be brought back with him. Hurry, therefore, and disembark, and when you find [the body],[777] return with both Paul and Païsios."

The honorable father Isidore and those with him went all around that desert looking for the body and when they found it they carried it and returned to the boat, carrying something more resplendent than gold and precious stones—what a strange and wonderful miracle![778] The great fathers Paul and Païsios in fact became rudders, guiding the ship the whole way as it sailed, delivering it from every danger in its path. In this way the ship was preserved unharmed until it reached Pisidia. The great[779] Isidore, carrying the honorable corpses while singing every hymn of praise,[780] placed the honorable remains in the monastery he had founded.

Conclusion and doxology

80. All those who were troubled by unclean spirits[781] or by any other kind of illness were taking hold of the remains of the saints and were being healed by merely touching them.[782] No one could possibly recount in full all the wondrous miracles God demonstrated and performed[783] after the burial of the holy men.

These few things, out of many, I <have related> to the best of my ability,[784] to the glory of the Father and the Son and the Holy Spirit, now and always, forever and ever. Amen.[785]

Notes

A text in English that does not indicate a manuscript is from Grec 1093.

1. I wish to thank Maged Mikhail and Jeff Russell for their helpful suggestions and Hany Takla for material from *The Red Monastery Church: Beauty and Asceticism in Upper Egypt*, ed. Elizabeth S. Bolman (New Haven: Yale Univesity Press, 2016). The introduction is a much-revised version of Tim Vivian, "A Spirituality of Desire: A Meditation on *The Life of Pshoi* vis-à-vis *The New Asceticism* by Sarah Coakley," *Cistercian Studies Quarterly* 53, no. 1 (2018): 9–31.
2. Simone Weil, *The Notebooks of Simone Weil*, trans. Arthur Wills (London: Routledge & Kegan Paul, 1976), 2:472; cited by Bernard McGinn, *The Foundations of Mysticism: Origins to the Fifth Century*, vol. 1 of *The Presence of God: A History of Western Christian Mysticism* (New York: Crossroad, 1991), 119.
3. On pleasure/pleasures (τέρπνα / *térpna*), "love" (ἀγάπη / *agápē*), "love," "loving desire" (ἔρως / *érōs*), and "lover" (ἐραστής /*erastḗs*), see the appendix to this introduction, "List of Three Key Terms in the *Life of Païsios*, with Quotations," pp. 46–49.
4. The *Life*, thus, runs counter to G.W.H. Lampe's general observation that *agápē*, "denoting esp. God's or Christ's love for [humanity], [humanity's] love for God, and fraternal charity of Christians," is "used in preference to [*érōs*] on account of the latter's undesirable associations." See Lampe, *A Patristic Greek Lexicon* (Oxford: Clarendon, 1961), 6a (hereafter: Lampe). *Phil-*, from *philía*, occurs in the *Life* only a few times, in compounds such as *philáretos*, "love of virtue" (*aretḗ*), and *philánthrōpos*. The definition for *agápē* comes from Walter Bauer, rev. and ed. Frederick William Danker, *A Greek–English Lexicon of the New Testament and Other Early Christian Literature*, 2nd ed. (Chicago: University of Chicago Press, 1979), 6a–7a (hereafter Bauer). Bauer continues its definition: "esteem, affection, regard, love," and "without limitation to very intimate relationships, and very seldom in general Greek of sexual attraction."
5. Sarah Coakley, *The New Asceticism: Sexuality, Gender and the Quest for God* (London: Bloomsbury, 2015). In the section "The Monastic Turn and Mysticism" in *The Foundations of Mysticism*, 131–39, Bernard McGinn does not mention *érōs* or *agápē*.
6. For a full discussion of the Païsios/Bishoi of history and tradition, see the general introduction, pp. 1–8.
7. Franco Montanari, ed., *The Brill Dictionary of Ancient Greek*, English eds. Madeleine Goh and Chad Schroeder (Leiden: Brill, 2015) (hereafter: Montanari), 991c.
8. Hippolyte Delehaye, *Les légendes hagiographiques* (Brussels: Société des Bollandistes, 1955), 107 (emphasis his); Delehaye, *The Legends of the*

Saints, trans. Donald Attwater (Dublin and Portland, OR: Four Courts Press, 1998), 90.
9 Delehaye, *Les légendes hagiographiques*, 108 (emphasis his); Delehaye, *The Legends of the Saints*, 91.
10 As Evelyn-White correctly observes (*The Monasteries of the Wadi 'N Natrun*, ed. Walter Hauser [New York: Metropolitan Museum of Art, 1926–32; repr. Arno Press, 1973], 2:111), the *Life*, as its Exordium shows, is a panegyric "intended (like most Coptic *Lives*) for recitation at the commemoration of the saint whose deed it records." He says it is not certain whether the *Life* was composed in the seventh century or earlier. See the general introduction.
11 Kent Nerburn, *Neither Wolf nor Dog: On Forgotten Roads with an Indian Elder* (Novato, CA: New World Library, 1994, 2002), 270.
12 Nerburn, *Neither Wolf nor Dog*, 273. One should remember that late antique Roman elites called Christianity a *superstitio*. See L.F. Janssen, "'Superstitio' and the Persecution of the Christians," *Vigiliae Christianae* 33, no. 2 (June 1979): 131–59.
13 I must emphasize that I do not use "myth" here in its current, derogatory sense, but rather as a term in religious studies for sacred story. See "Myth" in Jonathan Z. Smith, ed., *The HarperCollins Dictionary of Religion* (San Francisco: HarperSanFrancisco, 1995), 749a–751b, although I disagree with the article's overemphasis on "the deeds of superhuman beings" (although that emphasis can indeed apply often to Jesus in the Gospels and to the miracles and wonders in the *Life*). The symbolic theory of myth (750a) "denies that myths are false attempts to explain the world. In fact, myths are not explanations of anything. They are symbolic representations of abstract meanings, psychological repressions, complex collective structures, metaphysical archetypes, or a transcendent reality that is often defined as 'wholly other' or 'the Sacred.'" I also question "repressions." To my mind, metaphysical archetypes (here, how to live a *realized* life) are expressions of transcendent reality. Païsios, like Jesus, represents the sacred and calls on the sacred (scripture, God) for help.
14 Coakley, *The New Asceticism*, 5.
15 Virginia Burrus, "Introduction: Theology and Eros after Nygren," in *Toward a Theology of Eros: Transfiguring Passion at the Limits of Discipline*, ed. Virginia Burrus and Catherine Keller (New York: Fordham University Press, 2006), xiii. Burrus uses the term "theological erotics."
16 Burrus, "Introduction," xiii.
17 The title to ¶64 in one manuscript acknowledges the important theme of the will: "Concerning One Who Followed His Own Will."
18 Coakley, *The New Asceticism*, 5–6.

19 Coakley, *The New Asceticism*, 20.
20 Coakley, *The New Asceticism*, 4.
21 The literature is vast; for an introduction see Marilyn Dunn, *The Emergence of Monasticism: From the Desert Fathers to the Early Middle Ages* (Oxford: Blackwell, 2000), chapter 4, "The Meaning of Asceticism," 59–81, and Ewa Wipszycka, *The Second Gift of the Nile: Monks and Monasteries in Late Antique Egypt*, trans. Damian Jasiński (Warsaw: University of Warsaw, 2018). See also Vincent Wimbush, *Ascetic Behavior in Greco-Roman Antiquity* (Minneapolis: Fortress Press, 1990); William Harmless, *Desert Christians: An Introduction to the Literature of Early Monasticism* (Oxford: Oxford University Press, 2004); James E. Goehring, *Ascetics, Society and the Desert: Studies in Early Egyptian Monasticism* (Harrisburg, PA: Trinity, 1999); and Inbar Graiver, *Asceticism of the Mind: Forms of Attention and Self-transformation in Late Antique Monasticism* (Toronto: Pontifical Institute of Mediaeval Studies, 2018).
22 *Theosis* is traditionally translated "divinization"; it is a vital part of Eastern Orthodox Christian thought and spirituality. On its patristic use, see Lampe 649b–650a.
23 Aristotle Papanikolaou, "The Dance of Faith," *Christian Century* (February 15, 2017): 36–40. In publishing this article, the *Christian Century*, a mainstream magazine, brings the early monastic *politeía* into the present.
24 All quotations in this paragraph are from Coakley, *The New Asceticism*, 10. The metaphor of a tractor relies on an etymological play on words: Latin *traho* (*tractum* is the perfect passive participle), from which "tractor" evolves, means "to draw or drag."
25 See especially Coakley, *The New Asceticism*, 48–51 for Gregory's "appropriation" of Platonic eros. Burrus notes that, for Anders Nygren, Origen and Gregory "are prime examples of . . . erotic excess in the history of Christian thought" (Burrus, "Introduction," xv). On Nygren, see below.
26 Coakley, *The New Asceticism*, 51 (emphases hers). On mimesis, see below.
27 *Póthos* occurs five times in the *Life of Antony*, all positive; it marks the desire for divine or sacred realities. See the "Index des mots grecs" in *Athanase d'Alexandrie: Vie d'Antoine*, ed. and trans. G.J.M. Bartelink (Paris: Cerf, 1994), 416.
28 Anthony Meredith, *The Cappadocians* (Crestwood, NY: St Vladimir's Seminary Press, 1995), 55. On p. 98 n. 11, Meredith cites G. Horn, "L'amour divin. Note sur le mot 'Eros' dans saint Grégoire de Nysse," *Revue d'ascétique et de mystique* 8 (1927): 113–31. For brief discussions of Plato, Origen, and Gregory, see McGinn, *The Foundations of Mysticism*, 24–35, 108–30, and 139–42, respectively.

29 Burrus, "Introduction," xiv; Nygren, *Agape and Eros*, 31, cited by Burrus, xiv.
30 McGinn, *The Foundations of Mysticism*, 72. Contra Nygren's too "simple" bifurcation, McGinn suggests that "the New Testament's preference for *agapē* over *erōs* may apply only to what the philosophers came to call profane *erōs*, and not the heavenly or sacred version."
31 McGinn, *The Foundations of Mysticism*, 72.
32 In Luke 17:21, *entós* can mean either "among" or "within," but Bauer 340b gives only "inside, within."
33 Mt 22:34–40//Mk 12:28–34//Lk 10:25–28.
34 For three essays on Plato's Dialogue by Daniel Boyarin, Mark D. Jordan, and Mario Costa, see Burrus and Keller, *Toward a Theology of Eros*, part 1, "Restaging the Symposium on Love."
35 Daniel Boyarin, "What Do We Talk About When We Talk About Platonic Love?" in Burrus and Keller, *Toward a Theology of Eros*, 21. McGinn, *The Foundations of Mysticism*, 27, contra Nygren, says that for Plato, "rather, true *erōs* is love for the Good that seeks to beget the good, either the good of human offspring or of virtue." This latter is especially applicable to the *Life of Païsios*.
36 Boyarin, "What Do We Talk About," 22.
37 Alphabetical *Apophthegmata Patrum* (hereafter: AlphAP) Antony 24; see Tim Vivian, *The Sayings and Stories of the Desert Fathers and Mothers*, vol. 1 (Collegeville, MN: Cistercian Publications, 2021), 108.
38 Catherine Keller, "Afterword: A Theology of Eros, after Transfiguring Desire," in Burrus and Keller, *Toward a Theology of Eros*, 367.
39 On *psychē*, see Lampe 1542b–1553b.
40 Keller, "Afterword," 370 (italicization hers).
41 Keller, "Afterword," 373.
42 Coakley, *The New Asceticism*, 51.
43 Coakley, *The New Asceticism*, 6.
44 Aldous Huxley, "Distractions—I," in *Vedanta for the Western World*, ed. Christopher Isherwood (Hollywood, CA: Vedanta Press, 1946), 129.
45 Kent Nerburn, *Voices in the Stones: Life Lessons from the Native Way* (Novato, CA: New World Library, 2016), 156.
46 Coakley, *The New Asceticism*, 47. See Phil 3:13–14. See McGinn, *The Foundations of Mysticism*, 83, for a brief discussion of, and demurral from, A.-J. Festugière's explication of "two strands in Christian spirituality during the early centuries" centered on *érōs* and *agápē*.
47 Coakley, *The New Asceticism*, 47.
48 Quotations in this paragraph are from Coakley, *The New Asceticism*, 9. On demons, see David Brakke, *Demons and the Making of the Monk: Spiritual Combat in Early Christianity* (Cambridge, MA and London: Harvard University Press, 2006), and Graiver, *Asceticism of the Mind*.

49 Violence, psycho-somatic violence, does occur in the *Life*: violence from demons (¶59); violence in hell (22, 56); linguistic and theological violence against Jews (53, 55, 64–65); and verbal violence against women (65).
50 Coakley, *The New Asceticisim*, 20 (emphasis hers).
51 On myth, see n. 13.
52 See Bauer 497b.
53 Paul Evdokimov has commented that "[t]he ascetic of the desert offers a prodigious psychoanalysis followed by a psychosynthesis of the universal soul"; Evdokimov, *La nouveauté de l'esprit*, Spiritualité Orientale (Begrolles-en-Mauges: Bellefontaine, 1977), 207. See Graiver, *Asceticism of the Mind*.
54 Coakley, *The New Asceticisim*, 43 (Coakley's emphasis). The quotation from Freud is from Einstein and Freud, "Why War," 93 (Coakley's emphasis). The text may be found at http://www.public.asu.edu/~jmlynch/273/documents/FreudEinstein.pdf. Coakley dates the correspondence to 1933; the ASU site gives 1932 as the date of Freud's letter to Einstein.
55 See Romans 7.
56 See Coakley, *The New Asceticism*, 104. McGinn states that the "basic pattern of withdrawal-purgation-transformation was the structure that gave shape and purpose to the other values and practices of the first monastics" (*The Foundations of Mysticism*, 136).
57 Coakley, *The New Asceticism*, 111.
58 See, among several, Zech 13:9; Dan 12:10; Mal 3:3.
59 The *Life* always reserves *agápē* for divine love—God's or Christ's—and keeps *póthos*, "desire," and *erastēs*, "lover," primarily for humans.
60 Following Coakley, here and in our translation of the *Life*, except for two occasions, discussed in this introduction, *érōs* is "loving desire."
61 Coakley, *The New Asceticism*, 53 (emphasis hers).
62 On the desert mothers see Tim Vivian, "'We Sail by Day': Metaphor and Exegesis in the Sayings of Amma Syncletica of Egypt," *Cistercian Studies Quarterly* 54, no. 1 (2019): 3–24, and Vivian, "Courageous Women: Three Desert Ammas—Theodora, Sarah, and Syncletica," *American Benedictine Review* 71, no. 1 (2020): 75–107.
63 Dr. Rowan Williams, 104th Archbishop of Canterbury, the third, fourth, and fifth of five addresses given by the Archbishop of Canterbury during the retreat that began the Fourteenth Lambeth Conference, Fourth Address, "God's Mission and a Bishop's Discipleship," July 18, 2008, http://rowanwilliams.archbishopofcanterbury.org/articles.php/1739/the-archbishops-retreat-addresses-parts-iii-iv-v.
64 Evdokimov, *La nouveaueté de l'esprit*, 208.

65 *Life of Antony* 15.3 and 44.1 (95 and 151–53); see Bartelink, "Index des mots grecs," 391, in Athanasius of Alexandria, *Athanase d'Alexandrie: Vie d'Antoine*, 403. *Agápē* occurs ten times and its verbal form, *agapáō*, five. The noun and verb most often emphasize love for or by God and Christ, love for one's fellow monks, love for humankind, and, twice, Antony's love for his monastic way of life. All references to the English translation of the *Life of Antony* are to Tim Vivian and Apostolos N. Athanassakis, *The Life of Antony: The Coptic Life and the Greek Life*, Cistercian Studies Series 202 (Kalamazoo, MI: Cistercian Publications, 2003), with section numbers first, followed by page number(s), as in 16–43; 97–151.

66 Adulterer: Coptic *nnecnōik*, in paragraph 12, which is a midrash on Proverbs 7 (the Septuagint version does not use *erastés* for "lover"), and ultimately derives from *Lausiac History* 47. See Mikhail and Vivian, *The Holy Workshop of Virtue*, 80.

67 *Tiagapē, metmai, metmainouti, metmairōmi*. In his *Coptic Dictionary*, 156a, Crum lists ἐρᾶν and ἐραστής only with Proverbs 4:6 and Jeremiah 4:30, respectively. His Greek Index, 901c, lists ἐρᾶν only at 156a and ἐραστής at 156a-b and 285a with *poj*, "amorous (?)."

68 Tim Vivian, trans., *Witness to Holiness: Abba Daniel of Scetis*, Cistercian Studies Series 219 (Kalamazoo, MI: Cistercian Publications, 2008): God the lover of humanity (44), a Christ-loving person (45), God's merciful love for humankind (46), lovers of Christ (51), and almsgiving equals love (47). The Greek texts may be found in Léon Clugnet, "Vie et récits de l'Abbé Daniel, de Scété," *Revue de l'Orient Chrétien* 5 (1900): 49–73, 254–71, 370–91; *Revue de l'Orient Chrétien* 6 (1901): 56–87.

69 *Mikràs hēdonḗs*. The author of the Exordium is contrasting in this sentence inferior "pleasure" *(hēdonḗ)* and the passions with love, real love, loving desire. The entry on *hēdonḗ* in Lampe 601b is very instructive: a small portion of the entry (1–3) concerns types of pleasure, admissibility, and advisory or even monitory moderation; much of the rest of it is negative about pleasure (as in fact modern "hedonism" attests), for example: 4. in bad sense; 5. diabolical instigation; 6. life of pleasure incompatible with spiritual life; 7. evil effects of irrational pleasure; 7a. obscuring of judgment; 7b. hindrance to knowledge of God; 7c. psychological unrest; 7d. harm to soul; 8. ref. gluttony; 9b. sexual pleasure, illegitimate.

70 "Promised," Gk *epēngelménōn* < *epangéllō*: promised (by God); the root *-ángel* occurs in *euangélion*, "good news," "gospel."

71 That is, the *Life* presents an <u>onto</u>logy of the true life.

72 New Testament writers usually differentiate *páthēma*, "suffering, misfortune," from *páthos*, "experience of strong desire, *passion*." See Bauer 747b–748a and 748a–b.

73 Divine affection: *ho theíos póthos*, which can also mean "love, desire."
74 See Mt 16:25.
75 "With incorporeal forces" can go with "by always constraining nature" or with "they contend with the body," or both.
76 Coakley, *The New Asceticism*, 111 (emphasis hers).
77 Apposition: in grammar, "a syntactic relation between expressions, usually consecutive, that have the same function and the same relation to other elements in the sentence, the second expression identifying or supplementing the first" (Dictionary.com). The second expression in fact *identifies* the first, reveals its total character.
78 See Gen 3. On myth see n. 13.
79 Such invention would in fact represent a non-Judaic (and -Christian) radical dualism.
80 "Dark satanic mills": William Blake, "Jerusalem."
81 The *Life of Paísios* emphasizes the great themes discussed in the previous paragraphs and not quotidian asceticism, that is, day-to-day life in the cell, as does, for example, AlphAP Poemen 168 (John Wortley, trans., *Give Me a Word: The Alphabetical Sayings of the Desert Fathers* [Yonkers, NY: St Vladimir's Seminary Press, 2014], 254–55). See Lucien Regnault, *The Day-to-day Life of the Desert Fathers in Fourth-century Egypt*, trans. Étienne Poirier, Jr. (Petersham, MA: St. Bede's, 1999).
82 McGinn, *The Foundations of Mysticism*, 125: "Origen's mysticism centers on the transformation of eros ii, the power of yearning desire implanted in the soul by God who is EROS I."
83 To borrow from Martin Luther King Jr., the immoral arc of the universe. But this would be excruciatingly dualistic. May one say instead "the immoral arc of the 'worldly,'" that is, the realm of human "devices and desires," the passions?
84 *Tôn kalôn* does not occur as a substantive in the New Testament; it occurs adjectivally in such phrases as *tôn kalôn érgōn*, "good works."
85 The "Creator" here is the *dēmiourgós*, the Demiurge, the Creator of the World, of later Greek philosophy. See Henry George Liddell and Robert Scott, rev. Henry Stuart Jones, *Greek–English Lexicon* (Oxford: Clarendon, repr. 1977) (hereafter: LSJ), 386a, Lampe 342b, and Montanari 476a.
86 On mimesis, see ¶69: "someone who emulates" *(mīmētḗs)* and "emulating" *(mīmoúmenos < mīméomai)*.
87 Read the sentence twice, the first time inflecting "Jewish," the second time "woman," a double whammy. The *Life*, we need to note, like other early monastic literature, characterizes women—at least for monks—as the ultimate stumbling blocks: "The Enemy [that is, Satan] cannot possibly have at his disposal any device more suitable than a woman" (¶65).

88   In the *Life of Antony* (which quotes Jms 1:15), *epithymía*, "desire," occurs seven times, all negative: it is the desire, or even lust, connected with sin, anger, and possessions, more broadly (36.2, p. 137) a desire for evil. See the "Index des mots grecs" in Bartelink, 416.

89   See Acts 9:3; 26:12–13. Compare Gal 1:15.

90   See Is 49:2 and Song of Songs 2:5 (LXX). McGinn, *The Foundations of Mysticism*, 118, states that "Origen's use of erotic symbolism . . . introduces us to one of the most complex and controversial aspects of the history of Christian mysticism."

91   The term refers both to the future life and to those in this life "who have faith and charity," then specifically to the monastic life (Lampe 676a).

92   I have coined these two terms. Greek *iso-* means "equal to/with ("isosceles"); *isángelos*, "equal to/with the angels," is a common term for monks. *Sun-/syn-*, "with," equals Latin *cum* and Spanish *con*. In English see "synchronize," "synergy," "symphony," and "sympathy."

93   On Paul, see "Saint Paul of Tamma and the Life of the Cell," chapter 5 in Tim Vivian, *Words to Live By: Journeys in Ancient and Modern Egyptian Monasticism* (Kalamazoo, MI: Cistercian Publications, 2005), and the general introduction to this volume, 4–5.

94   It is almost as if the author of the *Life* fills the text with "loving desire" (*érōs*) eight times in the first nineteen chapters, only to forget about it until near the end. (Thus, there is an odd parallel with "signs" in John's Gospel. Many scholars suggest that John has multiple author-editors; perhaps the *Life* does, too.) *Érōs* occurs five times in ¶¶69–77 (the *Life* has eighty numbered paragraphs). But this is not quite fair: In ¶¶19–69, *póthos* occurs six times and forms of *philía*, *agápē*, and *storgḗ* occur thirteen times altogether.

95   See Coakley, *The New Asceticism*, 111.

96   Coakley, *The New Asceticism*, 115.

97   "The holy workshop of virtue" comes from Mikhail and Vivian, *Life of John the Little*, 9 (English, 77; Bohairic Coptic, 149). On the virtues in early monastic thought and spirituality, see also Vivian, "Ama Sibylla of Saqqara" in *Words to Live By*, 377–93.

98   Mikhail and Vivian, *Life of John the Little* 9 (English, 77; Bohairic Coptic, 149).

99   On this movement, see E.A. Judge, "The Earliest Use of Monachos for 'Monk' (P. Coll. Youtie 77) and the Origins of Monasticism," *Jahrbuch für Antike und Christentum* 10 (1977): 72–89, and James E. Goehring, "Through a Glass Darkly: Images of the Ἀποτακτικοί in Early Egyptian Monasticism," in *Ascetics, Society, and the Desert*, 53–72.

100 "Mystically instructed": *mystagōgētheís*; see *Life of Antony* 14:2 (p. 91, "having been initiated into the divine mysteries") and Lampe 890b–891a. Forms of *myst-* occur four times in the *Life*: ¶¶6, 35, 36, 40.
101 One could also add emphasis: *and ministers to others*.
102 Coakley, *The New Asceticism*, 117 (emphasis hers). She notes that such an understanding can be "contentious," "granted the smack of elitism that it inevitably suggests, especially to the suspicious Protestant investigator." She goes on (117–18) to adduce Evagrius of Pontus for support.
103 Coakley, *The New Asceticism*, 117 (emphasis hers). One wonders, while probably knowing, why this strand is "minority."
104 Lampe 1857a–1858b.
105 2 Cor 3:18: "From one degree of glory to another," lit. "from glory to glory."
106 Coakley, *The New Asceticism*, 122.
107 See Jean Daniélou, ed., *From Glory to Glory: Texts from Gregory of Nyssa's Mystical Writings* (Crestwood, NY: St Vladimir's Seminary Press, 1997).
108 Williams, "God's Mission and a Bishop's Discipleship."
109 Translated from BnF Grec 1093, 14th c., complete except for one folio page, vis-à-vis the text ed. by I. V. Pomialovskii [hereafter: Pom], *Zhitie prepodobnogo Paisiia Velikogo i Timofeia Patriarkha Alexandriiskogo* [*The Life of the Blessed Paḯsios and Timothy, Patriarch of Alexandria*], *Zapiski istoriko-filo-logicheskogo fakul'teta SPb U* [*Journal of the Historical-Philological Department of St. Petersburg University*], 2 [3?], vol. 50 (1902): 1–61; BnF Grec 1547 [1547], 1286 CE, folios 129–58 (digital pages 136–66) [complete]; and BnF suppl. gr. 0759 [759], folios 106–220, 12th c. [incomplete]. All the manuscripts are available online. Section numbering is generally Pomialovskii's (converted to Arabic numerals). Section titles, unless otherwise noted, are the translators'. Greek Paḯsios; his Coptic name is Pshoi, transliterated into Arabic as Bishoi or Bishoy. The title in Pom: The Life of Our Holy Father Paḯsios. Then "Bless, Father."
110 The Exordium uses a more sophisticated—or, at least, lengthier—syntax than the *Life* proper; we have chosen to follow it as best we can.
111 The delightful things of life: that is, "pleasures": *tà terpnà toû bíou*. There may be a play on words here emphasizing the transience of the delightful things: "delightful things" renders *terpná* while "subject to change" renders *treptá*. In addition, there may be a contrast between *bios*, "life," with *politeia*, "an ascetic/monastic way of life."
112 Lust, *érōs*. Transliterated Greek words are given mostly in their dictionary entry form.
113 Inferior pleasure: *mikrà hēdoné*.
114 Loving desire: *érōs*. Love is a major theme in the *Life*; see the introduction to this chapter. We have followed the lead of Sarah Coakley, *The New*

NOTES 97

Asceticism, and translated *érōs* as "loving desire" rather than "love." As Coakley asseverates, "When the ascetic life works, and works well, it unifies, intensifies, and ultimately purifies desire in the crucible of divine love, paradoxically imparting true freedom precisely by the narrowing of choices" (6).

115 Passions: *páthos*. In early Christian usage, the "passions" (from *páschō*, to suffer) connote "emotion, passion, impulse"; in Rom 1:26, Paul uses the phrase "degrading passions." Other uses in the New Testament (hereafter: NT) are 1 Th 4:5 and Col 3:5. See Lampe 992a–995a.

116 Loving desire: *érōs*.

117 Promised by God, *epangéllomai*: the root *-angel* occurs in *euangélion*, "good news," "gospel." An angel, therefore, is a messenger of the "good news."

118 Creator, *dēmiourgós*: see Lampe 342a and Heb 11:10.

119 "Divine affection": *ho theíos póthos*, which can also mean "love, desire."

120 Lovers: *erastés (érōs)*. In Classical Greek, *erastés* (the verb *éramai*) can mean "a lover," of sexual love; the verb in addition to "love" can mean "to love passionately, long for, lust after." See LSJ 681a. Neither the noun nor the verb appears in the NT, although a related verb, *eráō*, occurs in patristic literature; it is no longer deponent—reflexive or self-referential—and means "to feel passionately about, have a longing for, feel fervently about" (Bauer 389a). *Erastés* was Christianized by the fourth century and used, for example (and for us, perhaps, paradoxically), of Christ as a lover of chastity. Chrysostom (ca. 347–407), *Homily 62.5 on Matthew*, uses it for lovers of virtue. Patristic Greek frequently uses *eráō* interchangeably with *philéō (philía)* and *agapáō (agápē)*, though also of sexual love and passionate desire, used especially of God-loving creatures and creatures' love for God. See ¶36: "the lovers of this holy [monastic] way of life."

121 See Lk 18:29. Love: *philóō*.

122 See Mt 16:25.

123 Contend: Pom "contend together."

124 "By always constraining nature with incorporeal forces, they contend with the body" has a play on words: "incorporeal" renders *asōmátois* < *sôma* and "body" translates *sômati* < *sôma*.

125 Men: *andrôn* < *anér*, "man, male." When Greek uses the generic *ánthrōpos*, we use "human(s)," "human being(s)," or "person(s)."

126 See *Life of Antony*, Preface 3; *The Life of Antony*, 53.

127 Honor (*timḗ*) or love (*philía*): though classical terms and concepts, these words have significant and widespread coinage in the NT and patristic Greek. For *timḗ* see Bauer 1005a–1006a and Lampe 1393b–1394a (*tímios*); for *philía* and *philéō* see Bauer 1056b–1057a and 1057a–b and Lampe 1477a (*philéō*) and 1478a (*philía*).

128 It is interesting that although the Greek *Life* commonly uses "father" (πατήρ / *patḗr*), it never uses the common honorific "abba," "father" (see Mk 14:36; Rom 8:15; Gal 4:6).
129 See 1 Jn 1:1. In Greek "saw" and "heard" use the perfect aspect and could be translated "have seen" and "have heard." See for example the opening sentence of 1 Jn 1, which the *Life* here probably echoes: "We declare to you what was from the beginning, what we have heard, what we have seen with our eyes" where "what we have heard" and "what we have seen" use the perfect. The perfect aspect in Greek can emphasize that the effect of what has happened in the past continues still.
130 Pom, 1547 lack "and self-importance," ὑψηλότερος, the superlative of ὑψηλός (Montanari 2245c–2246a).
131 I will recount in full the praiseworthy things about this man: Pom "I will recount in full and in detail the praiseworthy and profitable things about this man."
132 See John of Shmūn, "An Encomium on Saint Antony" 6–9, in *Life of Antony*, 12–14.
133 Moses: one could infer from Lk 24:27 ("Then beginning with Moses and all the prophets Jesus interpreted to them the things about himself in all the scriptures") that Moses is a prophet; see Dt 18:18 and 34:10. Early Christian and rabbinic literature describe him as such, as does Islam.
134 Who saw God: *theoptḗs*; used by patristic authors of Abraham, Moses, and Isaiah.
135 The Scriptures: Pom, 759, 1547 "the Holy Scriptures."
136 Fearing the Lord: Pom, 759, 1547 "God-fearing."
137 See Dt 11:22; 19:9.
138 Prospered in everything: Pom, 759 "were filled with abundance" (lit. "multiplied all things"); *plēthúnousa*, "multiply," has biblical echoes: in Heb 6:14 God promises Abraham "I will surely bless you and multiply you," and Acts 12:24 says that "the word of God continued to advance and gain adherents."
139 See Job 29:12; Ps 10:14; Jer 7:6; Jms 1:27; among others.
140 See 1 Cor 1:27; 2 Cor 12:9.
141 The Lord's chosen: Pom "God's chosen."
142 Offered: Pom "proclaimed."
143 Me: lit. "us"; in Grec 1093 the plural often means the singular.
144 See Lk 1:38; Païsios' mother's use of *génoito* ("may") echoes that of Mary: "Here am I, the servant of the Lord; let it be [*génoito*] with me according to your word."
145 This passage appears to be modeled in part on the story of Samson in Jdg 13.

146 Lover: *erastḗs*; see ¶1.
147 The virtues: 1547 "what is holy."
148 Loving desire: *érōs*. On the "wound of love," see Is 49:2 and Song of Songs 2:5 (LXX).
149 This metaphorical use of being wounded by love (and fear), also classical in origin, is found in Origen, the *Pseudo-Macarian Homilies*, and Gregory of Nyssa. The adjective *theíō(i)* separates "fear" and "love" and probably applies to both: lit. "divine [*theîos*] fear and love."
150 Love: *érōs*.
151 The divine commandments: Pom "the Lord's divine commandments."
152 See Ex 12:5; Ex 12:1–28, the first Passover; 1 Pet 1:19; and the numerous references to "lamb" in Revelation.
153 Great Pambo: Pom, 1547 "holy." On Pambo, see Tim Vivian, *Four Desert Fathers: Pambo, Evagrius, Macarius of Egypt, and Macarius of Alexandria* (Crestwood, NY: St Vladimir's Seminary Press, 2004), 53–68.
154 The "spiritual" (*logikós*, which also means "rational") flock belongs to Christ, the Word (*lógos*), the "good shepherd."
155 Holiness and joy: Pom, 759, 1547 "goodness and joy."
156 Suitable: Pom, 1547 "upright" (lit. "straight").
157 Obedience: Grec 1093, 1547; Pom "patient obedience."
158 Obedience—and disobedience—is an important theme in the *Life*.
159 *Agōnistḗs* < *agōnízomai*, "engage in an athletic contest," then "fight, struggle," is important in the Pauline and deutero-Pauline literature: 1 Cor 9:25; Col 1:29; 1 Tim 6:12; 2 Tim 4:7; and then in early monasticism.
160 *Ánō*, "above," echoes "born from above" (*ánōthen*) in the story of Nicodemus (Jn 3:7; see also Jn 3:31 and 8:23).
161 Of the Creator: Pom "of the Creator, as to a benefactor." In the Late Antique world, *euergétēs*, "benefactor," had deep resonances from the patron–client social structure: "as a title of princes and other honored persons, esp. those recognized for their civic contributions" (Bauer 405A); then applied to the gods, such as Zeus and Osiris, and to God (see Lampe 564a). See Bruce J. Malina, *The New Testament World: Insights from Cultural Anthropology*, 3rd ed. (Louisville, KY: Westminster John Knox, 2001), esp. "The Honorable Person's Dyadic Alliances," 93–105. See Lk 22:25: "But [Jesus] said to them, 'The kings of the Gentiles lord it over them; and those in authority over them are called benefactors [*euergétai*].'" Bruce Malina and Richard L. Rohrbaugh, *Social-science Commentary on the Synoptic Gospels*, 2nd ed. (Minneapolis: Fortress, 2003), 317, note: "The title 'benefactor' was often given in the Hellenistic world to gods and kings. Both Caesar Augustus and Nero were so designated in inscriptions honoring their largesse."

162 Mystically instructed: *mystagōgētheís* < *mystagōgéō*. The word is used of Antony in *Life of Antony* 14:2 (91): "having been initiated into divine mysteries." See Lampe 890b–891a: "initiate into mysteries," "instruct in divine mysteries," "unfold the meaning of" such mysteries. Mystery, *mystérion*, has numerous meanings in patristic Greek: "mystery; secret rite; secret; secret purpose of God revealed or fulfilled; secret of God revealed by divine activity; that by which a secret is conveyed, object of mystical significance; sacrament" (Lampe 891b–893a).

163 He followed his teacher's instructions: lit. "he became one who fulfills [*plērōtḗs*]"; the word was used of someone completing the Law (Torah). In the next sentence, "order" translates *entolḗ*, which also means "command(ment)."

164 At that time, for three years he would carry out the godly father's order to the letter, not looking into the faces of the saints at all: Pom, 1547 "At that time, for three years he carried out this very order to the letter, not looking into anyone's face at all; instead, he devoted himself completely to reading the Holy Scriptures and searching out their meaning."

165 He would irrigate with their flowing streams his own soul: Pom, 1547 "He would irrigate with their flowing streams, giving his soul water to drink."

166 Like a tree that, flourishing when planted beside streams of water, bears ripe, sweet fruit in due and proper season: Pom, 1547 "like a tree that, flourishing when planted beside the watercourses, blossoms, laden, and from it grows ripe, sweet fruit in due and proper season." See Ps 1:3.

167 Pom continues: "adducing these words (for this passage was a favorite of his)."

168 Ps 118:103/119:103. When a psalm is given with two numbers, the first refers to the numbering in the Septuagint (LXX), the second to that of the NRSV. In antiquity the Psalms were attributed to David.

169 1 Thes 1:2.

170 2 Cor 6:5.

171 Instructing, *paidagogṓn* < *paidagogéō*: Pom, 1547 "subjugating," *doulagōgṓn* < *doulagōgéō*, lit. "make a slave [*doûlos*] of"; see 1 Cor 9:27.

172 See *Life of Antony* 3.4; 61–63.

173 Elder: *presbýtēs*, an elder, related to *presbýteros* (NT: "overseer"; "priest" is probably anachronistic) which also means "elder" or a "venerable person" in rank or years. The latter term, with some confusion, in patristic Greek came to mean either "priest" or "bishop" (Lampe 1129a–1131a). In the next paragraph "elder" translates *géronti* < *gérōn* (English "gerontology"), which means "old man" but in monastic terms an elder or spiritual elder who is wise and experienced but not necessarily chronologically old.

174 Spiritual discipline: *pneumatikḗ(i)* . . . *askḗsei*.
175 Desired: *epóthei*, cognate with *póthos*.
176 See 2 Kgs 2:13–14 (Elijah and Elisha) and *Life of Antony* 91.8–9; 253: Antony bequeaths his two sheepskin coats, one to Bishop Athanasius and one to Bishop Serapion.
177 See Heb 11:1.
178 See Acts 4:32.
179 Rule: *kanṓn*. In the NT, *kanṓn* means a "rule, standard" (Gal 6:16; Phil 3:16) and "assignment, formulation" (2 Cor 10:13, 15–18). In the second century it came to mean "rule of faith." See Bauer 507b–508a. According to Lampe 701a–702a, the word can indicate "rule of faith"; "canon of scripture"; and "canon of behavior," that is, a moral standard, as in Paul.
180 See Ps 132:1/133:1.
181 Loving desire: *érōs*.
182 Spiritual disciplines: *agōgṓn*.
183 He did not eat bread: Grec 1093, Pom; 1547 "he would engage in spiritual struggle."
184 As the rest of the paragraph makes clear, "prophecy" here refers to the book of the prophet Jeremiah, not to a particular prophecy by the seer; for this use of the word, see Lampe 1193a(III). Thus: prophecies.
185 To a loving desire: *érōs*.
186 See Phil 3:13.
187 Way of life: *diagōgḗ*; Pom here and in the title to the *Life* uses the usual monastic *politeía*, which has the same meaning.
188 Love: *érōs*.
189 Contemplative quiet: *hēsychía*, an important monastic term and practice. See Bauer 440b and Lampe 609a–610a. The practice involved—and involves—both contemplative quiet (or meditation) and solitude, so we have used two words to translate the term.
190 Contemplative quiet: *hēsychía*.
191 Love: *érōs*.
192 "Thought" here undoubtedly refers to those thoughts whose character the monks were always trying to discern. See *Life of Antony* 36; 37–139. See Antony Rich, *Discernment in the Desert Fathers: Διάκρισις in the Life and Thought of Early Egyptian Monasticism*, Studies in Christian History and Thought (Bletchley, UK: Paternoster Press, 2015). Evagrius especially emphasizes such scrutiny with regard to thoughts; for a recent study, see Brakke, *Demons and the Making of the Monk*, esp. chapter 3 on Evagrius, 48–77. See Graiver, *Asceticism of the Mind*.
193 After saying these things: Pom, 1557 "After exchanging these heartfelt words."

194 Lived: *kateskḗnōsen* here echoes *eskḗnōsen* (*skēnóō* < *skēnḗ*, "tent") of Jn 1:14, where the Logos "dwells" (lit. "pitches his tent") with humankind.
195 Virtue: Pom, 759, 1547 "virtues/the virtues."
196 A godly hymn on his lips: probably a psalm; "meditation" *(meletáō)* for the monks usually meant reciting a psalm or psalms sotto voce.
197 Peace be with you: see Jn 14:27.
198 Fear and trembling: see, among others, Ps 55:5; Mk 5:33; 1 Cor 2:3; and 2 Cor 7:15.
199 Who loves us: *philánthrōpos*. Pom "Christ, (our) Savior, who loves us"; Grec 1093, 1547 lack "Savior."
200 See Lk 1:38.
201 Monks: lit. "ascetics," those practicing asceticism. Perhaps an echo of God's promise to Abraham in Gen 17:5–6. See also *Life of Antony* 14.5; 93.
202 The Lord's chosen: Pom, 1547 "God's chosen."
203 Master: Pom, 1547 "Lord and Master."
204 Bivouacking *(aulizoménois)*: Pom, 1547 "contending" *(agōnizoménois < agṓn*, "struggle, contest, fight").
205 Desert: *érēmos* also means "wilderness," so the wilderness of the Exodus may be in the background here; the LXX uses *érēmos* at Ex 5:1, 3. An early reader or listener might also have thought of John the Baptist (Mk 1:3–4; Is 40:3) and/or Jesus (Mk 1:12–13//Mt 4:1–11//Lk 4:1–13).
206 Love: *agápē*. See Montanari 4a–6a and Lampe 7a–8b.
207 No one will lack anything: Pom, 1547 "no one will lack anything he needs."
208 Man: Pom, 1547 "Païsios."
209 Enemy, *echthrós*: Lk 10:19 may with "the enemy" be referring to Satan or the Devil.
210 Humility: Pom, 1547 "humility and righteousness."
211 With humility and a humble heart: Pom "with humility and righteousness and a humble heart."
212 See Lk 16:9.
213 See Jn 20:17.
214 Gnashed his teeth: among many biblical references, see Ps 112:10; Lam 2:16; Mt 8:12; 13:42.
215 Or "godly Power." "Power," *dýnamis*, occurs over one hundred times in the NT.
216 Form: *schḗma*: Pom, 1547 *próschēma*, "disguise," "false appearance." Ironically, the *schḗma* is also the monastic habit.
217 Wretched One *(deílaios)*: Grec 1093, 759; Pom, 1547 "Crafty/Deceitful/Treacherous One" *(dólios)*.
218 This story undoubtedly reflects what must have been a fairly common occurrence—the rich coming to the desert to bestow riches on the monks.

The offering—and rejection—of money is a topos in early monastic literature; for one example, involving Pambo and Melania the Elder, see *Lausiac History* 10.2–4.

219 See Ex 22:22; Dt 10:18; Ps 146:9; Is 1:17; Jms 1:27.
220 If you provide for them in God's name: Pom "If you provide for them from God's abundance."
221 Persuaded . . . need: Pom "Persuaded by the words of the saint [1547: "man"], the ruler returned home."
222 Shamelessly dared: Grec 1093, 1547; Pom "dared."
223 Devoting himself . . . incorporeal beings: Pom, 1547 "devoting himself to spiritual practices that differed in no way from the incorporeal beings."
224 <So the Holy Spirit, who dwelled in him>: Pom, 1547.
225 The delights of paradise *(paradeísou . . . terpná)* contrast here with "the delightful things of life" *(terpnà toû bíou)* that lead people astray, which the author highlights in the opening line of the *Life*.
226 First-born: *prōtótokos*. See Bauer 894a–b; Mt 1:25//Lk 2:7. "Church of the First-born": see Heb 12:22–23: "But you have come to Mount Zion and to the city of the living God, the heavenly Jerusalem, and to innumerable angels in festal gathering, and to the assembly [or: church *(ekklēsía)*] of the first-born [*ekklēsía(i) prōtotókōn*] who are enrolled in heaven."
227 The spiritual teaching: *mystagōgía*.
228 God, *dēmiourgós*: Demiurge, "craftsman, maker, author" (Lampe 342b). The term, popular in Gnostic and Manichean thought, occurs in the NT only in Heb 11:10 ("architect and builder" (NRSV): *technítēs kaì dēmiourgós*); patristic authors use it for "creator," and Basil (4th c.) uses *ho dēmiourgòs lógos*, "the creative Word," of the Son.
229 This sounds like Paῖsios is a semi-anchorite; that is, he lived apart from the community during the week and came in probably on Saturday, took part in the synaxis on Sunday, then returned to his *manshōpe*, dwelling.
230 The editor has mistakenly repeated the numeral "XVII" for this paragraph (p. 11). From here on we will put Grec 1093's numbering in parentheses.
231 Creative power: *dēmiourgía*.
232 The ability to transcend nature: Pom, 1547 "the ability to subject/control nature."
233 The lives of ill-fed children: Pom, 1547 "life for."
234 Three hundred years and more: Pom, 1547 "three hundred years."
235 On Elijah's assumption into heaven, see 2 Kgs 2:11–12; Sir 48:1–12; 1 Macc 2:58. See David Frankfurter, *Elijah in Upper Egypt: The Apocalypse of Elijah and Early Egyptian Christianity* (London: Bloomsbury T&T Clark, 1998).

236 <day>: Pom, 1547.
237 In his translation of Qur'ān 18:25 ("The Cave"), Ahmed Ali includes a note with the following sentence: "There is also the famous cave near Ephesus in Turkey known as the Cave of Seven Sleepers where, it is said, seven Christians slept two hundred years to escape persecution by the Romans." On the Seven Sleepers of Ephesus, see the article in the *Catholic Encyclopedia*: http://www.newadvent.org/cathen/05496a.htm.
238 <sought>: Pom, 1547.
239 See Ps 19:7–10.
240 Pleasure: *hēdonḗ*.
241 With godly eloquence: *enthéois . . . Seirêsi*, that is, the divine, charming eloquence of the Sirens, which demonstrates the transformative ability of language. The Sirens were originally mythological beings who lured men with their beautiful voices, as in *Odyssey* 1.2.39; a siren thus came to mean a deceitful woman and also "the Siren charm of eloquence" and "persuasiveness" (LSJ 1588b). Clement of Alexandria (2nd c.), *Stromateis* 1.10, uses the term; in patristic Greek the word came to mean "charm of words, felicity in expression" (Lampe, 1227b).
242 Monks: lit. "renunciants," *apotassoménōn*, those who renounce *(apotássomai)* the world. The word became a technical term for "monk"; see Lampe 216A(D) and 216B(D8) and Goehring, "Through a Glass Darkly," 53–72.
243 Life's pleasures: *bíou terpnoís*.
244 See Mt 11:29. Or "Gospel."
245 Loving desire: *érōs*.
246 Contemplative quiet: *hēsychía*.
247 Way of life, διαγωγή / *diagōgḗ*: Pom, 1547 "obedience," ὑποταγή / *hypotagḗ*. Obedience will be an important theme later in the *Life*; see ¶69. Pom: "the blessed way of life of obedience."
248 Brotherhood: *adelphótēs*. Not a common word in early Egyptian monastic literature but one that Basil the Great regularly uses in his monastic writings. See Palladius, *Lausiac History* 43.2. It occurs twice in 1 Pet 2:17 (NRSV: "family of believers") and 5:9 (NRSV: "brothers and sisters").
249 The virtues: Pom, 1547 "virtue."
250 <their>: Pom, 1547.
251 See Gen 3:19.
252 Loving affection, *philostorgía*: *philo-* + *storgḗ*; for *storgḗ*, see ¶21, n. 266.
253 He set down this rule above all others: Pom, 1547 "He set down this rule for everyone."
254 Accomplish: Pom, 1547 "seek/pursue."
255 But . . . father: Pom "but to accomplish everything with the advice and knowledge of one's spiritual father."

256 Contemplative silence: *hēsychía*.
257 Solitude, *anachōrésis*, lit. "withdrawal" (English "anchorite," one who withdraws).
258 Monks prayed standing, the *orans* position.
259 Love: *agápē*.
260 Or "by his love for Christ."
261 Rest and refreshment, *anápausis*. Or "inward stillness." *Anapaúō* and *anapaúomai* (vb.), *anápausis* (n.): a condition or state much desired by the monks. *Anápausis* comes to mean "cessation from wearisome activity for the sake of rest; rest, relief"; "repose, rest, refreshment," "a result of training in the practice of virtue" (Bauer 69a). It can mean "rest in eternity" and "tranquility, peace" (Lampe 115a–116a). Mt 11:29 gives us the biblical resonance: "Take my yoke upon you, and learn from me; for I am gentle and humble in heart, and you will find rest [*anápausis*] for your souls." For the synonym *katápausis*, see Heb 3:11, 18; 4:1–10.
262 See Jn 20:19; 21:4.
263 Desired: *potheinóteron* < *póthos*.
264 See Moses in Ex 3:1–5.
265 Stretched: stretched out, *epekteínas*; there may be an echo here of Phil 3:13, where Paul says "but this one thing I do: forgetting what lies behind and straining forward [*epekteinómenos*] to what lies ahead."
266 Love: *storgē̄*. See n. 252.
267 Worship: *therapóntas*; "servant," following, is *therapónti* (see Lampe 645a–b). The words are nouns of *therapeúō*, "worship, serve; heal."
268 See Jn 14:27.
269 <alarm>: Pom, 1547.
270 In such things *(toiaútois)*: Pom, 1547 "the things that you [are doing] *(toîs soîs)*." Things: *érgas*, lit. "works," so there may be an echo here of Jms 2:14–26, where "works" occurs eleven times; see esp. 2:26: "For just as the body without the spirit is dead, so faith without works is also dead."
271 Prayer: Pom, 1547 "zeal. "
272 See Jn 14:14; 15:7; 16:24; 20:23.
273 <Wretch that I am>: Pom, 1547; it is more likely that the phrase was dropped rather than added. "Wretch": *tálas*, which is related to *talaípōros*, which Paul uses in Rom 7:24.
274 <I need>: Pom, 1547.
275 See Mt 26:28; Rom 3:25; Eph 1:7; Heb 13:12.
276 How much suffering and how many deaths: Pom, 1547 "How many deaths."
277 Grec 1093 has this title.
278 Seized: Pom, 1547 "taken/conquered/caught," καταλαμβάνω / *katalambánō*; as an Attic Greek legal term: "convicted/condemned."

279 That is, the Devil.
280 Hades occurs ten times in the NT: Matthew (2x), Luke (2x), Acts (2x), and Revelation (4x).
281 It is necessary: Grec 1093, 1547; Pom "I have determined."
282 See Mt 24:31; 1 Cor 15:52; 1 Th 4:16.
283 See Mt 24:30; Rev 1:7. Or, depending on how one wants to emphasize words, "with angels and trumpets, and then he will receive the payment he deserves for his actions."
284 And now he heard: Grec 1093, 1547; Pom "Once again he was instructed in the divine mysteries by the voice." Divine mysteries: *memystagṓgētai* < *mystagōgéō*, *mystagōgía*. See *Life of Antony* 14.1; 91.
285 See Mt 24:30; 26:64; 1 Th 4:17.
286 Compassion: *tà splánchna* (lit. "guts"). See 2 Cor 6:12. The verb, *splanchnízomai*, occurs often in the Gospels (and, strikingly, not elsewhere in the NT), referring to Jesus' love and compassion.
287 Païsios: Pom, 1547 "Saint Païsios."
288 "Inner desert" means the more remote desert. In the *Life of Antony*, Antony moves to the inner desert.
289 Païsios: Pom, 1547 "Saint Païsios."
290 Speak openly: *parrēsía* and its verb *parrēsiázomai* occur often in the NT: "a use of speech that conceals nothing and passes over nothing, outspokenness, frankness, plainness" (Bauer 781b); "a state of boldness and confidence, boldness, fearlessness" (781b); "to express oneself freely, speak freely, openly, fearlessly" (782a).
291 On the theme of the holy man as intercessor, see Vivian, *Words to Live By*, 323–75.
292 Met him: Pom, 1547 "met him on the road."
293 The good elder: Pom, 1547 "the holy elder."
294 Holy father: *hierà kephalḗ*. *Kephalḗ*, "head," according to Lampe 749a(IIB2–4), can indicate a "chief, headman," "religious superior," such as a monastic superior or bishop.
295 <understands>: Pom, 1547; Grec 1093 "saw"; confusing οἶδε and εἶδεν, whose dipthongs at this time were pronounced the same.
296 Creator of the universe: *apántôn dēmiourgós*.
297 We who are your unworthy servants: Pom, 1547 "we who are your unworthy servants, Master, you who love us." You who love us: *philánthrōpos*. There is certainly one word play here, perhaps two: "to be regarded" translates *ophthḗnai* and "disregard" is *parophthḗnai*. "Worthless" translates *apráktous*, from *práxis*, "(monastic) practice." *Praktikós* has contending definitions in the early monastic world: it can be synonymous with "worldly" (*kosmikós*), "of active [qualities] opposing

contemplative qualities and way of life" (Lampe 1127a); more neutrally, it can mean "active, productive" and, positively, in a monastic context, ascetic practice. As John Eudes Bamberger notes (*Evagrius Ponticus: The Praktikos and Chapters on Prayer*, Cistercian Studies 4 [Kalamazoo, MI: Cistercian Publications, 1981], 3), Evagrius' "*Praktikos* confines itself to questions more directly concerned with the active life, with *ascesis*."

298 The elder's disciple: Grec 1093, 1547; Pom "the soul of your servant, the elder's disciple."
299 Presumably the sufferings of the disciple's elder.
300 Enjoy in Hades: Pom, 1547.
301 See Lk 16:19–31.
302 See Mt 24:30; 26:64; 1 Th 4:17.
303 Second coming: see Mt 24:44; Rev 1:7; 22:12; 1 Jn 2:28.
304 See Mt 24:31; 1 Cor 15:52; 1 Th 4:16.
305 Last day: Jn 6:39–40, 54.
306 See Mt 19:28; Col 1:16; Rev 20:4.
307 Judgment seat: see Mt 27:19; 2 Cor 5:10; Rom 14:10.
308 <Then his soul was entrusted to the elder>: Pom, required by the context; Grec 1093, 1547 lack.
309 Suddenly: Pom, 1547 lack.
310 Rest and peace: *anápausis*. Or "inward stillness."
311 Came: Pom, 1547 "immediately came."
312 Who loves, *philánthrōpos*: Grec 1093, 1547; Pom "who is wholly good (*panágathos*)."
313 Appeared to me: Pom, 1547 "appeared to me although I am a wretch" (reading οἰκτρῷ instead of Pom's οἰκτρός and 1547's οἶκτος, "pity, compassion"). In 1547 οἶκτος refers to God, who is compassionate.
314 Freed: Pom, 1547 "release/let loose." But "freed" (from *eleutheróō*) has the added implications of "setting (humankind) free (from sin)." *Eleuthería*, "liberty, freedom," and *eleutheróō*, "to set free," are key concepts for Paul. For the former, see 1 Cor 10:29; 2 Cor 3:17; Gal 5:13a; Rom 8:21; for the latter, see Rom 6:18, 22; 8:2, 21; Gal 5:1.
315 <me>: Pom, 1547.
316 Humble: see Mt 5:5; 11:29; 21:5; 1 Pet 3:4.
317 <about>: Pom, 1547.
318 And, coming to where Païsios was, found him: Pom, 1547 "and found him."
319 Offering hymns of thanksgiving: Pom, 1547 "offering hymns of thanksgiving to God."
320 Then the elder recounted: Pom, 1547 "Then the elder recounted with fear."
321 Seen and done: Pom, 1547 "seen and been taught."

322 Together the two of them declared their thanksgivings: Pom, 1547 "Together the two of them raised thankful voices to God." "Declare," *homologéō*, has a wide variety of meanings pertinent here: "confess, acknowledge, vow; confess (sins); declare, assert" (Lampe 957a–b).
323 Such great wonders: Pom, 1547 "such wonders."
324 Any sort of grace *(cháris)*: Grec 1093; 1547 "grace"; Pom "any kind of spiritual gift" (*chárisma*, a cognate).
325 Which bestows such assistance on those who ask with all their soul: Pom, 1547 "which supports those who ask with all their soul." "Bestows" and "supports" both render *oikonomoúsa* < *oikonoméō*; the difference is that Pom and 1547 lack *boētheías*, "help, assistance, aid."
326 <not>: Pom, 1547.
327 Love: *phíltron*.
328 Love: *agápē*.
329 Banished: *exostrakisthéntōn*. In ancient Greece an *óstrakon* was an earthen vessel, then a potsherd, and then the tablet or sherd used in voting. *Óstraka* (pl.) were used in votes of banishment, as with Socrates; thus the verb *ostrakízō* means "to banish by potsherds," from which we get "ostracize." The *ex-* in *exostrakízō*, "to banish by ostracism" may seem redundant but seems to be an intensifier.
330 This sentence may suggest a connection between the Evil One (Satan) and the serpent in the garden, a linking that in the Bible only Revelation 20:2 makes ("that ancient serpent, who is the Devil and Satan"). Four Maccabees 18:8, where a woman is speaking, is interesting: "No seducer corrupted me on a desert plain, nor did the destroyer, the deceitful serpent, defile the purity of my virginity." See Mt 5:37 and 6:13 (the Lord's Prayer), where "Evil One" (NRSV) is more likely a better translation than "evil" (the case ending of the noun is ambiguous). See Shawna Dolansky, "How the Serpent Became Satan: Adam, Eve and the Serpent in the Garden of Eden," Bible History Daily/Biblical Archaeology Society (https://www.biblicalarchaeology.org/daily/biblical-topics/bible-interpretation/how-the-serpent-became-satan/), and Elaine Pagels, *Adam, Eve, and the Serpent: Sex and Politics in Early Christianity* (New York: Vintage, 1989).
331 "He" here means both God and Christ as God.
332 See Is 53:5; Rom 5:21; Gal 5:1; 1 Pet 2:24.
333 Love: *agápē*.
334 See Jn 15:13.
335 Love: *agápē*.
336 <his>: Pom, 1547; Grec 1093 "my."
337 Rom 8:3 ("by sending his own Son in the likeness of sinful flesh") implies/assumes that "flesh" (the body here?) is sinful.

338 Who bestows all gifts: Grec 1093, Pom; 1547 "who bestows good things to everyone."
339 Our father Païsios was always zealous about the Apostle's precept: Grec 1093, 1547; Pom "Our father Païsios would zealously carry out the Apostle's precept."
340 Phil 3:13.
341 Spiritual struggles: *agōn*.
342 See Heb 11:38.
343 See Mt 6:4. In secret: Grec 1093, Pom; 1547 lacks.
344 Saved through him: thus, Païsios becomes a Christ figure; see Rom 5:9, for example.
345 See Mt 5:15.
346 Lovers: *erastēs*. This movement models that of Antony in the *Life*.
347 Teaching also models Antony's ministry; see *Life of Antony* 16–43; 97–151.
348 In Greek, "supervision," *episkopē* and *epískepsis*, are cognate with *epískopos*, which originally meant "supervisor," and in the NT means "bishop," "overseer," especially one who guards the apostolic tradition. See Lampe 532a–b. See 1 Pet 2:25 ("guardian"); Acts 20:28 ("overseers"); Phil 1:1 ("bishops," with a note, "overseers"); 1 Tim 3:2 ("bishop," with a note, "overseer"; for the author of 1 Timothy, perhaps fifty years later, it is clearly an office).
349 I am afraid that: Grec 1093, 1547; Pom "wretch that I am."
350 Thus Païsios exhibits the humility of the prophets when called by God; see Jer 1:6.
351 Pomialovskii skips from 32 to 34, omitting 33, so his numbering and Grec 1093's now agree again.
352 <to those you do here>: Pom, 1547.
353 But you will receive double the compensation, and even more, in the city above: Pom, 1547: "but your soul will receive double the resplendent compensation, and even more, in the heavenly Jerusalem." See Gal 4:21–31; Heb 12:22.
354 Teaching is a central part of early monastic *politeía*, life in community. See the long section on Antony's teaching in *Life of Antony* 16–43; 97–151.
355 Those who loved: *erastēs*.
356 With the advent of multitudes and with his teaching, Païsios models Antony.
357 Grec 1093 has in the left margin in abbreviations "Concerning the Appearance of Saint Constantine." Emperor Constantine "the Great" (272–337) ruled from 306 to 337. He is not a saint in the Western Churches but is in the Orthodox Churches. The Coptic-Arabic Synaxarium of the Coptic Church, understandably for the "Church of the

Martyrs," frequently mentions Constantine, who ended anti-Christian persecution, and his mother St. Helena.
358 Mystery: *mystḗrion*.
359 The holy man: Pom, 1547 "Païsios."
360 Just as he now arranged your arrival: Pom, 1547.
361 His Goodness *(autoû hē chrēstótēs)*: Pom, 1547 "His Goodness *(hē autoû agathótēs)*."
362 See Mt 11:30.
363 Constantine died in 337.
364 Lovers: *erastḗs*.
365 Good news: *euangélion*; also "gospel/Gospel."
366 <memory>: Pom, 1547.
367 <you>: Pom, 1547.
368 See Mt 20:16; Mt 22:1–14//Lk 14:15–24.
369 <their>: Pom, 1547.
370 See *Life of Antony* 60 (185–89), "Antony Sees Amoun Enter Heaven."
371 <as far as the holy walls of the heavenly Jerusalem>: Pom, 1547. See Heb 12:22–24; Gal 4:25–26.
372 Holy *(hierón)*: Grec 1093; Pom *euagōn*, which means "holy" but has the additional sense of "pure, undefiled."
373 <They>: Pom, 1547.
374 I find fault with myself: Pom, 1547 "I very much find fault with myself."
375 <us>: Pom, 1547.
376 Our God's judgment: Pom, 1547 "our good God's righteous judgment."
377 See Job 31:6 and 2 Cor 8:13.
378 Various <luxuries>: Grec 1093 "various kinds of food" *(trophḗ)*; Pom, 1547: "luxuries" *(truphḗ)*.
379 Delights: *terpná*.
380 Pleasure: *hēdonḗ*.
381 <wandering in deserts and mountains and caves and holes in the ground>: Pom, 1547. See Heb 11:37–38. In Late Antiquity many attributed Hebrews to Paul. Eusebius, *Ecclesiastical History* 3.3.5 and 6.20.3, acknowledges that some reject Paul's authorship; in 6.25.3, Eusebius says that Origen concluded that Paul was not the author.
382 This theme occurs in AlphAP Arsenius and elsewhere.
383 Reading καλῶς (as in Pom) instead of Grec 1093's καλῶν.
384 See Mt 7:15–20//Lk 6:43–44.
385 Go, then: Grec 1093, 1547; Pom "Go, then, John."
386 Mystery *(mystḗrion)*: Grec 1093, Pom; 1547 "astounding/miraculous mystery."
387 Demonstrate: Pom, 1547 "demonstrate for us."

388 Grec 1093 has this title.
389 In monastic literature, "Egypt" normally means not the country Egypt but rather non-monastic areas, such as Alexandria, the Delta, and Babylon (Cairo). The classic example of this in monastic literature is in AlphAP Achilles 3, where Abba Achilles says, "Come on, everyone! See Isaiah using sauce in Scetis! If you (sing.) want sauce, go back to Egypt!" See Vivian, *Sayings and Stories of the Desert Fathers and Mothers*, vol. 1:169–70. But since the monk here is from Syria, "Egypt" probably designates the country.
390 <asserting>: Pom, 1547. Greek *éphaske* can also mean "he was alleging."
391 See Athanasius, *To the Antiochenes* 3–7 (362 CE) and *Letter to Serapion* 1.1, 1.29, and 1.30 (358 CE). In *To the Antiochenes* 3, he "anathematizes" "the Arian heresy" and "also those who say that the Holy Spirit is a creature and separate from the essence of Christ"; these, Athanasius says, "blaspheme the Holy Spirit." See J. Stevenson, *Creeds, Councils, and Controversies: Documents Illustrative of the History of the Church A.D. 337–461* (London: S.P.C.K, 1966, 1981), 53. The Council of Nicaea in 325 focused on the Father and the Son, and its creed devotes only one sentence to the Holy Spirit (and has anathemas against heretics). The Council of Constantinople in 381 added an article on the Holy Spirit and an article about the Church, baptism, and the resurrection of the dead (and deleted the anathemas).
392 Paȋsios: Pom, 1547 "the divine Paȋsios."
393 Region: Pom, 1547 "region and whereabouts."
394 There is a sly play on words here: the elder has "a large number" of people following him, while Paȋsios makes "a number" of baskets, "number" twice translating *pléthos*.
395 Ungodly, *átheos*: Pom, 1547 "wicked" *(ponērós)*. *Átheos* (alpha-privative + *theós*): "separate from God, without God; ungodly, immoral; atheist; without the true God" (Lampe 44b). Opinion: *dógma*, which can also mean "fixed belief, tenet; system of belief, creed; precept, ordinance" (Lampe 377a–378a).
396 They then asked: Pom "they then asked, wishing to contradict him."
397 Friend and lover: *phílos . . . erastḗs*.
398 Holy Trinity: Pom, 1547 "supremely Holy Trinity."
399 *Hypostases: hypóstasis*, pl. *hypostáseis*, is a concrete manifestation of an abstract reality: being, substance, reality. For its many nuances, with patristic citations, see Lampe 1454–61. Pom lacks the term.
400 [manifested] *(emphainoménē)*: Pom, 1547, Grec 1093 *empheroménē*; *emphérō* in the passive voice, "bring in," can also mean "be accepted (as canonical)" (Lampe 458a), which would translate here as "the . . . Godhead is accepted [as canonical] in three forms or persons."

401 Form *(charáktēr)* and "person" *(prósōpon)* are technical Trinitarian language. For the former, see Lampe 1513a–b ("impress, stamp; picture, image; face, countenance; form, figure; person"); and the latter 1186a–1189b ("face, countenance; expression; sight, presence; the part that shows; representation; character in drama; guise, role; illustration, figure, type; visible presentation, outward appearance; individual self, person; particular individual; concrete presentation.")
402 [seeing that one is not greater or lesser in nature than the other]: Pom, 1547 "seeing that one is not greater or lesser than the other, nor does the Trinity work otherwise."
403 <the men>: Pom, 1547.
404 Very clear: Pom, 1547 "absolutely clear" (lit. "clearest").
405 Speaker: Pom, 1547 "speaker, filled with the Holy Spirit."
406 Heretics: *hairetikós*; Pom has *hairetizóntōn*, the progressive active participle of the verb *hairetízō*, so one could translate it simply "heretics," or it could have a more active meaning: "those who belong to heretical sects."
407 Their hearts: Pom, 1547 "the hearts of those who were ignorant."
408 Delineated: Grec 1093, 1547; Pom "he restored and delineated and imprinted." Restored: *anastēsas*, from *anístēmi*, cognate with *anástasis*, "resurrection." Thus, one could say that Paîsios resurrected the truth from the dead, that is, the death of heresy.
409 Citing: Grec 1093, 1547; Pom "clearly citing."
410 See 2 Tim 3:16.
411 Knowledge: *gnōsis*, which reminds us that both Christians such as Clement (ca. 150–ca. 215) and Origen (ca. 185–ca. 254) and Gnostics (and Christian-Gnostics) valued knowledge; see especially Romans and 1 and 2 Corinthians.
412 <their> ignorance *(ágnoian)*: Pom, 1547 "the Holy Trinity."
413 This passage echoes Antony's journey to combat Arian heretics in Alexandria; see *Life of Antony* 68–70; 203–207.
414 See Acts 9:3.
415 Diligently cares for everything (or, diligently guards/protects): or, diligently cares for everyone *(pántōn)*.
416 Had spread throughout the world: Pom, 1547 "had spread."
417 Love virtue: *philarétous* < *phil-* + *aretḗ*.
418 Seized with the desire: *póthos*.
419 Poemen *(poimḗn*: "shepherd") is a central figure in early Egyptian monasticism. He has 186 + 23 sayings in the AlphAP, 209, far more than anyone else. See Lucien Regnault, "Poemen, Saint," *CE* 6:1983a–1984b.
420 This is Paul of Tamma. See René-Georges Coquin, "Paul, of Tamma, Saint," *CE* 6:1923b–1925a, and Vivian, *Words to Live By*, 139–202.

421 <said>: Pom, 1547; Grec 1093 "I see."
422 Benefit: *ophéllō* in the active voice means "to cause to grow or increase, promote, enlarge, strengthen," and in the passive, "to be increased, become greater, prosper" (Montanari 1509a).
423 <his>: Pom, 1547.
424 Wretch: *tálas*; see n. 273.
425 The young man: Pom, 1547 "the young man (he had not yet seen him with human eyes)." "Young man," *néos*, as in "neophyte," according to Lampe 904b–905a, was not used specifically for a new monk. *The Shepherd of Hermas* (2nd c.) and Methodius (d. 311) use the word to mean "young in the faith; of new converts" (Lampe 904a(IB)). Marcellus of Ancyra (d. ca. 374) and the *Acts of Thomas* (904b(IIB)) use it to mean "new, of additions to an existing class," which applies here. "Human" eyes contrast with Païsios' "spiritual" eyes, that is, his prophetic foresight and insight.
426 <Where is your child and traveling companion?>: Pom, 1547.
427 See Mt 19:13–14; there Jesus says that the kingdom of heaven belongs to "little children" (*paideía* < *paîs*) such as those brought to him. When Païsios asks about Poemen, he refers to him as a "child" (*paîs*), and below. "Child" was a common monastic appellation for a young disciple.
428 <he took hold>: Pom, 1547.
429 <many>: Pom, 1547.
430 The hand of the Lord: see Acts 11:21.
431 He: Grec 1093, 1547; Pom "the great one."
432 God: Pom, 1547 "God. That concludes this story. The discourse will now continue with its narrative."
433 At the end of ¶46, Grec 1093 has this title. "Oversight," *episkopḗ*, cognate with *epískopos*.
434 Later Païsios says it has been twenty-two days.
435 Chosen one: see Ps 89:3; 106:23. The suffering of Christ (to be emulated) is a major theme in the NT: Mt 16:21; 8:31//Lk 9:22; Lk 17:25; Acts 1:3; Rom 5:3; 2 Cor 1:5; among many.
436 See Jms 1:17.
437 See Lk 10:7; 1 Tim 5:18.
438 Cave: Pom, 1547 "cave among those who dwell in the desert."
439 Champion: *agōnistḗs* < *agṓn*. Beneath the idea of "champion" (result) is one who competes or struggles for something (a cause); it may be an athletic prize, but in Classical Greek one could struggle for virtue, for example. In early Christian literature, the word can refer to all Christians in their spiritual lives (similar to Arabic *jihād*), and specifically to martyrs and ascetics.

440 Athlete: Grec 1093, 1547; Pom "suffering athlete."
441 Your Goodness: Pom "Your Reverent Goodness."
442 Has wasted away: Grec 1093, 1547; Pom "he is overcome."
443 Then Païsios said: Grec 1093, 1547 "Then Païsios said, 'Yes, it is obvious.'" Grec 1093 lacks "it is obvious." Perhaps the scribe saw it as sarcastic?
444 Pom, 1547.
445 You fast with strength and perseverance: Pom, 1547 "you fast with strength."
446 Desire: *póthos*.
447 And the Savior: Pom, 1547 "The Savior answered him."
448 See the Parable of the Workers in the Vineyard, Mt 20:1–16.
449 <that Gospel saying>: Pom, 1547.
450 Mt 25:21, 23.
451 See Mt 25:15–23.
452 Added: Pom, 1547 "always added."
453 Said: Pom, 1547 "said to him."
454 As quickly as possible: Pom, 1547 continue: "I cannot bear to be gone long, even for the sake of others."
455 This is a striking request. More than halfway through the *Life*, the narrative tells us that even this great saint, with all his ascetic accomplishments, still struggles with anger; a very human moment in the *Life*. See "Overcoming Anger" in Douglas Burton-Christie, *The Word in the Desert* (New York and Oxford: Oxford University Press, 1993), 267–73.
456 <If>: Pom, 1547.
457 <Do not hate anyone>: Pom, 1547.
458 English "denigrate" literally means "to blacken" (Latin *nigr-*); Greek *exoudenóō* here literally means to make nothing (*oudén*) of someone, to regard someone as nothing, a profoundly true etymology for denigration and vilification. See Mk 9:12; 2 Cor 10:10.
459 <your>: Pom, 1547.
460 Those who love: *agapáō* < *agápē*.
461 <them>: Pom, 1547; Grec 1093 "him."
462 <his> zeal: Pom, 1547; Grec 1093 "zeal."
463 See Dt 24:15.
464 In the heavenly Jerusalem: Pom "in heaven."
465 The editor has mistakenly numbered this paragraph the same as the last.
466 Struggles safe and sound: Pom "struggles."
467 Son and heir: κληρονόμος ἐστι καὶ υἱός / *klēronómos esti kaì huiós*. Both *klēronómos* (heir) and *huiós* (son) have acute biblical resonance: in Rom 8:14 Paul declares that "all who are led by the spirit of God are children

[*huioí*] of God" and in Rom 16:17 he says further that the Spirit bears witness that "we are children of God, and if children, then heirs [*klēronómoi*], heirs [*klēronómoi*] of God and joint heirs [*sunklēronómoi*] with Christ." In 8:17 Paul connects being "heirs of God and joint heirs with Christ" with suffering, an important theme in the *Life*. Those who suffer will be "glorified with Christ." In the NT Jesus is "Son of Man" and "Son of God."

468 Our narrative will now press ahead, proceeding: Pom, 1547 "our narrative has covered this topic. Our discourse will now press ahead, proceeding."
469 Grec 1093 supplies this title.
470 The elder later speaks Syriac, so this must be a vague reference to Syria. On this monk, see the general introduction, pp. 2, 14.
471 This is a common monastic theme.
472 Since the monk here is from Syria, "Egypt" here designates the country.
473 Love: *agápē*.
474 Monastic community: *óros*, lit. "mountain"; on this term see Tim Vivian, *Paphnutius*, rev. ed. (Kalamazoo, MI: Cistercian Publications, 2002), 18–26. In Exodus 19:2–3, the Septuagint uses *óros* for "mountain," so it is likely that the early monks made the connection between their sacred "mountains" and Mt. Sinai.
475 Nitria: see Antoine Guillaumont, "Nitria," *CE* 5:1794b–1796b, and Evelyn-White, *Monasteries*, 2:17–24. Nitria, along with Scetis (Wadi Natrun) and Kellia (Cells), was one of the major early monastic sites in Egypt. The *Life* earlier (¶4) identifies Paȋsios with Scetis.
476 Arrival, having been informed of it by divine grace: Pom, 1547 "arrival."
477 Paȋsios: Pom, 1547 "Paȋsios, appointed through God's grace."
478 Monks prayed standing, the *orans* position.
479 The language of the Egyptians: that is, Coptic; see Emile Maher Ishaq, "Coptic Language, Spoken," *CE* 2:604a–607a.
480 Sighing and groaning: see Job 3:24.
481 From the depths of his heart: Pom, 1547 "with all his heart."
482 The blessed one said: Pom, 1547 "he said."
483 Word: see Jn 1.
484 <being instructed alone by the godly Spirit>: Pom, 1547; the sense requires it.
485 The spiritual gifts and contemplative insight: Pom "the contemplative insight."
486 Both: Pom "On account of their conversation, both."
487 Six days: this may be an allusion to the six days of creation, Gen 1.
488 Holy and perfect: a possible allusion to 2 Cor 7:1: "holiness perfect in the fear of God."
489 Watchmen: *phylakós*, cognate with *phýlax*, "guard," and *phylássō/phyláttō*,

"to guard, protect, watch over." *Phylássō* is an important word in the AlphAP, and occurs 71 times in the systematic *Apophthegmata*. Isaiah and Jeremiah connect watchmen (NRSV "sentinels") with Jerusalem, sometimes positively, sometimes negatively.

490 His disciples: Pom "the disciples of the godly man."

491 Words: Pom, 1547 "word" (which here means "speech/discourse").

492 For Shenoute's flight on a cloud, see Besa, *Life of Shenoute* 17–19; *The Life of Shenoute by Besa*, trans. David N. Bell, Cistercian Studies 73 (Kalamazoo, MI: Cistercian Publications, 1983), 47–48.

493 The true God: possibly as opposed to the Arian God; see ¶41.

494 Astonished, *ekplḗttō/ekplḗssō*, "amazed, astonished, astounded, dumbfounded, shocked": the word occurs often in the Gospels in reference to Jesus' actions; Mt 19:25; Mk 10:26. Thus, another allusion to Paîsios as Christ-bearer. They were astonished: Pom, 1547 "They were astonished and praised God, who is wonderful among his saints."

495 Hope is an important theme in the Psalms, occurring 29 times, and to Paul, occurring 8 times in Romans and 9 times total in 1 and 2 Corinthians.

496 Love: *agapŏ̄ntas* < *agapáō* < *agápē*.

497 Blessing and giving glory to the one who gives glory to those who love him: Pom, 1547 "blessing and giving glory to God and to those who love him."

498 Jew: see also ¶¶64–65. One has to wonder, using the historical methodology of smoke and fire, what was going on between Jews and Christians in Egypt when this text was written (5th–8th c.). Early Christianity, from the NT on, is guilty of anti-Judaism. For just a few discussions, see Paula Fredriksen, "Jewish Romans, Christian Romans, and the Post-Roman West: The Social Correlates of the *Contra Iudeos* Tradition," in *Conflict and Religious Conversation in Latin Christendom: Studies in Honour of Ora Limor*, ed. Israel Jacob Yuval and Ram Ben-Shalom (Turnhout: Brepols, 2014), 23–53, and David Brakke, "Jewish Flesh and Christian Spirit in Athanasius of Alexandria," *Journal of Early Christian Studies* 9, no. 4 (2001): 453–81. Our thanks to Paula Fredriksen for these. See the discussion in the General Introduction, 12.

499 Grec 1093 has this title.

500 This is our numbering. Although Pomialovskii begins a new paragraph here, he does not give it a new number. Since the subject matter changes, a new number is warranted.

501 Egypt: see n. 389.

502 A certain, *tis*: or "some."

503 See Gen 3 and Rev 20:2.

504 The Expected One, *prosd[o]kōménō(i)* < *prosdokáō*: see Mt 11:3; Lk 7:18–23; 2 Pet 3:1–13. In patristic Greek the verb can indicate the expectation of Christ (Second Coming), of the future life, and of judgment (Lampe 1166b).

505 [The Messiah]: lit. "that one."

506 Immediately: reading παραχρῆμα, as does 1547, instead of Pom's παραχρῆμαι, which may be a typo.

507 Come near <him>: Grec 1093, 1547; Pom "approach him."

508 Without grace: *ácharis*. In the previous sentence the narrator says that the monk "fell from the grace [*cháris*] of baptism."

509 <not>: Pom, 1547.

510 Abomination, *bdélugma*: the term occurs often in the LXX (especially Ezekiel) and in the deuterocanonical works (the Apocrypha); see Lev 7:18. It occurs only four times in the NT, once in Luke and three times in Revelation.

511 <you>: Pom, 1547.

512 Shun me: Pom, 1547 "shun me as something execrable."

513 What happened to you?: Pom, 1547 "Tell me what happened to you."

514 "Nothing at all happened": Pom, 1547 "'Nothing at all happened. Forgive me.' In reply the elder said, 'Get away from me, child!'" The monk's lack of repentance in Grec 1093 gives a good reason for Païsios' anger. In Pom and 1547 "Forgive me" does not really fit.

515 <He said>: Pom, 1547.

516 <Shameful>: Pom, 1547; Grec 1093 *dunón* is corrupt.

517 Who did you speak to on the road?: Pom, 1547 "Who did you speak to on the road? Who did you talk with?"

518 The one whom you worship is not the Christ: Pom, 1547 "The one whom you accept as the Christ and worship is not the Christ."

519 I said, "Perhaps it's as you say": Pom, 1547 "I said, 'Perhaps it's as you say,' I quickly replied."

520 <What>: Pom, 1547.

521 Wretch: *áthlios*. There could be a play on words here: *áthlon* can mean "contest" and the prize won in a contest and *áthlos* means "contest." *Áthlēsis* means "contest, struggle," and can refer to martyrdom, and an *athlētḗs* (from which we get "athlete") is a "combatant, champion," especially for Christ. Monks often earned the monikers "athletes for Christ." See Lampe 46A. In the NT, the verb *athléō* occurs in 2 Tim 2:5 ("And in the case of an athlete, no one is crowned without competing according to the rules") and *áthlēsis* appears in Heb 10:32 ("But recall those earlier days when, after you had been enlightened, you endured a hard struggle [*pollḕn áthlēsin*] with sufferings").

522 Pom lacks "in Hell" (*ekeíse*, lit. "to that place"; in Classical Greek it can mean "to the other world").

523 Forgive my soul: Pom, 1547 "Have pity on my soul" (or: "Have compassion for my soul").
524 <carelessness>: Pom, 1547.
525 Abandoned: Pom, 1547 "pushed aside/rejected/renounced."
526 That is, baptism.
527 On this phrase and this subject, see Vivian, "Holy Men and Businessmen," in Vivian, *Words to Live By*, 323–75.
528 Wretch: *áthlion*. In Rom 7:24, for "wretch" Paul uses *talaipōros*.
529 Debt: *opheílēma*: see Mt 6:12, *opheílēma* ("Forgive us our debts"), both cognate with *opheílō*, "owe, be in debt to." Bauer 743a(2) suggests that *opheílēma* in Mt 6:12 means "obligation in the moral sense = debt"); compare Lk 11:4, which uses *hamartía*, "sin," in 4a and *opheílō* in 4b, suggesting that they're synonyms.
530 Restore: *apokatástasis*; later in the paragraph, in "the gift of regeneration, which will restore you," "restore" renders *apokatasthéntos*. Origen's idea of the ultimate restoration of all things *(apokatástasis pántōn)*, including, even ultimately, the demons and Satan, eventually led to his, quite posthumous, condemnation. See Lampe 195aB3.
531 Dove: see Mt 3:16//Mk 1:10//Lk 3:31–32//John 1:32.
532 See Mk 3:28–29; Mt 12:31–32//Mk 3:28–29//Lk 12:10.
533 Regeneration: *palingenesías*; see Lampe 998b. "Gift" translates *chárisma*, cognate with *cháris*, "grace." The word especially characterizes a spiritual gift; see Lampe 1518a–1519a.
534 Watch out for yourself from now on: Pom, 1547 "Watch out for yourself."
535 I will proceed: Pom, 1547 "we will proceed."
536 Grec 1093 has this section title.
537 <practicing>: Pom, 1547.
538 With the father: Pom, 1547 "with Father John."
539 So the disciple quickly prepared the table: Pom, 1547 "So the disciple, following Païsios' orders, quickly prepared the table for John."
540 Forgive me: Pom, 1547 "Forgive me, father."
541 The {evil} Spirit: Pom, 1547 "the Spirit." The former reading does not fit here.
542 A young man: Pom "a wicked young man"; which does not make sense.
543 Grec 1093 has this chapter title.
544 Ascetic: *askōn* < *askéō*. Usually only seasoned and tested monks withdrew by themselves to be anchorites or semi-anchorites; thus, this story may be monitory for young monks eager to leave the cenobium for the solitary life.
545 Discerned (*katanóēsas* < *katanoéō*: observed well, understood, perceived): Pom, 1547 "saw."
546 [Wickedness]: *ponērías*: Pom; Grec 1093, 1547 *porneías*, "sexual immorality." Further down Païsios uses *ponēroús*, "wicked thoughts," which suggests that *ponērías* is the better reading here.

547 Pom: "demons"; probably because of the following plural pronoun and participle; or, the singular here is a mistake.
548 Entreat always God's godly help: Pom, 1547 "entreat God's godly help."
549 Unharmed: Pom, 1547 continue: "And so it happened."
550 See 1 Pet 5:8.
551 What violence you do me, Païsios!: Pom, 1547 "What violence you do me!"
552 The Gerasene demoniac(s) says (say) this to Jesus in Mt 8:29//Lk 8:28.
553 [The Evil One] immediately disappeared: Pom, 1547 "He disappeared"; Grec 1093 "he immediately disappeared."
554 Live in the desert: Pom, 1547 "live in the desert, or not."
555 Laziness: *ra(i)thymía*. On the theme of monastic "laziness," see ¶61.
556 Frightful abuses: Pom, 1547 "frightful abuses and the assaults I have planned for him!"
557 <cast you>: Pom, 1547.
558 The reading is not clear; this is our conjecture. Pom lacks.
559 The Enemy's terrible assaults: "enemy" is *toū ponēroû* < *ponērós*; "evil" (neuter) or "the Evil One" (masculine), as probably in the Lord's Prayer (Mt 6:13).
560 This scene is common in early monastic literature, based ultimately on Jesus' temptation by and defeat of the Devil: Mt 4:1–17//Lk 4:1–13.
561 Ascetic struggles: *agōnizoménous* < *agonízomai* < *agōn*.
562 Beliar, or Belial: an evil spirit primarily in intertestamental literature, either under or identified with Satan. See 2 Cor 6:15. See Theodore J. Lewis, "Belial," in *The Anchor Bible Dictionary*, ed. David Noel Freedman (New York: Doubleday, 1992), 1.654a–656b.
563 <the novices>: Pom, 1547.
564 But when grace withdraws: ironically, grace's withdrawal uses the same verb, *anachōréō*, that lies at the root for "anchorite," *anachōrētés*, one who, because of grace, withdraws into solitude and silence.
565 Ready for me to seize: Pom, 1547 "ready for me to seize with my hands."
566 On this idea of the Devil biding his time, see the frightening line in Lk 4:13 (lacking in Matthew): "When the Devil had finished every test, he departed from him until an opportune time." Luke's verse is even more frightening because "opportune time" translates *kairós*, usually a positive term: "a moment or period as especially appropriate for the right, proper, favorable time" (Bauer 497b); see Mt 24:45; Jn 7:6–8; Rom 13:11; Col 4:5.
567 Fervently: Pom, 1547 "fervently and with grace."
568 <thus>: Pom, 1547.
569 Gehenna: Pom, 1547 "Gehenna. Then he will enjoy his just deserts: severe and abominable punishments." After Païsios said these words, both of the beings that had appeared to him left, the one in glory, the other in disgrace.

570 The latter did not have the ability: Pom, 1547 "the latter no longer had the ability."
571 The holy Païsios: Pom, 1547 "the godly Païsios."
572 Died a good death: this is a common monastic topos: the return of the prodigal monk, now repentant, who dies a sanctified death; see ¶67.
573 Grec 1093 has this title.
574 Came to him wanting to hear: Pom, 1547 "came to him to hear."
575 On disciples asking an abba or spiritual father for "a word," see Vivian, "Words to Live By," in Vivian, *Words to Live By*, 3–17.
576 Safeguard the tradition: Pom, 1547 "keep to the path." Tradition: *parádosis*, "teaching, received tradition." See 1 Cor 11:23 *(paradídomi)*.
577 Don't seek to do more than you're ordered: Pom, 1547 "don't seek to do more—anything more—than you're ordered."
578 *Páthēma*, related to *páthē*, the "passions" that disfigure the soul. The NT usually distinguishes between *páthē* (sing. *páthos*) "willful passions," and *pathḗmata* (sing. *páthēma*), "misfortunes," "sufferings" (Bauer 747b-748a).
579 Known only to God: Pom, 1547 "known only to God. All these things he has revealed to each of us. He has explained everything to us!"
580 When I had passed through ["trials and/or temptations" understood], *diabaínō*: Pom, 1547 "when I contemplated ["doing something" understood]." Pom, 1547 continue: "and when I proposed setting about doing it."
581 Judge: see Jn 8:50; 12:48; 2 Tim 4:8. God/Christ as "judge" (noun) is not common in the NT but God/Christ judging (verb) is.
582 Mt 12:37.
583 Mt 12:36.
584 <Believe me . . . I am telling you about the truth>: Pom; Grec 1093, 1547 omit.
585 What I have inwardly considered: Pom, 1547 "what I have often inwardly considered."
586 <me>: Pom, 1547.
587 They were saying: Pom, 1547 "They marveled and said."
588 Ps 67:35 (LXX).
589 They left him: Pom, 1547 "They left him, admiring the extravagance of God's gifts."
590 <baleful consequences>: Pom, 1547.
591 Grec 1093 has this section title. Given Prof. Mikhail's discussion in the General Introduction (p. 12) about anti-Muslim polemic appearing in Jewish guise, one wonders whether the story here and in ¶¶53B–57, if we date the text to the seventh-eighth century, are disguised anti-Muslim attacks.
592 <that>: Pom, 1547.

593 Erotic love: *érōs*. On fire, consumed: *kataphlégomai* means "to burn to the ground, consume with fire." Satanic and demonic: for "satanic," Lampe, 1227a, cites Chrysostom, 5th c., and Hyperchius, 6th c., as the earliest examples; for "demonic," 327a, he cites Ignatius of Antioch, 1st–2nd c., and Origen, 3rd c. Neither adjective occurs in the NT.

594 See Jms 1:15.

595 Thrice-accursed: possibly, if meant literally, because she is a woman, Jewish (¶¶53B–55), and a cause of apostasy.

596 Wretch, *áthlios*: see n. 521.

597 With "often," the (unanswerable) question is: If he has apostasized, left the faith, where is he getting/receiving Communion bread? A reminder that we are in the land of (sacred) story.

598 Help: Pom, 1547 "grace *(cháris)*." Help: *ropḗ*, "decisive influence, help," frequently of divine help (Lampe 1218b).

599 I will narrate, you too will marvel . . . without measure: Pom, 1547 "I will narrate, I trust that you too will marvel at the astounding compassion and heavenly oversight and godly grace that God has without exception for those who marvel at him without measure."

600 Was separated from the Christians because of his own impiety: Pom, 1547 "was separated from the Christians and had been cast down into the depths of Hades because of his own impiety."

601 Practiced the ascetic life: *askéō*, cognate with *áskēsis*.

602 There is a nice, perhaps intentional, play on words in this sentence. "Long ago" ("the man had long ago practiced the ascetic life") translates *pálai* (as in English "paleo-") whereas "ancient" ("he remembered that ancient and holy community") renders *palaiâs* ; in other words, in ancient days the monk had been part of an ancient (= venerable) and holy community. The play on words accents his apostasy.

603 Païsios: Pom, 1547 "the great one."

604 He fervently entreated . . . the machinations of the Enemy: Pom, 1547 "He fervently entreated them to ask the great elder to offer supplication on his behalf so the elder with his entreaties might entreat the Lord and propitiate him, so he would be freed from the machinations of the Enemy." "Entreated" renders Greek past progressive/imperfect, which means he was repeatedly asking them, not just once.

605 The painful events: Pom, 1547 "the events."

606 For just two "reminders," see the story of Adam and Eve (as traditionally understood) in Gen 3 and that of David and Bathsheba in 2 Sam 11. On Adam and Eve, see Pagels, *Adam, Eve, and the Serpent*.

607 Unfortunately, not an uncommon sentiment; in AlphAP Arsenius 28, Archbishop Theophilus berates a Roman woman, *a pilgrim to the monks*

of Egypt: "Don't you know you're a woman? Don't you know you should never go *anywhere*?" See Vivian, *The Sayings and Stories of the Desert Fathers and Mothers*, vol. 1:130–32.
608 This weapon: Pom, 1547 "this evil weapon." "Evil," *chalepós*, suggests a number of things: "hard to bear, grievous, serious, evil" (Lampe 1511b).
609 Descendants (ἐκγόνους / *ekgónous*): Pom, 1547 "grandsons" (ἐγγόνους / *engónous*).
610 We too must pray: Pom "we must always pray for ourselves."
611 See Jn 1:3.
612 Our: Grec 1093, 1547; Pom "my."
613 On denial see Mt 26:34, 69–75.
614 You who love us: *philánthrōpos*.
615 I look to your acts: Pom, 1547 "I look to all your acts."
616 See Ezek 18:23; 18:32; 33:11.
617 [call back]: Grec 1093 is deficient here; Pom, 1547: "call back."
618 See Mt 9:36; 10:6; 12:11. The story is also reminiscent of Mt 18:10–14.
619 My flock: Pom, 1547 "my angelic flock." "Angelic," Lampe notes, 9b(B7), can refer especially to the monastic life, as earlier with *isángelos*, "equal to/ with the angels" (see n. 92).
620 I am acceptable due to your grace each day: Pom, 1547 "I benefit from your grace each day."
621 Love: *agápē*.
622 <punishment>: Pom, 1547; Grec 1093 "reputation."
623 See Jn 20:17.
624 That is, the monastic life.
625 Love of virtue: *philáretos* < *aretē*.
626 He departed this life and went to the Lord: see ¶62.
627 We, hearing about such marvelous wonders, <must> glorify and exalt that saint's God: Pom, 1547: "we, hearing about such marvelous wonders, must glorify and sing praises to the Lord who makes that saint great."
628 Grec 1093 has this title.
629 The desert: Pom, 1547 "the monastery."
630 Worldly: *kosmikós* suggests "worldly, secular," and "non-monastic." Similarly at the end of this paragraph.
631 Inasmuch as he possessed neither a good spirit nor deep soil bearing the fruit of good words, he would make fun of the elder's words: Pom "Here is how the story ended: inasmuch as he possessed neither the good, nor an upright heart, not only did he not bear good fruit [Mt 7:17] but he would also make fun of the elder's words"; 1547 "Here is how the story ended: inasmuch as he neither possessed a good <heart,> nor bore the

fruit of good, he would also make fun of the elder's words." Good spirit: *noûs*; deep soil: see Lk 8:4–8.
632 The priest: Pom, 1547 "that priest."
633 *Adelphótēs*, a word employed for his community by Basil the Great in his *Questions and Answers* ("Long and Short Rules").
634 Virtues: *aretḗ*.
635 Through the assistance of the godly Païsios' prayers. We must now narrate another story, one that tells about the most awe-inspiring and astounding of wonders: Pom, 1547 "and the great forbearance of the Lord God. This concludes that story. We must now narrate another story, one that tells about the most awe-inspiring and astounding of wonders. Nothing in our narrative surpasses it in loftiness."
636 Pom has this title. Perhaps a better reading for ἐπιστασίας / *epistasías*, "control, authority," is παρουσίας / *parousías*, "appearance, personal visit." "Authority" could refer to God's judgment on Sodom and Gomorrah, although the *Life* does not mention that. But hospitality is the theme here.
637 See Gen 18.
638 Enjoying your hospitality if you oblige and welcome us: Pom, 1547 "your hospitality."
639 Païsios . . . [the hospitality] of that patriarch: Pom, 1547; Grec 1093 "Païsios, courteous, eagerly welcomed them, becoming someone who emulates that patriarch."
640 The author is contrasting the "carnal" nature of Abraham's hospitality (Gen 18:5) with the spiritual nature of Païsios.
641 <So>: Pom, 1547.
642 <in>: Pom, 1547.
643 See Jn 13:1–11.
644 Christ: Pom, 1547 "good Lord."
645 What great love: Pom, 1547 "With your love." Love: *phíltron*.
646 Those who love you: *erastḗs*.
647 Desire: *potheínos* < *póthos*.
648 Païsios: Pom, 1547 "It happened this way: Païsios."
649 Love for humankind: *philánthrōpos*.
650 Offering hospitality: Pom, 1547 "offering hospitality in accordance with the word" (1547 "words").
651 See Jn 14:27.
652 See Lk 24:13–32, esp. v. 32, which uses the same phrase *(kardía . . . kaioménē*, "heart on fire," and Jer 20:9.
653 Restrain himself: Pom, 1547 "restrain his soul." "Loving desire": *érōs*; Pom continues: "on account of his conversation with [the Lord.]"

654 Worthily propitious *(axióchrēston)*: Pom, 1547 "worthy of praise *(axiýmnēton)*." LSJ, Lampe, Bauer, and Montanari have neither, so each may be a *hapax legomenon*. Both words are eminently possible, the former combining *áxio-*, "worthy of," and *chrēstós* (at this time, due to itacizing, pronounced the same as *christós*, "Christ"), which has a wide variety of meanings: "useful, good; good, valiant, true; especially of the gods: propitious, merciful, bestowing health or wealth" (LSJ 2007a, esp. 2007a(II3)). The latter combines *axio-*, "worthy of," with *hymnētós* < *hymnéō*, "sing of, celebrate, praise" (LSJ 1849a), "to be praised," of God (Lampe 1431a).
655 <Christ>-loving: Pom, 1547: *philochrístou*; text *philochrḗstou*, "goodness-loving." See the previous note.
656 See Mt 19:19 and parallels.
657 The great one swooped down on him and gave him the reserved water to drink: Pom, 1547 "The great man scooped down." "Egypt" often indicates (non-monastic) places outside the Wadi Natrun.
658 While the answer was still in his mouth: lit. "he responded *(apephthénxato)* with his tongue"; Pom, 1547 "he contradicted *(anti-)* with his tongue *(antephthénxato)*."
659 Spiritual gifts: *chárisma*. Spiritual gifts, and the loss of them, will figure prominently below.
660 Godly: Pom, 1547 "divine/holy *(thespésios)*." Lampe notes, 646b, that *thespésios* is used especially "of inspired men": Moses, the prophets, John the Baptist, the evangelists, and the church fathers.
661 The patriarch Abraham: Pom, 1547 "Abraham"; see Gen 18.
662 The audacity of my base and unworthy hands!: Pom 1547 "The audacity of my base, rash, and unworthy hands!" Rash: *thrasús* can mean "bold, spirited, courageous, confident," but can also mean "overconfident."
663 Loving desire: *érōs*.
664 Commanded: Pom, 1547 "already commanded."
665 [madness] (ἀπόνοιας / *apónoias*): Pom, 1547; Grec 1093 ὑπόνοιας / *hypónoias*, which does not fit here: "suspicion, conjecture, guess; suggestion; deeper sense" (LSJ 1890b); "opinion, estimation; expectation; underlying meaning, deeper sense (in exegesis); allegory" (Lampe 1452a). But perhaps *hypónoias* means "*self*-estimation," that is, "too high a regard for oneself," but Greek has a late word for this: *hypérnoia*.
666 <lamented> (ἀποδύρετο): Pom, 1547; Grec 1093 ἐπωδύρετο, a misspelling.
667 He plaintively wailed: he plaintively lamented.
668 Wretch that I am!: lit. "Woe is me!" not Paul's cry at Rom 7:24.

669 What goodness I have robbed myself of: Pom, 1547: "What great good things I have been robbed of."
670 With these words, therefore: Pom, 1547 "With these and similar words."
671 Repentance: the word here is not the usual *metánoia*, but *metaméleia*, which also means "repentance, penitence" in patristic Greek.
672 See Rom 5:12–14.
673 Grace: *cháris*, which is etymologically—and, Païsios is saying, theologically—related to *chárisma*, "spiritual gift."
674 <to enjoy>: Pom, 1547.
675 Incessantly: (διηνεκώς / *diēnekṓs*): Pom, 1547 "fearfully, in terror" (δεινώς / *deinṓs*), but perhaps "with exaggeration," echoing δεινόω / *deinóō*: "to make terrible" = "to exaggerate."
676 <You seem to regret . . . protect it>: Pom, 1547; Grec 1093 lacks this sentence, probably due to homoteleuton.
677 Compassion: *splánchna*, lit. "guts," cognate with the verb, *splanchnízomai*, "to have compassion." See Lk 1:78; Phil 2:1; Mt 18:27; among many.
678 Pom, 1547 conclude the section: That concludes this story. God in compassion . . . bestows mercy on those who ask. See Mt 21:22; Mt 7:8//Mk 11:24//Lk 11:10.
679 <disciple>: Pom, 1547.
680 The godly elder: Pom, 1547 "the godly Païsios."
681 <my>: Pom, 1547.
682 At the walls of the city to the right you'll find a poor man sitting on a certain dunghill being stoned and mocked by children: Pom "You will find a man, poorly dressed, at the walls of the city to the right as you enter"; 1547 "You will find a poor man at the wall of the city to the right of where people enter."
683 He left quickly: Pom, 1547 "he left."
684 <would give up to him>: Pom, 1547.
685 <took>: Pom; Grec 1093, 1547 lack.
686 Loving: *axierásata*, lit. "worthy of love," related to *érōs* and *erastḗs*, "love" and "lover."
687 Him: Pom "the things he commands."
688 <your>: Pom, 1547.
689 <goes around>: Pom, 1547.
690 The great father: Pom, 1547 "the divine man and entreat him"; they continue: "and entreat him."
691 The great one: Pom "the godly man"; 1547 "godly Païsios."
692 Gifts: *chárisma*, the same "gift" that the disciple had lost.
693 Entered the tomb and went to his rest there: Pom, 1547 "entered the tomb with appropriate dignity and thanksgiving, offering up hymns to God, and went to his rest there."

694 <say>: Pom, 1547.
695 See Jn 11–12.
696 So you can say something appropriate for me: Pom, 1547 "so we can say something appropriate to you (pl.)."
697 <commands>: Pom; Grec 1093, 1547 "reasons/preaches." Paîsios, thus, like Christ, raises the dead.
698 The father: Pom, 1547 "your father."
699 [commandments]: Pom, 1547 διατάγμασι / *diatágmasi*; Grec 1093 διδάγμασι / *didágmasi*, "instructions, readings." See ¶¶71–72.
700 He once again fell asleep: Pom, 1547 "he once again fell asleep in his sepulcher."
701 The disciple returned: Pom, 1547 "Returning to the holy Paîsios, the disciple in amazement related in full everything that had happened."
702 This is what took place concerning him: Pom, 1547 "Our narrative has now recounted for those who praise God the marvelous events concerning the disciple and the dead man."
703 Our narrative . . . the dead man: Pom "This is what took place concerning him."
704 With regard to the rest, how shall I keep silent?: Pom, 1547 "But how can the narrative ask me to keep silent about other events and persons and not narrate in full wonderful things for those who love God?" "Those who love God": *philótheos*.
705 Troublesome matters: Pom, 1547 lack.
706 Pom has this section title.
707 Brotherhood: *adelphótēs*.
708 The great one: Pom, 1547 "the holy man."
709 Contemplative quiet: *hēsychía*.
710 Desired: *pothouménē* < *póthos*.
711 <them>: Pom, 1547.
712 Heard: Pom, 1547 "learned."
713 On the theme of a false seer, see the Coptic *Life of Macarius the Great* 6 in Vivian, *Four Desert Fathers*, 108–109.
714 He slandered: *diabállō*, which came to mean "slander" and "deceive by false accounts, mislead" (Lampe 390a); so *ho diábolos*, the Devil, means the Deceiver, the Slanderer.
715 *Laura*: a term more common in Palestine than in Egypt, *laúra* usually refers to a semi-anchoritic community (rather than a cenobium, a term the narrator uses in ¶77) where the monks live in separate dwellings but come together on Saturday and Sunday for communal prayer, liturgy, discussion, and meals. This may, as with the AlphAP, indicate Palestinian editing.

716 From there: Grec 1093; Pom, 1547 "from the monastery."
717 Our father: Pom, 1547 "the godly Païsios."
718 As Pom notes, 55 n. 32, after "everyone" a folio of Grec 1093 is missing; the manuscript begins again with ¶76. The text for the missing portion is taken from Pom and 1547, with Pom as the primary text.
719 Living in solitude: *hēsycházontas* < *hēsychía*.
720 Him: Pom, 1547 "them."
721 Spiritual gift: *chárisma*.
722 Gripped with fear, he fell at Païsios' holy feet: 1547 lacks.
723 Pig: since a demon is involved here, the pig may be a reference to the Gadarene (Garasene) demoniacs: Mt 8:28–34//Mk 5:1–13//Lk 8:26–33.
724 The godly man: 1547 "the father."
725 Abyss: lit. "chaos," *cháos*. As *An Intermediate Greek–English Lexicon* (Oxford: Clarendon, [1889] 1975) nicely puts it, 881b: "the nether abyss, infinite darkness." See Lk 8:26–39.
726 In AlphAP Ammonas 10, a delightful story, when it's rumored that a monk has a woman in his cell, he hides her "in a very large jar." A monastic mob enters his cell, with Ammonas. Ammonas sits on top of the jar and orders the cell searched. When the monks find nothing, Ammonas rebukes them and sends them away. To the brother he says only, "Watch out for yourself, brother." See Vivian, *The Sayings and Stories of the Desert Fathers and Mothers*, vol. 1:166–67.
727 <his>: 1547.
728 On Paul of Tamma, see the general introduction, 4–5.
729 Grec 1093 resumes here.
730 Each helped the other: Pom, 1547 "Each helped the other; waging war against the Enemy, they put him to shame."
731 The two of them brought forth [the] good things: Grec 1093, 1547; Pom "the two of them brought forth fruit."
732 Contemplative quiet: *hēsychía*. Pom "the good things of contemplative quiet."
733 New labors and loftier ascetic disciplines: there may be a play on words here: "labors" translates ἀγώνας / *agṓnas* and "ascetic disciplines" translates ἀγωγάς / *agōgás*.
734 Holy: Pom, 1547 "great."
735 Ancient in days: *palaiòs hēmerôn* is the same phrase in the Septuagint for the Ancient of Days in Daniel 7:9, 13, and 22.
736 <thoroughly>: Pom, 1547.
737 Most noble: Pom, 1547 "leader."
738 I follow your most noble advice: Pom, 1547 "I follow your praiseworthy and most noble advice."

739 With <your> prayers: Pom, 1547 "with your holy prayers."
740 Wonderworkers: *thaumátōn autourgoí*. Macarius the Great has the epithet "Wonderworker," *thaumatoúrgos*.
741 <They were called>: Pom, 1547.
742 Imitation: *mímēsis*.
743 Virtues: *aretḗ*.
744 See Mt 6:1–6.
745 Will: *thélēma*; thus there may be an allusion to doing God's will, as in the Lord's Prayer (Mt 6:10): "your will be done" *(tò thélēma sou)*. This undoubtedly does not refer to indiscriminant following of others' will but to submitting oneself to the ascetically practiced will of a spiritual father, which is obedience (*hypakoḗ* or *hypotagḗ*).
746 Contemplative quiet: *hēsychía*.
747 Lover who desired: *erôn* < *eráō*, cognate with *érōs* and *erastḗs*.
748 <godly>: Pom, 1547.
749 Loving desire: *erôn* < *eráō*.
750 Neighbors', *autôn*: Pom, 1547 "neighbor's," *autoû*.
751 Why have you resolved to act this way?: Pom, 1547 "Why have you resolved to act this way, father?"
752 Say: Pom, 1547 "reply."
753 <many are harmed by praise>: Pom, with "by praise" understood; Grec 1093, 1547 are deficient.
754 The Lord: Pom, 1547 "the Master."
755 Mt 6:3.
756 The narrative will now forego the details about his many teachings: Pom "That narrative will now continue, leaving aside the details about his many teachings"; 1547 "That narrative will now continue, leaving aside the successive details about his teachings."
757 His life: Pom, 1547 "the holy man's life."
758 Grec 1093 has this title between ¶¶67 and 68.
759 A great old age: Pom, 1547 "a great and inspired old age." Inspired, *kátochos*: Lampe 737a "possessed, inspired (by the Holy Spirit.)"
760 Pom adds "in this place" or "in that place," which one can perhaps translate "here on earth."
761 In the earth: Pom, 1547 lack.
762 Above, *ánōthen*, which has particular resonance in John (3:3, 7, 31; 19:11, 23): Pom, 1547 "in heaven." Which shows they are taking *ánōthen* as "from above" and not "again."
763 Rest: *anápausis*. Or "inward stillness."
764 <their>: Pom, 1547.
765 <the>: Pom, 1547.

766 For a discussion of the traditions surrounding the burial of Paul and Païsios and the role of Isidore, see the general introduction, 10.
767 Grec 1093 has this title.
768 Grec 1093 has this title. On Isidore and the relics, see Prof. Mikhail's discussion in the General Introduction, 10.
769 On relics, and the emergent cult of the saints, see Peter Brown, *The Cult of the Saints: Its Rise and Function in Latin Christianity* (Chicago: University of Chicago Press, 1981). On healings see ¶80.
770 <ship>: Pom, 1547.
771 <their>: Pom, 1547; Grec 1093 "the."
772 Were not able to at all: Pom, 1547 "were not able to."
773 <being held fast>, κατάσχεσιν / *katáschesin*: Pom, 1547; Grec 1093 "condemnation/blame/censure," κατάγνωσιν / *katágnōsin*.
774 From among the fathers: Pom, 1547 "from among the remarkable fathers."
775 <came down>: Pom, 1547.
776 Fellow lover: *synerastēs (erastēs)*.
777 Disembark and when you find [the body]: Grec 1093; 1547 "Disembark and when you find it"; Pom "disembark to look for him. Inquire where the body of the godly Paul has been placed and, when you find it."
778 Precious stones—what a strange and wonderful miracle: Pom, 1547 "precious stones. But the men, having a power to assist them that until then was invisibly hindering them, were not able to restrain the boat for—what a strange and wonderful miracle—!"
779 Great: Pom "divine."
780 Every hymn of praise: Pom continues: "and offering every spiritual gift, placed . . . ." See Rom 1:11; 1 Cor 1:7; 2:14; 12:1; 14:1, 12.
781 See Mk 3:11, 6:7.
782 All those who were troubled by unclean spirits or by any other kind of illness were taking hold of the remains of the saints and were being healed by merely touching them: Pom, 1547 "All those who were troubled by unclean spirits or by any other kind of illness were healed by merely touching the honorable caskets." See Brown, *The Cult of the Saints*.
783 Performed: Pom, 1547 "performed after the burial of the holy men."
784 These few things, out of many, I <have related> to the best of my ability: Pom, 1547 "These few things, out of many, to the best of my ability as they were available to me, I have related for the benefit of many"; Grec 1093 "These few things, out of many, I will relate to the best of my ability."
785 To the glory of the Father and the Son and the Holy Spirit, now and always, forever and ever. Amen: Pom, 1547 "to the glory of the Father and the Son and the Holy Spirit, one Deity in three, to whom it is fitting to give all glory, praise, and worship, now and always, forever and ever. Amen."

2
THE GREEK *LIFE OF PAÏSIOS*
BNF Grec 1093
Edited and Transcribed by Tim Vivian and Apostolos N. Athanassakis

Sigla

[ ] Translators' Content and Spelling Corrections
< > Corrections and Additions
{ } Deletions

¹Βίος² τοῦ ὁσίου πατρὸς ἡμῶν Παϊσίου³

Exordium
[165a]⁴ 1. Ὥσπερ τὰ τερπνὰ τοῦ βίου, καίπερ ὄντα τρεπτὰ καὶ λυόμενα, οἶδε⁵ τοὺς θελγομένους αὐτοῖς ἐφελκύσαι πρὸς ἔρωτα διά τε μικρᾶς ἡδονῆς τὴν αἴσθησιν σαίνεσθαι καὶ τὸν νοῦν πρὸς πάθη ἐπιρρέπεσθαι ποιοῦντα. Ὡς ὑπερφρονεῖν⁶ οὐ μόνον τὰ ἐπηγγελμένα ἀγαθά,⁷ ἀλλὰ καὶ αὐτὸν—φεῦ—τὸν δημιουργὸν τῆς ὄντως ζωῆς ἀποστρέφεσθαι, καὶ ταῦτα μᾶλλον προκρίνεσθαι τῶν ἐκείνου καλῶν. Τὸν ἀτελεύτητον καὶ χαλεπὸν ἑκουσίως ἐπισπ[ω]μένους θάνατον.

Οὕτω δὴ καὶ τοὺς ἐραστὰς τῶν μελλόντων καὶ τῶν ἐν ἐλπίσι κειμένων ὡς ἐκ διαμέτρου ὁ θεῖος κατεργάζ[ε]ται⁸ πόθος. Καὶ γὰρ ἡ μνήμη τῆς τῶν πόνων ἀντιδόσεως καὶ τῶν λαμπρῶν ἐκεῖσε ἐπάθλων τοῖς ἐκεῖσε⁹ κ[ε]καθαρμένοις οὐ μόνον διδάσκειν εἴωθε τῶν προσκαίρων καὶ ματαίων ὑπερορᾶν.¹⁰ Ἀλλὰ καὶ τὴν ζωὴν αὐτῶν παραβλέπειν¹¹ καὶ τὴν φιλουμένην, οἷα εἰκὸς, ἀπολέσαι ψυχήν. Ὡς ἐν τοῖς θείοις εἴρηται εὐαγγελίοις [ὑπὸ]¹² Χριστοῦ. Καὶ πάντων ἥδιστον καὶ τερπνότατον ἐκείνου ἕνεκα ἡγεῖσθαι τὸν θάνατον, κἂν μὴ [165b] τύχοιεν τούτου ὡς τάχιστα διὰ τὴν ἐρημίαν τῶν διωκόντων τὸ ἐργῶδες ἔχουσαν, ἀλλ᾽ οὖν τῆς ἐφέσεως ἄλλως ἀπολαῦσαι¹³ ἐπινοοῦσιν¹⁴ τὸν μακρότατον καὶ ἐπίπονον μηχανώμενοι θάνατον τὸν ἐν μυρίοις πόνοις καὶ καρτερίᾳ καθ᾽ ἑκάστην φερόμενον καὶ τῇ τε ἀσκήσει καὶ πολυτρόποις ἀγῶσι τοῖς ἀοράτοις μαχόμενοι καὶ τὴν φύσιν ἀεὶ βιαζόμενοι τοῖς ἀσωμάτοις {συν}αμιλλᾶσθαι[15] ἐν σώματι.

2. [165b11] Τῶν τοιούτων τοίνυν ἀρίστων καὶ θείων ἀνδρῶν τινὸς διηγήσασθαι μέλλοντι γέννησίν τε καὶ ἀνατροφὴν καὶ λαμπρότητα βίου—Παΐσιος ὄνομα τῷ ἀνδρὶ—μηδεὶς ἀπιστείτω τὰ ὑπὲρ φύσιν ἀκούων παράδοξα μηδὲ οἰέσθω με τιμῆς ἕνεκα <ἢ>[16] φιλίας τῷ τ[ο]ιούτῳ φιλτάτῳ πατρὶ[17] προσθεῖναί τι τραχύ τε καὶ ἀνώτατον, ὡς δόξαν τούτῳ χαριζόμενον παρ' ὃ τεθέαμαι οἰκείοις ὀφθαλμοῖς καὶ ὠσὶν ἠκηκόειν. Πορρωτάτω γὰρ ἐκεῖνος πάσης τιμῆς ἀνθρωπίνης καὶ ὑψηλοτέρας ὁ ἀνήρ.[18] <Οὐ>[19] χάριν γὰρ ἐκείνου εἴπερ μηδὲ τῶν χαμερπῶν δεῖται ἐπαίνων ὁ παρ' ἀγγέλοις ἐν ὕψει ἐπαινούμενος ἀλλὰ [166a1] τῆς τῶν ἀκουόντων ὠφελείας καὶ ζηλῶσαι ἐκείνου προ[αι]ρ[ου]μένων[20] τὴν ἀρετὴν διέξειμι τὰ αὐτοῦ[21] ἀξιέπαινα.[22]

Paΐsios' Birth and Parentage

3. [166a3] Τοῦτον τοίνυν τὸν μέγαν καὶ ἀοίδιμον ἄνδρα ἤνεγκεν Αἴγυπτος ἥτις πάλαι μὲν τὸν ἀκρ[έ]μονα τῶν προφητῶν Μωϋσῆν τὸν θεόπτην ἐνεγκαμένη διά τε τῆς ἐκείνου πρὸς θεὸν οἰκειώσεως καὶ τῶν μεγίστων τεραστίων περιβόητος ἐν [ταῖς] γραφαῖς ἐγεγόνει.[23] Οὐκ ἔλαττον δὲ ὕστερον, δειχθεῖσα εὐκλεὴς διὰ τοῦ ἱεροῦ Παϊσίου φαιδρὸν ὑπόδειγμα τῶν <ἀρετῶν>[24] τὸ ἐκείνου κατεπλούτησεν ὄνομα.

Γεννήτορες δὲ τούτῳ ἦσαν ἀμφότεροι εὐσεβεῖς καὶ φοβούμενοι τὸν Κύριον,[25] ἔν τε ταῖς ἐντολαῖς αὐτοῦ ἀμέμπτως πορευόμενοι καὶ τὰ χρηστὰ ἅπαντα κεκτημένοι. Τούτοις δὲ παῖδες ἑπτὰ ἐτύ[γ]χανον τῶν αὐτῶν[26] ἀντεχόμενοι ἀρετῶν. Πλοῦτος δὲ ἱκανὸς ὅσον τοῖς δεομένοις δαψιλῆ καὶ ὑπτί[α]ν τὴν χεῖρα τὰ πρὸς τὴν χρείαν ἑκάστῳ παρεχομένην ἐργάζεσθαι, ὅσον γὰρ οὗτοι τὰ προσόντα χερσὶ πενήτων διένεμον, πλείονα ἀντεδίδου τούτοις ἡ τοῦ θεοῦ ἄφθονος δωρεά, ὥς εὐθηνούμενα πάντα τὰ ἐν τῷ βίῳ τυγχάνειν.[27]

The Death of Paΐsios's Father; an Angel Appears to His Mother

Ἐπ[εὶ [166b1] δὲ τοῦ θανάτου ἄγευστος οὐδεὶς ὑπάρχει βροτῶν ἐξ ἀνθρώπων γίνεται, ὁ πατὴρ τῇ δὲ σεμνοτάτῃ γυναικὶ τῶν παίδων ἡ φροντ[ὶ]ς ἀπολέλειπται μόνῃ ὀδυνωμένῃ. Πάντων δὲ μικρότερος ἦν ὁ Παΐσιος, <καὶ>[28] [πλείονα][29] τῇ μητρὶ φροντίδα[30] διδούς. Ἀμέλει καὶ ἀωρὶ τῶν νυκτῶν γλυκ[ε]ῖα ὄψις ἄγγελος Κυρίου ἐπιστάς, "Τῶν ὀρφανῶν με," ἔφη, "ὁ πατὴρ ἀπέσταλκε[ν ὁ] θεός. Τί ἀθυμίας," φησίν, "ὑπόπλεως φαίνῃ τῆς τῶν παίδων ἕνεκα φροντίδος ὡς μόνη τούτων σὺ ᾖ φροντίζουσα καὶ οὐ θεός;[31] ἀλλά γε δὴ τὴν ἀθυμίαν ἔασον καὶ δίδου ἐκ τῶν σῶν υἱῶν ἕνα τῷ ὑψίστῳ θεῷ, δι' οὗ δοξασθήσεται τὸ ἀεὶ δοξαζόμενον καὶ πανάγιον αὐτοῦ ὄνομα."[32]

Ἡ δὲ, "Πάντες," ἔφη, "θεοῦ εἰσίν. Ὁποῖος ἂν καὶ εἴη εὐάρεστος <αὐτῷ>,³³ τοῦτον λάβοι."

Ὁ δὲ φανεὶς αὐτῇ ἄγγελος τὸν Παΐσιον, {ἔφη,}³⁴ χειρὶ κρατήσας, "Οὗτος," ἔφη, "ἐστὶ κυρίῳ ὁ εὐάρεστος."

Τὴν δὲ εἰποῦσαν μὴ εἶναι τοῦτον ἱκανὸν διὰ τὸ ἄωρον τῆς ἡλικίας πρὸς θεραπείαν θεοῦ· "Λάβε δὲ μᾶλλον τῶν μεγάλων, ὁποῖος ἂν εἴη ἱκανός."

Πρὸς αὐτὴν ἔφησεν³⁵ [167a1] ὁ θεῖος ἄγγελος, "'Αλλ' ἡ δύναμις τοῦ θεοῦ, ὦ καλλίστη γυναικῶν, ἐν τοῖς ἀσθενέσιν εἴωθε γίνεσθαι. Οὗτος γάρ ἐστιν ὁ ἐκλεκτὸς τοῦ Κυρίου,³⁶ ὅς μέλλει αὐτῷ εὐαρεστῆσαι." Ταῦτα εἰπών, ἀφίστατο.

Païsios Goes to Scetis

4. [167a6] Διυπνισθεῖσα³⁷ δὲ καὶ τὸ θεῖον ἀγαμένη τῆς ὄψεως παράγγελμα, ὕμνους τῷ θεῷ εὐχαριστηρίους φθεγγ[γ]ομένη.³⁸ "Γένοιτο," ἔλεγεν,³⁹ "ἐφ' ἡμᾶς, δέσποτα, καὶ τὸν δοῦλόν σου Παΐσιον τὸ ἔλεός σου." Καὶ ταῦτα μὲν αὐτὴ καὶ ἕτερα ῥήματα τῆς εὐχαριστίας τούτοις ὅμοια εἰποῦσα, προσευχομένη τὸν ἑαυτῆς παῖδα προσήνεγκε <τῷ> θεῷ καθιέρ[ω]μα.

Ὁ δὲ θεῖος Παΐσιος τῶν ἀρ[ε]τῶν⁴⁰ γενόμενος ἐραστὴς καὶ ἅμα τῇ τε ἡλικίᾳ καὶ τῇ χάριτι αὐξηθείς, φόβῳ θείῳ καὶ ἔρωτι τρ[ω]θεὶς τῆς μοναχικῆς⁴¹ ἤρα διαγωγῆς. Διϊππεύσαντος οὖν τοῦ χρόνου, ἐν ᾧ τὰς θείας ἐντολὰς τοῦ Κυρίου⁴² ἐχρῆν ἐργάζεσθαι, ὑπὸ τῆς θεϊκῆς χάριτος καθάπερ ἄμωμος ἀμνὸς εἰσφερόμενος ἐν τῇ ἐρήμῳ τῆς Σκήτεως, παρὰ τὸν ποιμένα τῶν λογικῶν προβάτων καθοδηγήθη τὸν μέγαν⁴³ Παμβώ.

Païsios, as Pambo's Disciple, Advances Spiritually

5. Ὁ δὲ [167b1] θεῖος πατὴρ⁴⁴ τοῦτον δεξάμενος ἐν πάσῃ ἁγιωσύνῃ⁴⁵ καὶ χαρμονῇ, τὸ ἅγιον σχῆμα <τοῦτον>⁴⁶ ἐνέδυσεν. Οὐκ ἄμοιρος γὰρ ἦν θείας γνώσεως, ἀλλὰ καὶ τὰ μέλλοντα⁴⁷ δι' ὁράσεως ἄνωθεν ἐμύ[η]το.⁴⁸ Ἐπ[ε]ὶ δὲ τῆς χάριτος σκεῦος ἦν ἐκλελεγμένος ὁ Παΐσιος καὶ ὑπ' αὐτῆς ὁδηγούμενος, πρὸς πᾶσαν ἀρετῶν ἰδέαν ἐπιτήδειος⁴⁹ γίνεται. Καὶ πρῶτον μὲν τὰ τῆς ὑπακοῆς⁵⁰ διανύσας, καλῶς κατ[ο]ρθώματα προθύμως τὰ δοκοῦντα τῷ πατρικῷ κελεύσματι ἐποιεῖτο πάντα. Ἐπ[ε]ιτα δὲ καὶ τῆς τῶν τελείων προσέθηκεν ἐπιβῆναι ἀναβάσεως τραχυτέρας ἐπιλαβόμενος ἀγωγῆς. Ὁ δὲ θεῖος πατὴρ ἡμῶν ἐκεῖνος τούτων τῶν κρειττόνων ἐφιέμενον ἑωρακὼς ἔφη πρὸς αὐτόν, "Τέκνον Παΐσιε, ἀρχαρίῳ τῷ ὄντι ἀγωνιστῇ προσώπῳ τινὸς οὐ δεῖ τὰς ὄψεις προσβάλλειν·⁵¹ ἀλλ' ἀεὶ τοῖς ποσὶ κάτω νεύοντα <τῷ>⁵² νοῒ ἄνω βλέπειν διηνεκῶς τοῖς διορατικοῖς⁵³ ὀφθαλμοῖς τὰ κάλλη τῆς ἀπορρήτου δόξης τοῦ Θεοῦ φανταζόμενον. Κἀντεῦθεν τὴν παντοδύναμον ἀγαθότητα τοῦ Δημιουργοῦ⁵⁴ δοξάζειν καὶ ὑμνεῖν.⁵⁵

⁵⁶6. Τούτοις [168a1] τοίνυν τοῖς τοῦ διδασκάλου Παΐσιος τοὺς ἐπωφελεῖς λόγους⁵⁷ μυσταγωγηθεὶς καὶ πόθου θείου⁵⁸ πλησθεὶς δι᾽ ἔργου πληρωτὴς γίνεται. Τηνικαῦτα γὰρ ἀκριβῶς διεφύλαττεν ἐντολὴν τρ[ε]ῖς χρόνους διανύσας ἁγίων πρόσωπον⁵⁹ μηδ᾽ ὅλως ἰδών, ἀλλ᾽ ἦν ὅλος τῇ τῶν θείων γραφῶν ἀναγνώσει προσ{σ}έχων καὶ τὰ νοήματα ἐξερευνῶν. Καὶ τοῖς αὐτῶν νάμασιν ἀρδεύων⁶⁰ τὴν οἰκείαν ψυχήν, καί, ἵν᾽ εἴπω Δα[υ]ιτικῶς, καθάπερ τι εὐθαλὲς τῶν φυτῶν ἐπὶ τὰς ἐξαγωγὰς⁶¹ τῶν ὑδάτων πεφυτευμένον καὶ⁶² πέπειρον καρπὸν φέρον ἐν τῷ καιρῷ τῷ προσήκοντι καὶ γλυκύν. Ὥστε καὶ τοῦτον,⁶³ "Ὡς γλυκέα," λέγειν, "τὰ λόγιά σου, κύριε τῷ λάρυγγί μου, ὑπὲρ μέλι τῷ στόματί μου."

Ἀλλ᾽ οὗτος μὲν οὕτως ἦν ἀδιαλείπτως κατὰ τὸν ἀπόστολον προσευχόμενος ἐν νηστείαις καὶ ἀγρυπνίαις τὸ σῶμα πιέζων καὶ παιδαγωγῶν,⁶⁴ καὶ οἷά τις ἔφη σοφὸς ἐν τῇ καρδίᾳ αὐτοῦ τὰς ἀρετὰς διατηρῶν.

7. [168a22] Ὁ δὲ θεῖος πρεσβύτης τοῦτον οὕτω <τῇ>⁶⁵ πνευματικῇ προκόπτοντα ἀσκήσει θεασάμενος καὶ ταῖς κατὰ θεὸν [168a1] ἀρεταῖς πατρικῶς αὐτῷ, προσεῖχε καὶ χεῖρα προσεκτικωτέρως τοῦτον ἐγείρουσαν καὶ ἐπὶ τὰ πρόσω κινοῦσαν παρεῖχεν ἀμέλει καὶ πρὸς πᾶσαν πρᾶξιν καὶ γνῶσιν εὐχερῶς διϊθύων καὶ διεξάγων⁶⁶ καλῶς πεπειραμένον αὐτὸν δείκνυσιν.

Ἐπ[ε]ὶ δὲ ὁ τῆς ἀναλύσεως ἐφε{ι}στήκει καιρὸς <τῷ γέροντι>⁶⁷ πρὸς λῆξιν οὐράνιον τοῦτον καλῶν καὶ πρὸς ἃ ἐπόθει ἐπ[ε]ιγόμενος πολ[λ]ῶν εὐλογιῶν ὁ ἱερὸς Παμβῶ⁶⁸ τὸν Παΐσιον καταξιώσας καὶ λόγους οὐ μετρίους προφητικοὺς περὶ αὐτοῦ διεξιὼν τῶν τῇδε πρὸς τὴν ἀΐδιον ἀπανίσταται ζωήν. Καὶ οὕτω μὲν οὗτος εὐκλεῶς τὰ τῶν ἐλπίδων ἐν οὐρανοῖς ἀπείληφε χρηστά.

After Pambo's Death, John Remains with Païsios

8. [168a16] Ἐγὼ δὲ ὁ ταπεινὸς Ἰωάννης ἀπολέλειμμαι⁶⁹ σὺν τῷ ἱερῷ Παϊσίῳ, ἀμφότεροι ὁμόστεγοι, τὴν γνώμην κατάλληλοι, ὁμοῦ μὲν συνδιαιτώμενοι, ὁμοῦ δὲ τὴν διαγωγὴν ὡς οἷόν τε διανύοντες καθ᾽ ὃν παρὰ⁷⁰ τοῦ πατρὸς ἡμῶν κανόνα παρειλήφαμεν. Θάτερος θατέρῳ στηριζόμενος καὶ Δα[υ]ιτικῶς εἰπεῖν οἷα εἰκὸς ἐπὶ τὸ αὐτὸ ἀδελφὰ φρονοῦντες καὶ τῶν οἰκείων ψυχῶν ἐπιμελούμενοι. Χρόνου τοίνυν [169a1] ἡμῖν⁷¹ οὐ βραχέως διανυσθέντος, οὕτω συνεζευγμένοις, ἐπ[ε]ὶ τὸν Παΐσιον ἄλλων ὑψηλοτέρων ἀγωγῶν ἔρως κατέσχεν, διαζεύξεως ἀνάγκη γίνεται, ὡς ἡμῖν διηγητέον.

Païsios's Spiritual Disciplines

9. [169a5] [Οἵ]δε⁷² μὲν οὖν τῷ {τῷ}⁷³ πνεύματι ζέοντι Παϊσίῳ [ἀγῶνες].⁷⁴ Τὸ διὰ τῆς ἑ[β]δομάδος ὅλης ἄρτον μὴ [ἐσθίειν],⁷⁵ διὰ δὲ

τοῦ σαββάτου ἄρτος καὶ ἅλ[ας]⁷⁶ ἡ τροφὴ αὐτῷ ἦν. Ἀντὶ ἄρτου γὰρ [αἰ]σθητοῦ νοητοῦ ταῖς λοιπαῖς κατετρύφα τῶν ἡμερῶν. Συνεχῶς δὲ καὶ τῇ προφητ[ε]ίᾳ τοῦ θεσπεσίου Ἰερεμίου διωμίλει καὶ αὐτῷ ἐκεῖνος πολλάκις ὀφθεὶς ὡς λέγεται τὰ τῆς προφητείας ἀπόρρητα διερμηνεύ[ων] καὶ διὰ τῶν κεκρ[υμ]μένων ἐννοιῶν διήγειρεν ἐκείνου τὸν νοῦν εἰς ἔρωτα τῶν ἐπηγγελμένων ἀγαθῶν.

10. [169a17] Ἐπ[ε]ὶ δὲ ἐπὶ τὰ πρόσω ἀεὶ ἐπεκτεινόμενος ἦν, τῆς προτέρας οὐκ εἴχετο⁷⁷ διαγωγῆς, ἀλλ' ἑτέρας ἀντέχεται·⁷⁸ τῇ προτέρᾳ ἑ[β]δομάδι⁷⁹ ἑτέραν προσθ[εὶ]ς,⁸⁰ καὶ [διοδεύων]⁸¹ νηστεύων τῇ ἀρχῇ, τῆς τρίτης μετεῖχε τροφῆς⁸² ἄρτου βραχέως σὺν ἅλατι. Καὶ τὸ δ[ὲ]⁸³ θαυμαστότερον ὅτι οὐδεὶς ἐκείνου [169b1] τὴν ἰσάγγελον διαγωγὴν⁸⁴ ἐγνωκὼς ἦν εἰ μὴ μόνος⁸⁵ ὁ τὰ κρυπτὰ βλέπων καὶ τὰ ἄδηλα ἐν ὀφθαλμοῖς ἔχων Θεός. Ἀμέλ[ει]⁸⁶ καὶ τῷ τῆς ἡσυχίας οὐκ ἀνάλωτος γίνεται ἔρωτι ἀλλ' ἐκείν<ῳ> φίλον εἶναι δοκεῖ τὸ καταμόνας τῷ μόνῳ Θεῷ προσφέρειν τὰς εὐχὰς καὶ προσομιλεῖν καὶ τῷ ἀκροτάτῳ τῶν ἐφετῶν οἰκειοῦσθαι⁸⁷ καὶ προσ[εγγίζειν]⁸⁸ διὰ τῶν ἐκεῖθεν ἐλ[λ]άμψεων.

Païsios and John the Little Separate

11. [169b10] Ταῖς τοιαύταις οὖν ἐκεῖνον ἀπασχολούμενον ἐννοίαις <κατανοῶν>,⁸⁹ καίπερ ἐμοὶ <τὸ>⁹⁰ τῆς ἐκείνου διαζεύξεως ἀνασχέσθαι πρᾶγμα οὐ⁹¹ φορητὸν ἀπόπειραν ποιούμενος τὸν τῆς ἡσυχίας ἐκείνης γνῶναι τρόπον κἄν τε εἴη κατὰ Θεὸν ἢ οἴκοθεν. "Ἀδελφέ," εἶπον, "Παΐσιε, ἰδοὺ σε ὁρῶ τῷ τῆς ἡσυχίας ἔρωτι κάτοχον ὄντα. Κἀγὼ εὖ ἴσθι τῷ αὐτῷ ἑάλω[ν] φίλτρῳ, ἀλλ' οὖν ὅστις εἴη καὶ ὅθεν ἥκοι ὁ τοιοῦτος λογισμός οὐκ ἐπίσταμαι. Δεῦρο, τοίνυν, τῶν τοῦ Θεοῦ δεηθῶμεν οἰκτιρμῶν καὶ κατὰ τὴν ἐκείνου περὶ ἡμᾶς θέλησιν ἀνενδ[ο]ιάστως μετερχ[ώ]μεθα· εἴτε ἐπὶ τὸ αὐτὸ ἀμφότεροι καρτεροῦντες ἔχοιμεν τὰς διατριβάς, εἴτε διακριθέντες ἀλλήλων ἀποσταίημεν."

[170a1] Καὶ ὅς, "Καλῶς ἔχει,⁹² ἠγαπημένε," ἀπεφθέγγετο. "Οὕτω[ς] δὴ καὶ ποιήσωμεν ὅπως εὐπρόσδεκτος εἴη ἡ περὶ ταύτην⁹³ σπουδὴ καὶ ἀνύποπτος."

Ταῦτα εἰπόντες,⁹⁴ τοῦ Θεοῦ ἐδεόμεθα Θεῷ δὲ τὰς ἡμῶν ἱκεσίας οὐκ ἦν παριδεῖν εὐσπλάγχους καὶ ἀγαθοὺς ἔχοντι τοὺς οἰκτιρμούς.⁹⁵

12. [169b7] Περὶ γὰρ τὸν ὄρθρον θεῖος, ἡμῖν ἄγγελος ἐπιστάς. "Ὑμῖν," ἔφη, "παρὰ Θεοῦ ἑκάστῳ οἴκησις⁹⁶ διορίζεται. Οὐκ ἔτι γὰρ ὑμῖν συνοδία μία, ἀλλ' ἑκατέρῳ οἰκεία ἔσται διατριβή.⁹⁷ Σὺ μεν, Ἰωάννη, ἐνθάδε καρτερήσας πολλῶν πρὸς σωτηρίαν γενοῦ ὁδηγός. Καὶ σύ, Παΐσιε, θεράπων Χριστοῦ, μετάβηθι τῶν ὧδε ἐπὶ δ[υ]σμὰς τῆς ἐρήμου. 'Λαός σοι,' λέγει Κύριος, 'συναθροισθήσεται ἄπειρος καὶ μοναστήριον θείᾳ κελεύσει οἰκοδομηθήσεται, καὶ τὸ ὄνομά μου διὰ σοῦ αὐτόθι δοξασθήσεται.'"

Καὶ ταῦτα μὲν ὁ φανεὶς εἰρηκώς, ἀπέστη τῆς ὁράσεως. Ἡμεῖς δὲ τῇ ἐκείνου κελεύσει εἴξαντες ἀπ᾽ ἀλλήλων ἐχωρίσθημεν. Καὶ ἐγὼ μὲν ἀπελείφθην, ὡς ἐτάχθην,[98] ἐν τῷ τόπῳ, Παΐσιος δὲ πορρωτάτω ὡς ὥριστο, ἐπὶ δ[υ]σμὰς [170b1] πορευθεὶς ἄντρον λατομ[ή]σας ἐν αὐτῷ κατεσκήνωσε καὶ τοσοῦτον ᾠκειώθη <τῷ> θεῷ διά τε τὴν ὑπερβάλλουσαν καθαρότητα καὶ [ἃς][99] ἔδειξεν ἀγωγάς, ὥστε καὶ τὸν Χριστὸν αὐτῷ πολλάκις ἐμφανίζεσθαι, ἰθύνοντά τε πρὸς ἀρετὴν[100] καὶ ὁδηγοῦντα, ὡς ἤδη τοῦ λόγου δηλώσει ἡ ἀκολουθ{ε}ία.

The Savior Appears to Païsios

13. [170b7] Ἐν μιᾷ γοῦν τῶν ἡμερῶν τῷ Παϊσίῳ καθεζομένῳ ἐν τῷ οἰκείῳ ἄντρῳ καὶ τὸν θεϊκὸν ἐπὶ[101] στόματος ἔχοντι ὕμνον, παρῆν αὐτῷ ὁ Σωτήρ, "Εἰρήνη σοι," λέγων, "τῷ ἠγαπημένῳ μοι θεράποντι Παϊσίῳ."

Ὁ δὲ ἐγερθεὶς φόβ[ῳ] καὶ τρόμῳ συνεχόμενος, "Χριστὲ φιλάνθρωπε,"[102] ἔφη, "ἰδοὺ ὁ δοῦλός σου. Τί τὸ περὶ ἐμέ, δέσποτα, δοκοῦν τῇ σῇ ἀγαθότητι, καὶ τί τὸ αἴτιον τῆς σῆς συγκαταβάσεως;"

Καὶ [ὁ]ς πρὸς αὐτόν, "Ὁρᾷς τὴν ἔρημον ταύτην," ἔφη, "ὅσον μῆκος καὶ πλάτος ἔχουσαν; Διὰ σοῦ τὸ ἐμὸν δοξαζόντων ὄνομα εὖ ἴσθι[103] ἐμπλήσω ἀσκητῶν."

Ὁ δὲ ἐκλεκτὸς τοῦ Κυρίου[104] ἐν τῷ ἐδάφει πεσών, "Πάντα," ἔφη, "Δέσποτα,[105] τῇ χειρί σου τῇ κραταιᾷ[106] ὑποτέτακται καὶ ἅμα τῷ βούλεσθαι ἔχειν[107] καὶ τὸ εἶναι. Δέομαι τῆς σῆς ἀγαθότητος γνῶναι [π]όθεν ἔσται ὁ τῶν{ί} ἀναγκαίων πορισμὸς [171a1] τοῖς ἐν αὐτῇ αὐλιζομένοις;"[108]

Ὁ δέ, "Π[ε]ίσθητι <μοι>[109] ὡς ἀληθῶς, ὅτι ἐὰν ἀγάπην τὴν μητέρα τῶν ἀρετῶν αὐτοὺς ἔχοντας εὕρω καὶ τὰς ἐμὰς τηροῦντας ἐντολάς, οὐδενὸς δεηθήσονται,[110] ἀλλ᾽ ἐγὼ τὴν φροντίδα πᾶσαν ἕξω περὶ αὐτῶν."

Εἶτα φησὶ πρὸς αὐτὸν ὁ θεῖος ἀνήρ,[111] "Ἔτι ἅπαξ ἐρωτήσω τὴν σὴν ἀγαθότητα πῶς μέλ[λ]ουσιν εὐμαρῶς τὰς παγίδας τοῦ ἐχθροῦ διελθεῖν καὶ τῶν δεινῶν ἐκείνου ἐπηρειῶν;"

Καὶ ὁ Σωτήρ, "Ἐὰν τὰς ἐμάς, ὡς εἴρηταί σοι, ἐντολὰς τηρήσωσιν ἐν πραότητι καὶ ταπεινώσει καρδίας,"[112] οὐ μόν[ο]ν τῶν ἐπηρ[τη]μένων[113] πολέμων καὶ πονηρῶν ἐπιβουλῶν ἀνωτέρους ποιήσω, ἀλλὰ καὶ βασιλείας οὐρανῶν ἐν ταῖς αἰωνίοις σκηναῖς[114] κληρονόμους δείξω."[115]

Ταῦτα εἰπὼν ὁ Σωτήρ, μετὰ δόξης εἰς οὐρανοὺς ἀνῆλθεν, ὁ δὲ ἱερὸς Παΐσιος πλείονα φόβον ἔκτοτε ἑαυτῷ ἐπεσπάσατο τὴν πρὸς αὐτὸν τοῦ Σωτῆρος αἰδούμενος συγκατάβασιν.

A Rich Ruler, Suborned by the Devil, Comes to Païsios with Money

14. Ὁ δὲ [171a25] τοῦ φθόνου πατὴρ καὶ μ[ι]σάνθρωπος ἐχθρός, τοῦτον ἀσφαλῶς τὰς ἐνέδρας διαβαίνοντα ὁρῶν ἀνάλωτόν τε ταῖς μηχαναῖς

καὶ ὑπέρτερον τῶν ἐπιβουλῶν σφόδρα διεπρίετο, καὶ μὴ δυνάμενος αὐτῷ προσελθεῖν[116] διὰ τὴν θείαν ἥν ἐκ θεοῦ εἴληφε δύναμιν μετῄει δι᾽ ἄλλων μεσιτείας τούτου περιγενέσθαι δολίως μηχανώμενος. Ὤετο γὰρ εὐχερῶς τὸν Παΐσιον ἁλῶναι τῇ τῶν χρημάτων λιχν[ε]ίᾳ καὶ ἐλεημοσύνης ἀφορμαῖς προσβαλεῖν τούτῳ[117] ἠπείγετο, ἵνα κἄν τούτῳ τῆς ἀκτημοσύνης ἐκείνου ἐκπεσόντος παραχωρηθείη κατ᾽ αὐτοῦ ἡ τῶν δ[ει]νῶν εἴσοδος.

Ὅθεν ὁ ποικίλος ἐχθρὸς πρόσεισί τινι τῶν τῆς Αἰγύπτου ἀρχόντων, ἀνδρὶ πλούτῳ κομῶντι, καὶ ἐν προσχήματι[118] ἀγγέλου ὁ δείλαιος[119] φανεὶς, φησὶ πρὸς αὐτόν, "Διαναστάς, ὦ οὗτος, πορεύθητι ἐν τῇ ἐρήμῳ καὶ εὑρήσεις ἄνδρα ὀνόματι Παΐσιον. Πτωχὸν μὲν τὸν βίον κ[ε]κτημένον ἀρεταῖς δὲ λαμπρῶς κ[ε]κοσμημένον καὶ τῆς θείας χάριτος σκεῦος [172a1] ἐκλελεγμένον. Τοῦτον εὑρών, χρήμασιν ἐπιεικῶς τίμησον καὶ ἀφειδῶς."

[120]15. [172a2] Ὁ δὲ ἄρχων ἐκεῖνος, μὴ ὑπονοήσας τὴν δαιμονικὴν πλάνην, ἀλλ᾽ ἀγγελικὴν εἶναι τὴν τοῦ φαινομένου δύναμιν πιστεύσας, φόρτον παντοδαπῶν χρημάτων λαβών, ἀπῄει πρὸς τὸν ἅγιον. Ἡ δὲ περιέ[χ]ουσα[121] τοῦτον θεϊκὴ δύναμις τὴν ἐπιβουλὴν κατάδηλον ἐποίει,[122] ὅπως τε εἴη καὶ τίνι τρόπῳ ὁ ἐχθρὸς διὰ τῆς δωρεᾶς τοῦ ἄρχοντος μεμηχάνηται τούτ[ῳ] διεξιοῦσα. Ὁ δὲ θεῖος ἀνὴρ εὐθὺς ἀναστάς, ἐπορεύετο πρὸς ἀπάντησιν τοῦ ἄρχοντος καὶ συνανατήσας ὑπ᾽ αὐτοῦ, ἠρωτήθη[123] τίς τε εἴη Παΐσιος καὶ ποῦ μένοι.

Ὁ δὲ, "Καὶ τίνος χάριν," ἀντεφθέγξατο, "ἐκεῖνον ζητεῖς;"

"Χρήματα," ὁ ἄρχων ἔφη, "καὶ χρυσὸν ἐνέγκας ἐκείνῳ δοῦναι βούλομαι τοῖς μοναχοῖς διανεῖμαι."

Καὶ ὅς, "Σύγγνωθι," φησίν, "ὦ φιλόχριστε, χρυσοῦ ἢ ἀργύρου οὐκ ἔστιν ἡμῖν χρεία τοῖς[124] τὴν ἔρημον ταύτην οἰκῆσαι θελήσασιν.[125] Ἀλλ᾽ ἄγε οὐδὲ τῶν ἐνθάδε οἰκούντων τις δέχεταί τι τῶν σῶν. Ἄπελθε τοιγαροῦν, καὶ μὴ λυποῦ, ὁ [172b1] θεὸς γὰρ τὴν σὴν προσεδέξατο δ[ω]ρεὰν ἐὰν {ἐὰν} τὰ προσενεχθέντα διανε[ί]μῃς πτωχοῖς καὶ ἐνδεέσιν, εἰσὶ γὰρ παρὰ τὰς κώμας τῆς Αἰγύπτου πολλοὶ ἐπιδεεῖς ὀρφανοί τε καὶ χῆραι. Τούτων προμηθούμενος πλείονας παρὰ θεοῦ,[126] ἕξεις τὰς ἀμοιβάς."

Ὁ δὲ τοῖς τοῦ θείου[127] ῥήμασι πεισθεὶς ἐπανιὼν ὡς ἐδιδάχθη ἐποίησε πάντα πτωχοῖς καὶ πένησι διανείμας τὰ χρήματα καὶ οἷς ταῦτα εἰς χρείαν καθέστηκεν.[128]

Païsios Defeats the Devil and Enjoys Spiritual Communion

[129]16. [172a11] Ἐπανιόντι δὲ τῷ Παϊσίῳ εἰς τὸ ἄντρον[130] φαίνεται αὐτῷ ὁ διάβολος, "Ὦ βία," λέγων, "Παΐσιε, τί σοι δρᾶσαι οὐκ ἔχω τὰς ἐμὰς ἀποκρουσαμένῳ μηχανάς;[131] Ἄπειμι λοιπὸν ἐφ᾽ ἑτέρους βαδίζων εἰς πόλεμον. Ἐπὶ σὲ γὰρ οὐδαμῶς ἔρχομαι ἡττημένος γὰρ γέγονώς." Ὁ δὲ θεῖος ἀνὴρ ἐπιτιμήσας αὐτῷ, "Φιμώθητι," ἔφη, "ὁ τὴν πονηρίαν πολύς."

Ὁ δὲ κατῃσχυμμένος διωχθείς, οὐκέτι τούτῳ ἀναιδῶς[132] με προσπελάσαι ἐτόλμα. Αὐτὸς δὲ τῇ ἐσωτέρᾳ πρόσεισιν ἐρήμῳ, ἐκεῖσε τῷ σώματι μὲν οἰκῶν ἦν τῷ δὲ πνεύματι τοῖς οὐρανίοις καὶ τῷ τούτ[ω]ν [δεσπότῃ][133] συναυλιζόμενος τραχείαις τε ἑαυτὸν ἐδίδου διαγωγαῖς ταῖς τῶν ἀσωμάτων [173a1] ἐν μηδενὶ διαφερούσαις διαγωγῆς ἀμέλει[134] καὶ τῶν οὐρανίων γενέσθαι θεατὴν τὸν Παΐσιον θησαυρῶν καὶ τῆς ἐκεῖσε τῶν δικαίων ἀγαλλιάσεως <τὸ ἐνοικοῦν ἐν αὐτῷ θεῖον πνεῦμα εὐδόκησαν.>[135]

17. [172b4] Ἐν προσευχῇ γὰρ γενόμενος ὑπόπτερος πρὸς οὐρανοὺς ἐγεγόνει. Καὶ πρῶτον μὲν τὰ τοῦ παραδείσου τερπνὰ ἑώρα πλησθεὶς ἀγγαλιάσεως, ἔπειτα δὲ καὶ τὴν <τῶν>[136] πρωτοτόκων ἐν οὐρανοῖς ἐκκλησίαν θεασάμενος καὶ τροφῆς ἀΰλου μετασχὼν ἐκ τῆς ἄνω μυσταγωγίας, τοῦ τῆς ἀσιτίας καὶ ἐγκρατείας κατηξιώθη[137] χαρίσματος. Ἅπαξ γὰρ τῇ ἑ[β]δομάδι ἐν τῇ τῶν ἡμερῶν κυρίᾳ τῆς θείας κοινωνίας μεταλαμβάνων μέχρι τῆς ἐρχομέν[ης] ἄσιτος ἦν. Καὶ ταύτην μὲν οὕτως πρὸς τοῦ δημιουργοῦ τῆς φύσεως καταπλουτήσας διαμένουσαν εἶχε τὴν χάριν.

18. (17)[138] [172b18] Ἐμοὶ δὲ ἀπειστείτω μηδεὶς τῶν πειθαρχούντων τῷ θείῳ νόμῳ[139] μάρτυρα τοῦτον τῆς ἀληθείας ἔχοντι, πάντα γὰρ ὑποτέτακται τῷ θείῳ νεύματι. Ῥηθήσεται <δὲ>[140] τἀληθές· ὅτι μετὰ τὴν φρικτὴν μετάληψιν ἐπὶ ἑ[β]δομήκοντα ἡμέραις ἄσιτος διετέλει, καὶ θαυμαστὸν οὐδὲν τῆς θείας [173b1] δυνάμεως τὸ κράτος ἀνείκαστον ἐχούσης. Ἡ γὰρ μετάληψ{ε}ις τῶν σιτίων ἀναπλήρωσίς ἐστι τῶν τοῦ σώματος κενουμένων τῆς φυσικῆς δυνάμεως τούτων δεομένης τῆς τῶν σωμάτων ἕνεκεν αὐξήσεώς τε καὶ ἀλλοιώσεως, τοῖς δὲ ὑψηλοτέροις καὶ τῆς φύσεως ἀνωτέροις πάντ[ω]ς ἡ δημιουργικὴ δύναμις τὸ ὑπὲρ φύσιν καὶ δύναμιν δίδωσιν ἀνενδεῶς ἔχουσα καὶ νόμῳ φύσεως μὴ ὑποκειμένη.[141] Οἴδαμεν γὰρ[142] καὶ ἐν τῇ γῇ ἐπὶ τριακοσίοις ἔτεσιν[143] ἀτρόφους ἐν Ἐφέσῳ παῖδας φυλάξαι ζῶντας,[144] τὸν δὲ Ἠλίαν ἐν οὐρανοῖς μέχρ[ι] τῆς ἐσχάτης <ἡμέρας.>[145] Ἀλλὰ ταῦτα μὲν ἅλις.

Paΐsios' Pastoral Care

19 (18). [173a14] Τῷ δὲ θείῳ Παϊσίῳ πλήθ[η] ἀριθμ[ὸ]ν ὑπερβαίνοντα κατ᾽ εὐδοκίαν Θεοῦ συνέρρει τῶν τε κοσμικῶν καὶ μοναστῶν συμπαραμένειν αὐτῷ ἐφιεμένων. Οἵ γε περινοστήσαντες αὐτὸν[146] καθάπερ σμῆνος μελισσῶν περὶ τὰ κηρία τῆς γλυκύτητος τοῦ θείου μέλιτος <γλιχόμενοι>[147] ἦσαν ἀκόρεστοι. Ὁ δὲ ἐκ τῆς ἀενάου καὶ θείας π[η]γῆς [αἰ]σθητοῦ παντὸς μέλιτος καὶ κηρίου ἡδύτερον νᾶμα βρυούσης τούτους ποτίσας πλήρεις ἀνέδειξεν ἡδονῆς. Καὶ ταῖς ἐνθέοις ἐκείνου Σειρῆσι,[148] πολλοῦ πλήθους τῶν ἀποτασ[σ]ομένων [174a1] ἁλόντος καὶ τοῖς τε τοῦ βίου τερπνοῖς χαίρειν εἰπόντος καὶ τὸν ζυγὸν τοῦ Χριστοῦ εὐαγγελικῶς ἐπ᾽ [ὤ]μ[ω]ν λαβόντος, προσθήκη καθ᾽ ἑκάστην <ἡμέραν>[149] οὐ[150] βραχεῖα γίνεται.

Καὶ οἷς μὲν τῆς ἡσυχίας <ὁ>¹⁵¹ ἔρως ἐξήφθη κατὰ μόνας Θεῷ προσομιλεῖν ἐδίδασκε διὰ προσευχῆς οἷς δὲ φίλον¹⁵² ἦν ἡ μακάρια διαγωγὴ¹⁵³ τῆς ὑποταγῆς συνᾴδειν ἑτέροις καὶ συμπαραμένειν ἔταξε τῇ ἀδελφότητι. Τισὶ δὲ καὶ ἐργόχειρον διωρίσατο, τοῦτο τὸ μὲν ἵνα μὴ ἀγύμναστοι πρὸς ἀρετὰς¹⁵⁴ ὦσι καὶ ἄνετοι, τοῦτο δὲ <ἵνα>¹⁵⁵ καὶ ἐκ τῶν οἰκείων ἰδρώτων οὐ μόνον τὸν <ἑαυτῶν>¹⁵⁶ ἄρτον ἐσθίωσιν ἀλλὰ <ἵνα>¹⁵⁷ καὶ φιλοστοργίαν περὶ τοὺς πένητας ὑποδεικνύωσι. Τὸ δὲ κ[ε]φάλαιον ἐκείνων¹⁵⁸ νενόμιστο τὸ μή τινι πράτ[τ]εσθαι τῶν ἁπάντων τῶν οὐδὲν τῶν ὅσα ἰδίῳ θελήματι γίνεσθαι δοκούντων¹⁵⁹ ἀλλὰ βουλῇ πατρικῇ καὶ γνώμῃ πάντα διαπράττεσθαι.¹⁶⁰

Καὶ ταῦτα μὲν τῆς ἐκείνου διδασκαλίας καὶ τῆς τῶν πλησίων¹⁶¹ ἐπιμελείας. Τὰ δὲ τῆς ἡσυχίας καὶ ἀναχωρ[ή]σεως, ἀκριβῶς οὐδεὶς λόγος ἐπεξελθεῖν ἐξισχύσειεν, ἐκ δὲ τῶν πολ[λ]ῶν ὀλίγα τινὰ καθ' ἑξῆς ῥηθήσεται.

20 (19). [173a24] Ἐγένετό ποτε τὸν θεῖον Παΐσιον ἐν τῇ ἐσωτέρᾳ ἐρήμῳ εἰσιέναι, καὶ [174b1] ἄντρον εὑρόντα [τρεῖς χρόνους]¹⁶² ἐν τούτ[ῳ] κατοικεῖν. Λίαν δὲ τὰς τρίχας τῆς κ[ε]φαλῆς ἐκταθείσας, πασ[σ]άλῳ τινὶ ἐν τῷ ἀνωτέρῳ μέρει τοῦ ἄντρου πεπ[η]γμένῳ, ταύτας μηχανᾶσθαι δεδεμένας, τὰς εὐχὰς ἀνυστ{ερ}ικώτερον ποιοῦντα. [Καὶ ἦν]¹⁶³ νύκτωρ καὶ μεθ' ἡμέραν ἐκεῖσε εἰς πολλοὺς ἀγῶνας καὶ κόπους ἑαυτὸν διαμερίζων, ὑπὸ τῆς ἀγάπης τοῦ Χριστοῦ θερμαινόμενος καὶ ἀνάπαυσιν τῶν πόνων λογιζόμενος. Ἀμέλει καὶ ὁ Σωτὴρ κατὰ τὸ λεχθὲν ἐν τοῖς ἱεροῖς εὐ[α]γγελίοις ἐμφανῆ ἑαυτὸν τούτῳ καθίστησιν.

21. (20) [174a18] Ἐν προσευχῇ γὰρ τῷ Παϊσίῳ ὄντι τὸ πάντων ποθ[ει]ν[ό]τερον αὐτῷ φαίνεται ὁ Σωτήρ. Καὶ ὃς μὴ φέρων τὴν μορφὴν ἐκείνου θεάσασθαι ἐν τῷ [175a1] ἐδάφ[ει], πεσὼν δέει καὶ φόβῳ συνείχετο. Εἶτα ὁ Σωτὴρ χεῖρα τούτῳ ἐπεκτείνας—<ὦ>¹⁶⁴ τῆς ἀφάτου σοῦ, Χριστὲ Βασιλεῦ, περὶ τοὺς σοὺς θεράποντας στοργῆς—κρατήσας ἤγειρεν, "Εἰρήνη σοι," ἐπ[ε]ιπών, "τῷ ἐμῷ θεράποντι. Μὴ φόβῳ περιληφθῇς, μηδὲ εἰς τὴν σ[ὴ]ν <δέος>¹⁶⁵ ἐπ[ε]ισίῃ καρδίαν. Τοιαύτοις¹⁶⁶ γὰρ ἔργοις σφόδρα ἥδεταί μου ἡ ἀγαθότης καὶ λίαν παρ' ἐμοὶ εὐπρόσδεκτός σου ἡ εὐχή.¹⁶⁷ Εὐφραίνου λ[ο]ιπὸν καὶ ὑπόδεξαι τὴν ὑπὲρ τούτου λαμπροτάτην ἀμοιβήν. Ἰδού σοι δίδωμ{ο}ι χάρισμα τοιοῦτον,¹⁶⁸ ἵν' ὅ τι ἂν αἰτήσῃ ἐν τῷ ὀνόματί μου δοθήσεταί σοι. Οὐ μὴν ἀλλὰ καὶ περὶ ὧν δε[ή{θη}ῃ]ῃ ἁμαρτιῶν ἀφεθήσεται τοῖς ἁμαρτάνουσιν."

Ὁ δὲ ἱερὸς Παΐσιος, "Τοιαύτης," ἔφη, "Φιλάνθρωπ[ε]¹⁶⁹ Χριστὲ καὶ θεέ, παρὰ τῆς σῆς ἀγαθότητος ἀξιωθεὶς [χάριτος] ὁ τάλας¹⁷⁰ ἐγὼ δέομαι τό γε νῦν ἔχον ἃ δεῖ μ[οι] [αἰ]τεῖν καὶ ὧν <ἡ> χρεία ἀναγκαία, εὐμαρῶς τε τὰς σωτηριώδεις τρίβους διανύσαι παρασχεθῆναί μοι καὶ τέλους ἐπιτυχεῖν ἀγαθοῦ, ἄνευ γὰρ τῆς σῆς προνοίας οὐδέν τι τῶν καλῶν ἡμῖν πράττεσθαι δυνατόν. Εἰ γὰρ τὸ αἷμά σου τὸ τίμιον ὑπὲρ ἡμῶν ἐξέχεας καὶ ταφὴν καὶ θάνατον κατεδέξω, τὴν σωτηρίαν ἡμῖν διὰ τῆς ἀναστάσεώς σου χαρισάμενος. [175b1] Πόσους πόνους καὶ θανάτους ἆρα γε <ἡμῖν>[171] ὑπὲρ σοῦ ὑπομεῖναι χρεών ἐστι;"

Ταῦτα οὕτως εἰπόντα τὸν Παΐσιον, ὁ Σωτὴρ εὐλογ[ή]σας εἰς οὐρανοὺς ἀνῆλθεν. Ἀποδείξεις δὲ τῶν εἰρημένων ἔστ[ω][172] ἐκ τῶν ἐφ' ἑξῆς λεχθησομένων.

Païsios Intercedes with God on Behalf of Another's Disciple
Περὶ τοῦ τελευτήσαντος μαθητοῦ γέροντος[173]
22 (21). [175a7]
Συνέβη τοίνυν τινὸς τῶν γερόντων τελευτῆσαι μαθητήν. Ὃς τῇ πλάνῃ κατασχεθεὶς τοῦ ἀεὶ βασκαίνοντος τοῖς ἀνθρώποις,[174] ἀπειθείᾳ καὶ παρακοῇ τὸν βίον ἀπέλιπε καὶ τὸ δὴ χαλεπώτερον ὅτι καὶ πτώματι πρὸ τοῦ θανάτου κατενεχθεὶς ἀμετανόητον πέρας τοῦ βίου. Διέβη περὶ τούτου οὖν πολλάκις γνῶναι δεηθέντα τὸν γέροντα ποῦ τοῦ ῥᾳθύμου κατέληξεν. Ἡ ψυχὴ ἐν τῷ ᾅδῃ συνέβη ταύτην ἰδεῖν[175] χαλεπαῖς βασάνοις τιμωρουμένη. Ὅθεν περὶ τοῦ μαθητοῦ σφοδρῶς τὴν καρδίαν πληγεὶς δάκρυσιν οὐκ ἔλιπε καθικετεύων, προσθεὶς δὲ καὶ νηστείαν ἐπὶ νηστεί[ᾳ] μέχρι τεσ[σ]αράκοντα ἡμερῶν ἄσιτος ἦν. Ἐπ[ε]ιτα φωνὴ ἤκουστο λέγουσα, "Ταύτην δὴ τὴν ψυχὴν περὶ ἧς θερμῶς καθικετεύεις[176] ἐν τῷ ᾅδῃ δεῖ[177] εἶναι ἄχρι τῆς ἐμῆς ἐλεύσεως ἐπὶ νεφελῶν μετὰ ἀγγέλων καὶ σαλπίγγων καὶ τότε λήψεται μισθὸν ἐπάξιον τῆς οἰκείας [176a1] ἐργασίας."[178]

23 (22). [175b1] Ταύτης οὖν ἀκούσας ὁ πρεσβύτερος[179] τῆς ἀποφάσεως λύπης καὶ κατηφείας μεστὸς γενόμενος ἑτέρας, πρὸς ταῖς προλαβούσαις προσέθηκε τεσσαράκοντα ἡμέρας νηστεύων καὶ ἐπὶ πλε[ῖ]ον τῇ δεήσει ἑαυτὸν κατατρύχων, ἀλλ' οὐδὲν πλε[ῖ]ον τῆς πρώτης ἀποφάσεως ἤκουσε. Πάλιν γὰρ ὡς: "Οὔπω ἐκείνῳ ἔσται ἄνεσις," ἤκουσεν,[180] "ἀλλ' ἐν τῷ ᾅδῃ μενέτω ἕως ἂν ἐπὶ νεφελῶν γέν{ν}ηταί μου ἡ ἔλευσις."

Ἐπ[ε]ὶ δὲ τὸ πείθειν οὐκ εἶχε τὰ σπλά[γ]χνα τὰ θεϊκὰ μηδὲν ἀκοῦσαι πλεῖ[ο]ν[181] οὗ ἤκουσε δυνηθείς—[182] προνοίας γὰρ ἴσως θεϊκῆς τῷ Παϊσίῳ[183] τ[ὸ] ἐγχείρημα τῆς ἐκείνου λυτρώσεως[184] ταμιευσαμένης— πρὸς τὸν Παΐσιον[185] ἐν τῇ ἐσωτέρᾳ ἐπείγεται ἐρήμῳ. Οὐκ ἄγνωστος γὰρ ἦν αὐτῷ ἡ πρὸς Θεὸν ἐκείνου παρρησία. Διὸ καὶ <ἐπ'>[186] αὐτῷ μόνῳ τὰς ἐλπίδας ἐσάλευε, πιστεύσας ἐπὶ τοῦ οἰκείου μαθητοῦ τὸν Θεὸν ἐξιλεώσασθαι δυναμένῳ.

24 (23). [175b20] Ὁ δὲ Παΐσιος ἐγνωκὼς διὰ τῆς χάριτος τὴν τοῦ γέροντος ἄφιξιν, συναντᾷ[187] τούτῳ πρὸς αὐτὸν ἐρχομένῳ καὶ περιπτυξάμενοι τὸν προσήκοντα ἀσπασμὸν θάτερος θατέρῳ ἀφωσιώσαντο. Εἶτα τῷ Παϊσίῳ εἰρηκότι, "Τίνος ἕνεκεν [176a1] πρὸς ἐμὲ τὸν εὐτελῆ καὶ ἁμαρτωλὸν ἐλήλυθας ταλ[αι]πωρῶν οὕτως, ὦ πάτερ;"

Ἀπεκρίνατο ὁ πρεσβύτης τὴν αἰτίαν διηγούμενος καὶ τὴν συμφορὰν τοῦ ἀπεγνωσμένου μαθητοῦ, ὅσα τε δ[υ]σωπήσας οὐδὲν διήνυσε καὶ ὅσα [ἠ]κηκόη παρὰ τῆς θείας φωνῆς ἐκεῖνον ἀποφαινομένης ἐν τῷ ᾅδῃ ὑποστῆναι μέχρι τῆς ἐλεύσεως τοῦ Κυρίου λυπηρά. Προσθεὶς δὲ καὶ ὅτι, "Δυσωπήσων τὴν σ[ὴ]ν ὁσιότητα ἀφικόμην ἵν᾽ ἐμοὶ τῷ ταλαιπώρῳ συμπάσχων ταῖς <σαῖς>[188] πρὸς <τὸν> θεὸν ἱκεσίαις σου[189] ἱκέτης γένῃ ὑπὲρ τοῦ ἐμοῦ ἀθλίου μαθητοῦ, πέπεισμαι γὰρ ὅτι ὑπὸ σοῦ δυσωπούμενος παρακληθήσεται ὁ Θεός. Δεήθητι, οὖν, μὴ ἀναβαλλόμενος μηδὲ τῇ λύπῃ με πολιορκεῖσθαι ἐάσῃς—εἰ δ᾽ οὖν ἀλλὰ τῶν τῇδε ὑποχωρῆσαι ἀδύνατον τῇ ἐμῇ ταπεινότητι."

25 (24). [176b19] Ταῦτα οὕτως ὁ ἀγαθὸς[190] πρεσβύτης ἐπεξιὼν δάκρυσι{ν} μᾶλλον ἢ ῥήμασι{ν}, πείθει τὸν μέγαν Παΐσιον ἱλεώσασθαι τοὺς οἰκτιρμοὺς τοῦ θεοῦ.

Καὶ ὅς, "Ἐμοὶ μὲν οὖν οὐκ ἐξόν," ἔφη, "ὦ ἱερὰ κ[ε]φαλὴ, τοιούτου ἐγχειρήματος ἐφάπτεσθαι. Σὸν γάρ ἐστι τοῦτο καὶ [177a1] τῆς σῆς μεγαλονοίας κα[ί]περ[191] ἀπαν[αί]ν[ε]ται ὁ Θεὸς νῦν, ὡς [οἶδε][192] μόνος αὐτὸς πολλὴν ἄβυσσον ἔχων τῶν κριμάτων, ὅμως <δ᾽ οὖν>[193] ἵνα μὴ γένωμαι τῷ σῷ κελεύσματι ἀντιταττόμενος, ἰδοὺ τῇ ἱκετείᾳ σὺν σοὶ ἐμαυτὸν δίδωμι τῷ Θεῷ δὲ ὃ δέδοκτ[αι][194] γίνηται. Ἀλλὰ σὺ μὲν ὧδε προσκα[ρ]τερῶν ἔσο, ἐγὼ δὲ ἐν τῇ ἐνδοτέρᾳ γίνομαι ἐρήμῳ[195] καὶ τὸν Θεὸν ἐκτενῶς ἀμφότεροι ἐκδυσωπήσομεν."[196]

Ταῦτα εἰπὼν πρὸς τὰ ἐνδότερα τῆς αὐτῆς ἐρήμου, ἀπῄει καὶ στὰς εἰς προσευχὴν καὶ χεῖρας ἅμα καὶ φρένας εἰς οὐρανὸν, ἀναπετάσας τ[ῷ] ἁπάντων δημιουργ[ῷ], "Ἔπιδε ἐπὶ τὰς δεήσεις ἡμῶν," ἔφη, "τῶν ἀναξίων δούλων σου[197] καὶ παράσχου, ὡς ἀγαθὸς, ἐκ τῶν δεσμῶν τοῦ ᾅδου ἐλευθερωθ[ῆ]ναι τὴν ψυχὴν τοῦ μαθητοῦ[198] τοῦ γέροντος."

26 (25). [176b18] Ταῦτα εἰπὼν καὶ τὰ τοιούτοις ὅμοια πρὸς τὸν φιλάνθρωπον θεὸν εὐχόμενος, οὐκ ἔμελλε τῆς ἀψευδοῦς ἀποτυχεῖν ὑποσχέσεως ἀλλ᾽ εὐθὺς ὁ πᾶσι παρὼν καὶ σωματικοῖς ἀπρόσ{σ}ιτος ὀφθαλμοῖς ἑαυτὸν τῷ Παϊσίῳ ἐμφανῆ καθίστησι καὶ "Τί, [ὦ] θεράπων μου Παΐσιος, ἐκτενῶς αἰτεῖται;" ἐπηρώτα.

27 (26). [176b25] Ὁ [177b1] δὲ, "Ὁ μόνος τὰ πάντα," ἔφη, "ἐπιστάμενος συμπαθὴς Θεός, ἐλέησον τὸν τῆς ὑπακοῆς ἀλογήσαντα καὶ ἔργοις ἀτόποις ἐμπεσόντα καὶ ταῖς τῆς γεέννης παραμένοντα τιμωρίαις, υἱοί, τὸν τοῦ γέροντος ταλαίπωρον μαθητήν. Μὴ οὖν τοὺς πόνους τοῦ σοῦ θεράποντος ἀπράκτους ὀφθῆναι σοι θελήσῃς μηδὲ ὑπὸ τῶν οἰκτιρμῶν σου παροφθῆναι ἐάσῃς ἡμᾶς."[199]

"Ἀλλ᾽ ἐγώ γε," φησὶ{ν} πρὸς αὐτὸν ὁ Σωτήρ, "Προιέμενος ἀπόφασιν ἀψευδῆ τῶν τῆς παρακοῆς καὶ ἀτόπου ἔργου ἀπολαύειν ἀμ[οι]βῶν[200] ἔταξα καὶ ἄνεσιν οὐκ ἀνίημι τοῦτο τῶν ὀδυνῶν[201] ἄχρι τῆς ἐμῆς ἐπὶ νεφελῶν ἐλεύσεως."

28 (27). [177a14] Ὁ δὲ ἐκλεκτὸς τοῦ Κυρίου, Παΐσιος, ἀποκριθεὶς ἱκετικῶς πρὸς αὐτὸν εἶπε, "Καὶ τί, δέσποτα τῶν ἁπάντων, τῇ σῇ θείᾳ οὐχ ὑποτάσσεται κελεύσει καὶ ὑπείκει κἂν ἐθελήσ[ε]ιας; Ῥᾷον γάρ σοι, τῷ δεσπόζοντι τῶν αἰώνων, καὶ ἐκ <τῶν> μὴ ὄντων <εἰς τὸ εἶναι>²⁰² τὰ πάντα παραγαγόντι, καὶ νῦν τὸν αὐτὸν ἐκείνης τῆς ἐλεύσεώς σου ἐλθεῖν τρόπον."

29 (28). [177b22] Ταῦτα εἰπόντος, ἀφανὴς <αὐτῷ>²⁰³ γενόμενος ὁ Σωτὴρ εἰς <τὸν>²⁰⁴ οὐρανὸν ἄνεισιν. Εἶτα μετὰ δόξης φρικτῆς, ἀγγέλων τε καὶ ἀρχαγγέλων καὶ σαλπίγγων, ἅμα δὲ καὶ δικαί[ων] χ[ο]ρῶν [178a1] καὶ ὅσα τῇ ἐσχάτῃ ἡμέρᾳ, διώρισται ἐκ τῶν οὐρανῶν ἐπὶ νεφελῶν κάτεισιν. Ἐπ[ε]ιτα καὶ θρόνοι τίθενται, καὶ καθέδρα φοβερὰ [δείκνυται]²⁰⁵ καὶ ἡ ψυχὴ τοῦ τεθνηκότος, ἐκ τοῦ ᾅδου ἀνακληθ[εῖ]σα, χερσὶ τοῦ Παϊσίου δίδοται. Εἶτα τῷ γέροντι μεταδίδοται,²⁰⁶ καὶ γὰρ ἐν τῷ οἰκείῳ ἦν τόπῳ αὐτ[ί]κα²⁰⁷ προσευχόμενος καὶ ἐναγώνιος,²⁰⁸ καθὼς ἀμφοτέροις νενόμιστ[αι] ὑπὸ τῆς συμβουλῆς.

Καὶ²⁰⁹ φωνῆς²¹⁰ ἄνωθεν ἐνεχθ[εί]σης, "Ἀπόλαβε," διακελευομένης, "τὴν τοῦ μαθητοῦ σου ψυχὴν διὰ τῶν χειρῶν τοῦ ἐμοῦ θεράποντος Παϊσίου," ἀκήκοεν, "ἐκ τῶν τοῦ ᾅδου βυθῶν ἀναδυθεῖσαν. Οὐκ ἔστι σοι ταύτην ἐν βασ{σ}άνοις ἀλλ' ἐν ἀναπαύσει ἔστιν ὁρᾶν."²¹¹

Εἶτα ἐρχομένην τὴν τοῦ μαθητοῦ ψυχὴν εὐθὺς παρεστάναι τῷ γέροντι καὶ εἰπεῖν ὁμολογοῦσαν ὅτι, "Πολλὰ ὑπέστην τῶν τῆς γεέννης [ὀ]δυνῶν²¹² τῆς παρακοῆς ἕνεκα, ἐπεὶ καὶ αὐτὴ ἐκείν[ης]²¹³ τῆς πτώσεως [αἴτιος]²¹⁴ γέγ[ο]νεν καὶ δι' αὐτῆ[ς] παρεχωρήθη τὰ δ[ει]νὰ ὑποστῆναι.²¹⁵ Ἀλλὰ διὰ τῶν σῶν καὶ τοῦ θείου Παϊσίου ἱκεσιῶν, συμπαθής²¹⁶ μοι φανεὶς ὁ φιλάνθρωπος²¹⁷ θεὸς ἐκ τῶν τοῦ ᾅδου δεσμῶν ἠλευθέρωσε²¹⁸ <με.>²¹⁹ Καὶ ἰδού, μετὰ τῶν [178b1] πραέων μετατίθεμαι." Ταῦτα φθεγξάμενος, ἐν ὄψει τοῦ γέροντος ἐν τῇ χώρᾳ τῶν δικαίων μετατ[ί]θεται ὁ μαθητής.

30 (29). [178a3] Καὶ ταῦτα μὲν τὰ [ὁ]ραθέντα τῷ γέροντι ἐν καιρῷ <τῆς> προσευχῆς. Ἐπεὶ δὲ καὶ πληροφ[ο]ρούμενος ἦν καὶ διστάζων οὐκέτι <περὶ>²²⁰ τῆς τοῦ μαθητοῦ σωτηρίας, αὐτ[ί]κα ὡς εἶχ[ε] τάχους ἀπῄει πρὸς τὸν μέγαν Παΐσιον καὶ εὗρεν²²¹ αὐτὸν εὐχαριστ[η]ρίους²²² ὕμνους ἀποδιδόντα ἕνεκα τῆς τοῦ τεθνηκότος σωτηρίας. Εἶτα πάντα²²³ διεξῄει τὰ τῆς ὀπτασίας ὁ γέρων κἀκεῖνος τὴν φρικτὴν τοῦ Κυρίου παρουσίαν καὶ πάντα <τὰ> [ὁ]ραθέντα καὶ πραχθέντα²²⁴ διηγεῖτο. Καὶ ὁμοῦ ἀμφότεροι τὰς εὐχαριστ{ε}ίας τῷ θεῷ ὁμολογοῦν τῷ²²⁵ ποιοῦντι θαυμάσια²²⁶ μόνῳ.

31 (30). [178a16] Ἔπ[ε]ιτα ὁ γέρων τῷ Παϊσίῳ, "Μεγάλην σοι," φησί, "χάριν ὁμολογῶ, θεῖε Παΐσιε, ὅτι διὰ τῶν σῶν εὐχῶν οὐ μόνον τὸν ἐμὸν ἀπεγνωσμένον μαθητὴν ἔσωσας,²²⁷ ἀλλὰ καὶ τὴν ἐμὴν διέσωσας ψυχὴν δεινῶς τῇ ἀθυμίᾳ κινδυνεύουσαν. Πλὴν δ[έ]ομαί σου

τῆς μεγαλονοίας, τίς ἡ θαυμαστὴ πρᾶξ{ε}ις καὶ τίνες οἱ ἀγῶνες δι᾽ ὧν τοιούτων ἠξιώθης τῶν χαρισμάτων; Ταῦτα ἐγώ γε γνῶναι ἐβουλόμην."

Καὶ πρὸς αὐτὸν ὁ μέγας ἀνὴρ φησὶ [179a1] Παΐσιος,[228] "Σύγγνωθι, τίμιε πάτερ, οὐδέν τι χάριτος[229] ἄξιον τῇ ἐμῇ εὑρίσκεται μετριότητι, ἀλ[λ]᾽ οὖν ἡ θεία πρόνοια, τοιαῦτα οἰκονομοῦσα τῆς ἐκ ψυχῆς δεομένοις βοηθείας,[230] οὐκ[231] ἔμελλε{ν} τὰς δεήσεις παρορᾶν οὐδὲ τ[ὸ] πολὺ φίλτρον ὅπερ ἐνεδείξω ὑπὲρ τοῦ παρηκόου μαθητοῦ. Ἔργῳ μ[ι]μούμενος δι᾽ ὑπερβολὴν ἀγάπης τὸν φιλάνθρωπον θεὸν ὡς ὑπὲρ ἡμῶν <τῶν>[232] ἐξοστρακισθέντων διὰ τὴν παρακοὴν καὶ ἐχθρῶν γεγονότων τῇ πλάνῃ τοῦ πονηροῦ. Κατενεχθεὶς καὶ τραφεὶς[233] καὶ παθὼν καὶ τῷ οἰκείῳ πάθει ἐλευθερώσας ἡμᾶς. Μεῖζ[ο]ν τῶν πάντων οὐδὲν εἶναι τῆς εἰλικρινοῦς ἀγάπης ἐθέσπισεν, [ἧ]ς ἕνεκα ὑπὲρ ἄλλου προθύμως τὴν ψυχὴν τέθεικας.[234] Αὕτη γὰρ γέγονεν αἴτι[ος] τῆς τοῦ μαθητοῦ σου, ὡς εἴρηται σωτηρίας. Ἄλλως δέ, οὐκ ἔστιν εἰπεῖν περὶ [τούτου].[235] Ἢ ὅτι ἀνὴρ ἁμαρτωλὸς πέφυκα μηδὲν ἐμαυτῷ συν[ει]δὼς[236] ἀναξίῳ ὄντι τῶν τοῦ Θεοῦ χαρισμάτων. Δεῦρο, οὖν, ὦ ἱερωτάτη ψυχή, συγγνώμην παρασχόμενος ἐκείνῳ μόνῳ δῶμεν εὐχαριστ{ε}ίαν καὶ αἶνον τῷ συμπαθεῖ καὶ φιλανθρώπῳ Θεῷ."[237]

Ταῦτα πρὸς ἐκεῖνον ταπεινόφρονως, διαλεγόμενος συνανύμν[η]σεν αὐτῷ τὸν πάροχον πά[ντ]ων τῶν δωρεῶν[238] Θεόν. Εἶτα [179b1] ἀλλήλων ὑπερευχόμενοι καὶ συνταξάμενοι ἀλλήλοις, ἐπὶ τὸ ἴδιον κατάλυμα ἕκαστος ἐπαν[ῄει].[239]

The Savior Tells Païsios to Strengthen and Teach the Brothers

32 (31). [179a3] Ὁ δὲ πατὴρ ἡμῶν Παΐσιος ἀεὶ σπουδάζων ἦν[240] ἀποστολικῶς, τῶν ὄπισθεν ἐπι[λ]ανθ[αν]όμενος καὶ τοῖς ἔμπροσθεν ἐπεκτεινόμενος, καὶ ἄλλοις τραχυτέροις ἑαυτὸν ἐκδιδοὺς ἀγῶσι. Τὴν ἄνυδρον γὰρ περι[ῄει][241] ἔρημον, τοὺς ἀνθρώπους λαθεῖν ἐπ[ε]ιγόμενος, ἵν᾽ ἐν τούτῳ ἅμα μὲν τὰ χρηστὰ ἐν τῷ κρυπτῷ πάντα δράσ[ειεν],[242] ἅμα δὲ τ[ῶ]ν τῆς ἡσυχίας καρπῶν ἀπαρενοχλήτως κατατρυφήσειεν. Καὶ οὗτος μὲν οὕτως.

33 (32). [179a12] Ὁ δὲ Θεός, ἐπεὶ τὸν Παΐσιον οὐ μόνον[243] ἀλλὰ καὶ ἑτέρους δι᾽ αὐτοῦ σωθῆναι βούλεται, οὐκ ᾤετο δεῖν τὸν λύχνον καταμόνας διαλάμποντα ἀφιέναι καὶ ἄλλους τ[ῶ]ν τούτου λαμπηδ[ό]νων δευμένους στερεῖσθαι.[244] Διὸ καὶ ἐκεῖθεν ἐξ[ι]έναι τὸν Παΐσιον πρὸς τὴν ἔξω ἔρημον κελεύει εἰς τοὺς ἐκεῖσε ἀδελφοὺς στηρίξαι καὶ διδάξαι καὶ μ[ι]μητὰς ποιῆσαι τῇ διδασκαλ[ί]ᾳ καὶ ἐραστὰς τῆς ἱερᾶς καὶ ἰσαγγέλου πολιτείας.[245] Καὶ ὅς, "Ὦ κύριε," φησί, "Τί μοι κέρδος τὰς ἐνταῦθα καταλ[ι]πόντι[246] διατριβάς, ἐν αἷς λίαν ἡδέως τῆς σῆς ἀπελαυσάμην ἐπισκοπῆς, καὶ ἄλλων εἰς ἐπίσκεψιν ἀπιόντι ὧν οὔπω γέγ[ο]να ἱκανὸς τῆς ἐπιστασίας; Δέδοικα γάρ, δέσποτα, μὴ {τῷ} τῇ ἐκείνων <ὁ τάλας>[247]

σχολῇ τὰ σὰ [180a1] προστάγματα πράττειν ὡς εἰκὸς μὴ δύνασθαι,²⁴⁸ ἔσομαι τῇ ἀμελείᾳ κατάκριτος ὁ ταλ[αί]πωρος."²⁴⁹

34. [179b3]²⁵⁰ Ταῦτα εἰπόντι, καὶ τὴν ἐκεῖσε ἄφιξιν συγχωρηθῆναι αἰτουμένῳ, "Οὐ μὲν οὖν," ἔφη ὁ Σωτὴρ, "Ὁ σὸς πόνος ὑπὲρ τῶν ἄλλων γενόμενος [ἴ]σο[ς] λογισθήσεται²⁵¹ <τούτων,>²⁵² ἀλλὰ διπλασίους καὶ πολυπλασίους ἐν τῇ ἄνω πόλει Ἰερουσαλὴμ ἀπολήψεται τὰς ἀντιδόσεις λαμπρᾶς ἡ σὴ ψυχή.²⁵³ Ἕνεκα τῶν σωζομένων διὰ τῆς σῆς διδασκαλίας."

Καὶ ταῦτα μὲν ὁ Σωτὴρ εἰρηκὼς, ἀφαν[ὴ]ς ἦν τοῖς ἐκείνου ὀφθαλμοῖς τὸ δὲ πέρας τῆς θείας διατάξεως τὸν Παΐσιον²⁵⁴ εἶχε παρὰ τὴν ἔρημον τὴν αὐτῷ δεδ[ε]ιγμένην. Ἐν αὐτῇ δὲ γενομέν[ῳ],²⁵⁵ οὐκ ἔλαθε τοὺς ἐραστὰς τῶν ἐκείνου καλῶν ἡ αὐτοῦ παρουσία, πλῆθος γὰρ αὐτῷ συνέρρε[ον], τῶν διψ[ώ]ντων ἐκείνου τὴν ἀρετὴν, π[η]γὴ γὰρ ἦν ἀέννοος πᾶσι νάμ[ατα]²⁵⁶ ἀθανασίας παρεχομένη. Κἀμὲ δὴ πόθος εἶχε τῆς ἐκείνου θέας, ὡς ἱκανὸν καὶ ἀπὸ μόνης γε μετασχεῖν χάριτος.

Emperor Constantine Appears to Païsios
Περὶ ὀπτασίας τοῦ ἁγίου Κωνσταντίνου²⁵⁷

35. [180a20] Καὶ ποτε τούτῳ παραβαλὼν, πρὸ τοῦ τῆς θύρας ἐπιβῆναι τοῦ οἰκιδίου αὐτοῦ, ἑτέρῳ ἀνδρὶ συνομιλοῦντος ἠκηκόειν. Εἶτα εὐλαβομένου μου τὴν ἐπιβάσιν²⁵⁸ ἔξω τε ἑστηκότος καὶ βοὴν πραεῖαν τοῦτον εἰς θέαν προσκαλουμένην ποιοῦντος, ἔξεισι τοῦ κελ[λ]ίου [180b1] ὁ τίμιος πατὴρ καὶ θεασάμενός με περιχυθεὶς ἀσμέν[ω]ς ἠσπάζετο. Κἀγὼ τὰ προσήκοντα ἐποίουν, ἔπ[ε]ιτα [συνεισελθὼν]²⁵⁹ ἐν τῷ καταγωγίῳ καὶ μηδένα ἕτερον ἑωρακὼς ἔνδον τίς ἂν καὶ εἴη ὁ πρὸ μικροῦ συλλαλῶν τῷ πατρὶ διηπόρουν ἐν τῷ ἐμῷ λογισμῷ, ἔνθεν κἀκεῖθεν ἐπισκεπτόμενος²⁶⁰ καὶ περιεργαζόμενος. Ὁ δὲ, "Τίνος ἕνεκεν τ[ῇ]δε²⁶¹ κἀκεῖσε περιεργάζῃ, ὥσπερ τι ξένον θεώμενος καὶ διανοούμενος;"

Κἀγὼ, "Καὶ ξένον ὄντως," ἀντέφησα, "καὶ παράδοξον πρᾶγμα λογίζ[ο]μαι, καὶ ἐκ τῆς ἀπορίας οὐκ ἔχω τί ἂν καὶ γένωμαι. Ἀρτίως γάρ μοι ἐληλυθότι ἑτέρου ἀνδρὸς ἤκουσταί μοι <ἡ> φωνὴ συνομιλοῦντός σοι καὶ συλλαλοῦντος, καὶ νῦν μοι οὔπω τις ἐν ὄψει ὁρᾶται. Τί δὴ πότε ἐστίν, ἀγνοῶ.²⁶² Δ[έ]ομαι οὖν γνῶναι παρὰ τῆς σῆς ὁσιότητος τοῦτο τὸ παράδοξον μυστήριον."

36. [180a22] Ὑπολαβὼν δὲ ὁ θεῖος ἀνὴρ,²⁶³ "Ὦ Ἰωάννη," ἔφη, "μυστήριον θεῖον καὶ παράδοξον ὁ Θεός σοι ἀποκαλύψαι βούλεται σήμερον,²⁶⁴ κἀμοὶ [προσ]ῆκόν ἐστιν ἐκεῖνό σοι ἐξ[ει]πεῖν ὅ περὶ ἡμᾶς ἔχ[ει] αὐτοῦ ἡ χρηστότης²⁶⁵ ἐφετόν.²⁶⁶ Αὐτὸς, φίλων ἄριστε, ὅν μοι συλλαλοῦντα [ἠ]κηκόεις, ἐκεῖνός ἐστιν ὁ μέγας τῶν χριστωνύμων ἄναξ Κωνσταντῖνος. Καὶ νῦν γὰρ πρός με οὐρανόθεν παρεγένετο

[181a1] καὶ συνομιλῶν μοι ἔφη, 'Μακάριοί ἐστε οἱ τῆς μοναχικῆς ἀξιωθέντες πολιτείας, ὄντ[ω]ς γὰρ [ὑ]μῖν ἐστιν οἰκ[εῖ]ος ὁ ἔνθεος τοῦ Σωτῆρος μακαρισμός.'
"Εἶτα καί, 'Τίς εἶ σ[ὺ], κύριε ἐμοῦ, ὁ ταῦτα λαλῶν καὶ μεγάλως ἡμᾶς μακαρίζων;'
"Εἰπόντι ἀντεφθέγξατό μοι, ' Εγὼ εἰμι,' εἰπὼν, 'ὁ μέγας Κωνσταντῖνος ὁ οὐρανόθεν ἀφ[ι]κόμενος καὶ τὴν δόξαν σοι ἐπαγγέλλομαι καὶ τὴν οἰκειοτάτην παρρησίαν ἣν ἔχουσιν οἱ τὸν ζυγὸν ἀράμενοι τοῦ Χριστοῦ ἐν οὐρανοῖς. Καὶ σοὶ μὲν οὖν τ[ῷ] διεγείροντι τοὺς ἐραστὰς ταύτης τῆς ἱερᾶς διαγωγῆς εὐαγγελίζομαι τὸν θεῖον μακαρισμόν. Ἐμαυτῷ δὲ, ὡς <τις>[267] μετάμελος, μέμφομαι τοιαύτης μεγίστης ἀποτυχόντι[268] τάξεως. Ὢ τῆς ζημίας ἧς οὐκ ἀνέχομαι <μνήμης>!'[269]

" Εμοῦ δὲ πάλιν εἰρηκότος, 'Καὶ τίνος ἕνεκεν, ὦ θαυμάσιε, σεαυτὸν καταγινώσκ[εις];'[270] "Ἄρα δ[ὴ] ἄμοιρος εἶ τῆς ἀειδίου δόξης ἐκείνης καὶ τῆς θείας ἐλλάμψεως;'

"' Ο δὲ, 'Οὐχί,' ἔφη, 'ἀλλ᾽ ἐπίσης τοῖς μοναχοῖς ἥκιστα τετύχηκα ἄνωθεν παρρησίας, οὐδαμῶς γὰρ ἐκείνοις ἐξισοῦμαι περὶ τὴν τιμήν. 37. [180b23] Ἐθε[ό]μην[271] γὰρ τινὰς τῶν μοναχῶν μετὰ τὴν τῆς ψυχῆς ἐκ <τοῦ>[272] σώματος ἐκδημίαν [ε]ἰς οὐρανοὺς θαρσαλέως ἀνιόντας[273] [181a1] ὀξυπετῶς[274] ἀετοῖς ἐοικότας τῷ δρόμῳ. Ἅμα γὰρ τῇ ἐξόδῳ πτέρυγες ἀναφύονται τούτοις ὀξυτάτως ἀνερχομένοις[275] <καὶ μέχρι τῶν ἱερῶν τειχῶν τῆς ἄνω Ἰερουσαλὴμ ἀφικνουμένοις>[276] πορρωτάτω τούτων πάσης ἀντικειμένης δυνάμεως ἀφισταμένης τὴν ὀξυτάτην ὁρμὴν εὐλαβουμένης.[277] Εἶτα τῶν τῆς πόλεως ἐκείνης ἱερῶν[278] ἐφαπτομένοις[279] θυρῶν καὶ εἴσω γενομένους τὴν τοιούτων [αἰ]δουμένων εἴσοδον τῶν θυρωρῶν καὶ μὴ[280] ἐπισχόντων τῷ οὐρανίῳ βασιλεῖ ὀφθῆναι. Παρρησία δὲ <τούτοις>[281] καὶ τῷ θείῳ θρόνῳ παρεστάναι. 38. [181b11] Ταύτης τοίνυν τῆς ἀξίας ἔγωγε ἀγασάμενος[282] ὑμᾶς τοὺς μοναχοὺς μὲν μακαρίζων ὡς ἀξίους πάρειμι ἐμαυτῷ δὲ καὶ μέμφομαι[283] τῶν τοιούτων βαθμῶν[284] ἀπαξιωθέντι. Καὶ εἴθε μοι ἂν εἴη πάντα τὰ τοῦ Βίου καὶ τῆς προσκαίρου Βασιλείας ἁλουργίδα τε καὶ διάδημα καταλιπόντι πενίας καὶ σάκκ[ου] καὶ ὅσα τῶν τῆς μοναχικῆς διαγωγῆς ἀντιποιήσασθαι.'[285]

39. [181a20] "Κἀγὼ πάλιν εἶπον αὐτῷ, 'Καλῶς, ὦ ἱερώ[τα]τε Βασιλεῦ, πάντα διεξῄεις οὕτω[ς] ψυχαγωγήσας <ἡμᾶς.>[286] Ἀλλ᾽ οὖν τοιαῦτα εἶναι πάντως προσήκει τὰ κρίματα τοῦ Θεοῦ ἡμῶν.[287] Καὶ πως ἂν ἔ{ι}χοι λόγος ἄλλως εἰπεῖν περὶ τῆς θείας δικαιοκρισίας ἢ οὕτως <γενέσθαι,>[288] [182a1] πάντα γὰρ ἐν σταθμῷ δικαιοσύνης ἑκάστῳ πρὸς ἀξίαν ὁ δίκαιος ἀντιμετρεῖ Θεὸς καὶ κατάλληλ[ο]ν τῶν πόνων δίδωσι καὶ τὴν ἀμοιβήν. Ὁ σὸς γὰρ βίος οὐκ ἴσους εἶχε πόνους, διαφέρων γὰρ ἦν τοῦ μονήρους· σοὶ γὰρ γυνὴ βοηθὸς[289] ὑπῆρχε καὶ παῖδες, καὶ ἀνδράποδα καὶ διάφορος τρ[υ]φή.[290] Οὗτοι δὲ τῶν τε ἡδ[ον]ῶν καὶ πάντων τῶν ἐν τῷ βίῳ τερπνῶν

καταφρονήσαντες τὸν Θεὸν ἀντὶ πάντων ἔλαβον. Πλοῦτον καὶ ἡδ[ο]νὴν <καὶ> τρυφὴν δὲ <καὶ> τὰ ἀρεστὰ αὐτ[ῷ] δρᾶν ἡγήσαντ[ο] καὶ ἦσαν κατὰ τὸν ἀπόστολον²⁹¹ "ὑστερούμενοι, θλιβόμενοι, κακοχούμενοι," καὶ τὰ ἑξῆς, "<ἐν ἐρημίαις πλανώμενοι καὶ ὄρεσι καὶ σπηλαίοις καὶ ταῖς ὀπαῖς τῆς γῆς." Πῶς>²⁹² σοι δὲ ἐκείνοις ἐξισοῦσθαι δυνατόν;'

40. [181b14] "Τοῦτ[ο]ν τοίνυν διὰ στόματος ἡμῶν ἐχόντων τὸν λόγον, ἀδελφέ μου Ἰωάννη, εὐθὺς σὺ μὲν καλ{λ}ῶς²⁹³ ἐπέστης κἀκεῖνος διαζευχ[θεὶς] εἰς οὐρανοὺς ἀνῆλθεν. Τοιγαροῦν, εἰ [ἐθέλης]²⁹⁴ γνῶναι, ὅσ[ω]ν οἱ τῆς ἀσκήσεως πόνοι πρόξενοι ἔσονται²⁹⁵ ἀγαθῶν ἤδη σοι σαφῶς θεόθεν δεδήλωται. Πορεύου, τοίνυν, καὶ στήριξον τοὺς ἀδελφοὺς διὰ τοῦ παρόντος²⁹⁶ μυστηρίου²⁹⁷ πειθόμενος."

Ταῦτα οὖν ἀκούσας ἐγὼ Ἰωάννης, μεγάλας τὰς εὐχαριστίας <τῷ> Θεῷ ἀπέπεμπον, εἶτα [182b1] ἱκανῶς τούτῳ συνομιλήσας καὶ συνταξάμενος ἐπανῆλθον χαίρων καὶ ἀγαλλόμενος. Καὶ ταῦτα μὲν ὧδε. Βούλεται δὲ τὸν τούτου περὶ τὴν πίστιν διάπυρον ζῆλον ὑποδεῖξαι²⁹⁸ ὁ λόγος.

Païsios Defends the Divinity of the Holy Spirit
Περὶ τοῦ κατὰ ἄγνοιαν πλανηθέντος ἀδελφοῦ καὶ εἰς ἀπιστίαν πεσόντος²⁹⁹

41. [182b8] Γέρων τις, ἔν τινι κώμῃ οἰκῶν τῶν γειτνιουσῶν τοῖς Αἰγύπτου μέρεσιν,³⁰⁰ ἀγνοίᾳ περιέπεσε,³⁰¹ τὴν γὰρ ἁγίαν τριάδα δυάδα <ἔφασκε>³⁰² σέβεσθαι χρῆναι ἔλεγεν, ἤτοι τὸν πατέρα καὶ τὸν υἱόν, τὸ δὲ πνεῦμα οὐ θεὸν λέγεσθαι. Πλῆθος δὲ τούτῳ συνηκολούθει ἱκανὸν τὸ αὐτὸ φρονοῦν. Ὁ δὲ Θεὸς τὸν τοῦ γέροντος ἀσκητικὸν πόνον καὶ ἱδρῶτα εἰς μάτην μὴ βουλόμενος ἀναλίσκεσθαι αὐτῷ, τῷ Παϊσίῳ³⁰³ δηλοῖ τὰ κατ' αὐτοῦ, ἐπισημάνας τὴν χώραν³⁰⁴ καὶ τὸν τόπον. Καὶ εὐθὺς³⁰⁵ διαναστὰς πλῆθος σπ[υ]ρίδων ποιησάμενος διὰ τριῶν ὠτίων κατασκευάζων, παραγίνεται πρὸς τὸν ἄνδρα ἐκεῖνον καὶ, τοῦτον καταλαβών, ξένον ἑαυτὸν προσεποιεῖτο. Πολλοὶ δέ τινες τῶν ἀφελεστέρων τούτῳ [183a1] συγκοινωνοὶ ἦσαν τοῦ ἀθέου δόγματος.³⁰⁶ Οἵ γε παραυτίκα³⁰⁷ εὑρεθέντες καὶ τῶν σκευῶν ἕκαστον ἀνὰ τρία κεκτημένον ὠτίων θεασάμενοι,³⁰⁸ τὸν δὲ Παΐσιον τίς τε εἴη καὶ πόθεν μὴ εἰδότες,³⁰⁹ ἐθαύμασαν λ{ε}ίαν ἀποροῦντες ἐπὶ τῇ κατασκευῇ τῶν σπυρίδων,³¹⁰ καὶ ἀνεπυνθάνοντο τί ἂν καὶ εἴη ταῦτα καὶ τί [βούλοιτο]³¹¹ τάδε ποιεῖν.

Ὁ δέ, "Π[ω]λῆσαι βούλομαι ταῦτα," φησι.

"Καὶ τί διὰ τριῶν ὠτίων ταῦτα πεποίηκας;" ἀντέφησαν.³¹²

"Ἐπειδή," <φησι>, "φίλος εἰμὶ τῆς ἁγίας τριάδος καὶ ἐραστής,³¹³ καὶ [δεῖ με]³¹⁴ διὰ τῶν ἔργων τοὺς χαρακτῆρας [ἀ]ποφαίνειν³¹⁵ καὶ τρισ[σ]ῶς ταύτην ἀνυμνεῖν διὰ χειρὸς τὰ τεκμήρια ἔχοντα. Καθάπερ γὰρ ἐκείνη μία φύσις ἐν τρισὶν ὑπάρχουσα χαρακτῆρσιν, ἄλλως οὐκ ὀρθῶς νοεῖται ἢ οὕτως³¹⁶ οὕτω δὴ καὶ ταῦτα ὑποληπτέον. Μίαν γὰρ οὐσίαν ἐν τρισὶν³¹⁷ ἕκαστον αὐτῶν κέκτηται,³¹⁸ ἐν ἑκάστῳ γὰρ τῶν τριῶν ὠτίων ὅλη ἡ οὐσία αὐτοῦ ἐπίσης ἐμφέρεται.³¹⁹ Οὕτως οὖν ἡ ἄϋλος φύσις καὶ ὑπερούσιος θεότης ἐν τρισὶ χαραχτῆρσιν ἤγουν προσώποις—πατρὶ <σὺν>³²⁰ υἱῷ καὶ ἁγίῳ πνεύματι—[ἐμφαινομένη]³²¹ καὶ ὅλη ἐν ἑκάστῳ διαμένουσα. Οὔτε μᾶλλον [183b1] οὔτε ἧττον [περὶ]³²² τὰ τρία λέγεται, ἅτε οὐ μᾶλλον τούτου ἐκείνου ἢ ἧττον ἐκείνου τούτου ὄντος."³²³

42. [183a3] Ταῦτα τοῦ Παϊσίου ἐν ἐπιτομῇ λόγου εἰπόντος τὴν ἀλήθειαν, <οἱ ἄνδρες>³²⁴ ἅμα τῷ ἀσκητῇ ἐκείνῳ, ἐθεάσαντο, διὸ καὶ [αἰ]δεσθέντες³²⁵ καὶ οὓς εἰς ἀκοὴν ἑτοιμάσαντες, "Εἰπὲ ἡμῖν," ἔφασαν, "ὦ θαυμάσιε, καὶ ἔτι περὶ ὀρθοδοξίας τρανότερον³²⁶ ἑτέρα[ι]ς τοιαύταις ἐναργέσι χρησάμενος ἀποδείξεσι, καὶ γὰρ ἡμᾶς ἐκ τῶν προοιμίων κατέπληξας."

43. [183a11] Ὁ δὲ θεῖος Παΐσιος, οἷά τις ἀριστεὺς ἔμπειρος θαρσαλέᾳ τῇ φωνῇ,³²⁷ πάντα τὰ τῶν αἱρετιζόντων³²⁸ βλάσφημα ῥήματα, κωμῳδήσας καὶ ἀράχνης τὰ περὶ αὐτῶν³²⁹ ἀποδείξας ἀσθενέστερα τήν τε ὀρθόδοξον πίστιν διεξοδικ[ώ]τερον τούτοις διαγνωρ[ί]σας³³⁰ καὶ ἐν ταῖς καρδίαις αὐτῶν³³¹ τὴν ἀλήθειαν ἀναζωγραφήσας³³² καὶ ἐντυπώσας, εἰς γνῶσιν ἤγαγεν ἀκριβῆ πολλὰς περὶ τοῦ ἁγίου πνεύματος ἐκ τῶν θεοπνεύστων γραφῶν ἀποδείξεις³³³ ἐκθέμενος. Ἔπ[ε]ιτα, νουθετήσας πάντας ὁμολογεῖν τε τὴν [ἁγίαν Τριάδα],³³⁴ διδάξας καὶ ὑπὲρ τῆς οἰκείας παροινίας μετανοεῖν ἰθύνας ἐπανῄει εἰς τὴν ἔρημον, ὕμνους εὐχαριστηρίους τῷ Θεῷ³³⁵ ἀναπέμπων.

An Angel Assures Païsios of God's Care

44. [183b25] Ἐν τῇ ἐρήμῳ [184a1] δὲ γενόμενος,³³⁶ φῶς ἀθρόον ἐξέλαμψεν ἐν ταῖς ὄψεσιν αὐτοῦ καὶ ἀτενίσας εἰς τὸ φῶς, ἀγγέλων τάγματα ἑώρα τὴν ἔρημον πληροῦντα καὶ θαυμάσας τί ἂν {καὶ} εἴη <τοῦτο,>³³⁷ διηπόρει γνῶναι <τί>³³⁸ τὸ φαινόμενον. Καὶ εὐθέως ὁ συμπορευόμενος αὐτῷ ἄγγε{γγε}λος πρὸς αὐτὸν εἶπε, "Καὶ παρόντος σου καὶ ἀπόντος,³³⁹ ὦ Παΐσιε, τοὺς ἐνταῦθα οἰκοῦντας μοναχοὺς³⁴⁰ φυλάττομεν, καθώ[ς] σοι ὁ πάντων ὑπέσχετο Θεός." Ὧδε³⁴¹ ἐν εὐχαριστηρίοις ᾠδαῖς τὸν πάντων ἐπιμελούμενο[ν] ἐδόξαζε Θεόν.

Paul and Poemen Come to Visit Païsios

45. [183b11] Καὶ ταῦτα³⁴² μὲν περὶ τούτων. Περὶ δὲ τῶν προφητ[ι]κῶν χαρισμάτων οἷος ἦν ὁ θεῖος Παΐσιος ὁ λόγος δηλώσ[ω]ν ἔρχεται.

Ἐπεὶ οὖν ὁ ἱερὸς οὗτος ἀνὴρ διὰ πάσης τῆς γῆς τῇ φήμῃ διέτρεχε³⁴³ καὶ τὰς φιλαρέτους εἰς ὄψιν καὶ εὐχὰς ἐξεκαλεῖτο ψυχὰς, οὐκ ἔμελλε τὸν μέγαν ἐν τοῖς πατράσιν ἄκλητον εἶναι³⁴⁴ Ποιμένα. Ἀλλ' ἤδη καὶ αὐτὸς νέος ὢν ἔτ[ι]³⁴⁵ τὴν ἡλικίαν κατ' ἐκείνου καιροῦ, ἑάλω τῷ πόθῳ τῆς ἐκείνου θέας.³⁴⁶

Περὶ τοῦ μεγάλου Ποιμένος

Ἀμέλει πρὸς τὸν ὅσιον Παῦλον παργενόμενος ἐδυσώπει αὐτὸν συναπελθεῖν αὐτῷ πρὸς τὸν μέγαν, συνήθης γὰρ ἦν ἐκείνῳ καὶ συχνῶς αὐτῷ προσέβαλλεν.[347]

Ὁ [184b1][348] δὲ πατὴρ ἡμῶν Παῦλος, "Νέον ὄντα σε, [ὁ]ρῶ,[349] τέκνον, αἰδοῦμαι πρὸς τὸν μέγαν ἐκεῖνον ἀγαγεῖν. Ὑψηλὸς γάρ ἐστιν ὁ ἀνὴρ καὶ ἁπλῶς οὐ παραβάλλομεν αὐτῷ οὐδ᾽ ἀσκέπτως, ἀλλ᾽ εὐλαβῶς, καὶ τοῦτ[ο] οὐκ ἀεὶ, ἀλλ᾽ ἐν καιρῷ τῷ προσήκοντι ὠφελείας χάριν."

"Ἀλλ᾽ ἔγωγε ἔξω τῆς κέλλης <ἐκείνου,>"[350] ἔφη, "στήσομαι σὺν σοὶ ἀπελθὼν καὶ ἡδ[ο]νὴ οὐ μετρία ἔσται μοι ἀκούοντι τῆς θείας φωνῆς αὐτοῦ συλλαλοῦντό[ς] σοι. Καὶ εὖγε τῆς τοιαύτης δωρεᾶς εἴγε τούτου,[351] τύχοιμι. Εἰ δέ γε καὶ τοῦτο οὐ ῥᾴδιον ἀλλ᾽ ἐργῶδες φανείη, κἂν[352] τῆς κέλλης αὐτοῦ ἅψ[ω]μαι, σωθήσομαι. Ἀλλὰ καὶ σοῦ τοῖς ποσὶ τοῖς ἔνδον βηματίσασιν, ἐξερχομένου περιπλακήσομαι ἀντὶ τοῦ ἐδάφους οὗπερ ἐκείνου, οἱ ὡραῖοι πόδες ἐπιβαίνουσιν κἂν τούτῳ[353] εὐλογίας ἀπολαύσ[ομαι][354] δαψιλοῦς."

46. [184a17] Ταῦτα εἰπόντα τῆς ταπεινώσεως καὶ τῆς πολλῆς πίστεως θαυμάσας,[355] ἔλαβε μεθ᾽ ἑαυτοῦ ὁ θεῖος Παῦλος καὶ ἄπεισι πρὸς τὸν μέγαν. Καὶ καταλαβόντες τὴν κέλλαν τοῦ ὁσίου, μόνος ὁ Παῦλος εἰσῄει. Ὁ δὲ φιλικῶς καὶ πατρικῶς τοῦτον ὑπὸ δεξάμενος, διεπυνθάνετο περὶ τοῦ νέου,[356] <"Ποῦ ἐστί," φάσκων, "ὁ συνοδοιπόρος σου παῖς;">[357]

Ὁ δὲ "Ἔξω, πάτερ, ἀπολ[ει]φθεὶς τὴν εἴσοδον εὐλαβεῖται."

Καὶ ὅς εἰσελθεῖν ἐκέλευσε καὶ,[358] "Οὐ καλὸν," ἔφη, "τοὺς τοιούτους ἡμῖν [185a1] παραβαλλόντας κωλύεσθαι τῆς ἐλεύσεως. Τοὺς γὰρ τοιοῦτος εἰς οὐρανὸν ῥᾷον εἰσιέναι ὁ Σωτὴρ ἡμῶν διακελεύεται."

Ταῦτα εἰπών, οἰκείαις χερσὶ λαβὼν τὸν νέον ἐνηγκαλίσατο εὐλογῶν αὐτὸν καὶ λέγων, "Πείσθητί μοι, ὦ φίλτατε Παῦλε, ὅτι ὁ παῖς οὗτος πολλῶν ἀνδρῶν μέλλει σώζειν ψυχὰς καὶ <πολλοὶ>[359] δι᾽ αὐτοῦ τῆς τοῦ παραδείσου ἀξιωθήσονται τροφῆς. Μετ᾽ αὐτοῦ γὰρ χεὶρ Κυρίου φαίνεται πρὸς θείας ὁδοὺς [ἰθύνουσά τε καὶ][360] περιέπουσα."

Ταῦτα εἰπών, χεῖρας αὐτῷ ἐπιθεὶς[361] καὶ εὐλογήσας,[362] ἀπέπεμψε σὺν τῷ ἱερῷ Παύλῳ, μεγάλως εὐλογοῦντας καὶ δοξάσαντας[363] τὸν θεόν.[364]

The Savior Visits Païsios and Teaches Him about Acceptable Good Work

Περὶ τῆς τοῦ Κυρίου ἐπισκοπῆς καὶ ὧν ὁ Σωτὴρ πρὸς αὐτὸν διεξῄειν.[365]

47. [184b15] Συνέβη τῷ ἱερῷ Παϊσίῳ μίαν πρὸς ταῖς εἴκοσιν ἡμέραις ἀσίτῳ ὄντι τὸν Χριστὸν πρὸς αὐτὸν παραγενέσθαι καὶ "Πολλὰ ἄρα κακοπαθῶν δι᾽ ἐμὲ," εἰρηκέναι, "ὁ ἐκλεκτός μου Παΐσιος <εἴη>."[366]

Ὁ δέ, "Καὶ τίς ἡ ἐμή, δέσποτα ἀγαθέ, αὕτη <ἡ>[367] μηδαμινὴ κακοπάθεια; Παρὰ σοὶ γὰρ πᾶσα δῶσις καὶ[368] πᾶν δώρημα τέλειον, τῷ τὴν ἰσχὺν διδόντι."

Καὶ ὁ Σωτήρ, "Εὐπρόσδεκτον παρ᾽ ἐμοί," φησιν, "ἅπαν ἔργον χρηστὸν καὶ ἐπίσης ἀντιμετρήσω τὸν μισθόν. Δεῦρο, οὖν, ἀκολούθει μοι."

Ὁ δὲ συνείπετο ἐν τῇ ἐρήμῳ τῷ Σωτῆρι μέχρι τινὸς τ[ῶ]ν τῆς [185b1] ἐρήμου σπηλαίων.[369] Εἶτα, "[Εἴσελθέ]"[370] φησι τῷ Παϊσίῳ, "καὶ θέασαι ἄνδρα τῷ ὄντι ἀγωνιστήν."

Ὁ δὲ εἰσελθών, ἄνδρα ἑώρακεν ἐπὶ <τῆς>[371] γῆς κυλινδο{υ}μενον, στόμα τε καὶ πρόσωπον τῷ ἐδάφει καταψήχοντα. Ἀπορῶν οὖν τὸν ἄνδρα τῆς τοῦ ἀγῶνος ὑπερβολῆς, εὐθὺς ἐξῄει γνῶναι παρὰ τοῦ Σωτῆρος δεόμενος τὸ [αἴ]τιον τῆ[ς] σφοδροτάτης ἀγωνίας τοῦ ἀνδρός. Καὶ ὅς, "Τὸν ἐμὸν εἶδες ἀθλητὴν[372] οἵους ὑπομένει δι᾽ ἐμὲ πόνους;"

Ὁ δὲ "Εἶδον, δέσποτα," ἔφη, "καὶ ἔφριξα τὰς ὀδύνας τῶν καμάτων. Τίνες δὲ τούτῳ οἱ ἀγῶνες ἐμοὶ μὲν ἄδηλοι, σοῦ δὲ ἡ ἀγαθότης δυσωπουμένη[373] δηλώσει<ς>;"

Καὶ ὁ Σωτήρ, "Δύο ἡμέρας νηστεύων μόνον διήν[υ]σε καὶ ἰδοὺ τῇ πείνῃ τηκόμενος[374] καὶ τῇ δίψῃ φλεγόμενος οὕτως ὁρᾶται."

Εἶτα ὁ Παΐσιος, "Καὶ πῶς[375] εἴκοσι καὶ δύο ἔγωγε ἡμέρας ἔχων ἄσιτος πάσχω οὐδὲν τοιοῦτον;"[376]

Πρὸς αὐτὸν πάλιν ὁ Σωτήρ,[377] "Σὺ μὲν οὖν τῇ χάριτι ἐνισχυ{ν}όμενος κραταιῶς νηστεύεις,[378] ἐκεῖνος δὲ ὡς ἀθλητὴς ἐκ τῆς οἰκείας προαιρέσεως ἐν ἀγωνίᾳ νηστεύει,[379] τῷ πόθῳ φλεγόμενος καὶ πάσχειν ὑπὲρ δύναμιν ἀνασχόμενος."

Ἔπειτα τὸν Παΐσιον ἐρέσθαι, "Καὶ τίνα, Κύριε, ἕνεκα τῶν δύο ἡμερῶν ἀμοιβὴν παρὰ τῆς σῆς χρηστότητος λήψεται οὗτος;"

Ὁ δὲ Σωτήρ,[380] "Ἴσην ταῖς σαῖς εἴκοσιν καὶ δύο ἡμέρας αὐτῷ ἀνταμείψομαι καὶ [186a1] ἀμφοτέροις ῥηθήσεται τὸ <εὐαγγέλιον ἐκεῖνο ῥητὸν τὸ>[381] εἴσελθε εἰς τὴν χαρὰν τοῦ Κυρίου σου, σοί τε τῷ τὰ πέντε τάλαντα εἰληφότι, κἀκείνῳ τῷ τὰ δύο, ἐπίσης γὰρ τὸ καλὸν ὤφθητε πεπραχότες καὶ σπουδαῖοι κατὰ δύναμιν."

Ταῦτα εἰπὼν ὁ Σωτήρ, ἀφίστατο.

48. [185b5] Ὁ δὲ πατὴρ ἡμῶν Παΐσιος ἔκτοτε[382] πλείονας ἀγῶνας προσέθηκε[383] τὸν Θεὸν ἐκδυσωπῶν ἀν[ώ]τερος γενέσθαι τροφῆς, καὶ ἦν αὐτῷ ἡ τροφὴ διὰ τῆς κυριακῆς ἡ μετάληψις τοῦ σώματος τοῦ Κυρίου ἡμῶν Ἰησοῦ Χριστοῦ καὶ τοῦ αἵματος. Ὁ δὲ Σωτὴρ πάλιν ὀφθεὶς φιλανθρώπως τῷ οἰκείῳ θεράποντι, φησι,[384] "Περὶ τροφῆς, τί," φησι, "πλεῖον αἰτεῖς μηδὲν ἐσθίων; Σχολὴ σοι δὲ περὶ ἄλλου[385] αἰτεῖσθαι;"

Καὶ ὅς, "Κύριε, θέλω ἵνα ἡνίκα ἂν ἐκ τῆς δὲ τῆς ἐρήμου εἰς ἐπίσκεψιν ἀδελφῶν παραγένωμαι ἐν τάχει ἀπελεύσομαι."[386]

Ὁ δὲ, "Μὴ λυποῦ. Οὐκ ἀφίσταμαί σου ταύτης ἐξιόντος."
Εἶτα, "Τοῦ θυμοῦ," ἔφη, " ἐλευθέρωσόν με, Χριστέ."
Ὁ δε, "[Εἰ]³⁸⁷ τὸν θυμόν," φησι, "νικῆσαι [ἐ]θέλεις καὶ τὴν ὀργὴν, μὴ ἐπιτιμήσης μηδενί, μηδὲ <μισήσης τίνα, μηδὲ>³⁸⁸ ἐξουδενώσης. Ταῦτα φυλάξας, οὐ θυμωθήσῃ."

Καὶ ὅς, "Φιλάνθρωπε δέσποτα καὶ μακρόθυμε κύριε, εἰ ἔστι τις ἐν ταῖς ἐντολαῖς³⁸⁹ πορευόμενος καὶ τοῖς ἀγαπῶσί σε παραβάλλων ἕνεκεν τῆς αὐτῶν θεραπείας, ἆρα κέρδος ἢ ζημίαν ἕξει ἡ περὶ τούτων³⁹⁰ σπουδή;"³⁹¹

Καὶ ὁ Σωτὴρ ἔφη, "Καθάπερ ἐργάτης εἰς ἀγρὸν ἀφικόμενος³⁹² ἔργου [186b1] ἕνεκεν μισθὸν παρὰ τοῦ κυρίου τοῦ ἔργου λήψεται μὴ ἀναβαλέσθαι ἔχοντος, οὕτω κἀγὼ ποιῶ περὶ τοὺς ποιοῦντας τὸ καλὸν καὶ διδάσκοντας ἢ ἀντιλαμβανομένους. Τοῖς τοιούτοις γὰρ λαμπροτέρας ἀμοιβὰς ἐν τῷ οὐρανῷ ἀποδώσω."³⁹³

49 (48).³⁹⁴ [186b6] Ἔπ[ε]ιτα ὁ Παΐσιος ἐπερωτᾷ,³⁹⁵ "Ἐάν τις εἴη ἀγωνιζόμενος³⁹⁶ καὶ ἄλλους θεραπεύων, ἄλλος δὲ ἀγωνιζόμενος, οὐ μέντοι θεραπεύει ἄλλους, τί δήποτε ἕτερος ἑτέρου διαφέρει πρὸς τὰς ἀμοιβάς;"

Καὶ ὁ Σωτὴρ, "Ὁ ἀγωνιζόμενος μόνον μαθητής ἐστιν, ὁ δὲ ἀγωνιζόμενος καὶ ἑτέρων ὢν θεραπευτὴς κληρονόμος ἐστι καὶ υἱός."

Τοῦ δὲ Παϊσίου πάλιν εἰπόντος, "Ἐάν τις εἴη σπουδαῖος περὶ τὴν τῶν ἄλλων θεραπείαν, ὡς οἷόν τε μὲν ἀγωνιζόμενος, <οὐ πάντως δὲ τοῖς ἀγωνιζομένοις>³⁹⁷ ἐξισούμενος, τῆς τῶν ἄλλων ἐπιμελείας τοὺς αὐτοῦ ἐπισχούσης σφοδροὺς³⁹⁸ ἀγῶνας, ἆρα ἐπίσης αὐτῷ ἔσται <ὁ>³⁹⁹ μισθός;"

"Ναὶ," φήσας ὁ Σωτὴρ, "εἰς οὐρανοὺς ἄνεις{ε}ι."

Καὶ ταῦτα μὲν περὶ τούτου εἴρηται, ἡμῖν δὲ ἐπὶ τὰ παράδοξα τῶν θαυμάτων ὁ λόγος βαδιεῖται.⁴⁰⁰

A Syrian Monk Visits Païsios
Περὶ τοῦ ἀνδρὸς τοῦ ἀρκτῴου

50. [186a22] Ἦν τις ἀρκτῷος ἀνὴρ ποικίλαις ἀρεταῖς κ[ε]κοσμημένος. Τούτου ἐν προσευχῇ γενομένῳ τοιαύτη ἔν[ν]οια ἐπεισῄει⁴⁰¹ ἆρα τίνι τῶν εὐαρεστησάντων τῷ Θεῷ ἐφάμιλλος εἴη.⁴⁰² [187a1] Ταῦτα διαλογιζομένῳ, θεία φωνὴ ἄνωθεν αὐτῷ ἠκούετο, "[Εἰς Αἴγυπτον]. [sic]⁴⁰³ ἄπελθε," λέγουσα, "καὶ εὑρήσεις ἄνδρα Παΐσιον ὄνομα τῇ κατὰ σὲ τυγχάνοντα ταπεινότητι⁴⁰⁴ καὶ ἀγάπῃ Θεοῦ κ[ε]χρημένον."

Ὁ δὲ τίμιος γέρων τῆς ὁδοῦ τὸ μῆκος περιφρονῶν, ὡς εἶχε ποδῶν τῆς ἐπὶ τὴν Αἴγυπτον εἴχετο πορείας. Εἶτα τῆς γῆ[ς] Ν[ι]τρίας τὸ ὄρος⁴⁰⁵ καταλαμβάνει, ποῦ ἄν καὶ εἴη Παΐσιος ἐρόμενος. Ἐπεὶ δὲ ἐν ἅπασι{ν} κεκήρυκτο τοῦ Παϊσίου τὸ ὄνομα, οὐκ ἔλαθεν τοῦτον ὁ τόπος τῆς ἐκείνου οἰκήσεως, οὐδὲ μὴν τὸν Παΐσιον ἡ τοῦ πρεσβύτου ἔλευσις.⁴⁰⁶ Ἐρχομένῳ γὰρ πρὸς αὐτὸν αὐτ[ί]κα ἐν τῇ ἐρήμῳ συναντᾷ θάτερος οὖν θατέρῳ τῇ χάριτι γνωρισθείς.⁴⁰⁷ Περιπλακέντες ἀλλήλοις ἡδέως περιεπτύξαντο, ἔπειτα ἐν τῷ καταγωγίῳ τοῦ ἱεροῦ Παϊσίου εἰσελθόντες καὶ εὐχὴν ποιησάμενοι ἐκαθέσθησαν. Λόγων δὲ ἀρξάμενος ὁ γέρων πρὸς τὸν θεῖον Παΐσιον διαλέγεται τῇ[ν] τῶν Σύρων διάλεκτον,⁴⁰⁸ ὁ δὲ Αἰγύπτιος ὢν τὴν τῶν Αἰγυπτίων μόνην ἐπιστάμενος⁴⁰⁹ ἐλυπεῖτο οὐ μετρίως τοιούτου γέροντος ἀποτυχεῖν λόγων ἐπωφελῶν.⁴¹⁰ Καὶ εὐθὺς εἰς οὐρανὸν ἀνασχὼν ὁ μακάριος ἅμα⁴¹¹ καὶ φρένας καὶ [187b1] στενάξας ἐκ βάθους καρδίας,⁴¹² "Υἱὲ θεοῦ καὶ Λόγε," φησί, "παράσχου μοι τῷ σῷ οἰκέτῃ γνῶναι τὴν δύναμιν τῶν ῥημάτων τοῦδε τοῦ γέροντος."

51. [187a3] Ταῦτα εἰπὼν—ὢ ταχείας ἐπισκέψεως!—αὐτίκα ἅμα τῷ λόγῳ καὶ λαλῶν καὶ νοῶν τὴν τῶν Σύρων διάλεκτον ἦν ὁ Παΐσιος <ὑπὸ μόνου τοῦ θείου πνεύματος διδασκόμενος>.⁴¹³ Εἶτα τῶν λόγων κατατρυφήσαντες ἀλλήλων θάτερος θατέρῳ ὧν ἠξιώθη θεωριῶν⁴¹⁴ διέξῃει καὶ οἵοις ἐνέτυχεν ἕκαστος πατράσιν τούτων τὰς ἀρετὰς ἐξεῖπεν ἑτέρῳ καὶ πλήρεις ἦσαν ἡδονῆς διὰ τῆς ὁμιλίας⁴¹⁵ ἀμφότεροι ἐπὶ ἓξ ἡμέραις τούτοις διηνυσμέν[οις].⁴¹⁶ Ἐπει[δὴ] τὸ τῆς ὁμιλίας πέρας τὸν πρεσβύτην⁴¹⁷ εἶχεν καὶ ἐπανιέναι ἐπὶ τὰ ἴδια ἔμελλε πάντας, προσκαλεῖται Παΐσιος τοὺς αὐτοῦ μαθητὰς καὶ "Ἰδού," φησι πρὸς αὐτούς, "ὦ φίλτατα τέκνα, ἀνὴρ ἱερὸς τῶν τελείων, πλήρης χαρίτων καὶ Πνεύματος Ἁγίου. Πάντες γ᾽οὖν ἀντὶ πύργων καὶ φυλάκων τοῖς ὑπεναντίοις ἀνθισταμένας αὐτοῦ τὰς εὐχὰς εὐσεβῶς προσλαμβάνεσθαι."⁴¹⁸

Ταῦτα εἰπόντος, πάντες τὴν προσκύνησιν χαμαὶ ποιήσαντες, τὴν προσήκουσαν ὑπὲρ αὐτῶν εὐχῶν τε καὶ εὐλογιῶν ἀξιωθῆναι ἐκείνου θερμῶς ᾐτοῦντο. Ὁ δὲ τούτων [188a1] ὑπερευξάμενος εὐλογ[ή]σας τε καὶ συνταξάμενος ἅπασι τῆς ὁδοῦ εἴχετο.

Coda: Païsios Sees the Syrian Monk Borne Home on a Cloud

52. [187b2] Βραχέος δὲ χρόνου διανυσθέντος ἐκείνου ὑποχωροῦντος, παρεγένετό τις τῶν ἀναχωρητῶν πρὸς τὸν μέγαν Παΐσιον. Οἱ δὲ μαθηταὶ τοῦ θείου ἀνδρός,⁴¹⁹ "Ὦ οὗτος," ἔφασκον, "οἷόν σε κέρδος ἂν ἐγένετο εἰ ταχεῖα πρὸς ἡμᾶ<ς> σου γέγονεν <ἡ>⁴²⁰ ἄφιξις, θεῖος γὰρ ἀνὴρ παρεγένετο πρὸς ἡμᾶς ἐκ τῆς γῆς τῶν Σύρων,⁴²¹ τὸν νοῦν καὶ τὴν καρδίαν κατηγλαϊσμένος, ὅς ἡμᾶς λόγοις⁴²² στηρίξας ἀρτίως ἀπῄει. Καὶ εἰ βούλῃ τοῦτον φθάσον,⁴²³ οὐ πόρρω ὄντα."⁴²⁴

Τῷ δὲ προθύμῳ ποδὶ φθάσαι κινήσαντι, "Παῦσαι,"⁴²⁵ ἔφη ὁ θεῖος Παΐσιος.⁴²⁶ "Ἐκεῖνος⁴²⁷ γὰρ ἤδη ἐπέκεινα τῶν ὀκτὼ καὶ δέκα μιλίων διήνυσε διάστημα ἐπὶ νεφέλης εἰς τὰ ἴδια φερόμενος." Ταῦτα ἐκείνου εἰρηκότος, πάντες τὸν ἀληθῆ Θεὸν δοξάσαντες ἦσαν ἐκπληττόμενοι.⁴²⁸

An Angel Watches over Païsios

53A.⁴²⁹ [187b18] Ἀδελφός τις ἦλθε{ν} πρὸς τὸν πατέρα ἡμῶν Παΐσιον, ἰδεῖν αὐτὸν βουλόμενος, καὶ εὑρὼν αὐτὸν κοιμώμενον καὶ φύλακα ἔχοντα πρὸς τῇ κεφαλῇ ἄγγελον εὐπρεπῆ,⁴³⁰ καὶ θαυμάσας, "Ὁ θεός," ἔφη, "ὄντως τοὺς εἰς αὐτὸν ἐλπίζοντας φυλάττει." Καὶ ἀπῆλθεν, εὐλογῶν καὶ δοξάζων τὸν δοξάζοντα θεὸν καὶ τοὺς ἀγαπῶντας αὐτόν.⁴³¹

Païsios' Disciple Is Deceived by a Jew
Περὶ τοῦ μαθητοῦ τοῦ γέροντος

53B. [188b2] Ἁπλοῦς τις τὴν διάνοιαν ἦν τῷ ἱερῷ Παϊσίῳ μαθητὴς καλῶς πειθαρχῶν τοῖς αὐτοῦ κ[ε]λεύσμασιν,⁴³² ὃς ἀπελθὼν εἰς Αἴγυπτον π[ω]λῆσαι <τὸ> ἐργόχειρον, Ἑβραίῳ τινὶ συναντήσας ἐν τῇ ὁδῷ,⁴³³ συνοδοιπόρει αὐτῷ. Ὁ δὲ τὴν τούτου ἁπλότητα καταμαθών, καὶ ὃν ἐν τῇ καρδίᾳ⁴³⁴ ἐκ τοῦ ψυχοφθόρου ὄφε[ω]ς εἶχεν ἰὸν διὰ τῆς μιαρᾶς <αὐτοῦ>⁴³⁵ γλώττης ἐκχέας, εἶπε τῷ μοναχῷ, "Ὦ οὗτος, τί τῷ ἐσταυρωμένῳ ἁπλῶς καὶ ὡς ἔτυχε πιστεύετ[ε] μὴ ὄντι τῷ προσδ[ο]κωμένῳ; Ἄλλος γάρ ἐστιν ἐκεῖνος, καὶ οὐχ οὗτος."

Ὁ δὲ μοναχὸς, γνώμης ἀκεραιότητι καὶ καρδίας ἁπλότητι <ἁλοὺς>⁴³⁶ πρὸς τὸν Ἑβραῖ[ο]ν, "Ἴσ[ω]ς οὕτ[ω]ς ἔχει," ἀναγκασθεὶς ἀντεφθέγξατο.

Ταῦτα εἰπών—φεῦ τῆς συμφορᾶς—παραχρῆμα, οἴμοι, ἐξέπεσε τῆς τοῦ βαπτίσματος χάριτος, ὡς διὰ τῶν ἐφεξῆς ἡμῖν δειχθήσεται.

Païsios Rebukes and Teaches the Monk

54. [188a18] Ἐπανιόντος γὰρ ἐν τῇ ἐρήμῳ καὶ τῷ θείῳ Παϊσίῳ⁴³⁷ ὀφθέντος, ἀπρόσιτος ἦν αὐτοῦ⁴³⁸ ἡ ἄφιξις καὶ ἄχαρις τοῖς τοῦ διδασκάλου ὀφθαλμοῖς. <Οὐ>⁴³⁹ γὰρ ἦν ἐκείνῳ προσχὼν οὐδαμῶς, ἀλλὰ τῇδε κἀκεῖσε ἀποστρεφόμενος, λόγων δὲ αὐτῷ ἥκιστα συμμετέχων. Ἐφ' ἱκανὸν οὖν χρόνον, τὸν γέροντα παρορ[ῶ]ντα αὐτὸν ὁ μαθητὴς ὁρῶν⁴⁴⁰ καὶ [189a1] ἀποστρεφόμενον, διηπόρει τὴν αἰτίαν. Ἡνιᾶτο τὴν ἀποστροφήν, ἤλγει τὴν συμφοράν. Εἶτα προσελθὼν αὐτῷ, τοῖς ποσὶ προσπίπτει, "Τί ἀποστρέφεις," λέγων, "τὰς χρηστάς σου ὄψεις, ὦ πάτερ,⁴⁴¹ ἐμέ τε τὸν ἄθλιον παρορᾷς σου μαθητὴν καὶ ὅπερ οὐδέπω⁴⁴² μοι εἴωθας δείκνυ[σ]θαι τοῦτο δρῶν ἀναφαίνῃ νυνὶ⁴⁴³ ὡς βδέλυγμα με⁴⁴⁴ ἀποστρεφόμενος;"

Τὸν δὲ γέροντα, "Καὶ τίς εἶ σύ," φάναι, "ὦ ἄνθρωπε; Καὶ γὰρ τὰ σὰ οὔπω συνίημι γνωρίσματα οὐδ' ἀκριβῶς <σε ἔγωγε>⁴⁴⁵ γινώσκω."

Ὁ δὲ, "Καὶ τί ἐν ἐμοὶ ξένον τεθέασαι, πάτερ, διὸ με ἀγνοεῖς⁴⁴⁶ παρωθούμενος;⁴⁴⁷ Οὐκ εἰμὶ ἐγὼ ὁ σὸς μαθητής, ὁ δ[εῖ]να;"⁴⁴⁸

Ὁ δὲ γέρων, "Ἐκεῖνος," ἔφη, "Χριστιανὸς ὑπῆρχε καὶ βάπτισμα εἶχε. Σὺ δὲ οὐχ οὕτως τυγχάνεις ἔχων. Εἰ δὲ ἄρα ἐκεῖνος εἶ, τὸ βάπτισμα ἀπὸ

σοῦ ᾤχετο καὶ τὰ τῶν Χριστιανῶν ἰδιώματα.⁴⁴⁹ Τί δὴ σοι τὸ συμβὰν διηγοῦ καὶ τὴν ἐπαγωγὴν σαφῶς.⁴⁵⁰ Τί πέπονθας ἐν τῇ ὁδῷ;"
Καὶ ὅς, "Μηδὲν πεπραχέναι," ἔλεγε.
Καὶ ὁ γέρων,⁴⁵¹ " Ἄπ[ι]θι," φησὶ, "τέκνον, πόρρωθεν, Θεὸν γὰρ ἀθετήσαντος ὁμιλίας οὐκ ἀνέχομαι. Εἰ σὺ γὰρ ἦς ἐκεῖνος, ἑώρων ἄν σε ὄντα⁴⁵² οἷος ἦσθα καὶ πρότερον."
Ὁ δὲ στενάξας καὶ δάκρυα⁴⁵³ εἰς οἶκτον κινοῦντα ἐκχέας ἐκεῖνον. <Ἔλεγεν αὐτὸν>⁴⁵⁴ εἶναι καὶ οὐκ ἄλλον ἔλεγε, καὶ ὅλως ἀγνοεῖν τὸ ἐγκαλούμενον, μηδὲν <αἰσχρὸν>⁴⁵⁵ [189b1] δεδρακέναι ἰσχυριζόμενος.⁴⁵⁶
55. [189b1] Καὶ ὁ μέγας, "Τίνι," φησὶν, "ἐν τῇ ὁδῷ προσωμίλησας;"⁴⁵⁷
Ὁ δὲ, " Ἑβραίῳ τινὶ, ἑτέρῳ δὲ οὐ οὐδενί."
Εἶτα, "Καὶ τί σοι ἐξεῖπε καὶ τί ἀπεκρίθης αὐτῷ;"
Καὶ ὅς,⁴⁵⁸ "Οὐδὲν μοι ἕτερον ἀπεφθέγξατο εἰ μὴ ὅτι, 'Τὸν Χριστὸν μὴ εἶναι ὃν ὑμεῖς προσκυνεῖτε.⁴⁵⁹ Ἐκεῖνος γάρ ἐστιν ὁ μέλλων ἔρχεσθαι.'⁴⁶⁰ Κἀγὼ εἶπον, 'Ἴσως οὕτως ἔχει.'"⁴⁶¹
56. [189a8] Ὑπολαβὼν δὲ ὁ γέρων, "[Τί]⁴⁶² χαλεπώτερον ἢ αἰσχρότερόν ἐστι τοῦδε τοῦ ῥήματος, ἄθλιε; Δι' οὗ καὶ τὸν Χριστὸν ἠθέτησας καὶ τὸ ἅγιον⁴⁶³ βάπτισμα ἀπεδύσω. Ταλαίπωρε! Λοιπόν, ἄπελθε, σεαυτὸν κλαῦσον ὡς βούλει. Μέρ[ο]ς οὐκ ἔστι σοι μετ' ἐμοῦ. Μετὰ γὰρ τῶν τὸν Χριστὸν ἀρνησα[μέν]ων,⁴⁶⁴ τὸ σὸν ὄνομα ἐγράφη καὶ μετὰ τούτων τὰς τιμωρίας ἐκείνων⁴⁶⁵ ὑποστήσῃ."
Ὁ δὲ οἰμ[ώ]ξας καὶ θρηνήσας, εἰς οὐρανὸν ἀνέπεμψε⁴⁶⁶ φωνὰς, "Ἐλέησόν με, πάτερ," βοῶν, "τὸν δύστηνον, καὶ τὴν ἐμὴν ἐλέησον⁴⁶⁷ ψυχήν. Τί γὰρ ἂν καὶ γένωμαι οὐκ οἶδα. Δι' ἀπροσεξίας τὸν θεῖον φωτισμὸν παρωσάμενος⁴⁶⁸ καὶ ἐπίχαρμα τοῖς ὀλεθρίοις δαίμοσι γενόμενος. Ἀλλ' ἐπὶ σὲ μετὰ <τὸν>⁴⁶⁹ Θεὸν ποιοῦμαι τὴν καταφυγήν. Μὴ οὖν παρίδῃς με τὸν ἄθλιον."

The Monk Importunes Païsios

57. (189b24) Οὕτω<ς> τῷ μαθητῇ⁴⁷⁰ δ[υ]σωποῦντι καὶ δάκρυσι μᾶλλον ἢ ῥήμασιν εἰς [190a2] οἶκτον διεγείροντι ἵλεως αὐτῷ ὁ πρεσβύτης γίνεται, "Ἀνάσχου," λέγων, "ὦ τέκνον. Τοὺς οἰκτιρμοὺς δυσωπεῖν ἡμᾶς χρὴ⁴⁷¹ τοῦ φιλανθρώπου Θεοῦ ὑπὲρ σοῦ."
Καὶ ταῦτα εἰπών, ἱκέτης γίνεται τοῦ Θεοῦ⁴⁷² θερμότατος ὑπὲρ ἐκείνου λύσιν τοῦ πλημμελήματος αἰτούμενος. Θεὸς δὲ οὐκ ἠμέλει ἀλ<λ'> εὐθέ[ω]ς τὴν τοῦ ὁσίου αἴτησιν ἀναπληροῖ. Πέρας γὰρ τῆς ἱκεσίας λύσις ἦν τοῦ τε ὀφλήματος <καὶ>⁴⁷³ ἀποκατάστασις τοῦ θείου βαπτίσματος. Τὸ γὰρ Ἅγιον Πνεῦμα ὡσεὶ περιστερὰ τῷ γέροντι ἑωρᾶτο διὰ στόματος τοῦ μαθητοῦ εἰσερχόμενον τὴν τοῦ Πνεύματος δωρεὰν ἐπανιοῦσαν ὑποδεικνύ[ο]ν,⁴⁷⁴ τὸ δὲ βλάσφημον πνεῦμα ἐξερχόμενον καπνῷ ἐοικὸς καὶ ἐν ἀέρι διαλυόμενον.

Ταῦτα ἰδὼν καὶ ἀδιστάκτως τετυχηκέναι τῆς αἰτήσεως πιστεύσας, ἐπιστραφεὶς ἔφη τῷ μαθητῇ, "Δὸς δόξαν τῷ Θεῷ καὶ εὐχαριστίαν, ὦ τέκνον, σὺν ἐμοί. Ἰδοὺ γὰρ τὸ ἀκάθαρτον τῆς βλασφημίας πνεῦμα ἀπὸ σου[475] ἔξεισι καὶ ἀντ' αὐτοῦ τὸ εὐθὲς εἴσεισι πνεῦμα τοῦ τῆς παλιγγενεσίας ἀποκατασταθέντος χαρίσματος. Σεαυτῷ οὖν πρόσεχε[476] καὶ μηκέτι δι' ἀπροσεξίας καὶ ῥᾳθυμίας ταῖς τῆς ἀσεβείας[477] ἐμπέσῃς παγίσι μηδὲ[ν] ὀλεθρίῳ ὀλισθήματι τὴν ψυχὴν προί[ει][478] τῷ τῆς γεέννης πυρὶ κατακαίεσθαι."

Καὶ ταῦτα μὲν περὶ τούτου, ἐφ' ἕτερον δὲ βαδιοῦμαι.[479]

Païsios Assists John the Anchorite with His Fasting
Περὶ τοῦ ἐλθόντος Ἰωάννου πρὸς τὸν Παΐσιον

58. [190a2] Ἦλθέ ποτε πρὸς τὸν ἱερὸν Παΐσιον τις τῶν γερόντων, Ἰωάννης ὀνόματι, ὃς ἐν τῇ ἐρήμῳ πολλὰς ἡμέρας διανύσας, πόνους ἀσκητικοὺς <ἐγγυμναζόμενος>[480] σφοδρῶς ταλαιπωρῶν ἐδεῖτο τροφῆς καί τινος τότε ψυχαγωγίας. Ἐπ[ε]ὶ δὲ ἀλλήλοις ἐντυχόντες[481] τῆς χαριεστάτης ἐφ' ἱκανὸν ἐνετρύφησαν[482] ὁμιλίας, εἰδὼς[483] ὁ Παΐσιος ὅτι Ἰωάννης λίαν τῇ ἐγκρατείᾳ ἦν πιεζόμενος καὶ ἀναγκαίας μεταλήψεως ἐπιδεόμενος,[484] φησὶ τῷ προσόντι αὐτῷ μαθητῇ, "Τάχ[ε]ιον τράπεζαν ἑτοιμασθῆναι καὶ τροφὴν παραχθῆναι διακελεύομαι[485] ἵνα τῷ πατρὶ[486] συνεστιασθῶμεν." Ὁ δὲ ἐν τάχει παρέθηκε τράπεζαν.[487] Εἶτα ὁ γέρων παρῄνει τῷ Ἰωάννῃ ἐσθίειν, λέγων, "Σὺ μὲν ὑπὸ τῆς ἄγαν ἐγκρατείας τροφῆς[488] ὑποδεὴς ὤν, ἀνάσχου μεταλήψεως."

Ὁ δέ, "Σύγγνωθι," ἔφη, "ὅτι[489] σήμερον νηστεία ἐστὶ καὶ δεῖ με νηστεύειν ἕνεκα τῶν πολλῶν μου ἁμαρτιῶν."

Ὁ δὲ γέρων, θαυμάσας τὸν τοῦ Ἰωάννου ἀκλινῆ λογισμόν, αὐτ[ί]κα διαναστὰς καὶ προσχὼν εἰς οὐρανούς, "Κύριε," ἐκ βάθους καρδίας, εἶπεν, "Ἐπίσκεψαι τὸν δοῦλόν σου Ἰωάννην τὸν ὑπερβαλλόντως ἀγωνιζόμενον ἕνεκεν τοῦ ὀνόματός σου."

Οὕτως προσευχομένου, [191a1] χρηστὸν καὶ παράδοξον δώρημα ἐδίδου τὸ τῆς εὐχῆς πέρας· τηνικαῦτα τῷ {πονηρῷ} πνεύματι[490] κάτοχος γενόμενος ὁ Ἰωάννης νεανίσκον ἑωρακέναι ἐδόκει τροφὴν καὶ ποτὸν ἐν χερσὶν[491] ἔχοντα αὐτῷ προσ[σ]ιόντα ταύτην διδόναι. Εἰς ἑαυτὸν δὲ γενόμενος, ἔμπλεως ἦν ἡδονῆς καὶ μέχρι κόρου τροφῆς ἐμφορούμενος. Ἐπ[ε]ὶ μηδ' ὁ ὑλικῆς ἐδεῖτο,[492] ὁ τῆς ἀγγελικῆς [πεπληρωμένος][493] τροφῆς. Ἄντικρυς ἀνέστη Θεῷ τε καὶ τῷ θείῳ Παϊσίῳ, χάριτας ὁμολογῶν, τὴν ἔρημον πάλιν νήστης καταλαμβάνει, ἑτέραν ἐπὶ τῇ προτέρᾳ προσθεὶς νηστείαν.[494] Καὶ ἦν ἑαυτῷ διαλεγόμενος,[495] "Ἡδέως," ἔφαγον, "νηστεύσω λοιπὸν προθύμως."[496] Καὶ οὕτω μὲν ὁ γεννάδας[497] παλαίων ἦν καὶ νικῶν, τῇ προσευχῇ τοῦ ἱεροῦ Παϊσίου ἰσχὺν ἀνακτώμενος.[498]

Βούλεται δὲ ὁ λόγος ἕτερον ἄνδρα δεῖξαι κατὰ μὲν τὴν σπουδὴν ἀπειρίας ἐχόμενον, ἐπίκουρον δὲ τὴν τοῦ θείου Παϊσίου προσευχὴν ἐσχηκότα καὶ νικητὴν τροπαιοῦχον γεγονότα.

Païsios Helps a Young Anchorite to Defeat the Devil
Περὶ τοῦ ἐνοχλουμένου ὑπὸ τῶν λογισμῶν

59. [190b19] Ἦν τις τῶν εἰσαγομένων ἀνὴρ καταμόνας ἐν τῇ ἐρήμῳ ἀσκῶν ὅς τ[ῇ] τῶν λογισμῶν ἐπαναστάσ[ε]ι δεινῶς ὀχληθείς, πρὸς τὸν θεῖον ἀφικνεῖται Παΐσιον καί φησι πρὸς αὐτόν, "Δυσωπῶ τὴν σὴν ὁσιότητα ἐν ταῖς ἱεραῖς [191b1] σου εὐχαῖς τῆς ἐμῆς ἐπιμνησθῆναι εὐτελείας, ὅτι δεινῶς ὑπὸ τῶν δαιμόνων πολεμοῦμαι."

Ὁ δὲ τοῦτον οἰκείῳ θελήματι ἐπόμενον κατανοήσας,[499] καὶ τῷ ποικίλῳ τῆς [πονηρίας][500] δαίμονι καὶ τῆς κενοδοξίας ἐξακολουθοῦντι ἐπισχεῖν, τὸν ν[έ]ον βουλόμενος[501] ἀτάκτως φέρεσθαι, ἔφη πρὸς αὐτόν, "Οὐκ οὕτ[ω]ς, ὦ τέκνον, ὡς ὑπέλαβες, ὑπὸ δαιμόνων πολεμούμενος ἦς,[502] ἄτε αὐτῶν μὴ αἰσθανομένων ἀκμὴν εἴγε ἐν τῇ ἐρήμῳ τῇδε παραγέγ[ο]νας, ἀλ[λ' οὖν] ἐξ οἰκείων λογισμῶν πεπολέμησαι. Ἀπελθε, τοιγαροῦν, ἀγωνιζόμενος καὶ τὴν θείαν ἀεὶ[503] ἐπισκέψεσθαί σε ῥοπὴν ἐκδυσωπῶν. Πειρασθῆναι γὰρ μέλλεις καὶ δ[ει]νῶς πολεμηθῆναι τηνικαῦτα καὶ εἴσῃ καλῶς τὰς τῶν δαιμόνων προσβολὰς καὶ οἷα ὑφίστανται οἱ ὑπ' αὐτῶν πολεμούμενοι χαλεπά."

Ταῦτα εἰπ[ὼ]ν, οἴκαδε τὸν νέον ἀπέπεμψεν, εἶτα ὑπερηύξατο ἐκτενῶς ἄτρωτον τὸν νέον[504] διαφυλαχθῆναι.[505]

60. [191a20] Ὁ δὲ ἄρχων τῶν δαιμόνων ἄντικρυς ὠρυόμενος ὤφθη λεοντοειδής, "Ὦ Βία," λέγων, "Τί ἐμοὶ καὶ σοί,[506] ὦ Παΐσιε;[507] Πάνυ με ἀδικεῖς, μηδὲν σε πολεμοῦντα."

Ὁ δὲ γέρων, "Ἀπόστηθι," ἔφη, "τοῦ {ν}νέου μοναχοῦ. Μὴ ὀχλήσῃς αὐτῷ πονηροὺς [192a1] διεγείρων λογισμούς."

Καὶ ὁ δαίμ[ω]ν θαρσαλέως καὶ ἀλαζ[ο]νικῶς, "Πείσθητί μοι," ἀντέλεγεν, "ὅτι ὁ νεανίας οὗτος οὔπω μοι ἐγνωρίσατο εἰ τῆς ἐρήμου γέγονεν οἰκήτωρ,[508] ἀλλ' ὑπὸ τῆς οἰκείας πολιορκεῖται ῥᾳθυμίας. Ἀπὸ δὲ τοῦ νῦν γενέσθω ἕτοιμ[ο]ς ὑποστῆναι τὰς ἐμὰς δεινὰς ἐπηρείας."[509]

Ὁ δὲ γέρων, "Ἐπιτιμήσας σε ὁ θεός," ἔφη, "τῆς ἀληθείας, ἐχθρέ, καὶ τῷ αἰωνίῳ διωθήσειε πυρί."

Ταῦτα εἰπόντος, εὐθὺς γέγονεν ἄφαντος,[510] ἀλλὰ τῆς κακίας οὐκ ἐπαύσατο[511] ὁ ταύτης ὑπηρέτης καὶ ἐραστής[512] ἀλλ' ἔργοις τὰ ῥηθέντα διαβ[ε]β[αι]οῖ κατὰ τοῦ νέου στρατεύσας μοναχοῦ καὶ πᾶν εἶδος δείκνυει[513] τῆς αὐτοῦ κακοτεχνίας. Ἐπ[ε]ὶ δὲ ταῖς τούτου ἐπινοίαις πειραζόμενος ὁ νέος στέγων οὐκ ἦν τὴν τοῦ ἐχθροῦ δεινότητα ἀλλὰ πρὸς τὸν ἄσειστον πύργον πάλιν καταφεύγει τὸν μέγαν Παΐσιον καὶ τὰ ἀφόρητα διηγεῖται τοῦ πονηροῦ πάντα καὶ ὅτι οὐδαμῶς ἀνεκτὰ[514] τὰ ἐκείνου δεινά.

Ὁ δὲ ἅγιος, "Οὐκ εἶπόν σοι," ἔφη, "ὦ τέκνον, ὅτι οὐκ ἔστι ἡ ἄφ[ι]ξίς σου[515] ἐν τῇδε τῇ ἐρήμῳ [ἀγνωστὸς εἶναι][516] ἐκείνῳ;" Εἶτα παραινῶν αὐτῷ καὶ ἐπαλ[εί]φων εἰς προσευχήν, [192b1] ἐτράπετο καὶ, "Κύριε, υἱὲ Θεοῦ καὶ Λόγε," εἶπε, "τὸ πλάσμα σου μὴ παρίδῃς ὑπὸ τοῦ δυσμενοῦς καταποθῆναι, ἀλλ' ἄνωθεν αὐτῷ χεῖρα ἀρ[ρ]ωγὸν παράσχου εἰς ἐπικουρίαν, ἀήττητον γάρ σου τὸ κράτος καὶ πάντα ὑποτέτακται τῇ δυνάμει σου."

61. [192a6] Ταῦτα εἰπόντος <καὶ>[517] προσευχομένου, θεῖος ἄγγελος εὐθὺς αὐτῷ ἐπιστάς, ἁλύσεσι τὸν διάβολον ἔχων δεδεμένον, "Λάβε τοῦτον," εἶπεν, "ὡς βούλῃ[518] τὸν ἀλιτήριον ἐξέτασον. Ἰδού σοι ὡς δέσμιος δ[ί]δοται ὁ ταῖς ποικίλαις αὐτοῦ μηχαναῖς πολλοὺς δεσμίους ἐσχηκώς."

Ὑπολαβὼν δὲ ὁ διάβολος τῷ γέροντί, φησι, "Φεῦ τῆς εὐχῆς σου, Παΐσιε, ἕως πότε με βασανίζων δι' αὐτῆς διατελεῖς πάντας περιέπων καὶ φυλάττων[519] τοὺς ταύτης τῆς ἐρήμου οἰκήτορας; Ἄθλιος ἐγώ γε εἰ τούτοις συνεδρεύων ἐνθάδε καρτερή[σαιμι].[520] Ἀναχωρήσω γὰρ ὄντως πορρωτάτω μεθ[ι]στάμενος."

Ὁ δὲ προσχὼν αὐτῷ, "Ἀποστάτα," ἔφη, "καὶ τοῦ ἀνθρωπ[ε]ίου γένους ἐχθρέ, ἵνα τί[521] ἐπέθου τῷ νεωτέρῳ δεινῶς μαχόμενος; Καὶ οὕτου χάριν τοὺς ἀγωνιζομένους ἐν τῇ ἀρχῇ ἐμμανῶς πολεμεῖς;"

Καὶ πρὸς αὐτὸν ὁ Βελίαρ ἀποκριθείς, "Ἐγώ," φησι, "τοῖς εἰσαγωκικοῖς <ἀρχαρίοις>[522] οὐ πρόσειμι [193a1] περὶ τὴν τῶν ἀγώνων ἀρχήν. Παραχωρηθῆναι μὲν γὰρ ὑπὸ τῆς χάριτος τούτοις προσεγγίζειν μηδαμῶς[523] συμβαίνει θερμῶς ἀγωνιζομένοις. Ἀναχωρούσης δὲ τῆς χάριτος ἕνεκεν τῆς τούτων[524] ῥαθυμίας, εὐθὺς προσχωρῶν, ὡς θήραμα ἕτοιμον κατασχὼν παίγνιον[525] τούτους, ὡς βούλομαι, ἔχω. Διὰ γὰρ ταύτην τὴν [αἰ]τίαν καταρχὰς μὲν ἀπαναίνομαι μάχεσθαι τούτο[ις]· μὲν ὑπὸ τῆς χάριτος καὶ τῆς θέρμης[526] καταφλεχθῆναι σκεπτόμενος, τοῦτο δὲ καὶ τῇ προσδοκίᾳ τῆς ὕστερον ῥαθυμίας τούτοις περιφρονῶ ἀναβαλλόμενος.[527] Ἐπ[ε]ιδὰν δὲ θερμοτέρους αὐτοὺς καὶ ἐπὶ τῷ πρόσω χωροῦντας ὁρῶ,[528] τηνικαῦτα τὰς κατ' αὐτῶν ὁρμὰς ἐπέχω, ἵνα μὴ τῇ διηνεκεῖ τοῦ ἀγῶνος σπουδῇ καὶ τῇ προσθήκῃ τῶν χρηστῶν ἀκαταγώνιστοι γένωνται καὶ ἄτρωτοι οἰκειωθέντες τῇ χάριτι."[529]

Καὶ ταῦτα μὲν <οὕτως,>[530] ὁ διάβολος διεξῄει καὶ μὴ βουλόμενος.

62. [192b19] Ὁ δὲ ἅγιος, "Λάβέ," φησι τῷ ἀγγέλῳ, "τοῦτον τὸν δέσμιον. Τὸν τῆς ἀληθείας ἐχθρὸν τοῖς ἡτοιμασμένοις αὐτῷ δεινοῖς ἐν πυρὶ γεέν[ν]ης ταμιευσάμενος." Ταῦτα[531] εἰπόντος <αὐτοῦ,>[532] ἀπῄει ὁ μὲν ἐν δόξῃ ὁ δὲ ἐν ἀτιμίᾳ.[533] Ἠλευθερώθη δὲ καὶ ὁ μοναχὸς ἔκτοτε τῆς τοῦ δαίμονος ὀχλήσεως καὶ οὐ [193b1] καὶ τούτῳ ὀφθῆναι

ἢ πολεμῆσαι ἴσχυσεν,⁵³⁴ ὅς καὶ θεαρέστως διανύσας τὸν ἀσκητικὸν αὐτοῦ βίον ἀνεπαύσατο⁵³⁵ καλῶς ταῖς τοῦ ἱεροῦ⁵³⁶ Παϊσίου εὐχαῖς ἐπερειδόμενος.

John Tells about Païsios's Insight
Περὶ τῶν μοναχῶν τῶν ἐλθ[ό]ντων πρὸς τὸν Παΐσιον

63. [193a5] Καθεζομένου μοῦ ποτ[ε] πρὸς αὐτὸν, προσελθόντες αὐτῷ τινες τῶν μοναχῶν λ[ό]γων τῶν ἐκείνου ἐπωφελῶν ἀκοῦσαι.⁵³⁷ "Εἰπὲ ἡμῖν," ἔφησαν, "[ὦ]⁵³⁸ πάτερ, λόγον ζωηρόν."

Ὁ δὲ γέρων, "Πορευθέντες," ἔφη, "φυλάξατε τὴν παράδοσιν⁵³⁹ τῶν πατέρων καὶ πλ[έ]ον τῶν διατεταγμένων δρᾶν μὴ ζητεῖτε."⁵⁴⁰

Οἱ δὲ, "Εἰπὲ ἡμῖν," καὶ αὖθις, λέγουσιν, "ἕτερον τι ψυχωφελὲς τῶν τοῖς καθ' ἡμᾶς προσηκ[ό]ντων."

Ὁ δὲ θεῖος ἀνὴρ τὰ τῶν ἐκείνων ψυχῶν ἐνορατικοῖς⁵⁴¹ ὀφθαλμοῖς ἑωρακὼς ἐνθυμήματα καὶ διανοήματα ἐπεξῄει ἑκάστῳ κατὰ μέρος τί ἄν καὶ [εἴη]⁵⁴² διανοούμενος καὶ τ[ί]να μὲν εἴη τῶν νοηθέντων χρηστὰ, τίνα δὲ τῶν ἐναντίων, καὶ ὅθεν αὐτοῖς ταῦτα συνέβη.

Οἱ δὲ λίαν [194a1] θαυμάσαντες, κατ' ἰδίαν μοι εἰρήκασιν,⁵⁴³ "Ὄντως, πάτερ Ἰωάννη, πάντα ἡμῖν διήγητ[αι] τὰ τῆς καρδίας παθήματα κατ' εἶδος καὶ τὰ μόνα τῷ θεῷ⁵⁴⁴ γνωστά."⁵⁴⁵

Κἀγὼ εἶπον αὐτοῖς, "Ἐξ ὧν πολλάκις διεβεβαιώθην⁵⁴⁶ <καὶ ἐν πείρᾳ γενόμενος τῇ τῶν αὐτῶν πραγμάτων. Πιστεύετέ μοι, οὐδὲν τῶν ἐκείνου φθέγξομαι τῆς ἀληθείας ἐκτός. Ἐπεὶ καὶ δικαστὴν ἐκδεχόμεθα αὐτὴν τὴν ἀλήθειαν ἡμῖν ζητούμενον, καθὼς ἐν τῷ ἁγίῳ εὐαγγελίῳ γέγραπται, ὅτι 'Ἀπὸ τῶν λόγων σου δικαιωθήσῃ καὶ ἀπὸ τῶν λόγων σου κατακριθήσῃ,' καὶ ὅτι 'Ὑπὲρ ἀργοῦ λόγου λόγον δώσομεν,' ἐῶ γὰρ λέγειν καὶ τὰς λοιπὰς ἐτάσεις ἃς ὑποστῆναι καὶ ἀπολογηθῆναι, μέλλομεν ἐν ἐκείνῳ τῷ φοβερῷ καὶ ἀστέκτῳ βήματι τοῦ ποιήσαντος ἡμᾶς θεοῦ. Καὶ οὐαὶ τοῖς, ὡς ἐμὲ, ἐν ἐκείνῃ τῇ ἡμέρᾳ εὑρεθεῖσιν. Οἴμοι, οἴμοι, αὐτοκατάκριτοι γὰρ εἰς κόλασιν πεμφθήσονται, μηδὲν τὸ παράπαν ἔχοντες ἀποφθέγξασθαι.

"Ὅμως τῶν τοιούτων ἐνθυμήσεων μικρὸν ἀναμείναντες τὴν ἄνωθεν τοῦ λόγου ὁρμὴν βαδίσωμεν καὶ αὐτὴν τὴν ἀλήθειαν ὑμῖν διηγετέον. Ἐπ' ἀληθείας δὲ λέγω ὑμῖν>⁵⁴⁷ ὅτι π[ε]ίσθητέ μοι, καὶ ἃ ἐνδιαθέτως πολλάκις λελόγισμαι⁵⁴⁸ καὶ ἃ ἐν ἰδίᾳ δέδρακα διεσάφησέ μοι χαριέντ[ω]ς⁵⁴⁹ συναντ[ή]σας <μοι>⁵⁵⁰ ὡς συμπαρὼν ἅπαντα ἐξιών."⁵⁵¹

Οἱ δὲ, "Θαυμαστὸς⁵⁵² ὁ θεὸς ἐν τοῖς ἁγίοις αὐτοῦ," ἔλεγ[ο]ν,⁵⁵³ ἀναχωροῦντες.⁵⁵⁴

Βούλεται δὲ ὁ λόγος ὑποδεῖξαι ἔργον τῆς ὑπακοῆς καὶ οἷα τοῖς παρηκό[οι]ς <ἡ> ἀπείθεια.⁵⁵⁵

Païsios Intercedes with God on Behalf of the Apostate Monk Isaac
Περὶ τοῦ ἐξακολουθοῦντος τὸ ἴδιον θέλημα

64. [194a15] Ἀδελφός τις ἐξ[η]κόλουθει τῷ ἰδίῳ θελήματι. Τῆς ἐρήμου καὶ τῶν ταύτης καλῶν ἀφ[ι]έμενος, ἀπελθὼν ᾤκησε πλ[η]σίον πόλεως. Ἐπεὶ δὲ συγεχῶς τῇ πόλει <ἐκείνῃ>[556] προσήρχετο τὸ ἐργόχειρον ἀπεμπολῆσαι, συνέβη τινὶ γυναικὶ γένους τῶν Ἑβραίων ὑπαρχούσῃ τοῦτον ἐντυχεῖν,[557] ἔρωτι σατανικῷ καταφλεγομένῃ, συνεργ[ε]ίᾳ δαιμονικῇ καὶ λογισμῶν ἀπάτῃ τ[ῇ] πάγῃ ἐκείνης—οἴμοι—ἑάλω ὁ μοναχός. Τὸ δὲ ἐντεῦθεν, συνέλαβε [194b1] πόνον καὶ ἔτεκεν ἀνομίαν, καὶ τὸ δὴ χαλεπ[ώ]τερον ὅτι καὶ τῆς οἰκείας—φεῦ—ἀποστὰς[558] πίστεως τῇ Ἰουδαϊκῇ προσετέθη[559] θρησκείᾳ.

Σύσκηνός τε καὶ συνόμιλος ταύτῃ γενόμενος τοσοῦτον τῇ ταύτης συναπάγεται γνώμῃ ὅσον καὶ τῆς ἀσε[β]είας ἐκείνη[ς] κοινωνὸς, ἐφάνη συγκαταθέμενος τῇ ὕβρει.[560] Γίνεται γὰρ τὸ τρισκατάρατον ἐκεῖνο γύναιον μέχρι τοσούτου κατενεχθὲν βυθοῦ τῆς ἀπ[ω]λείας καὶ ἀν[αι]δείας, ὥστε πολλάκις τὴν κεφαλὴν ἐκείνου τοῦ ἀθλίου <ἐν>[561] οἰκείοις κόλποις [λαβοῦσα][562] καὶ τὸ στόμα αὐτοῦ ἀνοίξασα καὶ ξύλον ἐγχειρισαμένη χερσὶ τοὺς ὀδόντας[563] ἐξεκάθηρε[ν] ἵνα μὴ λείψανον ἐκ τῆς ἀχράντου κοινωνίας—ὢ τῆς ἀθεΐας—τοῖς ὀδοῦσιν ἐκείνου ἀπολειφθῇ.[564]

Ἠλγήσατε, οἶδα, ὑμεῖς τοιαῦτα ἀκούσαντες, κἀγὼ τὴν τοῦ θεοῦ ἐκπλήττομαι ἀνοχὴν, ἀλλ' οὖν τῆς αὐτοῦ φιλανθρωπίας καὶ τῆς ἄνωθεν ἐπισκοπούσης[565] θείας ροπῆς[566] τοῖς ἀγαμένοις τὸ ἄμετρον λέξων ἔρχομαι τὸ παράδοξον.[567]

65. [194a23] Ὁ οὖν ἀνὴρ ἐκεῖνος ὁ τῶν χριστιανῶν τῇ παρακοῇ διαζευχθεὶς διὰ[568] τὴν οἰκείαν ἀσέβειαν ὀψὲ γοῦν ποτε ἑαυτοῦ κατέγνω [195a1] <τῇ>[569] τῆς θείας οἰκονομίας καταυγασθεὶς δᾳδουχίᾳ. Συνέβη γάρ τινας τῶν τῆς ἐρήμου ἐκείνης ἐν ᾗ πάλαι ὁ ἀνὴρ ἤσκει τὴν πόλιν ἐκείνην διά τινα χρείαν καταλαβεῖν καὶ κατὰ πάροδον τὸ δολερὸν <ἐκείνης>[570] οἴκημα διελθόντας ἐν ὄψει γενέσθαι τ[ῷ] ἀνδρὶ ὅς πληγεὶς τὴν καρδίαν καὶ τῆς παλαιᾶς καὶ ἱερᾶς ἐκείνης ἐπιμνησθεὶς συνοδίας, ἐπυνθάνετο τούτους πόθεν εἶεν καὶ τίνες, καὶ ὅτου χάριν αὐτόθι παρεγένοντο.

Οἱ δὲ, "Ἐκ τῆς Ν[ι]τρίας," ἔφασαν, "εἶναι τοῦ Παϊσίου τυγχάνοντες[571] μαθηταὶ καὶ χάριν χρ[ε]ίας ἀναγκαίας ἐν τῇ πόλ[ει] γενέσθαι."[572]

Καὶ ὅς θερμῶς αὐτοὺς παρεκάλει ὑπὲρ αὐτοῦ τῷ μεγάλῳ[573] ἱκεσίαν ἀναφέρειν ὅπως αὐτοῦ ταῖς λιταῖς τὸν Κύριον ἐξιλεώσας τῶν τοῦ ἐχθροῦ μηχανημάτων με ἐλευθερω[θείη].[574]

Οἱ δὲ, "Ὡς βούλει ποιήσομεν τὴν ὑπόμνησιν," ἔλεγον, ἅμα δὲ καὶ παρακαλέσαι τὸν μέγαν[575] ὑπέσχοντο ὑπὲρ αὐτοῦ εὔχεσθαι.

Ἐπανιόντες τοίνυν τὰ κατ' αὐτὸν τῷ θείῳ διεσάφησαν πατρί. Ὁ δὲ γέρων τὰ περὶ ἐκείνου ἀκούσας,[576] [βυθιόν τε][577] στενάξας εἶπεν, "Οἴ μοι, τέκνα ἀγαπητά, πόσοι τῶν ἀρίστων διὰ γυναικῶν [195b1] τῆς θείας ἐξέπεσον χάριτος, ὧν ὑπομνήματα ἐκ τῆς θείας γραφῆς ἄνωθεν ἐκ προγόνων ἔχ[ο]μεν; Τῆς γὰρ γυναικὸς ἐπιτηδειοτέρῳ ὀργάνῳ οὐκ ἐνῆν τ[ῷ] ἐχθρῷ ἑτέρῳ χρήσασθαι. Τοῦτο γὰρ χρ[ώ]μενος[578] τῷ ὅπλῳ, τῶν μεγάλων εἴθ[ι]σται περιγενέσθαι ἀνδρῶν ὡς καὶ[579] τὸν μέγαν Δαυὶδ καὶ τοὺς ἐκείνου προγόνους καὶ ἐκγόνους.[580] Διὸ καὶ ἡμᾶς ῥυσθῆναι τῶν τοιούτων μηχανημάτων ἀεὶ ὑπερεύχεσθαι χρή."[581]

Ταῦτα εἰπών, ὑπ[ε]ρηύξατο, λέγων, "Κύριε, υἱὲ Θεοῦ καὶ Λόγ[ε],[582] μὴ παρίδῃς τὸ πλάσμα τῶν χειρῶν σου εἰς τέλος βυθῷ τῆς ἀπωλείας καταποθῆναι, ἀλλ' ἀνεξικάκως ἐκ τῶν ἐπουρανίων σου κατοικητηρίων ἐπ[ί]βλεψον[583] καὶ τὰς ἐμάς[584] σοι προσαγομένας εὐχὰς [πρόσ]δεξαι[585] ὑπὲρ τοῦ ἀθετήσαντός σε καὶ πάλιν ἑαυτοῦ καταγνόντος. Ἀνακάλεσαι[586] τοῦτον πρὸς μετάνοιαν δέομαι τῆς σῆς ἀγαθότητος."

Οὕτω δὲ ἐπὶ συχναῖς[587] ἡμέραις προσευχόμενος οὐκ ἐπαύσετο[588] τοὺς οἰκτιρμοὺς τοῦ Θεοῦ δυσωπῶν.[589] [Ἐπεὶ δὲ ταῖς τούτου δεήσεσιν][590] τῶν θεϊκῶν σπλάγχνων δυσωπηθέντων οὐ παρορῶντο, ἐπιφαίνεται αὐτῷ ὁ Σωτήρ[591] [196a1] καὶ τίνος χάριν αὐτοῦ γεγενῆσθαι τὴν δέησιν ἐπυνθάνετο[592] ὁ πάντα εἰδώς, "Μὴ ὑπὲρ τοῦ ἀθετήσαντός με καὶ τῆς ἐμῆς ἀπολειφθέντος τάξεως καὶ τοῖς ὑπεναντίοις συναπαχθέντος[593] τοῦ ποτὲ μὲν ὑπάρχοντος μοναχοῦ, νυνὶ δὲ Ἑβραίου γεγονότος, ὁ ἐμὸς θεράπων δέεται Παΐσιος;"

Ὁ δέ, "Ναί," φησι, "φιλάνθρωπε Χριστέ, εἰς τοὺς σοὺς γὰρ ἀφορῶν οἰκτιρμοὺς ταύτας[594] ἀεὶ πρὸς μετάνοιαν καλοῦντος[595] καὶ μὴ βουλομένου τὸν θάνατον τοῦ ἁμαρτωλοῦ, ἀλλὰ τὴν ἐπιστροφὴν αὐτοῦ ἀναμένοντος. Τούτου χάριν τεθάρρηκα ἐξιλεώσασθαι ὑπὲρ ἐκείνου τὴν σὴν ἀγαθότητα. Ἀνάσχου οὖν δυσωπούμενος καὶ ἵλε[ω]ς γενοῦ καὶ τὸ πεπλανημένον γένος [κάλεσόν][596] σου πρόβατον."[597]

66. [196a18] Ταῦτα μὲν οὗτος. Ὁ δὲ Σωτήρ, "Εἰ βούλει ἐκεῖνον δέ," φησι, "τὸν οἰκειωθέντα <τῇ>[598] παρανομίᾳ καὶ τῆς ἀγγελικῆς ἀποστασίας ποίμνης[599] διὰ τῶν ἀτόπων ἔργων αὐτοῦ ἐλεῆσαι καὶ ἀνακαλέσαι, τῶν σῶν πόνων ἀνάσχου ἀφελεῖν τὰ πλεῖστα τῶν ἐπάθλων, δικαίως ἀντιμετροῦντος [196b1] ἐκείνῳ τὴν φιλανθρωπίαν μυρίων ὄντι τιμωριῶν ἀξίῳ."

"Ναί," φησιν, "ἡδέως ἀνάσχωμαι, ἀγαθὲ Χριστέ," ὁ μέγας Παΐσιος. "Εἰ οὖν ἐμοὶ ἔργον εὐάρεστον ἐνώπιόν σου, οὐκ οἶδα, ἐκ τῆς σῆς δὲ μᾶλλον χρηστότητος, δι' ἧς καθ' ἑκάστην ἐ[υ]αρεστούμενος[600] τὴν χάριν σου ὁμολογῶ, ἔκχεον ἐπ' αὐτὸν τὸ ἔλεός σου, ἐφετόν μοι γὰρ ἀντ' ἐκείνου τὰς ἐκείνου τιμωρίας ὑποστῆναι σωζομένου, ἢ τῶν σῶν ἀπολαῦσαι εὐεργεσιῶν ἀπολ[λ]υμένου."

67. [196b10] Καὶ ὁ Σωτὴρ εὐθὺς πρὸς αὐτόν, "Βαβαὶ⁶⁰¹ τῆς τοῦ θεράποντός μου εὐγνωμοσύνης τὴν ἀγάπην μου μ[ι]μουμένου. Ὑπὲρ τῆς σῆς <τιμωρίας>⁶⁰² προείλου ἐκπεσεῖν ὑπὲρ ἁμαρτωλοῦ σωτηρίας διὰ τοῦτο τῶν σῶν μὲν ἥκ[ε]ιστα ἐκπεσὼν ἔσῃ, τεύξ[εται] δὲ καὶ τῆς αἰτήσεως."⁶⁰³

Ταῦτα εἰπών, ὁ Σωτὴρ πρὸς οὐρανοὺς ἀνῆλθεν. Οὐ πολὺ τὸ ἐν μέσῳ καὶ τοῦ δεινοῦ ἐκείνου γυναίου θεηλάτῳ ὀργῇ τὸν βίον καταστρέψαντος, ὁ Ἰσαὰκ πάλιν—τοῦτο γὰρ ἦν ἐκείνῳ τὸ ὄνομα—τὴν ἔρημον καταλαμβάνει καὶ κατηχηθεὶς παρὰ τοῦ μεγάλου·⁶⁰⁴ τῆς τε πρώτης αὐτοῦ πίστεως καὶ τ[ῆ]ς ἀγγελικῆς πολιτείας ἀντείχετο, ἐν ὑπακοῇ τε καὶ σεμνῇ διαγωγῇ⁶⁰⁵ καὶ καταστάσει φιλαρέτως βιώσας πρὸς Κύριον ἐξεδήμησε. Καὶ τοιούτων μὲν ἐκεῖνος ἔτυχε λιταῖς τοῦ ἱεροῦ⁶⁰⁶ [197a1] Παϊσίου. Ἡμᾶς δὲ τὰ ἐκείνου παράδοξα ἀκούοντας δοξάζειν <χρὴ>⁶⁰⁷ καὶ τὸν ἐκείνου μεγαλύνειν Θεόν.⁶⁰⁸

Païsios Prays on Behalf of an Impudent Priest
Περὶ τοῦ πρεβυτέρου τοῦ κοσμ[ι]κὰ φρονοῦντος
68. [197a5] Πρεσβύτερός τις ἦν ἐν τῇ ἐρήμῳ⁶⁰⁹ ἐκείνῃ κοσμικὸν φρόνημα κεκτημένος.⁶¹⁰ Ὁ δὲ ἡνίκα ἂν πρὸς τὸν πατέρα ἡμῶν Παΐσιον ἀφίκοιντο οἱ μοναχοὶ εἰς ἀκρόασιν τῶν ἐκείνου ἐπωφελῶν λογίων,⁶¹¹ τῆς μὲν ἀκοῆς αὐτοῖς ἐκοινώνει, τῆς δὲ τῶν θείων ῥημάτων ὠφελείας ἄμοιρος ἦν. Μὴ ἔχων γὰρ νοῦν ἀγαθὸν μηδὲ γῆν βαθύγεων καὶ καρποφόρον τοὺς λόγους ἐκωμῴδει καὶ ἑτέροις λόγοις⁶¹² οὓς αἱ κοσμικαὶ συνήθειαι φέρειν εἰώθασι, χρώμενος τὰ καταβαλλόμενα διέφθειρεν.⁶¹³

Ὅθεν ἀγανακτοῦντες πρός τινα γέροντα θεοφ[ι]λῆ⁶¹⁴ παραγενόμενοι κατ[η]γόγγυσαν.⁶¹⁵ Ὁ δὲ ἅμα τούτοις πρὸς τὸν μέγαν ἔρχεται Παΐσιον. Μετέπειτα δὲ καὶ ὁ πρεσβύτερος⁶¹⁶ συνείπετο. Ἐν ἰδί[ᾳ] δὲ ὁ γέρων ἐκεῖνος τῷ θείῳ Παϊσίῳ φησί, "Γνωστὸν ἔστω σοι, πάτερ, ὅτι ὁ πρεσβύτερος οὗτος σκανδάλων αἴτιός ἐστι καὶ πρόσκομμα τοῖς ἀδελφοῖς καὶ δέονται ἵνα <ὅπως>⁶¹⁷ τὴν ἄτακτον αὐτοῦ ὁρμὴν ἐπισχὼν ἐπιτιμίοις δι[ορ]θ[ώ]σ[ε]ις αὐτόν."

"Καὶ μήν," ἀντέφησε ὁ μέγας, [197b1] "πάλαι ἂν τοῦτο ἐποιησάμην εἰ τοῦτον ὠφεληθῆναι ἔγνωκα. Ἰδοὺ γὰρ ὁ διάβολος ἕτοιμος αὐτῷ ἐπέστη εἰς ἀπ[ώ]λειαν προσκαλούμενος. Καὶ ἡνίκα ἂν ἡμῶν ἀκούσῃ λόγον ἀηδῆ καὶ αὐστηρόν, ἐκ μέσου γίνεται τῆς ἀδελφότητος καὶ πάλιν τὰ κοσμικὰ καταλαμβάνει, ἐγὼ δὲ ὁ ἐγ[γ]υητὴς Θεῷ ὡς ὑπεύθυνος ὀφθήσομαι καὶ τῆς ἀπ[ω]λείας παραίτιος ἑνὸς ἀδελφοῦ μὴ δυνάμενος ἀντέχεσθαι ὑπὸ τοῦ ἐχθροῦ πολεμουμένου. Πλὴν οὖν περὶ τοῦ τοιούτου πάθους εὔχεσθαι χρή."

Ταῦτα εἰπών, ὑπερηύξατο ἐκείνου καὶ εὐθὺς τὸν δαίμονα τῆς ἀν[αι]δ[ε]ίας ἀποδρᾶσαι ποιεῖ. Καὶ ὃς ἦν παραχρῆμα τοῖς τῆς

μεταμελείας κέντροις δεινῶς νυσόμενος⁶¹⁸ καὶ λίαν τῷ συνειδότι τὴν
ψυχὴν παθ[αι]νόμενος δάκρυσί τε μᾶλλον⁶¹⁹ ἢ λόγοις ἀπολογούμενος τὴν
ἐπὶ τὸ κρεῖσσον μετάθεσιν καὶ πάντων συγ[γ]νώμην τῶν παρελθ[ό]ντων
[αἰ]τούμενος, καὶ ἦν ἔκτοτε προσηνὴς <καὶ>⁶²⁰ ἀκροατὴς τῶν θείων
λογίων, ἡδέως μὲν ἀκούων, ἡδέως δὲ τὰ τοῖς⁶²¹ λόγοις δοκοῦντα
πράττων χρηστά, ὅθεν καὶ πολ[λ]οὺς ὑπερβὰς περὶ τὰς ἀρετὰς δόκιμος
γέγονε[ν] ἀναχωρητὴς εὐχῶν συνεργ[ε]ίᾳ τοῦ θείου Παϊσίου καὶ ἄλλο⁶²²
φρικωδέστερον⁶²³ τῶν θαυμάτων καὶ παραδοξότερον διηγητέον.⁶²⁴

Païsios Washes Christ's Feet
Περὶ τῆς Παρουσίας⁶²⁵ τοῦ Σωτῆρος
μετὰ τῶν Δύο Ἀγγέλων.
69. [197b1] Ἐν προσευχῇ γενομένῳ ποτέ τ[ῷ] Παϊσίῳ ἐν τῷ ἰδίῳ
ἄντρῳ, παρέβαλεν ὁ Σωτὴρ σὺν δυσὶν ἀγγέλοις οἷα πρὸς τὸν
πατριάρχην Ἀβραάμ, "Χαίροις, Παΐσιε," λέγων, "σήμερ[ον] παρὰ σοὶ
φιλοξενηθῆναι ἡμᾶς δεῖ."⁶²⁶

Ὁ δὲ προθύμως δεξάμενος, μιμητὴς ἐκείνου γίνεται τοῦ πατριάρχου
<φιλόξενος,>⁶²⁷ οὐ βρωμάτων καὶ πομάτων ἐπιμελούμενος, ἀλλὰ διαθέσει
εἰλικρινεῖ χρώμενος. Ξενίζει <οὖν>⁶²⁸ τὸν πανταχοῦ οἰκοῦντα, εἶτα ὕδωρ
<ἐν>⁶²⁹ νιπτῆρι βαλών—ὢ τῶν σῶν οἰκτιρμῶν, Χριστέ,⁶³⁰ οἷον φίλτρον
περὶ τοιαύτους⁶³¹ ἐραστὰς ἔχων συγκαταβαίνεις ποθεινῶς!—φιλοτίμως
τοὺς ἀχράντους [σ]ου πόδας νίπτει Παΐσιος. ⁶³²˙ Ὁ μὲν τῆς φιλοξενίας
ἐπιμελούμενος προθύμως, ὁ δὲ τῆς ἀγάπης φιλανθρώπως [ἀν]εχόμενος.⁶³³
(Τὸ δὲ ἐντεῦθεν ἐπ[ε]ὶ μηδέν τι τῶν τῆς φιλοξενίας⁶³⁴˙ ἐπιεικέστερον τοῦ
ἀποπλῦναι τοὺς πόδας τῶν παραβαλλόντων.) "Εἰρήνη σοι τῷ ἐκλεκτῷ
μου," φήσας ὁ Σωτήρ, ἄφαντος ἐγένετο.

Ἀναφλεχθεὶς δὲ τῷ θείῳ ἔρωτι τῆς ἐκείνου ὁμιλίας, ὁ ἱερὸς
Παΐσιος⁶³⁵ κἂν τούτῳ τὸν Κλεοπᾶν μιμούμενος ἦν καιομένην [ἔχων]⁶³⁶
[198b1] τὴν καρδίαν καὶ δυσκάθεκτον ἔχων.⁶³⁷ Ἀμέλει καὶ τῷ ὕδατι
προσδραμὼν ὅπερ ὁ Σωτὴρ ὡς μέγα τι καὶ ἀξιόχρηστον⁶³⁸ χρῆμα
τούτῳ κατέλιπεν, ἡδέως αὐτῷ ἔπιε βραχύ τι καταλιπὼν τῷ οἰκείῳ
μαθητῇ. Καὶ τοῦτο οὐκ ἄποθεν τῆς φιλοχρ[ί]στου⁶³⁹ ἐκείνου γνώμης
τοῦ μὴ μόνον ἑαυτῷ ἑλομένου τὸ ἀγαθόν, ἀλλὰ καὶ τ[ῷ] πλησί[ον]⁶⁴⁰
ταμιευσαμένου. Ἐλθόντι οὖν τῷ μαθητῇ ἐκ τῆς ὁδοιπορίας—ἦν γὰρ εἰς
Αἴγυπτον—σφόδρα κεκοπιακότι.⁶⁴¹ Ὁ δὲ μέγας τὸ καταλ[ει]φθὲν ὕδωρ
πιεῖν αὐτῷ ἐνέσκηψεν,⁶⁴² "Ἄπελθε," εἰπών, "ὦ τέκνον, εἰς τὸν νιπτῆρα
καὶ πιὼν τὴν ἐκ τοῦ καύματος δίψαν κατάπαυσον."⁶⁴³

Ὁ δέ, "Οὕτω ποιῶν ἔσομαι, πάτερ." Τῇ γλώττῃ μὲν ἀπεφθέγξατο,⁶⁴⁴
ἐναντίως δὲ τῇ διανοίᾳ ἐλογίζετο, "Τί οὕτω μοι," λέγων, "ὁ γέρων διὰ
<τοῦ>⁶⁴⁵ καύματος ἐλθόντι ἀηδὲς ὕδωρ πιεῖν ἀδιακρίτως κελεύει; ἔδει
γάρ με παρὰ τὴν πηγὴν ἀποστεῖλαι διειδὲς καὶ ψυχρὸ{υ}ν ὕδωρ πιεῖν."

Τ[ο]ιάδε οἴκοθεν ἐνθυμηθέντι πάλιν ὁ γέρων, "'Άπιθι, τέκνον," ἔφη, "πίε."

Ὁ δὲ "'Ως κελεύεις," εἰπὼν, ἐκ δευτέρου οὐκ [198a1] ἀπῆλθεν. Ἔτι δὲ καὶ τρίτον εἰπόντος, αὖθις οὐχ ὑπήκουσε.

Τότε ὁ γέρων πρὸς αὐτόν, "Τὸ τῆς παρακοῆς," φησὶ, "γέρας ἀπ[ε]ίληφας, τέκνον, τὴν τῶν χαρισμάτων στέρησιν."

Ταῦτα ἀκούσας, ὁ μαθητὴς, πληγεὶς τὴν καρδίαν καὶ τὴν διάνοιαν καὶ προσδραμὼν τῷ νιπτῆρι εὗρεν οὐδὲν καὶ φησι πρὸς τὸν γέροντα, "Οὐδέν τι, πάτερ, εὑρίσκω ὕδωρ πιεῖν."

"Καὶ πῶς εὕροις," ἔφη ὁ θεῖος⁶⁴⁶ Παΐσιος, "οὗ ἀνάξιον σεαυτὸν ἐποίησας;·Ἡ γὰρ ἀπείθεια τὸ χάρισμα διώκειν εἴωθεν, ὥσπερ τῇ πειθοῖ τοῦτο προξενεῖν εἴθισται."⁶⁴⁷

Πρὸς ταῦτα οὖν ἀδημονῶν ὁ μαθητὴς ἐκεῖνος τί ἂν καὶ εἴη τὸ μέγα ἐκεῖνο, καὶ διὰ τί, καὶ πῶς⁶⁴⁸ ἀνελ[ή]φθη ἐπηρώτα.

Ὁ δὲ μέγας ἀνὴρ ἔφη, "Ὁ τῶν ἀπάντων βασιλεὺς καὶ δεσπότης Χριστὸς σὺν δυσὶν ἀγγέλοις ὤφθη μοι ξένοις ἀνδράσιν ἐοικόσι καθάπερ πάλαι τῷ Ἀβραὰμ⁶⁴⁹ καὶ βιασάμενος αὐτοῦ τοὺς πόδας ἀποπλῦναι ἐτόλμησα. Ὢ τῶν ἐμῶν χαμερπῶν χειρῶν!⁶⁵⁰ Εἶτα ἐκεῖνον μὲν ἀναληφθέντα δέχεται ὁ οὐρανός, ἐμοὶ δὲ πλούτου παντὸς τιμι[ώ]τερον [199b1] τὸ ὕδωρ κατελείφθη, οὗπερ ἡδέως ἐμφορηθεὶς μέρος σοι ὡς ὁμόφρονι μαθητῇ κατέλιπον. Ἐπ[ε]ὶ δὲ τῷ τῆς ἀπειθείας κατηνέχθης πτώματι καὶ τῷ θείῳ ἔρωτι τῆς ὑπακοῆς οὐκ ἐτρώθης,⁶⁵¹ ἀλλ᾽ ἔμεινας τῇ παρακοῇ κ[ε]χρημένος⁶⁵² πιεῖν ὅ προσετάχθης μὴ ἀνασχόμενος, τούτου χάριν οὐρανόθεν⁶⁵³ ἀρτίως ἄγγελος καταβὰς ἐν πάσῃ εὐλαβείᾳ λαβὼν τὸ ἱερὸν ἐκεῖνο νᾶμα ἐν χερσὶν, αὖθις εἰς οὐρανοὺς ἀνῆλθε, σὲ δὲ ὡς ἀνάξιον ὑπέδειξε τῆς ἐκείνου μεταλήψεως, παρακοῆς καὶ [ἀ]πονίας⁶⁵⁴ ὀφθέντα ὑπόπλεον."

Ταῦτα ἀκούσαντα τὸν μαθητὴν φρίκη καὶ δέος ἐλάμβανε⁶⁵⁵ καὶ ἐπὶ πολὺ ἄφωνος ἦν κατασεισθεὶς τῷ διηγήματι. Ὀψὲ γοῦν ποτὲ εἰς νοῦν⁶⁵⁶ ἐπανελθὼν γεγωνοτέρᾳ φωνῇ τὴν οἰκείαν ἀπωδύρετο⁶⁵⁷ δυστυχίαν, "Οὐαί μοι," γοερῶς βοῶν,⁶⁵⁸ "Ὁποίου ἐμαυτὸν ὁ ἄθλιος, ἀγαθοῦ ἐστέρησα;⁶⁵⁹ Τίς μοι φθόνος πονηροτάτου βασκαίνων δαίμονος οὐκ εἴασε τῶν καλῶν ἀπολαῦσειν;"⁶⁶⁰

70. [199b24] Τούτοις οὖν⁶⁶¹ τὴν συμφορὰν κατατραγῳδήσας μεταμέλειας [200a1] ἦν ἐχόμενος καὶ δάκρυσι μᾶλλον ἢ ῥήμασι τὸν [ἔ]λεον θηρώμενος πρὸς οἶκτον τὸν πρεσβύτην ἐκάλει. Ὅθεν πρὸς αὐτὸν ὁ θεῖος ἀνήρ, "Τέκνον," ἔφη, "ὁ Ἀδὰμ διὰ τὴν παρακοὴν ἐκ τοῦ παραδείσου ἐξέπεσε[ν] ἀντὶ αἰωνίου ζωῆς θανάτου κτήτ[ω]ρ γενόμενος καὶ ὡς ἀνάξιος τῆς πρώτης δόξης καὶ τῶν ὑπὲρ ἐκείνην διω[χ]θεὶς ἐξόριστος γέγονεν. Οὕτω δὴ καὶ σὺ τὴν ἐμ[ὴ]ν ἐντολὴν ἀποσεισάμενος καὶ ἧς ἔμελλες <ἀπολαῦσαι>⁶⁶² χάριτος ἐκπεσὼν δυσχεραίν[ει]ς

[διηνεκῶς]⁶⁶³ μεταμελό{ύ}μενος. <Φαίνῃ περὶ πράγματος οἰχουμένου, οὗ πρὸ μικροῦ ἐν χερσὶν ὄντος οὐκ ἐφείδου ἐπιμελούμενος.>⁶⁶⁴

Ἀλλ᾽ ὅμως ἐν μετανοίᾳ καὶ ὑπακοῇ διανιστάμενος τὸν Θεὸν θερμῶς ἐξιλεοῦ τ[ε] ἄφεσιν,⁶⁶⁵ [αἰ]τούμενος τῶν τῆς παρακοῆς ὀλισθημάτων. Κάμπτεται γὰρ τὰ θεϊκὰ σπλάγχνα⁶⁶⁶ τοῖς μετανοοῦσι καὶ ἐλέους τοῖς δεομένοις μεταδίδωσιν."⁶⁶⁷

Païsios Sends His Despondent Disciple to a Holy Man

71. [199b18] Ὁ δὲ <μαθητὴς>⁶⁶⁸ βραχύν τινα χρόνον διεκαρτέρει τῇ παραινέσει τοῦ γέροντος παραμυθούμενος, ἔπ[ε]ιτα τῇ μνήμῃ τοῦ παρελθόντος δράματος κάτοχος ὢν λύπῃ καὶ ἀθυμίᾳ συνείχετο καὶ οὐκ εἶχεν ὅ τι καὶ γένηται. Καὶ δὴ πρόσεισι τ[ῷ] θείῳ γέροντι,⁶⁶⁹ "Οὐκ ἔστι <μοι,>⁶⁷⁰ πάτερ," λέγων, "τῶν λογισμῶν ἄνεσις τῷ τῆς ἀπογνώσεως βυθῷ βυθιζομένῳ κἀκείνης ἀεὶ τῆς δωρεᾶς [200b1] μεμνημένῳ καὶ χαλεπ[ώ]τατα τὴν ἐμὴν δυστυχίαν ὀδυρομένῳ καὶ τί ἂν καὶ γένωμαι οὐκ ἔχω. Ἔασόν με παρά τινα ἀπελθεῖν τῶν δοκιμωτέρων γερόντων ὃν δοκεῖς σύ,⁶⁷¹ ἴσως λύσιν εὑρὼν τῶν λογισμῶν ἐλευθεροῦμαι τῶν ἀνιαρῶν."

Ὁ δὲ γέρων ἄρτον βραχὺν λαβὼν ἐδίδου τῷ μαθητῇ, λέγων, "Λάβε τοῦτον τὸν ἄρτον καὶ παραγεν[ό]μενος ἐν τῇδε τῇ πόλ[ει] εὑρήσεις ἄνδρα πτωχὸν παρὰ τὸ τεῖχος τῆς πόλεως ἐν τοῖς δεξιοῖς μέρεσιν⁶⁷² ἐπί τινος κοπρίας καθεζόμενον καὶ λίθοις ὑπὸ τῶν παίδων καταλευόμενόν τε καὶ π[αι]ζόμενον. Τούτῳ τ[ὸ]ν ἄρτον ἐγχειρίσας τὰ περὶ σοῦ⁶⁷³ δοκοῦντα θεοπρεπῶς ἀκούεις." Ὁ δὲ τὸν ἄρτον λαβών, εὐθέως ἀπῄει.⁶⁷⁴

72. [200a16] Καταλαβὼν δὲ τὴν πόλιν ἐκείνην καὶ τὸν θεῖον ἄνδρα θεασάμενος ἐκεῖνον τὸν ἄρτον⁶⁷⁵ ἐν χερσὶ[ν] ἔχων εὐκαιρίαν ἐζήτει τῶν παιδίων [ἄθυρμον αὐτῷ ἀποδοῦναι].⁶⁷⁶ Ὁ δὲ <τὴν>⁶⁷⁷ ἀναβολὴν μὴ ἀναμείνας, "Εὐθὺς δεῦρο, πάριθι," ἔφη, "σταλεῖσαν ἡμῖν δοὺς εὐλογίαν."⁶⁷⁸

Τοῦ δὲ προσελθόντος, χερσὶν οἰκία[ι]ς τὸν ἄρτον <λαβὼν> [εἰ]ληφὼς⁶⁷⁹ καὶ καταφιλήσας, "Πῶς ἔχει ὁ ἱερὸς Παΐσιος;" ἐπυνθάνετο.⁶⁸⁰ "Λίαν τὰ κατ᾽ ἐκείνου [201a1] ἀκούειν ἐπόθουν ἀξιέραστα. Καὶ σύ, τέκνον, ἵνα τί ἐπιδ[ε]ιάζουν οὐκ ἐπείσθης [τοῖς] ἐκείνου κελεύσμασιν;⁶⁸¹ Οὐκ οἶδας ὅτι διὰ τὴν παρακοὴν <σου>⁶⁸² ἐστερήθης τοῦ θείου νάματος καὶ τῆς ἐξ αὐτοῦ δωρεᾶς; Τί ἔτι παρακοῆς ἀντεχόμενος πρὸς ἕτερον καταφεύγεις ἐκείνου οὐ προσμένων⁶⁸³ [201b1] τῇ βουλῇ; Ἔοικάς μοι τῷ ἐν χερσὶ διειδὲς ὕδωρ ἔχοντι καὶ ἑτέρωθι ζητῆσαι τὴν τοῦ δίψους κατάπαυσιν περιόντι. Ἄπιθι, τοιγαροῦν, ὑποτάγηθι τῷ μεγάλῳ πατρί,⁶⁸⁴ ὁ γὰρ ἐκείνῳ π[ε]ισθῆναι μὴ βουλόμενος αὐτὸς καὶ τοῖς προστάγμασι τοῦ Σωτῆρος⁶⁸⁵ μὴ εἶξαι ἀφηνιάζει."

Ταῦτα ἀκούσας ὁ μαθητής, τὸν Θεὸν εὐλογῶν καὶ δοξάζων, ἐπανῄει καὶ ἦν ἐν ὑπακοῇ τοῦ ἱεροῦ Παϊσίου τοῖς θελήμασιν ἑπόμενος.

The Disciple Goes to See the Holy Man Again
73. [201a10] Οὐ πολὺ τὸ ἐν μέσῳ καὶ πάλιν τῆς δωρεᾶς ἐπὶ μνησθεὶς ἐκείνης τὴν ζημίαν ἐθρήνει καὶ αὖθις ἐδεῖτο τοῦ μεγάλου[686] πρὸς ἐκεῖνον ἀπελθεῖν τὸν ἄνδρα τὸν προσχήματι ὄντα πτωχόν. Ὁ δὲ μέγας παραινέσας καὶ νουθετήσας ἐπ[ε]ὶ τὸ πείθειν οὐκ εἶχεν ἐκεῖνον,[687] τοῖς λογισμοῖς πολ[ι]ορκούμενον κἀκεῖνον προσφοιτᾶν ἐφιέμενον, ἔφη, "Ἐκεῖνος, ὦ τέκνον, ὁ ἀνὴρ πρὸς Κύριον ἐξεδήμησε[ν] ἀλλ' ὅμως ἐπεὶ εἰς ἐκεῖνον τὰς ἐλπίδας ἐπισαλεύοντά σε μόνον ὁρῶ καὶ τῇ ἐκείνου συμβουλίᾳ πειθόμενον παραχωρεῖταί σοι καὶ τὸ σπουδαζόμενον. Ἄπελθε οὖν ἐπὶ τὸ ἀρκτῷον μέρος τῆς πόλεως καὶ εὑρὼν τάφον μέγιστον. Ἐν τούτῳ εἴσιθι καὶ τρία σώματα θεασάμενος κείμενα ἁγίων ἀνδρῶν [202a1] προφητικῶν χαρισμάτων [ἀξιωθέντων],[688] οἵτινες τὸ τῆς ζωῆς πέρας προεγνωκότες ἐν τῷ καιρῷ τῆς ἀναλύσεως, τῷ τάφῳ προσῇεσαν.[689] Τ[ῷ] μεταξὺ τῶν δύο διαλέχθητι, 'Παΐσιος, ὁ τοῦ Χριστοῦ δοῦλος, δι' ἐκείνου τοῦ ἐγείραντος τὸν τετραήμερον Λάζαρον, διακελεύεταί σοι ἐγερθῆναι ὅπως τὰ προσήκοντά μοι διαλεχθήσῃ.'"[690] Ταῦτα μὲν ὁ θεῖος ἀνήρ.

74. [201b8] Ὁ δὲ μαθητὴς προθύμῳ ποδὶ ὡς εἶχε τὴν πόλιν καταλαμβάνει καὶ τὸν εἰρημένον ἐξερευνήσας τόπον καὶ εὑρών, ἐν τῷ τάφῳ εἴσεισι καὶ τῷ τεθνηκότ[ι] φησί, "Παΐσιος σοι [διακελεύεται],[691] Χριστοῦ δυνάμει τοῦ ἐγείραντος τοὺς νεκρούς, 'Ἀνάστηθι, καὶ ἃ δεῖ με ποιῆσαι διέξιθι ὡς ἂν[692] τῆς τῶν λογισμῶν τύχοιμι ἀνέσεως.'"

Ὁ δὲ νεκρὸς ἅμα τῷ λόγῳ—ὢ τοῦ θαύματος—ἀνέστη εὐθύς. "Τί μοι," εἰπών, "οὐκ ἐπείσθης, ὦ οὗτος, καθώς σοι πρότερον εἴρηκα ὑποταγῆναι τῷ πατρὶ[693] διακελευομέν[ῳ]; Ἄπιθι, οὖν, κἀκείνῳ πειθήνιος γενοῦ ἀδιστάκτως αὐτοῦ τῶν λόγων ἀκούων εἰ σωθῆναι βούλει.[694] Ὄντ[ω]ς γὰρ τοῖς ἐκείνου ῥήμασιν ὁ ἀπειθῶν τοῖς τοῦ Χριστοῦ ἐναντιοῦται [διατάγμασι]."[695]

Ταῦτα εἰπὼν ὁ τεθνηκώς, πάλιν[696] ἐκοιμήθη. Ὁ δὲ ἐπανιὼν πρὸς τὸν ἱερὸν Παΐσιον ἐκπληττόμενος πάντα διεξῄει καὶ[697] ἦν ἔκτοτε ἐν [202b1] πραότητι λογισμῶν τὰ χρηστὰ ἀνακτ[ώ]μενος καὶ ἐν προκοπῇ αὐξανόμενος.

Καὶ ταῦτα μὲν περὶ τούτου.[698] Τὰ δ' ἄλλα πῶς σιωπήσω;[699] Τὰ πλεῖστα γὰρ τῶν ἐκείνου θαυμάτων παραδραμεῖν ζημίαν μὲν οὐ μετρίαν ἡμῖν εἶναι[700] ἀνηγησαίμην ἐργῶδες δὲ τῷ λόγῳ οὐκοῦν[701] δύο ἢ τρία διηγησάμενοι τὸν λόγον καταπαύσομεν.

Paḯsios Intervenes to Absolve Two Young Monks of False Charges
Περὶ τῶν δύο αὐταδέλφων.
75. [202a10] Δύο αὐτάδελφοι παρὰ τὸν θεῖον ἀφίκοντο Παΐσιον συνοικήτορες τῇ ἐκείνου ἀδελφότητι γενόμενοι, ἱκανὸν δὲ χρόνον διηνυκότες ἐν τῇ ὑπακοῇ, καταμόνας τὴν ἔρημον οἰκῆσαι συχνῶς

ἐδέοντο τοῦ μεγάλου.⁷⁰² Ὁ δὲ τὴν σπουδὴν αὐτῶν διεγηγερμένην ὁρῶν καὶ πρὸς ἡσυχίαν ἱκανοὺς ὄντας ἐπιστάμενος, ταύτης ἐφάπτεσθαι αὐτοῖς ἐπέτρεψεν. Οἱ δὲ⁷⁰³ πρὸς τὴν ποθουμένην ἀναχωρήσαντες ἡσυχίαν, σπουδαῖοι καὶ ἄτρ[επ]τοι⁷⁰⁴ διεδείκνυ[ν]το, τὰς τῶν ὑπεναντίων ἀποκρουσόμενοι⁷⁰⁵ προσβολάς. Ὁ δὲ τοῖς ἀγαθοῖς ἀεὶ βασκαίνων ἐχθρός,⁷⁰⁶ οἷα ποικίλος ὢν καὶ πολυτρόπως τὰς μηχανὰς ἐπινοῶν ἐξ ὁμοφυῶν <αὐτοῖς>⁷⁰⁷ διεγείρει τὸν πόλεμον.

Τινὶ γὰρ τῶν τῆς ἐρήμου [202a1] οἰκητόρων συνέβη τὰ οἰκεῖα ἀφαιρεθῆναι πράγματα, καὶ τίς τε εἴη ὁ ταῦτα κλέψας ὑπ' ἐκείνου ἠρευνᾶτο.⁷⁰⁸ Καὶ ἐπ[ε]ι[δὴ] πανταχοῦ ζητήσας εὗρεν οὐδέν, περί τινος γέροντος ἀκηκοὼς⁷⁰⁹ φανερῶσαι δυναμένου πρὸς αὐτόν, ἀπῄει καὶ ἐδεῖτο παρ' αὐτοῦ γνῶναι τὰ συληθέντα, ποῦ ἂν εἴη. Ὁ δὲ γέρων ἐκεῖνος οὐκ ἦν ὡς ἀληθῶς τῇ χάριτι διορατικός, ἀλλ' ἐνεργείᾳ δαιμονικῇ προφητεύων. Οὗτος οὖν τῷ μοναχῷ ἐκείνῳ τοὺς νεωτέρους διαβάλων,⁷¹⁰ "Οἱ νεωστί," φησι, "ταύτης τῆς ἐρήμου οἰκήτορες γενόμενοι νέοι⁷¹¹ τῆς κλοπῆς αὐτουργοὶ γεγόνασιν. Οὓς λαβών, μὴ ἀνήσῃς⁷¹² ἕως οὗ τὰ σὰ δώσουσιν."

Ταῦτα ἀκούσας ἐκεῖνος, ὡς εἶχε δρόμου πρὸς τὸν τῆς λαύρας ἡγούμενον ἀφικόμενος καὶ χεῖρα <ἐκεῖθεν>⁷¹³ λαβὼν κραταιὰν πρὸς τοὺς μονάζοντας ἀδελφοὺς ἀπ[ῄει] καὶ τυπτομένους καὶ συρομένους <αὐτοὺς,>⁷¹⁴ πρὸς τὴν λαύραν ἤγαγεν, εἶτα τῇ εἱρκτῇ ἠτιμωμένοι καθειρχθέντες ὡς κάκιστοι τῶν φωρῶν κατεδικάσθησαν. Γνοὺς τοίνυν διὰ τῆς χάριτος ὁ θεῖος πατὴρ ἡμῶν Παΐσιος⁷¹⁵ τὴν τῶν ἀδελφῶν ἐπήρειαν, εὐθὺς ἀναστὰς ἐπορεύθη πρὸς αὐτούς. <Ἐν> πᾶσιν οὖν τῆς αὐτοῦ ἀφίξεως δήλης γεγ[ο]νυίας,⁷¹⁶ <ἅτε ὑψηλότερον ἐκείνου οὐκ ἄλλου ἦν ὄνομά τινος, συναχθέντες [οὖν] ἅπαντες πρὸς αὐτὸν ἀφικνοῦνται. Συνῆν δὲ τούτοις καὶ ὁ γέρων ἐκεῖνος ὁ τῇ πλάνῃ κάτοχος.

Ἐπεὶ δὲ πάντες αὐτῷ τὸν ἀσπασμὸν ἀφωσίουν, ἔφη πρὸς αὐτοὺς ὁ μέγας πατήρ, "Τί τοὺς νέους ἐποιήσατε τοὺς ἡσυχάζοντας, ἀδελφοί;"⁷¹⁷

Οἱ δέ, "Κλέπται εἰσίν, πάτερ," ἔφασαν, "καὶ διὰ τὴν ἄτοπον ταύτην ἐργασίαν ἐβλήθησαν ἐν τῇ φυλακῇ."

Ὁ δέ, "Καὶ τίς ἀνήγγειλεν ὑμῖν," ἔφη, "ὅτι κλέπται εἰσίν;"

"Οὗτος," ἀπεκρίθησαν, "ὁ διορατικὸς γέρων."

Εἶτα τὸν γέροντα ὁ μέγας ἐπηρώτα Παΐσιος, εἰ ἀληθῶς ἔχει τὰ λεγόμενα περὶ αὐτοῦ.⁷¹⁸ Καὶ ὃς ὡς καὶ ἀληθής ἐστιν αὐτοῦ ἡ προφητεία ἔλεγεν, καὶ κατὰ θεόν. Ἔπειτα ὁ ἱερὸς Παΐσιος, "Εἰ ἐκ θεοῦ," ἔφη, "καὶ θεῖον τὸ χάρισμα, καὶ μὴ δαιμονικὴ πλάνη ἄντικρυς, οὐκ ἂν ἐφαίνετο ὁ διάβολος διὰ στόματός σου."⁷¹⁹

Ταῦτα ἀκούσαντες,⁷²⁰ φόβῳ καὶ συγχύσει συνείχοντο, καὶ γὰρ τὰ ἀπὸ στόματος Παϊσίου⁷²¹ λεχθέντα πάσης ἀμφισβητήσεως ἀφεστηκέναι ἐδόκει ὄντως τοῖς πᾶσιν. Ἀμέλει δὲ τὸν γέροντα ὀνειδισμοῖς παίοντες, ἀναπείθουσιν συγγνώμην αἰτεῖσθαι. Ὁ δὲ τῷ δέει συσχεθεὶς προσέπεσε τοῖς ἱεροῖς αὐτοῦ ποσί,[722] "Σύγγνωθι," λέγων, "ἅγιε πάτερ, καὶ ὑπερεύχου τοῦ πεπλανημένου." Τοῦ δὲ ὑπερευξαμένου εὐθὺς ἐνώπιον πάντων ἐξῆλθεν ὁ τῆς κενοδοξίας δαίμων ἐκ στόματος τοῦ πρεσβύτου χοίρῳ ἐοικώς. Ὃς τὸν θυμὸν μανικῶς ἔχων, ἐν τῇ ἐξόδῳ ἐφώρμησε[723] κατὰ τοῦ δικαίου τοῖς ὀδοῦσι σπαράξαι βουλόμενος. Ὁ δὲ θεῖος ἀνὴρ[724] ἐπιτιμήσας, εἰς χάος ἀπέρριψεν.

Ὁ δὲ ἐπεὶ τῆς πλάνης οὐ μόνον ᾔσθετο ἐλευθερίας, ἀλλὰ καὶ τὴν πλάνην ἐξ αὐτοῦ ἀπιοῦσαν ἑώρα, καὶ καταγνοὺς ἑαυτοῦ λίαν ὠδύρετο καὶ δυσωπῶν τῇ γῇ κυλινδόμενος, οὐκ ἐπαύσατο τῶν παρελθόντων λύτρου τυχεῖν. Ὡσαύτως καὶ οἱ δι' ἐκείνου πλανηθέντες ἑαυτοὺς μεμφόμενοι συγγνώμην ᾐτήσαντο.

Εἶτα τοὺς νέους ἐκείνους τοὺς συκοφαντουμένους μετακλήτους ποιούμενοι καὶ ὑπὲρ ὧν πεπαρῳνήκεσαν εἰς αὐτοὺς πλημμελήσαντες συγγνώμην ᾐτοῦντο. Ὁ δὲ πατὴρ ἡμῶν Παΐσιος οἷα εἰκὸς τῶν πάντων φειδόμενος τὰ προσήκοντα πᾶσι παρῄνει, ἔπειτα τῆς[725] λαύρας ἐν ἰδίῳ λαβὼν τόπῳ τῷ προεστῶτι ἐν ᾧ τὰ κλαπέντα πράγματα τυγχάνει διεσάφησεν. Τοὺς δὲ κλέψαντες οὐκ ἐδήλωσεν. Εἶτα τῇ διδασκαλίᾳ[726] καταρτίσας καὶ προσευξάμενος τὴν ἔρημον καταλαμβάνει.>

"Agents of Salvation for Everyone": The Divine Paΐsios and the Holy Paul

76. [203b1][727] Ἀκούσας δὲ περὶ τοῦ ὁσίου Παύλου, ὅσα δι' αὐτοῦ ὁ Θεὸς τοῖς ἀνθρώποις ἔδειξε, παραγίνεται πρὸς αὐτόν, συντυχόντες ἀλλήλοις[728] ἀχώριστοι ἦσαν, ἕτερος ἑτέρου βοηθός, ὡς[729] πόλις ἰσχυρά,[730] ἀμφότεροι τ[ῶ]ν τῆς ἡσυχίας καλῶν κατὰ τρυφῶντος νέους[731] τε ἀγῶνας ἐπινοοῦντες καθ' ἑκάστην καὶ ὑψηλοτέρας ἀγωγάς. Καὶ ἦν τῷ γήρᾳ ὑπερβεβηκὼς καὶ παλαιὸς ἡμερῶν ὁ ἱερὸς[732] Παΐσιος καὶ τοῦ θείου Παύλου τὴν μὲν ἡλικίαν παραπλήσιος, τῇ δὲ ψυχῇ[733] διεγηγερμένος. Ὅθεν καὶ τούτῳ, "Πρὸς καμάτους ἑαυτοὺς ἀεὶ ἐγείρωμεν," ἔλεγεν, "ὡς ἔτι καιρὸν ἔχομεν. Ἀναβολῆς[734] γὰρ τῆς ἐργασίας ἐφ' ὅσον ἔχομεν ζωὴν ὁ κύριος ἡμῶν οὐκ ἀνέχεται καὶ δέος ἡμῖν ἐστι καὶ αἰσχύνη εἴγε ἐν τῷ καιρῷ τῆς ἀποδημίας ἠμελημένοι εὑρεθείημεν."

Καὶ ταῦτα μὲν ὁ θεῖος Παΐσιος. Ὁ δὲ ἱερὸς Παῦλος ἡδέως ἀκούων[735] τῆς ἐκείνου ἐνθέου συμβουλίας, "Ἰδοὺ ἐγώ," ἀντέλεγεν, "ὦ πατέρων ἄριστε,[736] τῇ ἀρίστῃ[737] ἕπομαί σου βουλῇ, πέποιθα γὰρ [τὰς σὰς][738] εὐχὰς[739] ἔχων ἐπικουρίαν παρεχομένας, ὅτι κατὰ τὴν σὴν γνώμην ἡμῖν[740] ὁ θεὸς δῴη καταντῆσαι τοῦδε τοῦ βίου τῷ πέρατι."

77. [203a25] Τοιγαροῦν [204a1] ἀμφότεροι ἦσαν τῶν θαυμάτων αὐτουργοί, τῶν παθῶν ῥῦσται, τῶν ψυχῶν ἀκέστορες ἔμπειροι, ὑπὲρ πάντων εὐχόμενοι, τοῖς πᾶσι σωτηρίας πρόξενοι <χρηματίζοντες.>[741]

Ἀλλὰ τὰ μὲν τοῦ ἱεροῦ Παύλου πολλὰ τὰ διηγήματα, τὰ δὲ τοῦ θείου Παϊσίου πάμπολ[λ]α⁷⁴² καὶ ἀκατάληπτα. Ἐκ πολλῶν δὲ ὀλίγα ἐλέχθη ταῦτα πρὸς εὐχαριστίαν καὶ μίμησιν τὸν πόθον διεγείροντα. Τῆς γὰρ ἐκείνου ὑψηλοτάτης διαγωγῆς ἀκριβῶς οὐδεὶς λόγος ἐφ[ί]κοιτο. Οὐ γὰρ ἐφίλει τὰ καθ᾿ ἑαυτὸν ἀριστεύματα ἑτέροις γνωσθῆναι δι᾿ ἄκραν ταπείνωσιν. Τοῖς γὰρ ἐρωτ[ῶ]σιν ἀεὶ ποία τῶν ἀρετῶν ὑψηλοτέρα ὑπάρχει, ἔλεγεν, "Ἡ ἐν κρυπτῷ γ[ι]νομέν[η]." Τὸ αὐτὸ καὶ πάλιν ἐρωτηθείς, εἶπε, "Τὸ τοῖς ἄλλοις ἕπεσθαι καὶ μὴ τῷ οἰκείῳ θελήματι."

Κἀντεῦθεν καὶ καιρὸν ἡσυχίας καὶ καιρὸν κοινωνίας ἦν διανύων καλῶς. Ἐκεῖ μὲν [ο]ἰκειώσεως καὶ <θείας> ἀναβάσεως⁷⁴³ ἐρῶν, ἔνθεν δὲ τῆς τῶν⁷⁴⁴ πλησίον σωτηρίας. Καὶ τὸ δὴ θαυμαστότερον ὅτι οὐδέποτε τὴν αὐτοῦ διαγωγὴν καταλαμβάνειν εἴασέ τινα ἐν κοιν[ο]βίῳ, ἀλλ᾿ ἡνίκα ἂν περί τινος πράξεως ἔμελλε [204b1] δοξασθῆναι, εὐθὺς ταύτην κατελίμπανεν⁷⁴⁵ ἑτέρᾳ χρώμενος⁷⁴⁶ δι᾿ ἧς ἡ προτέρα σῴζεται. Καὶ ἡνίκα παρ᾿ ἐμοῦ ἠρωτήθη, "Διὰ τί τοῦτο⁷⁴⁷ δρᾶν διέ{ι}γνως;" Χαριέντ[ω]ς ἔλεγε,⁷⁴⁸ "Διὰ τὸ φυλαχθῆναι ἀλώβητον τὴν τῶν παρῳχηκότων ἐργασίαν καὶ μὴ διὰ τῶν ἐπαίνων φθαρῆναι. Μέγας γὰρ ὄντως κίνδυνος ὁ παρὰ τῶν ἀνθρώπων ἔπαινος καὶ τοῖς διὰ τοῦτο[υ] πλέουσι βραχὺ τὸ κέρδος καὶ ὀλίγοι οἱ σῳζόμενοι, ὅθεν [μεγάλα βλάπτονται].⁷⁴⁹ Καλῶς εἴρηται [ὑπὸ] τοῦ Κυρίου,⁷⁵⁰ 'Μὴ γνωσθήτω⁷⁵¹ ἡ ἀριστερά σου τί ποιεῖ ἡ δεξιά σου.'"

Ἀλλὰ ταῦτα μὲν τῆς πολλῆς ἐκείνου⁷⁵² διδασκαλίας ὁ λόγος διεξῆλθε,⁷⁵³ νῦν δὲ ἐπὶ τὴν τελευτὴν τούτου ἥξειν [ὁ λόγος] βούλεται.⁷⁵⁴

The Deaths of Païsios and Paul
Περὶ τῆς τελευτῆς τοῦ ἁγίου Παϊσίου
78. [204b16] Ἤδη ἐν βαθυτάτῳ γήρᾳ γενόμενος⁷⁵⁵ ὁ μέγας ἐν βίῳ καὶ ταῖς ἀρεταῖς διαλάμψας Παΐσιος πέρας τῶν⁷⁵⁶ πόνων ἔλαβε{ν} κλῆσιν πρὸς τὴν ἐκεῖθεν μακαριότητα φέρουσαν. Καὶ τὸ μὲν σῶμα φιλοτίμως <ἐν> τῇ γῇ⁷⁵⁷ κατέκρυψεν ἡ τῶν μοναζόντων πλ[η]θὺς, τὸ δὲ πνεῦμα ἡ ἄνωθεν⁷⁵⁸ εἶχεν ἀΐδιος ζωή. Οὐ πολὺ τὸ ἐν μέσῳ καὶ ὁ ἀοίδιμος Παῦλος τῶν ἐνθένδε⁷⁵⁹ πρὸς τὴν ἀγήρω ζωὴν καὶ αὐτὸς μεταβαίνει καὶ συναυλίζεται ἐν τῇ [205a1] λαμπρότητι τῶν ἁγίων, ἔνθα ἡ τοῦ Παϊσίου χορεία, ἵν᾿ ὥσπερ τῶν πόνων, οὕτω καὶ τῆς ἐκεῖθεν ἀναπαύσεως συγκατατρυφήσωσιν αἱ τούτων μακάριαι ψυχαί. Οὐ μὴν δὲ ἀλλὰ καὶ τὰ σώματα <αὐτῶν>⁷⁶⁰ μικρόν τι ἐν διαφόροις τόποις διεμερίζοντο {τὰ}⁷⁶¹ ἑνὶ χωρίῳ συνήγοντο τοιούτῳ δὲ τρόπῳ γέγονεν ἡ συνάφεια.⁷⁶² Ἀλλὰ προσεκτέον τ[ῷ] διηγήματι, καὶ γὰρ <τὸ>⁷⁶³ τῶν θαυμάτων λίαν παράδοξόν τι ὁ λόγος⁷⁶⁴ διεξελεύσεται.

Païsios and Paul are Buried Together; The Translation of the Relics
79. [204b11] Τοῦ Παϊσίου ἤδη τὸν βίον ἐκλιπόντος,⁷⁶⁵ ὁ θεῖος Παῦλος ἐν τῇ ἐσωτέρᾳ γίνεται ἐρήμῳ κἀκεῖ μετ᾽ οὐ πολὺ καταλύει τὸν βίον καὶ ἐντίμως ἐκεῖσε τέθαπται.⁷⁶⁶

Ἕτερον θαῦμα τοῦ ὁσίου μετὰ τὴν τελευτὴν αὐτοῦ.

Ἔπειτα ὁ πατὴρ ἡμῶν Ἰσίδωρος ἀκούσας περὶ τοῦ θανάτου τοῦ μεγάλου Παϊσίου, καὶ διὰ τῆς θαλάσσης πλοίου ἐπιβὰς παρὰ τὸν τόπον ἀφ[ί]κετο τὸ σῶμα κατείχετο τοῦ θείου Παϊσίου. Ὁ δὲ ἐν πάσῃ τιμῇ λαβὼν καὶ περιπτυξάμενος καὶ ἐν γλωσσοκόμῳ θεὶς ὡς μέγα τι χρῆμα παντὸς πλούτου τιμιώτερον τὴν ἰ[δί]αν⁷⁶⁷ πατρίδα καταπλουτίσαι βουλόμενος ἐπάνεισι [205b1] κομιζόμενος. Ἐπιβάντων δὲ <τῇ νηῒ>⁷⁶⁸ καὶ ἐφ᾽ ἱκανὸν τῆς θαλάσσης <τὴν>⁷⁶⁹ πορείαν διαστειλαμένων ἐν ὕμνοις τε καὶ μεγάλῃ χαρμονῇ ἐπ[ε]ιγομένων, ἐπεὶ καταντικρὺ τῆς τοῦ Παύλου ἐρήμου οὗ ἦν τὸ τίμιον ἐκείνου σῶμα ἐγένοντο, ἀκίνητον τὸ πλοῖον ἐτύγχανεν ἑτέρωθεν τὰς ὁρμὰς ἔχον καὶ ὅλον ἐπὶ τὴν τοῦ Παύλου ἔρημον ὡς ἔμψυχόν τι ἐπινεῦον τὸν συνήθη {ἀμελίον} ἐπιζητοῦντος τοῦ ἱεροῦ Παϊσίου.⁷⁷⁰

Οἱ δὲ βιαζόμενοι οὐκ ἴσχυσαν⁷⁷¹ τὴν [ν]αῦ[ν]⁷⁷² ἀποκινῆσαι ἐπὶ τὰ πρόσω.⁷⁷³ Δύο δὲ ἤδη αὐτῇ διελθουσῶν ἡμερῶν⁷⁷⁴ ἔνθεν κἀκεῖθεν ἀγαγ[εῖ]ν ταύτην πειρώμενοι οὐχ οἷόν τε ὄντες, θεόθεν καὶ οὐκ ἄλλοθεν εἶναι τὴν τοῦ εἱρμοῦ [κατάσχεσιν]⁷⁷⁵ ἔγνωσαν καὶ τ[ί] ἂν καὶ γένοιντο μὴ εἰδότες τὴν [ν]αῦ[ν] ἀφέντες⁷⁷⁶ ἀπελθεῖν ἀκυβέρνητον ἐφ᾽ ὃν⁷⁷⁷ ἂν ὁρμήσειεν ἐρ[ή]μου{ν}.⁷⁷⁸ Ἡ δὲ ἀοράτῳ χειρὶ⁷⁷⁹ ἐπὶ τ[ὴ]ν ἤπειρον ἐλθοῦσα ἔστη ἀκίνητος τὸν ἴδιον φόρτον ἐκδεχομένη.

Ἐν τούτῳ δὲ ἦσαν ἀπορίας καὶ ἀθυμίας μεστοί, γέρων δέ τις τῶν ἐπισήμων πατέρων⁷⁸⁰ Ἱερεμίας καλούμενος τῆς ἐρήμου ἐκείνης [206a1] ἀφώρματο,⁷⁸¹ <ἦλθεν>⁷⁸² ἐπὶ τὸν αἰγιαλὸν καί, "Τί τῷ ὑπὲρ φύσιν ἀντιμάχεσθ[ε], ὦ οὗτοι;" ἔλεγεν. "Τὸν γὰρ αὐτοῦ συνεραστὴν Παῦλον ὁ θεῖος προσκαλεῖται Παΐσιος, σὺν αὐτῷ ἀνακομισθῆναι βουλόμενος. Τοιγαροῦν ταχύνατε εἰς ζήτησιν ἐκείνου ἐξιόντες,⁷⁸³ καὶ εὑρόντες τὸ σῶμα ἀμφοτέρων τὴν ἀνακομιδὴν ποιήσατε."⁷⁸⁴

Ὁ δὲ τίμιος πατὴρ Ἰσίδωρος καὶ οἱ σὺν αὐτῷ τὴν ἔρημον ἐκείνην περιόντες ζητοῦντες ἦσαν τὸ ἅγιον τοῦ θείου Παύλου σῶμα, ὁ δὴ καὶ εὑρόντες καὶ ἀναλαβόμενοι ἐν τῷ πλοίῳ ἐπανίεσαν χρυσοῦ καὶ λίθου τιμίου τηλαυγέστερον θησαυρὸν ἔχοντες.⁷⁸⁵ Καί—ὦ τοῦ θαύματος!⁷⁸⁶—οἴακες ἦσαν ἀτεχνῶς οἱ μεγάλοι πατέρες Παῦλός τε καὶ Παΐσιος⁷⁸⁷ διὰ τῆς πολλῆς ποντοπορίας τὴν ναῦ[ν] ἰθύνοντες ἀπηλλαγμένην παντὸς τοῦ ἐπιπροσθοῦντος. Ἀποσῴζεται τοίνυν ἡ ναῦς ἀβλαβὴς ἐπὶ τὴν Πισιδίαν καὶ ἐν⁷⁸⁸ τῇ ὑπ᾽ αὐτοῦ οἰκοδομηθείσῃ μονῇ φέρων ὁ μέγας Ἰσίδωρος ἐκο[ί]μ[η]σε τὰ τίμια λείψανα ἐν πάσῃ ὑμνῳδίᾳ καὶ δωρ[ο]φορίᾳ.⁷⁸⁹

Conclusion and Doxology
80. [205b23] Ὅσοι δὲ τῶν ὀχλουμένων ὑπὸ πνευμάτων ἀκαθάρτων[790] ἢ ἄλλης τινὸς ἀσθενείας τῶν ἁγίων προσήπτοντο [206b1] λειψάνων ἐκ τῆς ἁφῆς καὶ μόνης ἰῶντο ἐπεὶ δὲ ἐντίμως ἐναπέθεντο ὅσα τῶν παραδόξων θαυμάτων δι᾽ αὐτῶν.[791] Ὁ θεὸς ἐδείκνυτο ποιῶν, οὐδενὶ τῶν πάντων ἐφικτὸν καταλέγειν.

Ἐμοῦ δὲ τῇ μετριότητι ἐκ πολλῶν ὀλίγα ταῦτα εἰρήσθω εἰς δόξαν[792] πατρὸς καὶ υἱοῦ καὶ ἁγίου πνεύματος,[793] νῦν καὶ ἀεὶ καὶ εἰς τοὺς αἰῶνας τῶν αἰώνων. Ἀμήν.

Notes
A text that does not indicate a manuscript is from Grec 1093.
1   164b.
2   Pom Βίος καὶ πολιτεία.
3   Pom, 1547 Παϊσίου τοῦ μεγάλου συγγραφεὶς (sic; συγγραφέως) παρὰ τοῦ ὁσίου πατρὸς ἡμῶν Ἰωάννου τοῦ Κολοβοῦ. Pom ends the incipit with Εὐλόγησον πάτερ. 759 Βίος καὶ πολιτεία τοῦ ἁγίου ἡμῶν Παϊσίου τοῦ ὁσίου πατρὸς ἡμῶν τοῦ μεγάλου συγγραφεὶς (sic; συγγραφέως) παρὰ Ἰωάννου τοῦ Κολοβοῦ.
4   Except where noted, we have followed the numbering of Pomialovskii's Grec 1093. All the manuscripts are unnumbered. Numbers in brackets indicate the pages of the digital Grec 1093, column a or column b.
5   ὄντα τρεπτὰ καὶ λυόμενα, οἶδε: Grec 1093, Pom; 1547 ὄντα λυόμενα μικρᾶς ἡδονῆς οἶδε.
6   ὑπερφρονεῖν: Pom, 759, 1547 περιφρονεῖν.
7   τὰ ἐπηγγελμένα ἀγαθά: Pom, 759, 1547 τῶν ἐπηγγελμένων ἀγαθῶν.
8   Grec 1093 κατεργάζηται; Pom, 1547 κατεργάζεται; 759 κατεργάζεσθαι.
9   ἐκεῖσε: Pom, 759, 1547 ἐντεῦθεν.
10 ὑπερορᾶν: Pom, 759, 1547 παρορᾶν.
11 παραβλέπειν: Pom, 759, 1547 παριδεῖν.
12 ὑπέρ: Grec 1093, 759; Pom, 1547 ὑπό.
13 τῆς ἐφέσεως ἄλλως ἀπολαῦσαι: 759; Pom, 1547 τῆς ἐφέσεως τῆς ἀπὸ τούτων ἄλλως ἀπολαῦσαι.
14 ἐπινοοῦσιν: Pom ἐννοοῦσιν; 759 ἐπινοοῦσιν; 1547 lacks.
15 {συν}αμιλλᾶσθαι: Pom, 1547 ἀμιλλᾶσθαι, which is correct.
16 <ἤ>: Pom, 759, 1547.
17 φιλτάτῳ πατρί: Grec 1093, 759, 1547; Pom lacks.

18 ἐκεῖνος . . . ὁ ἀνήρ; Pom, 1547 ἐκεῖνος πάσης ἀνθρωπίνης τιμῆς ὁ ἀνήρ, which is most likely correct. καὶ ὑψηλοτέρας has crept into Grec 1093; neither LSJ nor Lampe nor Montanari cites it.
19 <Οὐ>: supplied from Pom, 759, 1547.
20 προ[αι]ρ[ου]μένων: Pom προαιρουμένων; 1547 προαιρουμένοις.
21 αὐτοῦ: 759; Pom, 1547 τούτου.
22 ἀξιέπαινα: Grec 1093, 1547; Pom ἀξιέπαινα καὶ ὀνησιμώτατα διηγήματα.
23 τεραστίων περιβόητος ἐν [ταῖς] γραφαῖς ἐγεγόνει: Pom, 759, 1547 τεραστίων ἐν ταῖς θείαις γραφαῖς περιβόητος ἐγεγόνει.
24 τῶν <ἀρετῶν>: Grec 1093 τῶν; Pom, 759, 1547 ἀρετῶν.
25 τὸν Κύριον: Pom, 759, 1547 τὸν Θεόν.
26 1547 breaks off here.
27 τυγχάνειν: Pom, 759 πληθύνουσα.
28 Supplied from Pom.
29 Grec 1093 and 759 πλέον; Pom πλείονα.
30 φροντίδα: Pom, 759 φροντίδα ἑαυτόν; ἑαυτόν is a mistake.
31 ὡς . . . θεός: Pom ὡς μόνη σὺ πάντων τούτων καὶ οὐ θεὸς φροντίζων. 759 also has φροντίζων.
32 τὸ ἀεὶ . . . ὄνομα: Pom τὸ πανάγιον αὐτοῦ ὄνομα τὸ καὶ ἀεὶ δοξαζόμενον; 759 ἀεὶ δοξαζόμενον καὶ πανάγιον αὐτοῦ ὄνομα.
33 <αὐτῷ>: Grec 1093 lacks, as does 759; Pom αὐτῷ.
34 759 also has ἔφη here.
35 ἔφησεν is a very late form, almost Modern Greek; 759 ἀντέφησεν.
36 τοῦ Κυρίου: Pom, 759 θεοῦ.
37 1547 resumes here with -θεῖσα.
38 εὐχαριστηρίους φθεγ[γ]ομένη: Pom, 759, 1547 εὐ. ἐδίδου.
39 ἔλεγεν: 759 φθεγγομένη: 1547 ἔφη.
40 ἀρ[ε]τῶν: 1547 ἱερῶν.
41 μοναχικῆς: Grec 1093, 759, 1547; Pom μοναδίκης, which came to be a synonym of the former.
42 τοῦ Κυρίου: Grec 1093, 759, 1547; Pom lacks.
43 μέγαν: Pom, 1547 θεῖον.
44 Ὁ δὲ θεῖος πατήρ: Pom, 759, 1547 Ὁ δὲ θεῖος οὗτος πατήρ.
45 ἁγιωσύνη: Pom, 759, 1547 ἀγαθοσύνη.
46 σχῆμα: Pom, 1547 σχῆμα τοῦτον; 759, like Grec 1093, has τοῦτον after πατήρ.
47 τὰ μέλλοντα: Pom, 759, 1547 τὰ μέλλοντα περὶ τούτου.
48 ἐμύ[η]το: Grec 1093 ἐμύειτο; Pom ἐμεμύητο; 759 ἐμοῖετο; 1547 ἐμύειτω.
49 ἐπιτήδειος: Pom, 1547 ἰθυνόμενος.
50 τὰ τῆς ὑπακοῆς: Grec 1093, 1547; Pom τὰ τῆς ὑπομονῆς καὶ ὑπακοῆς.
51 προσβάλλειν: Grec 1093, 1547; Pom ἐπιβάλλειν.

52 <τῷ>: Pom, 1547; Grec 1093 τῶν.
53 διορατικοῖς: 1547 ὁρατοῖς, clearly a mistake.
54 τὴν παντοδύναμον ἀγαθότητα τοῦ Δημιουργοῦ: Pom τὴν ἀγαθότητα τοῦ Θεοῦ τὴν παντοδύναμον; 1547 τὴν παντοδύναμον ἀγαθότητα τοῦ Θεοῦ.
55 καὶ ὑμνεῖν: Pom καὶ ὑμνεῖν ὡς εὐεργέτην.
56 The text of 759 for most of ¶¶6–7 is too faint to work with.
57 ἐπωφελεῖς λόγους: Pom, 1547 ἐπωφελέσι λόγοις.
58 πόθου θείου: Grec 1093, 1547; Pom πόθῳ θείῳ.
59 Τηνικαῦτα . . . πρόσωπον: Pom, 1547 Τηνικαῦτα γὰρ τρεῖς διανύσας χρόνους τὴν αὐτὴν ἀκριβῶς ἐφυλάττετο ἐντολὴν ἀνθρώπινον πρόσωπον.
60 ἀρδεύων: Pom, 1547 ἀρδεύων καὶ ποτίζων.
61 Taking ἐπὶ τὰς ἐξαγωγὰς [Pom, 1547 διεξαγωγάς] to equal the LXX's ἐφυλάττετο παρὰ τὰς διεξόδους.
62 πεφυτευμένον καί: Pom, 1547 πεφυτευμένον ἀνθοῦν καὶ προκύπτον καί. The digital copy of 1547 now repeats fol. 131 with the same enumeration.
63 τοῦτον: Pom, 1547: τοῦτον λέγειν οὕτως ἀναδεικνύμενον (ἐπιθυμητὸν γὰρ ἦν αὐτῷ τουτὶ τὸ ῥητόν), "Ὡς . . . .
64 παιδαγωγῶν: Pom, 1547 δουλαγωγῶν.
65 Pom, 1547.
66 διϊθύων καὶ διεξάγων: Pom δηθύνων καὶ διεξάγων; 1547 διεξάγων διϊθύων.
67 [τῷ γέροντι]: supplied from Pom, 1547; Grec 1093 lacks.
68 Grec 1093 Παμβῶης.
69 Pom ὑπολέλειμμαι, but in par. 12, ἀπολείπω occurs with the same meaning: ἀπελείφθην; 759, 1547 ἀπολέλειμμαι.
70 ὅν παρά: Pom, 759, 1547 ὅν τινα παρά.
71 Χρόνου τοίνυν ἡμῖν: Grec 1093, 759, 1547; Pom Χρόνου τινὸς ἡμῖν.
72 [Οἵ]δε Pom; Grec 1093, 759, 1547 Ἤδη.
73 759 also has the redundant τῷ.
74 Pom; Grec 1093 ἄγων ἦσαν; 759, 1547 ἄγωνες ἦσαν.
75 μὴ [ἐσθίειν]: Pom; Grec 1093 μὴ ἐσθίων; 759, 1547 οὐ ἐσθίειν.
76 ἅλ[ας]: Grec 1093 ἅλη.
77 εἴχετο: Pom, 759, 1547 ἠνέσχετο.
78 διαγωγῆς, ἀλλ' ἑτέρας ἀντέχεται: 1547 lacks.
79 Grec 1093. εὐθυμάθι.
80 προσθ[εί]ς: 759; Pom, 1547 προστιθείς.
81 [διοδεύων]; possibly by lectio difficilior. Grec 1093, 759, 1547 δύο δύο, which is M.Gr.
82 νηστεύων τῇ ἀρχῇ, τῆς τρίτης μετεῖχε τροφῆς: Grec 1093, Pom; 579 νηστεύων . . . μετεῖχε τροφῆς 1547 νηστεύων τῆς προλάβοις ἧς μετεῖχε τροφῆς;

83 δ[έ]: Pom, 759, 1547 δή.
84 διαγωγήν: Grec 1093, 759, 1547; Pom πολιτείαν.
85 μόνος: Pom ἐκεῖνος μόνος; 759, 1547 μόνος ἐκεῖνος.
86 Pom, 759, 1547; Grec 1093: ᾽Αμέλη.
87 Pom, 759, 1547 οἰκειωθῆναι.
88 προσ[εγγίζειν]: Pom, 759, 1547 προσεγγίζειν; Grec 1093: προσεγκήζειν.
89 Supplied from Pom, 759, 1547.
90 Supplied from Pom; 759, 1547 lack.
91 οὐ: 1547 lacks.
92 ἔχει: Pom, 759, 1547 ἔφης.
93 ταύτην: Pom ταύτης.
94 Ταῦτα εἰπόντες: Pom, 759, 1547 Ταῦτα εἰπόντες θερμότατα διανυκτερεύσαντες.
95 τοὺς οἰκτιρμούς: 1547 τοῖς οἰκτιρμοῖς.
96 ἑκάστῳ οἴκησις: Pom, 759, 1547 οἰκεία ἑκάστῳ.
97 ἑκατέρῳ οἰκεία ἔσται διατριβή: 1547 ἑκατέριος ἰδίᾳ ἔσται διατριβή.
98 ἐτάχθην: Grec 1093, 759; Pom, 1547 προσετάχθη.
99 Pom; Grec 1093, 759 οὕς; 1547 οἷς.
100 Pom, 759, 1547 ἀρετάς.
101 ἐπὶ: Pom, 759, 1547 διά.
102 Χρίστε φιλάνθρωπε: Grec 1093, 759, 1547; Pom Χρίστε φιλάνθρωπε Σωτήρ.
103 εὖ ἴσθι: Grec 1093, 759 (ἴσθη [sic]); Pom lacks.
104 Κυρίου: Grec 1093, 759, 1547; Pom θεοῦ.
105 Δέσποτα: Pom, 759, 1547 Δέσποτα Κύριε.
106 τῇ χειρί σου τῇ κραταιᾷ: Grec 1093, Pom; 759 τῇ ἰσχυροῦ σου τῇ κραταιᾷ.
107 ἔχειν: Pom, 759, 1457 ἔχεις.
108 αὐλιζομένοις: Pom, 759 ἀγωνιζομένοις.
109 Supplied from Pom, 1547; 759 lacks.
110 δεηθήσονται: Pom, 759, 1547 δεηθήσονται τῶν ἀναγκαίων.
111 ἀνήρ: Grec 1093, 759, 1547; Pom Παΐσιος.
112 ἐν πρᾳότητι καὶ ταπεινώσει καρδίας: Grec 1093, 759; Pom ἐν πρᾳότητι καὶ δικαιοσύνῃ καὶ ταπεινῇ καρδίᾳ.
113 ἐπηρ[τη]μένων: Pom ἐπηρτημένων; 759 ἠρ[τη]μένων.
114 βασιλείας οὐρανῶν ἐν ταῖς αἰωνίοις σκηναῖς: Grec 1093, 759; Pom, 1547 βασιλείας αἰωνίου ἐν ταῖς ἐπουρανίαις σκηναῖς.
115 δείξω: Grec 1093, 759; Pom, 1547 ἀναδείξω.
116 Pom, 759, 1547 προσπελάσαι.
117 προσβαλεῖν τούτῳ: Pom, 1547 τοῦτον προσβαλέσθαι; 759 προσβαλέσθαι τοῦτον.
118 προσχήματι: Grec 1093, 759; Pom, 1547: σχήματι.

119 δείλαιος: Grec 1093, 759; Pom, 1547 δόλιος.
120 Much of 759.113a-b is illegible or marginally legible, especially 113b.
121 Grec 1093, Pom, 1547 περιέ[π]ουσα.
122 Pom, 1547 ποίει.
123 ἠρωτήθη: Pom ἐπηρωτήθη.
124 τοῖς: Grec 1093, Pom; 1547 εἰς.
125 θελήσασιν: Pom, 759, 1547 θελήσωμιν.
126 πλείονας παρὰ θεοῦ: Grec 1093, 759; Pom, 1547 πρὸς θεοῦ (sic).
127 θείου: Grec 1093, 759; Pom ἁγίου; 1547 ἀνδρός.
128 πεισθείς . . . καθέστηκεν: Grec 1093, 759; Pom, 1547 lack ἐπανών . . . χρείαν and instead of καθέστηκεν have ὑπέστρεψεν.
129 759 folio 113 is mostly illegible or marginally legible. 114a is fully legible, but 759 does not continue the *Life of Païsios*. It does not appear that the *Life* continues at all.
130 εἰς τὸ ἄντρον: 1547 ἐν τῷ ἰδίῳ ἄντρῳ.
131 τί σοι δρᾶσαι οὐκ ἔχω τὰς ἐμὰς ἀποκρουσαμένῳ μηχανάς: Pom, 1547; Grec 1093 τί σε δράσω οὐκ ἔχω τὰς ἐμὰς ἀποκρουσάμενον μηχανάς.
132 τούτῳ ἀναιδῶς: Grec 1093, 1547; Pom τούτῳ.
133 τῷ τούτ[ω]ν [δεσπότῃ]: Pom 1547; Grec 1093 τοῦτον δεσπόζοντι.
134 ἐδίδου . . . διαφερούσαις: Pom, 1547; Grec 1093 ἐδίδου διαγωγαῖς τῆς τῶν ἀσωμάτων ἐν μηδενὶ διαφερούσαις ἀμέλει.
135 <τὸ ἐνοικοῦν ἐν αὐτῷ θεῖον πνεῦμα εὐδόκησαν>: Pom, 1547.
136 Supplied from Pom.
137 κατηξιώθη: Pom ἠξιώθη.
138 Pomialovskii mistakenly repeated the numeral "XVII" for this paragraph (p. 11). From here on we will put his numbering in parentheses.
139 νόμῳ: 1547 λόγῳ.
140 Pom, 1547.
141 φύσεως μὴ ὑποκειμένη: Pom, 1547 φύσεως ἥκιστα ὑποτέτακται.
142 Οἴδαμεν γὰρ: 1547 Οἶδε μέντοι.
143 ἔτεσιν: Pom, 1547 ἔτεσιν καὶ ἐπέκεινα.
144 φυλάξαι ζῶντας: Pom, 1547 διαφυλάξαι τὴν ζωήν.
145 Pom, 1547.
146 αὐτόν: Grec 1093, 1547; Pom αὐτῷ.
147 Pom, 1547.
148 Καὶ ταῖς ἐνθέοις ἐκείνου Σειρῆσι: Pom Καὶ δὴ ταῖς ἐνθέου ἐκείνης Σειρήνης; 1547 Καὶ δὴ ταῖς ἐνθέοις ἐκείνου Σηρίνοις.
149 Pom, 1547.
150 οὐ: Grec 1093, Pom; 1547 lacks.
151 Pom, 1547.
152 φίλον: Pom, 1547 οἰκεῖον.

153 ἡ μακάρια διαγωγή: Pom, 1547 ἡ μακάρια ὑποταγή; Pom, 1547 lack τῆς ὑποταγῆς.
154 ἀρετάς: Pom, 1547 ἀρετήν.
155 Pom; Grec 1093, 1547 lack.
156 Pom, 1547.
157 Pom; Grec 1093, 1547 lack.
158 Τὸ δὲ κ[ε]φάλαιον ἐκείνων: Pom, 1547 Τὸ δὲ κεφάλαιον πάντων ἐκεῖνο.
159 τῶν ἁπάντων . . . δοκούντων: Pom τῶν ἁπάντων οὐδὲν ὅσα θελήματι ἰδίῳ γίνεσθαι δοκοῦσιν; 1547 τῶν πάντων οὐδὲν τῷ ὅσα θελήματι ἰδίῳ γίνεσθαι δοκούντων.
160 ἀλλὰ . . . διαπράττεσθαι: Pom, 1547 ἀλλὰ βουλῇ καὶ γνώμῃ πατρικῇ τῶν δοκίμων πάντα μετέρχεσθαι.
161 τῆς τῶν πλησίων: Pom, 1547 τῆς πρὸς τὸν πλησίον.
162 Pom, 1547; Grec 1093 τῷ τρισὶ χρόνοις.
163 [Καὶ ἦν]: Pom, 1547; Grec 1093 εἶν καὶ ἦν.
164 <ὦ>: Pom, 1547.
165 Pom, 1547.
166 Τοιαύτοις: Pom, 1547 Τοῖς σοῖς.
167 εὐχή: Pom, 1547 σπουδή.
168 τοιοῦτον: Pom, 1547 τοιόνδε.
169 Pom; Grec 1093, 1547 Φιλανθρωπίας.
170 ἀξιωθεὶς χάριτος ὁ τάλας: Pom, 1547; Grec 1093 ἀξιωθεὶς ὁ τάλας.
171 Πόσους πόνους καὶ θανάτους ἆρα γε <ἡμῖν>: Pom, 1547 Πόσους ἆρα γε θανάτους ἡμῖν.
172 ἔστ[ω]: Pom, 1547; Grec 1093 ἔστοσαν.
173 The MS. has this heading between pars. XXI and XXII.
174 Ὅς . . . ἀνθρώποις: Pom, 1547 Ὅς τῇ πλάνῃ τοῦ ἀεὶ βασκαίνοντος τοῖς ἀνθρώποις ἀλώμενος.
175 ἐν τῷ ᾅδῃ . . . ἰδεῖν: Pom, 1547 ἐν τῷ ᾅδῃ ἆρα ταύτην ὁρᾷ.
176 καθικετεύεις: Grec 1093, 1547; Pom ἱκετεύεις.
177 δεῖ: Pom ὥρισα; 1547 ἐν τῷ ᾅδῃ εἶναι.
178 τῆς οἰκείας ἐργασίας: Pom, 1547 τῆς ἐργασίας.
179 πρεσβύτερος: Pom, 1547 πρεσβύτης.
180 ἤκουσεν: Pom, 1547 διὰ φωνῆς μεμυσταγώγηται.
181 ἀκοῦσαι πλεῖ(ο)ν: 1547 ἀκοῦσαι δέομεν πλεῖον.
182 πλεῖ[ο]ν . . . δυνηθείς: Pom, 1547 πλεῖ[ο]ν ὧν ἤκουσε.
183 τῷ Παϊσίῳ: Pom, 1547 τῷ ἱερῷ Παϊσίῳ.
184 Pom, 1547: ἀπολυτρώσεως.
185 πρὸς τὸν Παΐσιον: Grec 1093, 1547; Pom πρὸς τὸν ἱερὸν Παΐσιον.
186 Pom; Grec 1093, 1547 lack.
187 συναντᾷ: Pom, 1547 ἀνὰ τὴν ὁδὸν συναντᾷ.

188 Supplied from Pom, 1547.
189 Pom, 1547 lack σου.
190 ἀγαθός: Pom, 1547 ἱερός
191 Pom, 1547; Grec 1093 κἄνπερ.
192 Pom, 1547; Grec 1093 εἶδεν.
193 Pom, 1547.
194 Pom, 1547; Grec 1093 δέδοκτε.
195 τῇ ἐνδοτέρᾳ γίνομαι ἐρήμῳ: Pom, 1547 τῇ ἐσωτέρᾳ πορεύομαι ἐρήμῳ.
196 ἐκδυσωπήσομεν: 1547 δυσωπήσομεν.
197 τῶν ἀναξίων δούλων σου: Pom τῶν ἀναξίων δούλων σου φιλάνθρωπε δέσποτα; 1547 δέσποτα φιλάνθρωπε.
198 τὴν ψυχὴν τοῦ μαθητοῦ: Grec 1093, 1547; Pom τὴν ψυχὴν τοῦ δούλου σου τοῦ μαθητοῦ.
199 ὀφθῆναι σοι . . . ἡμᾶς: Pom, 1547 ὀφθῆναί σοι ἀνασχόμενος τοὺς σοὺς οἰκτιρμοὺς δυσωποῦντας παροφθῆναι ἐάσῃς ἡμᾶς.
200 ἐκεῖνον . . . ἀμ[οι]βῶν: Pom, 1547 ἐκεῖνον ἐν τῷ ᾅδῃ τῶν τῆς παρακοῆς καὶ ἀτόπων ἔργων ἀπολαύεσθαι ἀμοιβῶν.
201 ἀμ[οι]βῶν ἔταξα καὶ ἄνεσιν οὐκ ἀνίημι τοῦτο τῶν ὀδυνῶν: 1547 ἀμοιβῶν ἄνεσιν οὐκ ἀνίημι ἐκείνῳ [Pom ἐκεῖνον] τῶν ὀδυνῶν.
202 ἐκ καὶ τῶν μὴ ὄντων εἰς τὸ εἶναι>: Pom ἐκ τοῦ μὴ ὄντος εἰς τὸ εἶναι; 1547 καὶ ἐκ μὴ ὄντων.
203 Pom, 1547.
204 1547.
205 Pom, 1547; Grec 1093 δύται.
206 Εἶτα τῷ γέροντι μεταδίδοται: Pom; Grec 1093, 1547 lack; Pom points out, 18 n. 18, that another manuscript, M, also omits this.
207 αὐτ[ί]κα: Pom, 1547 lack.
208 ἐναγώνιος: Pom, 1547 ἐναγώνιος αὐτῇ τῇ ὥρᾳ.
209 καί: 1547 αὐτίκα.
210 φωνῆς: Pom lacks.
211 ἔστιν ὁρᾶν: 1547 ὁρᾶν ἦναι.
212 Grec 1093: ὀδυνῶν; Pom, 1547 κακῶν.
213 Pom, 1547; Grec 1093 ἐκείνῳ.
214 Pom, 1547; Grec 1093 ἐτία.
215 ὑποστῆναι: Grec 1093, Pom; 1547 lacks.
216 συμπαθής: Pom οἰκτρός, 1547 οἶκτος. Because in Pom οἰκτρός is next to μοι, we are taking it as οἰκτρῷ, "wretch," modifying "me," rather than 1547's οἶκτος, "compassionate," referring to God.
217 φιλάνθρωπος, Grec 1093, 1547; Pom πανάγαθος.
218 ἠλευθέρωσε: Pom, 1547 προίετο, "release, let loose." But ἐλευθερόω has the added implications of "setting (humankind) free (from sin)." Ἐλευθερία,

"liberty, freedom," and ἐλευθερόω, "to set free," are key concepts for Paul; for the former, see 1 Cor 10:29; 2 Cor 3:17; Gal 5:13a; Rom 8:21; for the latter, see Rom 6:18, 22; 8:2, 21; and Gal 5:1.
219 Pom, 1547.
220 Pom, 1547.
221 καὶ εὗρεν: Grec 1093 1547; Pom καὶ γενόμενος ἐν τῷ τόπῳ ᾧ ἦν εὗρεν.
222 εὗρεν . . . εὐχαριστ[η]ρίους: Pom, 1547 εὗρεν αὐτὸν τῷ θεῷ τοὺς εὐχαριστηρίους.
223 Εἶτα πάντα: Grec 1093, 1547; Pom Εἶτα μετὰ φόβου πάντα.
224 πραχθέντα: Pom, 1547 διδαχθέντα.
225 ἀμφότεροι τὰς εὐχαριστ{ε}ίας τῷ θεῷ ὁμολογοῦν τῷ: Pom, 1547 ἀμφότεροι θεῷ τὰς εὐχαριστηρίους φωνὰς ἀπεδίδουν τῷ.
226 θαυμάσια: Grec 1093, 1547; Pom θαυμάσια μεγάλα.
227 ἔσωσας: Pom, 1547 διέσωσας.
228 ὁ . . . Παΐσιος: Pom ὁ μέγας Παΐσιος ἔφη 1547 ὁ μέγας ἔφη Παΐσιος.
229 τι χάριτος: Grec 1093, 1547 (1547 lacks τι); Pom χαρίσματος.
230 τῆς ἐκ ψυχῆς δεομένοις βοηθείας: 1547 τοῖς ἐκ ψυχῆς δεομένοις (βοηθείας lacking).
231 οἰκονομοῦσα τῆς ἐκ ψυχῆς δεομένοις βοηθείας, οὐκ: Pom, 1547 οἰκονομοῦσα τοῖς ἐκ ψυχῆς διαμένοις, οὐκ.
232 Pom, 1547.
233 Κατενεχθεὶς καὶ τραφείς: Grec 1093, 1547; Pom Καὶ τεχθεὶς καὶ ἀνατρεφείς.
234 τέθεικας: Pom, 1547 τίθεμεν.
235 Pom, 1547; Grec 1093 ἐμαυτοῦ.
236 Grec 1093 συνηδώς; Pom, 1547 συνεγνωκώς.
237 φιλανθρώπῳ Θεῷ: Grec 1093, Pom; 1547 lacks φιλανθρώπῳ.
238 πάροχον πά[ντ]ων τῶν δωρεῶν: Grec 1093, Pom; 1547 πάροχον πᾶσι τῶν ἀγαθῶν θεόν.
239 ἐπαν[ήει]: Pom, 1547; Grec 1093 ἐπάνησι.
240 ἀεὶ σπουδάζων ἦν: Grec 1093, 1547; Pom ἐν σπουδῇ διήνυε.
241 Pom, 1547; Grec 1093: περιείη.
242 τὰ χρηστὰ ἐν τῷ κρυπτῷ πάντα δράσ[ειεν]: Grec 1093, Pom; 1547 τῶν χρηστῶν πάντα δράσ[ε]ιεν.
243 οὐ μόνον: Grec 1093, 1547; Pom οὐ μόνον αὐτόν.
244 στερεῖσθαι: Pom, 1547 lack.
245 πρὸς τὴν ἔξω ἔρημον κελεύει . . . πολιτείας: Pom ἐν τῇ ἔξω ἐρήμῳ πρὸς τοὺς . . . πολιτείας διακελεύεται; 1547 πολιτείας διακελεύεται.
246 Grec 1093: καταλυπόντι. Pom, 1547 καταλιπεῖν; Pom, 21 n.14, incorrectly states that our MS. has καταλιπεῖν and prints καταλιπεῖν.

247 Pom; Grec 1093, 1547 lack.
248 μὴ δύνασθαι: Pom, 1547 μὴ δυνάμενος.
249 ταλαίπωρος: Grec 1093, 1547; Pom lacks.
250 Pom's numbering skips from XXXII to XXXIV, omitting XXXIII, so his numbering and ours now agree again.
251 λογισθήσεται: Pom, 1547 λελόγισται.
252 Pom, 1547.
253 ἀλλὰ διπλασίους . . . ψυχή: Pom, 1547 ἀλλὰ διπλασίως καὶ πολυπλασίως ἐν τῇ ἄνω Ἰερουσαλὴμ ἀπολήψῃ τὰς ἀντιδόσεις.
254 Παΐσιον: Grec 1093, 1547; Pom lacks.
255 Pom, 1547; Grec 1093 γενομένου.
256 Pom, 1547; Grec 1093 νάμμα.
257 The MS. has this title in the left margin in abbreviations.
258 ἐπιβάσιν: Pom, 1547 εἴσοδον.
259 Pom, 1547; Grec 1093 συνεισίων.
260 ἐπισκεπτόμενος: Pom ἐπισκοπούμενος; 1547 ἐπισκοπούμεν.
261 Pom, 1547; Grec 1093 τῷδε.
262 Τί δὴ πότε ἐστιν, ἀγνοῶ: Pom, 1547 Τί δὴ πότε εἶναι τὸ αἴτιον, ἀγνοῶ.
263 ἀνήρ: Pom, 1547 Παΐσιος.
264 Grec 1093 lacks here Pom, 1547 εἴπερ ἀρτίως τὴν σὴν ᾠκονόμησεν ἄφιξεν.
265 αὐτοῦ ἡ χρηστότης: Pom, 1547 ἡ αὐτοῦ ἀγαθότης.
266 ἐφετόν: Grec 1093, 1547; Pom, Grec 1093 ἧκον.
267 Pom; Grec 1093, 1547 lack.
268 ἀποτυχόντι: Pom, 1547 ἀποτυχόντα.
269 <μνήμης>: Pom, 1547.
270 Pom, 1547; Grec 1093 καταγινώσκον φαίνη.
271 Ἐθεόμην: Grec 1093, 1547; before ἐθεόμην Pom has Ἔστιν οὕς.
272 Pom, 1547.
273 [ε]ἰς οὐρανοὺς θαρσαλέως ἀνιόντας: Grec 1093, Pom; 1547 lacks.
274 ὀξυπετῶς: Pom, 1547 ὀξυπέταις.
275 ἀνερχομένοις: Pom, 1547 διανερχομένοις.
276 Pom, 1547; Grec 1093 lacks, probably through homoioteleuton, ἀνερχομένοις . . . ἀφικνουμένοις.
277 εὐλαβουμένης: Grec 1093, Pom; 1547 εὐλαβουμέοις.
278 ἱερῶν. Grec 1093, 1547; Pom εὐαγῶν.
279 ἐφαπτομένοις: Grec 1093, 1547; Pom ἐφαπτομένους.
280 μή: Pom, 1547 μηδαμῶς.
281 Pom, 1547.
282 ἀγασάμενος: Pom, 1547 ἀγάμενος.
283 μέμφομαι: Pom, 1547 λίαν μέμφομαι.
284 βαθμῶν: Grec 1093, 1547; Pom ἀγαθῶν.

285 διαγωγῆς ἀντιποιήσασθαι: Pom ἀγωγῆς ἐπιτήδεια ἀντιποιήσασθαι; 1547 ἀγωγῆς ἐπιτήδεια ἀντιποιησαμένω.
286 Pom, 1547.
287 τὰ κρίματα τοῦ Θεοῦ ἡμῶν: Pom, 1547 τὰ κρίματα τῆς δικαιοσύνης τοῦ ἀγαθοῦ Θεοῦ ἡμῶν.
288 Pom, 1547.
289 σοὶ γὰρ γυνὴ βοηθός: Pom ἄτε γὰρ σοὶ καὶ γυνὴ βοηθός; 1547 σοὶ μὲν γὰρ καὶ γυνὴ βοηθός.
290 τρυφή: Pom, 1547; Grec 1093 τροφή. See below.
291 ἦσαν κατὰ τὸν ἀπόστολον: Pom ἦσαν ὡς παρὰ τῷ ἀποστόλῳ; 1547 ἦσαν ὡς παρὰ τῶν ἀποστόλων; <καί> and <καί> supplied from Pom, 1547.
292 ἐν ἐρημίας . . . Πῶς: supplied from Pom, 1547.
293 καλλῶς: Pom καλῶν; 1547 καλῶς.
294 Grec 1093, Pom, 1547: θέλεις, which is Modern Greek.
295 ἔσονται: Grec 1093, 1547; Pom γίνονται.
296 παρόντος: Grec 1093, 1547; Pom παρόντος ὦ Ἰωάννη.
297 μυστηρίου: Grec 1093, Pom; 1547 παραδόξου μυστηρίου.
298 ὑποδεῖξαι: Grec 1093, Pom; 1547 ὑποδεῖξαι ἡμῖν.
299 Grec 1093 has a title heading at the end of the previous paragraph. Pom and 1547 lack all of the section titles that Grec 1093 has.
300 οἰκῶν . . . μέρεσιν: Pom, 1547 οἰκῶν γειτνιούσῃ τοῖς Αἰγυπτίοις μέρεσιν.
301 περιέπεσε: Pom, 1547 περιπεσών.
302 Pom, 1547; Grec 1093 lacks.
303 τῷ Παϊσίῳ: Pom, 1547 τῷ θείῳ Παϊσίῳ.
304 δηλοῖ . . . χώραν: Pom, 1547 δηλοῖ ἐπισημάνας καὶ τὴν χώραν.
305 Καὶ εὐθὺς: Grec 1093, Pom; 1547 lacks.
306 Πολλοὶ . . . δόγματος: Pom Πολλοὶ δὲ τίνες συγκοινωνοὶ τῶν ἀφελεστέρων τοῦ πονηροῦ δόγματος ἦσαν τούτου; 1547 Πολλοὶ δε τίνες τῶν ἀφελεστέρων τούτῳ συγκοινωνοὶ ἦσαν τοῦ πονηροῦ δόγματος.
307 Οἵ γε παραυτίκα: Pom, 1547 Οἵ γε παρ' αὐτὸν τηνικαῦτα.
308 καὶ τῶν σκευῶν ἕκαστον ἀνὰ τρία κεκτημένον ὠτίων θεασάμενοι: Pom καὶ σκευῶν ἀνὰ τριῶν ὤτων κατασκευασμέων θεασάμενοι; 1547 καὶ τῶν σκευῶν ἀνὰ τριῶν ὤτων κατασκευασμέων θεασάμενοι.
309 τὸν δὲ Παΐσιον τίς τε εἴη καὶ πόθεν μὴ εἰδότες: Grec 1093, Pom; 1547 τὸν δὲ Παΐσιον τίς τε εἴη καὶ πόθεν γνῶναι.
310 ἀποροῦντες . . . σπυρίδων: Pom ἀποροῦντες τὴν τῶν σκευῶν κατασκευήν; 1547 ἀποροῦντες τὴν τῶν καλῶν σκευῶν κατασκευήν.
311 Pom, 1547; Grec 1093 Βούλεται.
312 Καὶ τί διὰ τριῶν ὠτίων ταῦτα πεποίηκας ἀντέφησαν: Pom εἶτα καὶ τί δὴ διὰ τριῶν ὤτων εἴη ἡ τούτων κατασκευὴ ἀνηρώτων, καὶ ὅς

ἀντέφησαν; 1547 εἶτα καὶ τί δὴ διὰ τῶν τριῶν ὤτων εἴη ἡ τούτων κατασκευὴ ἀνηρώτων, καὶ ὅς.
313 φίλος εἰμὶ τῆς ἁγίας τριάδος καὶ ἐραστής: Pom, 1547 φίλος τῆς τριάδος ὑπάρχω τῆς ὑπεραγίας καὶ ἐραστής.
314 δεῖ με: Pom, 1547; Grec 1093 δῆ μαι.
315 Pom, 1547 ἀποφαίνειν; Grec 1093 ὑποφαίνειν.
316 ἢ οὕτως: Grec 1093, Pom; 1547 lacks.
317 τρισίν: Grec 1093, 1547; Pom τρισὶν ὑποστάσεσι.
318 αὐτῶν κέκτηται: Pom, 1547 τῶν σκευῶν ἔχει.
319 ἐμφέρεται: Grec 1093, 1547; Pom εἶναι φέρεται.
320 Pom; Grec 1093, 1547 lack.
321 [ἐμφαινομένη]: Pom, 1547; Grec 1093 ἐμφερομένη. Lampe, 458a, does not cite any Trinitarian-theological uses of ἐμφέρω.
322 [περί]: Pom, 1547; Grec 1093 παρά.
323 ἄτε οὐ μᾶλλον τούτου ἐκείνου ἢ ἧττον ἐκείνου τούτου ὄντος: Pom, 1547 ἄτε οὐ μᾶλλον τοῦτο ἐκείνου τοῦ ἄλλου αὕτη οἰκειοῦται.
324 Pom, 1547; Grec 1093 lacks.
325 διὸ καὶ [αἰ]δεσθέντες: Grec 1093, Pom; 1547 lacks.
326 τρανότερον: Pom, 1547 τρανότατα.
327 τῇ φωνῇ: Pom, 1547 τῇ φωνῇ πλησθεὶς πνεύματος ἁγίου.
328 αἱρετιζόντων: Pom, 1547 αἱρετικῶν.
329 αὐτῶν: Pom, 1547 αὐτά.
330 διαγνωρ[ί]σας: Pom, 1547 διαγνωρίσας < διαγνωρίζω; Grec 1093 διαγνωρήσας, which would derive from διαγνωρέω, which is not listed in LSJ, Montanari, or Lampe. This is an example of itacizing in later Greek.
331 αὐτῶν: Pom τῶν ἀγνοούντων.
332 τὴν ἀλήθειαν ἀναζωγραφήσας: Grec 1093, 1547; Pom τὴν ἀλήθειαν ἀναστήσας καὶ ἀναζωγραφήσας.
333 ἀποδείξεις: Grec 1093, 1547; Pom ἀποδείξεις σαφῶς.
334 [ἁγίαν Τριάδα] Pom, 1547; Grec 1093 ἄγνοιαν.
335 τῷ θεῷ: Grec 1093, 1547; Pom lacks.
336 γενόμενος: Pom, 1547 γενομένῳ.
337 Pom, 1547.
338 Pom, 1547.
339 ἀπόντως: Pom, 1547 ἀπόντός σου.
340 τοὺς ἐνταῦθα οἰκοῦντες μοναχούς: Pom, 1547 τοὺς ἐνταῦθα μοναχούς.
341 Ὧδε: Pom, 1547 Ὁ δε.
342 ταῦτα: Grec 1093, Pom; 1547 οὕτως.
343 ὁ λόγος . . . διέτρεχε: Grec 1093, Pom; 1547 διὰ πάσης τῆς γῆς τῇ φημῇ διέτρεχε.
344 εἶναι: Pom, 1547 ἄνειναι.

345 Pom, 1547; Grec 1093 ἔτη.
346 Grec 1093 follows here, on the same line, with Περὶ τοῦ μεγάλου Ποιμένος.
347 προσέβαλλεν: Pom παρέβαλεν.
348 There are indecipherable marginalia at the top right of this page.
349 [ὁ]ρῶ: Grec 1093 ὡρῶ. Pom lacks.
350 Pom; Grec 1093 lacks.
351 τούτου: Pom τούτων.
352 κἄν: Grec 1093, 1547; Pom κἂν ὁ τάλας.
353 κἂν τούτῳ: Grec 1093, Pom; 1547 lacks.
354 Pom, 1547; Grec 1093 ἀπολαύσω.
355 θαυμάσας: Pom ἀγασθεὶς τοῦτον; 1547 lacks.
356 περὶ τοῦ νέου: Pom, 1547 περὶ τοῦ νέου ὀφθαλμοῖς αἰσθητοῖς οὔπω ἑωρακὼς αὐτόν (1547 lacks αὐτόν).
357 <"Ποῦ ἐστί," φάσκων, "ὁ συνοδοιπόρος σου παῖς;>": Pom, 1547.
358 εἰσελθεῖν ἐκέλευσε καί: Grec 1093, 1547; Pom ἥξειν ἔσω ἐκέλευσεν.
359 <πολλοί>: Pom, 1547.
360 [ἰθύνουσά τε καί] περιέπουσα: Pom, 1547; Grec 1093 ἰθυνουσάντες περιέπουσα.
361 ἐπιθείς: Grec 1093, 1547; Pom ὁ μέγας ἐπιθείς.
362 εὐλογήσας: Pom, 1547 εὐλογήσας ἐπανιέναι.
363 εὐλογοῦντας . . . δοξάσαντας: Pom εὐλογοῦντα καὶ δοξάζοντα.
364 Θεόν: Pom, 1547 Θεόν. Καὶ ταῦτα μὲν ὧδε. Ἐχέσθω δὲ τῆς οἰκείας ἀκολουθίας ὁ λόγος and have instead a title for chapter XLVII (see the next note).
365 The title is supplied at the end of chapter XLVI.
366 Pom, 1547.
367 Pom, 1547; Grec 1093 lacks.
368 πᾶσα δῶσις καί: Pom, 1547 lack; δῶσις δόσις is far more common.
369 σπηλαίων: Pom, 1547 οἰκητόρων σπηλαίων.
370 [Εἴσελθε]: Pom; Grec 1093, 1547 εἴσιθι.
371 Pom, 1547.
372 ἀθλητήν: Grec 1093, 1547; Pom κακοχοῦντα ἀθλητήν.
373 δυσωπουμένη: Grec 1093, 1547; Pom lacks.
374 τηκόμενος: Grec 1093, 1547; Pom νικώμενος.
375 Εἶτα καὶ ὁ Παΐσιος, "Καὶ πῶς: Grec 1093, 1547; Pom Εἶτα ὁ Παΐσιος, "Ῥᾷον" φησι, "Καὶ πῶς."
376 ἔχων ἄσιτος πάσχω οὐδὲν τοιοῦτον": Pom ἔχων ἄσιτος πάσχω οὐδὲν τῶν δεινῶν;" Τὸν Σωτῆρα ἀντεπυνθάνατο; 1547 ἔχων ἄσιτος πάσχω οὐδὲν τῶν τοιοῦτον τῶν δεινῶν;" Τὸν Σωτῆρα ἀντεπυνθάνατο.
377 Πρὸς αὐτὸν πάλιν ὁ Σωτήρ: Pom, 1547 Καὶ πάλιν πρὸς αὐτὸν ὁ Σωτὴρ ἀντέφησεν.

378 κραταιῶς νηστεύεις: Pom, 1547 κραταιῶς καὶ ἰσχυρῶς νηστεύεις.
379 προαιρέσεως ἐν ἀγωνίαν νηστεύει: Grec 1093, 1547; Pom προαιρέσεως νηστεύει.
380 Ὁ δὲ Σωτήρ: Pom, 1547 Πρὸς αὐτὸν ἀπεκρίνατο ὁ Σωτήρ.
381 Pom, 1547.
382 ἔκτοτε: Pom, 1547 ἔκτοτε πάλιν.
383 προσέθηκε: Pom, 1547 προσέθηκεν ἀεί.
384 φησι: Pom, 1547 φησι πρὸς αὐτόν.
385 ἄλλου: Pom, 1547 ἄλλων.
386 θέλω ἵνα ἡνίκα ἂν ἐκ τῆς δὲ τῆς ἐρήμου εἰς ἐπίσκεψιν ἀδελφῶν παραγένωμαι ἐν τάχει ἀπελεύσομαι: Pom, 1547 θέλω ἡνίκα ἂν εἰς ἐπίσκεψιν ἀδελφῶν ἐκ τῆσδε τῆς ἐρημίας παραγένωμαι ἵνα ἐν τάχει ἐναπελεύσομαι βραδύτητος ὑπὲρ ἄλλων μὴ ἀνεχόμενος.
387 Pom, 1547.
388 μισήσῃς τίνα μηδὲ: Pom, 1547.
389 ἐν ταῖς ἐντολαῖς: Pom, 1547 ἐν ταῖς ἐντολαῖς σου.
390 τούτων: Pom, 1547 τούτου.
391 σπουδή: Pom, 1547 σπουδὴ ἐκείνῳ.
392 ἀκόμενος: Pom, 1547 παραγενόμενος.
393 ἐν τῷ οὐρανῷ ἀποδώσω: Pom, 1547 ἐν τῇ οὐρανίῳ ἀποδώσω· Ἰερουσαλήμ.
394 The editor has mistakenly numbered this paragraph the same as the last.
395 ἐπερωτᾷ: Pom, 1547 ἐπερωτᾷ αὖθις.
396 ἀγωνιζόμενος: Grec 1093, 1547; Pom σῶος ἀγωνιζόμενος.
397 Pom, 1547.
398 σφοδρούς: Pom, 1547 σφοδροτάτους.
399 <ὁ>: Pom, 1547.
400 εἴρηται, ἡμῖν δὲ ἐπὶ τὰ παράδοξα τῶν θαυμάτων ὁ λόγος βαδιεῖται: Pom, 1547 εἴρηται διαδραμούσης ἡμῖν τῆς διηγήσεως. Ἐπὶ δὲ τὰ παράδοξα τῶν θαυμάτων ὁ λόγος ἡμῖν [1547 lacks ἡμῖν] βαδίζειν ἐπείγεται.
401 ἐπεισῄει: Grec 1093, 1547; Pom ἐπεισῄει εἰ.
402 ἆρα τίνι τῶν εὐαρεστησάντων τῷ Θεῷ ἐφάμιλλος εἴη: Grec 1093, Pom; 1547 lacks.
403 [Εἰς Αἰγύπτῳ]: Pom, 1547; Grec 1093 Ἐν τῇ Αἰγύπτῳ.
404 ταπεινότητι. Pom, 1547 ταπεινοφροσύνῃ.
405 τὸ ὄρος: Grec 1093, Pom; 1547 lacks.
406 ἔλευσις: Pom, 1547 ἔλευσις ὑπὸ τῆς θείας χάριτος διδαχθέντα (1547 διδαχθείς).
407 γνωρισθείς: Pom, 1547 ὁρισθείς.
408 διάλεκτον: Grec 1093, Pom; 1547 διάλεκτον ἔχωντα.
409 μόνην ἐπιστάμενος: Grec 1093, Pom; 1547 μόνην.

410 τοιούτου γέροντος ἀποτυχεῖν λόγων ἐπωφελῶν: Pom τοιούτου γέροντος ὠφελεὶς λόγων ἀποτυχεῖν; 1547 τοιούτου γέροντος ἐπωφελῶν τυχεῖν λόγων.
411 ἀνασχὼν ὁ μακάριος ἅμα: Pom, 1547 ἀνασχὼν ὄμμα.
412 ἐκ βάθους καρδίας: Grec 1093; Pom ἐκ ὅλης καρδίας; 1547 ἐκ πάσης καρδίας.
413 Pom, 1547. The sense of the sentence requires it.
414 ἠξιώθη θεωριῶν: Grec 1093, 1547; Pom ἠξιώθη δωρεῶν καὶ θεωριῶν.
415 ἡδονῆς διὰ τῆς ὁμιλίας: Grec 1093, 1547; Pom lacks διὰ τῆς ὁμιλίας.
416 Grec 1093 seems to have διηνυσμένας or διηνυσμένης; Pom, 1547 διηνυσμένοις.
417 πρεσβύτην . . . μαθητάς: Pom, 1547 πρεσβύτην ἐπανιέναι ἐπὶ τὰ ἴδια εἶχε πάντας τοὺς προσόντας αὐτῷ μαθητὰς προσκαλεῖται Παΐσιος.
418 εὐσεβῶς προσλαμβάνεσθαι: Pom προσλαμβάνεσθε.
419 τοῦ θείου ἀνδρός: Grec 1093, 1547; Pom αὐτοῦ.
420 ἡμᾶ<ς> and <ἡ>: Pom, 1547.
421 θεῖος . . . Σύρων: Pom, 1547 θεῖος γὰρ ἡμῖν παρέβαλεν ἀνὴρ ἐκ τῆς γαίας τῶν Σύρων.
422 λόγοις: Pom, 1547 λόγῳ.
423 καὶ φθᾶσον: Pom, 1547 καὶ εἰ τοῦτον φθᾶσαι θέλεις (1547 lacks θέλεις).
424 οὐ πόρρω ὄντα: Pom, 1547 οὐ πόρρω γεγονότα ἀλλ' ἐγγὺς ὄντα. Ἐπείχθητι καταλαβεῖν.
425 Παῦσαι: Pom, 1547 Παῦσαι εὐθύς.
426 ὁ θεῖος Παΐσιος: Pom, 1547 ὁ θεῖος ἀνὴρ Παΐσιος.
427 Ἐκεῖνος γὰρ ἤδη: Pom ʹΟ γὰρ ἀνὴρ ἐκεῖνος ἤδη.
428 Pom, 1547 continue: ἀνύμνησαν αὐτὸν ὡς θαυμαστὸν ὄντα ἐν τοῖς ἁγίοις αὐτοῦ.
429 Pom has two separate pericopes in his par. LIII; we have subdivided the chapter.
430 ἔχοντα πρὸς τῇ κεφαλῇ ἄγγελον εὐπρεπῆ: Pom, 1547 ἔχοντα ἄγγελον εὐπρεπῆ πρὸς τὴν κεφαλὴν ἑστηκότα.
431 δοξάζων . . . αὐτόν: Pom, 1547 δοξάζων τὸν θεὸν καὶ τοὺς ἀγαπῶντας αὐτόν.
432 κ[ε]λεύσμασιν: Pom, 1547; Grec 1093 καὶ λεύσμασιν or καιλεύσμασιν.
433 ἐν τῇ ὁδῷ: Grec 1093, 1547; Pom lacks.
434 ἐν τῇ καρδίᾳ: Grec 1093, Pom; 1547 ἐν τῇ καρδίᾳ αὐτοῦ.
435 <αὐτοῦ>: Pom, 1547.
436 <ἁλούς>: Pom, 1547; Grec 1093 lacks.
437 θείῳ Παϊσίῳ: Grec 1093, 1547; Pom ὁσίῳ Παϊσίῳ.
438 αὐτοῦ: Pom; Grec 1093, 1547 lack.
439 Pom, 1547; Grec 1093 καὶ γάρ.
440 ὁρῶν: Pom ὡς ἑώρα.

441 ὦ πάτερ: Grec 1093, Pom; 1547 lacks.
442 οὐδέπω: Pom οὐδέποτε; 1547 ὅπέρ μοι οὐδέποτε.
443 δρῶν ἀναφαίνῃ νυνί: Pom, 1547 δρᾶν ἀνασχόμενος φαίνῃ.
444 με: Pom, 1547 lack.
445 Pom, 1547.
446 ἀγνοεῖς: Pom, 1547 ἀγνοεῖς ὡς ἄγος.
447 παρωθούμενος: Pom, 1547 παρωσάμενος.
448 δ[εῖ]να: Pom, 1547; Grec 1093 δῦνα.
449 ἀπὸ σοῦ ᾤχετο καὶ τὰ τῶν Χριστιανῶν ἰδιώματα: Grec 1093, Pom; 1547 οὗτος εἴχετο καὶ τὰ τῶν Χριστιανῶν ἰδιώματα.
450 σαφῶς: Pom, 1547 διαλέχθητι σαφῶς.
451 "Μηδὲν . . . γέρων: Pom, 1547 "Μηδὲν πεπραχέναι. Σύγγνωθι," ἔφη. Εἶτα ὑπολαβών, ὁ γέρων.
452 1547 lacks ὄντα.
453 δάκρυα: Pom δάκρυα τε; 1547 δάκρυα οὔτε.
454 <Ἔλεγεν αὐτόν>: Pom, 1547 Ἔλεγεν; Pom notes, 35 n. 45, that one should add αὐτόν after Ἔλεγεν.
455 Pom, 1547; Grec 1093 δυνόν, which is corrupt; LSJ, Lampe, and Montanari do not list δυνός.
456 ἰσχυριζόμενος: Pom διϊσχυριζόμενος; 1547 μηδὲν εἰς χερσὶν δεδρακέναι διϊσχυριζόμενος.
457 προσωμίλησας: Pom, 1547 προσωμίλησας καὶ συνελάλησας.
458 Καὶ ὅς: Pom, 1547 Καὶ ὁ μαθητὴς.
459 ὑμεῖς προσκυνεῖτε: Pom, 1547 ὑμεῖς ὑπολαμβάνετε καὶ προσκυνεῖτε.
460 Ἐκεῖνος γὰρ ἐστιν ὁ μέλλων ἔρχεσθαι: Pom, 1547 Ἐκεῖνος γὰρ ὁ μέλλων ἐλθεῖν ἄλλος ἐστίν; 1547 continues κἀγὼ ἴσως οὔπως ἐλθεὶς ἀποκριμόνος.
461 οὕτως ἔχει: Pom οὕτως ἔχει εὐθὺς ἀπεκρινόμην.
462 Pom, 1547.
463 τὸ ἅγιον: Pom, 1547 τὸ θεῖον.
464 ἀρνησα[μέν]ων: Pom, 1547; Grec 1093 ἀρνησάντων.
465 τιμωρίας ἐκείνων: Pom, 1547 ἐκεῖσε τιμωρίας.
466 ἀνέπεμψε: Pom, 1547 ἀνέπεμπε.
467 ἐλέησον: Pom, 1547 οἰκτείρισον.
468 παρωσάμενος (< παρωθέω): Pom, 1547 προϊέμενος (< προΐημι).
469 Pom, 1547.
470 τῷ μαθητῇ: Grec 1093, 1547; Pom τῷ μαθητῇ τούτῳ.
471 χρή: Grec 1093, Pom; 1547 lacks.
472 τοῦ Θεοῦ: 1547 lacks.
473 Pom, 1547.
474 τὴν τοῦ Πνεύματος δωρεὰν ἐπανιοῦσαν ὑποδεικνύ[ο]ν: Grec 1093, Pom; 1547 lacks.

475 ἀπὸ σου: Grec 1093, 1547; Pom lacks.
476 Σεαυτῷ οὖν πρόσεχε: Pom, 1547 Σεαυτῷ οὖν πρόσεχε τοῦ λοιποῦ.
477 ἀσεβείας: 1547 here mistakenly repeats ῥᾳθυμίας.
478 Pom, 1547 προίει: Grec 1093 προίη.
479 ἐφ' ἕτερον δὲ βαδιοῦμαι: 1547 ἐφ' ἕτερον δὲ βαδιοῦμεν; Pom ἡμεῖς δὲ ἐφ' ἕτερον βαδιοῦμεν.
480 Pom, 1547.
481 ἐντυχόντες: Pom, 1547 ἐντυχόντες καὶ ἤδη.
482 ἐνετρύφησαν: Pom, 1547 κατατρυφῶντες, with essentially the same meaning.
483 εἰδώς: Pom, 1547 ἔγνω.
484 ἐπιδεόμενος: Grec 1093, Pom; 1547 δεόμενος.
485 παραχθῆναι διακελεύομαι: Pom, 1547 προσαχθῆναι.
486 τῷ πατρὶ: Pom, 1547 τῷ πατρὶ Ἰωάννῃ σήμερον.
487 Ὁ δὲ ἐν τάχει παρέθηκε τράπεζαν: Pom, 1547 Ὁ δὲ ἐν τάχει τῷ προστάγματι εἴξας παρέθηκε τῷ Ἰωάννῃ τράπεζαν.
488 τροφῆς: Grec 1093, Pom; 1547 lacks.
489 "Σύγγνωθι," ἔφη, "ὅτι: Pom, 1547 "Σύγγνωθι," ἔφη, πάτερ, ὅτι.
490 τῷ {πονηρῷ} πνεύματι: Pom, 1547 τῷ πνεύματι. Given the context, Grec 1093's πονηρός does not make sense here. Perhaps a scribe thought that the spirit here was enticing John to abrogate his fast. Or this may reflect the early monks' concerns about having young men among them.
491 ἐν χερσίν: Grec 1093, Pom; 1547 lacks.
492 Ἐπ[εὶ] μηδ' ὁ ὑλικῆς ἐδεῖτο: Pom, 1547 Ἐπεὶ μηδ' ὑλικῆς ἐδεῖτο. Given the parallelism in the sentence, the first phrase equals Ἐπ[εὶ] μηδ' ὁ ὑλικῆς ἐδεῖτο τροφῆς.
493 Pom, 1547 πεπληρωμένος; Grec 1093 πεπλησμένος.
494 ἑτέραν ἐπὶ τῇ προτέρᾳ προσθεὶς νηστείαν: Grec 1093, Pom; 1547 lacks.
495 Καὶ ἦν ἑαυτῷ διαλεγόμενος: Pom, 1547 Καὶ ἦν ἀεὶ ἐν αὐτῷ διαλεγόμενος.
496 Ἡδέως," ἔφαγον, "νηστεύσω λοιπὸν προθύμως: Grec 1093, Pom; 1547 lacks.
497 ὁ γεννάδας: Grec 1093, 1547; Pom οὗτος ὁ γεννάδας.
498 τῇ προσευχῇ τοῦ ἱεροῦ Παϊσίου ἰσχὺν ἀνακτώμενος: Pom, 1547 τῇ προσευχῇ ἰσχὺν ἀνακτώμενος τοῦ ἱεροῦ Παϊσίου.
499 κατανοήσας: Pom, 1547 ἰδών.
500 [πονηρίας]: Pom; Grec 1093, 1547 πορνείας. Further down, Pshoi uses πονηρούς, which suggests that πονηρίας is correct here.
501 τὸν ν[έ]ον βουλόμενος: Grec 1093, 1547; Pom τὸν ν[έ]ον βουλόμενος μή.
502 ἧς: Grec 1093, 1547; Pom εἴης.
503 ἀγωνιζόμενος καὶ τὴν θεῖαν ἀεί: Pom, 1547 ἀγωνιζόμενος ἔσο τὴν θεῖαν.
504 ἄτρωτον τὸν νέον: Pom, 1547 τοῦτον ἄτρωτον.

505 Pom, 1547 continue: Καὶ ταῦτα μὲν οὕτως.
506 Τί ἐμοὶ καὶ σοί: Pom, 1547 Τί κοινὸν ἐμοὶ καὶ σοί. Lk 8:28 Τί ἐμοὶ καὶ σοί.
507 ὦ Παῖσιε: Pom lacks.
508 οἰκήτωρ: Pom, 1547 οἰκήτωρ ἢ οὐ.
509 τὰς ἐμὰς δεινὰς ἐπηρείας: Pom, 1547 τὰς ἐμὰς δεινὰς ἐπηρείας καὶ ἃς ἐπινενόηκα προσβολάς.
510 Ταῦτα εἰπόντος, εὐθὺς γέγονεν ἀφάντος: Pom Ταῦτα εἰπόντος ὁ πονηροὺς γέγονεν ἀφανής.
511 ἀλλὰ . . . ἐπαύσατο: Pom, 1547 ἀλλ᾽ οὐ μὲν οὖν τῆς κακίας παύεται.
512 καὶ ἐράστης: Grec 1093, 1547; Pom lacks.
513 δείκνυει: Pom, 1547 ποιῶν.
514 οὐδαμῶς ἀνεκτά: Pom, 1547 ἀνεκτὰ ἥκιστα αὐτῷ.
515 ὅτι οὐκ ἔστι ἡ ἄφιξίς σου: Pom, 1547 ὅτι ἀκμὴν σου ἡ ἄφιξις.
516 [ἀγνωστός εἶναι]: Pom, 1547; Grec 1093 γνωστή ἐστι.
517 <καὶ>: Pom; Grec 1093, 1547 lack.
518 τὸν διάβολον ἔχων δεδεμένον, "Λάβε τοῦτον," εἶπεν, "ὡς βούλῃ: Grec 1093, Pom; 1547 lacks.
519 δι᾽ αὐτῆς . . . φυλάττων: Pom, 1547 δι᾽ αὐτῆς πάντας περιέπεις καὶ φυλάττεις.
520 καρτερή[σαιμι]: Pom; Grec 1093, 1547 καρτερῆσαι μοι. But there is an ἰ above the ο in -μοι, suggesting a correction to καρτερήσαιμι.
521 ἵνα τί: Grec 1093, Pom; 1547 ἵνα τί εἶπέ μοι.
522 <ἀρχαρίοις>: Pom, 1547.
523 μηδαμῶς: Grec 1093, Pom; 1547 lacks.
524 τούτων: Pom αὐτῶν.
525 κατασχὼν παίγνιον: Pom, 1547 κατασχὼν ἐν χερσὶ παίγνιον.
526 ὑπὸ τῆς χάριτος καὶ τῆς θέρμης: Pom, 1547 ὑπὸ τῆς θέρμης.
527 τῇ προσδοκίᾳ τῆς ὕστερον ῥαθυμίας τούτοις περιφρονῶ ἀναβαλλόμενος: Grec 1093, 1547; Pom τῇ προσδοκίᾳ τῆς ῥαθυμίας τῆς εἰς ὕστερον γενομένης τούτων περιφρονῶ ἀναβαλλόμενος.
528 Ἐπ[ε]ιδὰν δὲ . . . ὁρῶ: Pom Ἐπειδὰν δὲ θερμωτέρως αὐτοὺς ἐπὶ τὰ πρόσω χωροῦντας θεάσωμαι; 1547 Ἐπ[ε]ιδὰν θερμωτέρους ἐπὶ τὰ πρόσω χωροῦντας ὁρῶ.
529 ἀκαταγώνιστοι . . . χάριτι: Pom, 1547 ἀκαταγώνιστοι καὶ ἄτρωτοι γένοιντο οἰκειωθέντες τῇ χάριτι.
530 <οὕτως>: Pom, 1547.
531 ταμιευσάμενος. Ταῦτα: Pom and 1547 have the following between ταμιευσάμενος and Ταῦτα: ἐκεῖ γὰρ ἀπολαύσεται τῶν οἰκωεῖον ἀμοιβῶν, τῶν χαλεπῶν τε καὶ ἀπορρήτων τιμωριῶν.
532 <αὐτοῦ>: Pom, 1547.

533 ὁ μὲν ἐν δόξῃ ὁ δὲ ἐν ἀτιμίᾳ: Pom, 1547 ὁ μὲν ἐν δόξῃ ὁ δὲ ἐν ἀτιμίᾳ ἕκαστος τῶν φαινομένων.
534 ὀχλήσεως . . . ἴσχυσεν: Pom, 1547 ὀχλήσεως. Οὐκ ἔτι δὲ τούτῳ ἢ ὀφθῆναι ἢ πολεμῆσαι ἴσχυσεν.
535 ἀνεπαύσατο: Pom, 1547 ἐπανεπαύσατο.
536 ἱεροῦ: Pom, 1547 θείου.
537 λ[ό]γων . . . ἀκοῦσαι: Pom, 1547 λόγων ἀκοῦσαι βουλόμενοι τῶν ἐκείνου ἐπωφελῶν.
538 Pom, 1547.
539 παράδοσιν: Pom, 1547 ὁδόν.
540 μὴ ζητεῖτε: Pom, 1547 μὴ ζητεῖτε μηδέν.
541 ἐνορατικοῖς: Pom, 1547 διορατικοῖς.
542 [εἴη]: Grec 1093 ἤει; Pom, 1547 εἴη.
543 μοι εἰρήκασιν: Pom, 1547 μοι γενομένῳ εἰρήκασιν.
544 κατ᾽ εἶδος καὶ τὰ μόνα τῷ θεῷ: Pom, 1547 κατ᾽ εἶδος καὶ οἷα παρὰ μόνῳ τῷ θεῷ (1547 τούτῳ).
545 Pom, 1547 continue: Ταῦτα πάντα τὰ καθ᾽ ἡμᾶς ἐγνώρισε καὶ διεσάφησεν ἡμῖν πάντα.
546 διεβεβαιώθην: Pom, 1547 διανοηθείς.
547 καὶ ἐν πείρᾳ. . . .᾽Επ᾽ ἀληθείας δὲ λέγω ὑμῖν: supplied from Pom; Grec 1093, 1547 lack.
548 λελόγισμαι: Pom, 1547 διαλελόγισμαι.
549 χαριέντ[ω]ς: Pom, 1547; Grec 1093 χαριέντος.
550 <μοι>: Pom, 1547.
551 ἐξιών: Pom, 1547 ἐπεξιών.
552 Οἱ δὲ: Pom, 1547 Οἱ δὲ θαυμάσεντες, θαυμαστός.
553 ἔλεγ[ο]ν: Pom, 1547; Grec 1093 ἔλεγων.
554 ἀναχωροῦντες: Pom, 1547 ἀναχωροῦντες τοῦτον ἀγάμενοι τῆς ὑπερβολῆς τῶν χαρισμάτων.
555 ἀπείθεια: Pom, 1547 ἀπείθεια προξενεῖ λυπηρά. ἡ supplied from Pom, 1547.
556 Supplied from Pom, 1547.
557 ἐντυχεῖν: Pom, 1547 θεάσασθαι καί.
558 ἀποστάς: Pom, 1547 ἐφαστάμενος.
559 προσετέθη: Pom, 1547 προσέκειτο.
560 Σύσκηνος . . . τῇ ὕβρει: Pom Σύσκηνός τε καὶ συνόμιλος ταύτῃ γενόμενος τοσοῦτον αὐτῇ συνάπτεται γνώμῃ, ὅσῳ τῆς ἀσεβείας κοινωνὸς ἐκείνης ἐφάνη συγκαταθέμενος τῇ ὕβρει; 1547 lacks both readings.
561 Supplied from Pom.
562 [λαβοῦσα]: Pom, 1547; Grec 1093 βαλοῦσα.

563 ὀδόντας: Grec 1093, Pom; 1547 ὀδόντας αὐτοῦ.
564 ἐκείνου ἀπολειφθῇ: Pom, 1547 αὐτοῦ ἐγκαταλειφθῇ. Corrections in this paragraph supplied from Pom, 1547.
565 ἐπισκοπούσης: Pom, 1547 ἐπισκέψεως καί.
566 ῥοπῆς: Pom, 1547 χάριτος.
567 τὸ ἄμετρον . . . παράδοξον: Pom, 1547 τὸ ἄμετρον διὰ τῶν ἐφεξῆς λεχθησομένων πείσομαι τὸ παράδοξον.
568 διαζευχθεὶς διά: Pom, 1547 διαζευχθεὶς καὶ εἰς βάθη τοῦ ᾅδου κατενεχθεὶς διά.
569 Pom, 1547.
570 Pom; Grec 1093, 1547 lack.
571 εἶναι . . . τυγχάνοντες: Pom, 1547 τοῦ μεγάλου τυγχάνομεν.
572 γενέσθαι: Pom ἀφικόμεθα.
573 τῷ μεγάλῳ: Pom, 1547 τῷ μεγάλῳ γέροντι.
574 τὸν Κύριον . . . ἐλευθερω[θείη]: Pom, 1547 τὸν Κύριον ἐξιλεώσασθαι δυσωπηθέντος τῶν τοῦ ἐχθροῦ μηχανημάτων ἐλευθερωθείη. For Grec 1093's ἐλευθερώσῃ, Pom, 1547 have ἐλευθερωθείη.
575 τὸν μέγαν: Pom, 1547 τὸν γέροντα.
576 τὰ περὶ ἐκείνου ἀκούσας: Pom, 1547 τὰ περὶ ἐκείνου ἀκούσας λυπηρά.
577 [βύθιόν τε]: Pom, 1547; Grec 1093 βυθίοντι.
578 Τοῦτο γαρ χρ[ώ]μενος: Pom, 1547 χαλεπῷ τούτῳ γὰρ χρωμένῳ.
579 ὡς καί: Pom, 1547 ὡς ἴστε.
580 ἐκγόνους, descendants; Pom, 1547 ἐγγόνους, grandsons.
581 μηχανημάτων ἀεὶ ὑπερεύχεσθαι χρή: Pom, 1547 μηχανημάτων εὔχεσθαι χρή.
582 1547 is deficient here, omitting τῶν τοιούτων . . . κύριε υἱὲ Θεοῦ.
583 ἐπ[ί]βλεψον: Pom, 1547; Grec 1093 ἐπέβλεψον.
584 ἐμάς: Grec 1093, 1547; Pom ἡμῶν.
585 [πρόσ]δεξαι: Pom, 1547; Grec 1093 πάνδεξαι.
586 ἀνακάλεσαι: Pom, 1547 ἀνακαλείσθαι.
587 συχναῖς: Pom, 1547 πολλαῖς.
588 ἐπαύσετο: Pom, 1547 ἐπαύετο.
589 δυσωπῶν: Pom, 1547 δυσωπεῖν.
590 [Ἐπεὶ δὲ ταῖς τούτου δεήσεσιν]: Pom, 1547; Grec 1093 Ἐπὶ δὲ τούτου δεήσεις.
591 δυσωπηθέντων . . . ὁ Σωτήρ: Pom, 1547 δυσωπηθέντων οὐκ ᾠήθη γὰρ ὁ Σωτὴρ τὰς αἰτήσεις παριδεῖν ἐπιφαίνεται τούτῳ.
592 γεγενῆσθαι τὴν δέησιν ἐπυνθάνετο: 1547 is deficient here, lacking τὴν δέησιν and apparently having ἄν.
593 συναπαχθέντος: Pom, 1547 συναπαχθέντος δειλαίου.
594 ταύτας: Pom, 1547 πάντας.

595 καλοῦντος: Pom, 1547 παρακαλοῦντος.
596 [κάλεσον]: Grec 1093 κάλε κάλεσε; Pom ἀνακαλούμενος.
597 Ἀνάσχου . . . πρόβατον: Pom, 1547 Ἀνάσχου οὖν δυσωπούμενος καὶ τὸ πεπλανημένον ἀνακαλούμενός σου πρόβατον, ἱλέως τούτου γένου.
598 <τῇ>: Pom, 1547; Grec 1093 ταῦτα.
599 καὶ τῆς ἀγγελικῆς ἀποστασίας ποίμνης: Pom, 1547 καὶ τῆς ἐμῆς ἀποστάντα ποίμνης.
600 ἐ[υ]αριστούμενος: Pom, 1547 εὐεργετούμενος; Grec 1093 ἐβαριστούμενος, reflecting M.Gr. pronunciation.
601 Βαβαί: Pom, 1547 Βαβαί εἰρήκει.
602 <τιμωρίας>: Pom, 1547; Grec 1093 ἀξίας.
603 Ὑπὲρ τῆς σῆς <τιμωρίας> . . . αἰτήσεως: Pom, 1547 Ὑπὲρ ἁμαρτολοῦ σωτηρίας τιμωρίας προείλου, κἀντεῦθεν ἐκπεσὼν μὲν ἥκιστα τῶν σῶν ἔσῃ, τεύξεται δὲ τῆς αἰτήσεως.
604 τοῦ μεγάλου: Pom, 1547 τοῦ μεγάλου ἀνδρός.
605 διαγωγῇ: Pom πολιτείᾳ; 1547 σεμνῇ καταστάσει καὶ πολιτείᾳ.
606 ἱεροῦ: Pom, 1547 ὁσίου.
607 χρή: Pom, 1547.
608 Ἡμᾶς . . . Θεόν: Pom, 1547 Ἡμᾶς δὲ ἀκούοντας τὰ τοιαῦτα παράδοξα δοξάζειν χρὴ καὶ ἀνυμνεῖν τὸν ἐκείνον μεγαλύναντα Κύριον.
609 τῇ ἐρήμῳ: Pom, 1547 τῇ μονῇ.
610 φρόνημα κεκτημένος: Pom, 1547 ἔχων φρόνημα.
611 λογίων: Pom, 1547 λόγων.
612 Μὴ . . . λόγοις: Pom Πέρας γὰρ τῶν εἰρημένων ἅτε μὴ ἔχων τὸ ἀγαθὸν μηδὲ καρδίαν ὀρθὴν κτησάμενος, οὐ μόνον καρπὸν οὐκ ἔφερεν, ἀλλὰ καὶ τοὺς λόγους; 1547 Πέρας γὰρ τῶν εἰρημένων ἅτε μὴ ἔχων τὴν ἀγαθὴν μηδὲ καρπὸν φέρειν ἀνασχόμενος τοὺς λόγους ἐκωμῴδει καὶ ἑτέροις λόγοις.
613 αἱ κοσμικαὶ συνήθειαι φέρειν εἰώθασι, χρώμενος τὰ καταβαλλόμενα διέφθειρεν: Pom αἱ κοσμικαὶ συνήθειαι φέρουσι χρώμενος τὰ καταβαλλόμενα διέφθειρεν; 1547 αἱ κοσμικαὶ συνήθειαι φέρειν ὁμιλίας, χρώμενος τὰ καταβαλλόμενα διέφθειρεν.
614 θεοφιλῆ: Pom, 1547 θεοφιλῆ γέροντα.
615 κατ[η]γόγγυσαν: Pom, 1547 κατεγόγγυζον; Grec 1093 κατεγόγγυσαν.
616 ὁ πρεσβύτερος: Pom, 1547 ὁ πρεσβύτερος ἐκεῖνος.
617 Pom; Grec 1093 lacks. Pom notes, 47 n. 33, that Jernstadt emended to ἵνα ὅπως; 1547 lacks ἵνα ὅπως.
618 δ[ει]νῶς (Grec 1093: δυνῶς) νυσόμενος: Pom, 1547 βαλλόμενος.
619 καὶ λίαν . . . μᾶλλον: 1547 lacks.
620 Pom, 1547.
621 τοῖς: Grec 1093, Pom; 1547 τούτοις.

622 καὶ ἄλλο: Pom καὶ πολλῆς ἀνοχῆς Κυρίου τοῦ Θεοῦ. Καὶ τοῦτο μὲν ἕως ὧδε; 1547 καὶ πολλῆς ἀνοχῆς. Καὶ τοῦτο μὲν ὧδε ἡμῖν δὲ ἄλλο.
623 φρικωδέστερον: Grec 1093, 1547; Pom φρικωδέττατον.
624 παραδοξότερον διηγητέον: Pom, 1547 παραδοξότερον καὶ οὐδέν τι τῶν κατὰ λόγον διήγημα ὑψηλότερον διηγητέον.
625 [Παρουσίας]: Grec 1093 Ἐπιστασίας.
626 δεῖ: Pom, 1547 χρή εἰ φιλοφρόνως δέξῃ ἡμᾶς.
627 [φιλόξενος] Pom; Grec 1093 δεξιός; 1547 φιλόξενος δόξιος (sic).
628 Pom, 1547.
629 Pom, 1547.
630 Χριστέ: Pom, 1547 ἀγαθὲ κύριε.
631 τοιαύτους: Pom, 1547 τοὺς σούς.
632 Grec 1093 lacks at the beginning of this sentence Pom, 1547 καὶ ταῦτα μὲν οὕτως.
633 [ἀν]εχόμενος: Pom, 1547; Grec 1093 ἐχόμενος ἦσαν.
634 φιλοξενίας: Pom, 1547 φιλοξενίας κατὰ λόγον (1547 λόγων).
635 Ἀναθφλεχθεὶς ... Παΐσιος: Grec 1093, 1547; Pom Ἀναθφλεχθεὶς δὲ τῷ ἔρωτι, ὁ ἱερὸς Παΐσιος.
636 καιομένην ἔχων: Pom, 1547; Grec 1093 ἦν καιομένην.
637 καὶ δυσκάθεκτον ἔχων: Pom, 1547 καὶ δυσκάθεκτον τὴν ψυχήν.
638 ἀξιόχρηστον: Pom, 1547 ἀξιύμνητον.
639 φιλοχρ[ί]στου: Pom, 1547; Grec 1093 φιλοχρήστου.
640 τῷ πλησίον: Pom, 1547; Grec 1093 τὸ πλησίῳ.
641 σφόδρα κεκοπιακότι: Pom, 1547 σφόδρα ἤδη κεκοπιακότι τὸ καταλειφθέν.
642 Ὁ δὲ μέγας ... ἐνέσκηψεν: Pom, 1547 Ὁ μέγας ἀνὴρ ἐνέσκηψεν.
643 κατάπαυσον: Pom, 1547 ἀνάπαυσον.
644 ἀπεφθέγξατο: Pom, 1547 ἀντεφθέγγετο.
645 Pom, 1547.
646 θεῖος: Pom, 1547 θεσπέσιος.
647 εἴθισται: Pom, 1547 εἴθιστο.
648 καὶ διὰ τί, καὶ πῶς: Pom, 1547 καὶ τίνι τρόπῳ καὶ διὰ τί καὶ πῶς.
649 τῷ Ἀβραάμ: Pom, 1547 τῷ πατριάρχῃ Ἀβραάμ.
650 χαμερπῶν χειρῶν: Pom, 1547 χαμερπῶν θράσους χειρῶν.
651 καὶ ... ἐτρώθης: Pom, 1547 καὶ τῷ τῆς ὑπακοῆς θείῳ οὐκ ἐτρώθης ἔρωτι.
652 κ[ε]χρημένος: Pom, 1547 ἤδη κεχρημένος.
653 οὐρανόθεν: Grec 1093, Pom; 1547 lacks.
654 [ἀ]πονίας: Pom, 1547; Grec 1093 ὑπόνοιας.
655 ἐλάμβανε: Pom, 1547 ὑπελάμβανε.
656 ἄφωνος ... νοῦν: Pom, Grec 1093; 1547 lacks.
657 [ἀ]πωδύρετο: Pom, 1547; Grec 1093 ἐπωδύρετο.

658 βοῶν: Pom, 1547 ἐθρήνει.
659 Ὁποίου . . . ἐστέρησα: Pom, 1547 Τίνος ἐμαυτὸν ὁ ἄθλιος, εἰπὼν, τῶν μεγίστων ἀγαθῶν ἐστερήθην.
660 βασκαίνων . . . ἀπολαύσειν: Pom δαίμονος βασκήνας οὐκ εἴασεν τοιούτων ἀγαθῶν [1547 καλῶν] ἀπολαῦσαι.
661 οὖν: Pom, 1547 καὶ τοῖς τούτων ὁμοίοις.
662 Pom, 1547.
663 διηνεκῶς: Pom, 1547; Grec 1093 δεινῶς.
664 Pom, 1547; Grec 1093 lacks, probably due to homeoteleuton: μεταμελό{ύ}μενος . . . ἐπιμελούμενος.
665 θερμῶς ἐξιλεοῦ τ[ε] ἄφεσιν: Pom, 1547 ἐξιλεοῦ θερμῶς τε καὶ ἐπισταμένως ἄφεσιν.
666 σπλάγχνα: Grec 1093, Pom; 1547 σπλάγχνα ὄντως.
667 Grec 1093 lacks here Pom, 1547 Καὶ ταῦτα μὲν οὕτως.
668 <μαθητής>: Pom, 1547.
669 γέροντι: Pom, 1547 Παϊσίῳ.
670 <μοι>: Pom, 1547.
671 γερόντων ὃν δοκεῖς σύ (1547 οἷς) δοκεῖς σὺ γερόντων.
672 Εὑρήσεις ἄνδρα πτωχὸν παρὰ τὸ τεῖχος τῆς πόλεως ἐν τοῖς δεξιοῖς μέρεσιν: Pom Εὑρήσεις ἄνδρα πτωχὸν τῷ σχήματι ἐν τοῖς δεξιοῖς τῶν εἰσερχομένων τειχέων; 1547 Εὑρήσεις ἄνδρα πτωχὸν παρὰ τὸ τεῖχος τῆς πόλεως ἐν τοῖς δεξιοῖς τῶν εἰσερχόμενων.
673 σοῦ: Pom, 1547 σε.
674 εὐθέως ἀπῄει: Pom, 1547 ἀπῄει.
675 τὸν ἄρτον: Grec 1093, Pom; 1547 lacks.
676 [ἀθυρμὸν αὐτῷ ἀποδοῦναι]: Pom, 1547; Grec 1093 ἀθυρμάτων γενέσθαι.
677 Pom; 1547 lacks.
678 πάριθι," ἔφη, "σταλεῖσαν ἡμῖν δοὺς εὐλογίαν": Pom "πάριθι," ἔφη, "καὶ ἡμῖν τὴν σταλεῖσαν δὸς εὐλογίαν."
679 <λαβὼν> [εἰ]ληφώς: Pom; Grec 1093 ἠληφώς; 1547 εἰληφώς.
680 ἐπυνθάνετο: Pom ἔχει; 1547 ἔφη.
681 τοις ἐκείνου κελεύσμασιν: Pom αὐτῷ; 1547 τις ἐκείνου κελεύσμασιν.
682 διὰ τὴν παρακοήν σου: Pom τῇ σῇ παρακοῇ; 1547 διὰ τὴν σὴν παρακοήν.
683 The rest of page 200b is blank.
684 τῷ μεγάλῳ πατρί: Pom τῷ θείῳ ἀνδρί. Pom, 1547 continue καὶ ἱκέτευσον αὐτόν.
685 τοῦ Σωτῆρος: Grec 1093, Pom; 1547 lacks.
686 καὶ αὖθις ἐδεῖτο τοῦ μεγάλου: Pom, 1547 καὶ αὖθις τοῦ θείου Παϊσίου ἐδεῖτο.
687 καὶ . . . ἐκεῖνον: Pom, 1547 ἐπεὶ τὸ πείθειν ἐκεῖνον ἀρμὴν οὐκ εἶχεν.

688 [ἀξιωθέντων]: Pom; Grec 1093, 1547 ἠξιομένων.
689 ἀναλύσεως . . . προσῄεσαν: Pom, 1547 ἀναλύσεως αὐτῶν τῷ τάφῳ προσίασιν ἕκαστος μετὰ τῆς προσηκούσης τιμῆς καὶ εὐχαριστίας, ὕμνους ἀναπέμπων Θεῷ καὶ κοιμηθεὶς ἀνεπαύσατο.
690 μοι διαλεχθήσῃ: Pom, 1547 ἡμῖν διαλεχθήσομεν.
691 [διακελεύεται]: Pom; Grec 1093, 1547 διαλέγεται.
692 ὡς ἂν: Pom, 1547 ὡς ἂν ἔγωγε.
693 τῷ πατρί: Pom, 1547 τῷ πατρί σου.
694 βούλει: Pom, 1547 βούλοιο.
695 [διατάγμασι]: Pom, 1547; Grec 1093 διδάγμασι.
696 πάλιν: Pom, 1547 πάλιν ἐν τῷ ἰδίῳ σηκῷ.
697 ἐπανιὼν . . . καί: Pom ἐπανῄει καί; 1547 ἐπανῄει.
698 τούτου: Pom, 1547 τούτων τοῖς μεγαλύνουσι τὸν Θεὸν ὁ λόγος διέξεισι.
699 Τὰ δ᾿ ἄλλα πῶς σιωπήσω: Pom, 1547 Τῶν δ᾿ ἄλλων πῶς μοι σιωπὴν ὁ λόγος εἰσφέρει (ἐνεῖναι), μὴ τοῖς φιλοθέοις διεξιόντι παράδοξα.
700 ἡμῖν εἶναι: Pom lacks; 1547 εἶναι.
701 ἀνηγησαίμην ἐργῶδες δὲ τῷ λόγῳ οὐκοῦν: Pom ἡνηγσαίμην εἶναι. Τοίνυν; 1547 ἀνηγσαίμην τοίνυν.
702 μεγάλου: Pom, 1547 ἁγίου ἀνδρός.
703 ὁρῶν . . . Οἱ δε: Grec 1093, Pom; 1547 ὁρῶν ἐφάπτεσθαι ἐπετρεψάντοις. Οἱ δε.
704 ἄτρ[επ]τοι: Pom, 1547; Grec 1093 ἄτρωτοι, which may be a mistake for ἄτρυτοι.
705 ἀποκρουσόμενοι: Pom, 1547 παρωθούμενοι, with essentially the same meaning.
706 ἀγαθοῖς ἀεὶ βασκαίνων ἐχθρός: Pom, 1547 χρηστοῖς ἀεὶ βασκαίνων ἐχθρός.
707 <αὐτοῖς>: Pom, 1547.
708 ὁ ταῦτα . . . ἠρευνᾶτο: Pom ὁ ταῦτα κλέψας ἀνερευνᾶτο παρ᾿ ἐκείνου; 1547 ὁ ταῦτα κλέψας ὑπ᾿ ἐκείνου ἀνερευνᾶτο.
709 γέροντος ἀκηκοώς: Grec 1093, 1547; Pom ἀναμαθὼν γέροντος.
710 Οὗτος . . . διαβάλων: Pom Οὗτος οὖν τοὺς μοναχοὺς ἐκείνῳ διαβάλλων; 1547 Οὗτος οὖν τοῖς μοναχοῖς ἐκείνῳ τοὺς νεοτέρους διαβάλλων.
711 νέοι: Grec 1093, 1547; Pom lacks.
712 μὴ ἀνήσῃς: Pom, 1547 οὐκ ἀνιῇς.
713 <ἐκεῖθεν>: Pom, 1547.
714 <αὐτούς>: Pom; Grec 1093, 1547 lack.
715 πατὴρ ἡμῶν Παΐσιος: Pom, 1547 πατήρ.
716 As Pom notes, 55 n. 32, after γεγονυίας a folio is missing; the manuscript begins again with 76. (203a1). Grec 1093 for this missing section is taken from Pom and 1547, with Pom as the primary text.
717 ἀδελφοί: 1547 ἀδελφούς.

718 αὐτοῦ: 1547 αὐτῶν.
719 σου: 1547 αὐτοῦ.
720 Ταῦτα ἀκούσαντες: 1547 ἀκούσαντες.
721 τὰ ἀπὸ στόματος Παϊσίου: 1547 ὑπὸ τοῦ Παϊσίου.
722 Ὁ δὲ τῷ δέει . . . ποσι: 1547 lacks.
723 ἐφώρμησε: 1547 ἐφόρμαται [sic].
724 ἀνήρ: 1547 πατήρ.
725 τῆς: 1574 ταύτης.
726 τῇ διδασκαλίᾳ: 1547 τῇ αὐτοῦ διδασκαλίᾳ.
727 The manuscript resumes here.
728 ὅσα δι᾽ αὐτοῦ ὁ Θεὸς τοῖς ἀνθρώποις ἔδειξε, παραγίνεται πρὸς αὐτόν, συντυχόντες ἀλλήλοις: Grec 1093, Pom; 1547 καὶ αὐτοῦ οὗτος ἀλλήλοις.
729 ἕτερος . . . ὡς: Grec 1093, 1547; Pom ἕτερος ἑτέρου βοηθὸς πολεμούμενοι τὸν ἐχθρὸν ἐκατήσχυναν.
730 ἰσχυρά: Pom, 1547 ὀχυρά.
731 καλῶν κατὰ τρυφῶντους νέους: Pom; 1547 καρπῶν κατὰ τρυφῶντους νέους.
732 ἱερός: Pom, 1547 μέγας.
733 ψυχῇ: Pom, 1547 ψυχῇ ὅλως.
734 Ἀναβολῆς: Pom, 1547 ἀναβολήν.
735 ἀκούων: Pom, 1547 ἀκηκοώς.
736 ἄριστε: Grec 1093, 1547; Pom ἔξαρχε.
737 τῇ ἀρίστῃ: Pom, 1547 τῇ ἐπαινετῇ καὶ ἀρίστῃ.
738 [τὰς σάς]: Pom, 1547; Grec 1093 τὰ σάς.
739 εὐχάς: Grec 1093, 1547; Pom ἁγίας εὐχάς.
740 ἡμῖν: Grec 1093, Pom; 1547 lacks.
741 <χρηματίζοντες>: Pom, 1547.
742 πάμπολ[λ]α: Pom, 1547 πάμπολλα ὑπερφυῶς.
743 <θείας> ἀναβάσεως: Pom, 1547; Grec 1093 ἀναβάσεως.
744 τῶν: Pom, 1547 τοῦ.
745 κατελίμπανεν: Pom, 1547 ἀφῆκεν, with essentially the same meaning.
746 χρώμενος: Pom, 1547 χρησάμενος.
747 Διὰ τί τοῦτο: Pom, 1547 Διὰ τί τοῦτο, πάτερ.
748 ἔλεγε: Pom, 1547 ἀντίλεγε.
749 [μεγάλα βλάπτονται]: Pom; Grec 1093, 1547 μαλα, which does not exist.
750 [ὑπὸ] τοῦ Κυρίου: 1547; Grec 1093 παρὰ τοῦ Κυρίου; Pom ὑπὸ τοῦ Δεσπότου.
751 γνωσθήτω: Pom, 1547 γνώτω, which is the reading of Mt 6:3.
752 τῆς πολλῆς ἐκείνου: Grec 1093, 1547; Pom τῆς ἐκείνου.
753 ὁ λόγος διεξῆλθε: Pom ὁ λόγος λαθὼν διέξεισι; 1547 ὁ λόγος λαθὼν δι᾽ αὐτῆς ἀκολουθίας διέξεισι.

754 τὴν τελευτὴν τούτου ἥξειν βούλεται: Pom, 1547 τὴν τελευτὴν ἥξειν ὁ λόγος βούλεται τοῦ ὁσίου.
755 γενόμενος: Pom, 1547 κάτοχος γενόμενος.
756 πέρας τῶν: Pom, 1547 πέρας τῶν τῇδε.
757 τῇ γῇ: Pom, 1547 lack.
758 ἄνωθεν: Pom, 1547 ἐν οὐρανοῖς.
759 τῶν ἐνθένδε: Pom, 1547 τῶν ἐνθένδε ἀπάρας.
760 <αὐτῶν>: Pom, 1547.
761 {τά}: Pom lacks; 1547 εἶτα.
762 συνήγοντο τοιούτῳ δὲ τρόπῳ γέγονεν ἡ συνάφεια: Pom, 1547 συνήγοντο τρόπῳ τοιῳδε συναφθέντες.
763 <τό>: Pom, 1547.
764 ὁ λόγος: Grec 1093, Pom; 1547 ὁ λόγος τι.
765 ἐκλιπόντος: Pom ἀπολιπόντος; 1547 λειπόντος [sic].
766 ἐκεῖσε τέθαπται: Pom, 1547 ἐν αὐτόθι ἐτάφη.
767 ἰ[δί]αν: Pom, 1547 ἰδίαν; Grec 1093 ἰκείαν.
768 <τῇ νηὶ>: Pom, 1547.
769 <τήν>: Pom, 1547.
770 ὡς ἔμψυχον τι ἐπινεῦον τὸν συνήθη {ἀμελίον} ἐπιζητοῦντος τοῦ ἱεροῦ Παϊσίου: Pom ὡς ἔμψυχον τι ἐπινεῦον τὸν συνήθη τοῦ ἱεροῦ ἐπιζητοῦντος Παϊσίου; 1547 ὡς ἔμψυχον τὸν συνήθη τοῦ ἱερου ἐπιζητοῦντος Παϊσίου.
771 οὐκ ἴσχυσαν: Pom, 1547 οὐκ ἴσχυσαν ὅλως.
772 τὴν [ν]αῦ[ν]: Pom, 1547 τὴν ναῦν; Grec 1093 τηναῦ.
773 ἀποκινῆσαι ἐπὶ τὰ πρόσω: Pom, 1547 ἐπὶ τὰ πρόσω κινῆσαι.
774 Δύο . . . ἡμερῶν: Pom, 1547 Δύο δὲ ἡμερῶν διελθουσῶν.
775 [κατάσχεσιν], being held back: Pom, 1547; Grec 1093 κατάγνωσιν, condemnation, blame, censure.
776 ἀφέντες: Pom, 1547 ἀφήκαν.
777 ἐφ᾽ ὅν: Pom, 1547 ἐφ᾽ οὗ.
778 ἐρήμου{ν}: Grec 1093, 1547; Pom lacks. Ἔρημος is usually feminine, very rarely masculine. If it is masculine here, the form should not be ἐρήμουν but rather ἐρήμου.
779 χειρί: Pom, 1547 χειρὶ ἰθυνομένῃ.
780 πατέρων. Pom, 1547 lack.
781 ἀφωρμάτο: 1547 ἐφωρμάτο, a mistake.
782 <ἦλθεν>: Pom, 1547.
783 ἐξιόντες: Grec 1093, 1547; Pom ἐξιόντες ἐρόμενοι τὸ θεῖον Παύλου σῶμα ποῦ τέθειται.
784 καὶ εὑρόντες τὸ σῶμα ἀμφοτέρων τὴν ἀνακομιδὴν ποιήσατε: Grec 1093, Pom; 1547 lacks.

785 περιόντες . . . ἔχοντες: Pom περιόντες καὶ τοῦτο ζητοῦντες καὶ εὑρόντες ἀνεῖλαν τὸ αὐτὸ καὶ ἐπανήεσαν ἐν τῷ πλοίῳ χρυσοῦ καὶ λίθου τιμίου τηλαυγέστερον ἔχοντες. Πλὴν οὐκ ἔτι ἐπισχεσθῆναι τοὺς ἄνδρας ἐγένετο, συνεργοῦσαν ἔχοντες ἕως τότε ἀπείργουσαν ἀόρατον δύναμιν; 1547 περιόντες ὁρώμενοι τὸ τοῦ θείου Παύλου σῶμα τοῦ τέθηται καὶ εὑρόντες ἀναλαβόμενοι αὐτὸ καὶ ἐπανίεσαν ἐν τῷ πλοίῳ χρυσοῦ καὶ λίθου τιμίου τηλαυγέστερον ἔχοντες. Πλὴν οὐκ ἔτι ἐπισχεσθῆναι τοὺς ἄνδρας ἐγένετο, συνεργοῦσαν ἔχοντες μάλιστα τὴν ἕως τότε ἀπείργουσαν ἀόρατον δύναμιν.

786 τοῦ θαύματος: Grec 1093, 1547; Pom τοῦ ξένου θαύματος.

787 οἱ μεγάλοι πατέρες Παῦλος καὶ Παΐσιος: Pom, 1547 lack.

788 ἰθύνοντες . . . ἐν: Grec 1093, Pom; 1547 ἐπὶ δὲ τὴν Πισίδιαν καὶ τε λάβων ἐν.

789 ὁ μέγας Ἰσίδωρος . . . δωρ[ω]φορίᾳ: Pom ὁ θεῖος Ἰσίδωρος ἐν πάσῃ ὑμνῳδίᾳ τὰ τίμια λείψανα κατατίθησιν.

790 ἀκαθάρτων: Grec 1093, Pom; 1547 lacks.

791 ἄλλης τινὸς ἀσθενείας . . . αὐτῶν: Pom, 1547 ἄλλης τινὸς ἀσθενείας ἐκ τῆς ἁφῆς καὶ μόνης τῶν τιμίων σορῶν ἰάθησαν καὶ ὅσα δὲ τῶν θαυμάτων παράδοξα μετὰ τὴν τούτων ἀπόθεσιν.

792 Ἐμοῦ . . . εἰς δόξαν: Pom Καὶ ταῦτα μὲν ἐκ πολλῶν ὀλίγα τῇ ἐμῇ μετριότητι κατὰ τὸ ἐμοὶ ἐφικτὸν εἰς πολλῶν ὠφέλειαν εἴρηται εἰς δόξαν. (1547 lacks κατὰ τὸ ἐμοὶ ἐφικτόν.)

793 καὶ ἁγίου πνεύματος: Pom, 1547 καὶ ἁγίου πνεύματος, τῆς μιᾶς ἐν τριάδι θεότητος (1547 τῆς μιᾶς ἀδιαιρέτου θεότητος), ᾗ πρέπει πᾶσα δόξα, τιμὴ, καὶ προσκύνησις.

3

THE GE'EZ (ETHIOPIC) *LIFE OF ABBA BSOY* IN TRANSLATION

Translated by Robert A. Kitchen

Introduction
Abba Bsoy: The Ge'ez Life of a Desert Father
The versions of a desert father
"The desert a city" no longer describes Egypt, but one of the remaining and thriving monasteries is that of Anba Bishoi, located in Wadi al-Natrun, south of Alexandria and northwest of Cairo. Bishoi (320–417) was a beloved desert father whose exploits never made it into the traditional collections of the desert fathers, the *Apophthegmata Patrum* (AP). Instead, a lengthy biography of Bishoi is narrated in chronological episodes in a style familiar to the apophthegmatic genre (generally short stories in which he performs a miracle or dispenses wisdom and guidance). While Bishoi was a Copt, there is no extant text of his biography in Coptic, the principal one being written in Greek, as was also the AP.[1] This Greek text has been translated into English in this volume by Tim Vivian and Apostolos N. Athanassakis.

Three other versions would appear: a Syriac translation was published in Paul Bedjan's *Acta Martyrum et Sanctorum* series, and translated in this volume into English (based on a different manuscript) by Rowan Greer, Maged Mikhail, and myself.[2] The Syriac generally follows the episodic sequence of the Greek and its contents, although the Syriac does omit some episodes and adds a few not found in the Greek.

The third is the Arabic version which found its way to the Monastery of St. Antony and became the basis of a distinct recension of the text.[3] In this volume Maged Mikhail offers an English translation. A Garshuni version, Arabic text in Syriac script, is on the boundary, but is a translation of a Syriac manuscript.[4]

The fourth is the Ge'ez version, edited by Gérard Colin, *La version éthiopienne de l'Histoire de Bsoy*.[5] Ge'ez is the classical Ethiopic language, unique among the classical Semitic languages in being written left to right and fully vocalized. The Geʻez text is similarly based upon the Greek, but at two stages down the road, the first being the translation into Syriac, and the second through an Arabic translation, and then translated into Geʻez most likely from the Monastery of St. Antony in the fifteenth century—the Geʻez version edited by Colin is from two manuscripts which reflect two different Arabic manuscripts. The Geʻez omits episodes from both the Greek and the Syriac, but agrees with the Syriac additions. Yet in the case of Syriac omissions, the Geʻez agrees with the Greek. There are a number of variants in the Geʻez from the other two versions as well as several unique additions.

Distinctive readings of the Geʻez Bsoy

The focus here is on several episodes in which the Geʻez version provides distinctive readings. First is the development of Bsoy's spiritual disciplines after Bamwi (Pambo)'s death. This section is not recorded in the Syriac version. While the Greek and Geʻez versions generally agree in content, the Geʻez uses different language to summarize or epitomize the primary text and is distributed in a different sequence from the Greek.

There are minor differences in detail regarding Bsoy's fasting practices (17). Greek: "He did not eat bread all week; on Saturday his food was bread and salt. The rest of the week, instead of actual bread, he would enjoy spiritual bread." Geʻez: "After this he fasted every week. On Sunday he would receive the body and blood of Christ and not eat anything else and test his body." The key day of the week is different, but the texts are describing virtually the same regimen, with the Geʻez appearing to depict a more rigorous discipline.

Bsoy's enthusiasm for the solitary life and desire for humble anonymity is expressed similarly, but the freer paraphrase of the Geʻez is evident (10). Greek: "Even more remarkable is the fact that no one knew about his way of life equal to the angels except God alone, who sees what is hidden and has the unknown right before his eyes. And so his love for contemplative quiet became inexhaustible, but what he held dear seemed to be to offer prayers in solitude to God alone and to converse with him and be reconciled with the Supreme Judge and draw near to him through illuminations received in solitude." Geʻez: "Everything which he did—his excellent discipline and his superior combat—was in secret. He wanted solitude and hardship and wished to dwell in the desert alone because God had called him to hardship and had guided him to become an excellent refuge for the salvation of the soul of many." The Geʻez intimates that Bsoy's asceticism is a response to God's call to be a source for the salvation of others—which diverts him from absolute solitude.

Although the variants in the two texts are not unusual, it is obvious we are missing something. The Ge'ez version was not translated directly from the Greek, coming from Syriac through Arabic. Nevertheless, the paraphrasing and rearrangement of the narrative suggests the possibility of the Ge'ez editor/translator recording according to memory.

The longest story: Saving another abba's disciple

Another instance of the absence of a Syriac version in which the Ge'ez agrees in general terms with the Greek is the longest episode of the *Life*, a novella in which Bsoy intercedes with God on behalf of another abba's disciple (22–29, 31). This story immediately follows Christ's appearance to Bsoy in the desert during which he promises Bsoy that whatever sins he intercedes for will be forgiven of the one who has sinned.

As evidence of the efficacy of Christ's gift, Bsoy is implored to assist as a "third party" in redeeming the soul of a disobedient and now deceased disciple of another abba whose prayers and fasting were of no avail to the disciple. The Ge'ez version is 60 percent the length of the Greek and gives evidence of significant paraphrasing and abridgement. And yet, the Ge'ez expands the tale at points. The elder whose disciple is wallowing in Hades/Sheol because of his unrepentant sin is described at the beginning of the episode as one who lived near Bsoy and visited and consulted with him regularly—which the Greek does not mention. The elder in the Greek version fasts forty days in penance for his disciple, but the voice of Christ twice comes to him insisting that the soul of this man will remain in Sheol until Christ's coming on the clouds. The Ge'ez version stretches this penance to three stints of forty days' fasting, and three times he is rebuffed by Christ.

Going to Bsoy and pleading for his assistance, the elder convinces Bsoy to intercede. Bsoy prays for the disciple's release. In the Greek, God asks, "What is it that you are asking for yourself at such length, Païsios, my servant?" (Ge'ez: "O my beloved Bsoy, what do you want?") The Greek now switches to the Savior, whereas Ge'ez clearly identifies Christ as the one appearing to Bsoy. Greek: "The Savior said to him, 'No, I have already handed down my judgment, which is incontestable: I have determined that he is to enjoy in Hades his reward for his disobedience and unnatural activities. I will allow no remission for him from his sufferings until I come upon the clouds.'" Ge'ez: "Our Savior said to him, 'Look, a word has issued from my mouth that he will remain in Sheol until I come upon a cloud.'"

The Greek presents Païsios persuading in a circular fashion, "What, Lord of all, is not subject to your divine command and complies with whatever you wish? It is easy for you, master of the ages, who have brought everything into being from nonbeing, even now to come the same way as at your second coming." The Ge'ez is more playfully suggestive: "The holy man said to him, 'My Lord, if you so desire, make a cloud come and sit upon it and rescue this soul.' Our Lord commanded a cloud and it came and he ascended upon it."

The soul of the disciple is released and given first to Bsoy, who then brings him to the elder. The Ge'ez simplifies the events here. Whereas the Greek has him transferred to heaven, in the Ge'ez the redeemed disciple reports to his abba that he has already been transferred to a place of rest. Section 30 of the Greek text does not occur in the Ge'ez version, in which the abba, assured now of his disciple's salvation, decides to go to Paisios and tell him of all that had happened, and finds the latter already offering hymns of thanksgiving for the disciple. They rejoice together, but the Ge'ez version truncates the narrative to omit this brief scenario.

We witness here the end result of a series of translations which work hard to be faithful, yet along the way make their own adjustments. Since the intermediary Syriac and Arabic translations are missing, one can only estimate the decisions that the Ge'ez translator made in his recension. The result is a condensed, quasi-paraphrased translation, yet, in some instances, an embellishment of the original story. Other aspects of the story are reimagined and reinterpreted as the consequence of going through multiple translations, but with little damage to the intent of the principal story.

The Syrian solitary

An episode found in all three translations is that of the Syrian solitary who comes to visit Bsoy (50–52). The tale is admirably uniform in all versions, although varying details reveal different perceptions of Bsoy, whom the story is really about. The first variant is in the identification of the ascetical visitor. The Greek describes him as "a certain man to the north adorned with a variety of virtues." One version of the Syriac is not shy about pinpointing "in the land of Syria a certain holy solitary whose name was Ephrem." Nevertheless, that is the only Syriac version to name this solitary;[6] the others simply state, "Now in the land of Syria there was a certain holy solitary." The Ge'ez follows the majority of the Syriac versions, "There was in the country of Syria a solitary saint." The later Syriac *Vitas* of Ephrem identified him anachronistically as a monk, which was historically not the case.[7] In general, the Ge'ez omits most historical references from the earlier millennium.

Particularly for this company, the actual encounter between the Syrian and Bsoy is as much of a miracle as a healing elsewhere. The Syrian could speak only Syriac and Bsoy could not understand a word, being a Coptic speaker. Bsoy prays to God to help him understand: Greek: "'Son of God and Word, allow me to understand the force of this old man's words.' As soon as he said these words, Paisios was instructed by the divine Spirit alone in how to think and converse in Syriac." Syriac: "'I beseech you, Lord, make known to me what this elder is saying.' Immediately, God enlightened his understanding with the glorious Spirit, and he understood the confused words." Ge'ez: "'My Lord, [I] desire that you should reveal to me what this brother is saying.' Immediately, God enlightened his heart through the divine spirit and enabled him to understand the Syriac language." The Syriac translator knows it is not easy to learn Syriac quickly, so helps Bsoy to acquire the sense of the conversation. For Greek and Ge'ez, Pentecost is relivable for Bsoy so that he can speak the language now.

Barbarians at the gate and Bsoy's well

The following episode, also not in the Greek, recalls the attacks of so-called "barbarian" *(barbrāyē)* raiders in Scetis in the early fifth century in which many monks were killed. In the Syriac version, Bsoy's friend John speaks to him about leaving the region so that they may not be killed, and send their assailants to Gehenna in consequence, to which Bsoy agrees (γ). The Ge'ez follows the story closely, referring at first to "murderers" and then identifying them also as "barbarians" *(barbar)*.

Later, just before the conclusion of the *Vita*, a brief mention is again made of the barbarian encroachments, a notice mentioned neither in the Greek nor in the Syriac (λ). The barbarians found and killed forty-nine monks near a fortress, Piamoun/Beymon.[8] On their way back to their own country they stopped to rest near the well of Bsoy, and washed their bloody swords from the massacre in the water, and as a result that water became a remedy for all manner of illnesses up to today. This is an unusual historical reference for the Ge'ez translation, although its inclusion in the Ge'ez *Synaxarium* provides the impetus for this rare insertion of historical materials in this *Vita*.

The travails of transmission

These four translations of the Païsios/Bishoi/Bsoy/Bishay *Vita* give evidence of a normal sequence of transmitting a story through multiple languages, cultures, and time. A better part of a millennium separates the Greek from the Ge'ez, with Syriac and Arabic acting as intermediary languages of transmission, yet the story remains remarkably intact and faithful to its theological content in these translations. Variants do occur frequently, usually of no significant importance for the meaning of the episodes, but some do reveal local traditions and emphases. The gaps and omissions found in the four texts occur primarily because of the transmission of varying manuscripts, but the evidence is uneven. Especially with Ge'ez, the translator works for a more concise summarizing translation which often results in a slightly nuanced interpretation of an event or saying.

All the recensions project an image of the abba as a genuinely humble holy man who deflects attention away from his own needs and ego. His primary gift is being able to successfully intercede with Christ on behalf of other monks or individuals who have sinned greatly or perhaps fallen away from the orthodox Nicene faith—of which Bsoy is an ardent advocate and champion. Notable is how Bsoy is persistently portrayed assisting monks and other abbas who have fallen into some kind of mental and spiritual depression, and aiding them in restoring their balance.[9] The phenomena of depression and despondency among the desert fathers resulting from misapplied spiritual disciplines have been investigated from the insights of cognitive psychology by Inbar Graiver.[10]

The Ethiopic *Life of Bsoy*

The Eighth of Ḥamlē: Abba Bsoy

[12][11] In the name of the Father and the Son and the Holy Spirit, One Lord. The history of our holy father Bsoy, the great, beautiful, and pure solitary, who dwelt in the country of Egypt. This book was written after his death by the hand of the pure priest John the Little who was his [spiritual] brother when [Bsoy] came into the desert. Both of them became obedient disciples and doers of the desire of our holy and great father Bamoy.[12] May their prayer guard us all, Amen.

The foundation of his history and way of life was virtuous and gentle. His life was beautiful and prosperous, redeemed from sin and error. [His life] was close to God through his service, [accomplished] without ceasing or negligence, like the angels—blessed be the name of God. His death was on the eighth of Ḥamlē.[13] May peace and grace surround, protect, and fill the one who writes and reads and loves his life,[14] Amen.

Exordium

1. Greetings in our Lord the Christ, my brothers, friends of the living God. Pay attention and listen to me so that I can tell you about the [spiritual] combat and beautiful discipline of the honored, holy, and pure, our father Bsoy who chose God. He rejected everything that was in the world and fulfilled his mission and monastic life in purity and extraordinariness. He was a witness [of God] through his great combat and offered his soul and his body acceptable to God. He continued to circulate around the desert and caves in the interior of the land. He built up his body with purity and became the guardian of the commandments of his Lord, reveling in his combat. He taught and saved the souls of many and gathered them into the kingdom of heaven by the knowledge of divine power.

2. "My witness is God,"[15] said the one who wrote this book of his story. I will tell you what my eyes have seen regarding him from time to time. I have written this for the solace of your soul and for those who want to follow this teaching.

Bsoy's birth and parentage

3. The father and mother of this holy Abba Bsoy were virtuous people, righteous and pure for God, lovers of the church who gave a great deal of excellent alms. Their family [lived] in the land of Ḥegwāz, near the country of Egypt by the city whose name was Tāstalbtā. They were joyous people and pure in their bodies. And when [14] God saw their way of life he gave them male children and blessed their possessions.

The death of Bsoy's father; an angel appears to his mother

After some time,[16] their father died and their mother was left to bring them up and nourish them in the confidence of God. The holy Abba Bsoy was smaller than his brothers. One night, an angel of God appeared to her while the children were sleeping with her. The angel said to her, "Look, God has sent me to you and says to you, 'Give me one of your children who will sanctify my name among the peoples.'"[17] The mother of the child said, "Look, my Lord, all of them belong to God, so let him take the one whom he wishes from them." The angel stretched out [his hand] and took hold of the hand of Abba Bsoy and said, "This one will worship God with beautiful adoration and seek him." She said to the angel, "Take the one who is older and stronger than him, for this one is small and weak." The angel said to her, "This is the one who is fitting for God's service, for the strength of God will manifest itself over the weaknesses." He said this to her, and then vanished from her [sight].

Bsoy goes to Scetis

4. When the holy Abba Bsoy grew older and stronger, he went about with the confidence of God, and desired to take on[18] the monastic way of life. When God wished to fulfill what he had promised him, he led him like an innocent lamb and brought him into the desert of Skete [Scetis], the desert of Egypt. He brought him and entrusted him to the virtuous pastor, governor of souls, our father the holy Bamoy [Bamwi]. This person was [also] for me, John the Little, the redeemer and guide for my life.

Bsoy, as Bamoy's disciple, advances spiritually

5. Our father Bamoy received him joyously and clothed him in the holy habit[19] of the monastic life. Everything which he commanded [Bsoy] he would do and complete with great humility. Watching the pure ones who went about righteously, he would examine their struggles and conduct and rejoice in their beautiful life and their disdain for things of the flesh and all the desires of this world, and their resemblance to the angels. In everything he gave thanks to God, glorifying and praising him.

One day our teacher, our father Bamoy, said to him, "It is not fitting for the brothers to [walk around] looking up,[20] while pure people render their faces dull and do not look at anything [other than the ground]. May your gaze be down toward the earth and do not look at anything except your footprints. May your eyes be lifted up to the One God and your thought prostrate itself before him at all times."

6. When [Bsoy] heard this from the holy abba, he lowered his gaze for three years and did not look insolently at the face of anyone. But he [16] followed the Holy Scriptures and applied himself to reading them continually

and remembering them by heart. He quenched his soul with the words of life, the words of the Holy Spirit, just as was said, "The wise person keeps all the commandments in his heart and does them."[21] He prayed constantly without ceasing and idleness, as Paul the Apostle commanded.[22] He was steadfast in fasting and standing in vigil every night. The word of God was sweeter in his mouth than honey and sugar. Every day the benefit of [his] virtues was increasing. He grew up like a tree planted by a stream of water which gives its fruits according to each of its seasons and its foliage does not fall off.[23]

7. When the holy Bamwi saw his excellent discipline and humility, he loved him. He marveled and rejoiced spiritually and named him 'Seyā'[24]—its translation is "Orient,"[25] that is to say, on account of the light of his soul. [Bsoy] showed the abundance of his actions and the excellence of his combat. God wanted to visit him. Since he loved the holy Bsoy so much, he took him by himself and brought him to where they were praying constantly standing up, and established him in an excellent way of life.

After Bamoy's death, John remains with Bsoy

8. After this, our father Bamoy died and I remained, myself small and despicable, with the blessed brother holy Abba Bsoy. Both of us dwelt in spiritual love at the place which God had chosen.

Bsoy's spiritual disciplines

9. The holy Abba [Bsoy], overflowing [with virtues], adhered to fasting and prayer, and did not eat anything except once per week. He explored the Holy Scriptures, learning and interpreting [them]. He was constantly praying the prophecy of Jeremiah the prophet and when he was reading Jeremiah the prophet Jeremiah would come to him and interpret for him his book and speak with him and rejoice in his perspective. He revealed to him many teachings and was talking about the spiritual life.

10. [Bsoy] was improving every day and doubling [his effort] in his regimen and in deeds. He was fasting every other week and when he took [something] to eat after these days he took some dried bread and worn-out salt.[26] Everything which he did—his excellent discipline and his superior combat—was in secret. He wanted solitude and hardship, and wished to dwell in the desert alone because God had called him to hardship and had guided him to become an excellent refuge for the salvation of the soul of many.

Bsoy and John separate

11. [18] After some time, I said to him, "My brother, saint of God, I see that you love hardship and dwelling in solitude. I too love the same thing. Come

now, let us keep vigil this night and let us make prayer and petition. If God wishes in his pleasure, he will reveal and show us what will be useful to us and [what] he is preparing for us." He said to me, "You have spoken well," and we stood for prayer until after the night.

12. When morning approached, an angel of God appeared to us and said to us the following, "God says to you, 'Each of you dwell by yourself in your habitations to fulfill the gift which he has bestowed on you for the salvation of the souls of many. As for you, John, remain in this desert and I will send to you many people,' says the Lord." Then he spoke to holy Abba Bsoy, "As for you, separate yourself[27] a little [from one another] and make for yourself a dwelling and reside alone by yourself. 'I will gather many people and bring [them] to you,' says the Lord. There will be a monastery in this desert in which they will remember your name. They will sanctify the name of their God in the same way they sanctify the exalted [saints]. [The word] will be fulfilled which says, 'As for this one who dwells in this desert, God will gather for him a chosen people.' This is what [God] said concerning the holy Abba Macarius."[28] The angel having said this vanished from us.

Then, the holy Abba Bsoy separated himself from me. He went to the neighborhood of my dwelling and made for himself a dwelling two miles away and remained there, and God was with him. His excellence increased and multiplied. His reputation was spread into all the cities and many people asked him to put the monastic vestment on them. He received them and prepared them to be strong and courageous servants of the King Jesus Christ. There grew up among his disciples blessed branches loving God and loving their brothers. They wished to follow his way of life as much as they could see and act in accordance with his combat and obey his holy words. I went constantly to him as well and unveiled to him my thoughts. And in the same way, he also came to me and related to me his thoughts.

The Savior appears to Bsoy

13. After some time, while [Abba Bsoy] was sitting in his cell, the Lord Jesus Christ came to him and said to him, "Greetings to you, O Bsoy, my chosen one." [Bsoy] was astonished and stood up, and then prostrated himself before him. Our Lord said to him, "Have you not seen this desert from on high? From now on its exaltation[29] will be increased and the monks who sanctify my name will live in it." The holy Bsoy said to him, "My Lord, will you nourish them in this desert?" Our Lord said to Abba Bsoy, "In truth, I say [20] to you, when I find love among them, and they strive in the observance of my commandments, and they believe in me and endure hardship, after a little while, I will prepare for them here their nourishment

and give them grace." The holy Abba Bsoy said to him, "O my Lord, will you save them from temptation and from the battle of the Enemy which comes upon them?" Our Lord said to him, "If they observe my commandments, I will save them from temptation and from the Enemy; and whoever believes in me and trusts in my name I will make him inherit the kingdom of heaven." Our Lord said this to the holy Abba Bsoy, then ascended into the heavens with great glory.

A rich ruler, induced by the Devil, comes to Bsoy with money

14. After this, the holy Abba Bsoy multiplied his observance [of the commandments] in order to preserve his soul. He humbled himself, making himself a servant, disciplining and strengthening himself in the confidence of his Lord. An angel of God visited him constantly. Bsoy loved solitude. Satan set an ambush for him in order to trap and overpower him, but he was not able to defeat his strength. He laid hold [of him] to tempt him through the desire to honor him, and if through this [Bsoy had been tempted] he would have become weak and fallen from his strength. [Satan] went into the land of Egypt to a governor whose name was Mowamal[30] and appeared to him in the likeness of an angel and said to him, "In the desert of Egypt there is a man who does not possess anything, a very holy person, and everything which he asks God gives to him. Go to him and offer him a gift and a contribution so that he may bless you." The man said to him, "What is his name?" [Satan] said to him, "Bsoy is his name."

15. That man rose up and loaded much wealth and clothing and other precious items upon camels and went into the desert. God, who every day was going out to Abba Bsoy, came out and said to him, "Know that it is Satan who is laying a trap for you through the love of precious things and the reception of gifts and presents. Here Satan has gone into the country of Egypt to one of the important men and told him to bring out to you precious things and great wealth." The pure elder got up and went out to walk into the desert. The governor encountered him and said to him, "Do you know, O elder, in this desert the one whom they call Abba Bsoy?" The holy Bsoy said to him, "What do you want from him?" The governor said to him, "I wish to give him this gift which I have with me and this money to distribute to his brothers in the desert so that it may be a blessing in my house." The holy elder said to him, "In this desert there is no desire for the money with you, and as for those who dwell here they do not desire anything from this gift which is with you. Why are you tiring yourself out? God will receive your presents. Now, return to the regions of Egypt and distribute [22] this wealth which is with you to the poor and orphans and widows, and God will grant a blessing upon you and upon your house." That man returned to his house

and did just as the holy one had commanded.

Bsoy defeats the Devil and enjoys spiritual communion

16. When the saint returned to his dwelling, Satan appeared to him and said to him, "You have fooled me, O Bsoy." The chosen one of God, Bsoy, said to him, "Since you were created, you weary yourself for no reason, O enemy of what is good." Satan said to him, "But I say that you, you were not created after anything." The holy elder said to him, "May God devastate you and send [you] far away." [Satan] went away and did not return and did not appear to him again. The all-powerful one [Bsoy] broke the snare [Satan] had made and returned to his dwelling in peace. God was with him in all his works and rescued him from all his enemies.

17. After this, [Bsoy] got up and went into the inner desert and dwelt there alone. He strengthened his soul through onerous combat, and became strong as a fortress by his excellence. God commanded that they should take up his rational knowledge into the garden of delights so that he might see all the good things which are there, and he saw all the good things. These gave him spiritual nourishment and he ate; and by this he fortified himself from hunger and thirst. After this he fasted every week. On Sunday, he would receive the body and blood of Christ and not eat anything else and test his body.

18. Everything which he did, he did not appear to do [it] with his body. As our Lord said in the holy Gospel, "Whoever lives in me and loves me, my Father will love him, and I also will love him and I will show myself to him."[31] The work which I am doing he will do."[32] On account of this, it will happen that he will neither fall nor will he be divided. [God] said this regarding Abimelech who slept for seventy years [and] neither ate nor drank.[33] In the same way, the seven children[34] slept three hundred seventy-five years, neither eating nor drinking, and their souls were united with their bodies. In this way, it is written that the weak among people are the strong.[35]

Bsoy's pastoral care

19. Then the spiritual children assembled around the holy abba and surrounded [him] like a bee that circles a pot of honey. He gave them spiritual food to drink: the word of life which flowed forth from his mouth. They sanctified God constantly. He taught them without ceasing to love living in hardship in the desert, and to become poor and practice the vigil and the worship of the Lord, and to pray and make supplication night and day, and neither cease nor stop, nor omit nor neglect [these practices]. They should perform manual work by which to feed themselves [24] and receive the stranger and have mercy upon the poor. The fulfillment of this commandment [is] that they should leave behind their [own] will and do the will of their neighbor.

This and what is similar to it, the holy one of God taught them.

The Savior appears again to Bsoy

20. When he saw that the brothers who had gathered around him had multiplied, he went far away from them by himself into the inner desert. Entering a cave, he dwelt in it for three years and did not see a single person. His discipline extended and spread out over his body. He stood praying before God day and night and did not sleep on account of his love for his Lord. After this, he fastened a stake and tied down his hair and stood in prayer before God.

21. When he had completed three years in this combat our Lord Jesus Christ came out to him in that cave. When the elder saw him, he trembled and being afraid fell down on the ground. Our Savior fortified him and took him up by his hand and made him stand up. He said to him, "My peace be upon you, pure Bsoy. Look, I have seen your works and the hardship you have endured. I have given you a gift. Anyone who supplicates and requests from me in your name, and asks for forgiveness for his sins, I will forgive him and guard him." The holy one said, "O my Lord, I pray to you to make me strong by your awesome and holy name, for you alone are the Lord, the righteous Lord of the universe. You have suffered for the sake of your creation; you were dead, you were raised up, and you have saved us. How much is it necessary for us sinners to suffer on account of your name and to praise you?" Our Lord blessed him and gave him peace and ascended into the heavens.

Bsoy intercedes with God on behalf of another's disciple

22. There was an elder [who] had confidence in God and feared him. He dwelt near the abode of the holy Abba Bsoy, and many times would go and be instructed by him. This elder had a disciple whom he loved very much because he was holy. Satan, the enemy of good, threw an evil thought into that brother and made him fall into a sin, and he died in his sin and they cast him into Sheol. After this, that elder was praying and beseeching God night and day on behalf of his spiritual son. He fasted forty days, being saddened and grieving over him. A voice came and said to him, "He will remain in Sheol until our Lord comes on a cloud."

23. Again, that elder fasted for forty days, beseeching God to bring him out from Sheol. The voice came just as before and said to him, "He will remain until the Lord comes on a cloud." A third time he fasted forty days, and prayed and implored and petitioned on account of that brother. The voice came just as before and said to him, "He will remain in Sheol until the day our Lord comes upon a cloud."

[26] That elder arose and went into the desert and inquired regarding the dwelling of the holy Abba Bsoy.

24. The holy Bsoy knew by the Holy Spirit, and came out to meet the elder and comforted him and prostrated himself to him and they greeted[36] one another. The holy Bsoy said to him, "O my holy father, why are you tired and have searched for one who is deficient like me?" The elder told him about his coming out to him and about the story of his [spiritual] son, and how he was tormented on account of him, and how a voice came from God three times. Abba Bsoy said to him, "Rise up and let us pray, and whatever God wishes will be." The elder said to him, "I swear now that I will not separate myself from you, while prostrating myself before you, weeping and groaning, until you petition God and he turns toward me and has mercy on me and gladdens my heart with that brother and indicates to us whether he will bring him out from Sheol or not."

25. The holy man got up at that moment and entered into the inner desert and prayed, "Be merciful on your servant and rescue your servant from tribulation." 26. Christ appeared to him and said, "O my beloved Bsoy, what do you want?" 27. The holy man said to him, "My Lord, I am petitioning you on account of this elder's son so that you may pardon him his sins and bring him out of Sheol." Our Savior said to him, "Look, a word has issued from my mouth that he will remain in Sheol until I come upon a cloud." 28. The holy man said to him, "My Lord, if you so desire, make a cloud come and sit upon it and rescue this soul."

29. Our Lord ordered a cloud, which came and he ascended upon it. He commanded that the soul of that son should come out and it came out, and [then] gave him to the chosen one, Bsoy. The holy Bsoy took him and brought him to the elder. When the elder saw him, he was greatly amazed and asked him about the affliction that had fallen upon him in Sheol. [The monk] said to him, "I had much torment on account of my sins, but especially because I did not obey you, O my father. Then when you were afflicted and prayed, relief came to me and they transferred me to a place of rest." [30 *omitted in this recension*]

31. The heart of the elder rejoiced at that moment, and he went to Abba Bsoy and said to him, "You have bestowed upon me a great grace, O holy father. Because you have had mercy on this son, God has given him rest and he came back to me. Through your prayer [God] had mercy on him and forgave him just as was written, saying, 'God strengthens his holy ones and listens to their prayers.'[37] Now, O my father, I wish that you would tell me what you did so that God would grant you this great gift." Abba Bsoy said to the elder, "Forgive me, my father. This is the will of [28] God. From the beginning, he first granted his mercy upon people, and through his gentleness he has given mercy to [your] son. It is not on account of me, me the despicable one, nor is it on account of my deeds, nor on account of

my prayers which have brought into being this matter. It does not happen in this way, but it is on account of you, for you have fasted for forty days three times and have exposed yourself to death for the love of God. In as much as you had suffered in your heart on account of that brother and offered yourself in his place, God gave him to you. There is no greater love than to offer one's life, a person for his neighbor.[38] This is the gift you have received from Christ. This is the way it is for every one of the fathers on account of their deeds and each one according to the grace [granted] him." After this they praised God, sat down, and ate bread together, and each one of them returned to his dwelling in peace.

The Savior tells Bsoy to strengthen and teach the brothers

32. After this, the elder [Bsoy] established himself in [spiritual] combat. He went around the desert to [visit] those he could find there, but hid his deeds so that no one would know what they were. He applied himself to fasting and prayer, and when he ate he would not taste anything but rotten bread and drink salty water.

33. Our Lord appeared to him and conversed with him, "Go to the brothers who are in the desert to become a father to them and teach them the rule and the way of monasticism through which they will acquire life [eternal]." The Abba beseeched his God, "O my Lord, I do not have the strength for this task and I am afraid lest my actions be diminished which I have established on account of your great and holy name."

34. Our Lord said to him, "I will give to you the reward of your efforts in the holy heavenly Jerusalem and I will make your name great. Blessed is the person who keeps the commandments of God."[39] The name of our holy father Bsoy exuded a beautiful perfume, filling the entire desert. The brothers came to him from every place and, surrounding him, were greatly astonished at his humility. He taught all of them the fear of God and commanded them, and made them all better according to what was appropriate.

Emperor Constantine appears to Bsoy

35. After some days, I, John the Little, went to him to know how he was [doing]. When I came to the door of his cell, I heard the voice of a person conversing with Abba Bsoy and he was weeping. I knocked, and [Bsoy] opened [the door] to me and I entered and we prayed together and then sat down. I said to him, "Our father, who was it that was speaking that I just now heard?" 36. The holy one replied to me, "Since you have heard, I will tell you. It was Constantine, emperor[40] of the Romans. He came to me from heaven, crying and distressed of heart. He said, "I did not know that such honor was given to monks [30] on account of their poverty on

earth and their wandering for the sake of our Lord. If I had known this while I was on earth I would have abdicated the transitory kingdom and would have become a monk." I said to him, "What glory were you given in heaven, O king?" He said to me, "Certainly, it was given to me, but it did not reach the glory of the monks. 37. I saw some of them at the time of their departure from their bodies. [The Lord] sprouted wings for them and they were flying and elevating themselves above the heavenly Jerusalem and were entering [it]. No one was inhibiting them from the citadels which were there." [38 *omitted from this recension*]

39. I said to him, "Is [not] such a judgment appropriate for you? For you, have you [not] had a wife, children, and servants and treasures and a high throne? Should [God] make you equal with those who have abandoned homes and wealth? They are the ones who do not have anything, paupers and poor, the rejected and the despised, fasters and keepers of vigils. They are hungry and thirsty, and were rejected from the face of the earth." 40. I spoke to him in this way. When you knocked, he disappeared." When I heard this from the holy father, I said, "Blessed be the God who reveals his miracles to his saints."

Bsoy defends the divinity of the Holy Spirit

41. There was a solitary man in the city called Baswi in Thebes. Satan ensnared him in a trap and placed into his heart [the idea] to say that there is no Holy Spirit, but only the Father and the Son. [The man] declared this openly through his speech and through his teaching. God the Compassionate showed compassion, not wishing to wipe out the [good] deeds of this elder. He revealed this to the holy Abba Bsoy and told him in a vision, "Get up and go to the city of Baswi in Thebes, and find there a solitary who regards and proclaims through his proposition that there is no Holy Spirit." As for Abba Bsoy, the wisdom of God shone in his heart how he should respond to this solitary. He began to make baskets and for each one [of them] made three handles in the likeness of the Holy Trinity, and picking them up he went to that solitary. He entered into his [dwelling] in the guise of a stranger, and the holy Abba Bsoy began to serve just as our great and distinguished father had walked on [this path], the miracle worker, the holy spiritual Abba Macarius, who was an exorcist of demons, performed signs and great miracles, was the curer of souls, and a guide of wrongdoers. The holy Bsoy had written all this in his heart. He set out to go just as that one [Macarius] had walked, and imitated [Macarius] in everything he did. He went to find [32] that elder to bolster him and raise him up and pick him up from his fall to bring him back to the right [road], both him and those who were following him in his error. He spent that night with

him. When morning came, many people went to that solitary in order to be blessed by him. At that moment, Abba Bsoy brought out the baskets, and when the solitary saw that each one had three handles, he said to him, "What is this, our father?" The holy Abba Bsoy said to him, "These are the work of my hands to sell." That solitary said to him, "Why did you make this, baskets each with three handles? Everyone makes [them] with two [handles]." The holy Abba Bsoy said to him, while there were many people gathered who were listening, "As for me, the Holy Trinity is one Lord and I worship him. On account of this, I perform the work of my hands like this Holy Trinity." Those who were gathered said to him, "O, our father, are the Father and the Son with the Holy Spirit?" Our holy Abba Bsoy declared, "The Holy Spirit, my God, exists with the Father; and the Holy Spirit [is] first before eternity, who is neither created nor made."

He turned toward that solitary and said to him, "Do you know the Holy Scriptures?" The solitary said, "Yes." Our holy father said to him, "Have you not heard what Moses said in the Book of Genesis? 'In the beginning God created the heavens, but before the earth existed and had not yet appeared, the clouds were above it and the Spirit of God was hovering over the waters.'[41] Moreover, Isaiah the prophet said regarding the Son of God, 'The Spirit of God is upon me, on account of whom [God] anointed me. He has sent me to announce [the Good News] to the poor.'[42] And David said, 'You have sent your Spirit. They have been created and you renew the face of the earth.'[43] And Ezekiel said, 'In this way God spoke to me, "Call out and say by the Spirit, may [the winds] blow over these bones so that they may rise up living."'[44] John the Baptist, when he circulated around [the country] proclaiming the Son of God, said, 'I see the Holy Spirit, and it is sitting upon him.'[45] Again, our master Paul said, 'There is no one who speaks by the Spirit of God and says, "Anathema to Jesus." And there is no one who is able to say "Lord Jesus Christ" without the Holy Spirit being upon him.'[46] Daniel, a man agreeable to God, said, 'I see thrones placed, and seated upon the three [thrones] the ancient[47] of days speaking.'[48] This sign is for the One God in the Holy Trinity. Our Lord Christ commanded his holy Apostles and said to them, 'Go and baptize all the nations in the name of [34] the Father and the Son and the Holy Spirit.'[49] And now, is not this witness sufficient for you, which we have brought forth to you from the Holy Scriptures that proclaim about the Holy Spirit which is my Lord, without dispute or diversity?"

42–43. When they had heard this discourse from the mouth of our holy father Bsoy—this witness from the Holy Scriptures—that solitary believed, as well as those who were with him. He woke up [from his error], reaped great benefit, and underwent a righteous conversion, and believed in the Father, the Son, and the Holy Spirit. He knew the right faith and gave thanks to God. Our holy father Bsoy returned to his place, glorifying God.

An angel assures Bsoy of God's care
44. While he was walking to the desert, a great light shone before his eyes and he saw the desert [full] of all the angels of God. He was greatly astonished and said, "What is this?" One of the angels responded to him and said to him, "We are those who guard the saints in this desert." [Bsoy] was astonished and praised God who thinks about his servants at all times.

Bawri [Paul] and Banmun [Poemen] come to visit Bsoy
45. He was dwelling in the desert alone, working and holding fast to a rigorous way of life. His reputation had spread out into every place. Abba Banmun [Poemen] of Tamoytekul heard of his reputation and wished to see and meet with him and see his way of life and receive his blessing. He rose up and went to the holy Paul [Bawri] of Tamawi since he had heard him talking about holy Abba Bsoy's regimen. Since Paul continually was going [to meet with Bsoy] and knew his way of life, Abba Banmun said to Abba Paul, "Is it not possible for you to do a favor for me and take me with you to the holy one of God, our father Abba Bsoy, so that his blessing will be shared with me?" Abba Paul said to him, "I am afraid to take you to him because you are young." [Banmun] said to him, "Allow me, my lord, to go with you as far as the gate of [his] abode and I will sit down at his gate until you enter, and you will embrace him and come back out to me. Then I will embrace you so that his blessing will come upon me."

46. Abba Paul said to him, "Do [it that way]." The two of them went together down into the desert of Egypt. When they came to the place of Abba Bsoy, Abba Paul entered and embraced him, and they embraced each other and prayed and sat down together. Abba Bsoy said to him, "Why did that one who came with you not come in and [why] have you left him in the desert?" Abba Paul said to him, "Forgive me, O my holy father. For I said he is young and is not [able] to present himself as a peer to you." The holy father said to him, "Do not say, 'This one [is] a young child,' for our Lord said, 'To one who is like them is the kingdom of heaven.'[50] Truly, I say to you that many called will enter the garden of delights on account of the hands of this infant, for the strength of God [36] is with him. And he is not little, but is great and powerful." He ordered Abba Paul[51] to introduce [Banmun] to him, and he brought him in. He embraced him and blessed him. He prayed over them and they went out from being with him and returned to their places in peace, praising God.

The Savior visits Bsoy and teaches him about acceptable good work

47. After this, Abba Bsoy fasted twenty-one days. Our Lord Jesus Christ came to him and said to him, "O my chosen Bsoy, your soul has been very courageous." Bsoy said to him, "My Lord, my confidence [rests] upon you that you will strengthen me. Because of this, I do not have any weakness at all." Our Lord led him, directing him to a weak brother who had fasted for two days. Abba Bsoy saw him falling down upon the ground and stumbling this way and that, and looking for something cool and some air from the suffering of fasting. Without completing two days he wanted respite. Bsoy said to our Lord, "My Lord, what is the problem with this brother?" Our Lord said to him, "[It is] because he fasted the night." Bsoy said to him, "How many nights since he [began to] fast until he fell and was thrown [to the ground]?" Our Lord said to him, "From when I created him, I did not deprive him of a meal a single day except for this night, and see, I have sent upon him hunger and weakness. But as for you, having fasted for twenty-one days, did you perceive that the affliction was like this?" Bsoy said, "No, my Lord, but I wish that you would tell me what are you going to give to this brother, and what [will be] his reward." Our Lord said to him, "I will give him his wages such as I will give to you. As for you, I have strengthened you against fasting and hunger. This [wage] is apportioned to one who does not have the strength and who will suffer according to his measure for my name. I tell you, enter now into the joy of your Lord."

Christ again appears and teaches Bsoy about the nature of asceticism

48. From this day, Abba Bsoy set for himself a greater task. He asked God, "My Lord, I do not wish to eat much bread." Again, he asked, "My Lord, if I do not go out into the desert, I will become very weak." Our Lord said to him, "Do not do the will of your flesh and [you] will not be weak." Again, [Bsoy] asked, "My Lord, many times I have been defeated by anger." Our Lord said to him, "Do not curse or abuse, quarrel or belittle anyone. Then anger will not defeat you, and the Holy Spirit will abide over you." God was with our father, following him wherever he was going and speaking with him as a person speaks with his friend. Again, [Bsoy] asked his Lord, "O my Lord, what does one obtain who obeys your holy name and serves you, yet is involved with people and is useful to them?" Our Lord said to him, "Just as a worker who works with you in your land—do you not give to him his wages?—in the same way, I will give them their wages in the heavenly Jerusalem." [38]

49. Again, [Bsoy] asked, "O my Lord, if someone dwells among people and serves them, and comes and goes with them in humility, but does not suffer much, what will this one obtain?" Our Lord said to him, "This is my

commandment—if he accomplishes a lot, he will become an heir [of the kingdom of heaven]." Again, Abba Bsoy said to him, "If there is one person who accomplishes a lot and is afflicted for your name and is involved with your servants and serves them and is agreeable to you,[52] what will you give [him]?" Our Lord said to him, "His honor and his reward will be great, and he will become like one of my saints, and I will give to him benefits in the kingdom of heaven." Upon saying this, Our Lord then ascended up into heaven with great glory.

A Syrian monk visits Bsoy

50. There was in the country of Syria a solitary holy man. He served before God night and day and was rigorous in his regimen, and performed great deeds for the sake of God. One day, he was standing in prayer during the night, praising in his heart, "Will I find grace before God as one of the saints?" At that moment, a voice came from heaven which said, "There is in the desert of Egypt an old man [who] serves God and worships him with a beautiful adoration—his name is Bsoy—grace finds [him] in this way: his appearance changes and his face brightens before God." The solitary rose up with joy and went up by boat and came to Alexandria. He inquired of the place where Abba Bsoy resided, and they informed him that he was dwelling in the desert of Batira [Nitria]. He went directly and arrived there. The holy Abba Bsoy received and embraced him and they greeted one another. He brought him into his cell and they prayed together and sat down. That solitary's language was Syriac and Abba Bsoy did not know the Syriac language. He raised up his eyes to heaven and opened up his mind and said, "I bow down to your grandeur, my Lord, and desire that you should reveal to me what this brother is saying."

51. Immediately, God enlightened his heart through the divine spirit and enabled him to understand the Syriac language. They began to speak with one another of God's grandeur and grace. That Syrian asked about the rules which Abba Macarius had set for good discipline, and the good and righteous Abba Bsoy said to him, "This one who first dwelt in this desert is the one who has established this rule and these laws, and is the one who proclaimed the discipline publicly and has guided everyone who dwells there in the desert." He told him of many of [Macarius'] deeds and his rules and related to him the miracles which God had made known through his pure hands. Having heard this, that solitary was astonished [40] and did not [know] what to say. Then he said, "How great and constantly praiseworthy is one who imitates such a perfect person, Abba Macarius." The holy Bsoy said to the brothers, "Hasten to receive a blessing from this great man because I am a witness that divine strength is upon him and that he is full of grace." The brothers came so that they

might be blessed by him. He remained with our father one week and saw his way of life and came to know his excellence. His heart shone with his vision, and he offered praise to God and said to our father, "O my brother, pray for me and rest in peace, because I wish to go back to my country." They embraced one another and he departed from him and went back to his country.

Coda: Bsoy sees the Syrian monk borne home on a cloud

52. After this, one of the brothers departed in order to find our father. The brothers said to him, "If you [had come] earlier, you would have received the blessing of that excellent [and] great man who had come to us from Syria. If you go after him right away you will find him because he has gone [only] a single mile." Our holy father Bsoy answered that brother, "Do not go after him because you are not able [to catch up to him] since he has gone on a march of eighteen days on a cloud." When the brothers heard [this] they praised God who resides in his saints.

Bsoy sees an angel watching over a brother

53A. One day, holy Abba Bsoy went to the dwelling of a brother in order to understand what he was doing. He found him asleep, and above his head an angel was guarding him. He said, "Truly, God guards those who have confidence in Him," and he returned praising God.

Bsoy's disciple is deceived by a Jew

53B. Another [time], a certain brother went down into Egypt to sell his handiwork. A Jew met him, and while he was arguing, said to him, "You Christians say that the one who was crucified is the Christ. It was certainly not [him], but another who resembled him."[53] That brother said to him foolishly, "You have spoken well." Once he had spoken in this way, the grace of baptism distanced itself from him at that word which he had spoken foolishly in his heart.

Bsoy rebukes and teaches the monk

54. He returned and went back into the desert and our holy father observed that the grace of baptism had been taken from him, but he was silent for a good while. When that brother saw the face of Abba Bsoy, that it was not an accepting[54] face, smiling as was his custom, he said to him, "O my father, why do you turn your face away from me today?" The holy one of God Abba Bsoy said to him, "What is your name?" [The brother] said to him, "I am 'so-and-so.'" The elder said to him, "No, you are not, for I do not see upon you the grace of holy baptism." That brother said to him, "Why has it gone from me,

Father?" 55. The elder said to him, "On account of the word which you spoke to the Jew in Egypt." 56. [The brother] prostrated himself before [Bsoy] and said to him, "Forgive me, O my holy father, because I have sinned through my folly, for I did say that word." 57. The holy one said to him, [42] "Be careful, O my son. From now on do not accept the word of a stranger against this orthodox faith, but rather what you have received from the fathers, from the saints; let us hold on to [the faith] firmly." Our father prayed for him, "My Lord and my God, there is no one who has not sinned except you alone. I lift up [my eyes] toward you full of mercy and inclined toward restoration; forgive the sin of this brother who has become separated by his foolishness." By the prayer of the elder, God restored the grace of baptism to that brother.

Bsoy assists John with fasting

58. Another [time], an eminent elder whose name was John came to Bsoy. He fasted greatly night and day, and dwelt in the desert and neither ate nor drank. He performed a great deal of work, but his soul was oppressed by thirst and hunger. He said to himself, "I will go to Abba Bsoy in order to hear[55] his news." He got up and went out to him and knocked at the door. The holy Abba Bsoy came out to him and brought him into his dwelling. They prayed and sat down and consoled one another. God revealed through the Spirit to Abba Bsoy that John had fasted many days, and was burning up from thirst and was in torment. Abba Bsoy ordered his disciple to bring bread and water so that they might eat with Abba John in order to strengthen his soul which was weak with hunger and thirst. The disciple brought [bread and water] according to the order of his father. He said to Abba John, "Get up, eat the bread and drink a little water." But Abba John did not want to taste anything and he said to him, "Forgive me, I am not eating, for I am fasting for my sins." Abba Bsoy said to him, "O my brother, drink a little water because you are burning up from the heat." Abba John said to him, "Leave me [alone]." When our father Bsoy saw that he did not wish to eat or drink, he rose up and stretched out his hands and prayed before God and said, "Hasten, my Lord Jesus Christ, for the sake of your servant John, for he is dwindling and weak from fasting." At that moment, the spirit of Abba John was taken up and he saw four [beings] feeding him bread and giving him water to drink until he was satisfied. This vision really happened. After he had eaten and drunk and was satisfied, [John] returned to his dwelling and increased his fasting, and said to his soul, "Fast now, because, look, you were possessed by your abstinence."

Bsoy helps a young anchorite to defeat the Devil

59. There was a [spiritually] athletic man who was new in the monastic life.

The demons harassed him, so he got up and went to visit Abba Bsoy and said to him, "O Abba Bsoy, remember me in your holy prayer because the demons are harassing me and spoiling my life. They do not stop attacking me at any moment." Our holy father said to him, "Be strong in the Spirit and do not show them your weakness. Pray to Christ [44] and ask for compassion from him, and do not stop praying. He will chase them away from you and will give you rest. Know that with this attack you shall receive a reward from God. By this, we shall know that you are a strong athlete if you stand up against it with strength."

60. After this, Abba Bsoy called out the impure spirit which was dwelling in that brother, and it came out roaring like a lion. It said to our holy father, "You have hurt me!" The blessed elder said to him, "Distance yourself from this brother and do not perturb him [any more]." Satan said, "I swear to you, I did not know that this monk had strength, but instead I was tempting a weak spirit. From now on, I will attack him with everything of which I am able." The elder said, "May God curse you and destroy you and disperse you like smoke." After this, Satan placed some dirt on that brother and beat him repeatedly[56] and frightened him until he fled and went out naked from his dwelling. [The brother] went out to [visit] the elder and said to him, "O my holy father, help me and save me." The elder said to him, "What is the matter with you, my son?" That brother said to him, "You see that the demons have chased and driven me naked out of my dwelling." Abba Bsoy took him by his hand and brought him into his dwelling and left him so that he might find relief from his terror. The holy elder stood up to pray and raised up his hands toward heaven and beseeched God and said, "O Lord God, all-powerful and creator of the universe by [your] wisdom, you, Lord, [are] our guardian and our protection. O Lord of the universe, to you I bow down and plead for mercy so that you may rescue this your servant from the harassment of Satan and strengthen him so that he may dwell in this desert and fulfill your will, and become like a tree which yields its fruit and its foliage into your hands all the days of his life. You, Lord, have said, 'I will fill this desert with monks who sanctify my holy name.' On account of this, we implore you and bow down under your hand so that you may be our guardian and our protector and the upholder of our weakness, for you are capable of everything, the only Jesus Christ, for ever and ever, Amen."

61. When the righteous and virtuous Abba Bsoy had completed his prayer, he saw an angel of God [who] had tied up Satan with chains and had placed him before [Bsoy]. Satan howled and lamented, "Woe is me on account of you, O Bsoy, for you have greatly tormented me. God is alive before whom I shudder and am afraid. I am leaving this desert to you and those who dwell in it, and I will go to another country." The holy elder said

to him, "O enemy of the one who is righteous, do you ever relent attacking the servants of Christ whom he has rescued by his own precious blood? Why did you pursue and attack this brother?" Satan said to him, "I want to make him fall [46] rapidly. If I allow him to be free, he will become much stronger than me and my torments and afflictions will greatly increase." The holy one said to him, "May God curse you and drive you far away." Satan swore to him and said, "If you leave me in this desert, I will not come back to torment this brother."

62. After this, Abba Bsoy said to the angel, "Release and leave him until the day on which God judges and recompenses him according to his evil deeds." With this, [Bsoy] left and went out to that brother and made the sign of the holy cross upon his face in the name of the Father and the Son and the Holy Spirit. He consoled and affirmed him and sent him back to his dwelling, praising and glorifying God. By the prayer of the holy Abba Bsoy, the demons did not come back against this brother from that day and did not abuse [him]. He began to increase [his] combat every day, doubling it, glorifying and praising God. He came to know his grace that was upon him and praised Abba Bsoy.

John tells about Bsoy's insights

63. Another time, some brothers came while that brother was with Abba Bsoy, in order to hear his news, and they asked him regarding many teachings so that their souls might gain profit. [Bsoy] responded to them, "Do battle [spiritually] in order to guard the rule of monks which is fasting and prayer, purity and humility, and love for all. But as for doing something harmful, may no one think [about this], since it is not proper for Christians." He spoke to them many things similar to this and revealed to them the thought of their hearts. He exhorted them until they were deprived of speech and greatly amazed. The brothers said to Abba John, "Our father, truly this elder is a holy one of God, for he has revealed to us the thoughts of our hearts." [Bsoy] said again to them while Abba John was there, "Many times I have done by myself actions which people did not know." When he met with Abba John, there was nothing he concealed. When he had spoken like this, the brothers increased the praise of God who resides in his saints.

Bsoy intercedes with God on behalf of the apostate monk Isaac

64. There was one brother [who] was continually doing his own will. He did not take counsel with the fathers and did not ask them [for advice] and did not do their will. He rose up and settled alongside the dwelling of the brothers near Qastata [Fustat] in order to dwell living alone. After some

days, he entered the city of Qastata to sell his handiwork. A Jewish female magician saw him from her window, and Satan filled her heart with desire for him. She called out to him and brought him into her house as if to buy his handiwork. She took him into her nets and made him swear to [48] abandon his monastic life and to dwell with her. She converted him to the Jewish way like her and made him lie down at her feet. She took a splint of wood and placed it in the middle of his teeth so that he could not retain [anything] from the body of the Savior.

65. After this, some of the brothers went down to buy their necessities and entered into the city, and while they were buying [their goods] Isaac the Jew saw them and asked them, "Are you from the desert?" They said to him, "Yes." He said to them, "Do you know the holy Abba Bsoy?" They said to him, "We are his disciples." He said to them, "I implore you, when you return, speak to him and tell him, Isaac the Jew says to you, I am confiding [in you], O holy Abba, to pray for me because I have fallen into the traps of Satan." The brothers said to him, "We will tell him just as you have spoken to us." When the Jewish woman heard them talking, she knew that the holy Bsoy was able to rescue him from her hands. She looked out the window and said to the brothers, "Say to the solitary Bsoy, if I see him here, I will torment him and make him perish." When the brothers returned to the desert they went to visit Abba Bsoy in order to be blessed, [but] they forgot and did not tell him about Isaac. But holy Abba Bsoy, who truly was a prophet like Elijah and Elisha, said to the brothers, "Was there someone who spoke to you in Egypt that you should give me a message?"[57] They said to him, "There was no one," because Satan had made them forget. The holy Abba Bsoy said to them, "Was not Isaac the Jew the one who sent you to speak to me?" They said to him, "Yes, our father, he greets you in great peace and confides in you to pray for him because he has fallen into the nets of Satan. When he spoke to us like this, his wife watched us and she heard and spoke to us, 'Tell the solitary Bsoy, "If I see you here, I will torment you and burn you."'" They recounted everything to the holy Bsoy which had happened.

When he had heard this, he trembled and pulled together his feet, and recoiling backward, he grumbled for three breaths. He cried out in a loud voice, "O my Lord Jesus Christ, help me!" The brothers were disturbed and astonished, and said to him, "O, our father, why are you troubled and afraid?" The holy Abba Bsoy said to them, "Who is able to unravel the net of Satan that is put together by a woman unless God is with[58] him? Indeed, a woman led our father Adam into sin and made him depart from the garden of delights.[59] Joseph the righteous was thrown into prison by the subterfuge of a woman.[60] Elijah the prophet fled into the desert because of the fear of Jezebel.[61] The mighty and strong Samson was enchained by a woman.[62] On account of a woman, a spear came upon the children [50] of Israel and 230,000 men were killed in a single day.[63] John the Baptist's head was cut off by the counsel of a woman.[64] Solomon, the great and wise, who was the leader in his kingdom and was elevated above those who were kings before him, women obscured his heart and took away his wisdom.[65] Peter, the leader of the apostles, a woman berated him and he denied his Lord.[66] Why do I chastise the saints with this reprimand? Be it as it may, I have spoken with such examples, for God was with each one of them until God made them depart from the sea—and the waves—of this world." When the brothers heard this, they admired the greatness of his wisdom and the elder's discernment and they greatly glorified God. [Bsoy] had revealed to them about this woman that she was a magician, and by her magic she had cast a net over Isaac and made him an unbeliever.

From that day on, our father Abba Bsoy took to praying night and day. He asked God to rescue Isaac from that Jewish woman. God accepted the prayer of the holy Abba Bsoy, and appeared to him and said to him, "O my chosen Bsoy, why do you tire yourself out for Isaac? Because from his infancy, he kept doing what he wished [to do] until he fell into the traps of Satan and denied the baptism in which he was anointed." Abba Bsoy wept and said, "I will not stop from pleading and supplicating to you until you have mercy and return him to us and pardon him." 66. Our Lord said to him, "If I pardon him, should I take the reward from you and give it to him?" The elder said to him, "O Lord, you know what is in [our] hearts. Just as I desire salvation for myself, in the same way I desire salvation for everyone. It is not possible for me to see my brother in distress and suffering and I am living comfortably, for we are from one dust and all of us are the product of your holy hands. Yes, my Lord, have mercy on him and return him to your holy favor. I will not cease from beseeching and imploring you all the days of my life until you return him to me." 67. Our Lord said to him, "You have acted well, my beloved Bsoy. I know that you are surrendering your life for your neighbor, according to what I commanded to my apostles, 'There is no greater love than this, that one surrenders his life for his friends.'[67] Now, I will not take away from your compensation, but I will increase it for you and your reward will be great because you have loved my work. On account of you, I will have mercy on Isaac who has sinned and denied me, and I will lead him to you." Then our Lord gave the peace and ascended into heaven with great glory. He sent down a punishment upon the Jewish woman, and she was in anguish for a few days [52] and then died. Isaac got up and went out to the desert to our holy father and became his disciple. He returned to Christianity and became an accomplished monk and pleased God during all the days of his life.

A lesson about theft
[α]. After some time,[68] the saint walked into the desert and entered a cave, and found there an old dead person who had been wrapped up a long time ago and bound [with bandages]. He prayed and sat down and said, "O man, you have departed from this transitory world and are now separated from it." When he wished to go out [of the cave], he thought to himself, "I will take with me this *waltama*[69] so that the brothers will eat from it and remember this death," and he stretched out his hand and took it. He said, "When I took it and wanted to go out, a voice from that dead one came to me, saying, 'O Bsoy, put back the *waltama* in its place; it is not proper [to do that] in this desert of thieves.' At once, I left it and I went praising God. This is what God revealed to me, O brothers: it is not worthy for a person to take what is not his, and especially the wealth of a dead person."

Instructions to monks on attending festivals and visiting shrines
[β]. He commanded the brothers, "Do not search out too much food for yourselves and do not prepare too many banquets. Do not go to the festivals or to the commemorations of the martyrs and the righteous, and do not take part in a gathering of commemoration. But on the second day, go into the houses of the holy martyrs, and pray, 'O Lord of the holy martyrs, forgive us our sins and have mercy upon us so that we might do your will at all times,' and [then] return to your dwellings."

Bsoy and John leave Scetis
[γ]. After this, murderers came into the desert. As for me, John, I spoke to my holy brother, "I am not hiding from you what is in my heart, [for] when I saw the barbarians killing the fathers I was afraid of death and I said, 'I will go from here so that the barbarians do not kill me and go into hell on account of me.'" The holy man said to me, "If you go, I also will go with you." On account of this, we rose up and prayed, and departing, we went into Egypt. As for me, I found a cave and entered it. Abba Bsoy went up to the south, near to the village of Anṭınoē.[70] His renown and discipline were great. Those who lived close by him came out to [see] him.

Bsoy's instructions on dogma, sacrament, and love
[δ]. As for him, he was teaching them to keep the orthodox faith of the Holy Trinity—Father, Son, and Holy Spirit, one God—which is first without beginning and without end forever. He commanded them to

gather in the church and receive [54] the body and blood of the Lord, for his body and his blood are eternal life for anyone who receives it with orthodox faith.

Again, he said to them, "Love the work of God: anyone who loves the commandment of God will indeed love our Lord.[71] And whatever we do for our brothers for God's sake will wait for us there [in heaven]."

Bsoy tests the brothers; Isaac answers correctly

[ε]. While he was sitting with the brothers and talking with them about what is necessary for their souls, he wanted to test whether their faith was orthodox or if it were not. He said to them, "Satan approached me so that I would speak a word, and he responded that this word [is] in accord with orthodox faith: do not desire to say something like this again. Again, if he does some action similar to the monastic rule, is this our rule from which we take fruit? Now having done this, do not return to me. Having acted this way up until now, should you follow my will in this matter?"[72] Some among them said to him, "O, our father, are you not disturbed? If the worship of God exists, we will beseech you and place our trust in you." Others among the monks said to him, "We will not disobey you; in everything which you command us, we will obey you." Others also said, "Whatever you have told us, we will follow."[73] One of them contended before the fathers, "As for me, I am not coming to you except to know the orthodoxy which leads one to God. But if you doubt the orthodox faith, I will neither follow nor dwell with you." The holy Abba Bsoy stood up and kissed his head and said, "This is the one who guards the commandments of the Lord. This is Isaac who had become a Jew." After this, [Isaac] converted and became strong and steadfast in the faith. He became increasingly zealous for the love of his God, and the holy Abba Bsoy loved him. After the death of the saint, he became an abba to the brothers, an example and superior guide, and a cause of salvation. He taught the brothers constantly and strengthened them for the salvation of their soul.

Bsoy prays on behalf of an impudent priest

68. There was a priest who dwelt near Abba Bsoy. When the holy Bsoy was teaching the brothers, this priest would give them news of this world and make them doubt, as well as all who came out to be instructed by the holy Bsoy. Moreover, hearing the news of that priest regarding the glory of this world, they were scandalized by him. Some brothers went back to Abba Bsoy in order to meet with him. The brothers gathered together with another elder and told him the work of that priest and his lies and the turmoil he [created]. "All of us are perturbed and distressed on account of the doubt which he throws down before us. [56] And when we go back into our dwellings

Satan reminds us and terrifies us." The elder said to them, "Come, let us go to our father and when [the priest] is speaking a little, remind me so that I will ask him to banish [the priest] so that he will not disturb you [any more] with his talking." They rose up and went to see the holy father. That priest also went out according to his custom and began to speak before them and his talking was successful. Abba Bsoy did not rebuke him. The elder took Abba Bsoy aside [to where] they were alone, and told him how the brothers were murmuring about this priest, "When they wish to fill themselves with your teaching, this priest becomes for them a guide of scandal." Abba Bsoy said, "What do you want me to do with him? For Satan wishes to destroy him, and you too wish his affliction and expulsion. Has not [Satan] told me, 'Bsoy, I have given you a man and you have not been patient with him'? If I were to banish him and prevent him from talking according to his custom, he would be upset and go away from me. He would return to his city and become a lay person and destroy his soul. It is appropriate, however, that you should be patient with me and with him, in love. After this, your souls will be in peace." [All the monks] responded to him, "If he should abandon his custom and return to the monastic rule and leave behind this behavior and this obstinacy, we will be patient with him and celebrate with him[74] so that he will return to the light." After this, that priest recognized his sin and his foolishness. He abandoned his poor speech and offered his penance, and had a great reward. He was obedient to the elder all the days of his life.

Bsoy washes Christ's feet

69A. While the holy Abba Bsoy was dwelling in a cell in the desert of Thebes, our Lord Jesus Christ came to him with two of his angels, just as he had appeared to our father Abraham under the oak tree of Manbar.[75] Just as Abraham sanctified God, in the same way our father Bsoy sanctified God constantly, without ceasing. Christ said to him, "Peace be with you, O Bsoy the pure." The blessed elder got up quickly and prostrated himself before him. He took up some water and offered it to him and pleaded with him [to allow him] to wash him, and then he washed his feet. Then our Lord ascended up before him with great glory and ascended into the heavens.

Bsoy's disciple learns about the fruits of disobedience and obedience

69B. Abba Bsoy drank from that water and that which remained he left in a jar.[76] It remained there until his disciple came back from Egypt, so that he could drink of the blessing of Christ in order that the Scripture could be accomplished which said, "Love your neighbor as yourself."[77] When his disciple arrived, he said to him, "O my son, pick up and drink from [58] the receptacle. [The disciple] said to him, "O my father, I will go to drink." But his heart quibbled and he said, "Instead of saying to me, 'Drink some fresh water,' because I have come through this heat and am thirsty, he said to me, 'Drink water from this receptacle.'" He did not wish to drink from it. Again, the elder said to him, "Get up, my son, drink a little from the receptacle." [The disciple] said to him, "Pray for me and I will go do it." But he did not do it and said in his heart, 'I would like to drink fresh water from the pot.' [Bsoy] spoke to him a third time, "I am telling you to get up, drink a little water from the receptacle." [The disciple] said to him, "I am going to drink from it," but he did not go. The abba remained silent before him. The disciple looked at the face of our father;[78] his face returned to what it was before. He then got up and went to that water of the receptacle, but he could not find [any]. He returned to our father and said to him, "Have you made me a fool, O my father? I went, but could not find the water in the receptacle." [Bsoy] said to him, "The new Elijah, the second Elijah, has given the victory." Then the holy Abba Bsoy told a parable, and said to him, "This water has remained in the ground until now." His disciple said to him, "What is this water?" The virtuous [Bsoy] said to him, "Believe me, my son. Christ has come to one of the brothers, God loved him in this desert who is worthy of blessing to wash the feet of our Lord. [The brother] washed [Christ] with that water, and he brought to me some of that water and I drank. I had left you some of it, but you did not obey [my order] to drink, [and now] the angels have taken it away." When the disciple heard [this], he fell down at the feet of the holy abba and his heart was darkened for a full hour.

70. When his soul returned, the holy elder, a true prophet, picked him up and said to him, "Know this: Adam, because he did not obey his Creator, departed from the garden of delights. And if you had obeyed me, you also would have become associated with that gift, but it is a great help that it has been held back from you." That disciple was shocked and suffered greatly. He began to cry for himself because he had not obeyed his teacher. He suffered because he had not become associated with that gift. The holy elder consoled him, exhorted and affirmed him. He said to him, "Due to your affliction, today your sin is forgiven you."

Bsoy sends his despondent disciple to a holy man

71. But the heart [of the disciple] was not consoled. That disciple entreated [Bsoy] and said to him, "My lord and my father, have pity on me and send me to a person mature and strong in God so that I may ask him about my folly." After this our father gave him some bread of lupine seed and said to him, "Go to the village of Arsinoë,[79] and there you will find to the right of the fortress a man seated upon the rubbish, [60] resembling a fool, and the

children are throwing stones at him. Give him this seed in my name, and he will talk to you regarding what you should do."

72. The disciple got up and went according to what his master[80] had said to him. He found that man upon the rubbish, and the children surrounding him and throwing stones at him. He chased away the children and gave him the bread of lupine seed[81] upon which was [inscribed] the name of Abba Bsoy. The old man said, "Many times I have wished to hear of his news." He said to the disciple, "Because you have not obeyed your master and disobeyed his order, and have neglected something like this great gift after you were trembling and parched, may your trembling and your fear become your rule. Get up now and return to your abba and obey him. Know that anyone who does not obey the holy Abba Bsoy does not obey Christ." That disciple returned to the holy Abba Bsoy and told him how the prophet of God had spoken to him.

The disciple goes to see the holy man again

73. He dwelt with his [spiritual] father, but after some days the disciple was afflicted in his heart. He was weeping a great deal and constantly saying, "Woe is me. I would prefer to die than to live, because I did not drink the blessing [of the water] of the washing of the feet of Christ." Then the holy Abba Bsoy consoled him, "After you have shown your repentance and your affliction, God will have pity on you and will pardon your folly." But his heart was not consoled by this word. He asked his father to send him to that blessed elder so that he might heal him of his sorrow. Our holy [and] spiritual father Bsoy said, "That elder prophet to whom you went has died.[82] However, go to that village; at its edge you will find a large cave, its door being open, and enter there. You will find there three men who are dead and are sleeping together. This cave is the tomb of the prophets who have previously pleased God in their village and in the markets. When the moment has come for each one of them to depart from this world he climbs up to this place and returns his soul to God. Enter there and place your hand upon the one who is sleeping between those other two. He will get up and speak with you."

74. That disciple went and found the three men sleeping just as the holy Abba Bsoy had described to him. He placed his hand upon the middle one and said to him, "In this way the holy Abba Bsoy says to you, rise up so that I may talk with you." That dead prophet rose up and said to him, "Did I not speak to you before that you should obey your master? Why have you become the enemy of the faith like this? If you have the right faith, see what I have told you: anyone who obeys Abba Bsoy has obeyed Christ. And anyone who refuses to obey his master has refused [to obey] Christ, the Son of God. Rise up now and go back to your abba, because he is pleading and imploring

for your sake to God." That prophet said this to him and went back to sleep. [62] That disciple rose up and returned to Abba Bsoy and related to him what that prophet had said. That disciple was astonished at what he had seen and heard. Fear and trembling seized him in the presence of the greatness of Bsoy and he obeyed him all the days of his life. Hearing this, who would dare to believe that this is true? Our Lord said, "Whoever believes in me will do what I do, and will do that which is greater than that."[83]

Bsoy intervenes to absolve two young monks of false charges

75. There were two brother monks who came to Abba Bsoy and said to him, "Do for us a favor, our father, receive us so that we might be under the mantle of your prayer. Guide our souls and give them profit." Our holy father received them with joy and love and installed them with him, talking with them and teaching them how to beseech God. After this, our holy father wished to separate himself from people and dwell in solitude in order to fulfill his service to God in hardship and be vigilant in conduct. He said to the two brothers, "Rise up and go into this desert and dwell in hardship and apply yourselves to the reading of the Scriptures." The brothers responded to him, "To whom should we go, [for] the words of life are with you, O holy one of God?"[84] He said to them, "Yes, go, because the monk is not able to accomplish and fulfill [anything] without being in solitude and labor." They said, "Show us, our father, where we should go." He said to them, "Search out the desert of Daqwa," and he prayed over them. They received his blessing and went to the desert of Daqwa and dwelt there just as he had commanded them.

One day, thieves came and entered into the dwelling of one of the brothers and took his pot. There was an elder who dwelt in the desert whose heart Satan had clouded. When the goods of the people disappeared, he said to them, "'So and so' has taken it, for it is an angel who has spoken to me." Their abba went to the elder and said to him, "O, our father, tell me who has pillaged the dwelling of 'so and so'?" The elder said to him, "Those two brothers who have come here and settled in this desert, they are the ones who have taken [the pot]." All the brothers with the abba believed him. They seized the two brothers as the robbers and threw them into the prison. The holy Abba Bsoy, prophet above all, knew by the Holy Spirit that evil had come to these brothers. He rose up quickly and went to the desert of Daqwa and found the two brothers in the prison. He said to the abbot, "These fellows that you have imprisoned are not the robbers." The abbot said to him, "This elder prophet is the one who told us." Abba Bsoy said to him, [64] "Assemble all the brothers."

All of them assembled together, and when they saw the holy one, they were blessed by him and all of them prostrated themselves before him. The holy Abba Bsoy said to them, "What wrong have these foreign brothers whom you have imprisoned done against you?" That elder said to him, "Because they have stolen the property of the brothers." Our holy father groaned in his mind and said to the elder, "Do a favor for me and tell me, are you certain regarding this vision which has appeared to you?" The elder said to him, "I am not mistaken, for I have spoken to you truly." The holy Abba Bsoy said to him, "Do [for me] a favor [and listen to me], and believe that this is a temptation from Satan, so that the brothers will recognize that this is your error." Abba Bsoy was an upright prophet, a spiritual man. The brothers prostrated themselves to him. As for that elder, they rebuked him and struck his heart with terror. He said, "Satan has led me astray!" Once he had thus spoken, the spirit of Satan went out from him in the form of a desert pig, its long tusks coming out of his mouth. It wished to tear apart the elder, [but] Abba Bsoy prevented it and cursed it, and it disappeared like smoke. When the brothers saw what had happened, they prostrated themselves before Abba Bsoy and that elder prostrated himself with them. They said to him, "Forgive us, our holy father. God truly resides in you." At once, they brought out the two brothers from the prison. By the Holy Spirit which was revealed to him, he said to the abbot, "Go into such and such a place and in there you will find what had been stolen." He did not say who it was who had stolen and commanded him not to say to anyone that he had revealed to him [the place] in order to separate the praise from him. The abbot went and found [the pot] according to what the holy one had said. He glorified God who resides in his holy ones.

Bsoy teaches about anger

[ፘ]. Our father was exceedingly steadfast in his way of life, not angry, sweet and peaceful. A brother came to [visit] the holy one and a child was with him. He dwelt nearby the elder several days, but the child was walking about here and there. The brothers were scandalized many times and spoke to our father, "Here is something that has happened to us that could lead to scandal; now chastise this child." But our father did not say anything. Again, the brothers said to him, "Did you not rebuke him so that he would not bother all of us?" He said to them, "My children, why should I give him such a rule and order?" One of the brothers went to strike [the child], but the elder prevented him and said to them, "If I were to act like this, I would ruin all of my labor and all that I had accomplished in the days of my life." The brothers said to him, "Who would cause this ruin for you?" He said to them, "Everything that I have acquired would be destroyed if I become angry and quarrel. In this way, our father teaches us that we should not rebuke the disciple who comes to us and that we should not become angry [66] against him. Scripture says, 'Reprimand your child with a stick,'[85] because the child will not die by the discipline of his father. His soul will be blessed and he will become useful for you and for his God."

Bsoy as an abbot

[η]. All of a sudden, Our Lord came to [see] Abba Bsoy and encouraged him on account of his purity and his virginity. The Lord said to him, "You will have a monastery in this desert of Skete and numerous souls will gather to it, and they will offer sacrifice and offering for my name and you will become father over many brothers." The holy one said, "Forgive me, my Lord, I am an old man and am not able to continue in[86] this ministry. This work should be for holy people who guard your commandment but I am a sinner." Nevertheless, Our Lord assembled many brothers to dwell near him, and [Bsoy] dressed them in the habit[87] of monks, and they dwelt in the cells near to him. He would teach them every day the fear of God and the reading of the Holy Scriptures and the psalms of David. He said to them, "My children, work with your hands in order to give alms, and a reward will be waiting for you in heaven."

Bsoy teaches a disgruntled monk about work

[θ]. There was a brother who heard our father commanding the brothers to work with their hands. He thought in his heart, "If the abba is working with his hands, he may order us; but if he is not [working], why should he order us?" Our father [Bsoy] knew [about this] through the Spirit and said to him, "My son, are you thinking this and murmuring against me? Since I am teaching the brothers and strengthening them for work, the reading of the scriptures and of the psalms, the worship [of God] and prayers, do you not know that before God I am working for your souls at every moment?" Hearing that, the brother threw down the fibers of the palm leaves from his hands and bowed down before our father and said, "Forgive me, my father." Abba Bsoy said, "O my son, God knows if I have worked or if I have not worked. Since I came into this desert I have not ceased working and serving [God] day and night. When I finish praying I work with my hands and fatigue my body so that it does not defeat me and drive me into Gehenna. Whoever wears out his body and tests it by fasting, prayer, reading [the Scriptures], and the worship [of God] is rescued from Gehenna. But whoever here makes his flesh profit strengthens youthful desires against himself and he will inherit the fire of Gehenna." Hearing this, the brothers prostrated before him and said, "Forgive us, our father, for no one is able to do what you do, and your soul enjoys itself in spiritual work and you will call many [people] [68] into [eternal] life." Our holy father did many things in secret without anyone knowing it.

The enumeration of the four great monasteries

[ı]. Abba John said, "Many times, the brothers became worthy, having found the excellence of our holy father." Since many steadfast solitary hermits dwelt in this desert so that their name might be known and endure forever, they have received their reward. God wished that monasteries would be constructed for them, for each one of their names. Christian churches would be constructed in their locations where they lived in order to offer in it the sacrifice and the offering which shines like the sun that gives life to [our] soul and body. These are the pure ones whom God has chosen and revealed to them and placed them as a haven for the feeble in this world, so that they might save the souls of all who come to them with an upright heart like the city which has [around] it a strong wall and protects those who are inside it. First, the one who established the spiritual law is this prophet Abba Macarius, whose renown has spread out into all the earth. He was the refuge and the guide of life for all who dwelt in this desert. This one is our holy father Macarius. After him, it is me, John the Little. Why should I praise myself? I am writing this regarding someone whom God has chosen, about whom our holy father Bamwi had prophesied in the place where I planted a tree as my abba ordered me. This is Abba Bsoy who lived in the way of life and excellence. These are the holy fathers, from Rome,[88] Maximos, and Domdeyos [Maximus and Domitius], whom Abba Macarius had guided. He taught them the way of life of this holy one. These four holy ones are those who shone in the desert of Skete like a pearl of great price and like the four apostles who had proclaimed the Gospel in the entire world.

On the position of Bishoi's monastery in Wadi al-Natrun

[κ]. We have found written in the Gospel that Christ had chosen seventy-two disciples and sent them to preach in every place.[89] But he did not reveal to us their names. But he did reveal to us the names of the twelve Apostles because he had chosen them first and appointed them as a light to all the world. In the same way, he revealed to us the names of those four important saints who became greater than the other saints. As for the holy Abba Bsoy, his renown spread out into all the earth and God revealed a great grace in the place [where he dwelt].

The healing well at Bishoi's monastery

[λ]. [70] Some barbarians found forty-nine monks near a high tower which they called Piamoun[90] and killed them all. While returning to their country, they rested with their chariots near the well of Abba Bsoy. They took up their swords, full of the blood of the martyred monks, and washed them in the wells. The water became a remedy for all ailments up to today. Praise be to God who takes pleasure in his saints.

Bsoy and Paul accept a disciple

[μ]. The holy Abba Bsoy was constantly going to [visit] Abba Paul.[91] There was a young man whose name was Sirās who was from the village of Antinoë.[92] He wanted to receive their blessing and wished to put on their [monastic] garment and engage in [spiritual] combat just like their combat. Many times, he would go out into the desert and remain there. When the holy fathers came out, he saw the grace of God residing over them. Abba Paul and Abba Bsoy said to one another, "May our body be upon the earth in the same way of life, and may our souls in the world to come [be] in the same dwelling." They knew that God would carry [this] out for them and reunite many people.

Bsoy and Paul live together

76. For a long time, Abba Paul and Abba Bsoy lived in friendship. Bsoy went out continually to visit Paul, and they would discuss together the Holy Scriptures just as the prophets Elijah and Elisha. In this way, the Holy Spirit widens the soul of the prophets. Abba Bsoy said to Abba Paul, "My brother Paul, be steadfast in order to work and endure hardship while we are in the world before we depart from it." And Abba Paul said to him, "Pray for me, O holy one, so that I will accept gratefully from you all that you order me, and I will not hide from you anything of what is in me." Abba Bsoy said to him, "Let us praise God with all of our heart because he has taught us and come to us in this beautiful time. Let us do business with the five talents so that they might be doubled for us[93] with the Lord and not be lazy like the foolish [virgins], for the love of the Lord is over us. Let us guard his love with the five wise virgins who lit the oil of their lamps[94] so that he may have mercy upon us." Abba Paul said to him, "Pray for me so that I may fight with all my strength."

77A. During that time, Abba Bsoy was like a brass wall for all the monks who came out to be blessed by him. They would discuss a word of salvation and the hatred of the world. Let us prostrate ourselves before them in order that they may remember us before Christ our God so that he may have mercy upon us when we stand before him.

The death of Bsoy

77B. [72] When the time of the passing of the holy Bsoy approached and arrived, and his days were long and he had become very old, he offered up his body as a sacrifice acceptable to his God. Then he said to me, "Just as in the years which I dwelt in the desert of Skete, in the same way I have dwelt in the desert with the fathers . . .[95] in the south while serving them and glorifying my Lord. Abba Paul dwelt in the desert many years while sanctifying his God. His way of life and his deeds were [done] in excellence." 78A. Abba Bsoy said, "There is no greater combat than that of one who does not utter a word before his brother talks." He said again, "The years that I dwelt in the monastery, I performed a hidden deed of which no one knew [what I was doing]. But through this I hope for a reward. But if the people had known it, I would not expect anything." They said about him that every deed which he would do, if there were some who knew it, he would change and begin another. He said, "Vain praise is empty and its foliage falls off, but many are those who love this." But this holy one dismissed this [praise] and confided in God from his youth, and inherited the kingdom of heaven and entered into good things which are eternal.

78B. But now when the holy father had come to old age, his days were many and his body was failing, our Lord wanted to make him depart from the fetters of this world which are full of affliction. He passed away[96] on the eighth of the month of Ḥamlē and our Lord received his pure soul. The angels came to receive him, rejoicing in him. They crowned him and rejoiced with him until they brought him into the kingdom on high with honor and glory. The brothers who were dwelling with him wrapped up his holy body with great honor and buried him in a place where they would gather for prayer, glorifying and praising God.

Perhaps someone among the people knows how many years he dwelt in the desert, but we do not know [how many]. We have asked people many times to tell us, but no one knows [the number of years] since he fled from people so that they might not honor him. But this is what they said: he had dwelt seven years[97] praising God with a beautiful praise. Other years he dwelt in the south in the desert of Thebaid, and performed many miracles which could not be counted. God alone knows [how many] and rewards him. But as for us, while there are many things which could have been recounted, we have written [only] a little of the way of life of this strong [and] beneficent [man], full of the Holy Spirit, Abba Bsoy, the chosen one. Glory to God who has made this one strong. We need to follow his holy way of life.

Translation of relics

79. [74] Abba Paul also died on the seventh of Ḥamlē in 'Anṭorāwiniqi, in the desert where he was buried. When Abba Sirwes heard that these holy ones had died, he went by boat and traveled to Mukyāduḥ, and took the body of the holy Abba Bsoy and placed it upon the boat to bring it to Antinoē[98] in order to [bury] it in the place which he had constructed. When

they entered into the river and came to the place of Abba Paul, the boat stopped in the middle of the river for two days and refused to keep going. The sailors became weary as they were toiling to move forward, but were unable to make it move. There was an old monk living in a cave, a spiritual man, whose name [was] Abba Jeremiah.[99] He got up and went toward the boat and said to the people of the boat, "Do you know why your boat is not moving?" They said, "No." He said to them, "On account of the body of Abba Paul who is from Tamma,[100] because Abba Bsoy and Abba Paul made a pact between themselves while they were still living, saying, 'May our bodies be in one place in this world and our souls in the world to come.'" On the next day, the holy Abba Barnabas took with him some men, went into the desert, and brought out the body of the holy Paul from where he was and placed him in the boat with them. They went and came to the village of Antinoë[101] and carried them to the monastery with great honor and with vestments of very great expense. They honored them according to what was fitting for them. People came out and were blessed by them and embraced their bodies. Anyone who had the poison of an illness would go out there and be cured, just as we have narrated regarding the faithful people, for they came out from the village of Antinoë[102] to the place of holy Antony in order to pray there.

Conclusion and doxology
80. When I heard that the holy one of God, Abba Bsoy, had died, I grieved greatly. But I consoled myself in my heart because he had come to the honor and the joy for which he had dwelt hoping for it, and I praised my God and glorified his holy name. Right away, that which my eyes had seen and my ears had heard, words and actions, I have written down for you, friends of God, for the usefulness of your souls. This holy father, Abba Bsoy, is one who departed in truth toward the divinity in the kingdom on high. As for us, we are praying to God to render us relatives of his grandeur through prayer to the holy Abba Bsoy and Our Lady Mary, mother of joy. We offer glory and praise to our Lord Jesus Christ with his Father, the merciful and compassionate one, and the Holy Spirit, the Vivifier, now and always, in the generations of generations, and forever and ever, Amen and Amen, so it shall be.

I have written this book, I, Abraham, the sinner and transgressor. What I have omitted in my account, correct it by your [own] accounts.[103] For the sake of the love of Tanse'a Krestos, my [spiritual] father Abba Nob had me write it. May God have pity on us together in the kingdom of heaven, forever and ever, Amen.

Notes

1 See above, general introduction, 8–10; Greek versions are MS Family A.
2 General introduction, 10–14; BLOr. Syr. 971 [Add. 14735], ff. 113r–129v, is the base text for this translation.
3 General introduction, 16–17; MS Family C.
4 General introduction, 16–17.
5 General introduction, 16–17. *La version éthiopienne de l'Histoire de Bsoy*, ed. and trans. Gérard Colin, Patrologia Orientalis 49.3, no. 219 (Turnout: Brepols, 2002); Robert Beylot, "La version éthiopienne de 'l'Histoire de Besoy,'" *Revue de l'Histoire des Religions* 203, no. 2 (1986): 169–84. Both Beylot and Colin utilize the only two extant Ge'ez mss: Bibliothèque Nationale de France eth. Abbadie 126 (BnF Éth. 126), ff. 51ra–73ra (15th c.); and British Library Oriental 692 (BL.Or. (Eth.) 692), ff. 174r-202v (15th c.).
6 General introduction, 16.
7 See Sebastian P. Brock, *The Luminous Eye: The Spiritual World Vision of Saint Ephrem*, Cistercian Studies 124 (Kalamazoo, MI: Cistercian Publications, 1992), 131–33, for the erroneous tradition of Ephrem as a monk.
8 In the *Synaxarium*: Ṭūba 26 and Amshir 5.
9 Intercession with Christ for a disciple of another abba (22–31); Bsoy's disciple deceived by a Jew (53B–54); Bsoy assists John with fasting (58); Bsoy helps a young solitary to defeat the Devil (59–61); Bsoy intercedes with God for an apostate monk Isaac (64–67); Bsoy sends a despondent disciple to a holy man (69B–74).
10 Inbar Graiver, *Asceticism of the Mind: Forms of Attention and Self-transformation in Late Antique Monasticism*. ST 213 (Toronto: Pontifical Institute of Mediaeval Studies, 2018).
11 Bracketed numbers indicate the beginning of Ge'ez pages in Colin's critical edition.
12 Bamawi/Bamoy = Pambo.
13 July 15.
14 *gadl*: lit. "combat" or "struggle," often used as a depiction of the ascetical life.
15 Rom 1:9.
16 Lit. "after some days."
17 Is 29:23.
18 Lit. "approach."
19 Lit. "the appearance."
20 Lit. "lift up their gaze."
21 Prov 10:8.
22 1 Thes 5:17.
23 Jer 8:13.

24 From a Coptic word.
25 Or "Sunrise"; see the general introduction, 3, on the relevance of this sentence and the play on the saint's name.
26 Cf. Mt 5:13.
27 Lit. "distance yourself."
28 See the *Synaxarium* devoted to Macarius: "27 Maggābit," *Le synaxaire éthiopien: Mois de maggābit*, ed. and trans. Gérard Colin, PO 46.3, no. 207 (Turnhout: Brepols, 1994), 418–19 [122–23].
29 Lit. "altitude."
30 "Mowamal" is apparently a misunderstanding of Arabic *mumawwal*, the term for a governor.
31 Jn 15:5; 14:23; 14:21.
32 Jn 14:12.
33 See Paralipomena of Jeremiah or 4 Baruch, chapter 5. This book is received as canonical by the Ethiopian Orthodox Church.
34 That is, the Seven Sleepers of Ephesus.
35 See 2 Cor 12:10.
36 Lit. "gave the peace."
37 See Ps 102:18.
38 Jn 15:13.
39 Lk 11:28.
40 Lit. "king."
41 Gen 1:1–2.
42 Is 61:1.
43 Ps 104:30.
44 Ezek 37:9.
45 Jn 1:32.
46 1 Cor 12:3.
47 The word wrongly translated from Arabic for "ancient" is the term for "hypostases." It is uncertain whether the plural was intended to be a Trinitarian reference.
48 Dan 7:9.
49 Mt 28:19.
50 Lk 18:16.
51 Bawli.
52 Lit. "gives pleasure to your face."
53 Beylot, "La version éthiopienne de 'l'Histoire de Besoy,'" observes that this statement is more typical of a Muslim against Christianity in the early centuries AH than that of a Jew, implying that this section was a later addition to the Bsoy Vita.
54 Lit. "open."

55 Lit. "know."
56 Lit. "with many attacks."
57 Lit. "tell me a word."
58 Lit. "upon."
59 Gen 3:1–7.
60 Gen 39:7–20.
61 1 Kgs 19:1–10.
62 Jgs 16:4–22.
63 Num 25:1–9 and 1 Cor 10:8.
64 Mk 6:17–29.
65 1 Kgs 11:1–13.
66 Mk 14:66–72.
67 Jn 15:13.
68 Lit. "after these days."
69 Transliterated term, most likely a cup or receptacle.
70 'Anṭēnu.
71 Jn 14:21.
72 Uncertain text: lit. "follow my will that there is."
73 Lit. "we will do like it."
74 Lit. "we will carry him upon our heads."
75 Mamrē; Gen 18:12.
76 Lit. "in the heavens." Probably a case of dittography from the word used above.
77 Mt 19:19.
78 The text is apparently missing the phrase "and his face had changed."
79 'Ersenä.
80 Lit. "his lord."
81 Lit. "lupine seed of bread." Lupine are eaten with bread, but bread is not made from lupine.
82 Lit. "has been set free."
83 Jn 14:12.
84 See Jn 6:68.
85 Prov 23:13.
86 Lit. "to stand up to."
87 *Skemu*.
88 The text reads *Abrom* as the name of one of the saints, but is likely a scribal corruption of "from Rome," referring to the home country of the first two—Maximos (Maximus) and Domadius (Domitius).
89 Lk 10:1.
90 Beymon.
91 Bawli.

92 'Ansenā.
93 Mt 25:1–30.
94 Mt 25:2–4.
95 The text is missing a few words.
96 Lit. "crossed over."
97 The Arabic and Syriac versions give sixty (60) years before Bsoy/Bishoi went into the southern regions.
98 'Ensenā.
99 'Ērmeyās.
100 Tamwi.
101 'Ensenā.
102 'Ensenā.
103 Lit. "What I have omitted in my *word*, correct it by your *words*."

4

THE SYRIAC *LIFE OF ABBA BISHOI* IN TRANSLATION

Manuscript Family B
Recension SA Syr1
Introduction by Maged S.A. Mikhail
Translated by †Rowan A. Greer, Robert A. Kitchen, and Maged S.A. Mikhail

Introduction

Manuscripts belonging to MS *FamB, Rec. SA Syr*, form the basis for the English translation of the Syriac *Life of Abba Bishoi (LBsh)* in this study.[1] Paul Bedjan published a Syriac version of *LBsh* in 1892, which Monica Blanchard translated in her study of Beh Isho'.[2] In his version, Bedjan relied upon BnF Syr. 236, though he read it as a manuscript filled with "lacunae" that he supplied from a manuscript that belonged to his friend M. Salomon. Still, Bedjan's edition did not contain ¶¶22–31 (Syr. 236, fols. 25v–26r), which he appeared to have omitted intentionally,[3] and a section from ¶41[4] that corresponds to a missing folio in the Salomon Manuscript (which likely lacked the last folio as well). Eight years after Bedjan's edition appeared, V. Scheil published texts for both omissions based on a private manuscript he accessed in Qaraqosh (al-Hamdaniya) in northern Iraq.[5] The whereabouts of the Salomon and Qaraqosh manuscripts are unknown.

Although it is the only published text, Bedjan's edition suffers from a barrage of textual problems. Fundamentally, he misses the very essence of BnF Syr. 236,[6] a complete East Syrian manuscript without any missing folios or lacunae. All the pericopes documented in Syr. 236 are complete, though several are carefully abridged. Equally significant, the scribe typically inserted small decorative elements where whole pericopes were omitted. Hence, what is lacking in Syr. 236 is not due to an accident of scribal omission or the physical deterioration of the manuscript, but reflects deliberate choice. Syr. 236, which otherwise follows the structure of *Rec. SA Syr1*, is an abridged recension: *SA Syr1–Short1*. Moreover, the fact that the scribe retained the most theologically problematic account for Eastern Christians (¶¶22–31; see the general introduction) proves that he undoubtedly focused on abridging a lengthy biography, rather than conforming to an established concept of orthodoxy per se.[7]

Another problem is the way the Bedjan edition integrates the Salomon Manuscript with Syr. 236, which led to a host of irregularities. For example, the positioning of ¶53A in the printed edition (p. 597) does not conform to the structure of Syr. 236 (or the Salomon Manuscript). Furthermore, even when Bedjan is purportedly transcribing Syr. 236, he favors readings from the Salomon Manuscript. Many of these deviations are minor and are duly noted in the footnotes; still, undocumented readings of various lengths pepper the Bedjan edition.[8] Finally, in addition to the paragraphs Bedjan omitted (¶¶22–29 and 31) and that which is missing from the Salomon Manuscript (¶41), his edition lacks eleven pericopes attested in the available manuscripts: ¶¶58–60, ι–μ, 77A, 78A, 77B, 79. Hence, given these irregularities and shortcomings,[9] we decided to base our translation on BL.Or. Syr. (971) [Add. 14,735], which provides a complete text for *SA Syr1*. It was not possible to include an edition of that recension here, but we look forward to publishing it in the near future.

Manuscripts referenced

MS A: BL.Or. (Syr.) 971 [Add. 14,735], fols. 24v–50v. The basis for this translation

MS B: BL.Or. (Syr.) 963 [Add. 14,732.8], fols. 113r–129v

MS C: BnF Syr. 236, fols. 21r–33r (Based on the manuscript, not Bedjan's edition)

MS D: University of Cambridge Add. 2016, fols. 20r–36v

MS E: Syriac Orthodox Monastery of Saint Mark in Jerusalem 119A, fols. 66r–80r (Garshuni)

MS F: Salomon Manuscript (Based on P. Bedjan's edition)

The Syriac *Life of Abba Bishoi*
BL.Or. (Syr.) 971 [Add. 14,735], fols. 24v–50v

[24v] An account of the way of life of the ascetic and perfect solitary, our holy father Abba Bishoi, from the desert of Scetis. The venerable[10] priest Abba John the Little, who became his brother when he came to Scetis, wrote it after his departure. Both became obedient disciples to holy Abba Bemoi. It narrates the beginning of [Abba Bishoi's][11] excellent deeds and angelic life, and his departure on the eighth of the month of Abib of the Copts, which is the second of the month of Tammuz of the Syrians.[12]

May mercy and grace be with those who come upon it and read it.

Exordium
1. My brothers in Christ, beloved of the living God, hear from me what I shall begin to relay about the virtue, accomplishments, and way of life of the great holy man, our father Abba Bishoi, who was chosen by God. He abandoned everything in this world, conquered the passions, and perfectly fulfilled the monastic way of life. He was a true witness by his great labors and virtue, and he presented his soul and body as an acceptable oblation to God, as he dwelt in deserts, caves, and holes in the ground.[13] This is the one to whom [Christ][14] appeared because of the purity of his body. He was a chosen [25r] disciple who observed the Lord's commandments; he preached his gospel, saved many souls, and brought them to the kingdom of heaven by his divine teaching. 2. For God is my witness,[15] I shall tell you the truth about him; what I have seen with my own eyes from him time and again.[16] I am writing this [account][17] for the benefit of your souls, and the souls of those who, likewise, will come upon it in the future.

Bishoi's birth and parentage
3. Now the parents of Abba Bishoi were just, righteous, God-fearing people, who loved the church and loved to give alms.[18] By race, they were from the region of Arabia that is in Egypt,[19] from a village called Basenshayā.[20] They were chaste people, pure in their bodies, and because God saw their admirable deeds, he gave them seven male children and blessed their possessions.

The death of Bishoi's father; an angel appears to his mother
After some time, their father went to his rest from this temporal life. So their mother was left as a guide to bring them up in the complete fear of God. Now our father Abba Bishoi was the smallest of his brothers. One night, his mother saw a vision while her seven sons were with her;

the angel of God said to her, "The Lord has sent me to you, and he says to you, 'Give me one of your sons that he might sanctify my name among people.'"

His mother said to the angel, "My lord, they all belong to God; [25v] may he take whomever he desires among them." The angel stretched out his hand and gripped the hand of our father Abba Bishoi, and said, "This one will serve his Lord well"; that is to say, he will be useful to him.

His mother said to the angel, "Take one who is stronger than he, for this one is pitiful and weak." The angel said to her, "He is the one who is suitable and apt for the Lord's service; for the Lord's power is perfected in weakness."[21] [After] the angel said these things, he departed and was not seen by her.

Bishoi goes to Scetis

4. When the holy Abba Bishoi grew strong in his body, he set his intentions on the fear of God,[22] and he desired and longed to attain the monastic life. When the Lord willed, and the time came to fulfill all he ordained for him, he led him forth as a pure spotless lamb and brought him to Shihēt,[23] the Balance of the Heart,[24] that is, the desert of Scetis. He handed him over to the shepherd and savior of souls, our holy father Abba Bemoi,[25] who became a spiritual father and a guide to me, and a savior of my life; I, the worthless John.

Bishoi, as Bemoi's disciple, advances spiritually

5. Our father received him joyfully, and clothed him in the holy monastic habit. And whatever [Abba Bemoi] commanded or determined[26] for him, he obeyed and completed in faith and with great humility.

He would closely observe the countenance[27] and deeds of holy individuals, [26r] marveling at their angelic lives and praising God. One day, our holy father said to him, "It is inappropriate for the brothers to stare at the faces of holy individuals, and not pay attention to anything else. Therefore, constantly cast your sight down, focus solely on your own steps, and fix your mind on God at every moment."

6. When he heard this from our holy father, [Abba Bishoi] cast his sight down for three years, and did not gaze at the countenance of anyone at all, but rather meditated on the Holy Scriptures. Their remembrance was always in his heart, and he imbued[28] his soul with the living words of the Holy Spirit. In this way, the word of Scripture was perfected in him: "The wise of heart observes all commandments."[29] Moreover, he prayed constantly, without rest and without interruption, just as the Apostle Paul commanded.[30] And he persisted in fasting and vigils. He loved the words of

God more than honey or the honeycomb.[31] Every day he advanced in virtue, and he increased and flourished like a tree planted by streams of water, which brings forth fruit, and its leaves do not wither.[32]

7. When he saw his virtuous and well-pleasing deeds, our holy father Abba Bemoi [26v] loved him and rejoiced with him spiritually, and he called him Abba Shī'a.[33] That is, "Sunrise," because of the light of his soul and the brightness of his virtue and progress in good things. And when God willed it, he reposed our holy father Abba Bemoi from this temporal life, and on account of his great love for him and his mercy upon him, he raised him up on high to the place he had longed for.

After Bemoi's death, John remains with Bishoi

8. I, the insignificant one, remained with my brother, Abba Bishoi.[34] I lived together with him in spiritual love in that place which the Lord willed, where I planted the tree as my father had commanded me, as our holy father Abba Bemoi had prophesied to [me].[35]

Bishoi's spiritual disciplines

9. And so, blessed Abba Bishoi persisted in fasting, and he did not taste anything except from one week to the next.[36] He recited many writings of the Holy Scriptures, and he constantly meditated on the prophecies of Jeremiah the prophet. So when he read him, the prophet would come to him, converse with him, and explain his writings to him. The prophet took delight in appearing to him, and revealed to him the spiritual meaning of his words. 10. Abba Bishoi advanced day after day, and added to his deeds. He would fast for two weeks, and when he tasted something after this, he ate [27r] dried bread and crushed salt. He worked secretly to perfect all of his activities, and he constantly sought stillness[37] and desired to dwell in the wilderness as a solitary.[38] God, therefore, called him because of these [traits] to be a safe harbor for the salvation[39] of many souls.

Bishoi and John separate

11. One day I said to him, "My brother, holy one of God, I see that you have a desire for the solitary life and stillness. I, also, desire this. Let us, then, keep watch tonight in constant prayer and supplication and, if it is the Lord's will, we trust that he will reveal what is beneficial for us." He said to me, "You have spoken well." And we stood up to pray.

12. At the end of the night, the angel of the Lord appeared to us and said to us with joy, "The Lord says to you, 'Let each of you dwell in solitude in his own place in order to fulfill the way of life[40] designated for you, for the salvation of many souls. You, then, John, dwell in this

place; and I will send you an abundant following,' says the Lord." Then he said to holy Abba Bishoi, "You, too, Bishoi, depart a short [distance] from the dwelling of your brother, and build for yourself a cave, and live in it. I will gather and bring to you a large following,' says the Lord. 'And there will be a monastery at that place; your name will be upon it, [27v] and they will sanctify my name in it as it is sanctified on high.' By this what was promised to the one who first dwelt in this wilderness, the blessed Macarius, will be fulfilled; namely, that the Lord would gather to him a chosen people." The angel said these things to us and disappeared from our sight.

As a result of this, holy Abba Bishoi separated from me, and trekked north from my cell. He made a cave for himself two miles from me, and he dwelt in it. The Lord was with him, and he prospered in all his activities, and he attained many virtues at that place.

His well-pleasing account was preached everywhere; and his virtue was lauded. Many came to him, beseeching him to clothe them in the monastic habit. He received them, instructed them, and tonsured them, and established them as powerful servants of the great king, Christ. He raised up from his disciples blessed branches, ascetics who love God and who love their brothers, who are mature in love and perfect, as is the example they saw from [Abba Bishoi's] way of life, labors, and holy words.

So I would go to him constantly to reveal my thoughts. Likewise, he, also, would come to me and make known his thoughts.

The Savior appears to Bishoi

13. One day, while [Abba Bishoi] was sitting in his cave, [28r] our Lord Jesus Christ came to him and said to him, "Peace to you, my chosen Bishoi." And he got up in fear and worshiped him. Our Lord said to him, "Do you see this wilderness and the hills in it? From now on, I will multiply in them the monasteries in which they will sanctify my name."

The chosen Bishoi said to him, "My Lord, you will provide for them from this wilderness?" Our Lord said to him, "Truly I say to you, if I find love among them, and they observe my laws and commandments, and they believe in me, even if they do not toil much, I, myself, will provide for their necessities here, and will fill them with good things."

The holy Abba Bishoi said to him, "My Lord, will you save them from the temptations and the tribulations that will come upon them?" The Lord said to him, "If they will keep my commandments, I will deliver them from temptations, and I will make all who fear me heirs of the kingdom on high." Our Lord said this to our father, gave him the peace, and ascended to heaven with great glory.

A rich ruler, induced by the Devil, comes to Bishoi with money

14. After this, our father continued steadily in guarding his soul, and he excelled in the worship[41] of his Lord. The angel of the Lord constantly visited him and conversed with him. However, Satan, the enemy of what is well-pleasing, constantly spread traps to capture him in his snares, [28v] but he was unable to overcome him. He schemed to trap him by the desire for honors and goods,[42] so that he might by this be deceived and his resolve weakened. He went to a certain rich ruler who was in Egypt. He appeared to him in the form of an angel and said to him, "There is a man in the desert of Scetis, a virtuous ascetic, who is granted whatever he asks of the Lord. Go to him, and offer him goods and honors, so that he might bless you." The man said to him, "What is his name?" Satan said to him, "He is called Abba Bishoi."

15. So the man rose up, loaded many goods upon camels, and took money with him and traveled to the desert. But the angel of the Lord, who looked after Abba Bishoi, came and said to him, "Satan has spread a trap for you so that you may desire goods and be overcome by receiving gifts. Now, one of the magistrates of Egypt is coming to you; he has set out carrying goods and money, which he is bringing to you."

The holy elder got up and went out to walk in the desert. The ruler met him and said to him, "Do you know of a great elder who dwells in this desert who is called Abba Bishoi?" The chosen one said to him, "Why are you looking for him?" That ruler said, "I am looking for him to give him these gifts that are with me, as well as money, which he may share with the brothers, so that his blessing might come upon my household."

Then that elder said to him, "There is no need of money in this desert. [29r] Those who live here will not receive anything from these goods that are with you. Do not seek to trouble yourself in this manner. God has already received your offering. Now turn back, go to the towns of Egypt, and distribute what is with you among the poor, the orphans, and the widows; and God will bless you and your household." So that man returned to his home and fulfilled what the Lord's holy one had instructed him.

Bishoi defeats the Devil and enjoys spiritual communion

16. When our holy father returned to his cell, Satan appeared to him and said to him, "You have tormented me, Bishoi!" God's chosen one said to him, "Since your creation, you who hate what is good, your existence has been in vain." Satan said to him, "I regard you as though you were never created." The holy elder said to him, "May the Lord rebuke you, and destroy you!" Then [Satan] went away and disappeared, his deceitful traps having been shattered. And [Abba Bishoi] returned to his place in peace.

The Lord was with him in all his dealings, and he delivered him from all of his adversaries.

17. After this, he rose up and entered the inner desert. He remained there in solitude; he devoted himself to great toils, and he thrived tremendously. And the Lord commanded that his mind and heart be caught up into Paradise to see the good things there. He was taken to the church of the firstborn in heaven,[43] and he was given spiritual food, which he ate; thus, he overcame hunger and thirst. From then on, he fasted the whole week. On Saturday and Sunday, he partook of the body and blood of Christ; [29v] and he did not taste anything else. 18. He toiled with his body as though it were not his own. To the point, the Lord said in his gospel, "Whoever abides in me, I abide in him; and the works that I do, he also will do, and even greater than these."[44] Concerning this, it is inappropriate that anyone should doubt what I will be saying. Recall Abimelech of Moriah who slept for seventy years, without eating or drinking.[45] Likewise, the seven youths at Ephesus who slept three hundred seventy-five years without food or drink, while their souls remained in their bodies. For it is written that those who are weak among humans are strong in God.[46]

Bishoi's pastoral care

19. And so spiritual sons of our holy father congregated around him like bees encircling a honeycomb. He imbued their souls with spiritual wealth from the living words that flowed from his mouth. He constantly sanctified them to God. Indeed, he taught them to always love the stillness of the desert, to go far away from settled places, to give up worldly possessions, to become poor in the Spirit, and to persist in vigils with services,[47] supplications, and prayers without ceasing, and without interruption or negligence. [He also taught them] not to disregard their handiwork, nor to labor with their hands just enough to provide for their own needs, but [rather to also have enough] for welcoming [30r] strangers,[48] for having compassion [upon others], and to give alms from their labor. Moreover, [he taught them] that they should love estrangement and poverty, and that the perfection of all of these things is to abandon their own will and do the will of their brothers; this is the law and the prophets. These were the things that the Lord's holy one commanded them.

The Savior appears to Bishoi

20. So when he saw a multitude of brothers gathered around him, he separated himself from them and entered the inner desert, far from them. He found a certain cave and lived in it three years, and he was not seen by anyone. His hair grew long on his body by a hand span. He persisted in prayer

before God and kept watch night and day, and he did not sleep because of his love of the Lord. [He was able to do so because] he had driven a stake into that cave and tied his hair to it, and he would stand in prayer before God.

21. When he had lived this way of life for three years, Christ came to him at that cave. When the elder saw him, he trembled in fear and fell on the ground, but our Savior caught him, stood him up, and said to him, "Peace to you, my chosen Bishoi. I have seen the labors you have undertaken, and I have accepted them. I have given you a grace[49] that whoever asks me in your name, pleading for his sins, I will absolve and guard him."

The holy one said to him, "My Lord, I beseech you to strengthen me, so that I will labor for the sake of your mighty and holy name. For while you were innocent and Lord of all, you suffered for the whole world; [30v] you died, were resurrected, and saved us.[50] How much more appropriate is it for us sinners to suffer for your name and praise you?" And our Lord blessed him and left him in peace, as he ascended in glory to heaven.

Bishoi intercedes with God on behalf of another's disciple[51]

22. There was a certain elder, who greatly feared[52] the Lord. He lived within proximity to the cell of our father, holy Abba Bishoi, since his youth. He would often go to learn from him. Now that elder had a spiritual son, that is, a disciple. Satan, who hates what is good, attacked this brother with evil thoughts and made him fall into sin; and he died in his sin, and he was taken to Gehenna. Now the elder prayed and entreated God day and night on behalf of his son, and he fasted forty days, as he mourned and grieved for him. Then a voice came to him, saying, "He will remain in Gehenna until the Lord comes upon the clouds." 23. Again, [the elder] fasted another forty days, as he pleaded with the Lord to raise him from Gehenna. However, he heard the same voice. Again, he fasted forty days, and prayed and pleaded with the Lord concerning [his son]. But the same message came to him, saying, "He will remain in Gehenna until the Lord comes upon the clouds." The elder rose up and came to the wilderness and inquired as to [the whereabouts] of the Lord's holy one, our father Abba Bishoi.

24. He arrived at the place where [Abba Bishoi] lived (the blessed one had learned this by the blessed spirit) and went to meet the elder. [The elder] bowed and greeted [Abba Bishoi] and they blessed [31r] one another. The blessed Bishoi said to him, "My holy father, why have you done such a difficult thing and have come to my insignificance?" The elder informed him about his son and those labors he had done for him, and those voices he had heard. Abba Bishoi said to him, "Our holy father, rise; let us pray, and may the will of the Lord be done." That elder said to him, "As the Lord lives,[53] I will not leave here, but I will throw myself before you, weeping and in anguish,

until you ask God to have mercy upon me and gladden my heart concerning this brother, and inform us[, both you and me,] if he has departed from Gehenna or not." 25. Immediately, our father rose up and went into the inner desert, and prayed and said, "Lord, have mercy on your creation, and deliver your servant from torment." 26. At that moment, Christ the Savior appeared to him and said, "My chosen Bishoi, what are you asking for?" 27. The holy one said to him, "My Lord, the son of this elder, I am asking concerning him that you might forgive his sins and raise him from Gehenna." Our Savior said to him, "It has proceeded from my mouth that he will remain in Gehenna until I come upon the clouds." 28. The holy one said to him, "My Lord, if you desire, summon a cloud, sit upon it, and save that soul." 29. Our Savior commanded a luminous cloud to come and he ascended upon it. Likewise, he commanded, "Bring the soul of that youth, and give it to my chosen Bishoi." And the holy man received it,[54] and he sent it to the elder. When the elder saw it, he was greatly amazed, and asked it about the suffering it endured in Gehenna. It said to him, "I suffered a great deal because of my sins, [31v] and even more so because of my disobedience to you, my father." Then they brought the soul to a place of rest. [*30 lacking in this recension*]

31. The heart of the elder rejoiced, and he returned to our father Abba Bishoi and said to him, "I owe you a [great] favor, my father, for you have had compassion upon this brother, whom the Lord, because of your prayers, had compassion upon and spared. For it is written, 'the Lord aids his saints and answers them.'[55] I ask you, my father, tell me, what did you do so that God graced you with these great gifts?" Our father said to the elder, "Forgive me, our father. Since the beginning, the will of the Lord has been to extend his mercy to everyone. In his compassion, he had mercy on this brother. It was not because of me, I the insignificant one, or because I deserved such a thing. [Nor] should you suppose, my father, that I labored until this took place. God forbid! Rather, it was because of what you did—fasting for forty days on three occasions, giving yourself to death on three occasions on account of your love of God, as you grieved in your heart for this brother, and offering yourself on his behalf—that God delivered his [soul] to you. For there is no greater love than this: that one should lay down his life for his friend.[56] For each one of the fathers is given such things according to the grace[57] Christ grants him." And they gave thanks to the Lord, ate bread together, [32r] and each one returned to his cell in peace.

The Savior tells Bishoi to strengthen and teach the brothers

32. Our father, then, devoted himself to harsh and great ascetic practices. He wandered about in the empty wilderness where there was no one, concealing his activities so that they would not be known to anyone, and

continuing in fasting and prayer. When he ate, he did not eat anything other than dry bread, and he drank water.

33. Then the Lord, again, appeared to him and spoke with him and said that he should go out to the brothers in the wilderness and become their father, and teach them the canons and the standards of monasticism, and the commandments by which they should conduct their lives. However, our father pleaded with the Lord and said, "My Lord, I have no strength for this ministry, and I fear that the labors I have performed for the sake of your great and holy name will come to nothing."

34. The Lord said to him, "Do not be afraid; I will, indeed, give you remuneration for your labors in the heavenly Jerusalem, and I will magnify your name." Indeed, blessed is the one who keeps the Lord's commandments![58] For the sweet odor of the name of our holy father Abba Bishoi spread, and the whole desert of Nitria was filled with it. Multitudes visited him, and they came from everywhere to consult him. And they marveled at the greatness of his humility; he taught all of them the fear of the Lord, and he peacefully consoled each of them accordingly.

Emperor Constantine appears to Bishoi

35. One day, I, the insignificant John, went to [Abba Bishoi] to learn of his news. When I arrived at the door of his cave, I heard the voice of someone [32v] talking with the elder while weeping. I knocked on the door, and he came out and opened it for me, and I entered. We prayed and sat down, and I said to him, "My father, who was speaking with you just now?"

36. The holy one said to me, "In that you have heard him speaking, I will tell you that he was Constantine, the king of the Romans. He came to me from heaven, grieving in his heart, weeping, and saying, 'I did not know that this honor was prepared for monks, because of their poverty on earth and living as strangers for God's sake. Had I [known], I would have abandoned my kingship and become a monk.' And I said to him, 'Has not [God] given honor to your kingship in heaven?' He said to me, 'Yes. Nevertheless, I have not reached the honor of monks. 37. For I have seen how some among them, who have rested from the body, have grown wings and ascended as high as the walls of the heavenly Jerusalem, and they enter without being hindered by the gatekeepers there.' [38 *omitted from this recension*]

39. "And I said to him, 'Would it be appropriate that you, who had a wife, children, slaves, possessions, a kingdom, and the honor of your rank, be made equal with those who have left their homes and riches, have become poor, afflicted, and needy? They labor and keep vigils. They hunger and thirst, and lie on the ground. Those are the ones about whom Paul wrote: "People of whom the world was not worthy."'[59] 40. I was saying

these things to him, when you knocked on the door, and he left." When I heard this from the holy elder, I gained great strength, and I said, "Blessed be the Lord, who has revealed his wonders to his saints!"

Bishoi defends the divinity of the Holy Spirit

41. There was a certain elder, a solitary, in the region called Basway.[60] [33r] Satan set a snare for him and put it into his heart to say that there is no Holy Spirit, but only the Father and the Son, and he proclaimed this error openly. Now God, the compassionate, did not want to bring the elder's labors to nothing. He revealed his concern to our holy father Abba Bishoi and instructed him in a vision, "Get up and go to the region of Basway, in the Thebaid of Egypt. There you will find a certain solitary who says and proclaims that there is no Holy Spirit."

Now the holy elder, Abba Bishoi, took up the wisdom of God in his heart in order to attend to the matter and to admonish the elder. He fashioned baskets, each of which had three handles, as an example[61] of the Holy Trinity, and he took them to Egypt and brought them to where that elder dwelt. He settled there as though he were a stranger.

This elder, our holy father Abba Bishoi, followed down the same paths as the chosen one, the great one, the wonderworker, the perfect spiritual one, our holy father, the blessed Abba Macarius, the persecutor of unclean spirits and slayer of demons by his humility, and performed great wonders and glorious signs, who healed souls and bodies, and recovered the lost. He, who being instructed, "Rise, go to Wasim, a town near Fustat, to a heretic who is called Harkel,[62] and return him, by the power of the Holy Trinity, to the orthodox faith—him and all his fellow heretics," performed a great miracle there by the power of the Advocate,[63] who was with him. He raised a dead man, who had died in ancient times, and he brought him to the desert along with Harkel whom he turned from his error, and he instructed them and they remained with him until their death.[64] By this, our holy father Abba Bishoi came to resemble [Abba Macarius] and followed in his footsteps.

By the power of the Holy Trinity, he packed up and came to deliver that elder [33v] and raise him from his fall, and return him to the truth—he and all who followed his error. Now, after [Abba Bishoi] rested that night, when it was morning, many came to that solitary to be blessed by him. And they inspected the baskets of our father and saw that each had three handles. The solitary said to him, "What are these, our father?" The holy elder, our father Abba Bishoi, said to him, "These insignificant things are my handiwork; I want to sell them." The solitary said to him, "Why do your baskets have three handles?"—as mockery increased among the crowd. Our father said to him, while those who had gathered around the solitary were listening, "For my part, I worship a Holy Trinity in one Godhead. That is why I have made these handiworks as an example of the Holy Trinity."

Those who had gathered said to him, "Our father, is there a Holy Spirit with the Father and the Son?" [Our father] opened his mouth[65] in the spirit and preached to them about the Holy Spirit and said, "The Holy Spirit exists essentially with the Father and the Son; an eternal Trinity, uncreated, and indivisible."

He responded and said to that solitary, "Do you know some of the Holy Scriptures?" He said to him, "Yes." The righteous father said to him, "Have you not heard Moses say in the book of Genesis: 'In the beginning God created heaven and earth, and the earth was empty and chaotic, and darkness was over the face of the deep, and the Spirit of God hovered over the face of the waters?'[66] Also Isaiah the prophet said about the person of the Son of God: 'The Spirit of the Lord is upon me, because he has anointed me and sent me to preach good news to the poor.'[67] Again, David said: 'You send forth your Spirit, they are created, and you renew the face of the earth.'[68] [34r] Also, Ezekiel said: 'Thus the Lord said to me, "Cry to the Spirit that it may breathe on these bones, and many will rise up alive,"'[69] as a pledge[70] for what will take place in the resurrection. And John the Baptist, when he was proclaiming and preaching the good news about the Son of God, said: 'I saw the Spirit rest and remain over him.'[71] Also, our teacher Paul said: 'No one can say Jesus is Lord except by the Holy Spirit.'[72] And Daniel, in ecstasy,[73] said, 'I saw thrones that were set in place.' He identifies the thrones with the three persons[74] [of the Trinity]. 'And the Ancient of Days took his seat'.[75] with this he indicated the one Godhead in the Trinity.[76] Moreover, our Lord Jesus Christ commanded his holy apostles and said: 'Go, make disciples and baptize all peoples in the name of the Father and the Son and the Holy Spirit.'[77] Are these testimonies we have taken from the Holy Scriptures enough for you now, so that we may proclaim that the Holy Spirit exists eternally with the Father and the Son, without being separated from them?"

42–43. When they heard from the mouth of our holy father Abba Bishoi these testimonies from the Scriptures concerning the Holy Spirit, that elder and those with him believed and benefited greatly. And many were greatly helped by his teaching, and he strengthened them in the orthodox faith in the Trinity: Father, Son, and Holy Spirit. He established them in the true faith, and returned to his monastery praising God.

An angel assures Bishoi of God's care

44. Then it happened when he was walking in the desert that a light poured out on his eyes, and he saw the desert filled with angels. In great amazement

he said, "What is this?" An angel answered and said to him, [34v] "We are the ones who watch over the saints in this desert." He marveled and glorified God who takes such care of his servants at all times.

Paul and Bifimun come to visit Bishoi

45. Thus, he labored and dwelt in the wilderness, and he excelled in his works of virtue, and his fame spread everywhere. Abba Bifimun,[78] who was from Tamoqniqon,[79] heard of him and longed to see him and to receive his blessing. He rose up and went to Abba Paul, who was from Tamma.[80] For he had heard what he recounted about the holy Abba Bishoi's deeds, because Abba Paul constantly went to our father and learned of his news. Abba Bifimun said to Abba Paul, "Would you do me a favor and take me with you to the Lord's holy one, our father Abba Bishoi, that I might receive his blessing?"

Abba Paul said, "I fear bringing you to him since you are a youth."[81] [Abba Bifimun] said to him, "Then let me go with you only up to the door of his cell, and I will sit at the door until you enter and greet him with a kiss, and when you come out, I will greet you, and I believe his blessing will come upon me [in this manner]."

46. Abba Paul said, "Let it be done"; and the two of them went together down to the desert of Nitria.[82] When they arrived at the cell of our holy father Abba Bishoi, Abba Paul entered and greeted him with a holy kiss; and they prayed, and sat down. Our father said to Abba Paul, "Why did you not bring this brother in with you, but left him outside?"

Abba Paul said to him, "Forgive me, my holy father, because I said he is a youth, it is inappropriate [35r] to bring him in to you." Our holy father said to him, "Do not speak in this manner, 'that he is a youth and little.' For our Savior said that to those like them belongs the kingdom of heaven.[83] Indeed, I tell you that many will enter paradise at the hands of this youth, because the Lord's hand is with him. For he is not little, but great and virtuous."

And he instructed [Abba] Paul to bring [Abba Bifimun] in to him. He did, and [Abba Bishoi] embraced and blessed him. [Then, Abba Bishoi] prayed for them,[84] and they left him and returned to their places in peace, glorifying God.

The Savior visits Bishoi and teaches him about acceptable good work

47. One time, when our holy father Abba Bishoi was fasting, on the twenty-first day of his fast, our Lord came to him. He comforted him and said to him, "My chosen Bishoi, you have exhausted yourself greatly." Our father said to him, "My Lord, I trust in you to strengthen me, and because of this I am not weakened at all."

Our Lord brought [Abba Bishoi] with him to a certain weak brother who had been fasting two days. Abba Bishoi saw him throwing himself on the ground, stumbling—turning to and fro—pleading for a reprieve and a release from the pains of the fast, though up to that time he had not yet completed the second day. Our father said to the Lord, "My Lord, what is the matter with this man that he throws himself down this way?" Our Lord said to him, "He is fasting for me." Abba Bishoi said to him, "How many days has he been fasting that he is so weakened as to fall down?"

Our Lord said, "Since his creation, he has not endured a single day without eating, except for this night, and I allowed hunger and weakness to overpower him. When you had fasted twenty-one days, were you weakened like [35v] this [brother]?"

He said to him, "No, my Lord; but I beseech you, my Lord, tell me what you will do with this man, and what reward you will give him?" Our Lord said, "I have reckoned him a reward just like yours for these twenty-one days. Just like you, he will receive a reward because I have strengthened you for the fasting of these [days], and this man, according to the strength which I gave him, he [also] labored. Indeed, I will tell you just as I have said in the gospel, "Enter—both of you—into the joy of your Lord.""[85]

Christ again appears and teaches Bishoi about the nature of asceticism

48. From then on, our father Abba Bishoi devoted himself to great ascetic labors. He entreated God and said, "My Lord, I do not want to eat much bread." The Lord said to him, "Do not ask about food; you do not eat much."

Again, he asked him and said, "My Lord, whenever I leave the wilderness, I grieve greatly."[86] The Lord said to him, "I will not subject you to anything beyond what you need, in proportion to your endurance,[87] and you will not be grieved when you go anywhere."

Again, he asked him and said, "My Lord, I have often been overcome by anger." Our Lord said to him, "Do not be irate with anyone or scold him. Do not expel anyone or rebuke him, and anger will not overcome you, and the Holy Spirit will dwell within you." In such a manner, the Lord accompanied our father wherever he went, and he spoke with him as a man speaks with his friend.[88]

He asked the Lord and said, "My Lord, if there is someone who obeys your holy name and serves you, but does not interact with your creation, that is, the common people, would this be, indeed, a sin for him?" The Lord [36r] said to him, "Just as you pay the worker who works with you in your field without duplicity, likewise I will give those who work together with me their pay in the heavenly Jerusalem."

49. Again, he asked him and said, "My Lord, if there is someone who knows how to get along with people, comes and goes with them, socializes with your creation, and is pleasing to them, but does not labor much for the sake of your name, what happens to him?" Our Savior said to him, "Such a disciple is a servant,[89] but if he labors considerably, he will become an heir."[90]

Again, our holy father Abba Bishoi asked and said, "My Lord, if there is someone who has labored a great deal and has suffered for your name's sake, and who knows how to interact with your creation, and socializes with [the common people], is pleasing to your image, has labored a great deal for your name's sake, and is virtuous, what will he have?" The Lord said to him, "The one who has done these things is a son and an heir,[91] and his honor and reward will be great. He will be like one of the holy men, Anoup and Apollo,[92] and I will give him blessings and delight in the kingdom of heaven." Our Lord said these things to [Abba Bishoi] and ascended with glory into heaven.

A Syrian monk visits Bishoi

50. Now, in the land of Syria there was a certain holy solitary.[93] He lived on one of the mountains there, worshiping the Lord by night and day. He excelled in all his activities, accomplishing mighty deeds,[94] and he greatly feared God. One night, as he was standing in prayer, he reflected and said in his heart, "Will I find favor before God like one of the saints?"

Immediately, a voice from heaven came to him, saying, "There is in Egypt, [36v] in the desert of Nitria, an elder who serves God and worships him constantly; he is called Bishoi. You have the same boldness[95] before God as he does."

That solitary rose up in great joy, took a ship, sailed, and arrived at Alexandria. He traveled up south from Alexandria,[96] asking where the holy Abba Bishoi was living, and they informed him that he was in the desert of Nitria, and directed him toward it. When he arrived and met him, our holy father Abba Bishoi embraced him, and they greeted one another. Our father brought him into his cave, and they prayed and sat down. But that elder was speaking in Syriac, and our father Abba Bishoi did not understand what he was saying. 51. He groaned toward heaven and said, "I beseech you, my Lord, and I entreat your magnificence, let me understand what this elder is saying."

Immediately, God enlightened his understanding with his glorious Spirit, and he understood the Syriac language. As they were speaking with each other about the greatness of God and of his compassion, [the elder][97] asked our holy father about the virtues and way of life of the true Israelite in whom there is no deceit,[98] our holy father, the great Abba Macarius.

So the righteous and faithful Abba Bishoi said to him, "He was the first who started dwelling in the wilderness. He established laws and commandments, and showed the path of truth, in which he guided all who dwelt in this wilderness. And he was widely known on account of his godly deeds." And [Abba Bishoi] relayed to him stories about the glorious wonders [37r] that God worked through his holy hands. The solitary was astonished and marveled at the things he heard. And [the elder] said, "How great and glorious was the power of the Almighty that dwelt in that holy and perfect man, the great Abba Macarius!"

So our father, the perfect and holy saint, Abba Bishoi, recognized the great virtue of the elder and said to the brothers, "Come! Receive a blessing from this great man. For I see that divine power is with him, and he is filled with grace." All of the brothers came and were blessed by him.

[The elder] remained with our father for seven days. He saw his way of life and came to know our father's virtue; he was strengthened in his heart, and profited by what he saw, and he praised God. He, then, said to our father, "Farewell, my lord; I wish to return to my own land." They embraced one another, and [the elder] left him and traveled to his own land.

Coda: Bishoi sees the Syrian monk borne home on a cloud

52. [Later] that day, a certain brother came to visit our father. The brothers said to him, "If only you had come a little earlier, you would have received the blessing of the great and perfect man who came to our father from Syria. Nonetheless, if you hurry after him, you will catch up with him; for he has walked scarcely a mile."[99] Our holy father answered and said to that brother, "My son, do not pursue him, you will not catch up to him. He has traveled more than eighteen miles[100] upon a cloud. When the brothers heard this, they were amazed and praised God who dwells in his saints.

Bishoi sees an angel watching over a brother

53A. One time, our holy father went to the cell of one of the brothers to learn of his news. He saw that as the brother slept, an angel at his head was watching over him. He said, "Truly the Lord watches over those who trust [37v] in him."[101] And he went away glorifying God.

Bishoi's disciple is deceived by a Jew

53B. A certain brother, a simpleton, went to Egypt to sell his handiwork. He met a Jew who argued with him about Christ. He said to him, "You Christians[102] say that he who was crucified was the Christ; however, he was not, rather it was another who resembled him."[103]

That brother said to him in his simplicity, "You have spoken correctly." As he declared thus, immediately the grace of baptism was taken from him, because of the statement he professed in his simplicity.

Bishoi rebukes and teaches the monk

54. [That monk] returned to the wilderness, but when our father saw that the grace of baptism had been taken from him, he remained silent for a long time. When the brother saw the elder turning his face away from him, he said to him, "My father, why are you avoiding me now?" The holy one of the Lord, Abba Bishoi, said to him, "Who are you?" He answered and said, "I am so-and-so." The elder said to him, "You are not he; for the grace of holy baptism is not upon you." The brother said to him, "Why has it gone from me, father?"

55. The blessed elder said to him, "Because of the words you spoke to the Jew in Egypt." 56. And that brother bowed down and said, "Forgive me, holy father, for I have sinned; indeed, I said those words because of my simplicity."

57. The holy one said to him, "Look, my son, from now on, do not accept strange statements about the faith; rather, we vigilantly cling to what we have received from our holy fathers." And our holy father prayed over him, saying, "Lord God, there is no one who has not sinned except for you.[104] I beseech you, you who are plentiful in mercies, to forgive this brother the sin he committed in his simplicity." By the elder's prayer, God restored the grace of baptism to that brother.

Bishoi assists John the anchorite with his fasting

58. One time, [38r] a great elder called Abba John came to our father from Baqe. This [ascetic] would keep vigil for many nights and days, often fasting while he remained in the wilderness without food or drink, performing great labors. Now his spirit became exhausted from thirst and fatigue, and he said to himself, "Let me rise up and go to Abba Bishoi to learn of his news." He rose and came to him and knocked on his door. Our holy father opened to him, embraced him, and brought him into his cell, and they prayed and sat down. Now as they were discussing the words of God, the Holy Spirit then revealed to Abba Bishoi that Abba John had been fasting for many days, and was consumed with thirst and exhaustion. Our father instructed his disciple to bring some water and bread in order to eat with Abba John, to strengthen his soul, which was overtaken by hunger and thirst. The disciple brought everything asked of him. [Our father] urged Abba John and said to him, "Come, eat a little bread and drink a little water. You have been walking in the heat and are exhausted." But Abba John did not want to taste anything.

He said, "Forgive me for not eating; I am fasting for my sins." Abba Bishoi said to him, "Brother, drink a bit of water so you are not consumed by the heat. Abba John said to him, "Let me be on account of the fast."

When he saw that [Abba John] did not want to eat or drink, our holy father stood up, spread his hands, and prayed before God and said, "Come to me, my Lord Jesus Christ, answer me, and have compassion upon John your servant, who is frail and weakened by the fast." Immediately, as he prayed Abba John was taken up in the Spirit, and he saw one eating bread and drinking water until he was full—and, indeed, this is what happened to him. After he ate and drank and was full, he returned [38v] to his cell, and he increased his fasting, saying to himself, "Fast now, for you were taken to a banquet."

Bishoi helps a young anchorite to defeat the Devil

59. A certain seedling[105] was in the desert, who had recently joined the monastery. He was troubled by the demons that were stirred up against him. He got up and went to Abba Bishoi and said to him, "Blessed father, remember me in your holy prayers. For the demon has left everything and attacks and torments me." Our father said to him, "My son, the statement you made is suitable for those who have been perfected and strengthened by God, against whom Satan wages war by night and day, but Satan is not yet aware that you live in this desert. Now, go entreat God, and I trust that he will give you relief from this matter." The brother returned to his place, and our father prayed to God and entreated him to have compassion on that brother and give him relief. 60. Immediately, Satan appeared, enraged, in the form of a roaring lion,[106] and he responded, saying to our holy father, "Why do you trouble me?" The pious elder said to him, "Abandon that novice brother, and do not trouble him or disturb him." Satan said to him, "I swear to you that I was not yet aware that he lived in this desert, he who is now tempted by a weak spirit. However, starting today I will attack him with all my might." The elder said to him, "May God rebuke and reject you!" And [Satan] left him and disappeared.

Afterward, Satan waged war against [39r] that brother with many great battles until he fled and escaped from his cell naked[107] due to what the demons inflicted upon him. He returned to the elder and said to him, "Holy father, hear me and help me." The elder said to him, "What is your grievance,[108] my son?" The brother said to him, "Father, the demons chased me out of my cell, and threw me out of it exposed because of what I suffered." Our father took him by the hand and brought him to his cave, and left him to rest from his ordeal. And the holy elder stood up in prayer and lifted up his hands toward heaven and entreated God and said, "Lord

God, Almighty, who created everything by his wisdom. You brought into existence that which did not exist by the living word from your[109] mouth. You, Lord, are our guardian and our protector. Now to you, God of all and Lord, I supplicate and entreat your compassion to keep this brother from the attacks of the demons and to strengthen him so he can remain in this desert and fulfill your will. He will become a tree, offering good fruit to you all the days of his life. You, Lord, have said that you will fill this desert with monks who will sanctify[110] your holy name. We beseech you for this, that you may be our protector and guardian, and to be mindful of our weakness, because you are able to do anything; one God, Jesus Christ, forever and ever."

61. When our righteous, virtuous, and distinguished holy father Abba Bishoi said "Amen" and concluded his prayer, an angel of the Lord appeared to him with Satan bound by him with chains; and he stood before him. Satan spoke, saying [39v] "Woe to you, Bishoi! For you have tormented me a great deal. As the Lord God before whom I tremble lives,[111] I will leave this desert to you and to those who dwell in it, and I will depart for other regions."

The holy elder said to him, "You enemy of truth, do you not cease warring against the servants of God; those whom he has gathered in his holy name? What is your quarrel with this brother? Why do you fight against him in this manner?"

Satan said to him, "I wanted to weaken him and defeat him quickly. For if I ignore him[112] and let him mature, he will fight valiantly against me and increase my affliction." The holy one said to him, "May the Lord rebuke you and destroy you." Satan promised him and said, "If you release me at this time, I will not come back and humiliate the brother." 62. Then our father said to the angel, "Release him, and send him away until the day the Lord exacts retribution and pays him back according to his evil deeds." Right away, [the angel] set him free and sent him away.

Now our father went back to that brother and sealed him with the sign of the holy cross, in the name of the Father, the Son, and the Holy Spirit. He comforted him and strengthened him, and he sent him to his cell praising and glorifying God. And by the prayers of our holy father Abba Bishoi, the demons did not return to [that brother] from that day, nor did they attack him. He advanced day by day and excelled, glorifying God and praising him, thanking him, and receiving his grace and that of our father Abba Bishoi.

John tells about Bishoi's insight

63. One time, while I[113] was sitting next to our father, some brothers came to him to learn of his news. They asked him to speak words of exhortation for the profit of their souls. He answered and said to them, "Strive to

observe the rules of monasticism: prayer, fasting, purity, humility, love of humanity,[114] and love of the brothers." He advised them with many such things, and revealed to them the thoughts [40r] of their hearts, and they marveled greatly at him.

When they departed from the elder, those brothers said to me,[115] "Our father, this elder is holy indeed, for he revealed to us the thoughts of our hearts." I, John, said to them, "On many occasions, I had performed some deed by myself, and although no one was aware of it, whenever I met him and was able to speak confidentially[116] with him, he would say to me, 'Such and such a thing was done by you.'" The brothers glorified him all the more, and they praised God who dwells in his saints.

Bishoi intercedes with God on behalf of the apostate monk Isaac

64. There was a certain brother who constantly followed his own will; he did not consult with the elders, nor did he obey them. He rose up and went to Pnita Datroway,[117] which is a bit south of Fustat, to dwell there as a solitary. One day, he entered the city of Fustat to sell his handiwork, and a Jewish woman, a sorceress, looked out of a[118] house and saw him. Satan filled her eyes with lust, and she fell greatly in love. She called to [that brother] and brought him into her house, as though she were buying his goods, and she captured him in her snares. She made him leave his monastic habit and remain with her. And she made him convert to the religion of the Jews, and he became a Jew like her. She let him sleep on her leg, and she took up a toothpick and collected what was between his teeth so that no fragments of the body of our Savior Christ would be left between them—as he reported to me afterward.

65. Then a trip called upon the brothers, the monks from the desert, to enter the city for some purpose. When they went there, Isaac, who had become a Jew, saw them; he asked them, "Are you from the desert?" They said to him, "Yes." He said to them, "Do you know the holy Abba Bishoi?" They said to him, "He is our father." He said to them, "I adjure you, [40v] when you go back, tell him Isaac the Jew says, 'I adjure you, our holy father, to pray for me because I have fallen into the snare of Satan.'" They said, "We will inform[119] him about you."

Now that Jewish woman heard him as he was speaking with the brothers, and she knew that our holy father was able to save him from her hands. She looked out of her house and said to the brothers, "Tell Bishoi the solitary, if I see you here, I will harm you."

So when the brothers returned to the desert, they went to our father to be blessed by him, but they forgot and did not tell him anything about Isaac. Holy Abba Bishoi, the prophet—for he was indeed a prophet like Elijah and

Elisha—answered and said to the brothers, "No one in Egypt spoke with you about me?" They said to him, "No, our father," because Satan had made them forget. The Lord's holy one said to them, "Did not Isaac the Jew say something you were to relay to me?" They said to him, "Yes, our father. He earnestly asked about your well-being, and he adjures you to pray for him because he has fallen into the snare of Satan. And while he said this to us, his wife heard him speaking with us. She looked out of her house and said to us, 'Tell Bishoi the solitary, "If I see you here, I will harm you."'"

Now the holy one was seated, and when he heard this, he was shaken, brought his feet back toward himself, and shuffled back three times, shouting out and saying, "Our Lord Jesus Christ, help me!" The brothers were amazed and astonished, and they said to him, "Even you are disturbed, our father?"

The Lord's holy one said to them, [41r] "Who can overcome Satan's snares involving women, except for the one whom God is with and is in? A woman deceived our father, the first Adam, and made him depart from paradise.[120] Likewise, the righteous Joseph was incarcerated in prison because of a woman.[121] Elijah the prophet fled to the wilderness from fear of Jezebel.[122] Samson, the mighty man of valor, was shackled by a woman.[123] Again, because of a woman, twenty-three thousand of the sons of Israel were killed by the sword in one day.[124] John the Baptist was decapitated at the instigation of a woman.[125] Women led astray the heart of Solomon, the great sage, who prospered in his kingdom more than all the kings before him.[126] A woman caused Peter, the chief of the disciples, to deny his Lord.[127] Now, I certainly do not condemn the saints—God forbid! Indeed, I have already said that the Lord was with each one of them until he crossed the stormy sea of this passing age."

When the brothers heard this, they marveled at the elder's sharp mind, and they glorified God who dwells in his saints. Then the elder informed them that this Jewish woman was a sorceress, who entangled Isaac by her words and cunning in her snares, and seduced him [to do] her bidding.

From then on, our father entreated God, by praying night and day, to deliver Isaac from that Jewish woman. And the Lord heard the prayer of his holy one, Abba Bishoi, and he appeared to him, saying, "My chosen Bishoi, why do you lament like this for Isaac, who purposely followed his own will until he fell into the snares of Satan, and denied me and the baptism he had received?" Our holy father wept and said, "I will not rest from entreating [41v] and supplicating you to have mercy on him, to bring him back to us, and pardon him."

66. The Lord said to him, "If I pardon him, I will take from your labors and give to him." The elder said, "Lord, you, yourself, know what is in the heart of everyone. Therefore, just as I desire to be saved, I also plead for

all to be saved. For I cannot bear to see my brother oppressed and afflicted while I am at rest, since we are from the same dust and the work of your holy hands. Indeed, my Lord, have mercy on him and bring him back to your holy flock. For I will not cease weeping and entreating you every night and day for all the days of my life, until you bring him back."

67. The Lord said to him, "You have done well, my chosen Bishoi. I know that you would have laid down your life for the sake of your friend, just as I commanded my disciples. Indeed, there is no greater love than this: that one should lay down his life for the sake of his friend.[128] Therefore, I will not take anything from your labors; rather, I will increase your remuneration and great reward because of the mercy you have shown to my creation. And for your sake, I will have mercy on Isaac, who sinned and denied me, and I will bring him back to you here." And the Lord gave him the peace and ascended to heaven.

Now the Lord was angry with that Jewish woman. After a few days had passed, she died. Isaac rose up and went to the wilderness, to our holy father, and he became his disciple and returned to Christianity.[129] He became a perfect monk, who pleased God all the days of his life.

A lesson about theft

[α]. One day, as our father was walking in the wilderness, he found a certain hole on a hillside and he descended into it. [42r] He found in it someone who was long dead, wrapped with worn-out rags,[130] and a bowl set on the side. He prayed, sat down and wept, and said, "Man, [how] brief is your life in this passing age! You are [now] released from it and your lusts have ceased." As he prepared to leave, he thought to himself and said, "I will take this bowl so that the brothers may eat from it and be reminded of this dead man."[131]

He reached out his hand and took it, but as he was about to leave, a voice came to him from the wrappings of the dead man, saying, "Bishoi, put the bowl back in its place. It is unbecoming to have thieves in the wilderness." Immediately, I[132] put the bowl back, and I glorified God. For God desires to tell us by these things, my beloved, that it is inappropriate for anyone to take anything that does not belong to him, whether small or great, and all the more anything from the deceased.

Instructions to monks on attending festivals and visiting shrines

[β]. Our father commanded the brothers, saying, "Do not go to the mill or bake much bread, but satisfy yourselves with what God bestows on you from the work of your hands. Do not go out to a vineyard so you do not lose yourselves. Moreover, do not go to the festivals of martyrs to see the crowds—as this is not a [proper] assembly.[133] Go to the shrines[134] of the martyrs and saints, and pray and say, 'Lord of the saints, forgive us our transgressions, and teach us to do your will at all times.' And return to your cells glorifying God."

Bishoi and John leave Scetis after a barbarian invasion

[γ]. Afterward, the barbarians started coming into the desert, killing the holy elders in it, and throwing us into confusion. One day, while I was sitting by our holy father, I said to him, "My beloved brother, I do not hide what has come to my heart from you. Since I saw the barbarians destroying the desert and killing [42v] the fathers, I considered leaving so the barbarians would not kill me and go to Gehenna on my account." Then that holy one said to me, "If you leave, I will also leave with you."

For this reason, both of us stood up and prayed, and we departed for Egypt. I went to Clysma, and from there to the monastery of the holy Abba Antony, [where] I found a cave and remained in stillness by myself, and I continued beseeching God on account of my sins. As for the holy Abba Bishoi, he went to Upper Egypt,[135] to the city of Antinoë, which is Ansina.[136] He went to the desert there, and dwelt in it as a solitary. He vigorously pursued his way of life, as he observed stillness.

Bishoi instructs on dogma, sacrament, and love

[δ]. Then God magnified his name there because of his angelic way of life. But when the brothers gathered around our holy father, the prophet of the Lord, he constantly taught them to persist in brotherly love[137] and the true faith of the Holy Trinity. That is, that there is one God without division, without confusion, and without alteration. The creator of everything, Father, Son, and Holy Spirit, who are equally one Godhead, uncreated, existing from eternity. Moreover, he taught them not to neglect going to church and to constantly assemble there, and to partake of the body and blood of our Lord Jesus Christ, which give life to everyone who partakes of them.

He also gave them commandments about love, saying, "Love the whole creation of God; for everyone who loves his brother, loves God. For whatever we do for our brothers, we do for God and for our souls."

Bishoi tests the brothers; Isaac answers correctly

[ε]. On another occasion, while he was sitting with the brothers, speaking with them regarding the profit of their souls, he wanted to test them as to whether they were steadfast in the faith. He said to them, "[What if] Satan prompted me to make an inappropriate statement about the true faith; [something] that is not even appropriate to utter? Beyond that [43r], [what if] I have instituted something not in accordance with the rule of the brothers? Would you, then, agree with me and follow my will?"

Some among them said to him, "You, our father, have not gone astray, but if—God forbid—you err, we would be patient with you." Others among the brothers said, "We will never stop obeying you in everything." And others said, "Whatever we see you do, we will also do." Finally, one of them answered and said, "For my part, I have come to you to know the path of God, but if you go astray from God, I will not follow you, nor remain with you."

Our father Abba Bishoi rose up and kissed his head, and said, "This one observes the Lord's commandments." Now this man was Isaac, who had become a Jew, but repented and become virtuous and perfect. He was renowned in the days of our holy father Abba Bishoi, and after his departure.

Bishoi prays on behalf of an impudent priest

68. Therefore, our holy father was a sign in the desert, a well-pleasing example, and a source of guidance. He constantly instructed the brothers and strengthened them for the salvation of their souls. Now a certain priest lived near our father, and whenever our father spoke with the brothers and admonished them, that priest would speak vulgar words. The brothers were at a loss. Moreover, all who came to our father heard the profane words of that priest and suffered loss because of him, and they complained about him.

When a certain elder came to visit our father Abba Bishoi, the brothers assembled and told that elder the deeds of the priest, saying,[138] "All of us are disturbed by the profane words that he has previously spoken to us; and when we go to our cells, the Adversary reminds us of his words and disturbs us."

The elder said to them, "Get up and let us go to our father, and when I have conversed with him [43v] for a little while, remind me, and I will urge him to restrain [that priest] so that you will not be disturbed by his words."

So they rose up and went to the elder. That priest came, as was his custom, and he was speaking before them in his foolish way, but Abba Bishoi did not admonish him. The elder beckoned our father and stood with him to the side. He informed him of the brothers' trials and their complaints about that priest. "The brothers," he said, "want to hear the word of God from you constantly, but this priest is the cause of offense to them because of his words."

Abba Bishoi said to them, "What do you suggest I do to him? Satan wants to destroy him, and you want me to banish him. However, the Lord would condemn me because of him, saying, 'I gave you one man, Bishoi, and you have not been patient with him.' For if I am irate with him and forbid him from speaking, as is his custom, he will [feel] persecuted and leave here, return to his land, become secular, and lose his soul. Instead, you must be patient with me and with him in love. Hence, do not act [in this manner], and, in due course, your soul will be pleased with us."

The brothers answered and said, "If he is prepared to change his ways and return to the monastic rule, we would be patient and carry him upon our heads[139] until he returns to the light." After this, that priest recognized his faults and his foolishness, and ceased from his evil words. He offered repentance and attained a good end, and he was obedient to the elder all the days of his life.

Bishoi washes Christ's feet

69A. Now our holy father Abba Bishoi was sitting in a cave in the wilderness of the Thebaid in Upper Egypt,[140] when our Lord Jesus came to him with two angels, just as he appeared to our father Abraham [44r] under the oak of Mamre.[141] This is not such an astonishing thing, for just as Abraham sanctified God, so, too, our father was God's servant who was constantly sanctifying [God's] name. Christ said to him, "Peace to you, my precious chosen elder, Bishoi." Quickly, the blessed elder stood up, bowed down, and worshiped him. He took water and brought a basin, asked permission, and washed [the Lord's] feet. Then our Lord went up, away from him, in glory to heaven.

Bishoi's disciple learns about the fruits of disobedience and obedience

69B. Our father, indeed, drank from that water, and left the remainder in the basin for a brother[142] and covered it; thus, when his disciple would come from Egypt, he might drink from it to be blessed by Christ. In this manner, he fulfilled what is written, "Love your neighbor as yourself."[143] Now when his disciple came from outside, he said, "My son, get up and drink a bit of the water in the basin."

He said to him, "Yes, my father, I will go drink from it." However, he was grieved in his heart and said, "Instead of telling me, 'Drink cool water, my son,' when I have come suffering from the heat and exhaustion, my father tells me to drink the water in the basin." And he was unwilling to drink from it.

Again, the elder said to him, "Get up, my son; drink a bit of water from the basin." He said, "Pray for me; I will do so." But he did not, and he said in his heart, "If I want to drink water, I will drink cool [water] from the pitcher." Again, our father said to him a third time, "I am telling you: get up, drink a bit of the water of the basin." He replied, "I will drink"; but he did not go, and the elder ceased speaking to him.

70. The disciple saw that the face of our father was not cheerful toward him, as he had been before. Immediately he rose up, went to the basin, and

uncovered it, but he did not find water in it. So he turned back to our father and said to him, "You must be ridiculing me, my father. I have found no water in the basin."

The new Elijah and the second Elisha, that is our holy father Abba Bishoi, answered and said to him, "Such water would not last on earth until now." The disciple said to him, "What is this water?"

The true and righteous one said to him, [44v] "Believe me,[144] my son, Christ came to a God-loving brother in this wilderness, because he was worthy, and he blessed him. [The brother] asked [Christ] to give him his feet, and he washed them with this water, and he brought some of it to me. I drank a bit and left some for you, but when you would not obey me and drink from it, angels raised it from earth."

When the disciple heard this, he fell on the ground at our father's feet, and his soul deserted him for a long time. When he came back to himself, the holy elder and true prophet raised him up and said to him, "Now[145] because Adam did not obey his creator, he fell from the joy of paradise. You, too, because you did not obey me and transgressed my instruction to drink, a great benefit has been taken away from you."

Bishoi sends his despondent disciple to a holy man

71. The disciple was then greatly struck in his heart, and he lamented and wept because of his disobedience. He was contrite over his transgression, and grieved on account of the gift of which he was not allowed to drink. Then the holy elder comforted and encouraged him, saying, "Now that you have repented, your sin[146] is abolished." But he was unable to comfort his heart. So that disciple implored him and said, "My lord and my father, have pity on me and send me to a perfect man who is mighty in God, that I might question him about my transgression." Our father then gave him a round loaf of bread and said to him, "Go to the city of Antinoë, which is Ansina.[147] South of the [city] wall, you will find a man sitting on a dunghill like a fool, with children throwing stones at him. Give him this round loaf in my name, and he will speak with you."

72. [The disciple] rose up and went to the city just as his master had told him. He found a man sitting on a dunghill as children were encircling him and throwing stones at him. [45r] He drove away those children, and gave [the man] the loaf of bread in the name of Abba Bishoi. [The man] turned to him and said, "I greatly desire to hear of his news." He also said to the disciple, "Why did you not obey your master, and failed to obey your father that such a great gift was taken away from you, and you become disturbed, and caused [yourself] all this turmoil? Get up now and return to your father. Obey him and know that whoever disobeys the holy

Abba Bishoi disobeys Christ." The disciple returned to our father Abba Bishoi, and relayed everything that the prophet of God had said to him. And he remained with his father.

The disciple goes to see the holy man again

73. A few days later, he was [again] afflicted in his soul because of the grace he had lost. He wept constantly, saying, "Woe is me! I am dying due to the anxiety of my heart, for I did not drink the blessing of Christ's washing!" Our holy father Abba Bishoi would comfort him, saying, "You have already demonstrated repentance. For you have grieved, and God had compassion on you and has forgiven your transgression."

His heart was not at all comforted by these things, and once more he asked our Father to send him to that elder, "that holy man who consoled my passion." The holy and spiritual Abba Bishoi said to him, "That prophet, the elder to whom you went, has gone to his rest. Nonetheless, go to the east of the city of Antinoë. You will find a mortuary chapel facing the desert with its door open. Enter and you will find three dead men reposed together. For this mortuary chapel is the burial place of those prophets who were well-pleasing to God in monasteries and cities. As the time came for each one of them to depart, he would go up to this place and entrust his soul into God's hands. So enter there and put your hand on the one lying in the middle, and as he rises, he will speak with you."

74. The disciple went and found [45v] the three sleepers, just as our father had told him. And he put his hand on the one in the middle and spoke to him in this manner, "Holy Abba Bishoi says to you, 'Rise up,' so I may speak with you."

The dead prophet immediately rose up and said to the disciple, "Did I not already tell you to obey your master? Why are you lacking faith to such an extent? If, indeed, you had faith, I would tell you that whatever is accepted from Abba Bishoi, is accepted from Christ, and whoever does not obey that virtuous man, does not obey Christ, the Son of the living God. Get up now and go to your father, and obey him in everything he commands you, because he is the one who supplicates the Lord on your behalf." [The prophet] said this and lay back in his place.

The disciple returned to our father Abba Bishoi and relayed everything the prophet had said to him, while he was amazed and contrite on account of what he had seen and heard. He remained in fear and trembling of the word of Abba Bishoi, and he obeyed him all the days of his life.

Therefore, let no one lose faith, or disbelieve these things, or deny them. For the Lord said with his mouth, "Whoever believes in me, the works that I do, he will also do; and [he will do] more than these."[148]

Bishoi intervenes to absolve two young monks of false charges

75. Now two sibling monks heard of the virtue of Abba Bishoi. They rose up and went to him. They entreated him and said, "If you would,[149] our father, receive us so that we may be under the protection of your prayers. Guide our souls and advance them."

Our father joyfully received them because of his great love for humanity. And he allowed them [to stay] with him for many days, while he exhorted them and taught them how to please God. Afterward, our father wanted to retreat from among people, and to remain in solitude to fulfill his service [46r] to God in stillness, and to advance in his way of life. He said to those two brothers, "Rise; go enter this desert. Live in solitude and occupy yourselves with prayer and with reading the Scriptures."

They responded, "To whom will we go, our father? The words of life are with you, holy one of the Lord."[150] He said to them, "Indeed, go; for a monk is not perfected without stillness." They said to him, "Direct us, then, our father, to where we should go." He said to them, "Go to the desert of Tkow";[151] and he prayed over them. They received his blessing and departed for the desert of Tkow, and dwelt in it as he had commanded them.

One day, thieves came and entered the cell of one of the brothers and stole all of his possessions. Now there dwelt in that desert a certain elder who had been deceived by Satan. He was teaching that he could tell people about what they had lost, and he would say to them, "It was an angel who informed me about their [location]." And so the head of the monastery rose up, went to that elder, and said to him, "Our father, tell me who robbed the cell of that brother?"

The deceiving elder said to him, "Those two brothers who have come here recently, and have dwelt in the desert; they are the ones who took his [handi]works." All the brothers were convinced of this, and they rose up with the head of the monastery, and arrested those two brothers and imprisoned them as thieves.

Now our spiritual father, the Lord's prophet, Abba Bishoi, learned of this by the Spirit; [that is,] he was informed of the trial that came upon those brothers. He rose up and quickly traveled up south to the desert of Tkow. He found those brothers imprisoned, and said to the head of the monastery, "These men are not the thieves." The head of the monastery said to him, "An elder, a seer, told me about them." [46v] The elder [Abba Bishoi] said to him, "Assemble all the brothers for me." They assembled, and that elder was among them. When they saw our father, all of them bowed down to him and were blessed by him. Then the holy Abba Bishoi said to them, "What evil have these two foreigners done among you that you have imprisoned them?" That elder said to him, "[It is] because they stole and took away the possessions of one of the brothers."

Our father sighed in his heart and said to the elder, "If you would,[152] confess that you have been deceived by these revelations." The elder said to him, "I have not been deceived; I have only spoken the truth." Saint Abba Bishoi said to him, "If you would, confess that you were tempted, and disclose the truth [of the matter]."

The brothers, then, because they knew that Abba Bishoi was a true prophet and a spiritual man, put that elder to shame. And his heart shuddered as he said, "Indeed, demons have deceived me." As he said this, a spirit of Satan came out of him in the form of a sow, with its tusks protruding from its mouth. It charged the elder to injure him, but our holy father Abba Bishoi rebuked it, and it immediately vanished. When all the brothers saw this, they knelt and bowed down before him—with that elder among them.

They said, "Absolve us, our holy father; indeed, God dwells in you." Immediately, they released those two brothers who were imprisoned. And by the Holy Spirit who was in him, our father said to the head of the monastery, "Go to such and such a place, and you will find what was stolen from the brother." But he did not reveal who committed the theft. Moreover, he bound him with an oath, "Do not tell anyone what I revealed to you about the location of the stolen items." With this, he had driven vainglory out of himself. Right away the head of the monastery went and found [the items] just as our father had told him, and so they [47r] glorified God who dwells in his saints.

Bishoi teaches about anger

[ܙ]. So our father was mighty in his way of life and virtuous, patient, not given to anger, and serene. A certain brother accompanied by a youth[153] came to him, and he remained with the elder for a few days. But that youth went about here and there, and he greatly offended the brothers. Seeing him act in this manner, they entreated our father and said to him, "Admonish this [youth], father, because he offends us." The brothers hoped that he would rebuke and punish him, but [Abba Bishoi] did not speak with him.

Again, the brothers said to him, "Reprimand this youth and whip him so that he may not offend us." He responded to them, "No, my sons, it is not my place to reprimand him." [Then] one of the brothers went to whip him, but the elder would not permit him. He said to them, "If I considered doing this, I would lose everything I have labored for all the days of my life." The brothers said to him, "What would you lose?"

He said to them, "My willpower against giving in to anger. For if I spoke with this person in anger, I would lose all my labors. What, then, would I gain by reprimanding him if I should lose what I have?"

By this, our father taught us that we should not admonish a disciple who is not our own,[154] and should not be angry with him when he transgresses. As for a disciple who is our own, that is, a son, Scripture says, "Discipline your son with an iron rod; he will not die from a blow, and his soul will bless you."[155] For if you do not discipline your sons, their souls will be lost.

Bishoi as an abbot

[η]. Now, the Lord came to our father at all times and spoke with him because of his purity, chastity, and holiness. One time, the Lord said to him, "There will be a monastery for you in the desert of Scetis and many souls will congregate in it, offering the oblation[156] in your name. And you will be [47v] the father of many brothers forever. Amen."

The holy one said to him, "Excuse me [from this duty], my Lord; I am an old man and I am unable to take on this service. Such a task belongs to holy men who keep your commandments, and I am a sinner."

Nonetheless, the Lord gathered a multitude of brothers to dwell with him, and he clothed some of them with the monastic habit, and they dwelt in caves around him. He taught them to constantly fear the Lord and to read the Scriptures and the psalms. He used to say to them, "My sons, work with your hands so that you may live, and so that from your work you are able to give alms for your souls."[157]

Abba Bishoi teaches a disgruntled monk about work

[θ]. Now one of the brothers was sitting and listening to our father teaching the brothers, exhorting them to work with their hands; he reflected and said in his heart, "If only our father had worked with his hands, he would know the hardship of work, and would cease urging and pressuring us to work."[158]

Our father perceived this in the Spirit and said to him, "My son, these things you are criticizing and grumbling against me about—teaching the brothers and exhorting them to persist in the work of their hands, reading Scripture and psalms, services and prayers—do you not know that I am anxious for your souls before God at all times?"

When the brother heard this, a braided cord[159] fell from his hands, and he bowed down before our father, venerated him, and said, "Forgive me, father." Abba Bishoi said to him, "I, my son, even I work. Indeed, the Lord knows that since I came to this place I have not ceased working night and day while I completed my prayers. I labor with my hands, and weaken my body so that it may not overtake me and I be tormented there in Gehenna.[160]

For whoever toils here with his body, and weakens it by fasting, prayer, vigils, reading, and manual labor, [48r] is freed from Gehenna, but whoever rests his body here, fornication will overwhelm him and conquer him, and he will inherit the eternal Gehenna."

When the brothers heard this, they bowed down to him and said, "Forgive us, our holy father; for we cannot perform all these [labors]. For your soul rejoices greatly in spiritual works and is strengthened by them."

Our father performed the multitude of his deeds privately, so they might remain unknown. Thus, it can be easily said many times that he is more honored than many other holy men whose virtues are known.

The hierarchy of the four great monasteries

[ı]. However, while many Scetians, that is, virtuous ascetics [from Scetis], lived in this desert, we know [only] the names of those who drew intimately[161] close to God and have labored, and their memory will last forever and ever. Some among these [ascetics], by the command of God, have had monasteries built after their names, and churches at those locations, and radiant altars that illuminate the world more than the sun, upon which heavenly oblations are offered daily, granting life to our souls and bodies. These, the chosen among God's elect, he has revealed and rendered them a [safe] harbor for the whole world, to deliver the souls of whoever comes to them with upright hearts, like cities set apart as places of refuge. The first of these [monasteries] is that of the holy chosen one, the prophet and friend of God, the founder of the spiritual law, the great one, our father Abba Macarius, whose name became renowned throughout the whole earth. He became a guide,[162] a holy father, and the spiritual master to all who live in this desert. After him, I, the insignificant John, not to praise myself, not that, I have written [only] what the Lord willed, and what our holy father Abba Bemoi had foretold. Next [48v] is our holy father Abba Bishoi, whose excellent way of life we are narrating. After this are our holy fathers: the Roman fathers,[163] those whom our father Abba Macarius guided and taught the life of the holy monastic habit. These four holy [monasteries] shine in the desert of Scetis like precious stones, pearls sparkling in the darkness. They are like the four disciples who preached the gospel; those who evangelized the whole world.

On the position of Bishoi's monastery in Wadi al-Natrun

[ⲕ]. Moreover, we find it written in the gospels that Christ chose seventy-two disciples and he sent them to preach everywhere.[164] Their names were not revealed to us, because earlier he chose twelve and called them disciples,[165] and told us their names and identified them to us. In like manner, then, here also God has revealed the names of these four holy [places], who[se saints] are much greater than the rest of the other saints, as I have said previously. [The Lord] spread their fame throughout the whole world.

The healing well at Bishoi's monastery
[λ]. Moreover, God gave a great gift to the monastery of the holy Abba Bishoi in [the following way].[166] Barbarians had attacked forty-nine elder monks, near the great tower called Biamūn. They attacked and killed them all. Then, they changed direction to go to their country in the west. When they arrived at the water well at the monastery of Abba Bishoi, they rested along with their horses near the well. They took their swords, covered as they were with the blood of those monk-martyrs whom they had slain, and washed them in that well. [The water] from it became a cure for all diseases until this very day, for the praise of God, who is pleased by his saints.

Bishoi and Paul accept a disciple
[μ]. As our father aged, he struggled a great deal in the spirit, as if he were just beginning his monastic vocation,[167] and he loved stillness and excelled in his way of life. He rose up and went to Abba Paul of Tamma, who lived on a certain hill, and prayed before the Lord unceasingly, performing innumerable labors. He[168] had a son, Abba Sīraws, who came [49r] from the city of Ansina. He would faithfully go to Abba Paul and Abba Bishoi to receive their[169] blessing. In faith, he desired to touch their clothing to be blessed by them,[170] and to follow their ways. Many times, he would come to the wilderness and remain in stillness in it. And when he came to these holy men, they saw the divine blessing upon him, and they said to him, "Your body will not separate from our bodies in this world, nor will your soul separate from our souls in the world to come." And they told him, "God will establish a monastery in your name." Thus, he humbled himself to them all the days of his life.

The godly Bishoi and holy Paul
76. Now Abba Paul loved Abba Bishoi and even humbled himself to him. Our father Abba Bishoi would constantly go to Abba Paul and they would speak from the Holy Scriptures like Elijah and Elisha, the holy prophets. For it is written, "The spirit of the prophets is subject to prophets."[171] Abba Bishoi said to Abba Paul, "Brother Paul, we must labor a little as long as we remain in the world, before we depart from it." Abba Paul said to him, "Pray for me, my holy father, that I may implement[172] all you have instructed me, and not hide any of my private [thoughts] from you." Abba Bishoi said to him, "Let us worship God with our whole heart, for he had mercy upon us and brought us to this most pleasant time. And [let us] work with the five

talents, which the Lord will increase for us, and not be disheartened like the one who had the one talent,[173] and anger the Lord against us that he should place our portion with the hypocrites. Rather may we stand before him with a pure heart that he might remember our labors and have mercy upon us." Abba Paul said to him, "Pray for me, that I may struggle with all my might."

77A. Thus, they became at that time like a [protective] brass wall to all the monks who came to be blessed by them, and they prayed especially for the deliverance and preservation of the world. We also ask them now to remember us before God Christ that he may have mercy upon us when we stand before him.

Bishoi and Paul in the cave cell

78A. Now as the time of the departure of our father Abba Bishoi drew near, for his life was long and he became very old, he offered up his body as an acceptable offering to the Lord.

He said to me, "As many years as I have lived in the desert of Scetis, likewise I lived in the desert with the monastic fathers[174] in the south.[175] I went [49v] to them in faith, and I would consult with them, and praise God." He also lived with Abba Paul in the desert for many years, as he sanctified the Lord. The divine and excellent deeds he performed [then] were innumerable.

Sayings of Bishoi

77B. Abba Bishoi would say thus, "Of all the virtues, there is none like placing your word below the word of your friend, and placing what is his before what is yours."

Again, he said, "Those years I have spent at the monastery before anyone knew of my way of life are the ones that I am confident I will receive a reward for, but those [years] since people knew of me, I am not relying on anything from them."

They say about him that among all the deeds he performed, if anyone knew of it,[176] he would abandon it and take up another. Thus, at all times he would flee from vainglory. He said that as vainglory takes hold of an individual, it eats up all of his fruits; yet, many are those who love it, but this holy man fled from it. He had relied upon God since his youth, and [thus] he inherited the kingdom in heaven and attained the good eternal things.

Death of Bishoi

78B. As [Abba Bishoi] became old and increased in his days, his body grew weak from advanced age, and the Lord wanted to give rest to his servant and release him from the prison of this sorrowful world. He passed away on the eighth day of the Egyptian month of Abib, which is the second of Tammuz.[177] The Lord received his holy soul, and angels came out to meet him, rejoicing for him and accompanying him until they brought him into the kingdom on high with splendor and honor. Then the brothers who dwelt with him wrapped his holy body with great honor, and they buried him in Minyat Duwany,[178] while praising God and glorifying him.

Now, if someone implores and asks us about the years he spent in the desert, let him know that we do not know them. Indeed, we asked him on many occasions to tell us about them, but he did not [50r] want to, because he eschewed the honor of people. Nonetheless, we were told by trustworthy individuals that he lived sixty years in the desert, worshiping the Lord by night and day, praising his name. A portion of those years he dwelt in Upper Egypt,[179] that is, the Thebaid. He performed many [other] great wondrous deeds, which we have not written due to the deficiency of faith. God alone knows of [those deeds], and he rewarded him. Thus, we have written for you but a few of the many distinguished and virtuous deeds of the chosen and perfect one, our holy father Abba Bishoi. For the glory of his Lord, let us imitate his holy way of life, and follow in his steps.

Translation of relics
79. Now Abba Paul also departed on the seventh of Bābah, of the months of the Copts, which is the fourth of Teshrin I.[180] He died and was buried in a desert cave.[181] When Abba Sīraws learned of the passing of these saints, he immediately boarded a boat and came to Minyat Duwany. He took the body of the holy Abba Bishoi and placed it on the boat to bring him to Ansina, and place him in the monastery he had built. They sailed in the sea,[182] but when they reached the place where the body of Abba Paul was, the boat halted in the middle of the sea and would not proceed. They remained for two days in this manner. The sailors on the boat labored to make it sail, but it did not move from its spot.

Now there was a certain spiritual elder who lived in a cave at that location, called Abba Jeremiah. He rose up and went to the boat and said to the people in it, "Do you know why your boat is not moving?" They said to him, "No." He said to them, "It is on account of the body of Abba Paul of Tamma, because he and Abba Bishoi promised [50v] each other, while they were alive, that their bodies would remain in the same place in this world, and their spirits in the house of God." When the holy Abba Sīraws heard this, he took some people with him and went to the wilderness and brought the body of Abba Paul from where it was, and placed it with them on the boat. They sailed and arrived at Antinoë, that is

Ansina, and, immediately, he carried them to his monastery. He adorned them with great honor in expensive wrappings, and he kept them in befitting splendor.

People would come to be blessed by them and to embrace their holy bodies. And whoever had a disease, as he approached their bodies, would be cured. Faithful, honest people who came from the city of Ansina to the Monastery of the holy Abba Antony to pray had reported that to us;[183] it was they who informed me of these things.

Conclusion and doxology

80. When I heard the news about the repose of the God-loving one, the holy Abba Bishoi, I mourned him greatly. However, my heart was comforted in that he attained the good things he longed for, and I thanked the Lord and praised his name. Immediately, I sought to quickly write to you, God-loving ones, a few of the words and deeds that my eyes have seen and my ears have heard, for the benefit of your souls and for the commemoration of our holy father Abba Bishoi, who, indeed, went on to the kingdom on high.

Let us all be worthy of the prayer of our father, and let us render glory and praise to our Lord Jesus Christ with his compassionate Father and his life-giving Holy Spirit, now and always, and forever.
Amen.[184]

Notes

1   On this recension and the manuscripts, also see the general introduction, 15–16.
2   See the appendix in Monica Blanchard, "Beh Isho' Kamulaya's Syriac Discourses on the Monastic Way of Life: Edition, English Translation, and Introduction" (PhD diss., Catholic University of America, 2001).
3   See the general introduction, 15–16, and the following paragraph. These paragraphs were likely in the Salomon manuscript as well.
4   Paul Bedjan, *Acta Martyrum et Sanctorum*, vol. 3 (Leipzig: Otto Harrassowitz, 1892), 587. (Hereafter: Bedjan.)
5   V. Scheil, "Restitution de deux textes dans le récit syriaque de la vie de Mar Bischoi (ed. Bedjan)," *Zeitschrift für Assyriologie und verwandte Gebiete* 15 (1900), 104–106.
6   The contents of the manuscript are listed at http://archivesetmanuscrits.bnf.fr/ark:/12148/cc101803w; the manuscript is accessible at http://gallica.bnf.fr/ark:/12148/btv1b53115223f, accessed August 1, 2017.
7   See the general introduction, 2, 7, and 15.

8   For instance, Syr. 236 preserves an abbreviated version of ¶65; though relying on the Salomon manuscript, Bedjan provided the longer recension attested here.
9   This is a rough guide to the Bedjan edition (in italic) vis-à-vis BnF Syr. 236 and the Salomon Manuscript: p. *572*/¶¶1–3, Syr. 236; *573*/4, Syr. 236; *574*/5–6, Syr. 236; *575*/7–8, Syr. 236; *576*/9–11, Syr. 236; *577*/12, Syr. 236; *578*/13, Syr. 236; *579*/14, Syr. 236; *580*/15, Syr. 236; *581*/16–18, Syr. 236; *582*/19–20, Syr. 236; *583*/21, Syr. 236; *584*/32–35, Syr. 236; *585*/35 cont., Syr. 236; *586*/41, Sal. MS; *587*/41 cont., Sal. MS; *588*/42–43, Sal. MS; *589*/44–46, Sal. MS; *590*/47, Syr. 236; *591*/48, Syr. 236; *592*/49, Sal. MS; *593*/50, Sal. MS; *594*/51, Sal. MS; *595*/52 | | end 60–61, Sal. MS; *596*/62–63, Sal. MS; *597*/53A-54, Syr. 236; *598*/64, Syr. 236; *599*/65, Syr. 236; *600*/65 cont., Syr. 236; *601*/65 cont., Syr. 236; *602*/66–67, Syr. 236; *603*/α, Sal. MS; *604*/β, γ, Sal. MS; *605*/δ, ε, Sal. MS; *606*/68, Sal. MS; *607*/68 cont., Sal. MS; *608*/69A-B, Syr. 236; *609*/70, Syr. 236; *610*/71, Syr. 236; *611*/72–73, Syr. 236; *612*/74, Syr. 236; *613*/75, Sal. MS; *614*/75 cont., Sal. MS; *615*/75 cont., Sal. MS; *616*/ζ, Sal. MS; *617*/η, Syr. 236; *618*/θ, Sal. MS; *619*/78B, Syr. 236; *620*/80, Syr. 236.
10 Or "chaste."
11 MS A reads "their," but then switches to "his"; MS E retains the masculine singular, "his," throughout.
12 That is, July 15.
13 Heb 11:38.
14 "Christ" is lacking in MS A, where there appears to be an incomplete correction made to the text. The correct reading is preserved in MS B.
15 Rom 1:9.
16 Lit. "from time to time."
17 Lit. "these things."
18 "Churches" and "alms" are plural in the text.
19 Perhaps Tarabia in the western Delta, as M. Blanchard has suggested; see S. Timm, *Das christlich-koptische Ägypten in arabischer Zeit* (Wiesbaden: Dr. Ludwig Reichert Verlag, 1984–92), 6:2522–30.
20 MS B reads "Besīnīshyā"; MS C reads "Basinbīyā."
21 Cf. 2 Cor 12:9.
22 Lit. "set his face/himself on the fear/worship of God."
23 That is, Scetis.
24 This is the literal Arabic translation (*mizān al-qulūb*) of the Coptic etymology: Scetis < Cop. Shihēt: *shi* "to weigh" or "measure," and *bēt* "heart" or "mind."
25 The name is not vocalized in MSS A or D, but it is in the others: MS B, "Bemoi"; MS C, "Bamawi"; MS E, "Bamwa"; MS F, "Bimuḥ" or

"Bimuch"—the last letter is a *ḥēt*, a likely misreading of the *yod*, which is attested otherwise.
26 Or "forbade."
27 Or "appearance"; "demeanor."
28 Or "satiated"; lit. "watered."
29 See Prov 10:8.
30 1 Thes 5:17.
31 Ps 119:103.
32 Ps 1:3.
33 This corrupted form is likely "Abā Bāshaya." See the general introduction, 3.
34 Lit. "I, the insignificant one, remained with the one who is a brother to me, Abba Bishoi." MS B adds "John" after "insignificant one."
35 Although MSS A, C, E, F read "us," MS B, fol. 114r, reads "to me," which is the preferred reading here given that the tradition referenced involved only John the Little.
36 MS F (Bedjan, 576) adds: "On Sundays, he partook of the holy mysteries of the body and blood of Christ."
37 Here and below, Syr. *shelya*, which is often synonymous with Gr. *hēsychía*, hesychia.
38 Or "hermit/monk."
39 Or "deliverance"; "refuge."
40 Gr. *katástasis*; Geoffrey W.H. Lampe, *A Patristic Greek Lexicon* (Oxford: Clarendon, 1961), 720(B.5).
41 Lit. "fear."
42 Syr. *iqāre*.
43 Heb 12:23.
44 See Jn 15:5; 14:12.
45 See n. 60 to the English translation of the Arabic recension (chapter five).
46 On this theme, see 1 Cor 1:25–31; 2 Cor 12:9.
47 "Ministry," or "service," includes monastic and liturgical offices.
48 I.e., hospitality.
49 Lit. "gift."
50 MS C reads "saved me."
51 ¶¶22–31 are in MS C, though Bedjan omits them from his edition; see the general introduction, 16–17.
52 Or "worshiped."
53 This is an oath formula attested in the Old Testament; e.g., 1 Sam 14:45.
54 Lit. "her," that is, the soul of the disciple.
55 See Ps 99:6.
56 Jn 15:13.

57 Lit. "gift."
58 See Ps 119:2; 112:1. Lit. "man," Syr. *gabra*.
59 Heb 11:38.
60 Vowels were added to the text here. Unfortunately, there is a smudge in the middle of the word in MS A. MS B reads "Būsuy," and MS F reads "Basqi." It is not clear what "Basway" refers to; shortly below, the text notes that it was in the Thebaid, in Middle Egypt. The Greek text vaguely states that the elder lived "in a village near the borders of Egypt." MS E reads the word as the proper name of the solitary.
61 Gr. *túpos*.
62 Or "Hieracas"; lit. "Arqā."
63 Lit. "Paraclete," that is, the Holy Spirit; see Jn 14:16, 26; 15:26; 16:7.
64 The summary demonstrates knowledge of the *Life of Macarius*, ¶6 (Eng. trans. Tim Vivian, *St. Macarius the Spiritbearer* [Crestwood, NY: St Vladimir's Seminary Press, 2004]); cf. *Life of Paul of Tamma* (Ar. Long Rec.: Awad Wadi, "La recensione lunga della vita araba di Paolo di Tamma, presentazione, edizione e indice." *SOCC* 38 [2005]: 115–78), ¶¶85–92.
65 Cf. Mt 5:2.
66 Gen 1:1–2.
67 Is 61:1.
68 Ps 104:30.
69 See Ezek 37:5.
70 From Gr. *arrabōn*.
71 Cf. Jn 1:32–34.
72 1 Cor 12:3.
73 Lit. "clothed with God."
74 Reads *qnumi* (sg. *qnuma*): "hypostasis," "person."
75 Dan 7:9.
76 The proof depends upon the contrast to "thrones" in the plural and the fact that only one person takes his seat.
77 Mt 28:19. Here, they are identified, but "name" is singular.
78 Text reads Bīfīmūn; Greek reads Poemen.
79 MS B: Tamoneqon; MS F: Temoniqon.
80 MS A: Ṭamaway; MS B: Ṭamoi; MS F: Ṭamios.
81 Here and below, MS E reads "child."
82 Scetis and Nitria are often conflated as one region.
83 See Mt 18:2–4; Mk 10:13–16.
84 Here and in MS B, but MS F reads "him."
85 Mt 25:21, 23.
86 Or "troubled," "weary."
87 Cf. 1 Cor 10:13.

88 Cf. Ex 33:11.
89 Or "in bondage/enslaved."
90 Cf. Gal 4:1–7. These last few sentences are identical in MSS A and B, but they differ from MS E and the Ethiopic text.
91 Perhaps, "a true son"; lit. "a son-heir."
92 This sentence is attested only in MS A, B, and E, and in no other recension. On Apollo and Anoup, see Tim Vivian, "Monks, Middle Egypt, and Metanoia: The *Life of Phib by Papohe the Steward* (Translation and Introduction)," *Journal of Early Christian Studies* 7, no. 4 (1999): 547–71.
93 Only MS F, the Salomon Manuscript, adds "whose name was Ephrem." See the general introduction, 14. On Ephrem in Coptic literature, see Monica J. Blanchard, "Saint Ephrem's Coptic Friend, Apa Bishoi," *The Harp* 16 (2003): 43–55; and her "The Coptic Heritage of St. Ephrem the Syrian," in *Acts of the Fifth International Congress of Coptic Studies, Washington D.C., 12–15 August 1992*, ed. T. Orlandi and D.W. Johnson (Rome: C.I.M., 1993), 37–51.
94 MS F adds: "He was skilled in the knowledge and interpretation of Scripture and in the contemplation [*theoria*] of the Spirit."
95 Lit. "show your face before."
96 Since the Nile flows north, traveling south in Egypt is typically described as traveling "up."
97 Lit. "he." MS F reads "Ephrem."
98 See Jn 1:47.
99 In recension *SA Syr2*, according to MS F (Bedjan, 595), the contiguous text reads: "for he has walked scarcely a mile. Our holy father replied and said, 'Glory to your holy name'"—thus concealing a large gap from the end of ¶52 to the latter portion of ¶60. In that manuscript, the text should be read: "[¶52] for he has walked scarcely a mile . . . . [¶60] . . . Our holy father replied." MS B provides a slightly different, and likely earlier, form of *SA Syr2*. At the end of fol. 120r, it includes most of ¶52, concluding with "he has traveled more than eighteen miles," and then (fol. 120v) jumps to the middle of ¶60: "naked due to what the demons inflicted upon him." Some of the missing paragraphs (¶¶53A–57) are positioned elsewhere in Bedjan's edition based on the Salomon Manuscript; see Bedjan, 597–98.
100 The gap that demarcates Recension *SA Syr2*, according to MS B, begins after these words.
101 Cf. Ps 33:18.
102 Syr. *krīsṭyono*.
103 On this anachronistic passage, see the general introduction, 12.
104 2 Cor 5:21; Heb 4:15; 7:26; 1 Pet 2:22; 1 Jn 3:5.
105 Meaning a young, inexperienced monk.
106 See 1 Pet 5:8.

107 It is here that *SA Syr2*, as represented in MS B, resumes; top of fl. 120v.
108 Lit. "story"; "account"; "matter."
109 MS A and B read "his"; only MS E reads "your," which is the preferable reading.
110 It is here that the gap in *SA Syr2*, as represented in MS F, comes to an end. The odd transition is somewhat mitigated by the insertion of the word "glory": hence, "Our holy father answered and said, 'Glory to your holy name.'"
111 See n. 53, above.
112 Lit. "turn away from him."
113 MS F adds "John."
114 Or "philanthropy."
115 MS A reads "to him," but MS B retains the preferred reading, "to me."
116 Gr. *parrhesia*: "to speak confidently" or "candidly," but also, "boldness," "confidence," or "assurance."
117 MS B: "Pnita Datrowy"; MS F reads "Afaq Tarway."
118 MSS B and F read "her."
119 MSS B and E read "remind," which is the original reading in MS A, but it is crossed out and "inform" is in the margin.
120 Cf. 1 Tim 2:14.
121 Gen 39:20.
122 1 Kgs 19:3–4.
123 Judges 16:21.
124 1 Cor 10:7–8; cf. Ex 32:6; Num 25:1–9.
125 Mt 14:1–12.
126 1 Kgs 11:1–8.
127 See Mt 26:69–75; see Maged S.A. Mikhail, *The Legacy of Demetrius of Alexandria: The Form and Function of Hagiography in Late Antique and Islamic Egypt* (New York: Routledge, 2016), 66–69.
128 Jn 15:12–14.
129 Lit. *krīstonoutha*.
130 That is, in a burial shroud.
131 Or "remember [that is, pray for] that dead man."
132 There is an abrupt switch in grammatical person here from third to first person.
133 Or "where there is no church." "Assembly," "gathering," and "church" are all the same word here.
134 Or "churches."
135 Syriac: M-r-i-s (Mārīs) < Coptic *marēs*. See Timm, *Das christlich-koptische Ägypten*, 4:1590–92.
136 "Antinoë, which is Ansina," is also in MSS B and E.

137 Lit. "love of the brothers."
138 Lit. "namely," "that is."
139 That is, they will cater to him, or treat him with the utmost respect.
140 See n. 135, above.
141 Gen 18.
142 MS A reads "brothers," though, given the remainder of the account, the plural is likely a mistake. MSS B, C, and E lack the word altogether.
143 Mt 22:39.
144 While the Syriac text uses different words, the Gharshuni translator rendered this phrase with variations of the same verb: *fa-qāllā al-ṣiddīq al-ṣādiq, ṣaddiqnī ya ibnī*.
145 MSS E and F read "my son."
146 Or "foolishness."
147 The phrase is also in MSS B, C, and E.
148 See Jn 14:12.
149 Lit. "Do love/charity"; i.e., "please." This expression, likely of Greek origin, is also common in Christian Arabic hagiography.
150 See Jn 6:68.
151 Here and below: Daqū.
152 See n. 149, above.
153 MS F reads "child"; cf. Gr. *paîs*.
154 Lit. "our son."
155 See Prov 23:13–14.
156 Or "Eucharist."
157 Tobit 12:9. In general, see Tobit 2; 12; Sirach 3:30; Mt 6:2–4; Acts 10:4, 31.
158 The second half of this sentence is lacking in MS B.
159 Syr. *sīro*; MS C reads "knife."
160 See 1 Cor 9:27.
161 Lit. "greatly."
162 Lit. "path."
163 That is, Maximus and Domitius.
164 See Lk 10:1.
165 Mt 10:1–2; Mk 3:14.
166 Lit. "such as this."
167 Lit. "his way of life."
168 This is probably Paul, but the pronoun is ambiguous.
169 MS A reads "his"; MS B "their."
170 See Mt 9:20–21.
171 1 Cor 14:32.
172 Lit. "receive."
173 See Mt 25:14–30.

174 Lit. "fathers of the *iskīm*/monastic habit."
175 See n. 135, above.
176 That is, a particular deed or ascetic practice.
177 That is, July 15.
178 MS B reads "Mūnya Dūnī." "Munya" is the Arabic "Minya[t]" (< Gr. *monē*), but Duwany remains unknown.
179 See n. 135, above.
180 That is, October 17.
181 Gr. *antronikē*.
182 MS B "river."
183 See the general introduction, 5, on the importance of this sentence.
184 Scribal note: "The account of our holy father Abba Bishoi has concluded by the prayers of the Mother of God Mary and all the saints. Christ, Son of the living and holy God, have mercy on the children of the holy church. Amen. Amen. It is completed. Lord, by the prayers of Abba Bishoi, help us. Amen."

5

THE ARABIC *LIFE OF BISHOI* IN TRANSLATION

Manuscript Family C
Recension WN2 Ar1

Translated by Maged S.A. Mikhail

Introduction

All currently accessible Arabic manuscripts for *LBsh* adhere to *Rec. WN2 Ar1*. In 2012, Bartolomeo Pirone published a very detailed edition of *LBsh* based on four manuscripts.[1] For his main text, Pirone relied on BnF Ar. 4796 (nineteenth century),[2] which, in spite of its date, retains an early version of this recension; moreover, it was the manuscript Evelyn-White used in his *Monasteries of the Wadi 'N-Natrun*.[3] Having access to Pirone's edition and BnF Ar. 4796, this study relies upon Göttingen Ar. 114 (sixteenth century), which preserves earlier readings than those in BnF Ar. 4796. Still, Pirone's edition and BnF Ar. 4796 helped to clarify several readings in the Göttingen manuscript (and vice versa); such readings are duly noted in the editorial apparatus.

A third manuscript, Coptic Museum (New) 30B (eighteenth century),[4] reflects the evolution of this recension. The bulk of CM 30B survives (forty of fifty folios), though its quires have been rebound out of sequence, and several folios were lost in the process.[5] Still, it retains much of the wording of the other manuscripts, though it consistently makes alterations that clarify enigmatic passages, correct odd grammar, and replace archaic vocabulary with more common equivalents.

Other witnesses to this recension include MS Deir Abū Maqār Hag. 19 (Zanetti, 385), some portions of which have been published.[6] In his study, Fr. Zakariyā al-Baramūsī commented on three Arabic manuscripts at the Syrian Monastery: *Maymir* 290 (AD 1720), 308 (AD 1598?), and an unnumbered manuscript. All three adhere to *Rec. WN2 Ar1*. Furthermore, there are the manuscripts utilized in the editions by Fathers Mīṣā'īl Baḥr and Bishūy Kāmil, which were discussed in the general introduction, along with the recent (selective) edition of BnF Ar. 4796 by Fr. Makarī al-Bahnasawī.[7] Finally, Yūsuf Ḥabīb had read several manuscripts of *LBsh* at the Syrian and

Barāmūs monasteries.[8] It is difficult to draw definitive conclusions from his study, though it is clear that *Rec. WN2 Ar.1* dominates all the texts he accessed. Even ¶v is unattested in the manuscripts Ḥabīb surveyed, though he relayed the account based on Fr. Ṣamū'īl al-Suryānī's study (see appendix).[9]

Translation notes

Biblical verses have been translated as they appear in the Arabic text. When used as a title, *abū* (< Gr./Cop. *abba* or Cop. *apa*) has been rendered as "Abba," while "Anba" (< Gr./Cop. *abba*) has been retained as such. The nearly synonymous *barr* and *ṣiddīq* have been consistently translated as "pious" and "righteous." Finally, the ubiquitous *qāla*, "he said," has been translated with some latitude.

Editorial conventions

Göt.	Göttingen Ar. 114, fols. 150v–180r (16th c.), the text for this edition. An edition of this manuscript is forthcoming.
BnF	Bibliothèque nationale, Ar. 4796, fols. 119r–169v (19th c.)
CM	Coptic Museum, New 30B, fols. 123r–161v (18th c.)
‹ ›	Reading attested in BnF
« »	Reading attested in CM
< >	An attested reading that is likely a scribal error
[ ]	Editorial addition(s)

The Arabic *Life of Bishoi*
(Göttingen Ar. 114, fols. 150v–180r)

[150v]
In the Name of the Father, the Son, and the Holy Spirit; one God.[10]

Let us begin with the assistance of God, and the excellence of his guidance, to write the way of life[11] and [spiritual] struggle[12] of our saintly father, the chaste ascetic, the brilliant light, our saintly father Abba Bishoi[13] from the Mountain of Shihīt.[14] May the Lord have mercy on us through his prayers.

It was written by the virtuous, saintly father, the hegumen John the Little,[15] who became [Abba Bishoi's] spiritual brother from the time he came to the Mountain of Shihīt and both came under the direction of Saint Anba Bamwah.[16] He wrote it after [Anba Bishoi's] repose, revealing how he began [acquiring] virtues, and the completion of his angelic life. His repose was on the eighth day of the month of Abīb.[17]

In the Peace of God. Amen.

Exordium
1. My beloved in the Lord, the beloved of God, my God, on to eternity, listen to me today as I speak about the gems[18] of this saint and his marvelous deeds. He who is perfect in the Lord God, this champion who is victorious in battle, our pious, righteous father, the great Anba Bishoi, who offered his soul and body as a sacrifice to the living God.[19] This ascetic, who is mighty in virtue and the great [spiritual] warfare[20] that accompanies monasticism. A martyr by his labors; [151r] this prophet who saw the Lord God on account of the purity of his body, and his wandering in deserts, caves, and holes in the ground for many years.[21] This evangelizing apostle, who saved many souls, and ushered them into the kingdom of our Master Jesus Christ.

2. God is my witness; I have not embellished the account I am relaying to you. Rather, what I have written to you is but a portion of what I have seen with my own eyes, «that it may»[22] profit your souls, and those who will come after you.

Bishoi's birth and parentage
3. «The parents of our father» were righteous people, prophets among their peers,[23] who worshiped God, loved the churches, and loved to give charity in a village called Shanshā,[24] among the districts of the Delta of

Egypt. They enjoyed an exceedingly good reputation for purity and the love of God. When God saw their piety, he graced them with seven sons.

Death of Bishoi's father: An angel appears to his mother

When their father passed away, their mother reared them. Our pious father Abba Bishoi was the youngest of his siblings. On account of the purity of his pious parents, his mother saw a vision at night. Her seven children were with her when the angel of the Lord appeared and said to her, "The Lord says to you, 'Give me one of your sons that he may become my servant all the days of his life.'" She said to him, "They all belong to the Lord, master; [151v] let him take as he pleases." The angel stretched out his hand and gripped the head of the pious Saint Abba Bishoi, and said, "This one is a good laborer for his Master." Nonetheless, his mother said to the angel, "Take a strong, handsome one; this one is weak and unfortunate." The angel replied, "The power of the Lord is perfected in the weak."[25] When the angel said this, he departed from her.[26]

Bishoi goes to Scetis

4. When Saint Abba Bishoi increased in physical stature, he sought to enter ⟨into worship⟩ with great fervor; he desired the venerable way of life of monasticism. Now at the time God had appointed for him to complete all his affairs, he drew the saint, our father Anba Bishoi, like a spotless lamb,[27] and took him up to the Mountain of Shihīt, and presented him to the great shepherd, the savior of souls, our saintly father Anba Bamwah. He, who became my spiritual father, a counselor, and a guide unto righteousness—I the wretched ⟨John⟩.

Bishoi, as Bamwah's disciple, advances spiritually

5. Saint Anba Bamwah joyfully received Anba Bishoi, and clothed him in the holy monastic habit. [Anba Bishoi] would observe the instructions and [monastic] canons that [Anba Bamwah] instructed him in faith and great humility of heart. [Anba Bishoi] was always contemplative,[28] and would often gaze at the face of the saintly elder, [152r] and [be inspired by] his stillness and the serenity of his worship of God. He was in awe and would praise the eternal God for [Anba Bamwah's] way of life, which resembled the life of angels.

Our father said to him, "My son, it is not the discipline of the brothers to gaze at the face of the saints. Rather, the discipline of monks is to cast your face toward the ground to discern the path you are negotiating, and to focus your thoughts on God at all times." 6. When Abba Bishoi heard this from our father Bamwah, he cast his face toward the ground, and continued [in this manner] for three years without seeing the face of anyone at all. Rather, he persisted in his heart in reading the Holy Scriptures of the Lord, the God of Israel, in order to water his soul with the words of the Holy Spirit, until what is written was fulfilled in him: "the wise of heart accepts all commandments."[29] He would pray without ceasing, according to the instruction of Paul the Apostle.[30] He persisted in fasting and night vigils, and he loved the words of the Lord more than honey or honeycomb.[31] This pious man, Abba Bishoi, increased daily like a tree planted by the rivers of the water of life, giving fruit in all seasons.[32]

7. Father Anba Bamwah loved him greatly. As for me, I was desirous of his worship of God, the extent of his asceticism, and the labor [by which he attained] virtues. [152v] His father[33] often called him by this name, "the Shining Father,"[34] and would comfort him with spiritual joy. When the blessed Abba Bamwah pleased God, his soul was reposed and he ascended on high to Christ, whose servant he was.

After Bamwah's death, John remains with Bishoi
8. We lived with each other, in spiritual love, at the same place. That which God had appointed for us through his divine plan; the place where I had planted the tree as our saintly father Anba Bamwah had commanded.[35]

Bishoi's spiritual disciplines
9. As for the revered Anba Bishoi, he would not eat except once a week, and he memorized a great deal from the Holy Scriptures. He spent much of his time reading from the prophet Jeremiah. Every time he would read, the prophet would come and comfort him, and explain to him the expressions and the meanings ‹of the words› of the Holy Spirit. 10. On several occasions, he would not eat for twelve days. His nourishment was bread and salt, and he would persist in his handiwork. Each day Abba Bishoi would embark upon great [spiritual] combat,[36] ascetic practices of various sorts [153r], and great rigor. He would perform the majority of his practices[37] in private, seeking solitude, and especially [seeking] to live alone. For God was determined to call him to become a safe ‹harbor›, and a [means of] salvation for many souls.

Bishoi and John separate
11. Hence, I said to him, "My God-loving brother, I see that you prefer solitude and seek seclusion. I, likewise, desire this same state. Nonetheless, if you desire to surpass Moses,[38] let us keep vigil this whole night, praying and persisting in vigil and [ascetic] labors until tomorrow. For we believe that God, the Compassionate One, will let us know what is beneficial." And that is what we did.

12. When the night had passed, immediately the angel of the Lord appeared, and said to us joyfully, "This is what the Lord says, 'Let each of you live by himself to fulfill the divine plan[39] God has prepared for you, for the salvation of your souls. As for you, John, remain in this place, and I will send to you a great multitude.'" «Then he said to Saint Anba Bishoi, "As for you, Bishoi, separate a short distance from your brother, and make for yourself a cell and live in it. And I will gather to you great multitudes as well.» You will have many [children] in that place, and your name will be set upon it," says the Lord, "and they will worship in it in the same manner as the Powers on high. [153v] In this manner, I will fulfill what I have promised the leader of the congregation[40] in the wilderness that belongs to me," says the Lord, "he who is truly revered, the pious Abba Macarius."[41] After the angel said this, he departed from us. In this manner, Saint Anba Bishoi departed by the command of the Lord God, and built for himself a cell over the rock,[42] approximately two miles to the north of me, and he lived at that place.

Now the Lord was with him in all his deeds. He took on many [ascetic] practices[43] in that place to the extent that news of his miracles and way of life spread throughout the whole region. As a result, many would come to him eagerly seeking the holy words of monasticism, and he would fashion them into obedient soldiers for Christ the King. They became [as] spiritual branches to him—a chosen people, elect ascetics who loved one another in perfect love without hypocrisy. This blessed man became an example to them in word and deed.

I would constantly go to him and divulge my thoughts, and on various occasions he also came [154r] to me and provided me with his beneficial words in my cell, <and likewise in his holy cell>.[44]

The Savior appears to Bishoi

13. One day, our pious father Anba Bishoi was sitting in my cell working on his handiwork when, suddenly, he stood up—I mean the righteous Anba Bishoi—and he went out to his cell. Then our Lord Jesus Christ came and said to him, "Rejoice, my pure chosen one, Anba Bishoi." Immediately, he worshiped him, and the Lord said, "Do you see this mountain? I will fill it with monks as [densely] as dove towers,[45] and they will worship me in it." The saint said to him, "Lord, and you will sustain them in this wilderness?" [The Lord] said to him, "The truth, the truth I say to you.[46] If they truly love one another, keep my commandments and precepts, and work in simplicity as one, I will grant them their livelihood,[47] and will support them on every front." The pious one said, "Will you also save them from all the tribulations mentioned in the Gospel?"[48] The Lord answered him,

"Whoever fears me and follows my commandments, I will save; and I will rescue whoever obeys me from his temptations." The Lord [then] gave him peace,[49] and ascended into the heavens in unspeakable glory and honor.

A rich ruler, induced by the Devil, comes to Bishoi with money

14. [154v] As for the blessed Anba Bishoi, he persisted in great [ascetic] labor,[50] and the angel of the Lord would care for and comfort him. But Satan would try to entrap him, desiring to cast him under his feet, though he could not prevail against him. [Once, Satan] even came to him with worldly possessions, hoping to mislead the pious one, who is mighty indeed. It happened that Satan approached a rich official in Egypt[51] in the form of an angel, and said to him, "What are you doing sitting here? There is an anchorite on the Mountain of Shihīt; every blessing he will bestow upon you will come true." The notable[52] asked him, "What is his name?" He said, "His name is Anba Bishoi."

15. The notable rose up and took a great deal of gold in hand and loaded camels with gifts, and set out to the holy wilderness of Shihīt. Now the angel that accompanied the righteous Anba Bishoi said to him, "Satan has set a trap for you, to entice you to love possessions. He went to the notable in Egypt; he has loaded camels with gifts and, at this very moment, he is on his way with a large amount of gold to give to you." Saint Anba Bishoi rose up and went out into the mountain.[53] ⟨The notable met up with him⟩ and asked, "Do you know the great man on this mountain; [155r] that is, Anba Bishoi?" The saint said to him, "What do you want with him?" The notable said, "I want to give him this gold and these goods to distribute among the brothers so that their blessings may come upon me and my household." ⟨The saint⟩ answered and said to the notable, "Desert dwellers have no need of gold, and do not accept anything for this reason. Do not trouble yourself; the Lord has accepted your charity. Now go to the ⟨villages⟩ of Egypt and distribute [this wealth] to the poor and the infirm, and God will bless you, and all your relatives." The notable, then, returned to his home, and did as Saint Anba Bishoi had instructed him.

Bishoi defeats the Devil and enjoys spiritual communion

16. Now, as the pious Anba Bishoi was returning [to his cell], Satan came up to him and said, "I have labored a great deal with you, Bishoi." The saint said to him, "Since your creation,[54] your labor has been in vain." Satan said to him, "I will leave you as though you were never born." But the saint rebuked him, and [Satan] departed from him. By the help of God, our saintly father Anba Bishoi destroyed the snares of the hunter,[55] and returned to his place in peace.

17. Moreover, our father would instruct himself with many hardships and various [ascetic] practices.[56] The Lord provided him with spiritual nourishment at the hand of the angel [155v] who accompanied him.[57] On account of this nourishment, he persisted in fasting, not eating at all on several occasions.[58] 18. Such a feat is not difficult for God. Abimelech, the slave-king,[59] remained for seventy years without eating or drinking.[60] Likewise, the seven youths of Ephesus remained three hundred years serenely sleeping, without eating or drinking, with their souls in them.[61] For [what is limited by] human frailty is possible with God.[62]

Bishoi's pastoral care

19. Like bees swarming around wax, [visitors] surrounded our pious father and his spiritual children, learning from him the ways of monasticism. His greatest desire was to water their souls with the words of life that spring from the font within him.[63] He would imbue them so that they would love the solitude of the wilderness, asceticism, the love of estrangement and poverty, the rejection of the world, to labor in their handiwork, and especially to provide alms from their labor.[64] The completion of this is that he would instruct them that each one should be concerned ‹with his own affairs›, and do what is appropriate for his companion. For this is the fulfillment of the Law and the Prophets.[65]

Emperor Constantine appears to Bishoi

35.[66] [156r] One day, I, the wretched John, went to visit Saint Anba Bishoi. As I approached the door of the cell, I heard someone inside weeping as he spoke with the elder. When I knocked on the door, [Anba Bishoi] came and opened it for me. After I entered, prayed, and sat down with him, I said to him, "My father, who was speaking with you just now?" 36.[67] The saint said to me, "[The one] you heard was Constantine, the great king. He came to me from heaven with an aching heart, and said to me, 'Had I known about the great honor prepared for monks on account of their estrangement and poverty, I would have left my kingship and become a monk as well.'" I said to him, "Did you not receive your kingship in heaven?" He said to me, "Yes; but I did not receive the honor [given to] monks. 37. For I have looked on as a group of [monks] departed from their bodies; they did not attain the honor of those sitting at the gates [of heaven], but rather they received wings of fire, like those of eagles, and flew over the fortification until they entered the Holy City, the heavenly Jerusalem."[68] [38 *lacking in this recension*]. 39.[69] I said to him, "Indeed, you had a wife, children, servants, [156v] and luxuries; [how can] you be included among those who abandoned their homes and all their possessions, and were deprived of worldly goods? They sleep on the ground, keep night vigils, and fast with various types of asceticism. They are destitute, tormented, wandering in deserts, caves, and holes in the ground. Those about whom the pure apostle Paul said that the world was not worthy of them.[70] 40. At the moment I said this, you knocked on the door, and immediately [Constantine] ascended to heaven." When I heard this from the saintly elder, the pious Anba Bishoi, I was greatly consoled, and said, "Blessed be the Lord God who reveals his wonders through his saints everywhere."

Bishoi defends the divinity of the Holy Spirit

41. There was an anchorite living near Ibṣāy,[71] for whom Satan set a trap in this manner. He inclined his heart to believe and declare that there is no Holy Spirit, but only the Father and the Son. [The anchorite] would declare as much publicly. Now the merciful God, who loves humanity, ‹did not› wish the [previous] labors of this elder to go to waste, so he revealed his matter to Saint Anba Bishoi, saying, "Rise, go toward Ibṣāy, in southern Upper Egypt. [157r] You will find an elder anchorite there who declares that there is no Holy Spirit."

Saint Anba Bishoi placed the wisdom[72] of God in his heart, and proceeded to plait baskets with three handles, symbolizing the Holy Trinity. He took them with him throughout the districts of Egypt,[73] and brought them to where that anchorite lived. He met up with him as though he were a stranger. For he was following in the footsteps of the true star—he who performed venerable marvels and wonders, who banishes evil spirits, the healer of souls and bodies, who raised the dead and exorcised demons by the power of the Spirit of the Paraclete who is with him.[74] The prophet and great apostle, Abba Macarius, the spirit-bearer, when he traveled toward the city of Wasīm, and with the power of the Holy Trinity, returned the foolish [anchorite] and all who followed him from their error and polluted view to the orthodox faith.[75] Likewise our father, Saint Anba Bishoi, with the sign of the Holy Trinity, began to save another [foolish anchorite] from his error, along with all those who were influenced by him, from their grievous error.

[157v] In the morning, crowds came to the anchorite to be blessed by him. Now, when the anchorite and the whole crowd saw that the baskets of our pious father had three handles each, [the anchorite] asked him, "What are these, my father?" Our father said, "This is my handiwork; I came to sell it." The anchorite said to him, "What is the need for these three handles that you have fashioned for your baskets, which sets them apart from those of the brothers?" The pure father, Anba Bishoi, responded to those who were mocking him, both the brothers and the anchorite, saying, "I believe[76]

in a Trinity with a single divinity; thus, I manufacture my handiwork to symbolize the Holy Trinity." The crowd said, "Is there a Holy Spirit, father?" Our pious father opened his mouth and preached to them about[77] the Holy Spirit, saying, "The Holy Spirit exists since the beginning with the Father and the Son; an uncreated, inseparable Trinity."

Moreover, our pure father Anba Bishoi said to the anchorite, "Do you know the scriptures?" He said, "Yes." Then our pious father responded, saying, "Have you not heard the prophet Moses say in the Old Testament, 'In the beginning, God created the heavens and the earth, and the earth was invisible and unformed, and darkness was over the abyss, [158r] and the Spirit of God hovered over the water'?[78] Also, the prophet Isaiah, while in the majesty of God, said, 'The Spirit of the Lord is upon me, for this he anointed me and sent me to preach to the poor about a year of the Lord's favor.'[79] Additionally, David says, 'You send your Spirit, they will be created, and the face of the earth will be renewed again.'[80] Also, John the Baptist spoke, preaching about the Son of God, 'I have seen the Holy Spirit descend from heaven like a dove and rest on him.'[81] And our pure teacher, the apostle Paul, states, 'No one can say that Jesus is the Christ except by the Holy Spirit.'[82] The prophet Ezekiel also said, 'The Lord said to me, I will make my Spirit blow over these bones and they will all become alive in the resurrection.'[83] And the prophet Daniel also says, 'I looked, and thrones were set in place,'[84] in order to teach us that it is not a single throne, but three, as befitting of the Holy Trinity. And if all these witnesses do not convince you, our Lord Jesus Christ instructed the saintly apostles, saying, 'Go, make disciples of all nations, and baptize them in the name of the Father, the Son, and the Holy Spirit.'[85] Are you [still] not convinced by all these witnesses [158v] from the Holy Scriptures that the Holy Spirit exists from the beginning with the Father and the Son?'"[86]

42. When the anchorite, and those with him, heard these words, the breaths of God,[87] from our saintly father, the spirit-bearer, the great Anba Bishoi, they all believed and greatly benefited and confessed the Holy Trinity. 43. Once the saint, our pious father, confirmed them in the correct faith, he returned to his monastery,[88] praising the Lord Jesus Christ.

An angel assures Bishoi of God's care

44. Our righteous father Anba Bishoi was walking in the wilderness when the eyes of his intellect were opened. He saw the mountain filled with angels, and he marveled greatly, and said to himself, "Who are these?" One of them responded, "We are the ones who protect the saints in this place." Then he marveled greatly, and praised God for the great care he takes of all of his saints.

A Syrian monk visits Bishoi

50. There was a great anchorite from the lands of the Syrians ‹living› in a mountain cave in Syria, worshiping God by night and day, performing many [ascetic] austerities, and he was exceedingly mighty in all his deeds.[89] One time, as he stood praying at night, saying, "Will I find mercy with God like some of the saints?" a voice came to him, saying, [159r] "[There is] an elder in Egypt at the Mountain of Natrun who worships God constantly; his name is Anba Bishoi. You have the same intimacy[90] with God as he does." That elder joyfully rose up, boarded a ship, and came to Alexandria. Upon arrival, he inquired as to the whereabouts of Saint Anba Bishoi, and he learned that he resided at the Mountain of Natrun. So he went there and met with our pious father. They greeted one another;[91] then [Anba Bishoi] brought him into the cell and they prayed and sat down. Now the elder spoke Syriac, but our father Anba Bishoi did not know Syriac at all. He sighed toward heaven and said, "I ask you, my Master Jesus Christ, enable me to understand what this saintly elder is saying."

51. Then, suddenly, God opened his mind and he understood the words of the Syrian elder. They sat discussing the great deeds of God with great passion. The anchorite inquired from our father concerning the virtues[92] of the one who became a true Israelite,[93] our saintly father Abba Macarius. Saint Anba Bishoi informed him, ‹saying›, "He became a leader, a guide, and a lawgiver to all the saints. He then relayed to [the anchorite] many of the [ascetic] deeds and wonders [159v] God performed at his hands. The anchorite was amazed and said, "How great is the power of the Almighty, which dwelt with this pious one, the great Abba Macarius, who fulfilled the will of God." As for our pious father Anba Bishoi, he discerned many virtues in the anchorite, and he said to the brothers, "Come to receive a blessing from this great man, for I have seen the power of God with him." [The monks came] and bowed before the saintly elder and were blessed by him. The anchorite remained with our saintly father Abba Bishoi for a week. When he saw [Anba Bishoi's] labors and asceticism, he thanked the Lord God and took courage. Afterward, he bowed down to Saint Anba Bishoi, [saying], "I bid you farewell, my beloved father, for I desire to return to my district."

Coda. Bishoi sees the Syrian monk borne home on a cloud

52. After he greeted[94] [Anba Bishoi] and departed, another brother came to visit our father, and the brothers said to him, "Had you hurried a bit, you would have been blessed by a great man who came to our saintly father from Syria. Nonetheless, if you run, you will catch up to him, for he could not have traveled more than a mile by now." But our pious father said, "My son, do not run after him; you will not catch him. He has traversed thirteen

miles riding upon a cloud." When the brothers heard this, they were astonished and glorified our Master Jesus Christ and all his saints.

Bishoi sees an angel watching over a brother
53 A.[95] [160r] Our pious father Abba Bishoi came to the cell of a brother to visit him; he saw him sleeping while the angel of the Lord guarded him. He said, "Indeed, the Lord protects those who depend upon him." He departed as he glorified God, ‹our Lord› Jesus Christ.

Bishoi's disciple is deceived by a Jew
53 B. Once, a virtuous[96] brother went to Egypt to sell his handiwork. [On the road], he met a Jew who spoke with him about the faith[97] in our Master Jesus Christ. The Jew responded and said to the brother, "You Christians say that the Christ was crucified, but it was another who resembled him."[98] Naively, the brother said to him, "Your statement is correct." When the brother stated ‹this›, the grace of holy baptism was removed from him, on account of that single naïve utterance.

Bishoi rebukes and teaches the monk
54. When the brother returned to the monastery, our father saw that the grace of baptism had been removed from him. Our holy father Anba Bishoi remained silent for a long while, but when the brother saw the elder frowning at him, he said to him, "My father, what has changed your countenance toward me today?" He said to him, "Who are you?" He said, "I am brother so-and-so." The elder said to him, "You are not him; for the grace of baptism has departed from you." 55. The brother asked him, [160v] "On account of what, my father?" ‹The elder› replied, "On account of the words you spoke with the Jew in Egypt."[99] 56. The brother made a prostration of repentance,[100] saying, "Forgive me, my holy father, for I have sinned on account of my naïveté." 57. The elder said to him, "Be careful, my son, lest you make strange statements regarding the holy faith;[101] rather, what we have received from our holy fathers is what we cling to with firmness." Then our father prayed, saying, "Lord God, no one is without sin except you alone,[102] you who are full of compassion.[103] I ask you, my Master Jesus Christ, to forgive this brother the errors he has committed." Then, through the prayers of the elder, God granted the brother the grace of holy baptism.

The Savior appears to Bishoi
20. Our father Anba Bishoi remained for some time in the wilderness in his mountain cell. For three years he did not see anyone, and his hair grew out about a hand's width. He persisted in prayer night and day, with a constant

petition for the sake of the tremendous love of the compassionate God. He would keep vigils without sleeping. [To that end,] he made a crack in the rock, and placed a peg in it; hence, whenever nature moved him to sleep, he would tie the hair of his head [to it] and would stand praying to God unceasingly.

21. [161r] After the father spent three years in this manner, our Master Jesus Christ came to him in the mountain cell. Startled, Anba Bishoi fell to the ground, but the Savior gripped him, and raised him up and said, "My precious Bishoi, peace to you. I have seen your labors and your toils and I have granted you [the blessing] that whoever petitions me in your name, I will forgive his sins." Anba Bishoi said to him, "My master, ‹allow me to› labor for the sake of your holy name, for you have, likewise, accepted passion[104] on behalf of the whole world; you died and were resurrected to save us." The Lord gave him peace, and ascended to the heavens in great glory, and God graced him with [the gift] to heal many.

Bishoi intercedes with God on behalf of another's disciple

22.[105] There was an elder in one of the monasteries, a pious man, who had a son—a monk. Satan, the enemy of goodness, cast the aforementioned son into sin. Then he died, and was taken to [the place of] severe punishment. The elder would pray night and day for his sake, and he observed forty days of fasting and mourning for his sake. Afterward, a voice from heaven came to him, saying, "He will remain in punishment until the Lord comes upon the clouds."[106] 23. Now, the elder fasted [161v] another forty days so the Lord might spare [the young monk] from punishment. Yet, again, the voice came to him a second time: "He will remain in punishment until the Lord comes upon the clouds." The elder then fasted [yet] another forty days, pleading with God for the sake of his son. Then the voice came to him a third time: "He will remain in punishment until the Lord comes upon the clouds." When the elder heard this, he rose up quickly and went to the inner desert and sought out the friend of God,[107] Anba Bishoi.

24. When he arrived where he resided, [Abba Bishoi] learned through the Spirit [of his arrival], and he went and received the elder. They both bowed down, prostrating before one another. Our father Anba Bishoi then said to him, "My saintly father, why have you taken on such hardship to come to my insignificance?" The elder told him everything concerning the young monk, as well as his labors, and the voice that came to him on [the monk's] account. Our saintly father, Anba Bishoi, said to the elder, "My father, rise, let us pray." The elder said to him, "By the Son of God![108] I will not stand, but I will prostrate before you, and weep before you, until God has mercy on me and comforts my heart concerning the brother, [letting me know] whether he has been released from suffering or not."

25. [162r] Our saintly father, Anba Bishoi, stood up and went into the wilderness and prayed to the Lord, saying, "My Master, have mercy upon your creation and hear your servant." 26. Immediately, the Good Savior appeared to him and said, "Peace to you, my chosen Bishoi. What are you asking of me, you who are equal to my angels?" 27. [Anba Bishoi] said to him, "My Master, [I am praying] for the sake of the son of the elder that you may forgive him—for he had sinned; and that you may raise him from punishment." The Good Savior said, "It has proceeded from my mouth that he should remain in punishment until I come upon the clouds." 28. Then the saint said to the Good Savior, "My Master, if you so desire now, you may summon a cloud, ride it, and have mercy upon this soul." 29. The Good Savior had compassion. He called for a luminous cloud to come, and he stepped upon it, and commanded that the soul of the young monk be brought and given to Saint Anba Bishoi.[109] Anba Bishoi gripped it, and handed it over to the elder. When he saw it, he marveled greatly, and the elder asked about the punishment it[110] had endured. It said, "I have received a great deal of suffering in Hades, my father, on account of my sins, and even more so for disobeying you, my father." Then the soul of the young [monk] was taken to [the place of] repose. [30 *lacking in this recension*.]

31. The elder returned [162v] to our father Anba Bishoi and said to him, "You have had mercy on me. You pleaded with the Lord until he had compassion on the soul of the brother, as it is written, 'the Lord aids his saints.'"[111] Then he asked our father Anba Bishoi, "I entreat you, let me know what [ascetic] practice[112] you performed so that the Lord granted this tremendous blessing to you." Anba Bishoi said to him, "Forgive me, my saintly father. This was the commandment of the Lord since the beginning on account of his compassion;[113] because of this, he had mercy even on me; [still,] none of this happened on account of my humility or piety. Lest you, my father, say in your heart that I presented my soul to [the point of] death until this [grace] was granted to me. Rather, this took place because of you, my father, because you fasted for forty days on three occasions for the love of God. Thus, [God] granted this [grace] to you. For there is no greater love than this, that one sacrifice himself for his children."[114] The elder thanked God, and they discussed their [ascetic] practices[115] with one another, and each returned to his residence.

The Savior tells Bishoi to strengthen and teach the brothers

32. Afterward, our father Anba Bishoi was in the wilderness, [in] a place without anyone. He would punish himself, and would not let anyone [163r] know of his labors. He would increase his fasting by several days, completing twenty-one days before tasting anything, and he would eat only bread and salt.

33. The Lord instructed him to become a father to the brothers in the wilderness, [saying, "Go][116] and teach them all the virtues, and that they should not consider themselves human at all, or to even consider such [earthly] things."[117] Our father Anba Bishoi entreated the Lord, saying, "Lord, I am unable to carry out the duties required for this ministry, for I fear losing the labors I have accepted for the sake of your holy name."[118] 34. The Lord said to him, "Do not fear. I will multiply [the reward for] all your labors in my spiritual city, the heavenly Jerusalem." Blessed is the one who keeps the commandments of the Lord; such an individual is revered and pious.[119] As for Saint Anba Bishoi, his name and labors filled the whole Mountain of Natrun. Multitudes would seek him out every day as a father, and he would teach them the path of the Lord in humility.

Paul and Phoibammon come to visit Bishoi

45. Once, while our saintly father Anba Bishoi was in the wilderness, Anba Phoibammon[120] of the City of the Eagle[121] heard of the virtues of our father, and how people were blessed by him. Thus, he went to our father Paul of Tamma. [163v] He heard him speak of the honor of the pious Anba Bishoi, for he had visited him on several occasions, and he would speak about him with everyone. Anba Phoibammon said to Anba Paul, "Have mercy on me, and take me with you to be blessed by [Anba Bishoi]." Anba Paul said to him, "I fear [taking you], because you are a youth; I cannot take you at all." Then Anba Phoibammon said, "Let me come with you; I will sit at the door [of his cell] while you enter and greet him with a kiss.[122] When you come out, I will greet you with a kiss; for I believe that his blessing will come upon me." 46. Anba Paul said, "Yes."

Now, they journeyed together in the wilderness, and when they arrived at [Anba Bishoi's] cell, Anba Paul entered and greeted him, and they prayed and sat down. Then our father Anba Bishoi said to Anba Paul, "Why didn't the brother come in with you? But you left him outside the door." Anba Paul said to him, "Forgive me, my saintly father. I thought that [since] he is a youth I should not bring him to you." Anba Bishoi said to him, "Do not speak in this manner: 'He is a youth.' For our Savior said that the kingdom of heaven belongs to such as these.[123] Indeed, many will enter Paradise because of this father, for the hand of the Lord is with him; [164r] he is not small but great."[124] [Our father] instructed Anba Paul to bring [the youth] to him, and he greeted him with a kiss and blessed him. Then they departed from [his cell] and returned to their dwellings in peace, glorifying our Master Jesus Christ.

[*47–49 lacking in this recension.*]

Bishoi prays on behalf of an impudent priest

68. At [the monastery] of our saintly father, there was a priest who would administer Communion to the brothers. Whenever our father spoke with the brothers about what is beneficial for their souls, that priest would sit and speak useless words, sowing doubt in the souls of the brothers. Thus, the brothers who came to our saintly father Anba Bishoi would lose [spiritual benefit], and they would complain because of [that priest]. Once, when an elder came to visit our father Anba Bishoi, the brothers told the elder about the matter of the priest and said to him, "We are disturbed by the worthless words of this priest. Not only that, but, moreover, the Adversary reminds us of his words in our dwelling." The elder said to them, "Let me go to our father. After I speak with him a bit, remind me of the deeds[125] of the elder-‹priest›, so that I may ask him about his words and reproach him." When they rose and were on their way to our father Anba Bishoi, the priest also came, leading them, as was his custom, and he spoke. Nonetheless, Anba Bishoi remained quiet, and did not reprove him right away.

The [visiting] elder gestured[126] to our father and took him aside [164v] and relayed to him the suffering of the brothers and their dissatisfaction; for they desired to hear the words of the Lord, but the priest distracted them with secular words. Our father Anba Bishoi said to them, "What do you want me to do with him? For Satan seeks his destruction, and you want me to expel him. Nonetheless, the Lord will ask me about him, and will say, 'One man I have entrusted to Bishoi, and he could not bear with him.' I also fear that if I reproached him, he would return to his village, become a layman, and destroy his soul. However, if you are patient with me, brothers, and also with him, in love—for this is how you ought to behave—your hearts will be pleased with us." The brothers answered, saying, "If he would abandon his disposition and follow the monastic canons, we would support him[127] until he approaches the light once again." After this, the priest came to know his error and abandoned his former ways, and he repented before the brothers, who loved him, and his remaining days were greatly improved. He remained obedient to our father until the day of his passing.

‹ With this abundant grace and power, our father Anba Bishoi did not relent from his ascetic practices by night or day. ›[128]

Bishoi assists John the anchorite with his fasting

58. Afterward, a great elder came to our father Anba Bishoi. While in the desert, [that elder] would not eat or drink, [165r] but his soul became anxious due to the excess of labor in ‹hunger and› thirst. He thought to himself, "Rise, go to our father Anba Bishoi and consult him."[129] When the elder came and knocked on his door, Saint Anba Bishoi went out and

opened [it] for him. Once [Anba Bishoi] recognized him and greeted him, they went into his cell, prayed, sat down, and discussed the commandments of the Lord. Then the Holy Spirit informed our father Anba Bishoi that the elder had been fasting for several days and that he was parched. Anba Bishoi gestured to the disciple to bring a bit of water to drink and bread in order to eat with [the elder] so he might regain his strength; for he was wasting away from hunger and thirst. When the disciple set out [the provisions], [Anba Bishoi] said to [the elder], "Come, let us eat some bread and drink a bit of water since you have come in from the heat." The elder said to him, "Forgive me, my father, I do not eat or drink, but I fast and mourn for my sins until I please the compassionate God." Our father Anba Bishoi said to him, "Drink a bit of water, my brother, on account of the heat; I see you are fatigued by thirst." The elder said to him, "Forgive me, my father; it is a fast." When he realized that [the elder] would not eat or drink, the saintly father Anba Bishoi stood up and raised his hands to the Lord, saying, [165v] "Come to me, my Master Jesus Christ, to have mercy upon your servant; for he is wasting away from thirst." Immediately, as he was praying, his mind was caught up and he looked on as [the elder] was fed with bread and given water to drink until he was satisfied. Indeed, [that elder] truly ate and [his thirst] was quenched to satisfaction. That elder then rose up and went to his residence in peace. He fasted all the more, saying to himself, "You have received your desire, ‹poor› soul."

Bishoi as an abbot
[η].[130] Many brothers gathered around our father Saint Anba Bishoi, all desiring to live at his [monastery]. [To] some of them, he granted the monastic habit;[131] they lived around him, and he taught them about the fear of the Lord. He would say to all of them, "My children, persevere in your manual labor to provide for your necessities and to be able to give alms."

Bishoi teaches a disgruntled monk about work
[θ]. Now, one of the brothers was sitting, listening to our father Anba Bishoi as he instructed everyone to persist in their manual labor. He became disgruntled in his heart, and said thus: "Had our father performed manual labor, he would know the exhaustion of manual labor, and would not speak to us in this manner." As [the brother] was pondering this in his heart, our saintly father learned of this through the Spirit, so he responded and said to him, [166r] "My son, even you are thinking in this manner, and complain when I instruct the brothers to perform their manual labor along with their prayers, readings, and psalms. Do you not know that I am mindful of you and your souls before the Lord at all times?" Immediately, when

‹that brother› heard this from ‹our father›, he dropped the braided [cord] from his hands, and bowed his face to the ground and made a prostration of repentance, saying, "Forgive me, my saintly father." Anba Bishoi said to him, "My son, the Lord knows, since I came to this place, I have not ceased working by night or day, performing my prayers and my manual work simultaneously. I punish my body in this place, that I may escape eternal punishment. For whoever punishes his flesh here with prayer, fasting, readings, and vigils will be saved from eternal punishment. When the brothers heard this, they performed a prostration of repentance and said, "Forgive us, our saintly father, for we are unable to labor like you." And our saintly father would comfort the brothers through the power of the Holy Spirit.

Bishoi helps a young anchorite to defeat the Devil

59. There was a brother who was a new seedling in the wilderness, and the demons troubled him greatly. He rose and came to our father and said to him, "Remember me in your holy prayers! [166v] For Satan has left everyone, but he troubles and harasses me a great deal." The saint said, "My son, the words you speak are befitting of warriors[132] who are strengthened by the Lord God, those against whom Satan wages war by day and night. As for you, my son, Satan does not even know you are at this mountain.[133] Rather, go and entreat God, for we believe that he will comfort you." When the brother returned to his dwelling, our father Saint Anba Bishoi interceded with the Lord on behalf of the brother that he might have mercy upon him.

60. At that point, Satan roared in anger like a lion,[134] and said to the saint, "Why do you torment me?" The blessed elder said to him, "Get away from this new seedling; do not trouble him any longer." Satan said to him, "I swear to you, I did not even know that he resides on this mountain; perhaps he has a weak spirit that tempts him even now.[135] Nonetheless, starting today I will channel all my might against him." But the elder rebuked him, and he departed from him.

Satan then waged a mighty war against the brother, to the point that he fled from his cell naked due to the severity of the pains that [the demon] inflicted upon him. Straightaway, [167r] the brother returned [to Anba Bishoi], screaming, "My saintly father, rescue me!" The blessed elder said to him, "What happened to you, my son?" The brother said to him, "My father, Satan expelled me from my dwelling by the many tortures he inflicted upon me, my father." The elder grabbed the hand of the brother and took him to [his] cell to rest a bit from his troubles. Then our saintly father, the blessed Anba Bishoi, stood up and prayed, saying, "Lord God, Almighty, who created everything through his boundless wisdom and brought it into existence out of nothing by the word of your mouth alone, the will of your beloved Son, and the pleasure of your Holy Spirit,[136] [which is] particularly the case with regard to the human being, whom you created according to your rational image, and adorned with holy gifts. You, Lord, are the one who preserves and protects us from all things. Lord, master of everyone, I ask you to guard this brother from the evil deeds of Satan, that he may be established in this wilderness until your will [for him] is fulfilled. Let him become a fruitful tree, pleasing you all his days. For you have said, "I will fill this mountain with monks [167v] who will worship me all the days of their lives."[137] Because of this, we ask that you become our advocate and champion,[138] Lord, for you alone are Almighty,[139] along with our Master Jesus Christ, ‹and your Holy Spirit›, forever. Amen."

61. When our father Anba Bishoi said, "Amen," an angel of the Lord stood [before him] with Satan bound with an iron chain. Immediately, [Satan] screamed, "Woe to me! As the Lord God lives,[140] before whom I shudder, I will leave this mountain along with all who are in it to you, and I will go elsewhere." The saint said to him, "Enemy of all righteousness, will you ever cease warring against the servants of the Lord, those whom he gathered by his holy name? What did this new seedling do to you, ‹that you› should trouble him?" Satan replied, "I wanted to quickly humble him; for if I let him be, he will trouble me a great deal." The pious one said to him, "May the Lord punish you!" Satan retorted, saying, "If you let me go this time, I will no longer trouble him."

62. Then the saint said to the angel of the Lord, "Let him be until the day the Lord wishes to repay him in accordance with his evil deeds." Thus, the angel released [Satan]. Our father went to the brother and sealed his heart and his face [168r] with the holy cross, and sent him to his cell glorifying God through the prayers of Saint Anba Bishoi. The demons no longer bothered him after that day, and the brother grew each day [in virtue], thanking God for the prayers of our father Anba Bishoi.

John tells about Bishoi's insight

63. I was once seated [in the cell] of our father Anba Bishoi when some brothers came to visit him, seeking words of instruction for the benefit of their souls. He said to them, "Let us strive to keep the monastic canons, ‹which are› purity, fasting, prayer, humility, and our mutual love for one another." He then divulged the thoughts of their hearts, and they were greatly astonished. When they came out [of his cell], they said to me, "Our father, indeed, this elder is a righteous man;[141] he divulged all the thoughts of our hearts." I, the insignificant John, said to them, "Often I have done something in private, whether it be prayer or fasting or some work I've

performed, and when I would meet him, he would lean toward my ear and tell me the deed I had done." And the brothers glorified God all the more for the grace that God grants his saints.

Bishoi intercedes with God on behalf of the apostate monk Isaac

64. There was a brother who enjoyed seclusion.[142] He journeyed toward Qaw,[143] one of the provinces of Egypt, to live there in seclusion. One day, he went to Egypt[144] to sell his handiwork, [168v] when a Jewish woman, a sorceress, saw him from her home. Satan led her gaze toward him and she desired him, and she invited him to enter her home so she might buy his handiwork. Thus, she seduced him through her trickery, changed him into a layman, and kept him with her. She converted him from his creed to ‹the creed of› Judaism. [That woman] would let him recline on her hips,[145] and she would take a toothpick and pluck at his teeth, saying, "This is so no small particle from the body of Christ would remain in them"—as [that monk] later informed our father Anba Bishoi.

65. When some brothers, monks, traveled to Egypt for their necessities, the Jew saw them and called to them, saying, "Are you from the wilderness?" They answered, "Yes." He said to them, "Do you know Saint Anba Bishoi?" They said, "He is the father of us all." He said to them, "I implore you, when you return to the mountain, say to my holy father, 'Anba Bishoi, your son, Isaac the Jew, says to you: I beg you to pray for me, for I have fallen into the snare of Satan.'" They said to him, "We will remind him [of your plea]." Now when the woman heard these words from the brothers, she knew that the pious one was able to save [Isaac] from her hands. She peeked out of her house and said to the brothers, "Say to Bishoi the anchorite, 'If I see you, I will hurt you.'"

When the brothers reached the wilderness of Shihīt, to the father, and were blessed by him, [169r] they did not say anything to him. For they had forgotten [the matter]. Our holy father, the prophet Anba Bishoi—for he was truly a prophet like Elisha and Elijah—inquired[146] of the brothers, saying, "Did anyone ask you to relay anything to me?" They said, "No, father." For Satan had made them forget the message. The righteous one then asked, "Isaac the Jew didn't say anything to you?" They said, "Yes, father, he asked a great deal about you. He said to us, 'Say to my holy father, Anba Bishoi, to pray for me, for I have fallen into the snares of Satan.' Also, a woman peeked out of her house, and when she heard him speaking with us, she said, 'Say to Bishoi the anchorite, if I see you, I will harm you also.'"

[Our father] gathered his legs, for he was sitting, and shuffled back three times, and cried out saying, "My Master Jesus Christ, rescue me!" The brothers marveled, saying, "Are you also afraid, father?" The saint said to them, "Who among the saints was able to escape the deceptions of Satan and women, except for the one [strengthened] by God?[147] Our father, the first Adam, was misled by a woman. The chaste Joseph—[recall] how he was thrown into prison because of a woman.[148] The prophet Elijah fled into the wilderness for several days on account of Jezebel.[149] The mighty Samson, the strongman, [169v] [recall] how he would not have been ‹overcome if not› for a woman.[150] ‹Moreover›, because of a woman, twenty-three thousand Israelites fell on a single day.[151] Again, a woman made them take the head of John the Prophet,[152] the star of Jesus Christ, who is great among all the saints—the pure Saint John the Baptist. Likewise, Solomon the instructor,[153] who was more exalted in his kingdom than his predecessors in Jerusalem, women misled his heart. Lest we survey all the scriptures,[154] a woman, likewise, made the great one, the leader of the apostles,[155] the pure Peter, deny our Master.[156] Now, we do not reproach the saints—God forbid; rather, I had stated earlier that the Lord strengthened them. He was with each one of them, until he crossed over this great snare of Satan, and this vain world that has misled many." When the brothers heard all of this, they marveled at the great understanding and sharp mind of the righteous elder, Anba Bishoi, and they glorified God all the more, along with his saints.

The elder then informed them that that [170r] Jewish woman was a sorceress, who deceived [Isaac] with her words until she drew him into her snare. As for the blessed saint, who desires the well-being of everyone, he labored a great deal and spent many days in vigil, with great toil and abstinence, asking the Lord God with a confident heart to save Isaac the Jew from the woman. [66 *lacking in this recension*.] 67. God, who loves humanity, heard the petition of the saint, and saved that brother from the hands of that Jewish woman. He then returned to the mountain, to the elder, on account of the prayers of the saint.[157] He went on to become a distinguished, mighty monk, obedient to the elder with an exceedingly humble heart, thankful to our Master Jesus Christ for all he had done with him.[158]

A lesson about theft

[α]. Once, the great Abba Bishoi was walking in the wilderness, when he found a crevice chiseled into the rock. He entered it and found a dead man with a plate placed at his feet. He prayed and sat down weeping and saying, "How brief is your stay, you human, in this transitory world that you no longer inhabit!" He then said, "I will take this plate to my dwelling, and conceal this decrepit tomb. Whenever the brothers eat [170v] from this plate, they will remember the deceased." [He continued] and said, "I took it, but as I proceeded on my way, a voice came to me from that tomb, saying, 'Bishoi, return the plate to its place. Do not become a thief in this wilderness.'" He continued, "When I heard ‹that voice›, I left [the plate] in its place, and praised God." With this [account], brothers, he teaches us that no one should take an item[159] that does not belong to him, lest we nurture the habit of theft in us. This is particularly the case with the possessions of the deceased.

Instructions to monks on attending festivals and visiting shrines

[β]. Now he would say to the brothers, "Do not go to the crop harvest; rather, what you earn from your handiwork is sufficient for you. Nor should you go to the vineyards, lest you lose yourselves. Nor should you go to the festivals of the saints, eating, drinking, and amusing yourselves, for it was gluttony that exiled Adam from Paradise. Rather, if you go to the festival of a saint, a martyr, or a pure individual, go, but pray only in their shrine,[160] and say thus: 'God, the God of the saints, forgive us our sins and teach us to do your will at all times.' Then return to your residence, praising our Lord Jesus."

Bishoi and John leave Scetis

[γ].[161] Afterward, the Berbers raided the deserts, killing the saintly elders. Therefore, I sat with Saint Anba Bishoi, [171r] I, the insignificant John, and said to him, "My beloved brother, I will share with you what came to my heart. You see that the Berbers have destroyed the deserts and killed our fathers. I wish to leave this mountain, fearing that a Berber may come and kill me and go to Hades on my account." When I said this to him, he replied, "If you want to depart, I will come with you." For this reason, we both departed and went to Egypt.[162] I went to Clysma, and from there to the monastery of the great Saint Anba Antony; and I lived in seclusion there in a small cell, entreating God on account of my sins. As for the pious saint, Anba Bishoi, he headed toward Upper Egypt and traveled to the city of Ansina,[163] and lived on that mountain practicing asceticism and great [self-]restraint. Again, God spread his name throughout that region, so that his way of life, which resembles that of angels, may be substantiated.

Bishoi washes Christ's feet

69A.[164] One day, while our saintly father, Anba Bishoi, was sitting, he saw our Lord Jesus Christ approaching him along with his pure angels, as he had once come to the chief of the fathers at [171v] the Oak of Mamre.[165] This is not strange. For the one whom Abraham had served is the same whom [Abba Bishoi] served: that is God, the Lord of everyone. The Lord said to him, "My chosen Bishoi, he who has attained a venerable age, ‹Peace to you›." Immediately, the righteous one was strengthened; he worshiped [the Lord], and took water and placed it [in a basin] in front of him and washed his feet.[166] The Lord then comforted and blessed him, and ascended into the heavens with great glory.

Bishoi's disciple learns about the fruits of disobedience and obedience

69B. Our father Anba Bishoi drank a bit of that water and then placed the rest of it in a water bucket[167] and covered it until his disciple, who used to serve him, would come so he too might drink a bit and be blessed by Christ—implementing[168] what is written: "Love your neighbor as yourself."[169] When the disciple came, the father said to him, "My son, go to the water bucket and drink that bit of water in it." The brother said to him, "I will go, my father." But the disciple grumbled in his heart, saying, "Rather than saying to me to drink a bit of cool water because I came in from the heat, he now tells me to drink the water under [the lid] of the water bucket." And he did not go toward [the water bucket]. Again, the elder said to him, [172r] "Get up, my son; drink a bit of water from under [the lid] of the water bucket." The brother said to him, "Pray for me, my father," but he did not go [to the water bucket], and said in his heart, "If I were to drink water, I would drink cool water from the jar." Again, the saint said this a third time, "I am telling you, drink a bit of the water covered by [the lid] of the water bucket." The brother then said, "I will drink, my father"; and the elder remained silent.

When the disciple saw on the face of the elder that he was upset with him, he quickly proceeded to the covered water bucket, but when he uncovered it, he did not find any water in it. So he returned to the father and said to him, "Are you mocking me, my saintly father? I did not find any water in the water bucket." The new Elijah and Elisha, that is, Anba Bishoi, said, "Water such as that would not remain on earth this long." The disciple said to him, "What is the story with this water, my father?" The saint said to him, "Believe me, my son, our Master Jesus Christ came to a brother monk who loves God on this mountain, as he merits. [That monk] blessed [the Lord] and washed his feet with that water. Then he brought me a bit of it. I drank some [172v] and left the remainder for you. However, when you disobeyed, angels came and ascended with it to heaven." When the disciple heard this, he fell to the ground at the feet of our saintly father; he fainted for a long time. 70. As for the prophet who was born ‹a prophet, that is›, our saintly father Anba Bishoi, ‹he raised him up› and said, "My son, Adam would not have fallen from Paradise had it not been for his disobedience to God, and had you not ‹similarly› disobeyed, you would have been worthy of this exceedingly great salvation." The disciple was distraught and constantly wept on account of the disobedient act he had committed, and the elder would comfort him, saying, "You have regretted [your actions]; you are blameless."

Bishoi sends his despondent disciple to a holy man

71. Nonetheless, [Anba Bishoi] was unable to console him at all, but [the disciple] would ask him, saying, "My master, father, have mercy on me, send me to a perfect individual, who is mighty in God, that I may consult him lest I be blamed as you have said." Our saintly father, the anchorite Anba Bishoi, gave him some bread and said to him, "Get up, and go to the city of Ansina. [There] you will find a man to the south of the keep of the city, who is being stoned by youths like a crazy man. Give him this bread in my name, and he will speak with you."

72. The disciple rose up and went to [173r] the city as our father had told him, and he found an individual on top of the garbage heap with youths throwing stones at him. The disciple chased the youths away from him and gave him the bread in the name of the righteous Anba Bishoi. [The man] said to him, "I am exceedingly eager to hear news about [Anba Bishoi]." Then that holy man also said to him, "Why did you disobey your father and lose out on this great grace? Because of your disobedience, anxiety has stricken you in this manner. Now, rise and go to your father and obey him. For whoever disobeys Saint Anba Bishoi disobeys our Master Jesus Christ." The disciple rose up and returned to the place where our saintly father resided, and he repeated everything that the saintly man, the prophet, said to him, and he remained with our saintly father for a few days.

The disciple goes to see the holy man again

73. Afterward, he again grew anxious on account of the great salvation that eluded him. He sat weeping, saying, "Woe, woe to me! I will die of grief, for I did not deserve the blessing of Christ!" Our saintly father, Anba Bishoi, would comfort him, saying, "If you have regretted [your actions], then God has forgiven you."[170] Nonetheless, his heart was not soothed; rather, he would plead with [Anba Bishoi,] saying, "Send me [173v] to that aforementioned prophet so he may console me in this anxious state I am in." The saint said, "That prophet is reposed, but rise and head toward the city. You will find a tomb in the mountain. Open its door and you will find three men lying in it. They have died [there]; for it is the tomb of the prophets who have pleased God in that whole city. At the end of their time, each would release [his] spirit into the hand of the Lord [there]. Proceed, enter [the tomb], and place your hand on the one lying in the middle in my name; he will rise and converse with you."

74. The brother, the disciple, went and found three men [lying in the tomb] as [Anba Bishoi] had said to him. He placed his hand on the one lying in the middle, and said to him thus, "Saint Abba Bishoi said, rise that I may speak with you." Immediately, that prophet sat up and said to the disciple, "Did I not just tell you to obey your father? Why are you acting like an unbeliever? If you have faith in me, I have already told you that whoever obeys the prophet Anba Bishoi obeys God, and whoever disobeys that mighty one, it is Christ, the Son of God, whom he disobeys. Rise and go to your father and obey him in everything; for he is the one who intercedes for you before the Lord." [174r] Once he said this, he reclined. Then the disciple went to our father Anba Bishoi and repeated to him everything the prophet had said. The disciple would marvel and wonder at the sight he had seen, and he would revere the words of the elder and obey him in everything, in the fear of God, until the day of his repose. Let none of the faithful ‹disbelieve› these words. For our Master, to whom be glory, said from his divine mouth, "Whoever believes in me will do the works I do, and even greater than they."[171]

[v. Bishoi Carries Christ: see the appendix, 323–26]

Bishoi intervenes to absolve two young monks of false charges

75. Once, two brothers who were monks heard of the reputation of our saintly father Anba Bishoi. They came and asked him, saying, "If you would, our saintly father, accept us so we may remain under the shadow of your prayers, to be worthy of your holy blessing, and that you may guide our souls." The pious one joyfully accepted them, for he exceedingly loved people. He kept them with him for a few days, and taught them how to please God. After some days, our saintly father, Anba Bishoi, sought to briefly separate from people in order to perform his ministry and [ascetic] labors. He said to the brothers, "Rise, go to the wilderness of Upper Egypt and live in seclusion there [174v] to focus solely upon reading the Holy Scriptures." The two brothers said to him, "Where should we go, our saintly father?" He said to them, "Go to Mount Qaw[172] to live in seclusion. For without solitude, the monk does not make progress." The two brothers obeyed him. They received his blessing, departed from [his cell], and went to Mount [Qaw] and lived there.

Sometime later, thieves entered the cell of a brother and took all of his possessions. Now, there was at that place[173] an elder who had a contemptuous spirit that would inform him about everything, but he would say, "This was revealed to me through the angel of the Lord." The Father of the Monastery[174] went to him and said, "My father, tell us who robbed the cell of this brother." He said ‹to him›, "It was these two brothers who recently came to this mountain," and all the brothers believed him. Consequently, the Father of the Monastery seized the sibling monks and expelled them as thieves.

Our father the prophet, the spirit-bearer, Anba Bishoi, learned through the Spirit of the trials that had befallen the [two] brothers. He hurried to Mount Qaw, where he found the two brothers imprisoned. He said to the Father of the Monastery, "These individuals would not do any such thing." [175r] The Father of the Monastery said to the elder, "It was the seer-elder who informed us [of their guilt]." Our father Anba Bishoi responded and said, "Gather all the brothers for me." Hence, all the brothers gathered, and that elder came with them. When they saw [our] father, they all bowed down and were blessed by him. The saint said to them, "What evil deed have these foreign brothers committed?" The [seer-]elder said to him, "It was they who stole the possessions of this brother." Our father sighed in his soul, and said to the elder, "Kindly[175] say '[The demons] have deceived me.'" But the elder refused, and said, "They did not deceive me; I speak the truth." The righteous one again said, "Kindly say, '[The demons] have tempted me.'"

Now the brothers knew that our father Anba Bishoi was a prophet, so they pressured the elder until he said, "They tempted me." When he said this, immediately, that ‹vile› spirit came out of him like a sow with its tusks protruding out of its mouth. It charged to gore him, but our saintly father Anba Bishoi rebuked it, and it immediately disappeared. Seeing all that transpired, the brothers fell down and venerated him. Likewise, the ‹misguided› elder also [bowed down], and they said, "Forgive us, our saintly father; undoubtedly, God resides in you." Our saintly father, the pious Anba Bishoi, through the prophetic Spirit that resided in him, informed the head of that mountain,[176] saying, "Go [175v] to such and such a place and you will find the stolen goods." Nonetheless, [Anba Bishoi] did not divulge the identity of the thief; rather, he instructed [the Father of the Monastery] not to relay what he had divulged to him to anyone. For [our father] did not regard human glory. The Father of the Monastery ‹went and found› the goods as our saintly father Anba Bishoi had told him, and they praised God for this along with our holy father.

Bishoi's restraint from anger

[ζ].[177] Our revered father, the great Anba Bishoi, was mighty in divine attributes.[178] He was steady in his demeanor, refraining from anger in order [to present] to everyone filled with all goodness, loving of all, an image of God adorned with the Holy Spirit.[179]

[Paragraphs η and θ are positioned earlier in this recension, which also omits paragraphs δ and ε altogether.]

The hierarchy of the four great monasteries

[ı]. [Abba Bishoi] performed most of his virtues in secret. In short, I would say that he was exceedingly great, even more than many saints. He attained what they had attained, for many striving ascetics lived on this holy mountain, but those who drew near to God were not many. [Those saints, however,] their names have endured for all generations according to the command of God, and he founded monasteries after their names, and also churches were built after their names as well as glorious altars that shine many times brighter than the sun. Every day, they carry the rational sacrifices that give life to our souls [176r] and bodies, which is the body of Christ and his precious blood, which he presented as a flawless lamb for the life of the whole world.[180] A salvation for those who seek him earnestly, through the uprightness of their hearts.[181] Just like the Mighty One who chose them and called them.[182] [...][183] the law-giving prophet Moses, saying that whoever flees to these [cities of refuge] is free from reprisal.[184]

I speak of the star, the saintly prophet, the God-bearer, who truly laid down the law for us, the great one, the spirit-bearer, our father Abba Macarius the pious, whose name has ‹reached› the farthest ends of the earth. He has become a guide and a spiritual father to all who inhabit the wilderness. After that, [it is] I, the insignificant John. And I do not take pride in this, God forbid, but [it is due to] the providence of God and the prophecy of the one who became a spiritual father to me, Saint Anba Bamwah.[185] After that, the true saint, our father Anba Bishoi, about whom we speak now and whose precious memory we celebrate today. After that are the Roman saints, whom our father Abba Macarius established and directed well in the work of the monastic habit.[186] These are the four stars,[187] my beloved, that shine on the holy Mountain of Shihīt, like jewels and precious stones [176v] in a dark place. These resemble the four holy gospels, which illuminated the whole inhabited world.

On the position of Bishoi's monastery in Wadi al-Natrun

[κ].[188] I have strayed from what I have been relaying concerning the revered Anba Bishoi. For he is exceedingly great, even more than the saints. He has attained what those others have attained. We find this in the holy Gospels where it states, "Afterward, the Lord appointed another seventy and sent them to preach at every place,"[189] though their names were not recorded for us. However, he [also] chose twelve, those were called "apostles," and he informed us of their names.[190] Among those were the four evangelists, Saint[s] Matthew, Mark, Luke, and John.[191] Similarly, the four stars are the four monasteries of the Mountain of Shihīt. The Lord has revealed their names, and they are renowned, even more than many among the saints, as I have previously mentioned. And this is the tremendous grace that the Lord granted him, I mean the pious Anba Bishoi, at his holy place,[192] for he was worthy of such grace.

The healing well at Bishoi's monastery

[λ].[193] After the Berbers had killed the saintly elders in Shihīt at the Great Keep, which is called "the East," [177r] on their return to their country they reached the water well in the monastery of our saintly father Anba Bishoi. [The Berbers] and their pack animals rested there, and [the Berbers] washed their swords, which were smeared with the blood of the pure martyrs, in that well. Consequently, its waters became a source of healing for whoever bathes in it. All who are sick with various diseases, until this very day, are immediately healed and glorify God and his saints.[194]

Bishoi and Paul accept a disciple

[μ]. Afterward, our saintly father Anba Bishoi went to Anba Paul who is from Tamma, for he remained in a cave praying unceasingly, offering many prayers and great [ascetic] labor. Anba Athanasius of Ansina would go to Anba Bishoi and Anba Paul to receive their blessings and to consult them with great sincerity. He earnestly sought to [touch][195] their [monastic] garb and to follow their guidance. When he went to the saints and saw the grace of God that was upon them, they both said to him, "May you not physically separate from us in ‹this› world, nor your soul separate from us in the coming age." They also told him, "You will have a monastery, through God's will, and it will bear your name." He obeyed them in humility.

The godly Bishoi and holy Paul

76. Our saintly father Anba Bishoi would often go to our father Anba Paul, and they would comfort one another [177v] with the words of the Holy Scriptures, similar to Elisha and Elijah the prophet[s]. Our father Anba Bishoi would say to our father Anba Paul, "Let us labor a little as long as we remain in this world, while we remain in the flesh, before we are called for and summoned from this foreign place." Anba Paul said to him, "Pray for me, my saintly father, that I may obey you in everything and not hide any of [my inner thoughts] from you."[196] Our father Anba Bishoi said to him, "Worship the Lord simply from your heart. For we have reached a good age to invest in the five talents that they may be multiplied for us by the Lord.[197] Let us not be lazy like the owner of the single talent, so the Lord does not become angry with us and place our lot with the hypocrites." Our father Anba Paul said to him, "Pray for me, my saintly father, that I may do my utmost." 77A. At that time, they became a brass fortress to all the monks

who came to be blessed by them, and even more [because of] their petitions on behalf of the whole world.

Bishoi and Paul in the cave cell

78A. When the time of our saintly father Anba Bishoi drew near, after he had lived a long life and presented his body as an acceptable sacrifice to the Lord God,[198] he said—I mean Saint Anba Bishoi—"The years I resided [178r] in the wilderness of Shihīt have equaled the years I have resided in Upper Egypt—living faithfully among the fathers, consulting them." Our father Anba Paul also resided for many years on the mountain, and he would engage in innumerable [ascetic] labors on that mountain.

Sayings of Saint Bishoi

77B. Our father Anba Bishoi would say that of all the pious acts[199] performed by everyone, the greatest and most admirable is for one to delay his words and prefer the words of his friend over his own.

He also said, "The years I lived in the wilderness, before anyone knew of me or became acquainted with me, are the ones I am depending on; those are the ones for which I will receive a reward. However, from the time people have come to know of me, and have become acquainted with me, I have not expected to receive anything from those."

It was said about him that once any virtue[200] he performed was discovered by people, he would abandon it and perform another. He spent his whole life fleeing from human glory, saying, "Such a thing disturbs the individual and [results in] the loss of his fruit, though many prefer that." As for our father, he cast such things away from him and followed Christ with his whole heart.

The death of Bishoi

78B. As our pious father Anba Bishoi advanced in years, he was impaired by his age, [178v] and having crucified his body for a long time, his ‹body› would secrete a substance due to the extent of his asceticism,[201] struggle, and labor. The Lord sought to advance him and transfer him from the prison of this world and vain life. He was reposed on the eighth day of the month of Abīb.[202] The Lord received his holy soul, and the angels and the saints received him, rejoicing with him until they raised him to heaven in glory and dignity. The brothers who lived in that fort wrapped his body in a shroud with great respect, and they buried him in Minyat al-Saqr,[203] in the glory of God, the merciful.

If[204] one desired to know the years he lived in the wilderness, he would not be able to know them because [the saint] did not wish to inform us; for he fled human glory. We have learned this only from trustworthy individuals, that he remained in the wilderness of Shihīt for sixty years before he went down to the provinces of Egypt, worshiping God by night and day, performing great labors that no one would be able to hear of lest he lose faith. For this reason, we did not write about [those labors], but we have written for you a small portion of his struggles and the many virtues and deeds[205] he performed.

Translation of relics

79. As for our father Anba Paul, he was reposed on the seventh day of Bābah[206] in the inner desert. When Athanasius learned [179r] that the saints were reposed, he took a boat and ascended to Minyat al-Saqr[207] to bring the body of our father Anba Bishoi to the city of Ansina,[208] to place it in the monastery he had already built.[209] [Anba Athanasius obtained the body of Saint Anba Bishoi, placed it in the ship, and began to sail to his monastery.][210] However, when he reached the place where the body of Anba Paul was, the boat halted in the middle of the sea.[211] They remained stationary for two days; the boat did not move. The sailors[212] were astonished, and they were not able to move [the boat] anywhere. Now there was an elder, ‹a monk› filled with the Holy Spirit, named Jeremiah, who also lived at that same place in a mountain cell.[213] He came to the boat and said to the men, "Why is the boat not moving?" They said to him, "We do not know, father." He said to them, "This is on account of the body of Anba Paul of Tamma. For he had promised Saint Anba Bishoi while he was alive that they would remain with each other in this world, and that their bodies would not be separated from one another after their death."[214] When Saint Athanasius heard these words from Saint Jeremiah, he took the men with him and they brought [the body of] Saint Anba Paul from where it was placed, and brought it to the boat. [179v] Instantly, the boat then sailed until it reached Ansina; and he took [the bodies of the saints] to his monastery, and adorned them with great dignity.[215]

Athanasius ordered that their bodies be placed in an iron reliquary.[216] Then Athanasius said to his children ‹the monks, "Look›, I have built for you two bronze fortresses to guide you, and even all the districts of Egypt." Everyone would come and venerate the bodies of the saints. And these saints grant healing to the sick unto this very day—as I have learned from faithful, trustworthy people who came from the city of Ansina to the Monastery of Saint Abba Shenoute; they prayed in it,[217] and informed us concerning all things.

Conclusion and doxology

80. Hitherto, I was in great sorrow due to human weakness on account of the repose of Saint Abba Bishoi, but I was confident that he attained the

heavenly [rewards] and the good things he desired. Thus, I thanked the Lord and glorified his blessed name. Immediately, that which I saw with my eyes, learned about and verified through word and deed, I hastened to write down for the sake of your love of Christ to be a profit for your souls, and as a commemoration to the one who has, indeed, moved into the heavenly dwellings, our father [180r] Anba Bishoi. Through the grace, compassion, and love of humanity, which belong to our Master and Savior Jesus Christ, to whom is due glory, honor, might, and authority now, and at every age, and unto the ages of ages. Amen.

The life of the anchorite, the great saint, Anba Bishoi, is concluded.

[That is the life of] him whose monastery is third in rank in the wilderness of the great saint, the luminous star, Abba Macarius on the Mountain of Natrun. May the Lord Jesus Christ, Son of the living God, who, due to the multitude of his love, was incarnate of the Holy Spirit and the pure spotless Virgin, Saint Mary, for the salvation of the race of Adam and his progeny forgive the sins of the one who cared [to commission this manuscript],[218] [its] owner, the reader, the hearer, the scribe, and the rest of the children of the baptismal font,[219] through the prayers of the great Saint Anba Bishoi, the focus of this great life, along with all the martyrs and saints. Amen.

Glory be to God forever.

<Amen.>

Notes

1 Bartolomeo Pirone, ed., "Anbā Bishoy," *SOCC* 45 (2012), 7–104; Pirone, trans., *Vite di santi egiziani: Macario, Massimo e Domezio, Mose il Nero, Paolo di Tamma, Anba Bishoy, Arsenio, Apollo e Phib* (Milan: Edizioni Terra Santa, 2012).

2 Pirone's manuscripts are: *Codex M*, BnF Ar. 4796, fols. 119r–169v; *Codex B*, Monastery of al-Baramūs, Hagiography Nr.5/15, fols. 3v–40r; *Codex C*, MS Church of Our Lady Mary in the village Kafr al-Saʿīdī, fols. 1r–43r; *Codex S*, MS Church of St. Barbara in Old Cairo, 12 History, fols. 96v–112r.

3 B. Evetts provided H.G. Evelyn-White with his unpublished translation of this manuscript: Evelyn-White, ed. Walter Hauser, *The Monasteries of the Wadi 'N Natrun*, 2 vols (New York: Metropolitan Museum of Art, 1926–32; repr. Arno Press, 1973), 2:111 n. 4.

4 Simaika: 113(B); History 482(B); Old: 699(B); New 30(B) Graf 726(B); fol. 161v dates the MS: Friday, 1 Baramhāt 1431/March 10, 1714.

5 It should be read as follows: [1] 1 missing folio + 8 fols. (151r–158v), [2] 8 fols. missing, [3] 11 fols. (141r–150v), [4] 2 fols. (127r–128v), [5] 4 fols. (123r–126v), [6] 12 fols. (129r–140v), [7] 1 fol. missing + 3 fols. (159r–161v).

6 Monks of Shihīt (Scetis), *Firdaws al-abā'*, 3 vols., 2nd printing, expanded edition (N.p.: n.p., 2006–2007), 1:550–59. The monastery has another copy: MS Hag. 31 (Zanetti, 397).
7 Makarī al-Bahnasawī, ed., *Sīrat al-qiddīs al-ʿazīm al-Anbā Bishūy* (Cairo: Dār Nūbār, 2018). This edition skips over passages the editor deemed problematic or inaccurate.
8 Yūsuf Ḥabīb, *al-Qiddīsān Anbā Bishūy wā Anbā Būlā al-ṭāmūhī* (Cairo: n.p., 1971).
9 I was unable to locate Fr. Ibrāhīm al-Anbā Bishūy's edition of *LBsh*, though judging by Fr. Zakariyā's notes on that edition, it likely belongs to *WN2 Ar2*.
10 First attested in documentary texts in early Islamic Egypt, "one God" is a pervasive addition to the Trinitarian formula by which Christians contested the accusation of polytheism leveled at them under Islamic rule.
11 Arabic *sīrah*, "life" or "way of life." Similar to the Latin *vita* and Greek *bios* and *politeia*, *sīrah* denotes "biography," "manner of conduct," "reputation," and "fame."
12 Ar. *al-jihād al-ʿazīm*. *Jihād* may designate a literal or figurative "battle" or "war," as well as "labor," "exertion," or "effort." Hence, translating the word consistently with one term has proven awkward, if not impossible. In Christian-Arabic literature, it may indicate ascetic labors or spiritual warfare. The "Great Jihād" has an additional resonance within an Islamic environment in that Muslim authors often distinguish the "lesser *jihād*," which is physical warfare, from the "great" or "greater *jihād*," the internal battle *against* one's base passions.
13 Göt. prefers *b-sh-y-h*; the modern *b-y-sh-w-y* is hardly attested in any of the manuscripts surveyed. On the name, see the general introduction, 2–5.
14 That is, Scetis; also known in Arabic as Wadi Habib and Mizān al-qulūb. In monastic texts (regardless of the language), "mountain," Ar. *jabal*, like Gk. *óros*, may indicate a "monastery," "desert," or "wilderness."
15 For the Coptic *Life of John the Little*, see Maged S.A. Mikhail and Tim Vivian, ed. and trans., *The Holy Workshop of Virtue: The Life of John the Little by Zacharias of Sakhā* (Collegeville, MN: Cistercian Publications, 2010). Stephen Davis published the Arabic recension in "The Arabic Life of St. John the Little," *Coptica* 7 (2008): 1–185.
16 Ar. "Bāmūyah"; CM reads "Amūnah"; in Coptic he is referenced as "Amoi"; all are renderings of "Pambo" (see *Life of John the Little*).
17 That is, July 15.
18 That is, "virtues."
19 E.g., Deut 5:26; 1 Sam 17:26; Jer 10:10; Mt 16:16; Rom 9:26.

20 Ar. *al-jihād al-'aẓīm*; see n. 12, above.
21 See Heb 11:38.
22 See 1 Jn 1:1.
23 Lit. "in their generation." Cf. Sirach 44:1; 1 Macc 2:51.
24 BnF: "Bishlitnā"; CM: "Ashtashnā." Only in MS Göt. is "Shanshā" attested. S. Timm identifies two locations: *Das christlich-koptische Ägypten in arabischer Zeit*, 7 vols. (Wiesbaden: Dr. Ludwig Reichert Verlag, 1984–92), 5:2272–74.
25 1 Cor 1:27; 2 Cor 12:9. This is a recurring theme in the Old Testament, most explicitly in 1 Sam 17.
26 Cf. 1 Sam 16:1–13.
27 1 Pet 1:19.
28 Or "outstanding."
29 Prov 10:8.
30 1 Thess 5:17; Eph 6:18.
31 See Ps 119:103; 19:10.
32 See Ps 1:3; cf. Jer 17:8; Rev 22:2.
33 BnF: "Our spiritual father."
34 BnF: *al-āb al-mushrif*, the "supervising father" or the "father in charge." Nonetheless, Göt., CM, and the other manuscripts surveyed by Pirone have the correct pointing: *mushriq*. On the name, see the general introduction, 3.
35 Mikhail and Vivian, *Life of John the Little*, ¶25; *Apophthegmata Patrum*, John the Little 1 (Benedicta Ward, trans., *The Sayings of the Desert Fathers: The Alphabetical Collection* [Kalamazoo, MI: Cistercian Publications, 1975], 85–86).
36 Ar. *jihād 'aẓīm*; see n. 12, above.
37 Ar. *faḍāyil (faḍā'il)* "virtues," which also denotes "miracles" and "ascetic practices."
38 The phrase is unique to this Arabic recension; see the general introduction, 16. Another characteristic of this recension is the use of the expression, "the Lord God." It is used 11 times here. In contrast, the Geʻez text cites the expression once, and the Syriac recension uses it only on three occasions. It is not attested in the Greek version.
39 Ar. *al-tadbīr*, "divine dispensation/economy."
40 This may be read as "monastery"; see Maged S.A. Mikhail, "A Lost Chapter in the History of Wadi al-Natrun (Scetis): The Coptic *Lives* and Monastery of Abba John Khame," *Le Muséon* 127, no. 1–2 (2014): 162.
41 See *Life of Macarius of Scetis*: Ar. in B. Pirone, ed. and trans., *Vita di San Macario* (Cairo: Franciscan Centre of Christian Oriental Studies, 2008),

¶28–29; S. Toda, *Vie de S. Macaire l'Egyptien* (Piscataway, NJ: Gorgias Press, 2012), Coptic text, 152–54; Tim Vivian, *St. Macarius the Spiritbearer* (Crestwood, NY: St Vladimir's Seminary Press, 2004), ¶8.

42 Possible allusion to Mt 7:24.
43 Or "spiritual battles," *ijtihādan*; see n. 12, above.
44 This clause is odd. CM 30B, fol. 155v, reads: "then he would return to his holy cell."
45 The image is of a cluster of dove towers with hundreds of birds flying around them, coming and going through fist-size holes that dot the whole façade of the towers.
46 The nuance is Johannine; cf. Jn 6:47; 8:34, 51, 58; 13:16.
47 Lit. "lives."
48 Mt 24; Mk 13; Lk 21; 17:20–37.
49 Or "the peace" (cf. Jn 14:27) used here as in to "bid farewell."
50 Ar. *jihād ʿazīm*; see n. 12, above.
51 The use of "Egypt" *(Miṣr)* for Babylon, Fustat, and/or Cairo is common and persists until today.
52 Ar. *arkhun* (< Gr. *archōn*), "notable," typically designated a government-appointed administrator in earlier texts. During the Arabic era, the term expanded to include any affluent patron or lay leader.
53 That is, the desert of Scetis/Wadi al-Natrun. See n. 14, above.
54 Göt. *khuliqt*, "created." BnF reads *khālift*, "disobeyed" or "rebelled."
55 Cf. 1 Tim 3:7.
56 BnF adds: "God looked to his great struggle *(jihād al-ʿazīm)* in the wilderness."
57 Several Orthodox icons and wall paintings depict Is 6:6–7 as an Old Testament type of the Eucharist. Here, Bishoi provides a literal fulfillment.
58 BnF reads: "did not eat at all. On several occasions he observed the forty days and more without eating."
59 Or "king of slaves." This designation possibly stems from Judges 9:18.
60 The Short Recension of the *Paralipomena of Jeremiah* (Baruch 4), 5.2; the Long Recension reads 66 rather than 70.
61 The account of the Seven Sleepers of Ephesus is of fifth-century Syrian origins. See Qurʾān 18:9–26; Ernest Honigmann, "Stephen of Ephesus (April 15, 448–October 29, 451) and the Legend of the Seven Sleepers," in *Patristic Studies: Studi e testi* 173 (Vatican City: Biblioteca Apostolica Vaticana, 1953), 125–68; S. P. Brock, "Jacob of Serugh's Poem on the Sleepers of Ephesus," in *"I Sowed Fruits into the Hearts" (Odes Sol. 17:13): Festschrift for Professor Michael Lattke*, ed. P. Allen, M. Franzmann, and R. Strelan (Strathfield: St. Paul's Publications, 2007), 13–30; Matthias Vogt, "Die Siebenschläfer: Funktion einer Legende," *Hallesche Beiträge*

zur Orientwissenschaft 38 (2004): 223–47; James Drescher, *Three Coptic Legends: Hilaria, Archellites, the Seven Sleepers* (Cairo: IFAO, 1957).

62 Cf. Mt 19:26; Mk 10:27; Lk 1:37; 18:26.
63 Cf. Jn 4:14.
64 BnF adds: "and to persist in fasting and prayer without ever ceasing" (1 Thess 5:17).
65 See Mt 22:39–40.
66 See the discussion of this recension in the general introduction, 16–17.
67 BnF adds: "Did you hear him?" I said, "Yes, my father."
68 For the heavenly Jerusalem as a walled city, see Rev 21:9–14; 22:14; Ezk 48:31.
69 This is reminiscent of John Chrysostom's *A Comparison between a King and a Monk*, trans. D.G. Hunter (Lewiston, NY: Edwin Mellen Press, 1988).
70 Heb 11:37–38.
71 Ibṣāy is likely Ptolemais Hermiou or Ptolemais in the Thebaid; Timm, *Das christlich-koptische Ägypten*, 3:1140–47.
72 BnF reads *kalimah*, "word." Doubtless, *ḥikmah*, "wisdom," is the original reading; cf. Is 11:2; 1 Cor 12:8; Eph 1:17; Wis. 7:7. Here, Bishoi, armed with the Holy Spirit, the Spirit of Wisdom, is about to prudently defend the divinity of the Holy Spirit before a hostile crowd.
73 See n. 51, above.
74 See Jn 14:16, 26; 15:26; 16:7.
75 Cf. *Life of Macarius*; Ar. Pirone, *Vita di San Macario*, ¶¶140–53; Toda, *Vie de S. Macaire*, Coptic appendix 2; Syr. 329–37; also see Toda's discussions and tables on pp. 28–31, 101–104; Vivian, *Four Desert Fathers: Pambo, Evagrius, Macarius of Egypt, and Macarius of Alexandria* (Crestwood, NY: St Vladimir's Seminary Press, 2004), 97–100; *Synaxarium* (ed. R. Basset), 27 Baramhāt, pp. 261–62.
76 Lit. "have."
77 Or "By."
78 Gen 1:1–2 (LXX).
79 Is 61:1–2; lit. "a year that is acceptable to the Lord."
80 Ps 104:30.
81 Jn 1.32.
82 1 Cor 12:3. CM, fol. 141r, reads: "No one can say that Jesus Christ is the Son of God except by the Holy Spirit."
83 Cf. Ezk 37:5 (LXX). BnF reads: "The Lord said to me, the Spirit shall blow over these bones and they will all live and rise."
84 Dan 7:9.
85 Mt 28:19.

86 BnF, fol. 132r, has a scribal error: "since *(min)* the beginning, the Holy Spirit exists from *(min)* the Father and the Son." CM, fol. 141r, reads: "For the Holy Spirit exists with *(kāyin [kā'in] ma'a)* the Father and the Son since the beginning."
87 BnF: "the Holy Scriptures that God breathed through our father."
88 This is the first explicit reference to Bishoi's monastery.
89 See the general introduction, 2, 14.
90 Ar. *idlāl*; reading it as *dalāl* (cf. *dallah*). Similar to the Greek *parrēsia*, it indicates confidence and freedom of access due to personal closeness and intimacy.
91 Lit. "kissed one another"; see Rom 16:16; 1 Cor 16:20; 2 Cor 13:12; 1 Thess 5:26; 1 Pet 5:14. It is unclear how early the practice began, but typically when Coptic monks greet each other, they kiss one another on the shoulders or the hands.
92 Ar. *faḍāyil (faḍā'il)*; see n. 37, above.
93 Jn 1:47.
94 Lit. "kissed," *qabbiluh*; see n. 91, above.
95 Cf. *Life of John the Little* (Mikhail and Vivian), ¶55.
96 Ar. *'afīf*, also "chaste" or "righteous."
97 In Christian Arabic, *al-amānah* is the "deposit of faith," or "doctrine," that each generation is "entrusted" with. It is not typically a reference to personal faith or trust *(īmān)*.
98 This is not a Jewish critique of Christianity, but an Islamic one (see Qur'ān 4:157); see the general introduction, 12.
99 For "Egypt," see n. 51, above.
100 In a monastic context, "to perform a *metanoia*" carries the double meaning of spiritual repentance and a physical prostration.
101 BnF: "do not accept ideas that are foreign to the holy faith."
102 This is an echo of Rom 3:3 and Heb 4:15; see also Rom 11:32; 2 Cor 5:21; 1 Pet 1:18–19, 2:22; 1 Jn 3:5.
103 Cf. Eph 2:4; Jas 5:11.
104 Lit. "labored"; BnF: "passion," or "experienced pain."
105 On this pericope, see the general introduction, 6, 9. The intriguing means by which the divine command was maintained while Saint Bishoi's prayers to the contrary were, nonetheless, answered should not be overlooked.
106 See Mk 13:26; 14:62; 1 Thess 4:16; Rev 1:7.
107 Reading *ṣ-d-ī-q* as *ṣadīq*, the likely reading (see James 2:23). Describing the holy man as a "friend of God" is common in monastic literature. Still, the vocalization may be *ṣiddīq*, "the righteous one."
108 BnF: "By the *righteousness* of God!" It reads *birr* rather than *ibn*, "son."

109 Referencing the soul as a physical object is common in patristic and medieval writings.
110 Several shifts in grammatical gender here and in the next sentence have been harmonized.
111 Cf. Ps 37:28; 67:36; 97:10 (LXX).
112 Ar. *ijtihād*; cf. n. 12, above.
113 Perhaps a reference to Gen 3:15, where justice and mercy, punishment and promise, are conjoined.
114 Cf. Jn 15:13; 1 Jn 3:16.
115 Ar. *ijtihādahum*.
116 Sharp grammatical shifts indicate a missing clause here.
117 CM 30B, fol. 147v, reads similarly. BnF, fol. 139v, reads, "and teach them all the virtues. And not to think of this at all. Our Father then prayed God."
118 Cf. Mk 10:20–30.
119 Cf. Deut 11:27; Lk 11:28.
120 Here and below, "Bīfāmān." Gr. reads "Poemen"; BnF: "Yanqanun"; CM: "Binyāmīn" (Benjamin). Two notable individuals had that name. One is Phoibammon of Koptos/Qift, who attended the Council of Ephesus (AD 431); see Timm, *Das christlich-koptische Ägypten*, 4:2141. The other, and likely, subject here (see the following note)—though the dates are harder to justify—is Phoibammon of Panopolis/Akhmin, the mid-sixth-century author of the *Second Encomium on Colluthus* (Timm, *Das christlich-koptische Ägypten*, 1:83–84). Peter Grossmann, "Phoibammon von Panopolis und das Kolluthos *Martyrium* in Pnewit," *Journal of Coptic Studies* 12 (2010): 19–31; G. Schenke, *Das koptische hagiographische Dossier des Heiligen Kolluthos—Arzt, Märtyrer und Wunderheiler*, CSCO 650 Subsidia 132 (Louvain: Peeters, 2013), 151–91.
121 Ar. Madīnat al-ʿiqāb. This is most likely Panopolis/Akhmim, a major site for the ancient Egyptian cult of the eagle, or the Horus falcon: see Karolien Geens, "Panopolis, a Nome Capital in Egypt in the Roman and Byzantine Period" (PhD diss., Katholieke Universiteit Leuven, 2007; repr. 2014), 117, 318–19, 368, 449, 468. The lost city by that name mentioned by al-Masʿūdī, *Murūj al-dhahab*, and more fully described in al-Maqrīzī's *Khiṭaṭ*, is much farther north and would hardly figure here: al-Maqrīzī, *al-Mawāʿiẓ wa-l-iʿtibār fī dhikr al-khiṭaṭ wa-l-athār*, ed. Ayman Fuʾad Sayyid, 5 vols. (London: al-Furqān Islamic Heritage Foundation, 2002–2004).
122 See n. 91, above.
123 Mt 18:3; 19:14; Mk 10:14; Lk 18:16.
124 Lit. "he is not small/young but large/great."
125 Lit. "the way"; less literally "manner," "character," "habit."

126 Ar. *fa-ashār*, "gestured"; CM 30B, fol. 149v reads *fa-sār*, "he went."
127 Lit. "raise him above our heads." This could also mean "to honor" or "to celebrate."
128 This sentence is likely misplaced.
129 Perhaps, "come under his care."
130 This is shorter than the Ethiopic and Syriac recensions.
131 Ar. *al-iskīm*.
132 Ar. *rijāl mujahidin*, "men of combat/battle."
133 See n. 14, above.
134 See 1 Pet 5:8. BnF: "Satan appeared to him, angry as a lion."
135 The spiritual ideal implicit here is that demons fight only against those who have already conquered basic vices.
136 CM, fol. 124r, "your very word and the pleasure of your only Son, and the pleasure of your Holy Spirit."
137 See ¶¶12 and 13, above.
138 Lit. "to fight on our behalf"; see Jn 14:16, 26; 15:26; 16:7.
139 BnF, fol. 146v: *al-qādir wahdak*; CM 30B, fol. 124v: *al-qādir 'alā kull shay'*, "Almighty." E.g., Gen. 48:3; Is 13:6; 2 Cor 6:18; Rev 16:14.
140 Lit. "Living is the Lord God." This is an oath formula; see Is 37:4; Jer 10:10; 23:36.
141 BnF: "friend of God."
142 BnF: "only followed his own will."
143 BnF: "Babylon"; see Timm, *Das christlich-koptische Ägypten*, 5:2120–32.
144 See n. 51, above.
145 BnF: "knees."
146 Ar. *ajāb*.
147 Or "accompanied." On the misogynistic tone of this paragraph, see Maged S.A. Mikhail, *The Legacy of Demetrius of Alexandria: The Form and Function of Hagiography in Late Antique and Islamic Egypt* (New York: Routledge, 2016), 66–69. This tone increased in Ḥabīb's edition in which he listed even more biblical passages to that end (*al-Qiddīsān*, 25–27).
148 Gen 39:20.
149 1 Kgs 19:1–9.
150 Judg 16.
151 See Num 25:9; 1 Cor 10:8.
152 Mt 14:1–12; BnF: "the Baptist."
153 Ar. *al-kanayysī (kana'ysī)*, the "ecclesiastic." This may be a literal rendering of the Greek (LXX) *ekklēsiastēs*: "teacher" or "preacher," which renders the Hebrew *qōheleth*: the one who "gathers" or "calls" an assembly. See 1 Kgs 8:1; Ecc 1:1.

154 1 Kgs 11:1–8. BnF misreads the clause: "so that he did not enter the books." CM omits it.
155 Ar. *muqaddim al-rusul*; CM, *kabīr al-rusul*. On the historical position of Saint Peter in the Coptic Orthodox Church (and the current distortion of that view), see Maged S.A. Mikhail, "A Reappraisal of the Current Position of St. Peter the Apostle in the Coptic Orthodox Church," *Bulletin of the St. Shenouda the Archimandrite Coptic Society* 5 (1999): 53–72. For the Orthodox East more generally, see John Meyendorff, ed., *The Primacy of Peter: Essays in Ecclesiology and the Early Church* (Crestwood, NY: St Vladimir's Seminary Press, 1992); John Chryssavgis, *Primacy in the Church: The Office of Primate and the Authority of Councils*, 2 vols. (Crestwood, NY: St Vladimir's Seminary Press, 2016).
156 Mt 26:69–75.
157 "The elder" and "the saint" are one and the same—Bishoi.
158 The Ethiopic recension of ¶ε names Isaac as Bishoi's successor.
159 Lit. "vessel."
160 Lit. "place."
161 Cf. *Life of John the Little* (Mikhail and Vivian), ¶76.
162 See n. 51, above.
163 Ancient Antinoopolis or Antinoë, six miles south of Bani Hassan, near the village of Shaykh ʿIbādah; see Timm, *Das christlich-koptische Ägypten*, 1:111–28.
164 On this passage, see the introduction to the appendix, 323–25.
165 Gen 18; cf. Jn 13:1–11. The association with Jn 13 is explicit in the Greek recension.
166 See Gen 18:4.
167 Ar. *qaṣriyyah* is typically a vessel used as a toilet or washbasin.
168 Göt.: *ʿāmilan bi-ẓikr al-maktūb*; BnF: *ʿājilan*, "quickly"; CM: *ʿāliman*, "knowing."
169 Mt 22:39; Mk 12:31, 33; Lk 10:27.
170 Lit. "had mercy upon."
171 Jn 14:12.
172 See n. 143, above.
173 Cop./Gr. *topos*, lit. "place," often indicates "monastery" or "church." BnF reads "monastery."
174 On this title, see Benjamin I, *On Cana of Galilee: A Sermon by the Coptic Patriarch Benjamin I. A Revised Expanded Edition*, trans. Maged S.A. Mikhail (Los Angeles: Saint Athanasius and Saint Cyril Theological School, 2019), section v of the sermon and n. 147.
175 Lit. "Do love," a common expression in Syriac, Coptic, and Greek for "please," "kindly," "if you will."

176 Ar. *ra'īs dhālk al-jabal*; cf. nn. 14 and 173, above.
177 This is a much shorter recension than in Syriac or Ethiopic manuscripts.
178 Or "divine essence," *dhāt allah*; cf. 2 Pet 1:4.
179 Cf. Col 1:28–29 and 2 Tim 3:16.
180 See 1 Pet 1:19; Jn 1:29.
181 See Heb 11:6.
182 See 1 Pet 2:9.
183 An abrupt grammatical shift indicates a missing passage; cf. the other recensions.
184 Ex 21:12–14; Num 35:9–34; Deut 19:1–13; Josh 20:1–3.
185 See n. 16, above.
186 Ar. *al-iskīm*.
187 BnF, "these are the four monasteries, the bright stars."
188 See the general introduction, 4, 6, concerning this paragraph and the hierarchy among the monasteries. This passage is poorly worded and poorly informed. Compare it with the analogous paragraph in the appendix in Mikhail, "A Lost Chapter," and the Arabic *Life of Macarius*, ¶¶172–77 (Pirone, *Vita di San Macario*). Both passages retain similar problems and the same analogy—truncated here—comparing the monasteries to the cities of refuge mentioned in Josh 20:1–9.
189 Lk 10:1, 17.
190 Mt 10:1–4; Mk 3:14–19; Lk 6:13–16.
191 Luke and Mark were not among the Twelve; see n. 188, above.
192 See n. 173, above.
193 The incident would have taken place in 444; see Evelyn-White, *Monasteries*, 2:164–67, 269–71.
194 See Jn 5:2–7.
195 Göt.: "wear" (*yalbis*); BnF retains a better reading, "touch" (*yalmis*).
196 Lit. "no part of my bones may be hidden."
197 Cf. Mt 25:14–30; Lk 19:11–27.
198 See Rom 12:1.
199 See n. 37, above.
200 Likely "ascetic discipline" here; see n. 37, above.
201 BnF: *al-shakka*, "thorn"; CM: *al-nusk*, "asceticism"; cf. 2 Cor. 12:7–9; Acts 19:11–12.
202 That is, July 15.
203 See the general introduction, 5.
204 This paragraph is not in CM 30B, fol. 160r. Here, and in the parallel passages in the Syriac and Ethiopic recensions, the text presents a slightly different version of the tradition in 78A.

205 See n. 37, above.
206 That is, October 18.
207 See the general introduction, 5.
208 See n. 163, above.
209 The monastery prophesied about in ¶μ.
210 This sentence is needed for the flow of the narrative; the Greek, Syriac, Garshuni, and Ethiopic recensions retain an analogous sentence.
211 Ar. *baḥr*, "ocean" or "sea"; the use of *baḥr* for the Nile is common in Egyptian Arabic.
212 Lit. "men."
213 This is most likely Anba Herminā; see the general introduction, 5.
214 In general, see Claudia Rapp, *Brother-making in Late Antiquity and Byzantium: Monks, Laymen, and Christian Ritual* (Oxford and New York: Oxford University Press, 2016), ch. 3.
215 This is most likely Dayr Anba Bishoi at al-Barsha; also known as Dayr al-Barsha or Dayr al-Nakhla.
216 Lit. "casket."
217 CM: "Monastery of Saint Bishoi," but that would not make sense given the context of the passage. On this important sentence, see the general introduction, 5.
218 Lit. "the one who cared," meaning "the one who commissioned this manuscript," is a fixed expression in Coptic and Copto-Arabic manuscript colophons.
219 Or "baptism."

APPENDIX: CARRYING CHRIST ¶V
Maged S.A. Mikhail
Manuscript Family C
Recension WN2 Ar2

Two accounts in the *LBsh* are especially noted and serve as the basis for the saint's modern Coptic iconography. The first, in which Bishoi washes the feet of Christ, is attested in every manuscript and recension surveyed in this volume (¶69A). Still, details of that account changed in later recensions. In the older versions, Bishoi immediately identifies his visitor, and the visitation and the foot-washing are juxtaposed against the background of Abraham's actions in Genesis 18. These details are minimized in later and contemporary renderings. In one version, Jesus comes to Bishoi's cell as an anchorite who had lost his way in the desert; in another, he is a poor visitor who happens to knock on Bishoi's cell.[1] In those recensions, as in the second account discussed below, Christ initially appears as a stranger,[2] and it is only when Bishoi proceeds to wash the feet of his guest (in one version, his thumb detecting the hole made by the nail on the cross) that he discerns the true identity of his mysterious visitor. By and large, the later versions are far more interested in the saint's humility as expressed through the act of foot-washing, and the revelation of the mysterious visitor's identity, than in depicting Bishoi as a new Abraham.

The second prominent account, in which Bishoi carries Christ, is not attested in any of the manuscripts or recensions directly studied here, and it was wholly lacking in the Coptic Arabic *Synaxarium* until the 2012 ecclesiastical edition. Still, it is quoted in several studies based on late Arabic manuscripts of the *LBsh*;[3] where this account is found constitutes *Rec. WN2 Ar2*. In it, the saint carries an individual who is ultimately revealed to be Jesus. Hitherto, three versions of this narrative are identified; in two (below) the saint carries an old man, in a third he carries a youth (*ṣabīy*) over his shoulders.[4] A memorable narrative, the

323

true significance of the pericope is habitually overlooked in light of the miraculous, enigmatic encounter. At its core, the account provides the basis for the belief in the incorruptibility of the saint's body. In spite of major discrepancies, in all three versions the identity of Christ is progressively revealed, and he blesses Bishoi by telling him that his body will not see corruption.

This belief was first documented ca. AD 1400, in the Ethiopic *Synaxarium*, and it reached its zenith in the nineteenth century, when the saint was believed to have, on occasion, physically reached out of his reliquary to greet pious visitors and pilgrims.[5] The tradition most likely originated in the mid-fourteenth century, when Patriarch Benjamin II (1327–39) came to Wadi al-Natrun in AD 1330 and consecrated the Holy Oil of Chrism *(al-mayrūn)* at the Monastery of Saint Macarius, and personally oversaw the restoration of Bishoi's monastery. At least one account positively links the two events, maintaining that Benjamin II discovered that Bishoi's body appeared as though he had just passed away.[6] Significantly, what appears to be the oldest version of ¶ v *(Version A)* is situated within the context of the consecration of a church at the Monastery of St. Macarius, which, although positioned in the early fifth century, would fit in well with Patriarch Benjamin II's much later visit to that monastery.

Two versions of the account are provided below. *Version A* is shorter and provides (albeit convoluted) historical clues. The text is provided from a passage quoted by the late Bishop Ṣamū'īl of Shibīn al-Qanāṭir.[7] There, the context is the consecration of a "church" at the Monastery of St. Macarius. *Version B* is drawn from a booklet published by the late Fr. Bishūy Kāmil in 1972.[8] Although he does not provide the complete vita, Fr. Bishūy quotes substantial passages from an unidentified Arabic manuscript that follows much of the wording and structure of the Arabic manuscripts surveyed here, though it appends the notable passage translated below. The opening sentence of the account would position it after the foot-washing narrative that concludes with ¶74.[9] Yet in Fr. Bishūy's edition, it is oddly positioned between ¶¶52 and 53A. This is either due to the manuscript Fr. Bishūy utilized or, perhaps, it was repositioned by him for the edition. Further support for placing ¶v after ¶74 is found in Fr. Zakariyā's book; there, he places ¶v after ¶74 based on an Arabic publication accessible to him.[10] In all, the account in that publication is a polished rendition of *Version B*. Significantly, the orthography (and vocalization) of the saint's name in both versions is the more modern *b-y-sh-w-y*, not the older *b-sh-y-h* or even *b-y-sh-ā-y*.

Version A[11]	Version B[12]
[v] When the church of Saint Macarius was constructed, and the elders of the wilderness determined a specific day for its consecration, monks from the various parts of the valley hurried to it.	[v] When the fathers in the wilderness heard about the appearance of the Lord Christ to his chosen one, Anba Bishoi, their souls longed for such a holy revelation. Thus, the saint asked the Lord to appear to the brothers that their faith might increase, and that they might be filled with power and fervor. The Lord promised to appear at a certain time, and [the saint] informed the brothers about that time, and they all rejoiced greatly. Early, on the morning of that day, the monks raced—young and old—to the [designated] mountain so that no one would miss the blessed opportunity.
As Anba Bishoi was making his way to [the church], he saw a frail[13] elder, who approached him taking slow steps. The pious one approached him, and asked him where he was going. He said that he wanted to go to the church of Saint Macarius to witness the consecration, and to receive the blessing of the fathers who were gathered in it.	As Anba Bishoi trailed a bit behind, he saw a frail[14] elder, walking, taking slow steps. [The saint] approached him and asked where he wanted to go. [The elder] said, "To the church."[15]
When Bishoi saw that exhaustion was clearly setting upon the elder, he offered to carry him wherever he desired. Initially he refused, but then he accepted his [offer]. The saint placed him on his shoulder, and he began to cross the valley of Scetis as though he were not carrying anything. But then, the old monk became increasingly heavy until the one carrying him could not proceed. At that [moment], Bishoi realized that that elder was none other than the one who is the Ancient of Days, who existed before all ages.[16] [Bishoi] looked up at him, saying, "The heavens cannot contain you, and the earth quakes because of your glory. How then can a sinner like me carry you?" Right then, the Lord smiled at him, and granted him peace to his spirit and a blessing to his body; he then left him and departed.	When [Bishoi] saw that exhaustion began to set upon [the elder], he was moved with compassion, and he offered to carry him. Initially, [the elder] refused, but after the saint insisted, he accepted [the offer]. [Anba Bishoi] lifted [the elder] up on his shoulder and began to cross long distances without tiring; it was as though he were not carrying anything. But then, [the elder] began to become increasingly heavy to the extent that [Bishoi] was unable to proceed. At that [moment], he realized through the Spirit that this elder was the Lord Jesus; the Ancient of Days.[17] [Bishoi] looked up at him and cried out: "My Master Jesus Christ, heaven cannot contain you and earth quakes because of your glory.[18] How then can a sinner like me carry you?" Right then, the Lord smiled at him and said, "Because you have carried me, my beloved Bishoi, your body will not see corruption."

Version A[11]	Version B[12]
	As for the saint, he continued on his path, overwhelmed with tremendous joy, until he reached the mountain. He found the brothers eagerly awaiting the appearance of the Lord of Glory,[19] with their eyes fixed at the east.[20] He informed them that [the Lord] had appeared, and that they had all seen him, but because they had shut their spiritual eyes[21] they did not recognize him.

Notes

1 Anonymous/A Monk from the Monastery, *Qiṣṣat dayr al-qiddīs al-ʿaẓīm al-Anbā Bīshūy: bayn al-ams wa al-yawm* (Cairo: al-Anba Ruways al-Ufsit, 1991), 108; Ṣamūʾīl of the Syrian Monastery [later, Bishop Ṣamūʾīl of Shibīn al-Qanāṭir], *al-Adurah al-maṣriyah al-ʿāmirah* (Cairo: al-Matbaʿat al-Tujāriyah al-ḥadīthah, 1968), 119.

2 Cf. post-Resurrection appearances in Mk 16:12–13; Lk 24:13–35; Jn 20:1–16.

3 Ṣamūʾīl, *al-Adurah al-maṣriyah*, 118–19; Anonymous, *Qiṣṣat dayr al-qiddīs*, 109.

4 This version of the tradition is noted by Yūsuf Ḥabīb based on unidentified manuscripts that he read (*al-Qiddīsān Anbā Bishūy wā Anbā Būlā al-ṭāmūhī* [Cairo: n.p., 1971], 55).

5 Ṣamūʾīl, *al-Adurah al-maṣriyah*, 123, relays the account with caution and implicitly criticizes it.

6 Anonymous, *Qiṣṣat dayr al-qiddīs*, 118. I have not found the exact passage alluded to in the *Book of Chrism* (the *Book* has an extended discussion of Benjamin II's visit). Perhaps the reference is in one of the monastery's manuscripts of that book. Also see Ṣamūʾīl, *al-Adurah al-maṣriyah*, 127. On Benjamin II in general, see Y.N. Youssef, "A Letter from the Patriarch Benjamin II to the Monks of Saint Macarius," in *Eastern Christians and Their Written Heritage: Manuscripts, Scribes and Context*, ed. J.P. Monferrer-Sala, H. Teule, and S.T. Tovar (Leuven: Peeters Publishing, 2012), 135–52.

7 Ṣamūʾīl, *al-Adurah al-maṣriyah*, 118–19; Yūsuf Ḥabīb published the same account based on Bishop Ṣamūʾīl's edition in his *al-Qiddīsān*, 54–55. Ṣamūʾīl begins the account with: "It is stated in some of the recorded lives [of the saints] (*al-siyyar*), which are common among monks." Notably, copies circulating among monks would not be the older, fragile manuscripts, but

more recent copies. The tradition of copying manuscripts by hand continued in Coptic monasteries into the twentieth century.

8   Bishūy Kāmil, *al-Anbā Bishūy* (Alexandria: Kanīsat Marī Jirjis Sbūrting, 1972; repr. 1979), 17–18.
9   Cf. Ḥabīb, *al-Qiddīsān*, 54–55.
10 Zakariyā al-Baramūsī, *al-Qiddīs al-'azīm al-Anbā Bishūy* (Cairo: Markaz al-Diltā lil-ṭibaʿah, 2002), 71–73, is citing the passage from a book by Fr. Ibrāhīm al-Anbā Bishūy (*Tarīkh al-qiddīs al-Anbā Bishūy*, 1970), which I was unable to locate. That longer version places the account in Ansina rather than Wadi al-Natrun, and it stipulates that the mysterious elder wanted to go to the mountain, not "the church"; on the importance of that gloss, see n. 15, below.
11 See n. 7, above.
12 See n. 8, above.
13 Lit. "an elder whose bones gave way," or "with weak bones."
14 See n. 13.
15 In this version, this appears to have been an altogether different direction. Is "church" here a fragment from an older tradition, perhaps *Version A*, or is this the crux of the account? That is, that the saint decided to go completely out of his way to have mercy on another, rather than to proceed to the mountain and see Jesus.
16 "Ancient of Days," cf. Dan 7:9, 13, 22. "Before all ages," cf. Jude 1:25.
17 "Ancient of Days," cf. Dan 7:9, 13, 22.
18 This echoes several biblical verses: 1 Kgs 8:27; 2 Chr 2:6; 6:8; Ps 97:4; 104:32.
19 Cf. 1 Cor 2:8.
20 Or "at the dawning sun."
21 Lit. "The eyes of their innards."

Bibliography

Manuscripts Referenced
Berlin, Königliche Bibliothek, Syr. 201 (Sachau 165)
BL.Or. (Eth.) 692
BL.Or. (Syr.) 963 [Add. 14,732.8]
BL.Or. (Syr.) 971 [Add. 14,735]
BnF Ar. 100 "Book of the Consecration of the Mayrūn"
BnF Ar. 4796
BnF Éth. 126
BnF Grec 1093
BnF Grec 1547
BnF suppl. gr. 759
BnF Syr. 234
BnF Syr. 236
Church of Our Lady Mary in the village Kafr al-Saʿidi, fols. 1r–43r.
Church of St. Barbara in Old Cairo, 12 History
Coptic Museum, New 30B
Damascus Patriarchate 12/17
Deir Abū Maqār Hag. 19 (Zanetti, 385)
Deir Abū Maqār Hag. 31 (Zanetti, 397)
Deir al-Zaʿfarān, cod. pap. 71 (Dolabany)
Göttingen Ar. 114
Mingana Syr. 83
Monastery of al-Baramūs, Hagiography Nr.5/15
Monastery of the Syrians, Syr. 30.D
Salomon Manuscript (according to P. Bedjan's 1892 edition; current whereabouts are unknown)
Syriac Orthodox Monastery of St. Mark in Jerusalem 199A

University of Cambridge Syr. Add. 2016
Vat. Syr. 117

Texts and Editions of the Life of Bishoi

Bedjan, Paul. *Acta Martyrum et Sanctorum*, vol. 3. Leipzig: Otto Harrassowitz, 1892.

Blanchard, Monica. "Beh Isho' Kamulaya's Syriac Discourses on the Monastic Way of Life: Edition, English Translation, and Introduction." PhD diss., Catholic University of America, 2001. Appendix I contains a translation of the Syriac text according to P. Bedjan's edition.

Colin, Gérard, ed. and trans. *La version éthiopienne de l'Histoire de Bsoy: Édition critique et traduction française*, PO 49.3. Turnhout: Brepols, 2002.

Pirone, Bartolomeo, ed. "Anbā Bishoy." *SOCC* 45 (2012): 7–104.

———, trans. *Vite di santi egiziani: Macario, Massimo e Domezio, Mose il Nero, Paolo di Tamma, Anba Bishoy, Arsenio, Apollo e Phib*. Milan: Edizioni Terra Santa, 2012.

Pomialovskii, I.V. *Zhitie prepodobnogo Paisiia Velikogo i Timofeia Patriarkha Alexandriiskogo* [*The Life of the Blessed Païsios and Timothy, Patriarch of Alexandria*], *Zapiski istoriko-filologicheskogo fakul'teta SPb U* [*Journal of the Historical-Philological Department of St. Petersburg University*] 50, no. 3 (1902): 1–61.

Scheil, V. "Restitution de deux textes dans le récit syriaque de la vie de Mar Bischoi (ed. Bedjan)." *Zeitschrift für Assyriologie und verwandte Gebiete* 15 (1900): 104–106.

Zakariyā al-Baramūsī. *al-Qiddīs al-'azīm al-Anbā Bishūy: tārīkh dayrahu wā āthāruh bi-Anṣinā ma'a sīratuh ḥasab al-naṣṣayn al-yūnāni wā al-'arabī*. Cairo: Markaz al-Diltā li-l-ṭiba'ah, 2002.

Editions Containing Portions and Summaries of the Life Based on Arabic MSS

Baḥr, Mīşā'īl. *Tārīkh al-qiddīs al-Anbā Yūḥannis al-qaṣīr wā manṭiqat Anṣinā*. N.p.: n.p., 1957.

Kāmil, Bishūy. *al-Anbā Bishūy*. Alexandria: Kanīsat Marī Jirjis Sbūrting, 1972; repr. 1979.

Ḥabīb, Yūsuf. *al-Qiddīsān Anbā Bishūy wā Anbā Būlā al-ṭāmūhī*. Cairo: n.p., 1971.

Makarī al-Bahnasawī, ed. *Sīrat al-qiddīs al-'azīm al-Anbā Bishūy*. Cairo: Dār Nūbār, 2018. Based on BnF 4796, but omits what is deemed theologically problematic.

Monks of Shihīt (Scetis). *Firdaws al-abā'*. 3 vols. 2nd printing, expanded ed. 1: 550–59. N.p: n.p., 2006–2007.

Primary Sources

Athanasius of Alexandria. *Athanase d'Alexandrie: Vie d'Antoine*. Edited and translated by G.J.M. Bartelink. Paris: Cerf, 1994.

Benjamin I. *On Cana of Galilee: A Sermon by the Coptic Patriarch Benjamin I. A Revised Expanded Edition*. Translated by Maged S.A. Mikhail. Los Angeles: Saint Athanasius and Saint Cyril Theological School, 2019. Coptic text and English translation.

Besa. *The Life of Shenoute by Besa*. Translated by David N. Bell. Cistercian Studies 73. Kalamazoo, MI: Cistercian Publications, 1983.

Cassian, John. *John Cassian: The Conferences*. Edited and translated by Boniface Ramsey. New York: Paulist, 1997.

Clugnet, Léon. "Vie et récits de l'Abbé Daniel, de Scété." *Revue de l'Orient Chrétien* 5 (1900): 49–73, 254–71, 370–91; *Revue de l'Orient Chrétien* 6 (1901): 56–87.

Evagrius Ponticus. *Evagrius Ponticus, The Praktikos and Chapters on Prayer*. Translated by John Eudes Bamberger. Cistercian Studies 4. Kalamazoo, MI: Cistercian Publications, 1981.

Evetts, B.T.A. *The Churches and Monasteries of Egypt and Some Neighbouring Countries*. Oxford: Clarendon Press, 1895; repr. Gorgias Press, 2001.

———, ed. and trans. *History of the Patriarchs* I (Vulgate): *History of the Patriarchs of the Coptic Church of Alexandria*. PO 1.2, 1.4, 5.1, 10.5. Paris, 1904–15; repr. Paris: Firmin-Didot, 1947–59.

John Chrysostom. *A Comparison between a King and a Monk*. Translated by David G. Hunter. Lewiston, NY: Edwin Mellen Press, 1988.

John of Shmūn. "An Encomium on Saint Antony." In Vivian and Athanassakis (trans.), *Life of Antony* (Athanasius of Alexandria), 1–35.

(Pseudo-) John III. *Les "Questions de Théodore": Texte sahidique, recensions arabes et éthiopienne*. Edited and translated by A. Van Lantschoot. Vatican City: Biblioteca Apostolica Vaticana, 1957.

Khater, A., and O.H.E. Khs-Burmester, eds. and trans. *History of the Patriarchs of the Egyptian Church*. V, 2.1–3. Cairo: Publications de la Société d'Archéologie Copte, 1948–59; vol. 3.3. Cairo: Publications de la Société d'Archéologie Copte, 1970.

Life of Ephrem: Joseph P. Amar, ed. and trans., *The Syriac "Vita" Tradition of Ephrem the Syrian*. 2 vols. CSCO 629 and 630, Scr. Syr. 242 and 243. Louvain: Peeters, 2011.

Life of Harmina: Makarī of the Monastery of Saint Macarius, *Sīrat al-qiddīs al-ʿazīm al-Anbā Hirmīnā al-sāʾiḥ*. Cairo: Dār Yūsuf Kamāl li-l-ṭibaʿā, n.d. [after 2012].

Life of John the Little: Coptic text and translation in Maged S.A. Mikhail and Tim Vivian, eds. and trans., *The Holy Workshop of Virtue: The Life of John the Little by Zacharias of Sakhā*. Collegeville, MN: Cistercian Publications,

2010. Arabic text and translation in Stephen Davis, "The Arabic Life of St. John the Little," *Coptica* 7 (2008).

Life of Macarius of Scetis: Arabic in Bartolomeo Pirone, ed. and trans., *Vita di San Macario*. Cairo: Franciscan Centre of Christian Oriental Studies, 2008. Coptic and Syriac texts, Satoshi Toda, *Vie de S. Macaire l'Egyptien*. Piscataway, NJ: Gorgias Press, 2012. Eng. trans., T. Vivian, *St. Macarius the Spiritbearer*. Crestwood, NY: St Vladimir's Seminary Press, 2004.

Life of Maximus and Domitius: Tim Vivian, trans., "The Bohairic *Life of Maximus and Domitius*." *Coptic Church Review* 26, no. 2–3 (2005): 34–63.

Life of Paul of Tamma (Short Recension: Arabic): A. Wadi, "La recensione breve della vita araba di Paolo di Tamma." *Aegyptus Christiana: Mélanges d'hagiographie égyptienne et orientale dédiés à la mémoire du P. Paul Devos, Bollandiste*, edited by U. Zanetti and E. Lucchesi. *Cahiers d'Orientalisme* 25, 195–210. Geneva: Patrick Cramer Editeur, 2004.

———. (Long Recension: Arabic): A. Wadi, "La recensione lunga della vita araba di Paolo di Tamma, presentazione, edizione e indice." *SOCC* 38 (2005): 115–78.

———. (Coptic Fragments): T. Orlandi, ed. and trans., *Paolo di Tamma: Opere*. Rome: C.I.M., 1988; Vivian, *Words to Live By*, 154–62.

al-Maqrīzī. *al-Mawāʿiẓ wa-l-iʿtibār fī dhikr al-khiṭaṭ wa-l-athār*. Edited by Ayman Fuʾād Sayyid. 5 vols. London: al-Furqān Islamic Heritage Foundation, 2002–2004.

al-Nabulsī, ʿUthmān. [*Taʾrīkh al-Fayyūm wā bilāduh*] *Description du Fayoum au VIIme siècle de l'Hégire par Abou ʿOsmân il Naboulsi iṭl Ṣafadi*. Edited by B. Moritz. Cairo: National Press/al-Maṭbaʿah al-Ahliyah, 1899 [1898]; Fr. trans. M. G. Salmon, "Répertoire géographique de la province du Fayoum, d'apres le *Kitāb Tārīkh al-Fayyoām* d'an-Nāboulsī." *Bulletin de l'Institut Français d'Archéologie Orientale* (1901): 29–77.

Palladius: The Lausiac History. Translated by Robert T. Meyer. New York: Newman Press, 1965.

Palladius of Aspuna: The Lausiac History. Translated by John Wortley. Collegeville, MN: Cistercian Publications, 2015.

Schenke, G. *Das koptische hagiographische Dossier des Heiligen Kolluthos—Arzt, Märtyrer und Wunderheiler*. CSCO 650 Subsidia 132. Louvain: Peeters, 2013.

Stevenson, J. *Creeds, Councils, and Controversies: Documents Illustrative of the History of the Church A.D. 337–461*. London: S.P.C.K, 1966, 1981.

Le synaxaire arabe-jacobite (rédaction copte). Edited and translated by R. Basset. PO 1, 3, 11, 16, 17. Paris: Firmin-Didot, 1905–28.

Le synaxaire éthiopien: les mois de sané, hamlé et nahasé. Edited by I. Guidi. PO 7.3. Paris: Firmin-Didot, 1907.

Le synaxaire éthiopien: Mois de maggābit. Edited and translated by Gérard Colin. PO 46.3. Turnhout: Brepols, 1994.

Vivian, Tim. *Four Desert Fathers: Pambo, Evagrius, Macarius of Egypt, and Macarius of Alexandria.* Crestwood, NY: St Vladimir's Seminary Press, 2004.

———. *Paphnutius.* Rev. ed. Kalamazoo, MI: Cistercian Publications, 2002.

———. *The Sayings and Stories of the Desert Fathers and Mothers*, vol. 1. Cistercian Studies Series 287. Collegeville, MN: Cistercian Publications, 2021.

———, trans. *Witness to Holiness: Abba Daniel of Scetis.* Cistercian Studies Series 219. Kalamazoo, MI: Cistercian Publications, 2008.

Vivian, Tim, and Apostolos N. Athanassakis. *The Life of Antony: The Coptic Life and the Greek Life.* Cistercian Studies Series 202. Kalamazoo, MI: Cistercian Publications, 2003.

Vivian, Tim, and Maged S. A. Mikhail. *The Holy Workshop of Virtue: The Life of John the Little by Zacharias of Sakha.* Cistercian Studies 234. Kalamazoo, MI: Cistercian Publications, 2010.

Ward, Benedicta, trans. *The Sayings of the Desert Fathers: The Alphabetical Collection.* Kalamazoo, MI: Cistercian Publications, 1975.

Wortley, John, trans. *Give Me a Word: The Alphabetical Sayings of the Desert Fathers.* Yonkers, NY: St Vladimir's Seminary Press, 2014.

Wüstenfeld, H. Ferdinand, trans. *Synaxarium, das ist Heiligen-Kalender der coptischen Christen.* Gotha: F.A. Perthes, 1879.

Secondary Sources

Allen, Pauline, and C.T.R. Hayward. *Severus of Antioch.* New York: Routledge, 2005.

Amar, Joseph P. "Byzantine Ascetic Monachism and Greek Bias in the Vita Tradition of Ephrem the Syrian." *Orientalia Christiana Periodica* 58 (1992): 136–56.

Anonymous/A Monk from the Monastery. *Qiṣṣat dayr al-qiddīs al-ʿaẓīm al-Anbā Bīshūy: bayn al-ams wa al-yawm.* Cairo: al-Anba Ruways al-Ufsit, 1991.

Atiya, Aziz S. *The Coptic Encyclopedia.* 8 vols. New York: Macmillan, 1991. (Abbreviated *CE); Claremont Coptic Encyclopedia (CCE),* https://ccdl.claremont.edu/digital/collection/cce/search.

Ayoub, Mahmoud M. "Toward an Islamic Christology II: The Death of Jesus, Reality or Delusion (A Study of the Death of Jesus in Tafsīr Literature)." *Muslim World* 70 (1980): 91–121.

Bauer, Walter. *A Greek–English Lexicon of the New Testament and Other Early Christian Literature.* Revised and edited by Frederick William Danker. Chicago: University of Chicago Press, 1979.

Beylot, Robert. "La version éthiopienne de 'l'Histoire de Besoy.'" *Revue de l'Histoire des Religions* 203, no. 2 (1986): 169–84.

Blanchard, Monica J. "The Coptic Heritage of St. Ephrem the Syrian." In *Acts of the Fifth International Congress of Coptic Studies, Washington, 12–15 August 1992*, edited by T. Orlandi and D.W. Johnson, 37–51. Rome: C.I.M., 1993.

———. "Saint Ephrem's Coptic Friend, Apa Bishoi." *The Harp* 16 (2003): 43–55.

Bolman, Elizabeth S., ed. *The Red Monastery Church: Beauty and Asceticism in Upper Egypt*. New Haven, CT: Yale University Press, 2016.

Boyarin, Daniel. "What Do We Talk About When We Talk About Platonic Love?" In *Toward a Theology of Eros: Transfiguring Passion at the Limits of Discipline*, edited by Virginia Burrus and Catherine Keller, 3–22. New York: Fordham University Press, 2006.

Brakke, David. *Demons and the Making of the Monk: Spiritual Combat in Early Christianity*. Cambridge, MA and London: Harvard University Press, 2006.

———. "Jewish Flesh and Christian Spirit in Athanasius of Alexandria." *Journal of Early Christian Studies* 9, no. 4 (2001): 453–81.

Brock, Sebastian P. "Jacob of Serugh's Poem on the Sleepers of Ephesus." In *"I Sowed Fruits into the Hearts" (Odes Sol. 17:13): Festschrift for Professor Michael Lattke*, edited by Pauline Allen, Majella Franzmann, and Rick Strelan, 13–30. Early Christian Studies 12. Strathfield: St. Paul's Publications, 2007.

———. *The Luminous Eye: The Spiritual World Vision of Saint Ephrem*. Cistercian Studies 124. Kalamazoo, MI: Cistercian Publications, 1992.

Brock, Sebastian P., and L. van Rompay. *Catalogue of the Syriac Manuscripts and Fragments in the Library of Deir al-Surian, Wadi al-Natrun (Egypt)*. Louvain: Peeters, 2014.

Brown, Peter. *The Cult of the Saints: Its Rise and Function in Latin Christianity*. Chicago: University of Chicago Press, 1981.

———. "The Rise and Function of the Holy Man in Late Antiquity." *Journal of Roman Studies* 61 (1971): 80–101.

———. "The Rise and Function of the Holy Man in Late Antiquity, 1971–1997." *Journal of Early Christian Studies* 6, no. 3 (1998): 353–76.

Burrus, Virginia. "Introduction: Theology and Eros after Nygren." In *Toward a Theology of Eros: Transfiguring Passion at the Limits of Discipline*, edited by Virginia Burrus and Catherine Keller, xiii–xxii. New York: Fordham University Press, 2006.

Burrus, Virginia, and Catherine Keller, eds. *Toward a Theology of Eros: Transfiguring Passion at the Limits of Discipline*. New York: Fordham University Press, 2006.

Burton-Christie, Douglas. *The Word in the Desert*. New York and Oxford: Oxford University Press, 1993.

Chitty, Derwas. *The Desert a City.* Crestwood, NY: St Vladimir's Seminary Press, 1977.

Chryssavgis, John. *Primacy in the Church: The Office of Primate and the Authority of Councils.* 2 vols. Crestwood, NY: St Vladimir's Seminary Press, 2016.

Coakley, Sarah. *The New Asceticism: Sexuality, Gender and the Quest for God.* London: Bloomsbury, 2015.

Constas, Nicholas. "An Apology for the Cult of Saints in Late Antiquity: Eustratius Presbyter of Constantinople, *On the State of Souls after Death* (CPG 7522)." *Journal of Early Christian Studies* 10 (2002): 267–85.

———. "'To Sleep, Perchance to Dream': The Middle State of Souls in Patristic and Byzantine Literature." *Dumbarton Oaks Papers* 55 (2001): 91–124.

Coquin, René-Georges. "Paul, of Tamma, Saint." *Coptic Encyclopedia* 6:1923b–1925a.

———. "Pshoi of Scetis." *Coptic Encyclopedia* 6:2029a–2030a.

———. "Pshoi of Tud." *Coptic Encyclopedia* 6:2030.

———. "Tutun." *Coptic Encyclopedia* 7:2283a–b.

Coquin, René-Georges, and Maurice Martin. "Dayr Anba Abshay." *Coptic Encyclopedia* 2:718b–719a.

Cox, Patricia. *Biography in Late Antiquity: A Quest for the Holy Man.* Berkeley: University of California Press, 1983.

Crum, W.E. *A Coptic Dictionary.* Oxford: Clarendon Press, 1939.

Daniélou, Jean, ed., *From Glory to Glory: Texts from Gregory of Nyssa's Mystical Writings.* Crestwood, NY: St Vladimir's Seminary Press, 1997.

Delehaye, Hippolyte. *Les légendes hagiographiques.* Brussels: Société des Bollandistes, 1955.

———. *The Legends of the Saints.* Translated by Donald Attwater. Dublin and Portland, OR: Four Courts Press, 1998.

den Heijer, J. "Relations between Copts and Syrians in the Light of Recent Discoveries at Dayr as-Suryân." In *Coptic Studies on the Threshold of a New Millennium, I–II: Proceedings of the Seventh International Congress of Coptic Studies,* edited by M. Immerzeel and J. van der Vliet, 923–38. Louvain: Peeters, 2004.

Desprez, Vincent. *Le monachisme primitif: Des origins jusqu'au concile d'Éphèse.* Bégrolles-en-Mauges: Bellefontaine, 1998.

Dolabany, Filoksinos Yohanna. *Catalogue of Syriac Manuscripts in Za'faran Monastery (Dairo Dmor Hananyo),* edited by G.Y. Ibrahim. Aleppo: Mardin Publishing House, 1994.

Drescher, James. *Three Coptic Legends: Hilaria, Archellites, the Seven Sleepers.* Supplément aux Annales du Service des antiquités de l'Egypte 4. Cairo: Institut français d'archéologie orientale du Caire, 1957.

Dunn, Marilyn. "The Meaning of Asceticism." In *The Emergence of Monasticism: From the Desert Fathers to the Early Middle Ages*, 59–81. Oxford: Blackwell, 2000.

Efthymiadis, Stephanos, ed. *The Ashgate Research Companion to Byzantine Hagiography*. 2 vols. Burlington, VT: Ashgate, 2011–14.

Emmel, Stephen, and Bentley Layton. "Pshoi and the Early History of the Red Monastery." In Bolman, *The Red Monastery Church*, 11–15.

Evdokimov, Paul. *La nouveauté de l'esprit*. Spiritualité Orientale. Begrolles-en-Mauges: Bellefontaine, 1977.

Evelyn-White, H.G. *The Monasteries of the Wadi 'N Natrun*. Edited by Walter Hauser. 2 vols. New York: Metropolitan Museum of Art, 1926–32; repr. Arno Press, 1973.

Fiey, J.M. "Coptes et Syriaques, contacts et échanges." *SOCC* 15 (1972–73): 295–365.

Frankfurter, David. *Elijah in Upper Egypt: The Apocalypse of Elijah and Early Egyptian Christianity*. London: Bloomsbury T&T Clark, 1998.

Fredriksen, Paula. "Jewish Romans, Christian Romans, and the Post-Roman West: The Social Correlates of the *Contra Iudeos* Tradition." In *Conflict and Religious Conversation in Latin Christendom: Studies in Honour of Ora Limor*, edited by Israel Jacob Yuval and Ram Ben-Shalom, 23–53. Turnhout: Brepols, 2014.

Gabra, Gawdat. "Perspectives on the Monastery of St. Antony: Medieval and Later Inhabitants and Visitors." In *Monastic Visions: Wall Paintings in the Monastery of St. Antony at the Red Sea*, edited by Elizabeth S. Bolman, ch. 10. New Haven, CT: Yale University Press, 2002.

Gardiner, Eileen. "Hell, Purgatory, and Heaven." In *Handbook of Medieval Culture*, vol. 1, edited by Albrecht Classen, 653–73. Berlin: De Gruyter, 2015.

Geens, Karolien. "Panopolis, a Nome Capital in Egypt in the Roman and Byzantine Period." PhD diss., Katholieke Universiteit Leuven, 2007, repr. 2014.

Goehring, James E. *Ascetics, Society, and the Desert: Studies in Early Egyptian Monasticism*. Harrisburg, PA: Trinity, 1999.

———. "Through a Glass Darkly: Images of the Ἀποτακτικοι in Early Egyptian Monasticism." In *Ascetics, Society, and the Desert: Studies in Early Egyptian Monasticism*, 53–72. Harrisburg, PA: Trinity, 1999.

Graiver, Inbar. *Asceticism of the Mind: Forms of Attention and Self-transformation in Late Antique Monasticism*. ST 213. Toronto: Pontifical Institute of Mediaeval Studies, 2018.

Griffith, Sidney H. *The Church in the Shadow of the Mosque: Christians and Muslims in the World of Islam*. Princeton, NJ: Princeton University Press, 2008.

Grossmann, Peter. "Phoibammon von Panopolis und das Kolluthos *Martyrium* in Pnewit." *Journal of Coptic Studies* 12 (2010): 19–31.

Guillaumont, Antoine. "Nitria." *Coptic Encyclopedia* 5:1794b–1796b.
Hägg, Tomas, and Philip Rousseau, eds. *Greek Biography and Panegyric in Late Antiquity*. Berkeley: University of California Press, 2000.
Hambye, Édouard René. "Pishay, anachorète: une commémoraison peu connue du calendrier de l'Eglise syrienne d'Antioche." *L'Orient syrien* 7 (1962): 255–59.
Harmless, William. *Desert Christians: An Introduction to the Literature of Early Monasticism*. Oxford: Oxford University Press, 2004.
Honigmann, Ernest. "Stephen of Ephesus (April 15, 448–October 29, 451) and the Legend of the Seven Sleepers." In *Patristic Studies: Studi e testi* 173, 125–68. Vatican City: Biblioteca Apostolica Vaticana, 1953.
Huxley, Aldous. "Distractions—I." *Vedanta for the Western World*. Edited by Christopher Isherwood. Hollywood, CA: Vedanta Press, 1946.
An Intermediate Greek–English Lexicon. Oxford: Clarendon, [1889] 1975.
Ishaq, Emile Maher. "Coptic Language, Spoken." *Coptic Encyclopedia* 2:604a–607a.
Ishaq, Shenouda [Imīl] Mahir. *al-Khalāṣ al-ladhī nuntaẓiruh*. Vol. 2, *Ḥālat arwāḥ al-rāqidīn*. 3rd printing. Cairo: al-Anbā Rūways al-'Ufset, 2002.
Janssen, L.F. "'Superstitio' and the Persecution of the Christians." *Vigiliae Christianae* 33, no. 2 (June 1979): 131–59. http://www.jstor.org/stable/1583266.
Judge, E.A. "The Earliest Use of Monachos for 'Monk' (P. Coll. Youtie 77) and the Origins of Monasticism." *Jahrbuch für Antike und Christentum* 10 (1977): 72–89.
Keller, Catherine. "Afterword: A Theology of Eros, after Transfiguring Desire." In *Toward a Theology of Eros: Transfiguring Passion at the Limits of Discipline*, edited by Virginia Burrus and Catherine Keller, 366–74. New York: Fordham University Press, 2006.
Lampe, G.W.H. *A Patristic Greek Lexicon*. Oxford: Clarendon, 1961.
Le Goff, Jacques. *The Birth of Purgatory*. Translated by Arthur Goldhammer. Chicago: University of Chicago Press, 1986.
Lewis, Theodore J. "Belial." In *The Anchor Bible Dictionary*, edited by David Noel Freedman, 1:654a–656b. New York: Doubleday, 1992.
Liddell, Henry George, and Robert Scott. *Greek–English Lexicon*. Revised by Henry Stuart Jones. Oxford: Clarendon, repr. 1977.
Malina, Bruce J. *The New Testament World: Insights from Cultural Anthropology*. 3rd ed. Louisville, KY: Westminster John Knox Press, 2001.
Malina, Bruce J., and Richard L. Rohrbaugh. *Social-science Commentary on the Synoptic Gospels*. 2nd ed. Minneapolis: Fortress Press, 2003.
Martin, Maurice, S.J. "Dayr Harmina." *Coptic Encyclopedia* 2:808.

Mattā al-Miskīn. *al-Rahbanah al-qibṭiyah fī 'asr al-qiddīs Anbā Maqqār.* 3rd expanded ed. Wadi al-Natrun: Maṭba'at Dayr al-Qiddīs al-Anbā Maqqār, 1995.

McGinn, Bernard. *The Foundations of Mysticism: Origins to the Fifth Century.* Vol. 1 of *The Presence of God: A History of Western Christian Mysticism.* New York: Crossroad, 1991.

McGuckin, John Anthony. *Westminster Handbook to Patristic Theology.* Louisville, KY and London: Westminster John Knox Press, 2004.

Meinardus, Otto F.A. "Aethiopica in Aegypto." *Journal of Ethiopian Studies* 3, no. 1 (1965): 23–35.

———. "St. Bishoi: A Coptic Christophorus." *Orientalia Suecana* 48 (1999): 67–73.

Meredith, Anthony. *The Cappadocians.* Crestwood, NY: St Vladimir's Seminary Press, 1995.

Meyendorff, John, ed. *The Primacy of Peter: Essays in Ecclesiology and the Early Church.* Crestwood, NY: St Vladimir's Seminary Press, 1992.

Mikhail, Maged S.A. *From Byzantine to Islamic Egypt: Religion, Identity, and Politics after the Arab Conquest.* London and New York: I.B. Tauris, 2014.

———. *The Legacy of Demetrius of Alexandria: The Form and Function of Hagiography in Late Antique and Islamic Egypt.* New York: Routledge, 2016.

———. "A Lost Chapter in the History of Wadi al-Natrun (Scetis): The Coptic *Lives* and Monastery of Abba John Khame." *Le Muséon* 127, no. 1–2 (2014): 149–85.

———. "A Reappraisal of the Current Position of St. Peter the Apostle in the Coptic Orthodox Church." *Bulletin of the St. Shenouda the Archimandrite Coptic Society* 5 (1999): 53–72.

Mirsanu, Dragos. "Dawning Awareness of the Theology of Purgatory in the East: A Review of the Thirteenth Century." *Studii Teologice* 4 (2008): 179–93.

Montanari, Franco, ed. *The Brill Dictionary of Ancient Greek.* English editors, Madeleine Goh and Chad Schroeder. Leiden: Brill, 2015.

Moreira, Isabel. *Heaven's Purge: Purgatory in Late Antiquity.* Oxford: Oxford University Press, 2010.

Moss, Yonatan. *Incorruptible Bodies: Christology, Society, and Authority in Late Antiquity.* Berkeley: University of California Press, 2016.

Nerburn, Kent. *Neither Wolf nor Dog: On Forgotten Roads with an Indian Elder.* Novato, CA: New World Library, 1994, 2002.

———. *Voices in the Stones: Life Lessons from the Native Way.* Novato, CA: New World Library, 2016.

O'Leary, De Lacy. *The Saints of Egypt.* London: SPCK, 1937; Amsterdam: Philo Press, 1974.

Pagels, Elaine. *Adam, Eve, and the Serpent: Sex and Politics in Early Christianity*. New York: Vintage, 1989.

Papaconstantinou, Arietta. "Hagiography in Coptic." In *The Ashgate Research Companion to Byzantine Hagiography*, vol. 1, *Periods and Places*, edited by Stephanos Efthymiadis, 323–43. Burlington, VT: Ashgate, 2011.

Papadopoulos, Leonidas, and Georgia Lizardos, trans. *Saint Païsios the Great by Saint John the Dwarf of Egypt*. Jordanville, NY: Holy Trinity Monastery, 1998.

Papanikolaou, Aristotle. "The Dance of Faith." *Christian Century* (February 15, 2017): 36–40.

Pletruschka, Ute. "Some Observations about the Transmission of Popular Philosophy in Egyptian Monasteries after the Islamic Conquest." In *Ideas in Motion in Baghdad and Beyond: Philosophical and Theological Exchanges between Christians and Muslims in the Third/Ninth and Fourth/Tenth Centuries*, edited by Damien Janos, ch. 3. Leiden: Brill, 2016.

Rapp, Claudia. *Brother-making in Late Antiquity and Byzantium: Monks, Laymen, and Christian Ritual*. Oxford and New York: Oxford University Press, 2016.

Regnault, Lucien. *The Day-to-day Life of the Desert Fathers in Fourth-century Egypt*, translated by Étienne Poirier, Jr. Petersham, MA: St. Bede's, 1999.

———. "Poemen, Saint." *Coptic Encyclopedia* 6:1983a–1984b.

Regnault, Lucien, and Michel Van Esbroeck. "John Colobos, Saint." *Coptic Encyclopedia* 5:1359b–1362a.

Rich, Antony. *Discernment in the Desert Fathers:* Διάκρισις *in the Life and Thought of Early Egyptian Monasticism*. Studies in Christian History and Thought. Bletchley: Paternoster Press, 2015.

Samir, Samir Khalil, and Jorgen Nielsen, eds. *Christian Arabic Apologetics during the Abbasid Period (750–1258)*. Leiden: Brill, 1994.

Samuel [Ṣamū'īl] of the Syrian Monastery [later, Bishop Samuel of Shibīn al-Qanatir]. *al-Adurah al-maṣriyah al-'āmirah*. Cairo: al-Matba'at al-Tujāriyah al-ḥadīthah, 1968.

Sanders, Johannes. "Introduction to the Life of Mar Bishoi (Siglum MB)." *The Harp* 8–9 (1995–96): 277–88. [This is Beh Isho', not Bishoi of Scetis]

Secretarial Committee. *al-Qarārāt al-majma'iyah fī 'ahd ṣāhib al-qadāsah al-Bābā Shinūdah al-thālith*. 3rd printing. N.p.: al-Markaz al-Thaqāfī al-Qibṭī al-Urthūdhuksī, 2011.

Smith, Jonathan Z., ed. *The HarperCollins Dictionary of Religion*. San Francisco: HarperSanFrancisco, 1995.

Soldati, Agostino. "Some Remarks about Coptic Colophons and Their Relationship with Manuscripts: Typology, Function, and Structure." *Comparative Oriental Manuscript Studies Bulletin* 4, no. 1 (2018): 115–19.

Stewart, Randall. "Daqahlah." *Coptic Encyclopedia* 2:693a.

Suciu, Alin. "Sitting in the Cell: The Literary Development of an Ascetic Praxis in Paul of Tamma's Writings. With an Edition of Some Hitherto Unknown Fragments of *De Cella*." *Journal of Theological Studies* n.s. 68, no. 1 (2017): 141–71.

Timm, S. *Das christlich-koptische Ägypten in arabischer Zeit*. 7 vols. Wiesbaden: Dr. Ludwig Reichert Verlag, 1984–92.

Vivian, Tim. "Ama Sibylla of Saqqara." In *Words to Live By: Journeys in Ancient and Modern Egyptian Monasticism*, 377–93. Kalamazoo, MI: Cistercian Publications, 2005.

———. "Courageous Women: Three Desert Ammas—Theodora, Sarah, and Syncletica." *American Benedictine Review* 71, no. 1 (2020): 75–107.

———. "Monks, Middle Egypt, and Metanoia: The *Life of Phib by Papohe the Steward* (Translation and Introduction)." *Journal of Early Christian Studies* 7, no. 4 (1999): 547–71.

———. "A Spirituality of Desire: A Meditation on *The Life of Pshoi* vis-à-vis *The New Asceticism* by Sarah Coakley." *Cistercian Studies Quarterly* 53, no. 1 (2018): 9–31.

———. "'We Sail by Day': Metaphor and Exegesis in the Sayings of Amma Syncletica of Egypt." *Cistercian Studies Quarterly* 54, no. 1 (2019): 3–24.

———. *Words to Live By: Journeys in Ancient and Modern Egyptian Monasticism*. Kalamazoo, MI: Cistercian Publications, 2005.

Vogt, Matthias. "Die Siebenschläfer: Funktion einer Legende." *Hallesche Beiträge zur Orientwissenschaft* 38 (2004): 223–47.

Weil, Simone. *The Notebooks of Simone Weil*. Translated by Arthur Wills. 2 vols. London: Routledge & Kegan Paul, 1976.

Williams, Rowan. 104th Archbishop of Canterbury. "God's Mission and a Bishop's Discipleship," 18 July 2008. http://aoc2013.brix.fatbeehive.com/articles.php/1739/the-archbishops-retreat-addresses-parts-iii-iv-v.

Wimbush, Vincent. *Ascetic Behavior in Greco-Roman Antiquity*. Studies in Antiquity & Christianity. Minneapolis: Fortress Press, 1990.

Wipszycka, Ewa. *The Second Gift of the Nile: Monks and Monasteries in Late Antique Egypt*. Translated by Damian Jasiński. Warsaw: University of Warsaw, 2018.

Wright, W. *Catalogue of the Syriac Manuscripts of the British Museum*. Vol. 3. London: Longmans/British Museum, 1872.

Youssef, Y.N. "A Letter from the Patriarch Benjamin II to the Monks of Saint Macarius." In *Eastern Christians and Their Written Heritage: Manuscripts, Scribes and Context*, edited by J.P. Monferrer-Sala, H. Teule, and S.T. Tovar, 135–52. Leuven: Peeters Publishing, 2012.

Zanetti, Ugo. *Les Manuscrits de Dair Abû Maqâr: inventaire*. Geneva: P. Cramer, 1986.

INDEXES

Topics

abbot 20n24, 228, 267, 297
Abimelech 206, 244, 288
Abraham 80, 81, 99n134, 103n201, 124n640, 125n661, 223, 232, 262, 302, 323
Abrom 235n88
abstinence 57, 73, 216
Achilles, Abba 112n389
Adam 82, 219, 224, 258, 263, 301, 302, 303
Adam and Eve 122n606
adversary 40, 261, 296
affection 51, 58
affection, divine 40, 41, 42, 95n73, 98n119
affection, loving 105n252
Alexandria 214, 252, 291
alms, almsgiving 39, 56, 228, 244, 267, 273n18, 288, 297
Ammonas 128n726
Amoi *see* Pambo
anchorite 71, 74, 80, 106n257, 119n544, 120n564, 255, 287, 289, 290, 291, 298, 323
Ancient of Days 128n735, 249, 325, 327n16, 327n17

angel xvi, 43, 52, 55, 56, 61, 66, 71, 75, 76, 80, 81, 82, 96n92, 98n117, 123n619, 202, 204, 205, 212, 215, 217, 218, 231, 239, 240, 241, 242, 243, 249, 250, 253, 256, 262, 265, 271, 284, 286, 287, 288, 290, 292, 299, 303
anger xvii n1, 69, 115n455, 213, 227, 251, 261, 266, 267, 306
Anoup 252, 276n92
anti-Judaism xvi, 117n498
anti-Muslim 121n591
Antony 35, 43, 94n65, 101n162, 102n176, 110n346, 110n347, 110n354, 110n356, 113n413, 232
Aphthartodocetists 1, 18n3
Apollo 252, 276n92
apophthegmata 34, 39, 117n489
apostasy 122n595, 122n597
apostle 37, 110n339, 211, 220, 229, 249, 307
Arabic 2, 3, 5, 7, 12, 16, 18n7, 195, 196, 197, 198, 234n30, 234n47, 236n97, 273n24, 274n45, 278n149, 279n178, 281, 312n11, 312n12, 312n14, 312n16, 313n20, 313n36, 313n37, 313n38, 314n50, 314n52, 316n90, 316n92, 316n97, 317n112,

317n115, 317n121, 318n126,
    318n131, 318n132, 318n139,
    318n146, 318n153, 319n155,
    319n167, 320n176, 320n186,
    320n201, 321n211, 323, 324
archetype 8, 9
Arianism 112n391, 113n413, 117n493
Arqā (for Hieracas) 275n62
Ascesis 32, 34, 108n297
ascetic xvi, 38, 39, 74, 93n53, 103n201,
    114n439, 119n544, 122n601,
    122n602, 242, 254, 268, 286, 307
asceticism 29, 32, 35, 38, 44, 69,
    95n81, 213, 251, 285, 288, 289,
    302, 309, 320n201
ascetic practices 35, 51, 246, 313n37
Athanasius of Alexandria 7, 39, 94n65,
    102n176, 112n391, 310
Athanasius of Ansina 5, 308
athlete 32, 68, 115n440, 217
authority 63, 124n636
authorship 8, 9

Bamawi *see* Pambo
Bamoy *see* Pambo
Bāmūyah *see* Pambo
Bamwa *see* Pambo
Bamwah *see* Pambo
Bamwi *see* Pambo
Banmun (Poemen) 212
baptism 73, 112n391, 119n526, 215,
    220, 249, 254, 258, 292, 321n219
barbarian 5, 199, 221, 229, 260, 269,
    302, 308
Barnabas, Abba 232
Baruch 234n33
Basil (the Great) 104n228, 105n248,
    124n633
basin 262, 263, 302, 319n167
baskets 45, 65, 66, 112n394, 210, 211,
    248, 289
battle 312n12, 318n132

battles, spiritual 314n43
bees 58, 206, 288
beginner 53, 76
Beh Ishoʿ 4, 22n48, 237
Belial (Beliar) 75, 120n562
Bemoi *see* Pambo
Benjamin (Binyāmīn) 317n120
Benjamin I, Patriarch 319n174
Benjamin II, Patriarch 6, 17, 21n36,
    324, 326n6
Berbers 302, 308; *see also* barbarians
Besa 117n492
Beymon (Piamoun) 199, 235n90
Biamūn (Poemen) 269
Bīfāmān (Poemen) 317n120
Bifimun (Poemen) 250
Bīfīmūn (Poemen) 275n78
Bimuch (Poemen) 274n25
Bimuḥ (Poemen) 273n25
Bishāra of Aleppo 15
Bishoi/Bsoy/Païsios: birth 52, 201, 239,
    283; body 6, 12, 17, 88, 231, 271,
    310, 324, 325, *see also* relics; burial
    5, 10, 88, 130n766, 130n783, 271;
    carrying Jesus xv, 11, 17, 323–27;
    death 5, 87, 230, 270, 271, 309;
    family 52, 201, 202, 239, 240, 283,
    284; forms of the name 1–4, 30,
    97n109, 199, 274n33, 312n13,
    324; mother 52, 99n144, 202;
    successor 222, 319n158; title of
    "Shining Father" 3, 285
Bishoi (Bishay) Anub 4
Bishoi of Akhmim (Sohag) 4
Bishoi (Païsios) of Constantinople 4,
    10, 23n56
Bishoi of Jeremiah 4, 19n13
Bishoi of Scetis 3, 10, 19n13, 23n56
Bishoi of Tud 4
blessing 17, 117n497, 212, 214, 230,
    243, 250, 252, 253, 264, 269, 287,
    289, 291, 295, 304, 305, 325

blood 229, 269, 308
boat 5, 87, 130n778, 232, 271, 310
body 88, 95n75, 98n124, 130n777, 231, 232, 269, 270, 271, 272, 309, 310
Body of Christ 300, 307
Book of Chrism 326n6
brass 230, 270, 308
bread 54, 58, 83, 102n183, 122n597, 203, 209, 213, 224, 225, 235n81, 241, 246, 247, 251, 254, 255, 259, 263, 285, 294, 297, 304
bronze 310
brother 84, 85, 226, 227, 251, 253, 255, 257, 259, 261, 262, 265, 267, 271, 278n142, 296, 297, 298, 305
brotherhood 58, 105n248, 127n707
Bsoy 3, 30, 195–236; *see also* Bishoi

care, pastoral 58, 206, 243, 288
cave, crevice 2, 58, 68, 80, 114n438, 201, 207, 221, 225, 232, 242, 244, 245, 252, 260, 267, 270, 271, 283, 301, 309
cell 67, 96n93, 116n475, 128n726, 228, 242, 243, 245, 246, 250, 253, 254, 255, 260, 265, 270, 286, 288, 291, 292, 293, 297, 298, 302, 305, 309, 314n44, 323
cenobium 87, 119n544, 127n715
charges, false 84, 265, 305
child(ren) 83, 114n427, 115n467, 116n467, 206, 212, 227, 228, 239, 263, 275n81, 278n153
children, spiritual 206
Christ, Jesus xvi, 34, 58, 59, 68, 69, 72, 78, 79, 80, 81, 90n13, 98n120, 100n154, 103n205, 106n260, 109n331, 110n344, 114n435, 116n467, 117n494, 118n504, 118n518, 118n521, 121n581, 124n644, 125n654, 127n697, 197, 204, 207, 209, 213, 217, 223, 224, 225, 229, 230, 242, 245, 246, 249, 251, 253, 255, 262, 263, 264, 273n14, 286, 290, 292, 293, 302, 303, 305, 323, 324, 325, 327n15
Christian xv, xvi, 72, 218, 237, 253, 292, 312n9, 312n12
Chrysostom, John 15n69, 122n593, 398n120
church(es) 104n226, 222, 229, 268, 273n18, 277n133, 277n134, 307, 319n173, 325, 327n10, 327n15
Church, Coptic Orthodox 110n357, 319n155
Church, Ethiopian Orthodox 234n33
Church of the First-born 57, 244
Church, Roman Catholic 7
cities of refuge 307, 320n188
city 10, 23n56, 35, 38, 42, 77, 78, 83, 84, 110n353, 126n682, 223, 257, 263, 264, 304, 315n68
Clement (of Alexandria) 7, 105n241, 113n411
Cleopas 81
cloud xvi, 6, 59, 60, 61, 71, 117n492, 197, 198, 207, 208, 215, 245, 246, 253, 290, 291, 292, 293, 294
combat 203, 206, 207, 209, 230, 231, 233n14, 285, 318n132
commandment 53, 56, 84, 100n151, 101n163, 261
Communion 57, 69, 77, 296
community 122n602, 124n633, 127n715
community, monastic 116n474
compassion 73, 78, 79, 82, 107n286, 108n313, 126n677, 126n678, 210, 217, 244, 246, 255, 256, 264, 294
Constantine xvi, 63, 64, 110n357, 111n363, 209, 247, 288, 289
Copt(-ic) xv, 1–4, 9, 17, 21n35, 30, 39, 90n10, 94n66, 94n67, 116n479,

INDEXES   343

195, 234n24, 273n24, 277n135, 312n15, 312n16, 319n173, 319n175, 321n218, 323, 327n7
Council of Constantinople 112n391
Council of Ephesus 317n120
Council of Nicaea 112n391
Creator 95n85, 98n118, 100n161, 104n228, 107n296

Daniel (Prophet) 211, 249, 290
Daniel of Scetis, Abba 39
David 53, 54, 78, 101n168, 122n606, 211, 249, 290
Dayr (monastery) *see* monasteries *and individual entries below*
dead people 83, 84, 221, 225, 248, 259, 264, 301, 302, 304, 305
death 38, 51, 52, 54, 59, 87, 106n276, 121n572, 202, 221, 231, 232, 246, 271, 284, 285
death of Bamoy/Bamwah/Bemoi/Pambo 54, 203, 241, 285
death of Paul/Bawli/Bawri of Tamma 87, 310
demiurge 95n85, 104n228
demon 37, 73, 74, 75, 76, 80, 84, 85, 93n49, 120n547, 128n723, 217, 218, 255, 256, 266, 298, 299, 306, 318n135
desert xvi, 38, 55, 56, 57, 60, 63, 66, 68, 69, 70, 71, 73, 74, 75, 77, 78, 84, 85, 88, 103n205, 111n381, 120n554, 123n629, 197, 201, 202, 204, 206, 207, 209, 212, 213, 214, 215, 216, 217, 219, 221, 223, 224, 226, 228, 229, 230, 231, 240, 243, 244, 248, 249, 250, 252, 255, 256, 257, 260, 261, 265, 267, 268, 270, 271, 283, 287, 289, 302, 312n14, 314n53, 323; *see also* wilderness
Desert Fathers 195, 200

desert, inner/interior 57, 60, 87, 107n288, 206, 207, 208, 244, 246, 293, 310
Desert Mothers 93n62
desert, outer 63
desire xvi, 29, 32, 33, 34, 35, 36, 38, 39, 40, 41, 42, 44, 51, 68, 95n73, 95n82, 96n88, 98n119, 98n120, 113n418, 115n446, 124n647, 219, 228, 243, 300
desire, loving 36, 38, 39, 40, 41, 42, 44, 45, 51, 53, 54, 58, 81, 82, 87, 93n60, 94n69, 96n94, 97n114, 98n116, 100n148, 102n181, 102n185, 105n245, 124n653, 125n663, 129n749
Devil 37, 43, 56, 57, 59, 71, 74, 75, 76, 80, 84, 85, 95n87, 103n209, 107n279, 109n330, 119n530, 120n560, 120n566, 127n714, 205, 206, 210, 216, 217, 233n9, 243, 255, 287, 298
disciple 44, 53, 59, 60, 61, 62, 69, 70, 71, 72, 73, 78, 81, 82, 83, 84, 108n298, 108n299, 114n427, 117n490, 119n539, 121n575, 126n679, 127n701, 197, 198, 201, 202, 204, 207, 208, 216, 219, 223, 224, 225, 226, 227, 229, 233n9, 240, 242, 244, 245, 246, 249, 252, 254, 259, 262, 263, 264, 267, 268, 269, 290, 292, 293, 297, 303, 304, 305
disciple, despondent 82, 224, 225, 263, 264, 304
discipline 53, 54, 86, 128n733, 201, 203, 207, 214, 228, 267, 284
discipline, ascetic 55, 86, 320n200
discipline, spiritual 54, 102n174, 102n182, 200, 203, 241, 285
disobedience *see* obedience
divinization 91n22

Domitius (Domadius/Domdeyos) 229, 235n88, 278n163
dove 73, 119n531, 286, 290, 314n45
drink 244, 254
dungheap, dunghill 83, 126n682, 263, 304
dwelling 67, 70, 104n229, 127n715, 204, 217, 221, 242, 298, 301

Egypt xv, 3, 10, 25n77, 52, 56, 57, 65, 70, 71, 112n389, 116n472, 116n475, 117n498, 117n501, 125n657, 127n715, 195, 201, 202, 205, 212, 214, 215, 216, 219, 221, 223, 239, 243, 248, 252, 253, 254, 258, 260, 276n96, 284, 287, 291, 292, 300, 302, 310, 312n10, 314n51; *see also* the Geographic Index
elder 59, 60, 61, 62, 65, 70, 71, 72, 73, 74, 83, 84, 88, 101n173, 107n293, 108n298, 108n299, 108n308, 112n394, 116n470, 118n514, 122n604, 123n631, 197, 198, 207, 208, 210, 226, 227, 245, 246, 248, 249, 253, 260, 261, 264, 265, 266, 271, 284, 289, 291, 293, 294, 296, 302, 305, 306, 308, 325, 327n10
Elijah 58, 104n235, 219, 224, 258, 301
Elijah and Elisha 102n176, 219, 230, 257, 263, 269, 300, 303, 308
eloquence 58, 105n241
endurance 251
enemy 43, 56, 75, 78, 80, 84, 95n87, 103n209, 120n559, 122n604, 128n730, 205, 218, 243
Ephesus 58, 105n237
Ephrem 2, 14, 16, 18n4, 25n76, 26n77, 198, 233n7, 276n93, 276n97
'Ērmeyās 236n99
Ethiopic (language) 2, 3, 14, 195, 276n90, 318n130, 319n158, 320n177, 320n204, 321n210, 324

Eucharist 278n156, 314n57
Eusebius 111n381
Evagrius of Pontus 97n102, 102n192, 108n297
Evil One 75, 109n330, 120n553, 120n559
Exordium 40, 41, 42, 51, 90n10, 94n69, 97n110, 201, 239, 283
eyes 53, 114n425, 202, 214, 240, 284, 326
Ezekiel 118n510, 211, 249, 290

faith 66, 264, 289
fasting xvi, 44, 54, 57, 59, 60, 68, 69, 73, 74, 115n445, 196, 197, 203, 206, 207, 209, 213, 216, 218, 228, 233n9, 240, 241, 244, 245, 246, 247, 250, 251, 254, 255, 257, 268, 285, 288, 293, 294, 297, 298, 299, 315n64
father 52, 70, 99n128, 105n255, 107n294, 119n538, 126n690, 127n698, 130n774, 202, 209, 228, 279n174, 305, 313n33, 313n34
Father of the Monastery 305, 306
al-Fayyum, 13, 24n67
fear 100n149, 103n198, 128n722, 226
feet 80, 81, 128n722, 223, 224, 225, 262, 263, 302, 303, 323
festival 221, 259, 302
flesh 109n337, 213, 228, 298
food xvi, 54, 57, 58, 69, 73, 74, 80, 111n378, 221, 244, 251, 254
food, immaterial 57
food, spiritual 206, 244
forgiveness 59, 73, 80, 82, 85, 86, 207, 208, 224, 264, 292, 293, 294
form 103n216, 113n401
fortress 308, 310

Garshuni 2, 3, 15, 26n80, 195, 278n144, 321n210

INDEXES 345

Ge'ez xvii n6, 2, 195, 196, 197, 198, 199, 200, 233n5, 233n11, 313n38
Gehenna 6, 61, 73, 76, 120n569, 199, 228, 245, 246, 260, 267, 268
Genesis 211, 249
gift 56, 57, 74, 82, 83, 103n218, 104n218, 110n338, 116n485, 119n533, 121n589, 126n692, 197, 205, 207, 209, 224, 225, 243, 246, 263, 274n49, 275n57, 287
gifts, prophetic 67, 83
gifts, spiritual 70, 81, 83, 85, 125n659, 126n673, 128n721
glory 51, 97n105, 117n497, 210, 277n110, 309
Gnostics 24n64, 104n228, 113n411
God 100n161, 104n228, 109n331, 114n432, 117n493, 121n581
God-bearer 307
Godhead 66
goodness 111n361, 115n441
goods 243, 288
Gospel 30, 34, 37, 51, 58, 68, 76, 90n13, 105n244, 111n365, 115n449, 117n494, 206, 229, 244, 251, 268, 307
grace 43, 44, 53, 72, 118n508, 120n564, 122n598, 123n620, 126n673, 245
Great Keep 308
Gregory of Nyssa 33, 34, 35, 37, 91n25, 91n28, 100n149

habit, monastic 103n216, 240, 242, 257, 267, 279n174, 284, 297, 307
Hades 43, 59, 60, 61, 62, 107n280, 108n300, 122n600, 197, 294, 302
hagiography 18n8, 25n73, 30, 39, 41
hair xv, 2, 58, 207, 244, 245, 293
Ḥamlē 231

handiwork 77, 215, 219, 244, 248, 249, 253, 257, 265, 285, 286, 288, 289, 300, 302
handles 210, 211, 248
hands 75, 83, 120n565, 125n662, 211, 228, 244, 259, 267, 316n91
hardship 203, 204, 206, 207, 226
hate 37, 69, 115n457
healing 88, 130n769, 199, 229, 232, 269, 272, 308, 310
heart 113n407, 116n481, 124n652
heaven 7, 8, 64, 69, 79, 104n235, 114n427, 115n353, 129n762, 198, 205, 244, 252
Hebrew 318n153
hegumen 283
Ḥegwāz 201
heir 115n467, 252, 276n91
Hell 72, 93n49, 118n522, 221
heresy 66, 112n391, 113n408
heretic 66, 113n406, 248
Herminā, Anba 321n213
Hieracas 10, 275n62
History of the Patriarchs 6, 23n60
holy man 82, 83, 224, 225, 263, 264, 304
Holy Spirit 43, 65, 73, 104n224, 112n391, 113n405, 116n467, 203, 208, 210, 211, 212, 213, 226, 227, 230, 240, 248, 249, 251, 254, 266, 267, 275n63, 285, 289, 290, 298, 315n72, 315n82, 316
honey 58, 203, 206, 241, 244, 285
hospitality 80, 81, 124n636, 124n638, 124n640, 124n650, 274n48
humility xvi, 67, 70, 84, 86, 103n210, 103n211, 110n350, 202, 209, 213, 218, 240, 247, 257, 294, 295, 299, 323
hunger 68, 206, 213, 216, 244, 251, 254, 296, 297
hypocrisy, hypocrites 270, 286, 308

Ignatius of Antioch 122n593
ignorance 65, 66, 113n412
immorality, sexual 32, 119n546
impiety 77, 122n600
incorruptibility 6, 17, 18n3
insight 70, 76, 116n485, 256, 299
instruction 53, 58, 59, 77, 101n163, 101n171, 127n699, 207, 218, 221, 244, 259, 263, 284, 293, 299, 300, 302
intellect 41, 51
intercession 6, 8, 59, 61, 77, 79, 107n291, 197, 200, 207, 208, 218, 233n9, 244, 246, 293, 294, 300
Isaac 222, 260
Isaac (the Jew) xvi, 14, 77, 78, 79, 219, 220, 222, 233n9, 257, 258, 259, 261, 300, 301, 319n158
Isaiah 99n134, 112n389, 117n489, 211, 249, 290
Isidore 23n55, 87, 88, 130n766, 130n768
Islam 12, 312n10, 312n12, 316n98
Israelite 252, 291, 301

Jeremiah xvi, 4, 47, 54, 88, 102n184, 117n489, 203, 241, 285, 310
Jeremiah, Abba 5, 232, 271
Jerusalem, heavenly 69, 110n353, 111n371, 115n353, 209, 210, 247, 251, 288, 295, 315n68
Jews, Judaism xvi, 12, 42, 44, 71, 72, 77, 78, 93n49, 95n87, 117n498, 122n595, 215, 216, 219, 220, 233n9, 234n53, 253, 254, 257, 259, 261, 292, 300, 301, 316n98
Jezebel 220, 258, 301
John (anchorite) 73, 74, 216, 233n9, 254, 255, 296
John, Apostle 34, 96n94
John of Shmūn 99n132

John the Baptist 103n205, 211, 220, 249, 258, 290, 301
John the Little 2, 5, 8, 12, 18n6, 44, 54, 64, 65, 76, 77, 199, 201, 202, 203, 209, 218, 221, 229, 239, 240, 241, 247, 257, 268, 274n34, 274n35, 283, 284, 286, 288, 299, 302, 307
John III (Pseudo-) 22n45
Joseph 219, 258, 301
judge 79, 121n581
judgment 7, 60, 61, 65, 108n307, 111n376, 118n504, 197, 210
Julian of Halicarnassus 1, 18n3

Kellia (Cells) 116n475
kiss 250, 295, 316n91
Kneeling Prayer *(sajdah)* 7
knowledge 113n411

labor 51, 58, 63, 65, 68, 86, 87, 128n733, 226, 227, 244, 245, 247, 248, 252, 254, 258, 259, 267, 268, 270, 283, 285, 287, 288, 289, 294, 295
labor, ascetic 65, 73, 251, 312n12; *see also* labor
labor, manual 244, 267, 268, 297
lamb 53, 100n152
language 26n77, 70, 198
Latin 312n11
laura 85, 86, 127n715
Lausiac History 94n66, 104n218, 105n248
Law (Jewish) 101n163
Lazarus 83
laziness 75, 76, 120n555
life, ascetic 98n114, 233n14
life, monastic 96n91, 123n619, 123n624, 240
Life of Abba Hermina (Hirmīnā) 20n27

Life of Antony 37, 39, 91n27, 94n65, 96n88, 97n100, 98n126, 99n132, 101n162, 101n172, 102n176, 102n192, 103n201, 107n284, 107n288, 110n346, 110n347, 110n354, 111n370, 113n413
Life of Ephrem 14, 26n77
Life of John Khame 24n62
Life of John the Little 12, 20n29, 24n62, 24n63, 25n70, 27n89, 39, 312n15, 312n16, 316n95, 319n161
Life of Macarius 22n45, 25n70, 127n713, 275n64, 315n75, 313n41, 320n188
Life of Maximus and Domitius 4, 10, 23n56, 25n70
Life of Paîsios 29, 31, 32, 33, 34, 35, 37, 38, 39, 40, 41, 45, 46
Life of Paul of Tamma 4, 5, 19n13, 19n18, 19n19, 19n20, 20n25, 22n45, 275n64
life, solitary 241
lion 255, 298, 318n134
Lord of Glory 326
love 29, 34, 37, 38, 39, 45, 62, 80, 89n4, 92n35, 93n59, 94n65, 94n68, 94n69, 95n73, 97n114, 98n119, 98n127, 100n149, 100n150, 102n188, 102n191, 103n206, 106n259, 106n260, 106n266, 107n286, 108n312, 109n327, 109n328, 109n333, 109n335, 110n355, 115n460, 116n473, 117n496, 123n614, 123n621, 123n625, 124n645, 124n646, 124n649, 126n686, 127n704, 223, 257, 260, 262, 278n137, 278n149, 293, 296, 299, 319n175
love, erotic 42, 77, 122n593
love, sexual 98n120
love, spiritual 285

lover 29, 36, 39, 40, 41, 42, 45, 93n59, 94n66, 94n68, 98n120, 100, 110n346, 111n364, 112n397, 126n686, 129n747, 130n776
loving 125n655, 126n686
Luke, Apostle 37, 118n510, 320n191
lust 42, 44, 51, 96n88, 97n112, 257

Macarius 4, 10, 11, 12, 13, 129n740, 204, 210, 214, 229, 234n28, 242, 248, 252, 253, 268, 286, 289, 291, 307, 311, 325
madness 125n665
magician 219, 220
Mamrē 235n75, 262, 302
manuscript xv, 1–18, 23n49, 23n53, 25n73, 25n77, 26n78, 26n80, 26n81, 32, 195–200, 237–38, 276n99, 281–82, 313n38, 321n218, 323–27; *see also* Salomon Manuscript
Marcellus of Ancyra 114n425
Mark, Apostle 37, 320n191
martyr 114n439, 221, 260, 269, 283, 308
Matthew, Apostle 37
Mawhub ibn Mansur, 21n34
Maximos (Maximus) 229, 235n88, 278n163
mercy 78, 79, 82, 126n678, 208, 220, 246, 254, 259, 270, 291, 293, 294, 317n113, 319n170, 327n15
Messiah 71, 72, 118n505
Methodius 114n425
mimesis 42, 43, 44, 91n26, 95n86
Minya(t) 279n178
miracle 12, 30, 51, 52, 84, 88, 90n13, 130n778, 198, 210, 231, 248, 286, 313n37
misogyny xvi, 24n61, 318n147
monastery, monasteries 1, 8, 13, 55, 88, 123n629, 128n716, 204, 228, 229, 242, 255, 265, 267, 268, 269,

270, 271, 272, 297, 307, 308, 310,
    311, 312n14, 313n40, 316n88,
    319n173, 320n188, 321n209,
    324, 327n7; *see also* entries for
    individual monasteries
Monastery of al-Barāmūs 1, 282
Monastery of al-Barsha 2, 5, 11, 13,
    20n23, 321n215
Monastery of al-Nakhla 321n215
Monastery of al-Zaʿfarān 15
Monastery of Anba Antunyus (Antony) 13–14, 195–96, 260, 272, 302
Monastery of Anba Bishūy 2, 6, 17,
    21n36, 24n69, 321n215, 321n217
Monastery of Anba Harmina 5
Monastery of Anba Macarius 18n2,
    21n35, 324
Monastery of Anba Shenoute 13, 310
Monastery of Ansina 24n66
Monastery of Jeremiah 5
Monastery of John the Little 18n2
Monastery of the Syrians (*al-Suryān*) xv,
    1, 2, 14, 18n2, 25n74, 26n77, 281
Monastery, Red 4
monasticism 35, 41, 209, 247, 283,
    284, 286, 288
money 56, 104n218, 205, 243
monk 40, 55, 58, 64, 65, 66, 71, 73, 75,
    76, 78, 79, 84, 85, 87, 102n192,
    103n201, 105n242, 106n258,
    114n425, 116n478, 118n514,
    118n521, 119n544, 121n572,
    122n602, 204, 226, 228, 229,
    247, 256, 257, 259, 265, 269, 270,
    276n105, 286, 293, 294, 299, 300,
    305, 316n91, 325
monks, falsely accused 84, 226, 265,
    305
monks of Shihīt (Scetis) 312n6
monk, Syrian 71, 214, 252, 291
Moses 16, 52, 99n133, 99n134,
    106n264, 211, 249, 285, 290, 307

mountain 116n474, 252, 286, 287,
    290, 293, 298, 299, 300, 301, 302,
    303, 304, 306, 307, 309, 312n14,
    325, 326, 327n10, 327n15
Mowamal 205, 234n30
murderers 199, 221
Murūj al-dhahab 317n121
Muslims 12, 234n53
mystery 101n162, 111n358, 386
mystery, divine 107n284

nakedness 217, 255, 298
Native American 30, 36
Natrun, Mountain of 291, 295, 311
nature 95n75, 104n232
New Testament 34, 37, 107n286,
    107n290, 116n467, 117n498,
    118n510, 121n578, 121n581,
    122n593
Nicodemus 100n160
Nile 23n52, 276n96, 321n211
Nob, Abba 232
north, "man to the" 70, 198
novice 74, 75, 120n563, 255

oath 318n140
obedience 44, 53, 61, 62, 77, 79, 81,
    82, 83, 84, 100n157, 100n158,
    105n247, 129n745, 222, 223, 224,
    225, 246, 262, 263, 264, 294, 296,
    303, 304, 305
oblation 267, 268
Old Testament 274n53, 290, 313n25,
    314n57
Origen 7, 34, 35, 36, 41, 91n25,
    91n28, 95n82, 96n90, 100n149,
    111n381, 113n411, 119n530,
    122n593

Païsios *see* Bishoi
Palladius 105n248
palm leaves 228

INDEXES 349

Pambo 34, 44, 47, 53, 54, 100n153, 104n218, 196, 233n12; Amoi 3, 18n6, 312n16; Bamawi 233n12, 273n25; Bamoy 201, 202, 203, 233n12; Bāmūyah 312n16; Bamwa 273n25; Bamwah 283, 284, 285, 307; Bamwi 96, 202, 203, 229; Bemoi 239, 240, 241, 268, 273n25

Paraclete 275n63, 289

paradise 57, 104n225, 244, 295

Paralipomena of Jeremiah 234n33, 314n60

passion 33, 41, 51, 80, 94n69, 94n72, 95n83, 98n115, 121n578

patience 223, 261, 262, 296

patriarch 6, 21n35

Paul, Apostle 33, 42, 46, 67, 106n265, 108n314, 111n381, 117n495, 125n668, 203, 211, 240, 247, 249, 278n168, 285, 289, 290

Paul of Tamma 2, 4, 5, 10, 11, 23n52, 23n57, 43, 67, 68, 86, 87, 88, 96n93, 113n420, 128n728, 130n766, 230, 231, 232, 250, 269, 270, 271, 295, 308, 309, 310; variations of the name: 212, 234n51, 235n91

perfume 209

Peter, Saint 220, 258, 301, 319n155

Phantasiasts 18n3

Phoibammon 295

Phoibammon of Koptos/Qift 317n120

Phoibammon of Panopolis/Akhmin 317n120

Piamoun 199, 229

pig 85, 128n723, 227, 266, 306

Plato 34, 91n28, 92n34, 92n35

pleasure 51, 94n69, 97n111, 97n113, 105n240, 105n243, 111n380

Poemen 67, 68, 95n81, 113n419, 114n427, 212, 275n78, 317n120

polytheism 312n10

poverty 56, 64, 209, 244, 247, 288

power, creative 104n231

power, divine 103n215, 253

praise 87, 125n654, 129n753, 231

prayer 54, 55, 58, 59, 60, 62, 70, 74, 75, 78, 80, 86, 106n271, 124n635, 129n739, 196, 203, 204, 206, 207, 208, 209, 214, 218, 226, 228, 232, 240, 241, 244, 245, 246, 247, 252, 256, 257, 265, 267, 268, 285, 293, 294, 298, 299, 315n64, 316n105

Prayer, Lord's 129n745

praying 57, 61, 70

pride 270, 309

priest 80, 101n173, 124n632, 223, 262

priest, impudent 79, 222, 261, 296

prison 85, 226, 227

prophecy 54, 85, 102n184, 241

prophesying 67, 84, 114n425, 321n209

prophet 219, 225, 226, 227, 230, 263, 264, 266, 269, 285, 300, 303, 304, 305, 306

prostration 316n100

Psalm 103n196, 228, 267

Pshōi *see* Bishoi

punishment 79, 123n622, 293, 294, 298, 317n113

purgatory and purgation 6, 7, 8, 22n42

purity 201, 228, 257, 283, 299

quiet, contemplative 38, 54, 55, 58, 84, 86, 102n189, 102n190, 105n246, 127n709, 128n732, 129n746, 196

Qur'ān 12, 105n237, 314n61, 316n98

raising the dead 127n697, 248

receptacle 223, 224, 235n69

relics 2, 4, 5, 6, 8, 10–13, 17, 20n32, 21n34, 23n60, 26n77, 87, 130n769, 231, 271–72, 310

reliquary 310, 324
remains 5, 21n34, 88, 130n782
repentance 42, 78, 80, 82, 118n514, 126n671, 225, 262, 263, 264, 292, 298, 304, 316n100
repose 87, 106n261, 272, 283, 294, 305, 309, 310
rest 106n261, 108n310, 129n763
restoration 119n530
resurrection 112n391, 113n408
Revelation, Book of 118n510
reward 59, 220, 251, 252, 259, 309, 311
riches 103n218, 247
righteousness 316n108
river 279n182, 232
Roman Fathers 1, 268
Rome 229, 235n88
rule 79, 102n179, 105n253
rule, monastic 222, 223, 257, 262
Rule of Saint Benedict 44
ruler, rich 56, 205, 243, 287

saint 83, 130n769, 130n782, 235n88, 252, 260, 269, 327n15
Salomon Manuscript 14, 15, 237, 238, 272n3, 273n8, 273n9, 276n93, 276n99
salt 51, 196, 203, 241, 285, 294
salvation 62, 63, 79, 86, 87, 203, 220, 285, 304
Samson 99n145, 220, 258, 301
Satan xvi, 40, 43, 95n87, 103n209, 109n330, 119n530, 205, 206, 207, 210, 217, 218, 219, 220, 222, 223, 226, 227, 243, 245, 248, 255, 256, 257, 258, 260, 261, 265, 287, 289, 293, 296, 298, 299, 300, 301, 307, 318n134
Saturday 196, 244
Savior 55, 56, 58, 59, 61, 62, 63, 64, 68, 69, 79, 80, 81, 103n199, 115n447,
197, 204, 207, 209, 242, 245, 246, 250, 252, 286, 292, 294, 295
scandal 80, 223, 227
Scetis *see* Geographic Index
scribal error 26n83, 316
scribe 26, 115, 184n490, 237, 311
Scripture 53, 66, 78, 99n135, 101n164, 202, 203, 211, 226, 227, 228, 240, 241, 249, 265, 267, 269, 276n94, 285, 290, 301, 305, 308, 316n87
sea 271, 321n211
seclusion 285, 300, 302, 305
Second Coming 108n303, 118n504
seedling 255, 298, 299
seed, lupine 224, 225, 235n81
seer 127n713, 265, 306
semi-anchorite 104n229
Serapion, Bishop 102n176
servant 106n267, 107n297, 252
Seven Sleepers/Youths of Ephesus 105n237, 234n34, 244, 288, 314n61
Severus of Antioch 1
sexuality 35, 38
Seyā 203
Shenouda III, Pope 1
Shenoute of Atripe, Saint 4, 117n492
Sheol 197, 207, 208
shepherd 100n154, 113n419
Shepherd of Hermas 114n425
ship 5, 10, 87, 88, 130n770, 130n778, 252, 291, 310
shrine 221, 259, 302
shroud 277n130, 309
silence, contemplative 58, 106n256
Silas 230
Sīraws, Abba 269, 271
Sirwes, Abba 231
Siyrwūs 5
slander 127n714
sleep 244, 245, 288, 293
socializing 252

INDEXES 351

Sodom and Gomorrah 124n636
solitary, solitaries xvii, 85, 198, 210, 211, 214, 233n9, 241, 248, 249, 252, 257, 258, 260
solitude xvi, xvii, 45, 48, 58, 63, 84, 85, 86, 102n189, 106n257, 128n719, 196, 203, 226, 244, 265, 285, 288, 305
Solomon 220, 258, 301
son 115n467, 246, 252, 267, 276n91, 278n145, 278n154, 293, 316n108
Song of Songs 43
sorceress 257, 258, 300, 301
soul 7, 8, 59, 61, 317n109
sow 266, 306
speech 107n290
spirit 74, 119n541, 130n782, 217, 266
Spirit-bearer 289, 290, 306
stillness, inward 106n261, 108n310, 129n763, 241, 244, 260, 265, 269
stones 88, 130n778, 225, 263, 268, 304, 307
struggle 44, 100n159, 102n183, 103n204, 114n439, 115n355, 118n521, 233n14, 269, 270, 314n56
struggle, ascetic 58, 62, 75, 120n561; see also labor
struggle, spiritual 68, 69, 76, 110n341; see also labor
suffering 94n72, 106n276, 108n299, 114n435, 116n467, 121n578, 213, 246, 252
Sunday 69, 196, 206, 244, 274n36
sunrise 3, 234n25, 241
superior 85, 107n294
supervision 110n348
sword 199, 229, 269, 308
Synaxarium (Synaxarion) 4, 5, 6, 14, 17, 19n17, 20n32, 21n36, 21n38, 22n49, 199, 233n8, 234n28, 323, 324

Syria, Syrian 71, 112n389, 116n470, 116n472, 198, 214, 215, 237, 239, 252, 253, 274n37, 274n42, 275n58, 276n102, 278n159, 291, 314n61
Syriac 2, 3, 8, 14, 25n73, 70, 116n470, 195, 196, 197, 198, 199, 214, 236n97, 237, 252, 277n135, 278n144, 291, 313n38, 318n130, 319n175, 320n177, 320n204, 321n210

talents 230, 270, 308
Tammuz 239, 271
Tamwi (Tamma) 236n100
Tanse'a Krestos 232
teacher xvii, 53, 71, 202, 318n153
teaching 63, 104n227, 110n347, 110n354, 110n356, 129n756, 223
tears 59, 60, 72, 73, 80, 82
teeth 103n214, 219, 257, 300
temptation 37, 43, 205, 242
Teshrin I 271
theft 84, 85, 86, 221, 226, 227, 259, 265, 266, 301, 302, 305, 306
Theophilus, Archbishop 122n607
thirst 68, 81, 83, 206, 216, 244, 254, 296, 297
thought 75, 76, 102n192, 245
Timothy of Gargar 22n47
tomb 83, 84, 126n693, 225, 301, 304, 305
toothpick 257, 300
Touton 13
tower 269, 286, 314n45
transgression 263, 264
tree 23n54, 101n166, 203, 223, 229, 241, 256, 285, 299
Tree of Ephrem 2, 26n77
Trinitarian 234n47, 312n10
Trinity 12, 45, 65, 66, 112n298, 112n400, 113n401, 113n402,

113n412, 210, 211, 221, 248, 249, 260, 289, 290
Ṭūba 233n8

vainglory xvii n1, 266, 270
vestments 232
vigil xv, 55, 204, 206, 254, 285, 293, 298
vineyard 259, 302
violence 93n49, 120n551
virginity 109n330, 228
virgins 230
virtue 39, 44, 53, 58, 79, 80, 86, 100n147, 105n249, 113n417, 123n625, 124n634, 129n743, 241, 242, 253, 268, 270, 285, 309, 312n18, 313n37
vision 53, 239, 248, 284

wages 68, 213
walking stick 26n77
wall 126n682, 229, 247, 263, 270, 288
wall, brass 230
water 80, 81, 82, 83, 101n165, 101n166, 125n657, 199, 209, 216, 223, 224, 225, 230, 241, 247, 254, 255, 262, 263, 269, 285, 297, 302, 303, 308
weakness 240, 251
wealth 43, 65, 205
weapon 123n608
well 199, 229, 269, 308
wickedness 32, 119n546
wife 51, 219, 258
wilderness 103n205, 246, 250, 251, 253, 254, 259, 262, 269, 286, 287, 290, 292, 294, 300, 301, 305, 307, 309, 310, 312n14, 314n56, 325, *see also* desert

will 42, 58, 74, 86, 129n745, 206, 213, 218, 235n72, 244, 245, 246, 257, 258, 261, 318n142
wings 64, 210, 247, 288
woman, Jewish xvi, 42, 44, 77, 218, 257, 259, 300, 301
women xvi, 77, 78, 93n49, 95n87, 105n241, 109n330, 122n595, 122n607, 123n607, 128n726, 219, 220, 257, 258, 259, 300, 301
wonders 109n323, 123n627
wonderworker 86, 129n740, 248
wood 77, 219
word xvii, 79, 80, 116n483, 121n575, 126n670, 236n103, 244
words, vulgar 261
work 68, 69, 216, 228, 267, 298
work, good 68, 213, 250
work, manual 58, 206, 267, 298; *see also* labor
works 76, 95n84, 106n270, 206, 207, 244, 250, 264, 265, 268, 305
worship 106n267, 206, 222, 228, 273n22, 284, 285
wretch 106n273, 108n313, 110n349, 114n424, 118n521, 119n528, 122n596, 125n668

Yanqanun 317n120
yoke of Christ 58, 64, 106n261
youth 250, 266, 295, 304, 323
Yusāb (Joseph), Patriarch 6

Zacharias of Sakhā 12
zeal 55, 65, 69, 74, 76, 84, 106n271, 115n462

Authors
Ali, Ahmed 105n237
Allen, Pauline 18n3
Amar, Joseph P. 25n77

Anonymous/A Monk from the Monastery 326n1, 326n3, 326n6
Athanassakis, Apostolos 94n65, 195

Ayoub, Mahmoud M. 24n64

Baḥr, Fr. Mīṣā'īl 16, 17, 21n39, 26n85, 27n88, 281, 321n211
Bamberger, John Eudes 108n297
Bartelink, G.J.M. 91n27, 94n65, 96n88
Basset, René 20n32
Bedjan, Paul 2, 7, 15, 21n41, 22n48, 195, 237, 238, 272n4, 273n8, 273n9, 274n36, 274n51, 276n99
Beylot, Robert 233n5, 234n53
Blake, William 40, 95n80
Blanchard, Monica J. 19n16, 22n48, 237, 272n2, 273n19, 276n93
Boyarin, Daniel 34, 35, 92n34, 92n35, 92n36
Brakke, David 92n48, 102n192, 117n498
Brock, Sebastian P. 19n14, 25n73, 25n74, 25n76, 233n7, 314n61
Brown, Peter 130n769, 130n782
Burrus, Virginia 32, 34, 90n15, 90n16, 91n25, 92n29
Burton-Christie, Douglas 115n455

Chryssavgis, John 319n155
Clugnet, Léon 94n68
Coakley, Sarah 29, 31, 32, 33, 34, 35, 37, 38, 39, 40, 44, 45, 46, 90n14, 90n18, 91n19, 91n20, 91n24, 91n25, 91n26, 92n42, 92n43, 92n46, 92n47, 92n48, 93n50, 93n54, 93n56, 93n57, 93n60, 93n61, 95n76, 96n95, 96n96, 97n102, 97n103, 97n106, 97n114
Colin, Gérard 2, 14, 25n71, 195, 196, 233n5, 233n11, 234n28
Constas, Nicholas 22n44
Coquin, René-Georges 19n15, 24n68, 113n420
Costa, Mario 92n34
Cox, Patricia 18n8

Daniélou, Jean 97n107
Davis, Stephen 25n74, 312n15
Delahaye, Hippolyte 30, 89n8, 90n9
Dolansky, Shawna 109n330
Drescher, James 315n61
Dunn, Marilyn 91n21

Efthymiadis, Stephanos 19n8
Evdokimov, Paul 39, 93n53, 93n64
Evelyn-White, H.G. 3, 18n1, 18n3, 18n5, 20n26, 20n32, 21n34, 21n36, 23n57, 25n70, 26n77, 26n84, 30, 90n10, 116n475, 281, 311n3, 320n193
Evetts, B.T.A. 20n31, 24n66, 311n3

Festugière, A.-J. 92n46
Frankfurter, David 104n235
Fredriksen, Paula 117n498
Freud, Sigmund 37, 93n54

Gabra, Gawdat 25n72, 25n75
Gardiner, Eileen 21n42
Geens, Karolien 317n121
Goehring, James E. 91n21, 96n99, 105n242
Graiver, Inbar 91n21, 92n48, 93n53, 102n192, 200, 233n10
Greer, Rowan 195
Griffith, Sidney H. 24n65
Grossman, Peter 317n120
Guidi, I. 21n36
Guillaumont, Antoine 116n475

Ḥabīb, Yūsuf 21n39, 281, 282, 312n8, 318n147, 326n3, 326n7, 327n9
Hägg, Tomas 19n8
Hambye, Édouard René 19n12
Harmless, William 18n1, 91n21
Hayward, C.T.R. 18n3
Honigmann, Ernest 314n61
Horn, G. 91n28
Huxley, Aldous 36, 92n44

Ibrahīm al-Anbā Bishūy, Fr. 17, 312n9, 327n10
Ishaq, Emile Maher (Fr. Shenouda) 22n45, 116n479

Janssen, L.F. 90n12
Jordan, Mark D. 92n34
Judge, E.A. 96n99

Kāmil, Fr. Bishūy 17, 21n39, 27n88, 281, 324, 327n8
Keller, Catherine 35, 92n38, 92n40, 92n41
Kitchen, Robert A. 14, 195

Lambdin, Thomas 18
Le Goff, Jacques 21n42
Lewis, Theodore J. 120n562
Lizardos, Georgia 21n40, 22n49

Makarī of the Monastery of Saint Macarius 20n27
Makarī al-Bahnasawī, Fr. 21n39, 281, 312n6
Malina, Bruce J. 100n161
al-Maqrīzī, 317n121
Martin, Maurice 19n15, 20n27
al-Masʿūdī, 317n121
Mattā al-Miskīn, Fr. 20n32
McGinn, Bernard 91n28, 92n30, 92n31, 92n35, 92n46, 93n56, 95n82, 96n90
McGuckin, John Anthony 7, 22n43
Meinardus, Otto F.A. 25n72, 26n86
Meredith, Anthony 34, 91n28
Meyendorff, John 319n155
Mikhail, Maged S.A. 19n9, 20n28, 20n29, 20n30, 21n35, 24n61, 24n62, 24n65, 25n70, 30, 89n1, 94n66, 96n97, 96n98, 121n591, 130n768, 195, 237, 277n127, 281, 312n15, 313n35, 313n40, 316n95, 318n147, 319n155, 319n161, 320n188
Mikhail, Ramez 25n74
Mirsanu, Dragos 22n42
Moreira, Isabel 22n44
Moritz, B. 24n67
Moss, Yonatan 18n3

al-Nabulsī, 24n67
Nerburn, Kent 90n11, 90n12, 92n45
Nielsen, Jorgen 24n65
Nygren, Anders 34, 35, 91n25, 92n29, 92n30, 92n35

Oberly, John 36
O'Leary, De Lacy 20n32

Pagels, Elaine 109n330, 122n606
Papaconstantinou, Arietta 19n8
Papadopoulos, Leonidas 21n40, 22n49
Papanikolaou, Aristotle 33, 91n23
Pirone, Bartolomeo 17, 27n90, 281, 311n1, 311n2, 313n34, 313n41, 315n75, 320n188
Pletruschka, Ute 25n72
Pomialovskii, I.V. 2, 97n109, 117n500, 119n351

Rapp, Claudia 18n6, 23n51, 321n214
Regnault, Lucien 95n81, 113n419
Rich, Antony 102n192
Rohrbaugh, Richard L. 100n161
Rousseau, Philip 19n8
Russell, Jeffrey 89n1

Salmon, M. Georges 24n67
Salomon, M. 15, 237
Samir, Samir Khalil 24n65
Ṣamūʾīl of Shibīn al-Qanāṭir, Bishop (Ṣamūʾīl al-Suryānī) 17, 21n39, 282, 324, 326n1, 326n3, 326n5, 326n6, 326n7

Sanders, Johannes 19n16
Scheil, V. 21n41, 237, 272n5
Schenke, G. 317n120
Scott, Robert 95n85
Smith, Jonathan Z. 90n13
Soldati, Agostino 22n45
Stevenson, J. 112n391
Suciu, Alin 19n13, 19n18, 20n26
Swanson, Mark 25n74

Takla, Hany 89n1
Timm, S. 273n19, 277n135, 313n24, 315n71, 317n120, 318n143, 319n163
Toda, S. 314n41, 315n75

Van Rompay, L. 19n14, 25n73, 25n74, 25n76
Vivian, Tim 20n29, 23n56, 89n1, 92n37, 93n62, 94n65, 94n66, 94n68, 96n93, 96n97, 96n98,
100n153, 107n291, 112n389, 116n474, 119n527, 121n575, 123n607, 127n713, 128n726, 195, 275n64, 276n92, 312n15, 313n35, 314n41, 315n75, 316n95, 319n161
Vogt, Matthias 314n61

Weil, Simone 29
Williams, Rowan xvii n9, 38, 46, 93n63, 97n108
Wimbush, Vincent 91n21
Wipszycka, Ewa 91n21
Wright, W. 14, 26n78
Wüstenfeld, H. Ferdinand 20n32

Youssef, Y.N. 326n6

Zakariyā al-Baramūsī, Fr. 20n32, 21n33, 21n40, 23, 26n87, 281, 312n9, 324, 327n10

Transliterated Names and Terms

Āb, al-Āb al-Mushrif 313n34
ácharis 118n508
adelphótēs 105n248, 124n633, 127n707
'*afīf* 316n96
agapáō 34, 48, 94n65, 98n120, 115n460, 117n496
agápē 29, 34–36, 38, 39, 45, 46, 47, 48, 89n4, 92n30, 92n46, 93n59, 94n65, 96n94, 98n120, 103n206, 106n259, 109n328, 109n333, 109n335, 115n460, 116n473, 117n496, 123n621
agápēn 47, 48
agápēs 47
agapētoí 42
agapṓntas 48, 117n496
agapṓsi 47
ágnoian 113n412
agōgás 128n733
agōgṓn 102n182
agṓn 103n204, 114n439, 119n341, 120n561
agṓnas 128n733
agōnistḗs 114n439
agonízomai 100n159, 120n561
agōnizoménois 103n204
agōnizoménous 120n561
amānah 316n97
anachōréō 120n564
anachōrḗsis 106n257
anachōrētḗs 120n564
anapaúō 106n261
anapaúomai 106n261
anápausis 106n261, 108n310, 129n763
anástasis 113n408
anastḗsas 113n408

andrôn 98n125
anḗr 98n125
-angel (root) 94n70, 98n117
anístēmi 113n408
ánō 100n160
ánōthen 100n160, 129n762
antephthénxato 125n658
ánthrōpos 98n125
anti- 125n658
antronikē 279n181
apántōn dēmiourgōs 107n296
apephthénxato 125n658
apokatástasis 119n530
apokatástasis pántōn 119n530
apokatasthéntos 119n530
apónoias 125n665
apotássomai 105n242
apotassoménōn 105n242
apráktous 107n297
archōn (arkhun) 314n52
aretḗ 89n4, 113n417, 123n625, 124n634, 129n743
arrabōn 275n70
Ashtashnā 313n24
askéō 119n544, 122n601
askḗsei (áskēsis) 32, 40, 44, 102n174, 122n601
askṓn 119n544
asōmátois 40, 98n124
átheos 112n395
áthlēsis(-ḗs) 118n521
áthlio(s) 118n521, 119n528, 122n596
áthlon(-os) 118n521
aulizoménois 103n204
autôn 129n750
autoû 129n750
autoû hē chrēstótēs 111n361
axierásata 48, 126n686
áxio- 125n654
axióchrēston 125n654
axiýmnēton 125n654

barbar (barbrāyē) 199
bārr 282
bdélugma 118n510
bíos 97n111, 312n11
bíou terpnoís 46, 105n243
birr 316n108
boētheías 109n325

chalepós 123n608
cháos 128n725
charáktēr 113n401
cháris 109n324, 118n508, 119n533, 122n598, 126n673
chárisma 109n324, 119n533, 125n659, 126n673, 126n692, 128n721
chrēstós 125n654
christós 125n654

dalāl (dallah) 316n90
deílaios 103n217
deinós(-ō) 126n675
dēmiourgía 104n231
dēmiourgós 95n85, 98n118, 104n228, 107n296
dhāt allāh 320n178
diabaínō 121n580
diabâllō 127n714
diagōgḗ 102n187, 105n247
diatágmasi 127n699
didâgmasi 127n699
didáskalos 45
diēnekṓs 126n675
dógma 112n395
dólios 103n217
doulagōgḗō(-n) 101n171
dunón 118n516
dýnamis 103n215

echthrós 103n209
efči ouōini 44
eis érōta 47
ekeíse 118n522

INDEXES 357

ekgónous 123n609
ekklēsí 104n226
ekklēsiastḗs 318n153
ekplḗssō 117n494
ekplḗttō 117n494
eleuthería 108n314
eleutheróō 108n314
emphainoménē 112n400
emphérō 112n400
empheroménē 112n400
engónous 123n609
enthéois 105n241
entolḗ 101n163
entós 92n32
epangéllō 94n70
epangéllomai 98n117
epekteínas 106n265
epektenómenos 106n265
epēngelménōn 94n70
éphaske 112n390
epískepsis 119n348
episkopḗ 114n433, 119n348
epískopos 114n433, 119n348
epistasías 124n636
epithymía 42, 96n88
epóthei 47, 102n175
éramai 98n120
eráō 45, 48, 98n120, 129n749
erastás 40, 41, 47, 48, 49
erastḗs 36, 40, 42, 45, 47, 48, 49, 93n59, 94n66, 98n120, 100, 111n364, 112n397, 119n346, 119n355, 124n646, 126n686, 129n747, 130n776
érēmos 103n205
érgas 106n270
érōn 45, 48, 129n747, 129n749
eros (érōs) xvi, 23n51, 29, 32–48, 89n4, 91, 92n30, 92n35, 92n46, 93n60, 95n82, 96n94, 97n112, 97n114, 98n116, 98n120, 100n148, 100n150, 102n181, 102n185, 102n188, 102n191, 105n245, 122n593, 124n653, 125n663, 126n686, 129n747
érōta 39, 41, 46
érōti 42, 44, 47, 48
'Ersenä 235n79
eskḗnōsen 103n194
ethike 38
euagṓn 111n372
euangélion 94n70, 98n117, 111n365
euergétaí(-ēs) 100n161
exostrakisthéntōn 109n329
exostrakízō 109n329
exoudenóō 115n458

faḍāyil (faḍā'il) 313n37, 316n92

gabra 275n58
gadl 233n14
génoito 99n144
géron(-ti) 101n173
gnṓsis 113n411

hairetikós 113n406
hairetízō 113n406
hairetizóntōn 113n406
hamartía 119n529
hē autoû agathótēs 111n361
hēdonḗ 46, 94n69, 105n240, 111n380
hēsycházontas 128n719
hēsychía xvi, 38, 45, 47, 48, 102n189, 102n190, 105n246, 106n256, 127n709, 128n719, 128n732, 129n746, 274n37
hēt (ḥēt) 273n24, 274n25
hierà kephalḗ 107n294
hierṓn 111n372
historéō 29, 30
historía 29, 30
ho dēmiourgòs lógos 104n228
ho diâbolos 127n714

homologéō 109n322
homoteleuton 126n676
ho theíos póthos 40, 41, 47, 48, 95n73, 98n119
huioí 116n467
huiós 115n467
hymnéō 125n654
hymnētós 125n654
hypakoḗ 129n745
hypér- 45
hyperchius 122n593
hypérnoia(-s) 125n665
hypostáseis 112n399
hypostases 66, 112n399, 234n47
hypóstasis 112n399, 275n74
hypotagḗ 105n247, 129n745

idlāl 316n90
ijtihād 314n43, 317n112, 317n115
īmān 316n97
iqāre 274n42
isángelos 43, 96n92, 123n619
iskīm 279n174, 318n131, 320n186
iso- 96n92
isóchristos 43

jabal 312n14
jihād 114n439, 312n12
jihād ʿazīm 312n12, 313n20, 313n36, 314n50, 314n56

kabīr al-rusul 319n155
kaioménē 124n652
kairós 37, 120n566
kanayysī (kanaʾysī) 318n153
kunōn 102n179
kardía 124n652
katágnōsin 130n773
katalambánō 106n278
katanaoëō 119n545
katanóēsas 119n545
katápausis 106n261

kataphlégomai 122n593
katáschesin 130n773
katástasis 274n40
kateskḗnōsen 103n194
kátochos 129n759
kephalḗ 107n294
klēronómoi(-os) 115n467, 116n467
klēronómos esti kaì huiós 115n467
kosmikós 107n297, 123n630
krīsṭonoutha 277n129
krīsṭyono 276n102

laúra 127n715
logikṓs 100n154
lógos 100n154, 103n194

manshōpe 104n229
mayrūn 324
meletáō 103n196
memystagṓgētai 107n284
metaméleia 126n671
metánoia 126n671, 316n100
metmai 94n67
metmainouti 94n67
metmairōmi 94n67
mikrà hēdonḗ 97n113
mikràs hēdonḗs 39, 94n69
miméomai 95n86
mímēsis 129n742
mimētás 42
mimētḗs 95n86
mimoúmenos 95n86
minyā 20n21
monḗ 279n178
mumawwal 234n30
muqaddim al-rusul 319n155
mushriq 313n34
mutakallimūn 12
myst- 97n100
mystagōgéō 101n162, 107n284
mystagōgētheís 97n100, 101n162
mystagōgía 104n227, 107n284

mystérion 101n162, 111n358, 386

néos 114n425
nnecnōik 94n66
noûs 124n631
nusk 320n201

oikonoméō 109n325
oikonomoúsa 109n325
óntos 41
opheílēma 119n529
opheílō 119n529
ophéllō 114n422
ophthḗnai 107n297
orans 106n258, 116n478
óros 116n474, 312n14
óstrak(-a/-on/-ízō) 109n329
oudén 115n458

paidagogêō 101n171
paidagogṓn 101n171
paideía 114n427
paîs 114n427, 278n153
pálai 122n602
palaiâs 122n602
palaiòs hēmerṓn 128n735
palingenesías 119n533
panágathos 108n312
pántōn 113n415
paradeísou 46, 104n225
paradídomi 121n576
parádosis 121n576
parophthḗnai 107n297
parousías 124n636
parrēsía 107n290, 316n90
parrēsiázomai 107n290
parrhesia 277n116
páschō 98n115
patḗr 99n128
páthē 39, 46, 121n578
páthēma(ta) 94n72, 121n578
páthos 94n72, 98n115, 121n578

peirasmós 37
phil- (root) 113n417
philánthrōpos 89n4, 103n199, 107n297, 108n312, 123n614, 124n649
philáretos 47, 48, 89n4, 113n417, 123n625
philéō 98n120, 98n127
philía 39, 46, 47, 89n4, 96n94, 98n120, 98n127
philochrḗstou 125n655
philochrístou 125n655
philóō 98n121
phílos 45, 49, 112n397
philostorgía 105n252
philothéois 48
philótheos 127n704
philoumenen 40
phíltron 46, 47, 48, 49, 109n327, 124n645
phōtismós 44
phōtízō 44
phylakós 116n489
phylássō 116n489
phyláttō 116n489
phýlax 116n489
phýsis 40
plērōtḗs 101n163
plḗthos 112n394
plēthúnousa 99n138
pneûma 31
pneumatikḗ(i) 102n174
poimḗn 113n419
poj 94n67
pólis 38
politeía 38, 42, 91n23, 97n111, 102n187, 119n354, 312n11
pollḕn áthlēsin 118n521
ponērías 32, 119n546
ponērós 112n395, 120n559
ponēroús 119n546
porneías 32, 119n546
potheínos 48, 49, 124n647

potheinóteron 47, 106n263
pothéō 47, 48
póthō(i) phlegómenos 47
póthos 34, 42, 45, 46, 47, 48, 49, 91n27,
    93n59, 96n94, 102n175, 106n263,
    113n418, 115n446, 124n647,
    127n710
pothouménē 48, 127n710
praktikós 107n297
práxis 107n297
presbýteros 101n173
presbýtes 101n173
próschēma 103n216
prosdokáō 118n504
prosdokōménō 118n504
prósōpon 113n401
prōtotókōn(-os) 104n226
psychḗ 35, 92n39

qnuma(-i) 275n74
qōheleth 318n153

ra'īs dhālk al-jabal 320n176
ra(i)thymía 120n555
rijāl mujahidīn 318n132
ropḗ 122n598
ruah 31

ṣalāt al-sajdah 7
schḗma 103n216
Seirêsi 105n241
Seyā 203
Shai 3
shelya 274n37
shi 273n24
Shī'a 241
shōi 3, 19n10
ṣiddīq 282, 316n107
sīrah 312n11
sīro 278n159
skema 235n87
skēnḗ 103n194

skēnóō 103n194
sôma(-ti) 35, 40, 98n124
splánchna 126n677
splanchnízomai 107n286, 126n677
storgḗ(s) 46, 47, 96n94, 105n252,
    106n266
sun- 96n92
sunerastḗs 49
sunklēronómoi 116n467
superstitio 90n12
syn- 96n92
sýnchristos 43
synerastḗs 130n776

tadbīr 313n39
talaípōros 106n273, 119n528
tálas 106n273, 114n424
tà splánchna 107n286
tà térpna toû bíou 39, 97n111
technítēs kaì dēmiourgós 104n228
terpná(-ois) 46, 97n111, 104n225,
    111n379
terpnà toû bíou 104n225
tḗs óntōs zōḗs 39
thánatos 40
thaumátōn autourgoí 129n740
thaumatoúrgos 129n740
theíō 100n149
theîos 100n149
thélēma 129n745
theoptḗs 99n134
theoría 276n94
theosis 33, 91n22
therapeúō 106n267
therapóntas(-i) 106n267
thespésios 125n660
thrasús 125n662
tiagapē 94n67
timḗ 98n127
tímios 98n127
tis 117n502
toiaútois 106n270

toîs soîs 106n270
tò kosmikón 35, 38
tôn kalôn 41, 95n84
tôn kalôn ekeínou 39
tôn kalôn érgōn 95n84
topos 319n173
tò thélēma sou 129n745
toū ponēroû 120n559
tractum 91n24
traho 91n24
treptá 97n111

trophḗ 111n378
truphḗ 111n378
túpos 275n61

vita 312n11

waltama 221

yalbis 320n195
yalmis 320n195
yod 274n25

Geographic Names

Afaq Tarway 277n117
Akhmim 317n121
Ansina 2, 5, 12, 13, 16, 23n53, 24n66, 31, 236n92, 260, 263, 269, 271, 272, 277n136, 302, 304, 310, 327n10; *see also* 'Ensenā
Antaiopolis 5
'Anṭēnu 235n70
Antinoë 2, 5, 12, 16, 23n53, 221, 230, 231, 232, 260, 263, 264, 271, 277n136, 319n163
Antinoopolis 319n163
'Anṭorāwiniqi 231
Arsinoë 224
Aswan 5, 22

Babylon 314n51, 318n143
Basenshayā 239
Basinbīyā 273n20
Basqi 275n60
Basway 248, 275n60
Baswi 210
Batira (Nitria) 214
Besīnīshyā 273n20
Būsuy 275n60

Clysma 260, 302
Constantinople 4

Daqū 278n151
Daqwa 226
Duwany 279n178

Egypt, Lower 6
Egypt, Middle 2, 10, 18n6, 275n60
Egypt, Upper 4, 20, 260, 262, 271, 289, 302, 305, 309
'Ensenā 236n98, 236n101, 236n102; *see also* Ansina

Fustat 23n53, 248, 257, 314n51

Hierakonopolis 20n22

Ibṣāy 289, 315n71
Ibshāy 3
Iraq 237

Kawm al-Aḥmar 20n22
Kellia (Cells) 116n475

Madīnat al-'iqāb 317n121
Madīnat al-Ṣaqr 20n22
Manbar 223
Marēs (Mārīs) 277n135
Minyat al-Ṣaqr 5, 309, 310
Minyat Duwany 271; *see also* Mūnya Dūnī
Miṣr 314n51

Mizān al-qulūb (Scetis) 273n24, 312n14
Mukyāduḥ 5, 231
Mūnya Dūnī 279n178; see also Minyat Duwany

Nitria (Batira) 70, 78, 116n475, 247, 250, 252, 275n83

Palestine 127n715
Panopolis 317n121
Pisidia 10, 23n53, 23n56
Pnita Datroway 257, 277n117
Ptolemais Hermiou 315n71
Ptolemais in the Thebaid 315n71

Qaraqosh (al-Hamdaniya) 237
Qastata (Fustat) 218, 219
Qaw 5, 300
Qaw, Mount 305, 306

Scetis (Skete/Shihēt/Shihīt/Wadi al-Natrun/Wadi Ḥabib/Mizān al-qulūb) xv, 1, 2, 4, 5, 6, 8, 18n6, 24n63, 31, 52, 53, 112n389, 116n475, 199, 202, 228, 239, 240, 243, 267, 268, 270, 273n23, 273n24, 275n83, 284, 312n14, 314n53, 325; see also individual entries

Shanshā (village) 283, 313n24
Shaykh 'Ibādah (village) 319n163
Shihēt (Ar. Shihīt) 1, 8, 240, 273n24, 300, 308, 309, 310
Shihīt, Mountain of 283, 284, 287, 307

Ṭamaway 275n80
Tamios 275n80
Ṭamoi 275n80
Tamoneqon 275n79
Tamoqniqon 250
Tamoytekul 212
Tarabia 273n19
Tastalbtā 201
Temoniqon 275n79
Thebaid 231, 248, 262, 271, 275n60
Thebes 210, 223
Tkow 265

Wadī al-Naṭrūn xv, 1, 2, 4, 5, 6, 9, 11, 12, 13, 14, 16, 17, 21n34, 23n54, 24n69, 31, 116n475, 125n657, 195, 229, 268, 307, 314n53, 324, 327n10; see also Scetis
Wadī Ḥabīb 312n14; see also Scetis; Wadi al-Natrun
Wasīm 248, 289

Scripture

Genesis
1	116n487
1:1–2	234n41, 275n66
1:1–2 (LXX)	315n78
2:4–3:24	36
3	95n78, 117n503, 122n606
3:1–7	235n59
3:15	317n113
3:19	105n251
17:5–6	198n201
18	124n637, 125n661, 278n141, 319n165, 323
18:4	319n166
18:5	124n640
18:12	235n75
39:20	277n121, 318n148
48:3	318n139

Exodus
3:1–5	106n264
5:1 (LXX)	198n205
5:3 (LXX)	198n205
12:1–28	100n152
12:5	100n152

19:2–3	116n474	2 Samuel	
21:12–14	320n184	11	122n606
22:22	104n219		
32:6	277n124	1 Kings	
33:11	276n88	8:1	318n153
		8:27	327n18
Leviticus		11:1–8	277n126, 319n154
7:18	118n510	11:1–13	235n65
		19:1–9	318n149
Numbers		19:1–10	235n61
25:1–9	235n63, 277n124	19:3–4	277n122
25:9	318n151, 318n152		
35:9–34	320n184	2 Kings	
		2:11–12	104n235
Deuteronomy		2:13–14	102n176
5:26	312n19		
10:18	104n219	2 Chronicles	
11:22	99n137	2:6	327n18
11:27	317n119	6:8	327n18
18:18	99n133		
19:1–13	320n184	Job	
19:9	99n137	1:5	7
24:15	115n463	3:24	116n480
34:10	99n133	29:12	99n139
		31:6	111n377
Joshua			
20:1–3	320n184	Psalms	
20:1–9	320n188	1:3	101n166, 274n32, 313n32
		10:14	99n139
Judges		19:7–10	105n239
9:18	314n59	19:10	313n31
13	99n145	33:18	276n101
16	318n150	37:28	317n111
16:4–22	235n62	55:5	198
16:21	277n123	67:35 (LXX)	121n588
		67:36	317n111
1 Samuel		89:3	114n435
14:45	274n53	97:4	327n18
16:1–13	313n26	97:10 (LXX)	317n111
17	313n25	99:6	274n55
17:26	312n19	102:18	234n37

104:30	234n43, 275n68, 315n80	7:6	99n139
104:32	327n18	8:13	233n23
106:23	114n435	10:10	312n19, 318n140
112:1	275n58	17:8	313n32
112:10	198n214	20:9	124n652
118:103	101n168	23:36	318n140
119:2	275n58		
119:103	101n168, 274n31, 313n31	Lamentations	
132:1	102n180	2:16	198n214
133:1	102n180		
146:9	104n219	Ezekiel	
		18:23	123n616
Proverbs		18:32	123n616
4:6	94n67	33:11	123n616
7	94n66	37:5	275n69, 315n83
10:8	233n21, 274n29, 313n29	37:9	234n44
23:13	235n85	48:31	315n68
23:13–14	278n155		
		Daniel	
Ecclesiastes		7:9	128n735, 234n48, 275n75, 315n84, 327n16, 327n17
1:1	318n153		
		7:13	128n735, 327n16, 327n17
Song of Songs		7:22	128n735, 327n16, 327n17
2:5	96n90, 100n148	12:10	93n58
Isaiah		Zechariah	
1:17	104n219	13:9	93n58
6:6–7	314n57		
11:2	315n72	Malachi	
13:6	318n139	3:3	93n58
29:23	233n17		
37:4	318n140	Tobit	
40:3	198n205	2	278n157
49:2	96n90, 100n148	12	278n157
53:5	109n332	12:9	278n157
61:1	234n42, 275n67		
61:1–2	315n79	Wisdom	
		7:7	315n72
Jeremiah			
1:6	110n350	Sirach	
4:30	94n67	3:30	278n157

44:1	313n23	10:1–4	320n190
48:1–12	104n235	10:6	123n618
		10:25	44

1 Maccabees
2:51	313n23	11:3	118n504
2:58	104n235	11:29	105n244, 106n261, 108n316
		11:30	111n362

2 Maccabees
12:42–44	7	12:11	123n618
		12:31–32	119n532
		12:36	121n583

4 Maccabees
18:8	109n330	12:37	121n582
		13:42	198n214
		14:1–12	277n125

Matthew
1:25	104n226	16:16	312n19
3:16	119n531	16:21	114n435
4:1–11	37, 198n205	16:25	95n74, 98n122
4:1–17	120n560	18:2–4	275n83
5:2	275n65	18:3	317n123
5:5	108n316	18:10–14	123n618
5:13	234n26	18:27	126n677
5:15	110n345	19:13–14	114n427
5:37	109n330	19:14	317n123
6:1–6	129n744	19:19	125n656, 235n77
6:2–4	278n157	19:25	117n494
6:3	129n755, 192n751	19:26	315n62
6:4	110n343	19:28	108n306
6:10	129n745	20:1–16	115n448
6:12	119n529	20:16	111n368
6:13	109n330, 120n559	21:5	108n316
7:8	126n678	21:22	126n678
7:15–20	111n384	22:1–14	111n368
7:17	123n631	22:34–40	92n33
7:24	314n42	22:39	278n143, 319n169
8:12	198n214	22:39–40	315n65
8:28–34	128n723	24	314n48
8:29	120n552	24:12	34
8:31	114n435	24:30	107n283, 107n285, 108n302
9:20–21	278n170	24:31	107n282, 108n304
9:36	123n618	24:44	108n303
10:1–2	278n165	24:45	120n566

25:1–30	236n93	16:12–13	326n2
25:2–4	236n94		
25:14–30	278n173, 320n197	Luke	
25:15–23	115n451	1:37	315n62
25:21	115n450, 275n85	1:38	99n144, 198n20
25:23	115n450, 275n85	1:78	126n677
26:28	106n275	2:7	104n226
26:34	123n613	3:31–32	119n531
26:64	107n285, 108n302	4:1–13	37, 120n560, 198n205
26:69–75	123n613, 277n127, 319n156	4:13	120n566
		6:13–16	320n190
27:19	108n307	6:40	44
28:19	234n49, 275n77, 315n85	6:43–44	111n384
		7:18–23	118n504
Mark		8:4–8	124n631
1:3–4	198n205	8:26–33	128n723
1:10	119n531	8:26–39	128n725
1:12–13	37, 198n205	8:28	120n552
3:11	130n781	9:22	114n435
3:14	278n165	10:1	235n89, 278n164, 320n189
3:14–19	320n190		
3:28–29	119n532	10:7	114n437
5:1–13	128n723	10:17	320n189
5:33	198	10:19	198n209
6:7	130n781	10:25–28	92n33
6:17–29	235n64	10:27	319n169
9:12	115n458	11:4	119n529
10:13–16	275n83	11:10	126n678
10:14	317n123	11:28	234n39, 317n119
10:20–30	317n118	11:42	34
10:26	117n494	12:10	119n532
10:27	315n62	14:15–24	111n368
11:24	126n678	16:9	198n212
12:28–34	92n33	16:19–31	108n301
12:31	319n169	17:20–37	314n48
12:33	319n169	17:21	34, 92n32
13	314n48	17:25	114n435
13:26	316n106	18:16	234n50, 317n123
14:36	99n128	18:26	315n62
14:62	316n106	18:29	98n121
14:66–72	235n66	19:11–27	320n197

21	314n48	14:26	275n63, 315n74, 318n138
22:25	100n161	14:27	103n197, 106n268, 124n651, 314n49
24:13–32	124n652		
24:13–35	326n2	15:5	234n31, 274n44
24:27	99n133	15:7	106n272
		15:12–14	277n128
John		15:13	109n334, 234n38, 235n67, 274n56, 317n114
1	116n483		
1:3	123n611	15:26	275n63, 315n74, 318n138
1:5	7	16:7	275n63, 315n74, 318n138
1:14	103n194	16:24	106n272
1:29	320n180	19:11	129n762
1:32	119n531, 234n45, 315n81	19:23	129n762
1:32–34	275n71	20:1–16	326n2
1:47	276n98, 316n93	20:17	123n623, 198n213
3:3	129n762	20:19	106n262
3:7	100n160, 129n762	20:23	106n272
3:16	317n114	21:4	106n262
3:31	100n160, 129n762		
4:14	315n63	Acts of the Apostles	
5:2–7	320n194	1:3	114n435
6:39–40	108n305	2:7–11	26n77
6:47	314n46	4:32	102n178
6:54	108n305	9:3	96n89, 113n414
6:68	235n84, 278n150	10:4	278n157
7:6–8	120n566	10:31	278n157
8:23	100n160	11:21	114n430
8:34	314n46	12:24	99n138
8:50	121n581	19:11–12	320n201
8:51	314n46	20:28	110n348
8:58	314n46	26:12–13	96n89
11:12	127n695		
12:48	121n581	Romans	
13:1–11	124n643, 319n165	Romans	113n411
13:16	314n46	1:9	233n15, 273n15
14:12	234n32, 235n83, 274n44, 278n148, 319n171	1:11	130n780
		1:26	98n115
14:14	106n272	3:3	316n102
14:16	275n63, 315n74, 318n138	3:25	106n275
14:21	234n31, 235n71	5:3	114n435
14:23	234n31	5:9	110n344

5:12–13	126n672	15:52	107n282, 108n304
5:21	109n332	16:20	316n91
6:18	108n314, 176n218		
6:22	108n314, 176n218	2 Corinthians	
7	93n55	1:5	114n435
7:24	106n273, 119n528, 125n668	3:17	108n314, 176n218
8:2	108n314, 176n218	3:18	97n105
8:3	109n337	5:10	108n307
8:14	115n467	5:21	276n104, 316n102
8:15	99n128	6:5	101n170
8:17	116n467	6:12	107n286
8:21	108n314, 176n218	6:15	120n562
8:38–39	33	6:18	318n139
9:26	312n19	7:1	116n488
11:32	316n102	7:15	198
12:1	320n198	8:13	111n377
13:11	120n566	10:10	115n458
14:10	108n307	10:13	102n179
16:16	316n91	12:7–9	320n201
16:17	116n467	12:9	99n140, 273n21, 274n46, 313n25
1 Corinthians		12:10	234n35
1:7	130n780	13:12	316n91
1:25–31	274n46	15–18	102n179
1:27	99n140, 313n25		
2:3	198	Galatians	
2:14	130n780	1:15	96n89
9:25	100n159	4:1–7	276n90
9:27	101n171, 278n160	4:6	99n128
10:7–8	277n124	4:21–31	110n353
10:8	235n63, 318n151, 318n152	4:25–26	111n371
10:13	275n87	5:1	108n314, 109n332, 176n218
10:29	108n314, 176n218	5:13a	108n314, 176n218
11:23	121n576	6:16	102n179
12:1	130n780		
12:3	234n46, 275n72, 315n82	Ephesians	
12:8	315n72	1:7	106n275
13:13	42	1:17	315n72
14:1	130n780	2:4	316n103
14:12	130n780	6:18	313n30
14:32	278n171		

Philippians
1:1   110n348
2:1   126n677
3:13   102n186, 106n265,
       110n340
3:13–14   92n46
3:16   102n179

Colossians
1:16   108n306
1:28–29   320n179
1:29   100n159
3:5   98n115
4:5   120n566

1 Thessalonians
1:2   101n169
4:5   98n115
4:16   107n282, 108n304,
       316n106
4:17   107n285, 108n302
5:17   233n22, 274n30, 313n30,
       315n64
5:26   316n91

1 Timothy
2:14   277n120
3:2   110n348
3:7   314n55
5:18   114n437
6:12   100n159

2 Timothy
2:5   118n521
3:16   113n410, 320n179
4:7   100n159
4:8   121n581

Hebrews
3:11   106n261
3:18   106n261
4:1–10   106n261
4:15   276n104, 316n102
6:14   99n138
7:26   276n104
10:32 118n521
11:1   102n177
11:6   320n181
11:10 98n118, 104n228
11:37–38   111n381, 315n70
11:38 110n342, 273n13, 275n59,
       313n21
12:22 110n353
12:22–23   104n226
12:22–24   111n371
12:23 274n43
13:12 106n275

James
1:15   42, 96n88, 122n594
1:17   114n436
1:27   99n139, 104n219
2:14–26   106n270
2:23   316n107
2:26   106n270
5:11   316n103

1 Peter
1:18–19   316n102
1:19   100n152, 313n27,
       320n180
2:9   320n182
2:17   105n248
2:22   276n104, 316n102
2:24   109n332
2:25   110n348
3:4   108n316
5:8   43, 120n550, 276n106,
       318n134
5:9   105n248
5:14   316n91

2 Peter
1:4   320n178
3:1–13   118n504

1 John
1:1   99n129, 313n22
2:28   108n303
3:5   276n104, 316n102
5:16–17   8

Jude
1:25   327n16

Revelation
1:7   107n283, 108n303,
           316n106
16:14   318n139
20:2   109n330, 117n503
20:4   108n306
21:9–14   315n68
22:2   313n32
22:12   108n303
22:14   315n68